I0018875

GNU Emacs 24.5 Reference Manual

A catalogue record for this book is available from the Hong Kong Public Libraries.

Published in Hong Kong by Samurai Media Limited.

Email: info@samuraimedia.org

ISBN 978-988-8381-95-1

Copyright 1985–1987, 1993–2015 Free Software Foundation, Inc.
Permission is granted to copy, distribute and/or modify this document under the terms of the GNU Free Documentation License, Version 1.3 or any later version published by the Free Software Foundation; with the Invariant Sections being "The GNU Manifesto," "Distribution" and "GNU GENERAL PUBLIC LICENSE," with the Front-Cover Texts being "A GNU Manual," and with the Back-Cover Texts as in (a) below. A copy of the license is included in the section entitled "GNU Free Documentation License." (a) The FSF's Back-Cover Text is: "You have the freedom to copy and modify this GNU manual. Buying copies from the FSF supports it in developing GNU and promoting software freedom."

Minor modifications for publication Copyright 2015 Samurai Media Limited.

Background Cover Image by https://www.flickr.com/people/webtreatsetc/

Short Contents

Table of Contents

Preface

This manual documents the use and simple customization of the Emacs editor. Simple Emacs customizations do not require you to be a programmer, but if you are not interested in customizing, you can ignore the customization hints.

This is primarily a reference manual, but can also be used as a primer. If you are new to Emacs, we recommend you start with the integrated, learn-by-doing tutorial, before reading the manual. To run the tutorial, start Emacs and type C-h t. The tutorial describes commands, tells you when to try them, and explains the results. The tutorial is available in several languages.

On first reading, just skim chapters 1 and 2, which describe the notational conventions of the manual and the general appearance of the Emacs display screen. Note which questions are answered in these chapters, so you can refer back later. After reading chapter 4, you should practice the commands shown there. The next few chapters describe fundamental techniques and concepts that are used constantly. You need to understand them thoroughly, so experiment with them until you are fluent.

Chapters 14 through 19 describe intermediate-level features that are useful for many kinds of editing. Chapter 20 and following chapters describe optional but useful features; read those chapters when you need them.

Read the Common Problems chapter if Emacs does not seem to be working properly. It explains how to cope with several common problems (see Section 34.2 [Dealing with Emacs Trouble], page 444), as well as when and how to report Emacs bugs (see Section 34.3 [Bugs], page 448).

To find the documentation of a particular command, look in the index. Keys (character commands) and command names have separate indexes. There is also a glossary, with a cross reference for each term.

This manual is available as a printed book and also as an Info file. The Info file is for reading from Emacs itself, or with the Info program. Info is the principal format for documentation in the GNU system. The Info file and the printed book contain substantially the same text and are generated from the same source files, which are also distributed with GNU Emacs.

GNU Emacs is a member of the Emacs editor family. There are many Emacs editors, all sharing common principles of organization. For information on the underlying philosophy of Emacs and the lessons learned from its development, see *Emacs, the Extensible, Customizable Self-Documenting Display Editor*, available from `ftp://publications.ai.mit.edu/ai-publications/pdf/AIM-519A.pdf`.

This version of the manual is mainly intended for use with GNU Emacs installed on GNU and Unix systems. GNU Emacs can also be used on MS-DOS, Microsoft Windows, and Macintosh systems. The Info file version of this manual contains some more information about using Emacs on those systems. Those systems use different file name syntax; in addition MS-DOS does not support all GNU Emacs features. See Appendix G [Microsoft Windows], page 505, for information about using Emacs on Windows. See Appendix F [Mac OS / GNUstep], page 502, for information about using Emacs on Macintosh (and GNUstep).

Distribution

GNU Emacs is *free software*; this means that everyone is free to use it and free to redistribute it under certain conditions. GNU Emacs is not in the public domain; it is copyrighted and there are restrictions on its distribution, but these restrictions are designed to permit everything that a good cooperating citizen would want to do. What is not allowed is to try to prevent others from further sharing any version of GNU Emacs that they might get from you. The precise conditions are found in the GNU General Public License that comes with Emacs and also appears in this manual[1]. See Appendix A [Copying], page 459.

One way to get a copy of GNU Emacs is from someone else who has it. You need not ask for our permission to do so, or tell any one else; just copy it. If you have access to the Internet, you can get the latest distribution version of GNU Emacs by anonymous FTP; see `http://www.gnu.org/software/emacs` on our website for more information.

You may also receive GNU Emacs when you buy a computer. Computer manufacturers are free to distribute copies on the same terms that apply to everyone else. These terms require them to give you the full sources, including whatever changes they may have made, and to permit you to redistribute the GNU Emacs received from them under the usual terms of the General Public License. In other words, the program must be free for you when you get it, not just free for the manufacturer.

If you find GNU Emacs useful, please **send a donation** to the Free Software Foundation to support our work. Donations to the Free Software Foundation are tax deductible in the US. If you use GNU Emacs at your workplace, please suggest that the company make a donation. To donate, see `https://my.fsf.org/donate/`. For other ways in which you can help, see `http://www.gnu.org/help/help.html`.

We also sell hardcopy versions of this manual and *An Introduction to Programming in Emacs Lisp*, by Robert J. Chassell. You can visit our online store at `http://shop.fsf.org/`. The income from sales goes to support the foundation's purpose: the development of new free software, and improvements to our existing programs including GNU Emacs.

If you need to contact the Free Software Foundation, see `http://www.fsf.org/about/contact/`, or write to

> Free Software Foundation
> 51 Franklin Street, Fifth Floor
> Boston, MA 02110-1301
> USA

Acknowledgments

Contributors to GNU Emacs include Jari Aalto, Per Abrahamsen, Tomas Abrahamsson, Jay K. Adams, Alon Albert, Michael Albinus, Nagy Andras, Benjamin Andresen, Ralf Angeli, Dmitry Antipov, Joe Arceneaux, Emil Åström, Miles Bader, David Bakhash, Juanma Barranquero, Eli Barzilay, Thomas Baumann, Steven L. Baur, Jay Belanger, Alexander L. Belikoff, Thomas Bellman, Scott Bender, Boaz Ben-Zvi, Sergey Berezin, Stephen Berman,

---

[1] This manual is itself covered by the GNU Free Documentation License. This license is similar in spirit to the General Public License, but is more suitable for documentation. See Appendix B [GNU Free Documentation License], page 470.

Karl Berry, Anna M. Bigatti, Ray Blaak, Martin Blais, Jim Blandy, Johan Bockgård, Jan Böcker, Joel Boehland, Lennart Borgman, Per Bothner, Terrence Brannon, Frank Bresz, Peter Breton, Emmanuel Briot, Kevin Broadey, Vincent Broman, Michael Brouwer, David M. Brown, Stefan Bruda, Georges Brun-Cottan, Joe Buehler, Scott Byer, Włodek Bzyl, Bill Carpenter, Per Cederqvist, Hans Chalupsky, Chris Chase, Bob Chassell, Andrew Choi, Chong Yidong, Sacha Chua, Stewart Clamen, James Clark, Mike Clarkson, Glynn Clements, Andrew Cohen, Daniel Colascione, Christoph Conrad, Ludovic Courtès, Andrew Csillag, Toby Cubitt, Baoqiu Cui, Doug Cutting, Mathias Dahl, Julien Danjou, Satyaki Das, Vivek Dasmohapatra, Dan Davison, Michael DeCorte, Gary Delp, Nachum Dershowitz, Dave Detlefs, Matthieu Devin, Christophe de Dinechin, Eri Ding, Jan Djärv, Lawrence R. Dodd, Carsten Dominik, Scott Draves, Benjamin Drieu, Viktor Dukhovni, Jacques Duthen, Dmitry Dzhus, John Eaton, Rolf Ebert, Carl Edman, David Edmondson, Paul Eggert, Stephen Eglen, Christian Egli, Torbjörn Einarsson, Tsugutomo Enami, David Engster, Hans Henrik Eriksen, Michael Ernst, Ata Etemadi, Frederick Farnbach, Oscar Figueiredo, Fred Fish, Steve Fisk, Karl Fogel, Gary Foster, Eric S. Fraga, Romain Francoise, Noah Friedman, Andreas Fuchs, Shigeru Fukaya, Xue Fuqiao, Hallvard Furuseth, Keith Gabryelski, Peter S. Galbraith, Kevin Gallagher, Fabián E. Gallina, Kevin Gallo, Juan León Lahoz García, Howard Gayle, Daniel German, Stephen Gildea, Julien Gilles, David Gillespie, Bob Glickstein, Deepak Goel, David De La Harpe Golden, Boris Goldowsky, David Goodger, Chris Gray, Kevin Greiner, Michelangelo Grigni, Odd Gripenstam, Kai Großjohann, Michael Gschwind, Bastien Guerry, Henry Guillaume, Dmitry Gutov, Doug Gwyn, Bruno Haible, Ken'ichi Handa, Lars Hansen, Chris Hanson, Jesper Harder, Alexandru Harsanyi, K. Shane Hartman, John Heidemann, Jon K. Hellan, Magnus Henoch, Markus Heritsch, Dirk Herrmann, Karl Heuer, Manabu Higashida, Konrad Hinsen, Anders Holst, Jeffrey C. Honig, Tassilo Horn, Kurt Hornik, Tom Houlder, Joakim Hove, Denis Howe, Lars Ingebrigtsen, Andrew Innes, Seiichiro Inoue, Philip Jackson, Martyn Jago, Pavel Janik, Paul Jarc, Ulf Jasper, Thorsten Jolitz, Michael K. Johnson, Kyle Jones, Terry Jones, Simon Josefsson, Alexandre Julliard, Arne Jørgensen, Tomoji Kagatani, Brewster Kahle, Tokuya Kameshima, Lute Kamstra, Ivan Kanis, David Kastrup, David Kaufman, Henry Kautz, Taichi Kawabata, Taro Kawagishi, Howard Kaye, Michael Kifer, Richard King, Peter Kleiweg, Karel Klíč, Shuhei Kobayashi, Pavel Kobyakov, Larry K. Kolodney, David M. Koppelman, Koseki Yoshinori, Robert Krawitz, Sebastian Kremer, Ryszard Kubiak, Igor Kuzmin, David Kågedal, Daniel LaLiberte, Karl Landstrom, Mario Lang, Aaron Larson, James R. Larus, Vinicius Jose Latorre, Werner Lemberg, Frederic Lepied, Peter Liljenberg, Christian Limpach, Lars Lindberg, Chris Lindblad, Anders Lindgren, Thomas Link, Juri Linkov, Francis Litterio, Sergey Litvinov, Leo Liu, Emilio C. Lopes, Martin Lorentzon, Dave Love, Eric Ludlam, Károly Lőrentey, Sascha Lüdecke, Greg McGary, Roland McGrath, Michael McNamara, Alan Mackenzie, Christopher J. Madsen, Neil M. Mager, Ken Manheimer, Bill Mann, Brian Marick, Simon Marshall, Bengt Martensson, Charlie Martin, Yukihiro Matsumoto, Tomohiro Matsuyama, David Maus, Thomas May, Will Mengarini, David Megginson, Stefan Merten, Ben A. Mesander, Wayne Mesard, Brad Miller, Lawrence Mitchell, Richard Mlynarik, Gerd Möllmann, Dani Moncayo, Stefan Monnier, Keith Moore, Jan Moringen, Morioka Tomohiko, Glenn Morris, Don Morrison, Diane Murray, Riccardo Murri, Sen Nagata, Erik Naggum, Gergely Nagy, Nobuyoshi Nakada, Thomas Neumann, Mike Newton, Thien-Thi Nguyen, Jurgen Nickelsen, Dan Nicolaescu, Hrvoje Nikšić, Jeff Norden, Andrew Norman, Edward O'Connor, Kentaro Ohkouchi, Christian Ohler, Kenichi Okada, Alexandre Oliva, Bob Olson, Michael Olson, Takaaki Ota, Pieter E. J. Pareit, Ross

Patterson, David Pearson, Juan Pechiar, Jeff Peck, Damon Anton Permezel, Tom Perrine, William M. Perry, Per Persson, Jens Petersen, Daniel Pfeiffer, Justus Piater, Richard L. Pieri, Fred Pierresteguy, François Pinard, Daniel Pittman, Christian Plaunt, Alexander Pohoyda, David Ponce, Francesco A. Potortì, Michael D. Prange, Mukesh Prasad, Ken Raeburn, Marko Rahamaa, Ashwin Ram, Eric S. Raymond, Paul Reilly, Edward M. Reingold, David Reitter, Alex Rezinsky, Rob Riepel, Lara Rios, Adrian Robert, Nick Roberts, Roland B. Roberts, John Robinson, Denis B. Roegel, Danny Roozendaal, Sebastian Rose, William Rosenblatt, Markus Rost, Guillermo J. Rozas, Martin Rudalics, Ivar Rummelhoff, Jason Rumney, Wolfgang Rupprecht, Benjamin Rutt, Kevin Ryde, James B. Salem, Masahiko Sato, Timo Savola, Jorgen Schäfer, Holger Schauer, William Schelter, Ralph Schleicher, Gregor Schmid, Michael Schmidt, Ronald S. Schnell, Philippe Schnoebelen, Jan Schormann, Alex Schroeder, Stefan Schoef, Rainer Schöpf, Raymond Scholz, Eric Schulte, Andreas Schwab, Randal Schwartz, Oliver Seidel, Manuel Serrano, Paul Sexton, Hovav Shacham, Stanislav Shalunov, Marc Shapiro, Richard Sharman, Olin Shivers, Tibor Šimko, Espen Skoglund, Rick Sladkey, Lynn Slater, Chris Smith, David Smith, Paul D. Smith, Wilson Snyder, William Sommerfeld, Simon South, Andre Spiegel, Michael Staats, Thomas Steffen, Ulf Stegemann, Reiner Steib, Sam Steingold, Ake Stenhoff, Peter Stephenson, Ken Stevens, Andy Stewart, Jonathan Stigelman, Martin Stjernholm, Kim F. Storm, Steve Strassmann, Christopher Suckling, Olaf Sylvester, Naoto Takahashi, Steven Tamm, Jan Tatarik, Luc Teirlinck, Jean-Philippe Theberge, Jens T. Berger Thielemann, Spencer Thomas, Jim Thompson, Toru Tomabechi, David O'Toole, Markus Triska, Tom Tromey, Enami Tsugutomo, Eli Tziperman, Daiki Ueno, Masanobu Umeda, Rajesh Vaidheeswarran, Neil W. Van Dyke, Didier Verna, Joakim Verona, Ulrik Vieth, Geoffrey Voelker, Johan Vromans, Inge Wallin, John Paul Wallington, Colin Walters, Barry Warsaw, Christoph Wedler, Ilja Weis, Zhang Weize, Morten Welinder, Joseph Brian Wells, Rodney Whitby, John Wiegley, Sascha Wilde, Ed Wilkinson, Mike Williams, Roland Winkler, Bill Wohler, Steven A. Wood, Dale R. Worley, Francis J. Wright, Felix S. T. Wu, Tom Wurgler, Yamamoto Mitsuharu, Katsumi Yamaoka, Masatake Yamato, Jonathan Yavner, Ryan Yeske, Ilya Zakharevich, Milan Zamazal, Victor Zandy, Eli Zaretskii, Jamie Zawinski, Andrew Zhilin, Shenghuo Zhu, Piotr Zieliński, Ian T. Zimmermann, Reto Zimmermann, Neal Ziring, Teodor Zlatanov, and Detlev Zundel.

Introduction

You are reading about GNU Emacs, the GNU incarnation of the advanced, self-documenting, customizable, extensible editor Emacs. (The 'G' in GNU (GNU's Not Unix) is not silent.)

We call Emacs *advanced* because it can do much more than simple insertion and deletion of text. It can control subprocesses, indent programs automatically, show multiple files at once, and more. Emacs editing commands operate in terms of characters, words, lines, sentences, paragraphs, and pages, as well as expressions and comments in various programming languages.

Self-documenting means that at any time you can use special commands, known as *help commands*, to find out what your options are, or to find out what any command does, or to find all the commands that pertain to a given topic. See Chapter 7 [Help], page 37.

Customizable means that you can easily alter the behavior of Emacs commands in simple ways. For instance, if you use a programming language in which comments start with '<**' and end with '**>', you can tell the Emacs comment manipulation commands to use those strings (see Section 23.5 [Comments], page 249). To take another example, you can rebind the basic cursor motion commands (up, down, left and right) to any keys on the keyboard that you find comfortable. See Chapter 33 [Customization], page 412.

Extensible means that you can go beyond simple customization and create entirely new commands. New commands are simply programs written in the Lisp language, which are run by Emacs's own Lisp interpreter. Existing commands can even be redefined in the middle of an editing session, without having to restart Emacs. Most of the editing commands in Emacs are written in Lisp; the few exceptions could have been written in Lisp but use C instead for efficiency. Writing an extension is programming, but non-programmers can use it afterwards. See Section "Preface" in *An Introduction to Programming in Emacs Lisp*, if you want to learn Emacs Lisp programming.

1 The Organization of the Screen

On a graphical display, such as on GNU/Linux using the X Window System, Emacs occupies a "graphical window". On a text terminal, Emacs occupies the entire terminal screen. We will use the term *frame* to mean a graphical window or terminal screen occupied by Emacs. Emacs behaves very similarly on both kinds of frames. It normally starts out with just one frame, but you can create additional frames if you wish (see Chapter 18 [Frames], page 162).

Each frame consists of several distinct regions. At the top of the frame is a *menu bar*, which allows you to access commands via a series of menus. On a graphical display, directly below the menu bar is a *tool bar*, a row of icons that perform editing commands if you click on them. At the very bottom of the frame is an *echo area*, where informative messages are displayed and where you enter information when Emacs asks for it.

The main area of the frame, below the tool bar (if one exists) and above the echo area, is called *the window*. Henceforth in this manual, we will use the word "window" in this sense. Graphical display systems commonly use the word "window" with a different meaning; but, as stated above, we refer to those "graphical windows" as "frames".

An Emacs window is where the *buffer*—the text you are editing—is displayed. On a graphical display, the window possesses a *scroll bar* on one side, which can be used to scroll through the buffer. The last line of the window is a *mode line*. This displays various information about what is going on in the buffer, such as whether there are unsaved changes, the editing modes that are in use, the current line number, and so forth.

When you start Emacs, there is normally only one window in the frame. However, you can subdivide this window horizontally or vertically to create multiple windows, each of which can independently display a buffer (see Chapter 17 [Windows], page 156).

At any time, one window is the *selected window*. On a graphical display, the selected window shows a more prominent cursor (usually solid and blinking); other windows show a less prominent cursor (usually a hollow box). On a text terminal, there is only one cursor, which is shown in the selected window. The buffer displayed in the selected window is called the *current buffer*, and it is where editing happens. Most Emacs commands implicitly apply to the current buffer; the text displayed in unselected windows is mostly visible for reference. If you use multiple frames on a graphical display, selecting a particular frame selects a window in that frame.

1.1 Point

The cursor in the selected window shows the location where most editing commands take effect, which is called *point*[1]. Many Emacs commands move point to different places in the buffer; for example, you can place point by clicking mouse button 1 (normally the left button) at the desired location.

By default, the cursor in the selected window is drawn as a solid block and appears to be *on* a character, but you should think of point as *between* two characters; it is situated *before* the character under the cursor. For example, if your text looks like 'frob' with the cursor over the 'b', then point is between the 'o' and the 'b'. If you insert the character '!'

---

[1] The term "point" comes from the character '.', which was the command in TECO (the language in which the original Emacs was written) for accessing the editing position.

at that position, the result is 'fro!b', with point between the '!' and the 'b'. Thus, the cursor remains over the 'b', as before.

If you are editing several files in Emacs, each in its own buffer, each buffer has its own value of point. A buffer that is not currently displayed remembers its value of point if you later display it again. Furthermore, if a buffer is displayed in multiple windows, each of those windows has its own value of point.

See Section 11.20 [Cursor Display], page 86, for options that control how Emacs displays the cursor.

1.2 The Echo Area

The line at the very bottom of the frame is the *echo area*. It is used to display small amounts of text for various purposes.

The echo area is so-named because one of the things it is used for is *echoing*, which means displaying the characters of a multi-character command as you type. Single-character commands are not echoed. Multi-character commands (see Section 2.2 [Keys], page 11) are echoed if you pause for more than a second in the middle of a command. Emacs then echoes all the characters of the command so far, to prompt you for the rest. Once echoing has started, the rest of the command echoes immediately as you type it. This behavior is designed to give confident users fast response, while giving hesitant users maximum feedback.

The echo area is also used to display an *error message* when a command cannot do its job. Error messages may be accompanied by beeping or by flashing the screen.

Some commands display informative messages in the echo area to tell you what the command has done, or to provide you with some specific information. These *informative* messages, unlike error messages, are not accompanied with a beep or flash. For example, `C-x =` (hold down `Ctrl` and type `x`, then let go of `Ctrl` and type `=`) displays a message describing the character at point, its position in the buffer, and its current column in the window. Commands that take a long time often display messages ending in '. . .' while they are working (sometimes also indicating how much progress has been made, as a percentage), and add '`done`' when they are finished.

Informative echo area messages are saved in a special buffer named `*Messages*`. (We have not explained buffers yet; see Chapter 16 [Buffers], page 147, for more information about them.) If you miss a message that appeared briefly on the screen, you can switch to the `*Messages*` buffer to see it again. The `*Messages*` buffer is limited to a certain number of lines, specified by the variable `message-log-max`. (We have not explained variables either; see Section 33.2 [Variables], page 420, for more information about them.) Beyond this limit, one line is deleted from the beginning whenever a new message line is added at the end.

See Section 11.23 [Display Custom], page 88, for options that control how Emacs uses the echo area.

The echo area is also used to display the *minibuffer*, a special window where you can input arguments to commands, such as the name of a file to be edited. When the minibuffer is in use, the text displayed in the echo area begins with a *prompt string*, and the active cursor appears within the minibuffer, which is temporarily considered the selected window. You can always get out of the minibuffer by typing `C-g`. See Chapter 5 [Minibuffer], page 26.

1.3 The Mode Line

At the bottom of each window is a *mode line*, which describes what is going on in the current buffer. When there is only one window, the mode line appears right above the echo area; it is the next-to-last line in the frame. On a graphical display, the mode line is drawn with a 3D box appearance. Emacs also usually draws the mode line of the selected window with a different color than that of unselected windows, in order to make it stand out.

The text displayed in the mode line has the following format:

```
cs:ch-fr  buf      pos line   (major minor)
```

On a text terminal, this text is followed by a series of dashes extending to the right edge of the window. These dashes are omitted on a graphical display.

The *cs* string and the colon character after it describe the character set and newline convention used for the current buffer. Normally, Emacs automatically handles these settings for you, but it is sometimes useful to have this information.

cs describes the character set of the text in the buffer (see Section 19.5 [Coding Systems], page 183). If it is a dash ('-'), that indicates no special character set handling (with the possible exception of end-of-line conventions, described in the next paragraph). '=' means no conversion whatsoever, and is usually used for files containing non-textual data. Other characters represent various *coding systems*—for example, '1' represents ISO Latin-1.

On a text terminal, *cs* is preceded by two additional characters that describe the coding systems for keyboard input and terminal output. Furthermore, if you are using an input method, *cs* is preceded by a string that identifies the input method (see Section 19.3 [Input Methods], page 181).

The character after *cs* is usually a colon. If a different string is displayed, that indicates a nontrivial end-of-line convention for encoding a file. Usually, lines of text are separated by *newline characters* in a file, but two other conventions are sometimes used. The MS-DOS convention uses a "carriage-return" character followed by a "linefeed" character; when editing such files, the colon changes to either a backslash ('\') or '(DOS)', depending on the operating system. Another convention, employed by older Macintosh systems, uses a "carriage-return" character instead of a newline; when editing such files, the colon changes to either a forward slash ('/') or '(Mac)'. On some systems, Emacs displays '(Unix)' instead of the colon for files that use newline as the line separator.

The next element on the mode line is the string indicated by *ch*. This shows two dashes ('--') if the buffer displayed in the window has the same contents as the corresponding file on the disk; i.e., if the buffer is "unmodified". If the buffer is modified, it shows two stars ('**'). For a read-only buffer, it shows '%*' if the buffer is modified, and '%%' otherwise.

The character after *ch* is normally a dash ('-'). However, if the default-directory for the current buffer is on a remote machine, '@' is displayed instead (see Section 15.1 [File Names], page 122).

fr gives the selected frame name (see Chapter 18 [Frames], page 162). It appears only on text terminals. The initial frame's name is 'F1'.

buf is the name of the buffer displayed in the window. Usually, this is the same as the name of a file you are editing. See Chapter 16 [Buffers], page 147.

pos tells you whether there is additional text above the top of the window, or below the bottom. If your buffer is small and all of it is visible in the window, *pos* is 'All'. Otherwise, it is 'Top' if you are looking at the beginning of the buffer, 'Bot' if you are looking at the end of the buffer, or 'nn%', where nn is the percentage of the buffer above the top of the window. With Size Indication mode, you can display the size of the buffer as well. See Section 11.18 [Optional Mode Line], page 84.

line is the character 'L' followed by the line number at point. (You can display the current column number too, by turning on Column Number mode. See Section 11.18 [Optional Mode Line], page 84.)

major is the name of the major mode used in the buffer. A major mode is a principal editing mode for the buffer, such as Text mode, Lisp mode, C mode, and so forth. See Section 20.1 [Major Modes], page 199. Some major modes display additional information after the major mode name. For example, Compilation buffers and Shell buffers display the status of the subprocess.

minor is a list of some of the enabled minor modes, which are optional editing modes that provide additional features on top of the major mode. See Section 20.2 [Minor Modes], page 200.

Some features are listed together with the minor modes whenever they are turned on, even though they are not really minor modes. 'Narrow' means that the buffer being displayed has editing restricted to only a portion of its text (see Section 11.5 [Narrowing], page 73). 'Def' means that a keyboard macro is currently being defined (see Chapter 14 [Keyboard Macros], page 114).

In addition, if Emacs is inside a recursive editing level, square brackets ('[...]') appear around the parentheses that surround the modes. If Emacs is in one recursive editing level within another, double square brackets appear, and so on. Since recursive editing levels affect Emacs globally, such square brackets appear in the mode line of every window. See Section 31.10 [Recursive Edit], page 404.

You can change the appearance of the mode line as well as the format of its contents. See Section 11.18 [Optional Mode Line], page 84. In addition, the mode line is mouse-sensitive; clicking on different parts of the mode line performs various commands. See Section 18.5 [Mode Line Mouse], page 165.

1.4 The Menu Bar

Each Emacs frame normally has a menu bar at the top which you can use to perform common operations. There's no need to list them here, as you can more easily see them yourself.

On a display that supports a mouse, you can use the mouse to choose a command from the menu bar. An arrow on the right edge of a menu item means it leads to a subsidiary menu, or submenu. A '...' at the end of a menu item means that the command will prompt you for further input before it actually does anything.

Some of the commands in the menu bar have ordinary key bindings as well; if so, a key binding is shown in parentheses after the item itself. To view the full command name and documentation for a menu item, type C-h k, and then select the menu bar with the mouse in the usual way (see Section 7.1 [Key Help], page 39).

Instead of using the mouse, you can also invoke the first menu bar item by pressing F10 (to run the command menu-bar-open). You can then navigate the menus with the arrow keys. To activate a selected menu item, press `RET`; to cancel menu navigation, press `C-g` or `ESC ESC ESC`.

On a text terminal, you can optionally access the menu-bar menus in the echo area. To this end, customize the variable `tty-menu-open-use-tmm` to a non-`nil` value. Then typing `F10` will run the command `tmm-menubar` instead of dropping down the menu. (You can also type `M-'`, which always invokes `tmm-menubar`.) `tmm-menubar` lets you select a menu item with the keyboard. A provisional choice appears in the echo area. You can use the up and down arrow keys to move through the menu to different items, and then you can type `RET` to select the item. Each menu item is also designated by a letter or digit (usually the initial of some word in the item's name). This letter or digit is separated from the item name by '`==>`'. You can type the item's letter or digit to select the item.

2 Characters, Keys and Commands

This chapter explains the character sets used by Emacs for input commands, and the fundamental concepts of *keys* and *commands*, whereby Emacs interprets your keyboard and mouse input.

2.1 Kinds of User Input

GNU Emacs is primarily designed for use with the keyboard. While it is possible to use the mouse to issue editing commands through the menu bar and tool bar, that is not as efficient as using the keyboard. Therefore, this manual mainly documents how to edit with the keyboard.

Keyboard input into Emacs is based on a heavily-extended version of ASCII. Simple characters, like 'a', 'B', '3', '=', and the space character (denoted as SPC), are entered by typing the corresponding key. *Control characters*, such as RET, TAB, DEL, ESC, F1, Home, and LEFT, are also entered this way, as are certain characters found on non-English keyboards (see Chapter 19 [International], page 177).

Emacs also recognizes control characters that are entered using *modifier keys*. Two commonly-used modifier keys are Control (usually labeled Ctrl), and META (usually labeled Alt)[1]. For example, Control-a is entered by holding down the Ctrl key while pressing a; we will refer to this as C-a for short. Similarly META-a, or M-a for short, is entered by holding down the Alt key and pressing a. Modifier keys can also be applied to non-alphanumerical characters, e.g., C-F1 or M-LEFT.

You can also type Meta characters using two-character sequences starting with ESC. Thus, you can enter M-a by typing ESC a. You can enter C-M-a by typing ESC C-a. Unlike META, ESC is entered as a separate character. You don't hold down ESC while typing the next character; instead, press ESC and release it, then enter the next character. This feature is useful on certain text terminals where the META key does not function reliably.

On graphical displays, the window manager might block some keyboard inputs, including M-TAB, M-SPC, C-M-d and C-M-l. If you have this problem, you can either customize your window manager to not block those keys, or "rebind" the affected Emacs commands (see Chapter 33 [Customization], page 412).

Simple characters and control characters, as well as certain non-keyboard inputs such as mouse clicks, are collectively referred to as *input events*. For details about how Emacs internally handles input events, see Section "Input Events" in *The Emacs Lisp Reference Manual*.

2.2 Keys

Some Emacs commands are invoked by just one input event; for example, C-f moves forward one character in the buffer. Other commands take two or more input events to invoke, such as C-x C-f and C-x 4 C-f.

A *key sequence*, or *key* for short, is a sequence of one or more input events that is meaningful as a unit. If a key sequence invokes a command, we call it a *complete key*; for

---

[1] We refer to Alt as META for historical reasons.

example, `C-f`, `C-x C-f` and `C-x 4 C-f` are all complete keys. If a key sequence isn't long enough to invoke a command, we call it a *prefix key*; from the preceding example, we see that `C-x` and `C-x 4` are prefix keys. Every key sequence is either a complete key or a prefix key.

A prefix key combines with the following input event to make a longer key sequence. For example, `C-x` is a prefix key, so typing `C-x` alone does not invoke a command; instead, Emacs waits for further input (if you pause for longer than a second, it echoes the `C-x` key to prompt for that input; see Section 1.2 [Echo Area], page 7). `C-x` combines with the next input event to make a two-event key sequence, which could itself be a prefix key (such as `C-x 4`), or a complete key (such as `C-x C-f`). There is no limit to the length of key sequences, but in practice they are seldom longer than three or four input events.

You can't add input events onto a complete key. For example, because `C-f` is a complete key, the two-event sequence `C-f C-k` is two key sequences, not one.

By default, the prefix keys in Emacs are `C-c`, `C-h`, `C-x`, `C-x RET`, `C-x @`, `C-x a`, `C-x n`, `C-x r`, `C-x v`, `C-x 4`, `C-x 5`, `C-x 6`, `ESC`, `M-g`, and `M-o`. (`F1` and `F2` are aliases for `C-h` and `C-x 6`.) This list is not cast in stone; if you customize Emacs, you can make new prefix keys. You could even eliminate some of the standard ones, though this is not recommended for most users; for example, if you remove the prefix definition of `C-x 4`, then `C-x 4 C-f` becomes an invalid key sequence. See Section 33.3 [Key Bindings], page 428.

Typing the help character (`C-h` or `F1`) after a prefix key displays a list of the commands starting with that prefix. The sole exception to this rule is `ESC`: `ESC C-h` is equivalent to `C-M-h`, which does something else entirely. You can, however, use `F1` to display a list of commands starting with `ESC`.

2.3 Keys and Commands

This manual is full of passages that tell you what particular keys do. But Emacs does not assign meanings to keys directly. Instead, Emacs assigns meanings to named *commands*, and then gives keys their meanings by *binding* them to commands.

Every command has a name chosen by a programmer. The name is usually made of a few English words separated by dashes; for example, `next-line` or `forward-word`. Internally, each command is a special type of Lisp *function*, and the actions associated with the command are performed by running the function. See Section "What Is a Function" in *The Emacs Lisp Reference Manual*.

The bindings between keys and commands are recorded in tables called *keymaps*. See Section 33.3.1 [Keymaps], page 429.

When we say that "`C-n` moves down vertically one line" we are glossing over a subtle distinction that is irrelevant in ordinary use, but vital for Emacs customization. The command `next-line` does a vertical move downward. `C-n` has this effect *because* it is bound to `next-line`. If you rebind `C-n` to the command `forward-word`, `C-n` will move forward one word instead.

In this manual, we will often speak of keys like `C-n` as commands, even though strictly speaking the key is bound to a command. Usually we state the name of the command which really does the work in parentheses after mentioning the key that runs it. For example, we will say that "The command `C-n` (`next-line`) moves point vertically down", meaning that the command `next-line` moves vertically down, and the key `C-n` is normally bound to it.

Since we are discussing customization, we should tell you about *variables*. Often the description of a command will say, "To change this, set the variable `mumble-foo`." A variable is a name used to store a value. Most of the variables documented in this manual are meant for customization: some command or other part of Emacs examines the variable and behaves differently according to the value that you set. You can ignore the information about variables until you are interested in customizing them. Then read the basic information on variables (see Section 33.2 [Variables], page 420) and the information about specific variables will make sense.

3 Entering and Exiting Emacs

This chapter explains how to enter Emacs, and how to exit it.

3.1 Entering Emacs

The usual way to invoke Emacs is with the shell command `emacs`. From a terminal window running in the X Window System, you can run Emacs in the background with `emacs &`; this way, Emacs won't tie up the terminal window, so you can use it to run other shell commands.

When Emacs starts up, the initial frame displays a special buffer named '`*GNU Emacs*`'. This *startup screen* contains information about Emacs and *links* to common tasks that are useful for beginning users. For instance, activating the '`Emacs Tutorial`' link opens the Emacs tutorial; this does the same thing as the command `C-h t` (`help-with-tutorial`). To activate a link, either move point onto it and type `RET`, or click on it with `mouse-1` (the left mouse button).

Using a command line argument, you can tell Emacs to visit one or more files as soon as it starts up. For example, `emacs foo.txt` starts Emacs with a buffer displaying the contents of the file '`foo.txt`'. This feature exists mainly for compatibility with other editors, which are designed to be launched from the shell for short editing sessions. If you call Emacs this way, the initial frame is split into two windows—one showing the specified file, and the other showing the startup screen. See Chapter 17 [Windows], page 156.

Generally, it is unnecessary and wasteful to start Emacs afresh each time you want to edit a file. The recommended way to use Emacs is to start it just once, just after you log in, and do all your editing in the same Emacs session. See Chapter 15 [Files], page 122, for information on visiting more than one file. If you use Emacs this way, the Emacs session accumulates valuable context, such as the kill ring, registers, undo history, and mark ring data, which together make editing more convenient. These features are described later in the manual.

To edit a file from another program while Emacs is running, you can use the `emacsclient` helper program to open a file in the existing Emacs session. See Section 31.5 [Emacs Server], page 393.

Emacs accepts other command line arguments that tell it to load certain Lisp files, where to put the initial frame, and so forth. See Appendix C [Emacs Invocation], page 478.

If the variable `inhibit-startup-screen` is non-nil, Emacs does not display the startup screen. In that case, if one or more files were specified on the command line, Emacs simply displays those files; otherwise, it displays a buffer named `*scratch*`, which can be used to evaluate Emacs Lisp expressions interactively. See Section 24.10 [Lisp Interaction], page 279. You can set the variable `inhibit-startup-screen` using the Customize facility (see Section 33.1 [Easy Customization], page 412), or by editing your initialization file (see Section 33.4 [Init File], page 437).[1]

You can also force Emacs to display a file or directory at startup by setting the variable `initial-buffer-choice` to a string naming that file or directory. The value of

---

[1] Setting `inhibit-startup-screen` in `site-start.el` doesn't work, because the startup screen is set up before reading `site-start.el`. See Section 33.4 [Init File], page 437, for information about `site-start.el`.

`initial-buffer-choice` may also be a function (of no arguments) that should return a buffer which is then displayed. If `initial-buffer-choice` is non-`nil`, then if you specify any files on the command line, Emacs still visits them, but does not display them initially.

3.2 Exiting Emacs

C-x C-c   Kill Emacs (`save-buffers-kill-terminal`).

C-z   On a text terminal, suspend Emacs; on a graphical display, "minimize" the selected frame (`suspend-emacs`).

Killing Emacs means terminating the Emacs program. To do this, type C-x C-c (`save-buffers-kill-terminal`). A two-character key sequence is used to make it harder to type by accident. If there are any modified file-visiting buffers when you type C-x C-c, Emacs first offers to save these buffers. If you do not save them all, it asks for confirmation again, since the unsaved changes will be lost. Emacs also asks for confirmation if any subprocesses are still running, since killing Emacs will also kill the subprocesses (see Section 31.4 [Shell], page 383).

C-x C-c behaves specially if you are using Emacs as a server. If you type it from a "client frame", it closes the client connection. See Section 31.5 [Emacs Server], page 393.

Emacs can, optionally, record certain session information when you kill it, such as the files you were visiting at the time. This information is then available the next time you start Emacs. See Section 31.9 [Saving Emacs Sessions], page 403.

If the value of the variable `confirm-kill-emacs` is non-`nil`, C-x C-c assumes that its value is a predicate function, and calls that function. If the result of the function call is non-`nil`, the session is killed, otherwise Emacs continues to run. One convenient function to use as the value of `confirm-kill-emacs` is the function `yes-or-no-p`. The default value of `confirm-kill-emacs` is `nil`.

To kill Emacs without being prompted about saving, type M-x kill-emacs.

C-z runs the command `suspend-frame`. On a graphical display, this command *minimizes* (or *iconifies*) the selected Emacs frame, hiding it in a way that lets you bring it back later (exactly how this hiding occurs depends on the window system). On a text terminal, the C-z command *suspends* Emacs, stopping the program temporarily and returning control to the parent process (usually a shell); in most shells, you can resume Emacs after suspending it with the shell command `%emacs`.

Text terminals usually listen for certain special characters whose meaning is to kill or suspend the program you are running. **This terminal feature is turned off while you are in Emacs.** The meanings of C-z and C-x C-c as keys in Emacs were inspired by the use of C-z and C-c on several operating systems as the characters for stopping or killing a program, but that is their only relationship with the operating system. You can customize these keys to run any commands of your choice (see Section 33.3.1 [Keymaps], page 429).

4 Basic Editing Commands

Here we explain the basics of how to enter text, make corrections, and save the text in a file. If this material is new to you, we suggest you first run the Emacs learn-by-doing tutorial, by typing C-h t (help-with-tutorial).

4.1 Inserting Text

You can insert an ordinary *graphic character* (e.g., 'a', 'B', '3', and '=') by typing the associated key. This adds the character to the buffer at point. Insertion moves point forward, so that point remains just after the inserted text. See Section 1.1 [Point], page 6.

To end a line and start a new one, type RET (newline). (The RET key may be labeled Return or Enter on your keyboard, but we refer to it as RET in this manual.) This command inserts a newline character into the buffer, then indents (see Chapter 21 [Indentation], page 205) according to the major mode. If point is at the end of the line, the effect is to create a new blank line after it and indent the new line; if point is in the middle of a line, the line is split at that position. To turn off the auto-indentation, you can either disable Electric Indent mode (see Section 21.4 [Indent Convenience], page 207) or type C-j, which inserts just a newline, without any auto-indentation.

As we explain later in this manual, you can change the way Emacs handles text insertion by turning on *minor modes*. For instance, the minor mode called Auto Fill mode splits lines automatically when they get too long (see Section 22.5 [Filling], page 212). The minor mode called Overwrite mode causes inserted characters to replace (overwrite) existing text, instead of shoving it to the right. See Section 20.2 [Minor Modes], page 200.

Only graphic characters can be inserted by typing the associated key; other keys act as editing commands and do not insert themselves. For instance, DEL runs the command delete-backward-char by default (some modes bind it to a different command); it does not insert a literal 'DEL' character (ASCII character code 127).

To insert a non-graphic character, or a character that your keyboard does not support, first *quote* it by typing C-q (quoted-insert). There are two ways to use C-q:

- C-q followed by any non-graphic character (even C-g) inserts that character. For instance, C-q DEL inserts a literal 'DEL' character.

- C-q followed by a sequence of octal digits inserts the character with the specified octal character code. You can use any number of octal digits; any non-digit terminates the sequence. If the terminating character is RET, that RET serves only to terminate the sequence. Any other non-digit terminates the sequence and then acts as normal input—thus, C-q 1 0 1 B inserts 'AB'.

  The use of octal sequences is disabled in ordinary non-binary Overwrite mode, to give you a convenient way to insert a digit instead of overwriting with it.

To use decimal or hexadecimal instead of octal, set the variable read-quoted-char-radix to 10 or 16. If the radix is 16, the letters a to f serve as part of a character code, just like digits. Case is ignored.

Alternatively, you can use the command C-x 8 RET (insert-char). This prompts for the Unicode name or code-point of a character, using the minibuffer. If you enter a name, the command provides completion (see Section 5.4 [Completion], page 28). If you enter a code-point, it should be as a hexadecimal number (the convention for Unicode), or a number with a specified radix, e.g., #o23072 (octal); See Section "Integer Basics" in *The Emacs Lisp Reference Manual*. The command then inserts the corresponding character into the buffer. For example, both of the following insert the infinity sign (Unicode code-point U+221E):

```
C-x 8 RET infinity RET
C-x 8 RET 221e RET
```

A numeric argument to C-q or C-x 8 RET specifies how many copies of the character to insert (see Section 4.10 [Arguments], page 23).

4.2 Changing the Location of Point

To do more than insert characters, you have to know how to move point (see Section 1.1 [Point], page 6). The keyboard commands C-f, C-b, C-n, and C-p move point to the right, left, down, and up, respectively. You can also move point using the *arrow keys* present on most keyboards: RIGHT, LEFT, DOWN, and UP; however, many Emacs users find that it is slower to use the arrow keys than the control keys, because you need to move your hand to the area of the keyboard where those keys are located.

You can also click the left mouse button to move point to the position clicked. Emacs also provides a variety of additional keyboard commands that move point in more sophisticated ways.

C-f   Move forward one character (forward-char).

RIGHT   This command (right-char) behaves like C-f, with one exception: when editing right-to-left scripts such as Arabic, it instead moves *backward* if the current paragraph is a right-to-left paragraph. See Section 19.19 [Bidirectional Editing], page 197. If visual-order-cursor-movement is non-nil, this command moves to the character that is to the right of the current screen position, moving to the next or previous screen line as appropriate. Note that this might potentially move point many buffer positions away, depending on the surrounding bidirectional context.

C-b   Move backward one character (backward-char).

LEFT   This command (left-char) behaves like C-b, except it moves *forward* if the current paragraph is right-to-left. See Section 19.19 [Bidirectional Editing], page 197. If visual-order-cursor-movement is non-nil, this command moves to the character that is to the left of the current screen position, moving to the previous or next screen line as appropriate.

C-n
DOWN   Move down one screen line (next-line). This command attempts to keep the horizontal position unchanged, so if you start in the middle of one line, you move to the middle of the next.

C-p
UP   Move up one screen line (previous-line). This command preserves position within the line, like C-n.

C-a
Home   Move to the beginning of the line (`move-beginning-of-line`).

C-e
End   Move to the end of the line (`move-end-of-line`).

M-f   Move forward one word (`forward-word`).

C-RIGHT
M-RIGHT   This command (`right-word`) behaves like M-f, except it moves *backward* by one word if the current paragraph is right-to-left. See Section 19.19 [Bidirectional Editing], page 197.

M-b   Move backward one word (`backward-word`).

C-LEFT
M-LEFT   This command (`left-word`) behaves like M-b, except it moves *forward* by one word if the current paragraph is right-to-left. See Section 19.19 [Bidirectional Editing], page 197.

M-r   Without moving the text on the screen, reposition point on the left margin of the center-most text line of the window; on subsequent consecutive invocations, move point to the left margin of the top-most line, the bottom-most line, and so forth, in cyclic order (`move-to-window-line-top-bottom`).

                A numeric argument says which screen line to place point on, counting downward from the top of the window (zero means the top line). A negative argument counts lines up from the bottom (−1 means the bottom line). See Section 4.10 [Arguments], page 23, for more information on numeric arguments.

M-<   Move to the top of the buffer (`beginning-of-buffer`). With numeric argument *n*, move to *n*/10 of the way from the top.

M->   Move to the end of the buffer (`end-of-buffer`).

C-v
PageDown
next   Scroll the display one screen forward, and move point onscreen if necessary (`scroll-up-command`). See Section 11.1 [Scrolling], page 69.

M-v
PageUp
prior   Scroll one screen backward, and move point onscreen if necessary (`scroll-down-command`). See Section 11.1 [Scrolling], page 69.

M-g c   Read a number *n* and move point to buffer position *n*. Position 1 is the beginning of the buffer.

M-g M-g
M-g g   Read a number *n* and move point to the beginning of line number *n* (`goto-line`). Line 1 is the beginning of the buffer. If point is on or just after a number in the buffer, that is the default for *n*. Just type RET in the minibuffer to use it. You can also specify *n* by giving M-g M-g a numeric prefix argument. See Section 16.1 [Select Buffer], page 147, for the behavior of M-g M-g when you give it a plain prefix argument.

M-g TAB   Read a number *n* and move to column *n* in the current line. Column 0 is the leftmost column. If called with a prefix argument, move to the column number specified by the argument's numeric value.

C-x C-n   Use the current column of point as the *semipermanent goal column* for C-n and C-p (`set-goal-column`). When a semipermanent goal column is in effect, those commands always try to move to this column, or as close as possible to it, after moving vertically. The goal column remains in effect until canceled.

C-u C-x C-n

   Cancel the goal column. Henceforth, C-n and C-p try to preserve the horizontal position, as usual.

When a line of text in the buffer is longer than the width of the window, Emacs usually displays it on two or more *screen lines*. For convenience, C-n and C-p move point by screen lines, as do the equivalent keys **down** and **up**. You can force these commands to move according to *logical lines* (i.e., according to the text lines in the buffer) by setting the variable `line-move-visual` to `nil`; if a logical line occupies multiple screen lines, the cursor then skips over the additional screen lines. For details, see Section 4.8 [Continuation Lines], page 22. See Section 33.2 [Variables], page 420, for how to set variables such as `line-move-visual`.

Unlike C-n and C-p, most of the Emacs commands that work on lines work on *logical* lines. For instance, C-a (`move-beginning-of-line`) and C-e (`move-end-of-line`) respectively move to the beginning and end of the logical line. Whenever we encounter commands that work on screen lines, such as C-n and C-p, we will point these out.

When `line-move-visual` is `nil`, you can also set the variable `track-eol` to a non-`nil` value. Then C-n and C-p, when starting at the end of the logical line, move to the end of the next logical line. Normally, `track-eol` is `nil`.

C-n normally stops at the end of the buffer when you use it on the last line in the buffer. However, if you set the variable `next-line-add-newlines` to a non-`nil` value, C-n on the last line of a buffer creates an additional line at the end and moves down into it.

4.3 Erasing Text

DEL
BACKSPACE

   Delete the character before point, or the region if it is active (`delete-backward-char`).

Delete   Delete the character after point, or the region if it is active (`delete-forward-char`).

C-d   Delete the character after point (`delete-char`).

C-k   Kill to the end of the line (`kill-line`).

M-d   Kill forward to the end of the next word (`kill-word`).

M-DEL   Kill back to the beginning of the previous word (`backward-kill-word`).

The DEL (`delete-backward-char`) command removes the character before point, moving the cursor and the characters after it backwards. If point was at the beginning of a line, this deletes the preceding newline, joining this line to the previous one.

If, however, the region is active, DEL instead deletes the text in the region. See Chapter 8 [Mark], page 45, for a description of the region.

On most keyboards, DEL is labeled BACKSPACE, but we refer to it as DEL in this manual. (Do not confuse DEL with the `Delete` key; we will discuss `Delete` momentarily.) On some text terminals, Emacs may not recognize the DEL key properly. See Section 34.2.1 [DEL Does Not Delete], page 444, if you encounter this problem.

The `Delete` (`delete-forward-char`) command deletes in the "opposite direction": it deletes the character after point, i.e., the character under the cursor. If point was at the end of a line, this joins the following line onto this one. Like DEL, it deletes the text in the region if the region is active (see Chapter 8 [Mark], page 45).

`C-d` (`delete-char`) deletes the character after point, similar to `Delete`, but regardless of whether the region is active.

See Section 9.1.1 [Deletion], page 52, for more detailed information about the above deletion commands.

`C-k` (`kill-line`) erases (kills) a line at a time. If you type `C-k` at the beginning or middle of a line, it kills all the text up to the end of the line. If you type `C-k` at the end of a line, it joins that line with the following line.

See Chapter 9 [Killing], page 52, for more information about `C-k` and related commands.

4.4 Undoing Changes

C-/   Undo one entry of the undo records—usually, one command worth (`undo`).

C-x u
C-_   The same.

Emacs records a list of changes made in the buffer text, so you can undo recent changes. This is done using the `undo` command, which is bound to `C-/` (as well as `C-x u` and `C-_`). Normally, this command undoes the last change, moving point back to where it was before the change. The undo command applies only to changes in the buffer; you can't use it to undo cursor motion.

Although each editing command usually makes a separate entry in the undo records, very simple commands may be grouped together. Sometimes, an entry may cover just part of a complex command.

If you repeat `C-/` (or its aliases), each repetition undoes another, earlier change, back to the limit of the undo information available. If all recorded changes have already been undone, the undo command displays an error message and does nothing.

To learn more about the `undo` command, see Section 13.1 [Undo], page 109.

4.5 Files

Text that you insert in an Emacs buffer lasts only as long as the Emacs session. To keep any text permanently, you must put it in a *file*.

Suppose there is a file named `test.emacs` in your home directory. To begin editing this file in Emacs, type

```
C-x C-f test.emacs RET
```

Here the file name is given as an *argument* to the command C-x C-f (`find-file`). That command uses the *minibuffer* to read the argument, and you type RET to terminate the argument (see Chapter 5 [Minibuffer], page 26).

Emacs obeys this command by *visiting* the file: it creates a buffer, copies the contents of the file into the buffer, and then displays the buffer for editing. If you alter the text, you can *save* the new text in the file by typing C-x C-s (`save-buffer`). This copies the altered buffer contents back into the file `test.emacs`, making them permanent. Until you save, the changed text exists only inside Emacs, and the file `test.emacs` is unaltered.

To create a file, just visit it with C-x C-f as if it already existed. This creates an empty buffer, in which you can insert the text you want to put in the file. Emacs actually creates the file the first time you save this buffer with C-x C-s.

To learn more about using files in Emacs, see Chapter 15 [Files], page 122.

4.6 Help

If you forget what a key does, you can find out by typing C-h k (`describe-key`), followed by the key of interest; for example, C-h k C-n tells you what C-n does.

The prefix key C-h stands for "help". The key F1 serves as an alias for C-h. Apart from C-h k, there are many other help commands providing different kinds of help.

See Chapter 7 [Help], page 37, for details.

4.7 Blank Lines

Here are special commands and techniques for inserting and deleting blank lines.

C-o   Insert a blank line after the cursor (`open-line`).

C-x C-o   Delete all but one of many consecutive blank lines (`delete-blank-lines`).

We have seen how RET (`newline`) starts a new line of text. However, it may be easier to see what you are doing if you first make a blank line and then insert the desired text into it. This is easy to do using the key C-o (`open-line`), which inserts a newline after point but leaves point in front of the newline. After C-o, type the text for the new line.

You can make several blank lines by typing C-o several times, or by giving it a numeric argument specifying how many blank lines to make. See Section 4.10 [Arguments], page 23, for how. If you have a fill prefix, the C-o command inserts the fill prefix on the new line, if typed at the beginning of a line. See Section 22.5.3 [Fill Prefix], page 214.

The easy way to get rid of extra blank lines is with the command C-x C-o (`delete-blank-lines`). If point lies within a run of several blank lines, C-x C-o deletes all but one of them. If point is on a single blank line, C-x C-o deletes it. If point is on a nonblank line, C-x C-o deletes all following blank lines, if any exists.

4.8 Continuation Lines

Sometimes, a line of text in the buffer—a *logical line*—is too long to fit in the window, and Emacs displays it as two or more *screen lines*. This is called *line wrapping* or *continuation*, and the long logical line is called a *continued line*. On a graphical display, Emacs indicates line wrapping with small bent arrows in the left and right window fringes. On a text terminal, Emacs indicates line wrapping by displaying a '\' character at the right margin.

Most commands that act on lines act on logical lines, not screen lines. For instance, C-k kills a logical line. As described earlier, C-n (next-line) and C-p (previous-line) are special exceptions: they move point down and up, respectively, by one screen line (see Section 4.2 [Moving Point], page 17).

Emacs can optionally *truncate* long logical lines instead of continuing them. This means that every logical line occupies a single screen line; if it is longer than the width of the window, the rest of the line is not displayed. On a graphical display, a truncated line is indicated by a small straight arrow in the right fringe; on a text terminal, it is indicated by a '$' character in the right margin. See Section 11.21 [Line Truncation], page 87.

By default, continued lines are wrapped at the right window edge. Since the wrapping may occur in the middle of a word, continued lines can be difficult to read. The usual solution is to break your lines before they get too long, by inserting newlines. If you prefer, you can make Emacs insert a newline automatically when a line gets too long, by using Auto Fill mode. See Section 22.5 [Filling], page 212.

Sometimes, you may need to edit files containing many long logical lines, and it may not be practical to break them all up by adding newlines. In that case, you can use Visual Line mode, which enables *word wrapping*: instead of wrapping long lines exactly at the right window edge, Emacs wraps them at the word boundaries (i.e., space or tab characters) nearest to the right window edge. Visual Line mode also redefines editing commands such as C-a, C-n, and C-k to operate on screen lines rather than logical lines. See Section 11.22 [Visual Line Mode], page 87.

4.9 Cursor Position Information

Here are commands to get information about the size and position of parts of the buffer, and to count words and lines.

M-x what-line
> Display the line number of point.

M-x line-number-mode
M-x column-number-mode
> Toggle automatic display of the current line number or column number. See Section 11.18 [Optional Mode Line], page 84.

M-=
> Display the number of lines, words, and characters that are present in the region (count-words-region). See Chapter 8 [Mark], page 45, for information about the region.

M-x count-words
> Display the number of lines, words, and characters that are present in the buffer. If the region is active (see Chapter 8 [Mark], page 45), display the numbers for the region instead.

C-x =   Display the character code of character after point, character position of point, and column of point (`what-cursor-position`).

M-x `hl-line-mode`
            Enable or disable highlighting of the current line. See Section 11.20 [Cursor Display], page 86.

M-x `size-indication-mode`
            Toggle automatic display of the size of the buffer. See Section 11.18 [Optional Mode Line], page 84.

M-x `what-line` displays the current line number in the echo area. This command is usually redundant, because the current line number is shown in the mode line (see Section 1.3 [Mode Line], page 8). However, if you narrow the buffer, the mode line shows the line number relative to the accessible portion (see Section 11.5 [Narrowing], page 73). By contrast, `what-line` displays both the line number relative to the narrowed region and the line number relative to the whole buffer.

M-= (`count-words-region`) displays a message reporting the number of lines, words, and characters in the region (see Chapter 8 [Mark], page 45, for an explanation of the region). With a prefix argument, C-u M-=, the command displays a count for the entire buffer.

The command M-x `count-words` does the same job, but with a different calling convention. It displays a count for the region if the region is active, and for the buffer otherwise.

The command C-x = (`what-cursor-position`) shows information about the current cursor position and the buffer contents at that position. It displays a line in the echo area that looks like this:

```
Char: c (99, #o143, #x63) point=28062 of 36168 (78%) column=53
```

After 'Char:', this shows the character in the buffer at point. The text inside the parenthesis shows the corresponding decimal, octal and hex character codes; for more information about how C-x = displays character information, see Section 19.1 [International Chars], page 177. After 'point=' is the position of point as a character count (the first character in the buffer is position 1, the second character is position 2, and so on). The number after that is the total number of characters in the buffer, and the number in parenthesis expresses the position as a percentage of the total. After 'column=' is the horizontal position of point, in columns counting from the left edge of the window.

If the buffer has been narrowed, making some of the text at the beginning and the end temporarily inaccessible, C-x = displays additional text describing the currently accessible range. For example, it might display this:

```
Char: C (67, #o103, #x43) point=252 of 889 (28%) <231-599> column=0
```

where the two extra numbers give the smallest and largest character position that point is allowed to assume. The characters between those two positions are the accessible ones. See Section 11.5 [Narrowing], page 73.

4.10 Numeric Arguments

In the terminology of mathematics and computing, *argument* means "data provided to a function or operation". You can give any Emacs command a *numeric argument* (also called a *prefix argument*). Some commands interpret the argument as a repetition count. For example, giving C-f an argument of ten causes it to move point forward by ten characters instead of one. With these commands, no argument is equivalent to an argument of one, and negative arguments cause them to move or act in the opposite direction.

The easiest way to specify a numeric argument is to type a digit and/or a minus sign while holding down the META key. For example,

```
M-5 C-n
```

moves down five lines. The keys M-1, M-2, and so on, as well as M--, are bound to commands (`digit-argument` and `negative-argument`) that set up an argument for the next command. M-- without digits normally means −1.

If you enter more than one digit, you need not hold down the META key for the second and subsequent digits. Thus, to move down fifty lines, type

```
M-5 0 C-n
```

Note that this *does not* insert five copies of '0' and move down one line, as you might expect—the '0' is treated as part of the prefix argument.

(What if you do want to insert five copies of '0'? Type M-5 C-u 0. Here, C-u "terminates" the prefix argument, so that the next keystroke begins the command that you want to execute. Note that this meaning of C-u applies only to this case. For the usual role of C-u, see below.)

Instead of typing M-1, M-2, and so on, another way to specify a numeric argument is to type C-u (`universal-argument`) followed by some digits, or (for a negative argument) a minus sign followed by digits. A minus sign without digits normally means −1.

C-u alone has the special meaning of "four times": it multiplies the argument for the next command by four. C-u C-u multiplies it by sixteen. Thus, C-u C-u C-f moves forward sixteen characters. Other useful combinations are C-u C-n, C-u C-u C-n (move down a good fraction of a screen), C-u C-u C-o (make "a lot" of blank lines), and C-u C-k (kill four lines).

You can use a numeric argument before a self-inserting character to insert multiple copies of it. This is straightforward when the character is not a digit; for example, C-u 6 4 a inserts 64 copies of the character 'a'. But this does not work for inserting digits; C-u 6 4 1 specifies an argument of 641. You can separate the argument from the digit to insert with another C-u; for example, C-u 6 4 C-u 1 does insert 64 copies of the character '1'.

Some commands care whether there is an argument, but ignore its value. For example, the command M-q (`fill-paragraph`) fills text; with an argument, it justifies the text as well. (See Section 22.5 [Filling], page 212, for more information on M-q.) For these commands, it is enough to specify the argument with a single C-u.

Some commands use the value of the argument as a repeat count, but do something special when there is no argument. For example, the command C-k (`kill-line`) with argument *n* kills *n* lines, including their terminating newlines. But C-k with no argument is special: it kills the text up to the next newline, or, if point is right at the end of the line, it kills the newline itself. Thus, two C-k commands with no arguments can kill a nonblank line, just like C-k with an argument of one. (See Chapter 9 [Killing], page 52, for more information on C-k.)

A few commands treat a plain C-u differently from an ordinary argument. A few others may treat an argument of just a minus sign differently from an argument of −1. These unusual cases are described when they come up; they exist to make an individual command more convenient, and they are documented in that command's documentation string.

We use the term *prefix argument* to emphasize that you type such arguments before the command, and to distinguish them from minibuffer arguments (see Chapter 5 [Minibuffer], page 26), which are entered after invoking the command.

4.11 Repeating a Command

Many simple commands, such as those invoked with a single key or with `M-x command-name RET`, can be repeated by invoking them with a numeric argument that serves as a repeat count (see Section 4.10 [Arguments], page 23). However, if the command you want to repeat prompts for input, or uses a numeric argument in another way, that method won't work.

The command `C-x z` (`repeat`) provides another way to repeat an Emacs command many times. This command repeats the previous Emacs command, whatever that was. Repeating a command uses the same arguments that were used before; it does not read new arguments each time.

To repeat the command more than once, type additional `z`'s: each `z` repeats the command one more time. Repetition ends when you type a character other than `z`, or press a mouse button.

For example, suppose you type `C-u 2 0 C-d` to delete 20 characters. You can repeat that command (including its argument) three additional times, to delete a total of 80 characters, by typing `C-x z z z`. The first `C-x z` repeats the command once, and each subsequent `z` repeats it once again.

5 The Minibuffer

The *minibuffer* is where Emacs commands read complicated arguments, such as file names, buffer names, Emacs command names, or Lisp expressions. We call it the "minibuffer" because it's a special-purpose buffer with a small amount of screen space. You can use the usual Emacs editing commands in the minibuffer to edit the argument text.

5.1 Using the Minibuffer

When the minibuffer is in use, it appears in the echo area, with a cursor. The minibuffer starts with a *prompt*, usually ending with a colon. The prompt states what kind of input is expected, and how it will be used. The prompt is highlighted using the `minibuffer-prompt` face (see Section 11.8 [Faces], page 74).

The simplest way to enter a minibuffer argument is to type the text, then `RET` to submit the argument and exit the minibuffer. Alternatively, you can type `C-g` to exit the minibuffer by canceling the command asking for the argument (see Section 34.1 [Quitting], page 443).

Sometimes, the prompt shows a *default argument*, inside parentheses before the colon. This default will be used as the argument if you just type `RET`. For example, commands that read buffer names usually show a buffer name as the default; you can type `RET` to operate on that default buffer.

If you enable Minibuffer Electric Default mode, a global minor mode, Emacs hides the default argument as soon as you modify the contents of the minibuffer (since typing `RET` would no longer submit that default). If you ever bring back the original minibuffer text, the prompt again shows the default. Furthermore, if you change the variable `minibuffer-eldef-shorten-default` to a non-`nil` value, the default argument is displayed as '`[default]`' instead of '`(default default)`', saving some screen space. To enable this minor mode, type `M-x minibuffer-electric-default-mode`.

Since the minibuffer appears in the echo area, it can conflict with other uses of the echo area. If an error message or an informative message is emitted while the minibuffer is active, the message hides the minibuffer for a few seconds, or until you type something; then the minibuffer comes back. While the minibuffer is in use, keystrokes do not echo.

5.2 Minibuffers for File Names

Commands such as `C-x C-f` (`find-file`) use the minibuffer to read a file name argument (see Section 4.5 [Basic Files], page 20). When the minibuffer is used to read a file name, it typically starts out with some initial text ending in a slash. This is the *default directory*. For example, it may start out like this:

    Find file: /u2/emacs/src/

Here, '`Find file: `' is the prompt and '`/u2/emacs/src/`' is the default directory. If you now type `buffer.c` as input, that specifies the file `/u2/emacs/src/buffer.c`. See Section 15.1 [File Names], page 122, for information about the default directory.

You can specify the parent directory with `..`: `/a/b/../foo.el` is equivalent to `/a/foo.el`. Alternatively, you can use `M-DEL` to kill directory names backwards (see Section 22.1 [Words], page 208).

To specify a file in a completely different directory, you can kill the entire default with `C-a C-k` (see Section 5.3 [Minibuffer Edit], page 27). Alternatively, you can ignore the default, and enter an absolute file name starting with a slash or a tilde after the default directory. For example, you can specify `/etc/termcap` as follows:

    Find file: /u2/emacs/src//etc/termcap

Emacs interprets a double slash as "ignore everything before the second slash in the pair". In the example above, `/u2/emacs/src/` is ignored, so the argument you supplied is `/etc/termcap`. The ignored part of the file name is dimmed if the terminal allows it. (To disable this dimming, turn off File Name Shadow mode with the command `M-x file-name-shadow-mode`.)

Emacs interprets `~/` as your home directory. Thus, `~/foo/bar.txt` specifies a file named `bar.txt`, inside a directory named `foo`, which is in turn located in your home directory. In addition, `~user-id/` means the home directory of a user whose login name is *user-id*. Any leading directory name in front of the `~` is ignored: thus, `/u2/emacs/~/foo/bar.txt` is equivalent to `~/foo/bar.txt`.

On MS-Windows and MS-DOS systems, where a user doesn't always have a home directory, Emacs uses several alternatives. For MS-Windows, see Section G.5 [Windows HOME], page 508; for MS-DOS, see Section "MS-DOS File Names" in *the digital version of the Emacs Manual*. On these systems, the `~user-id/` construct is supported only for the current user, i.e., only if *user-id* is the current user's login name.

To prevent Emacs from inserting the default directory when reading file names, change the variable `insert-default-directory` to `nil`. In that case, the minibuffer starts out empty. Nonetheless, relative file name arguments are still interpreted based on the same default directory.

You can also enter remote file names in the minibuffer. See Section 15.13 [Remote Files], page 142.

5.3 Editing in the Minibuffer

The minibuffer is an Emacs buffer, albeit a peculiar one, and the usual Emacs commands are available for editing the argument text. (The prompt, however, is *read-only*, and cannot be changed.)

Since `RET` in the minibuffer submits the argument, you can't use it to insert a newline. You can do that with `C-q C-j`, which inserts a `C-j` control character, which is formally equivalent to a newline character (see Section 4.1 [Inserting Text], page 16). Alternatively, you can use the `C-o` (`open-line`) command (see Section 4.7 [Blank Lines], page 21).

Inside a minibuffer, the keys `TAB`, `SPC`, and `?` are often bound to *completion commands*, which allow you to easily fill in the desired text without typing all of it. See Section 5.4 [Completion], page 28. As with `RET`, you can use `C-q` to insert a `TAB`, `SPC`, or '?' character.

For convenience, `C-a` (`move-beginning-of-line`) in a minibuffer moves point to the beginning of the argument text, not the beginning of the prompt. For example, this allows you to erase the entire argument with `C-a C-k`.

When the minibuffer is active, the echo area is treated much like an ordinary Emacs window. For instance, you can switch to another window (with `C-x o`), edit text there, then return to the minibuffer window to finish the argument. You can even kill text in another window, return to the minibuffer window, and yank the text into the argument. There are some restrictions on the minibuffer window, however: for instance, you cannot split it. See Chapter 17 [Windows], page 156.

Normally, the minibuffer window occupies a single screen line. However, if you add two or more lines' worth of text into the minibuffer, it expands automatically to accommodate the text. The variable `resize-mini-windows` controls the resizing of the minibuffer. The default value is `grow-only`, which means the behavior we have just described. If the value is `t`, the minibuffer window will also shrink automatically if you remove some lines of text from the minibuffer, down to a minimum of one screen line. If the value is `nil`, the minibuffer window never changes size automatically, but you can use the usual window-resizing commands on it (see Chapter 17 [Windows], page 156).

The variable `max-mini-window-height` controls the maximum height for resizing the minibuffer window. A floating-point number specifies a fraction of the frame's height; an integer specifies the maximum number of lines; `nil` means do not resize the minibuffer window automatically. The default value is 0.25.

The `C-M-v` command in the minibuffer scrolls the help text from commands that display help text of any sort in another window. You can also scroll the help text with `M-prior` and `M-next` (or, equivalently, `M-PageUp` and `M-PageDown`). This is especially useful with long lists of possible completions. See Section 17.3 [Other Window], page 157.

Emacs normally disallows most commands that use the minibuffer while the minibuffer is active. To allow such commands in the minibuffer, set the variable `enable-recursive-minibuffers` to `t`.

When not active, the minibuffer is in `minibuffer-inactive-mode`, and clicking `Mouse-1` there shows the `*Messages*` buffer. If you use a dedicated frame for minibuffers, Emacs also recognizes certain keys there, for example `n` to make a new frame.

5.4 Completion

You can often use a feature called *completion* to help enter arguments. This means that after you type part of the argument, Emacs can fill in the rest, or some of it, based on what was typed so far.

When completion is available, certain keys (usually `TAB`, `RET`, and `SPC`) are rebound in the minibuffer to special completion commands (see Section 5.4.2 [Completion Commands], page 29). These commands attempt to complete the text in the minibuffer, based on a set of *completion alternatives* provided by the command that requested the argument. You can usually type `?` to see a list of completion alternatives.

Although completion is usually done in the minibuffer, the feature is sometimes available in ordinary buffers too. See Section 23.8 [Symbol Completion], page 254.

5.4.1 Completion Example

A simple example may help here. `M-x` uses the minibuffer to read the name of a command, so completion works by matching the minibuffer text against the names of existing Emacs commands. Suppose you wish to run the command `auto-fill-mode`. You can do that by typing `M-x auto-fill-mode RET`, but it is easier to use completion.

If you type `M-x a u TAB`, the `TAB` looks for completion alternatives (in this case, command names) that start with 'au'. There are several, including `auto-fill-mode` and `autoconf-mode`, but they all begin with `auto`, so the 'au' in the minibuffer completes to 'auto'. (More commands may be defined in your Emacs session. For example, if a command called `authorize-me` was defined, Emacs could only complete as far as 'aut'.)

If you type `TAB` again immediately, it cannot determine the next character; it could be '-', 'a', or 'c'. So it does not add any characters; instead, `TAB` displays a list of all possible completions in another window.

Next, type `-f`. The minibuffer now contains 'auto-f', and the only command name that starts with this is `auto-fill-mode`. If you now type `TAB`, completion fills in the rest of the argument 'auto-fill-mode' into the minibuffer.

Hence, typing just `a u TAB - f TAB` allows you to enter 'auto-fill-mode'.

5.4.2 Completion Commands

Here is a list of the completion commands defined in the minibuffer when completion is allowed.

`TAB`   Complete the text in the minibuffer as much as possible; if unable to complete, display a list of possible completions (`minibuffer-complete`).

`SPC`   Complete up to one word from the minibuffer text before point (`minibuffer-complete-word`). This command is not available for arguments that often include spaces, such as file names.

`RET`   Submit the text in the minibuffer as the argument, possibly completing first (`minibuffer-complete-and-exit`). See Section 5.4.3 [Completion Exit], page 30.

`?`   Display a list of completions (`minibuffer-completion-help`).

`TAB` (`minibuffer-complete`) is the most fundamental completion command. It searches for all possible completions that match the existing minibuffer text, and attempts to complete as much as it can. See Section 5.4.4 [Completion Styles], page 31, for how completion alternatives are chosen.

`SPC` (`minibuffer-complete-word`) completes like `TAB`, but only up to the next hyphen or space. If you have 'auto-f' in the minibuffer and type `SPC`, it finds that the completion is 'auto-fill-mode', but it only inserts 'ill-', giving 'auto-fill-'. Another `SPC` at this point completes all the way to 'auto-fill-mode'.

If `TAB` or `SPC` is unable to complete, it displays a list of matching completion alternatives (if there are any) in another window. You can display the same list with `?` (`minibuffer-completion-help`). The following commands can be used with the completion list:

`Mouse-1`
`Mouse-2`   Clicking mouse button 1 or 2 on a completion alternative chooses it (`mouse-choose-completion`).

`M-v`
`PageUp`
`prior`   Typing `M-v`, while in the minibuffer, selects the window showing the completion list (`switch-to-completions`). This paves the way for using the commands

below. `PageUp` or `prior` does the same. You can also select the window in other ways (see Chapter 17 [Windows], page 156).

RET   While in the completion list buffer, this chooses the completion at point (`choose-completion`).

RIGHT   While in the completion list buffer, this moves point to the following completion alternative (`next-completion`).

LEFT   While in the completion list buffer, this moves point to the previous completion alternative (`previous-completion`).

5.4.3 Completion Exit

When a command reads an argument using the minibuffer with completion, it also controls what happens when you type RET (`minibuffer-complete-and-exit`) to submit the argument. There are four types of behavior:

- *Strict completion* accepts only exact completion matches. Typing RET exits the minibuffer only if the minibuffer text is an exact match, or completes to one. Otherwise, Emacs refuses to exit the minibuffer; instead it tries to complete, and if no completion can be done it momentarily displays '[No match]' after the minibuffer text. (You can still leave the minibuffer by typing `C-g` to cancel the command.)

  An example of a command that uses this behavior is `M-x`, since it is meaningless for it to accept a non-existent command name.

- *Cautious completion* is like strict completion, except RET exits only if the text is already an exact match. If the text completes to an exact match, RET performs that completion but does not exit yet; you must type a second RET to exit.

  Cautious completion is used for reading file names for files that must already exist, for example.

- *Permissive completion* allows any input; the completion candidates are just suggestions. Typing RET does not complete, it just submits the argument as you have entered it.

- *Permissive completion with confirmation* is like permissive completion, with an exception: if you typed TAB and this completed the text up to some intermediate state (i.e., one that is not yet an exact completion match), typing RET right afterward does not submit the argument. Instead, Emacs asks for confirmation by momentarily displaying '[Confirm]' after the text; type RET again to confirm and submit the text. This catches a common mistake, in which one types RET before realizing that TAB did not complete as far as desired.

  You can tweak the confirmation behavior by customizing the variable `confirm-nonexistent-file-or-buffer`. The default value, `after-completion`, gives the behavior we have just described. If you change it to `nil`, Emacs does not ask for confirmation, falling back on permissive completion. If you change it to any other non-`nil` value, Emacs asks for confirmation whether or not the preceding command was TAB.

  This behavior is used by most commands that read file names, like `C-x C-f`, and commands that read buffer names, like `C-x b`.

5.4.4 How Completion Alternatives Are Chosen

Completion commands work by narrowing a large list of possible completion alternatives to a smaller subset that "matches" what you have typed in the minibuffer. In Section 5.4.1 [Completion Example], page 28, we gave a simple example of such matching. The procedure of determining what constitutes a "match" is quite intricate. Emacs attempts to offer plausible completions under most circumstances.

Emacs performs completion using one or more *completion styles*—sets of criteria for matching minibuffer text to completion alternatives. During completion, Emacs tries each completion style in turn. If a style yields one or more matches, that is used as the list of completion alternatives. If a style produces no matches, Emacs falls back on the next style.

The list variable `completion-styles` specifies the completion styles to use. Each list element is the name of a completion style (a Lisp symbol). The default completion styles are (in order):

basic   A matching completion alternative must have the same beginning as the text in the minibuffer before point. Furthermore, if there is any text in the minibuffer after point, the rest of the completion alternative must contain that text as a substring.

partial-completion
             This aggressive completion style divides the minibuffer text into words separated by hyphens or spaces, and completes each word separately. (For example, when completing command names, 'em-l-m' completes to 'emacs-lisp-mode'.)

             Furthermore, a '*' in the minibuffer text is treated as a *wildcard*—it matches any character at the corresponding position in the completion alternative.

emacs22   This completion style is similar to basic, except that it ignores the text in the minibuffer after point. It is so-named because it corresponds to the completion behavior in Emacs 22.

The following additional completion styles are also defined, and you can add them to `completion-styles` if you wish (see Chapter 33 [Customization], page 412):

substring
             A matching completion alternative must contain the text in the minibuffer before point, and the text in the minibuffer after point, as substrings (in that same order).

             Thus, if the text in the minibuffer is 'foobar', with point between 'foo' and 'bar', that matches 'afoobbarc', where *a*, *b*, and *c* can be any string including the empty string.

initials   This very aggressive completion style attempts to complete acronyms and initialisms. For example, when completing command names, it matches 'lch' to 'list-command-history'.

There is also a very simple completion style called `emacs21`. In this style, if the text in the minibuffer is 'foobar', only matches starting with 'foobar' are considered.

You can use different completion styles in different situations, by setting the variable `completion-category-overrides`. For example, the default setting says to use only `basic` and `substring` completion for buffer names.

5.4.5 Completion Options

Case is significant when completing case-sensitive arguments, such as command names. For example, when completing command names, 'AU' does not complete to 'auto-fill-mode'. Case differences are ignored when completing arguments in which case does not matter.

When completing file names, case differences are ignored if the variable read-file-name-completion-ignore-case is non-nil. The default value is nil on systems that have case-sensitive file-names, such as GNU/Linux; it is non-nil on systems that have case-insensitive file-names, such as Microsoft Windows. When completing buffer names, case differences are ignored if the variable read-buffer-completion-ignore-case is non-nil; the default is nil.

When completing file names, Emacs usually omits certain alternatives that are considered unlikely to be chosen, as determined by the list variable completion-ignored-extensions. Each element in the list should be a string; any file name ending in such a string is ignored as a completion alternative. Any element ending in a slash (/) represents a subdirectory name. The standard value of completion-ignored-extensions has several elements including ".o", ".elc", and "~". For example, if a directory contains 'foo.c' and 'foo.elc', 'foo' completes to 'foo.c'. However, if *all* possible completions end in "ignored" strings, they are not ignored: in the previous example, 'foo.e' completes to 'foo.elc'. Emacs disregards completion-ignored-extensions when showing completion alternatives in the completion list.

Shell completion is an extended version of filename completion, see Section 31.4.7 [Shell Options], page 390.

If completion-auto-help is set to nil, the completion commands never display the completion list buffer; you must type ? to display the list. If the value is lazy, Emacs only shows the completion list buffer on the second attempt to complete. In other words, if there is nothing to complete, the first TAB echoes 'Next char not unique'; the second TAB shows the completion list buffer.

If completion-cycle-threshold is non-nil, completion commands can "cycle" through completion alternatives. Normally, if there is more than one completion alternative for the text in the minibuffer, a completion command completes up to the longest common substring. If you change completion-cycle-threshold to t, the completion command instead completes to the first of those completion alternatives; each subsequent invocation of the completion command replaces that with the next completion alternative, in a cyclic manner. If you give completion-cycle-threshold a numeric value n, completion commands switch to this cycling behavior only when there are n or fewer alternatives.

5.5 Minibuffer History

Every argument that you enter with the minibuffer is saved in a *minibuffer history list* so you can easily use it again later. You can use the following arguments to quickly fetch an earlier argument into the minibuffer:

M-p
UP   Move to the previous item in the minibuffer history, an earlier argument
                (previous-history-element).

M-n

DOWN   Move to the next item in the minibuffer history (`next-history-element`).

M-r *regexp* RET

         Move to an earlier item in the minibuffer history that matches *regexp*
         (`previous-matching-history-element`).

M-s *regexp* RET

         Move to a later item in the minibuffer history that matches *regexp*
         (`next-matching-history-element`).

While in the minibuffer, `M-p` or `UP` (`previous-history-element`) moves through the minibuffer history list, one item at a time. Each `M-p` fetches an earlier item from the history list into the minibuffer, replacing its existing contents. Typing `M-n` or `DOWN` (`next-history-element`) moves through the minibuffer history list in the opposite direction, fetching later entries into the minibuffer.

If you type `M-n` in the minibuffer when there are no later entries in the minibuffer history (e.g., if you haven't previously typed `M-p`), Emacs tries fetching from a list of default arguments: values that you are likely to enter. You can think of this as moving through the "future history" list.

If you edit the text inserted by the `M-p` or `M-n` minibuffer history commands, this does not change its entry in the history list. However, the edited argument does go at the end of the history list when you submit it.

You can use `M-r` (`previous-matching-history-element`) to search through older elements in the history list, and `M-s` (`next-matching-history-element`) to search through newer entries. Each of these commands asks for a *regular expression* as an argument, and fetches the first matching entry into the minibuffer. See Section 12.6 [Regexps], page 97, for an explanation of regular expressions. A numeric prefix argument n means to fetch the nth matching entry. These commands are unusual, in that they use the minibuffer to read the regular expression argument, even though they are invoked from the minibuffer. An upper-case letter in the regular expression makes the search case-sensitive (see Section 12.9 [Search Case], page 102).

You can also search through the history using an incremental search. See Section 12.1.7 [Isearch Minibuffer], page 94.

Emacs keeps separate history lists for several different kinds of arguments. For example, there is a list for file names, used by all the commands that read file names. Other history lists include buffer names, command names (used by `M-x`), and command arguments (used by commands like `query-replace`).

The variable `history-length` specifies the maximum length of a minibuffer history list; adding a new element deletes the oldest element if the list gets too long. If the value is `t`, there is no maximum length.

The variable `history-delete-duplicates` specifies whether to delete duplicates in history. If it is non-`nil`, adding a new element deletes from the list all other elements that are equal to it. The default is `nil`.

5.6 Repeating Minibuffer Commands

Every command that uses the minibuffer once is recorded on a special history list, the *command history*, together with the values of its arguments, so that you can repeat the entire command. In particular, every use of M-x is recorded there, since M-x uses the minibuffer to read the command name.

C-x ESC ESC

> Re-execute a recent minibuffer command from the command history (`repeat-complex-command`).

M-x list-command-history

> Display the entire command history, showing all the commands C-x ESC ESC can repeat, most recent first.

C-x ESC ESC re-executes a recent command that used the minibuffer. With no argument, it repeats the last such command. A numeric argument specifies which command to repeat; 1 means the last one, 2 the previous, and so on.

C-x ESC ESC works by turning the previous command into a Lisp expression and then entering a minibuffer initialized with the text for that expression. Even if you don't know Lisp, it will probably be obvious which command is displayed for repetition. If you type just RET, that repeats the command unchanged. You can also change the command by editing the Lisp expression before you execute it. The executed command is added to the front of the command history unless it is identical to the most recent item.

Once inside the minibuffer for C-x ESC ESC, you can use the usual minibuffer history commands (see Section 5.5 [Minibuffer History], page 32) to move through the history list. After finding the desired previous command, you can edit its expression as usual and then execute it by typing RET.

Incremental search does not, strictly speaking, use the minibuffer. Therefore, although it behaves like a complex command, it normally does not appear in the history list for C-x ESC ESC. You can make incremental search commands appear in the history by setting `isearch-resume-in-command-history` to a non-nil value. See Section 12.1 [Incremental Search], page 90.

The list of previous minibuffer-using commands is stored as a Lisp list in the variable `command-history`. Each element is a Lisp expression that describes one command and its arguments. Lisp programs can re-execute a command by calling `eval` with the `command-history` element.

5.7 Entering passwords

Sometimes, you may need to enter a password into Emacs. For instance, when you tell Emacs to visit a file on another machine via a network protocol such as FTP, you often need to supply a password to gain access to the machine (see Section 15.13 [Remote Files], page 142).

Entering a password is similar to using a minibuffer. Emacs displays a prompt in the echo area (such as 'Password: '); after you type the required password, press RET to submit it. To prevent others from seeing your password, every character you type is displayed as a dot ('.') instead of its usual form.

Most of the features and commands associated with the minibuffer can *not* be used when entering a password. There is no history or completion, and you cannot change windows or perform any other action with Emacs until you have submitted the password.

While you are typing the password, you may press `DEL` to delete backwards, removing the last character entered. `C-u` deletes everything you have typed so far. `C-g` quits the password prompt (see Section 34.1 [Quitting], page 443). `C-y` inserts the current kill into the password (see Chapter 9 [Killing], page 52). You may type either `RET` or `ESC` to submit the password. Any other self-inserting character key inserts the associated character into the password, and all other input is ignored.

5.8 Yes or No Prompts

An Emacs command may require you to answer a "yes or no" question during the course of its execution. Such queries come in two main varieties.

For the first type of "yes or no" query, the prompt ends with '(y or n)'. Such a query does not actually use the minibuffer; the prompt appears in the echo area, and you answer by typing either 'y' or 'n', which immediately delivers the response. For example, if you type `C-x C-w` (`write-file`) to save a buffer, and enter the name of an existing file, Emacs issues a prompt like this:

    File 'foo.el' exists; overwrite? (y or n)

Because this query does not actually use the minibuffer, the usual minibuffer editing commands cannot be used. However, you can perform some window scrolling operations while the query is active: `C-l` recenters the selected window; `M-v` (or `PageDown` or `next`) scrolls forward; `C-v` (or `PageUp`, or `prior`) scrolls backward; `C-M-v` scrolls forward in the next window; and `C-M-S-v` scrolls backward in the next window. Typing `C-g` dismisses the query, and quits the command that issued it (see Section 34.1 [Quitting], page 443).

The second type of "yes or no" query is typically employed if giving the wrong answer would have serious consequences; it uses the minibuffer, and features a prompt ending with '(yes or no)'. For example, if you invoke `C-x k` (`kill-buffer`) on a file-visiting buffer with unsaved changes, Emacs activates the minibuffer with a prompt like this:

    Buffer foo.el modified; kill anyway? (yes or no)

To answer, you must type 'yes' or 'no' into the minibuffer, followed by `RET`. The minibuffer behaves as described in the previous sections; you can switch to another window with `C-x o`, use the history commands `M-p` and `M-f`, etc. Type `C-g` to quit the minibuffer and the querying command.

6 Running Commands by Name

Every Emacs command has a name that you can use to run it. For convenience, many commands also have key bindings. You can run those commands by typing the keys, or run them by name. Most Emacs commands have no key bindings, so the only way to run them is by name. (See Section 33.3 [Key Bindings], page 428, for how to set up key bindings.)

By convention, a command name consists of one or more words, separated by hyphens; for example, `auto-fill-mode` or `manual-entry`. Command names mostly use complete English words to make them easier to remember.

To run a command by name, start with `M-x`, type the command name, then terminate it with `RET`. `M-x` uses the minibuffer to read the command name. The string 'M-x' appears at the beginning of the minibuffer as a *prompt* to remind you to enter a command name to be run. `RET` exits the minibuffer and runs the command. See Chapter 5 [Minibuffer], page 26, for more information on the minibuffer.

You can use completion to enter the command name. For example, to invoke the command `forward-char`, you can type

        M-x forward-char RET

or

        M-x forw TAB c RET

Note that `forward-char` is the same command that you invoke with the key `C-f`. The existence of a key binding does not stop you from running the command by name.

To cancel the `M-x` and not run a command, type `C-g` instead of entering the command name. This takes you back to command level.

To pass a numeric argument to the command you are invoking with `M-x`, specify the numeric argument before `M-x`. The argument value appears in the prompt while the command name is being read, and finally `M-x` passes the argument to that command.

When the command you run with `M-x` has a key binding, Emacs mentions this in the echo area after running the command. For example, if you type `M-x forward-word`, the message says that you can run the same command by typing `M-f`. You can turn off these messages by setting the variable `suggest-key-bindings` to `nil`.

In this manual, when we speak of running a command by name, we often omit the `RET` that terminates the name. Thus we might say `M-x auto-fill-mode` rather than `M-x auto-fill-mode RET`. We mention the `RET` only for emphasis, such as when the command is followed by arguments.

`M-x` works by running the command `execute-extended-command`, which is responsible for reading the name of another command and invoking it.

7 Help

Emacs provides a wide variety of help commands, all accessible through the prefix key C-h (or, equivalently, the function key F1). These help commands are described in the following sections. You can also type C-h C-h to view a list of help commands (help-for-help). You can scroll the list with SPC and DEL, then type the help command you want. To cancel, type C-g.

Many help commands display their information in a special *help buffer*. In this buffer, you can type SPC and DEL to scroll and type RET to follow hyperlinks. See Section 7.4 [Help Mode], page 41.

If you are looking for a certain feature, but don't know what it is called or where to look, we recommend three methods. First, try an apropos command, then try searching the manual index, then look in the FAQ and the package keywords.

C-h a *topics* RET
> This searches for commands whose names match the argument *topics*. The argument can be a keyword, a list of keywords, or a regular expression (see Section 12.6 [Regexps], page 97). See Section 7.3 [Apropos], page 40.

C-h i d m emacs RET i *topic* RET
> This searches for *topic* in the indices of the Emacs Info manual, displaying the first match found. Press , to see subsequent matches. You can use a regular expression as *topic*.

C-h i d m emacs RET s *topic* RET
> Similar, but searches the *text* of the manual rather than the indices.

C-h C-f   This displays the Emacs FAQ, using Info.

C-h p   This displays the available Emacs packages based on keywords. See Section 7.5 [Package Keywords], page 42.

C-h or F1 mean "help" in various other contexts as well. For instance, you can type them after a prefix key to view a list of the keys that can follow the prefix key. (You can also use ? in this context. A few prefix keys don't support C-h or ? in this way, because they define other meanings for those inputs, but they all support F1.)

Here is a summary of help commands for accessing the built-in documentation. Most of these are described in more detail in the following sections.

C-h a *topics* RET
> Display a list of commands whose names match *topics* (apropos-command).

C-h b   Display all active key bindings; minor mode bindings first, then those of the major mode, then global bindings (describe-bindings).

C-h c *key* Show the name of the command that the key sequence *key* is bound to (describe-key-briefly). Here c stands for "character". For more extensive information on *key*, use C-h k.

C-h d *topics* RET
> Display the commands and variables whose documentation matches *topics* (apropos-documentation).

C-h e   Display the *Messages* buffer (`view-echo-area-messages`).

C-h f *function* RET

> Display documentation on the Lisp function named *function* (`describe-function`). Since commands are Lisp functions, this works for commands too.

C-h h   Display the HELLO file, which shows examples of various character sets.

C-h i   Run Info, the GNU documentation browser (`info`). The Emacs manual is available in Info.

C-h k *key* Display the name and documentation of the command that *key* runs (`describe-key`).

C-h l   Display a description of your last 300 keystrokes (`view-lossage`).

C-h m   Display documentation of the current major mode (`describe-mode`).

C-h n   Display news of recent Emacs changes (`view-emacs-news`).

C-h p   Find packages by topic keyword (`finder-by-keyword`). This lists packages using a package menu buffer. See Chapter 32 [Packages], page 408.

C-h P *package* RET

> Display documentation about the specified package (`describe-package`).

C-h r   Display the Emacs manual in Info (`info-emacs-manual`).

C-h s   Display the contents of the current *syntax table* (`describe-syntax`). The syntax table says which characters are opening delimiters, which are parts of words, and so on. See Section "Syntax Tables" in *The Emacs Lisp Reference Manual*, for details.

C-h t   Enter the Emacs interactive tutorial (`help-with-tutorial`).

C-h v *var* RET

> Display the documentation of the Lisp variable *var* (`describe-variable`).

C-h w *command* RET

> Show which keys run the command named *command* (`where-is`).

C-h C *coding* RET

> Describe the coding system *coding* (`describe-coding-system`).

C-h C RET   Describe the coding systems currently in use.

C-h F *command* RET

> Enter Info and go to the node that documents the Emacs command *command* (`Info-goto-emacs-command-node`).

C-h I *method* RET

> Describe the input method *method* (`describe-input-method`).

C-h K *key* Enter Info and go to the node that documents the key sequence *key* (`Info-goto-emacs-key-command-node`).

C-h L *language-env* RET

> Display information on the character sets, coding systems, and input methods used in language environment *language-env* (describe-language-environment).

C-h S *symbol* RET

> Display the Info documentation on symbol *symbol* according to the programming language you are editing (info-lookup-symbol).

C-h .   Display the help message for a special text area, if point is in one (display-local-help). (These include, for example, links in *Help* buffers.)

7.1 Documentation for a Key

The help commands to get information about a key sequence are C-h c (describe-key-briefly) and C-h k (describe-key).

C-h c *key* displays in the echo area the name of the command that *key* is bound to. For example, C-h c C-f displays 'forward-char'.

C-h k *key* is similar but gives more information: it displays a help buffer containing the command's *documentation string*, which describes exactly what the command does.

C-h K *key* displays the section of the Emacs manual that describes the command corresponding to *key*.

C-h c, C-h k and C-h K work for any sort of key sequences, including function keys, menus, and mouse events. For instance, after C-h k you can select a menu item from the menu bar, to view the documentation string of the command it runs.

C-h w *command* RET lists the keys that are bound to *command*. It displays the list in the echo area. If it says the command is not on any key, that means you must use M-x to run it. C-h w runs the command where-is.

7.2 Help by Command or Variable Name

C-h f *function* RET (describe-function) displays the documentation of Lisp function *function*, in a window. Since commands are Lisp functions, you can use this method to view the documentation of any command whose name you know. For example,

        C-h f auto-fill-mode RET

displays the documentation of auto-fill-mode. This is the only way to get the documentation of a command that is not bound to any key (one which you would normally run using M-x).

C-h f is also useful for Lisp functions that you use in a Lisp program. For example, if you have just written the expression (make-vector len) and want to check that you are using make-vector properly, type C-h f make-vector RET. Because C-h f allows all function names, not just command names, you may find that some of your favorite completion abbreviations that work in M-x don't work in C-h f. An abbreviation that is unique among command names may not be unique among all function names.

If you type C-h f RET, it describes the function called by the innermost Lisp expression in the buffer around point, *provided* that function name is a valid, defined Lisp function. (That name appears as the default while you enter the argument.) For example, if point is located following the text '(make-vector (car x)', the innermost list containing point is the one that starts with '(make-vector', so C-h f RET describes the function make-vector.

C-h f is also useful just to verify that you spelled a function name correctly. If the minibuffer prompt for C-h f shows the function name from the buffer as the default, it means that name is defined as a Lisp function. Type C-g to cancel the C-h f command if you don't really want to view the documentation.

C-h v (describe-variable) is like C-h f but describes Lisp variables instead of Lisp functions. Its default is the Lisp symbol around or before point, if that is the name of a defined Lisp variable. See Section 33.2 [Variables], page 420.

Help buffers that describe Emacs variables and functions normally have hyperlinks to the corresponding source code, if you have the source files installed (see Section 31.11 [Hyperlinking], page 405).

To find a command's documentation in a manual, use C-h F (Info-goto-emacs-command-node). This knows about various manuals, not just the Emacs manual, and finds the right one.

7.3 Apropos

The *apropos* commands answer questions like, "What are the commands for working with files?" More precisely, you specify an *apropos pattern*, which means either a word, a list of words, or a regular expression.

Each of the following apropos commands reads an apropos pattern in the minibuffer, searches for items that match the pattern, and displays the results in a different window.

C-h a   Search for commands (apropos-command). With a prefix argument, search for noninteractive functions too.

M-x apropos

        Search for functions and variables. Both interactive functions (commands) and noninteractive functions can be found by this.

M-x apropos-user-option

        Search for user-customizable variables. With a prefix argument, search for non-customizable variables too.

M-x apropos-variable

        Search for variables. With a prefix argument, search for customizable variables only.

M-x apropos-value

        Search for variables whose values match the specified pattern. With a prefix argument, search also for functions with definitions matching the pattern, and Lisp symbols with properties matching the pattern.

C-h d   Search for functions and variables whose documentation strings match the specified pattern (apropos-documentation).

The simplest kind of apropos pattern is one word. Anything containing that word matches the pattern. Thus, to find commands that work on files, type C-h a file RET. This displays a list of all command names that contain 'file', including copy-file, find-file, and so on. Each command name comes with a brief description and a list of keys you can currently invoke it with. In our example, it would say that you can invoke `find-file` by typing `C-x C-f`.

For more information about a function definition, variable or symbol property listed in an apropos buffer, you can click on it with `Mouse-1` or `Mouse-2`, or move there and type `RET`.

When you specify more than one word in the apropos pattern, a name must contain at least two of the words in order to match. Thus, if you are looking for commands to kill a chunk of text before point, you could try `C-h a kill back backward behind before RET`. The real command name `kill-backward` will match that; if there were a command `kill-text-before`, it would also match, since it contains two of the specified words.

For even greater flexibility, you can specify a regular expression (see Section 12.6 [Reg-exps], page 97). An apropos pattern is interpreted as a regular expression if it contains any of the regular expression special characters, '`^$*+?.\[`'.

Following the conventions for naming Emacs commands, here are some words that you'll find useful in apropos patterns. By using them in `C-h a`, you will also get a feel for the naming conventions.

> char, line, word, sentence, paragraph, region, page, sexp, list, defun, rect, buffer, frame, window, face, file, dir, register, mode, beginning, end, forward, backward, next, previous, up, down, search, goto, kill, delete, mark, insert, yank, fill, indent, case, change, set, what, list, find, view, describe, default.

If the variable `apropos-do-all` is non-`nil`, the apropos commands always behave as if they had been given a prefix argument.

By default, all apropos commands except `apropos-documentation` list their results in alphabetical order. If the variable `apropos-sort-by-scores` is non-`nil`, these commands instead try to guess the relevance of each result, and display the most relevant ones first. The `apropos-documentation` command lists its results in order of relevance by default; to list them in alphabetical order, change the variable `apropos-documentation-sort-by-scores` to `nil`.

7.4 Help Mode Commands

Help buffers provide the same commands as View mode (see Section 11.6 [View Mode], page 73); for instance, `SPC` scrolls forward, and `DEL` or `S-SPC` scrolls backward. A few special commands are also provided:

`RET`   Follow a cross reference at point (`help-follow`).

`TAB`   Move point forward to the next hyperlink (`forward-button`).

`S-TAB`   Move point back to the previous hyperlink (`backward-button`).

`Mouse-1`
`Mouse-2`   Follow a hyperlink that you click on.

`C-c C-c`   Show all documentation about the symbol at point (`help-follow-symbol`).

`C-c C-b`   Go back to the previous help topic (`help-go-back`).

When a function name, variable name, or face name (see Section 11.8 [Faces], page 74) appears in the documentation in the help buffer, it is normally an underlined *hyperlink*. To view the associated documentation, move point there and type RET (`help-follow`), or click on the hyperlink with Mouse-1 or Mouse-2. Doing so replaces the contents of the help buffer; to retrace your steps, type C-c C-b (`help-go-back`).

A help buffer can also contain hyperlinks to Info manuals, source code definitions, and URLs (web pages). The first two are opened in Emacs, and the third using a web browser via the `browse-url` command (see Section 31.11.1 [Browse-URL], page 405).

In a help buffer, TAB (`forward-button`) moves point forward to the next hyperlink, while S-TAB (`backward-button`) point back to the previous hyperlink. These commands act cyclically; for instance, typing TAB at the last hyperlink moves back to the first hyperlink.

To view all documentation about any symbol in the text, move point to there and type C-c C-c (`help-follow-symbol`). This shows all available documentation about the symbol—as a variable, function and/or face.

7.5 Keyword Search for Packages

Most optional features in Emacs are grouped into *packages*. Emacs contains several hundred built-in packages, and more can be installed over the network (see Chapter 32 [Packages], page 408).

To make it easier to find packages related to a topic, most packages are associated with one or more *keywords* based on what they do. Type C-h p (`finder-by-keyword`) to bring up a list of package keywords, together with a description of what the keywords mean. To view a list of packages for a given keyword, type RET on that line; this displays the list of packages in a Package Menu buffer (see Section 32.1 [Package Menu], page 408).

C-h P (`describe-package`) prompts for the name of a package, and displays a help buffer describing the attributes of the package and the features that it implements. The buffer lists the keywords that relate to the package in the form of buttons. Click on a button to see other packages related to that keyword.

7.6 Help for International Language Support

For information on a specific language environment (see Section 19.2 [Language Environments], page 179), type C-h L (`describe-language-environment`). This displays a help buffer describing the languages supported by the language environment, and listing the associated character sets, coding systems, and input methods, as well as some sample text for that language environment.

The command C-h h (`view-hello-file`) displays the file etc/HELLO, which demonstrates various character sets by showing how to say "hello" in many languages.

The command C-h I (`describe-input-method`) describes an input method—either a specified input method, or by default the input method currently in use. See Section 19.3 [Input Methods], page 181.

The command C-h C (`describe-coding-system`) describes coding systems—either a specified coding system, or the ones currently in use. See Section 19.5 [Coding Systems], page 183.

7.7 Other Help Commands

C-h i (`info`) runs the Info program, which browses structured documentation files. The entire Emacs manual is available within Info, along with many other manuals for the GNU system. Type h after entering Info to run a tutorial on using Info.

With a numeric argument *n*, C-h i selects the Info buffer '`*info*<n>`'. This is useful if you want to browse multiple Info manuals simultaneously. If you specify just C-u as the prefix argument, C-h i prompts for the name of a documentation file, so you can browse a file which doesn't have an entry in the top-level Info menu.

The help commands C-h F *function* RET and C-h K *key*, described above, enter Info and go straight to the documentation of *function* or *key*.

When editing a program, if you have an Info version of the manual for the programming language, you can use C-h S (`info-lookup-symbol`) to find an entry for a symbol (keyword, function or variable) in the proper manual. The details of how this command works depend on the major mode.

If something surprising happens, and you are not sure what you typed, use C-h l (`view-lossage`). C-h l displays your last 300 input keystrokes. If you see commands that you don't know, you can use C-h c to find out what they do.

To review recent echo area messages, use C-h e (`view-echo-area-messages`). This displays the buffer *Messages*, where those messages are kept.

Each Emacs major mode typically redefines a few keys and makes other changes in how editing works. C-h m (`describe-mode`) displays documentation on the current major mode, which normally describes the commands and features that are changed in this mode.

C-h b (`describe-bindings`) and C-h s (`describe-syntax`) show other information about the current environment within Emacs. C-h b displays a list of all the key bindings now in effect: first the local bindings of the current minor modes, then the local bindings defined by the current major mode, and finally the global bindings (see Section 33.3 [Key Bindings], page 428). C-h s displays the contents of the syntax table, with explanations of each character's syntax (see Section "Syntax Tables" in *The Emacs Lisp Reference Manual*).

You can get a list of subcommands for a particular prefix key by typing C-h, ?, or F1 (`describe-prefix-bindings`) after the prefix key. (There are a few prefix keys for which not all of these keys work—those that provide their own bindings for that key. One of these prefix keys is ESC, because ESC C-h is actually C-M-h, which marks a defun. However, ESC F1 and ESC ? work fine.)

7.8 Help Files

Apart from the built-in documentation and manuals, Emacs contains several other files describing topics like copying conditions, release notes, instructions for debugging and reporting bugs, and so forth. You can use the following commands to view these files. Apart from C-h g, they all have the form C-h C-*char*.

C-h C-c   Display the rules under which you can copy and redistribute Emacs (`describe-copying`).

C-h C-d   Display help for debugging Emacs (`view-emacs-debugging`).

C-h C-e   Display information about where to get external packages (`view-external-packages`).

C-h C-f   Display the Emacs frequently-answered-questions list (`view-emacs-FAQ`).

C-h g   Display information about the GNU Project (`describe-gnu-project`).

C-h C-m   Display information about ordering printed copies of Emacs manuals (`view-order-manuals`).

C-h C-n   Display the "news" file, which lists the new features in this version of Emacs (`view-emacs-news`).

C-h C-o   Display how to order or download the latest version of Emacs and other GNU software (`describe-distribution`).

C-h C-p   Display the list of known Emacs problems, sometimes with suggested workarounds (`view-emacs-problems`).

C-h C-t   Display the Emacs to-do list (`view-emacs-todo`).

C-h C-w   Display the full details on the complete absence of warranty for GNU Emacs (`describe-no-warranty`).

7.9 Help on Active Text and Tooltips

In Emacs, stretches of "active text" (text that does something special in response to mouse clicks or RET) often have associated help text. This includes hyperlinks in Emacs buffers, as well as parts of the mode line. On graphical displays, as well as some text terminals which support mouse tracking, moving the mouse over the active text displays the help text as a *tooltip*. See Section 18.17 [Tooltips], page 174.

On terminals that don't support mouse-tracking, you can display the help text for active buffer text at point by typing C-h . (`display-local-help`). This shows the help text in the echo area. To display help text automatically whenever it is available at point, set the variable `help-at-pt-display-when-idle` to t.

8 The Mark and the Region

Many Emacs commands operate on an arbitrary contiguous part of the current buffer. To specify the text for such a command to operate on, you set *the mark* at one end of it, and move point to the other end. The text between point and the mark is called *the region*. The region always extends between point and the mark, no matter which one comes earlier in the text; each time you move point, the region changes.

Setting the mark at a position in the text also *activates* it. When the mark is active, we say also that the region is active; Emacs indicates its extent by highlighting the text within it, using the `region` face (see Section 33.1.5 [Face Customization], page 416).

After certain non-motion commands, including any command that changes the text in the buffer, Emacs automatically *deactivates* the mark; this turns off the highlighting. You can also explicitly deactivate the mark at any time, by typing `C-g` (see Section 34.1 [Quitting], page 443).

The above default behavior is known as Transient Mark mode. Disabling Transient Mark mode switches Emacs to an alternative behavior, in which the region is usually not highlighted. See Section 8.7 [Disabled Transient Mark], page 50.

Setting the mark in one buffer has no effect on the marks in other buffers. When you return to a buffer with an active mark, the mark is at the same place as before. When multiple windows show the same buffer, they can have different values of point, and thus different regions, but they all share one common mark position. See Chapter 17 [Windows], page 156. Ordinarily, only the selected window highlights its region; however, if the variable `highlight-nonselected-windows` is non-`nil`, each window highlights its own region.

There is another kind of region: the "rectangular region". See Section 9.5 [Rectangles], page 60.

8.1 Setting the Mark

Here are some commands for setting the mark:

C-SPC   Set the mark at point, and activate it (`set-mark-command`).

C-@   The same.

C-x C-x   Set the mark at point, and activate it; then move point where the mark used to be (`exchange-point-and-mark`).

Drag-Mouse-1
     Set point and the mark around the text you drag across.

Mouse-3   Set the mark at point, then move point to where you click (`mouse-save-then-kill`).

'Shifted cursor motion keys'
     Set the mark at point if the mark is inactive, then move point. See Section 8.6 [Shift Selection], page 49.

The most common way to set the mark is with C-SPC (set-mark-command)[1]. This sets the mark where point is, and activates it. You can then move point away, leaving the mark behind.

For example, suppose you wish to convert part of the buffer to upper case. To accomplish this, go to one end of the desired text, type C-SPC, and move point until the desired portion of text is highlighted. Now type C-x C-u (upcase-region). This converts the text in the region to upper case, and then deactivates the mark.

Whenever the mark is active, you can deactivate it by typing C-g (see Section 34.1 [Quitting], page 443). Most commands that operate on the region also automatically deactivate the mark, like C-x C-u in the above example.

Instead of setting the mark in order to operate on a region, you can also use it to "remember" a position in the buffer (by typing C-SPC C-SPC), and later jump back there (by typing C-u C-SPC). See Section 8.4 [Mark Ring], page 48, for details.

The command C-x C-x (exchange-point-and-mark) exchanges the positions of point and the mark. C-x C-x is useful when you are satisfied with the position of point but want to move the other end of the region (where the mark is). Using C-x C-x a second time, if necessary, puts the mark at the new position with point back at its original position. Normally, if the mark is inactive, this command first reactivates the mark wherever it was last set, to ensure that the region is left highlighted. However, if you call it with a prefix argument, it leaves the mark inactive and the region unhighlighted; you can use this to jump to the mark in a manner similar to C-u C-SPC.

You can also set the mark with the mouse. If you press the left mouse button (down-mouse-1) and drag the mouse across a range of text, this sets the mark where you first pressed the mouse button and puts point where you release it. Alternatively, clicking the right mouse button (mouse-3) sets the mark at point and then moves point to where you clicked. See Section 18.1 [Mouse Commands], page 162, for a more detailed description of these mouse commands.

Finally, you can set the mark by holding down the shift key while typing certain cursor motion commands (such as S-RIGHT, S-C-f, S-C-n, etc.). This is called *shift-selection*. It sets the mark at point before moving point, but only if there is no active mark set via shift-selection. The mark set by mouse commands and by shift-selection behaves slightly differently from the usual mark: any subsequent unshifted cursor motion command deactivates it automatically. For details, See Section 8.6 [Shift Selection], page 49.

Many commands that insert text, such as C-y (yank), set the mark at the other end of the inserted text, without activating it. This lets you easily return to that position (see Section 8.4 [Mark Ring], page 48). You can tell that a command does this when it shows 'Mark set' in the echo area.

Under X, every time the active region changes, Emacs saves the text in the region to the *primary selection*. This lets you insert that text into other X applications with mouse-2 clicks. See Section 9.3.2 [Primary Selection], page 58.

---

[1] There is no C-SPC character in ASCII; usually, typing C-SPC on a text terminal gives the character C-@. This key is also bound to set-mark-command, so unless you are unlucky enough to have a text terminal that behaves differently, you might as well think of C-@ as C-SPC.

8.2 Commands to Mark Textual Objects

Here are commands for placing point and the mark around a textual object such as a word, list, paragraph or page:

M-@   Set mark after end of next word (`mark-word`). This does not move point.

C-M-@   Set mark after end of following balanced expression (`mark-sexp`). This does not move point.

M-h   Move point to the beginning of the current paragraph, and set mark at the end (`mark-paragraph`).

C-M-h   Move point to the beginning of the current defun, and set mark at the end (`mark-defun`).

C-x C-p   Move point to the beginning of the current page, and set mark at the end (`mark-page`).

C-x h   Move point to the beginning of the buffer, and set mark at the end (`mark-whole-buffer`).

M-@ (`mark-word`) sets the mark at the end of the next word (see Section 22.1 [Words], page 208, for information about words). Repeated invocations of this command extend the region by advancing the mark one word at a time. As an exception, if the mark is active and located before point, M-@ moves the mark backwards from its current position one word at a time.

This command also accepts a numeric argument n, which tells it to advance the mark by n words. A negative argument moves the mark back by n words.

Similarly, C-M-@ (`mark-sexp`) puts the mark at the end of the next balanced expression (see Section 23.4.1 [Expressions], page 246). Repeated invocations extend the region to subsequent expressions, while positive or negative numeric arguments move the mark forward or backward by the specified number of expressions.

The other commands in the above list set both point and mark, so as to delimit an object in the buffer. M-h (`mark-paragraph`) marks paragraphs (see Section 22.3 [Paragraphs], page 210), C-M-h (`mark-defun`) marks top-level definitions (see Section 23.2.2 [Moving by Defuns], page 241), and C-x C-p (`mark-page`) marks pages (see Section 22.4 [Pages], page 211). Repeated invocations again play the same role, extending the region to consecutive objects; similarly, numeric arguments specify how many objects to move the mark by.

C-x h (`mark-whole-buffer`) sets up the entire buffer as the region, by putting point at the beginning and the mark at the end.

8.3 Operating on the Region

Once you have a region, here are some of the ways you can operate on it:

- Kill it with C-w (see Chapter 9 [Killing], page 52).
- Copy it to the kill ring with M-w (see Section 9.2 [Yanking], page 55).
- Convert case with C-x C-l or C-x C-u (see Section 22.6 [Case], page 216).
- Undo changes within it using C-u C-/ (see Section 13.1 [Undo], page 109).

- Replace text within it using M-% (see Section 12.10.4 [Query Replace], page 105).
- Indent it with C-x TAB or C-M-\ (see Chapter 21 [Indentation], page 205).
- Fill it as text with M-x fill-region (see Section 22.5 [Filling], page 212).
- Check the spelling of words within it with M-$ (see Section 13.4 [Spelling], page 111).
- Evaluate it as Lisp code with M-x eval-region (see Section 24.9 [Lisp Eval], page 278).
- Save it in a register with C-x r s (see Chapter 10 [Registers], page 64).
- Save it in a buffer or a file (see Section 9.4 [Accumulating Text], page 59).

Some commands have a default behavior when the mark is inactive, but operate on the region if the mark is active. For example, M-$ (ispell-word) normally checks the spelling of the word at point, but it checks the text in the region if the mark is active (see Section 13.4 [Spelling], page 111). Normally, such commands use their default behavior if the region is empty (i.e., if mark and point are at the same position). If you want them to operate on the empty region, change the variable use-empty-active-region to t.

As described in Section 4.3 [Erasing], page 19, the DEL (backward-delete-char) and delete (delete-forward-char) commands also act this way. If the mark is active, they delete the text in the region. (As an exception, if you supply a numeric argument *n*, where *n* is not one, these commands delete *n* characters regardless of whether the mark is active). If you change the variable delete-active-region to nil, then these commands don't act differently when the mark is active. If you change the value to kill, these commands *kill* the region instead of deleting it (see Chapter 9 [Killing], page 52).

Other commands always operate on the region, and have no default behavior. Such commands usually have the word region in their names, like C-w (kill-region) and C-x C-u (upcase-region). If the mark is inactive, they operate on the "inactive region"— that is, on the text between point and the position at which the mark was last set (see Section 8.4 [Mark Ring], page 48). To disable this behavior, change the variable mark-even-if-inactive to nil. Then these commands will instead signal an error if the mark is inactive.

By default, text insertion occurs normally even if the mark is active—for example, typing a inserts the character 'a', then deactivates the mark. If you enable Delete Selection mode, a minor mode, then inserting text while the mark is active causes the text in the region to be deleted first. To toggle Delete Selection mode on or off, type M-x delete-selection-mode.

8.4 The Mark Ring

Each buffer remembers previous locations of the mark, in the *mark ring*. Commands that set the mark also push the old mark onto this ring. One of the uses of the mark ring is to remember spots that you may want to go back to.

C-SPC C-SPC

> Set the mark, pushing it onto the mark ring, without activating it.

C-u C-SPC   Move point to where the mark was, and restore the mark from the ring of former marks.

The command C-SPC C-SPC is handy when you want to use the mark to remember a position to which you may wish to return. It pushes the current point onto the mark ring, without activating the mark (which would cause Emacs to highlight the region). This is actually two consecutive invocations of C-SPC (set-mark-command); the first C-SPC sets the mark, and the second C-SPC deactivates it. (When Transient Mark mode is off, C-SPC C-SPC instead activates Transient Mark mode temporarily; see Section 8.7 [Disabled Transient Mark], page 50.)

To return to a marked position, use set-mark-command with a prefix argument: C-u C-SPC. This moves point to where the mark was, and deactivates the mark if it was active. Each subsequent C-u C-SPC jumps to a prior position stored in the mark ring. The positions you move through in this way are not lost; they go to the end of the ring.

If you set set-mark-command-repeat-pop to non-nil, then immediately after you type C-u C-SPC, you can type C-SPC instead of C-u C-SPC to cycle through the mark ring. By default, set-mark-command-repeat-pop is nil.

Each buffer has its own mark ring. All editing commands use the current buffer's mark ring. In particular, C-u C-SPC always stays in the same buffer.

The variable mark-ring-max specifies the maximum number of entries to keep in the mark ring. This defaults to 16 entries. If that many entries exist and another one is pushed, the earliest one in the list is discarded. Repeating C-u C-SPC cycles through the positions currently in the ring.

If you want to move back to the same place over and over, the mark ring may not be convenient enough. If so, you can record the position in a register for later retrieval (see Section 10.1 [Saving Positions in Registers], page 64).

8.5 The Global Mark Ring

In addition to the ordinary mark ring that belongs to each buffer, Emacs has a single *global mark ring*. Each time you set a mark, this is recorded in the global mark ring in addition to the current buffer's own mark ring, if you have switched buffers since the previous mark setting. Hence, the global mark ring records a sequence of buffers that you have been in, and, for each buffer, a place where you set the mark. The length of the global mark ring is controlled by global-mark-ring-max, and is 16 by default.

The command C-x C-SPC (pop-global-mark) jumps to the buffer and position of the latest entry in the global ring. It also rotates the ring, so that successive uses of C-x C-SPC take you to earlier buffers and mark positions.

8.6 Shift Selection

If you hold down the shift key while typing a cursor motion command, this sets the mark before moving point, so that the region extends from the original position of point to its new position. This feature is referred to as *shift-selection*. It is similar to the way text is selected in other editors.

The mark set via shift-selection behaves a little differently from what we have described above. Firstly, in addition to the usual ways of deactivating the mark (such as changing the buffer text or typing C-g), the mark is deactivated by any *unshifted* cursor motion command. Secondly, any subsequent *shifted* cursor motion command avoids setting the mark anew. Therefore, a series of shifted cursor motion commands will continuously adjust the region.

Shift-selection only works if the shifted cursor motion key is not already bound to a separate command (see Chapter 33 [Customization], page 412). For example, if you bind S-C-f to another command, typing S-C-f runs that command instead of performing a shift-selected version of C-f (forward-char).

A mark set via mouse commands behaves the same as a mark set via shift-selection (see Section 8.1 [Setting Mark], page 45). For example, if you specify a region by dragging the mouse, you can continue to extend the region using shifted cursor motion commands. In either case, any unshifted cursor motion command deactivates the mark.

To turn off shift-selection, set shift-select-mode to nil. Doing so does not disable setting the mark via mouse commands.

8.7 Disabling Transient Mark Mode

The default behavior of the mark and region, in which setting the mark activates it and highlights the region, is called Transient Mark mode. This is a minor mode that is enabled by default. It can be toggled with M-x transient-mark-mode, or with the 'Active Region Highlighting' menu item in the 'Options' menu. Turning it off switches Emacs to an alternative mode of operation:

- Setting the mark, with commands like C-SPC or C-x C-x, does not highlight the region. Therefore, you can't tell by looking where the mark is located; you have to remember.

  The usual solution to this problem is to set the mark and then use it soon, before you forget where it is. You can also check where the mark is by using C-x C-x, which exchanges the positions of the point and the mark (see Section 8.1 [Setting Mark], page 45).

- Some commands, which ordinarily act on the region when the mark is active, no longer do so. For example, normally M-% (query-replace) performs replacements within the region, if the mark is active. When Transient Mark mode is off, it always operates from point to the end of the buffer. Commands that act this way are identified in their own documentation.

While Transient Mark mode is off, you can activate it temporarily using C-SPC C-SPC or C-u C-x C-x.

C-SPC C-SPC

> Set the mark at point (like plain C-SPC) and enable Transient Mark mode just once, until the mark is deactivated. (This is not really a separate command; you are using the C-SPC command twice.)

C-u C-x C-x

> Exchange point and mark, activate the mark and enable Transient Mark mode temporarily, until the mark is next deactivated. (This is the C-x C-x command, exchange-point-and-mark, with a prefix argument.)

These commands set or activate the mark, and enable Transient Mark mode only until the mark is deactivated. One reason you may want to use them is that some commands operate on the entire buffer instead of the region when Transient Mark mode is off. Enabling Transient Mark mode momentarily gives you a way to use these commands on the region.

When you specify a region with the mouse (see Section 8.1 [Setting Mark], page 45), or with shift-selection (see Section 8.6 [Shift Selection], page 49), this likewise activates Transient Mark mode temporarily and highlights the region.

9 Killing and Moving Text

In Emacs, *killing* means erasing text and copying it into the *kill ring*. *Yanking* means bringing text from the kill ring back into the buffer. (Some applications use the terms "cutting" and "pasting" for similar operations.) The kill ring is so-named because it can be visualized as a set of blocks of text arranged in a ring, which you can access in cyclic order. See Section 9.2.1 [Kill Ring], page 55.

Killing and yanking are the most common way to move or copy text within Emacs. It is very versatile, because there are commands for killing many different types of syntactic units.

9.1 Deletion and Killing

Most commands which erase text from the buffer save it in the kill ring. These are known as *kill* commands, and their names normally contain the word 'kill' (e.g., kill-line). The kill ring stores several recent kills, not just the last one, so killing is a very safe operation: you don't have to worry much about losing text that you previously killed. The kill ring is shared by all buffers, so text that is killed in one buffer can be yanked into another buffer.

When you use C-/ (undo) to undo a kill command (see Section 13.1 [Undo], page 109), that brings the killed text back into the buffer, but does not remove it from the kill ring.

On graphical displays, killing text also copies it to the system clipboard. See Section 9.3 [Cut and Paste], page 57.

Commands that erase text but do not save it in the kill ring are known as *delete* commands; their names usually contain the word 'delete'. These include C-d (delete-char) and DEL (delete-backward-char), which delete only one character at a time, and those commands that delete only spaces or newlines. Commands that can erase significant amounts of nontrivial data generally do a kill operation instead.

You can also use the mouse to kill and yank. See Section 9.3 [Cut and Paste], page 57.

9.1.1 Deletion

Deletion means erasing text and not saving it in the kill ring. For the most part, the Emacs commands that delete text are those that erase just one character or only whitespace.

DEL
BACKSPACE

> Delete the previous character, or the text in the region if it is active (delete-backward-char).

Delete   Delete the next character, or the text in the region if it is active (delete-forward-char).

C-d   Delete the next character (delete-char).

M-\   Delete spaces and tabs around point (delete-horizontal-space).

M-SPC   Delete spaces and tabs around point, leaving one space (just-one-space).

C-x C-o   Delete blank lines around the current line (delete-blank-lines).

M-^   Join two lines by deleting the intervening newline, along with any indentation
            following it (`delete-indentation`).

We have already described the basic deletion commands `DEL` (`delete-backward-char`),
`delete` (`delete-forward-char`), and `C-d` (`delete-char`). See Section 4.3 [Erasing],
page 19. With a numeric argument, they delete the specified number of characters. If the
numeric argument is omitted or one, they delete all the text in the region if it is active (see
Section 8.3 [Using Region], page 47).

The other delete commands are those that delete only whitespace characters: spaces, tabs
and newlines. `M-\` (`delete-horizontal-space`) deletes all the spaces and tab characters
before and after point. With a prefix argument, this only deletes spaces and tab characters
before point. `M-SPC` (`just-one-space`) does likewise but leaves a single space before point,
regardless of the number of spaces that existed previously (even if there were none before).
With a numeric argument n, it leaves n spaces before point if n is positive; if n is negative, it
deletes newlines in addition to spaces and tabs, leaving -n spaces before point. The command
`cycle-spacing` acts like a more flexible version of `just-one-space`. It does different things
if you call it repeatedly in succession. The first call acts like `just-one-space`, the next
removes all whitespace, and a third call restores the original whitespace.

`C-x C-o` (`delete-blank-lines`) deletes all blank lines after the current line. If the
current line is blank, it deletes all blank lines preceding the current line as well (leaving one
blank line, the current line). On a solitary blank line, it deletes that line.

`M-^` (`delete-indentation`) joins the current line and the previous line, by deleting a
newline and all surrounding spaces, usually leaving a single space. See Chapter 21 [Indentation], page 205.

The command `delete-duplicate-lines` searches the region for identical lines, and
removes all but one copy of each. Normally it keeps the first instance of each repeated line,
but with a `C-u` prefix argument it keeps the last. With a `C-u C-u` prefix argument, it only
searches for adjacent identical lines. This is a more efficient mode of operation, useful when
the lines have already been sorted. With a `C-u C-u C-u` prefix argument, it retains repeated
blank lines.

9.1.2 Killing by Lines

C-k   Kill rest of line or one or more lines (`kill-line`).

C-S-backspace
            Kill an entire line at once (`kill-whole-line`)

The simplest kill command is `C-k` (`kill-line`). If used at the end of a line, it kills the
line-ending newline character, merging the next line into the current one (thus, a blank line
is entirely removed). Otherwise, `C-k` kills all the text from point up to the end of the line;
if point was originally at the beginning of the line, this leaves the line blank.

Spaces and tabs at the end of the line are ignored when deciding which case applies. As
long as point is after the last visible character in the line, you can be sure that `C-k` will kill
the newline. To kill an entire non-blank line, go to the beginning and type `C-k` twice.

In this context, "line" means a logical text line, not a screen line (see Section 4.8 [Continuation Lines], page 22).

When `C-k` is given a positive argument *n*, it kills *n* lines and the newlines that follow them (text on the current line before point is not killed). With a negative argument −*n*, it kills *n* lines preceding the current line, together with the text on the current line before point. `C-k` with an argument of zero kills the text before point on the current line.

If the variable `kill-whole-line` is non-`nil`, `C-k` at the very beginning of a line kills the entire line including the following newline. This variable is normally `nil`.

`C-S-backspace` (`kill-whole-line`) kills a whole line including its newline, regardless of the position of point within the line. Note that many text terminals will prevent you from typing the key sequence `C-S-backspace`.

9.1.3 Other Kill Commands

`C-w`	Kill the region (`kill-region`).
`M-w`	Copy the region into the kill ring (`kill-ring-save`).
`M-d`	Kill the next word (`kill-word`). See Section 22.1 [Words], page 208.
`M-DEL`	Kill one word backwards (`backward-kill-word`).
`C-x DEL`	Kill back to beginning of sentence (`backward-kill-sentence`). See Section 22.2 [Sentences], page 209.
`M-k`	Kill to the end of the sentence (`kill-sentence`).
`C-M-k`	Kill the following balanced expression (`kill-sexp`). See Section 23.4.1 [Expressions], page 246.
`M-z char`	Kill through the next occurrence of *char* (`zap-to-char`).

One of the commonly-used kill commands is `C-w` (`kill-region`), which kills the text in the region (see Chapter 8 [Mark], page 45). Similarly, `M-w` (`kill-ring-save`) copies the text in the region into the kill ring without removing it from the buffer. If the mark is inactive when you type `C-w` or `M-w`, the command acts on the text between point and where you last set the mark (see Section 8.3 [Using Region], page 47).

Emacs also provides commands to kill specific syntactic units: words, with `M-DEL` and `M-d` (see Section 22.1 [Words], page 208); balanced expressions, with `C-M-k` (see Section 23.4.1 [Expressions], page 246); and sentences, with `C-x DEL` and `M-k` (see Section 22.2 [Sentences], page 209).

The command `M-z` (`zap-to-char`) combines killing with searching: it reads a character and kills from point up to (and including) the next occurrence of that character in the buffer. A numeric argument acts as a repeat count; a negative argument means to search backward and kill text before point.

9.1.4 Options for Killing

Some specialized buffers contain *read-only text*, which cannot be modified and therefore cannot be killed. The kill commands work specially in a read-only buffer: they move over text and copy it to the kill ring, without actually deleting it from the buffer. Normally, they also beep and display an error message when this happens. But if you set the variable `kill-read-only-ok` to a non-`nil` value, they just print a message in the echo area to explain why the text has not been erased.

If you change the variable `kill-do-not-save-duplicates` to a non-`nil` value, identical subsequent kills yield a single kill-ring entry, without duplication.

9.2 Yanking

Yanking means reinserting text previously killed. The usual way to move or copy text is to kill it and then yank it elsewhere.

C-y   Yank the last kill into the buffer, at point (`yank`).

M-y   Replace the text just yanked with an earlier batch of killed text (`yank-pop`). See Section 9.2.2 [Earlier Kills], page 55.

C-M-w   Cause the following command, if it is a kill command, to append to the previous kill (`append-next-kill`). See Section 9.2.3 [Appending Kills], page 56.

The basic yanking command is `C-y` (`yank`). It inserts the most recent kill, leaving the cursor at the end of the inserted text. It also sets the mark at the beginning of the inserted text, without activating the mark; this lets you jump easily to that position, if you wish, with `C-u C-SPC` (see Section 8.4 [Mark Ring], page 48).

With a plain prefix argument (`C-u C-y`), the command instead leaves the cursor in front of the inserted text, and sets the mark at the end. Using any other prefix argument specifies an earlier kill; e.g., `C-u 4 C-y` reinserts the fourth most recent kill. See Section 9.2.2 [Earlier Kills], page 55.

On graphical displays, `C-y` first checks if another application has placed any text in the system clipboard more recently than the last Emacs kill. If so, it inserts the clipboard's text instead. Thus, Emacs effectively treats "cut" or "copy" clipboard operations performed in other applications like Emacs kills, except that they are not recorded in the kill ring. See Section 9.3 [Cut and Paste], page 57, for details.

9.2.1 The Kill Ring

The *kill ring* is a list of blocks of text that were previously killed. There is only one kill ring, shared by all buffers, so you can kill text in one buffer and yank it in another buffer. This is the usual way to move text from one buffer to another. (There are several other methods: for instance, you could store the text in a register; see Chapter 10 [Registers], page 64. See Section 9.4 [Accumulating Text], page 59, for some other ways to move text around.)

The maximum number of entries in the kill ring is controlled by the variable `kill-ring-max`. The default is 60. If you make a new kill when this limit has been reached, Emacs makes room by deleting the oldest entry in the kill ring.

The actual contents of the kill ring are stored in a variable named `kill-ring`; you can view the entire contents of the kill ring with `C-h v kill-ring`.

9.2.2 Yanking Earlier Kills

As explained in Section 9.2 [Yanking], page 55, you can use a numeric argument to `C-y` to yank text that is no longer the most recent kill. This is useful if you remember which kill ring entry you want. If you don't, you can use the `M-y` (`yank-pop`) command to cycle through the possibilities.

If the previous command was a yank command, M-y takes the text that was yanked and replaces it with the text from an earlier kill. So, to recover the text of the next-to-the-last kill, first use C-y to yank the last kill, and then use M-y to replace it with the previous kill. M-y is allowed only after a C-y or another M-y.

You can understand M-y in terms of a "last yank" pointer which points at an entry in the kill ring. Each time you kill, the "last yank" pointer moves to the newly made entry at the front of the ring. C-y yanks the entry which the "last yank" pointer points to. M-y moves the "last yank" pointer to a different entry, and the text in the buffer changes to match. Enough M-y commands can move the pointer to any entry in the ring, so you can get any entry into the buffer. Eventually the pointer reaches the end of the ring; the next M-y loops back around to the first entry again.

M-y moves the "last yank" pointer around the ring, but it does not change the order of the entries in the ring, which always runs from the most recent kill at the front to the oldest one still remembered.

M-y can take a numeric argument, which tells it how many entries to advance the "last yank" pointer by. A negative argument moves the pointer toward the front of the ring; from the front of the ring, it moves "around" to the last entry and continues forward from there.

Once the text you are looking for is brought into the buffer, you can stop doing M-y commands and it will stay there. It's just a copy of the kill ring entry, so editing it in the buffer does not change what's in the ring. As long as no new killing is done, the "last yank" pointer remains at the same place in the kill ring, so repeating C-y will yank another copy of the same previous kill.

When you call C-y with a numeric argument, that also sets the "last yank" pointer to the entry that it yanks.

9.2.3 Appending Kills

Normally, each kill command pushes a new entry onto the kill ring. However, two or more kill commands in a row combine their text into a single entry, so that a single C-y yanks all the text as a unit, just as it was before it was killed.

Thus, if you want to yank text as a unit, you need not kill all of it with one command; you can keep killing line after line, or word after word, until you have killed it all, and you can still get it all back at once.

Commands that kill forward from point add onto the end of the previous killed text. Commands that kill backward from point add text onto the beginning. This way, any sequence of mixed forward and backward kill commands puts all the killed text into one entry without rearrangement. Numeric arguments do not break the sequence of appending kills. For example, suppose the buffer contains this text:

    This is a line *of sample text.

with point shown by *. If you type M-d M-DEL M-d M-DEL, killing alternately forward and backward, you end up with 'a line of sample' as one entry in the kill ring, and 'This is text.' in the buffer. (Note the double space between 'is' and 'text', which you can clean up with M-SPC or M-q.)

Another way to kill the same text is to move back two words with M-b M-b, then kill all four words forward with C-u M-d. This produces exactly the same results in the buffer and in the kill ring. `M-f M-f C-u M-DEL` kills the same text, all going backward; once again, the result is the same. The text in the kill ring entry always has the same order that it had in the buffer before you killed it.

If a kill command is separated from the last kill command by other commands (not just numeric arguments), it starts a new entry on the kill ring. But you can force it to combine with the last killed text, by typing `C-M-w` (**append-next-kill**) right beforehand. The `C-M-w` tells its following command, if it is a kill command, to treat the kill as part of the sequence of previous kills. As usual, the kill is appended to the previous killed text if the command kills forward, and prepended if the command kills backward. In this way, you can kill several separated pieces of text and accumulate them to be yanked back in one place.

A kill command following `M-w` (**kill-ring-save**) does not append to the text that `M-w` copied into the kill ring.

9.3 "Cut and Paste" Operations on Graphical Displays

In most graphical desktop environments, you can transfer data (usually text) between different applications using a system facility called the *clipboard*. On X, two other similar facilities are available: the primary selection and the secondary selection. When Emacs is run on a graphical display, its kill and yank commands integrate with these facilities, so that you can easily transfer text between Emacs and other graphical applications.

By default, Emacs uses UTF-8 as the coding system for inter-program text transfers. If you find that the pasted text is not what you expected, you can specify another coding system by typing `C-x RET x` or `C-x RET X`. You can also request a different data type by customizing `x-select-request-type`. See Section 19.10 [Communication Coding], page 189.

9.3.1 Using the Clipboard

The *clipboard* is the facility that most graphical applications use for "cutting and pasting". When the clipboard exists, the kill and yank commands in Emacs make use of it.

When you kill some text with a command such as `C-w` (**kill-region**), or copy it to the kill ring with a command such as `M-w` (**kill-ring-save**), that text is also put in the clipboard.

When an Emacs kill command puts text in the clipboard, the existing clipboard contents are normally lost. Optionally, you can change `save-interprogram-paste-before-kill` to `t`. Then Emacs will first save the clipboard to its kill ring, preventing you from losing the old clipboard data—at the risk of high memory consumption if that data turns out to be large.

Yank commands, such as `C-y` (**yank**), also use the clipboard. If another application "owns" the clipboard—i.e., if you cut or copied text there more recently than your last kill command in Emacs—then Emacs yanks from the clipboard instead of the kill ring.

Normally, rotating the kill ring with `M-y` (**yank-pop**) does not alter the clipboard. However, if you change `yank-pop-change-selection` to `t`, then `M-y` saves the new yank to the clipboard.

To prevent kill and yank commands from accessing the clipboard, change the variable `x-select-enable-clipboard` to `nil`.

Many X desktop environments support a feature called the *clipboard manager*. If you exit Emacs while it is the current "owner" of the clipboard data, and there is a clipboard manager running, Emacs transfers the clipboard data to the clipboard manager so that it is not lost. In some circumstances, this may cause a delay when exiting Emacs; if you wish to prevent Emacs from transferring data to the clipboard manager, change the variable `x-select-enable-clipboard-manager` to `nil`.

Prior to Emacs 24, the kill and yank commands used the primary selection (see Section 9.3.2 [Primary Selection], page 58), not the clipboard. If you prefer this behavior, change `x-select-enable-clipboard` to `nil`, `x-select-enable-primary` to `t`, and `mouse-drag-copy-region` to `t`. In this case, you can use the following commands to act explicitly on the clipboard: `clipboard-kill-region` kills the region and saves it to the clipboard; `clipboard-kill-ring-save` copies the region to the kill ring and saves it to the clipboard; and `clipboard-yank` yanks the contents of the clipboard at point.

9.3.2 Cut and Paste with Other Window Applications

Under the X Window System, there exists a *primary selection* containing the last stretch of text selected in an X application (usually by dragging the mouse). Typically, this text can be inserted into other X applications by `mouse-2` clicks. The primary selection is separate from the clipboard. Its contents are more "fragile"; they are overwritten each time you select text with the mouse, whereas the clipboard is only overwritten by explicit "cut" or "copy" commands.

Under X, whenever the region is active (see Chapter 8 [Mark], page 45), the text in the region is saved in the primary selection. This applies regardless of whether the region was made by dragging or clicking the mouse (see Section 18.1 [Mouse Commands], page 162), or by keyboard commands (e.g., by typing `C-SPC` and moving point; see Section 8.1 [Setting Mark], page 45).

If you change the variable `select-active-regions` to `only`, Emacs saves only temporarily active regions to the primary selection, i.e., those made with the mouse or with shift selection (see Section 8.6 [Shift Selection], page 49). If you change `select-active-regions` to `nil`, Emacs avoids saving active regions to the primary selection entirely.

To insert the primary selection into an Emacs buffer, click `mouse-2` (`mouse-yank-primary`) where you want to insert it. See Section 18.1 [Mouse Commands], page 162.

MS-Windows provides no primary selection, but Emacs emulates it within a single Emacs session by storing the selected text internally. Therefore, all the features and commands related to the primary selection work on Windows as they do on X, for cutting and pasting within the same session, but not across Emacs sessions or with other applications.

9.3.3 Secondary Selection

In addition to the primary selection, the X Window System provides a second similar facility known as the *secondary selection*. Nowadays, few X applications make use of the secondary selection, but you can access it using the following Emacs commands:

`M-Drag-Mouse-1`

> Set the secondary selection, with one end at the place where you press down the button, and the other end at the place where you release it (`mouse-set-secondary`). The selected text is highlighted, using the `secondary-selection`

face, as you drag. The window scrolls automatically if you drag the mouse off the top or bottom of the window, just like `mouse-set-region` (see Section 18.1 [Mouse Commands], page 162).

This command does not alter the kill ring.

`M-Mouse-1`

Set one endpoint for the *secondary selection* (`mouse-start-secondary`).

`M-Mouse-3`

Set the secondary selection, with one end at the position clicked and the other at the position specified with `M-Mouse-1` (`mouse-secondary-save-then-kill`). This also puts the selected text in the kill ring. A second `M-Mouse-3` at the same place kills the secondary selection just made.

`M-Mouse-2`

Insert the secondary selection where you click, placing point at the end of the yanked text (`mouse-yank-secondary`).

Double or triple clicking of `M-Mouse-1` operates on words and lines, much like `Mouse-1`.

If `mouse-yank-at-point` is non-`nil`, `M-Mouse-2` yanks at point. Then it does not matter precisely where you click, or even which of the frame's windows you click on. See Section 18.1 [Mouse Commands], page 162.

9.4 Accumulating Text

Usually we copy or move text by killing it and yanking it, but there are other convenient methods for copying one block of text in many places, or for copying many scattered blocks of text into one place. Here we describe the commands to accumulate scattered pieces of text into a buffer or into a file.

`M-x append-to-buffer`

Append region to the contents of a specified buffer.

`M-x prepend-to-buffer`

Prepend region to the contents of a specified buffer.

`M-x copy-to-buffer`

Copy region into a specified buffer, deleting that buffer's old contents.

`M-x insert-buffer`

Insert the contents of a specified buffer into current buffer at point.

`M-x append-to-file`

Append region to the contents of a specified file, at the end.

To accumulate text into a buffer, use `M-x append-to-buffer`. This reads a buffer name, then inserts a copy of the region into the buffer specified. If you specify a nonexistent buffer, `append-to-buffer` creates the buffer. The text is inserted wherever point is in that buffer. If you have been using the buffer for editing, the copied text goes into the middle of the text of the buffer, starting from wherever point happens to be at that moment.

Point in that buffer is left at the end of the copied text, so successive uses of `append-to-buffer` accumulate the text in the specified buffer in the same order as they were copied.

Strictly speaking, `append-to-buffer` does not always append to the text already in the buffer—it appends only if point in that buffer is at the end. However, if `append-to-buffer` is the only command you use to alter a buffer, then point is always at the end.

`M-x prepend-to-buffer` is just like `append-to-buffer` except that point in the other buffer is left before the copied text, so successive prependings add text in reverse order. `M-x copy-to-buffer` is similar, except that any existing text in the other buffer is deleted, so the buffer is left containing just the text newly copied into it.

The command `M-x insert-buffer` can be used to retrieve the accumulated text from another buffer. This prompts for the name of a buffer, and inserts a copy of all the text in that buffer into the current buffer at point, leaving point at the beginning of the inserted text. It also adds the position of the end of the inserted text to the mark ring, without activating the mark. See Chapter 16 [Buffers], page 147, for background information on buffers.

Instead of accumulating text in a buffer, you can append text directly into a file with `M-x append-to-file`. This prompts for a filename, and adds the text of the region to the end of the specified file. The file is changed immediately on disk.

You should use `append-to-file` only with files that are *not* being visited in Emacs. Using it on a file that you are editing in Emacs would change the file behind Emacs's back, which can lead to losing some of your editing.

Another way to move text around is to store it in a register. See Chapter 10 [Registers], page 64.

9.5 Rectangles

Rectangle commands operate on rectangular areas of the text: all the characters between a certain pair of columns, in a certain range of lines. Emacs has commands to kill rectangles, yank killed rectangles, clear them out, fill them with blanks or text, or delete them. Rectangle commands are useful with text in multicolumn formats, and for changing text into or out of such formats.

To specify a rectangle for a command to work on, set the mark at one corner and point at the opposite corner. The rectangle thus specified is called the *region-rectangle*. If point and the mark are in the same column, the region-rectangle is empty. If they are in the same line, the region-rectangle is one line high.

The region-rectangle is controlled in much the same way as the region is controlled. But remember that a given combination of point and mark values can be interpreted either as a region or as a rectangle, depending on the command that uses them.

C-x r k   Kill the text of the region-rectangle, saving its contents as the "last killed rectangle" (`kill-rectangle`).

C-x r M-w   Save the text of the region-rectangle as the "last killed rectangle" (`copy-rectangle-as-kill`).

C-x r d   Delete the text of the region-rectangle (`delete-rectangle`).

C-x r y   Yank the last killed rectangle with its upper left corner at point (`yank-rectangle`).

C-x r o   Insert blank space to fill the space of the region-rectangle (`open-rectangle`). This pushes the previous contents of the region-rectangle to the right.

C-x r N   Insert line numbers along the left edge of the region-rectangle (`rectangle-number-lines`). This pushes the previous contents of the region-rectangle to the right.

C-x r c   Clear the region-rectangle by replacing all of its contents with spaces (`clear-rectangle`).

M-x delete-whitespace-rectangle

Delete whitespace in each of the lines on the specified rectangle, starting from the left edge column of the rectangle.

C-x r t *string* RET

Replace rectangle contents with *string* on each line (`string-rectangle`).

M-x string-insert-rectangle RET *string* RET

Insert *string* on each line of the rectangle.

C-x SPC   Toggle Rectangle Mark mode (`rectangle-mark-mode`). When this mode is active, the region-rectangle is highlighted and can be shrunk/grown, and the standard kill and yank commands operate on it.

The rectangle operations fall into two classes: commands to erase or insert rectangles, and commands to make blank rectangles.

There are two ways to erase the text in a rectangle: `C-x r d` (`delete-rectangle`) to delete the text outright, or `C-x r k` (`kill-rectangle`) to remove the text and save it as the *last killed rectangle*. In both cases, erasing the region-rectangle is like erasing the specified text on each line of the rectangle; if there is any following text on the line, it moves backwards to fill the gap.

"Killing" a rectangle is not killing in the usual sense; the rectangle is not stored in the kill ring, but in a special place that only records the most recent rectangle killed. This is because yanking a rectangle is so different from yanking linear text that different yank commands have to be used. Yank-popping is not defined for rectangles.

`C-x r M-w` (`copy-rectangle-as-kill`) is the equivalent of `M-w` for rectangles: it records the rectangle as the "last killed rectangle", without deleting the text from the buffer.

To yank the last killed rectangle, type `C-x r y` (`yank-rectangle`). The rectangle's first line is inserted at point, the rectangle's second line is inserted at the same horizontal position one line vertically below, and so on. The number of lines affected is determined by the height of the saved rectangle.

For example, you can convert two single-column lists into a double-column list by killing one of the single-column lists as a rectangle, and then yanking it beside the other list.

You can also copy rectangles into and out of registers with `C-x r r r` and `C-x r i r`. See Section 10.3 [Rectangle Registers], page 65.

There are two commands you can use for making blank rectangles: `C-x r c` (`clear-rectangle`) blanks out existing text in the region-rectangle, and `C-x r o` (`open-rectangle`) inserts a blank rectangle.

`M-x delete-whitespace-rectangle` deletes horizontal whitespace starting from a particular column. This applies to each of the lines in the rectangle, and the column is specified by the left edge of the rectangle. The right edge of the rectangle does not make any difference to this command.

The command `C-x r N` (`rectangle-number-lines`) inserts line numbers along the left edge of the region-rectangle. Normally, the numbering begins from 1 (for the first line of the rectangle). With a prefix argument, the command prompts for a number to begin from, and for a format string with which to print the numbers (see Section "Formatting Strings" in *The Emacs Lisp Reference Manual*).

The command `C-x r t` (`string-rectangle`) replaces the contents of a region-rectangle with a string on each line. The string's width need not be the same as the width of the rectangle. If the string's width is less, the text after the rectangle shifts left; if the string is wider than the rectangle, the text after the rectangle shifts right.

The command `M-x string-insert-rectangle` is similar to `string-rectangle`, but inserts the string on each line, shifting the original text to the right.

The command `C-x SPC` (`rectangle-mark-mode`) toggles whether the region-rectangle or the standard region is highlighted (first activating the region if necessary). When this mode is enabled, commands that resize the region (`C-f`, `C-n` etc.) do so in a rectangular fashion, and killing and yanking operate on the rectangle. See Chapter 9 [Killing], page 52. The mode persists only as long as the region is active.

9.6 CUA Bindings

The command `M-x cua-mode` sets up key bindings that are compatible with the Common User Access (CUA) system used in many other applications.

When CUA mode is enabled, the keys `C-x`, `C-c`, `C-v`, and `C-z` invoke commands that cut (kill), copy, paste (yank), and undo respectively. The `C-x` and `C-c` keys perform cut and copy only if the region is active. Otherwise, they still act as prefix keys, so that standard Emacs commands like `C-x C-c` still work. Note that this means the variable `mark-even-if-inactive` has no effect for `C-x` and `C-c` (see Section 8.3 [Using Region], page 47).

To enter an Emacs command like `C-x C-f` while the mark is active, use one of the following methods: either hold `Shift` together with the prefix key, e.g., `S-C-x C-f`, or quickly type the prefix key twice, e.g., `C-x C-x C-f`.

To disable the overriding of standard Emacs binding by CUA mode, while retaining the other features of CUA mode described below, set the variable `cua-enable-cua-keys` to `nil`.

CUA mode by default activates Delete-Selection mode (see Section 18.1 [Mouse Commands], page 162) so that typed text replaces the active region. To use CUA without this behavior, set the variable `cua-delete-selection` to `nil`.

CUA mode provides enhanced rectangle support with visible rectangle highlighting. Use `C-RET` to start a rectangle, extend it using the movement commands, and cut or copy it using `C-x` or `C-c`. `RET` moves the cursor to the next (clockwise) corner of the rectangle, so you can easily expand it in any direction. Normal text you type is inserted to the left or right of each line in the rectangle (on the same side as the cursor).

You can use this rectangle support without activating CUA by calling the `cua-rectangle-mark-mode` command. But see also the standard `rectangle-mark-mode`. See Section 9.5 [Rectangles], page 60.

With CUA you can easily copy text and rectangles into and out of registers by providing a one-digit numeric prefix to the kill, copy, and yank commands, e.g., `C-1 C-c` copies the region into register 1, and `C-2 C-v` yanks the contents of register 2.

CUA mode also has a global mark feature which allows easy moving and copying of text between buffers. Use `C-S-SPC` to toggle the global mark on and off. When the global mark is on, all text that you kill or copy is automatically inserted at the global mark, and text you type is inserted at the global mark rather than at the current position.

For example, to copy words from various buffers into a word list in a given buffer, set the global mark in the target buffer, then navigate to each of the words you want in the list, mark it (e.g., with `S-M-f`), copy it to the list with `C-c` or `M-w`, and insert a newline after the word in the target list by pressing `RET`.

10 Registers

Emacs *registers* are compartments where you can save text, rectangles, positions, and other things for later use. Once you save text or a rectangle in a register, you can copy it into the buffer once, or many times; once you save a position in a register, you can jump back to that position once, or many times.

Each register has a name that consists of a single character, which we will denote by *r*; *r* can be a letter (such as 'a') or a number (such as '1'); case matters, so register 'a' is not the same as register 'A'.

A register can store a position, a piece of text, a rectangle, a number, a window configuration, or a file name, but only one thing at any given time. Whatever you store in a register remains there until you store something else in that register. To see what register *r* contains, use M-x view-register:

M-x view-register RET *r*
> Display a description of what register *r* contains.

All of the commands that prompt for a register will display a "preview" window that lists the existing registers (if there are any) after a short delay. To change the length of the delay, customize `register-preview-delay`. To prevent this display, set that option to `nil`. You can explicitly request a preview window by pressing C-h or F1.

Bookmarks record files and positions in them, so you can return to those positions when you look at the file again. Bookmarks are similar in spirit to registers, so they are also documented in this chapter.

10.1 Saving Positions in Registers

C-x r SPC *r*
> Record the position of point and the current buffer in register *r* (point-to-register).

C-x r j *r* Jump to the position and buffer saved in register *r* (jump-to-register).

Typing C-x r SPC (point-to-register), followed by a character *r*, saves both the position of point and the current buffer in register *r*. The register retains this information until you store something else in it.

The command C-x r j *r* switches to the buffer recorded in register *r*, and moves point to the recorded position. The contents of the register are not changed, so you can jump to the saved position any number of times.

If you use C-x r j to go to a saved position, but the buffer it was saved from has been killed, C-x r j tries to create the buffer again by visiting the same file. Of course, this works only for buffers that were visiting files.

10.2 Saving Text in Registers

When you want to insert a copy of the same piece of text several times, it may be inconvenient to yank it from the kill ring, since each subsequent kill moves that entry further down the ring. An alternative is to store the text in a register and later retrieve it.

`C-x r s r`   Copy region into register *r* (`copy-to-register`).

`C-x r i r`   Insert text from register *r* (`insert-register`).

`M-x append-to-register RET` *r*

Append region to text in register *r*.

When register *r* contains text, you can use `C-x r +` (`increment-register`) to append to that register. Note that command `C-x r +` behaves differently if *r* contains a number. See Section 10.5 [Number Registers], page 66.

`M-x prepend-to-register RET` *r*

Prepend region to text in register *r*.

`C-x r s r` stores a copy of the text of the region into the register named *r*. If the mark is inactive, Emacs first reactivates the mark where it was last set. The mark is deactivated at the end of this command. See Chapter 8 [Mark], page 45. `C-u C-x r s r`, the same command with a prefix argument, copies the text into register *r* and deletes the text from the buffer as well; you can think of this as "moving" the region text into the register.

`M-x append-to-register RET` *r* appends the copy of the text in the region to the text already stored in the register named *r*. If invoked with a prefix argument, it deletes the region after appending it to the register. The command `prepend-to-register` is similar, except that it *prepends* the region text to the text in the register instead of *appending* it.

When you are collecting text using `append-to-register` and `prepend-to-register`, you may want to separate individual collected pieces using a separator. In that case, configure a `register-separator` and store the separator text in to that register. For example, to get double newlines as text separator during the collection process, you can use the following setting.

```
(setq register-separator ?+)
(set-register register-separator "\n\n")
```

`C-x r i r` inserts in the buffer the text from register *r*. Normally it leaves point before the text and sets the mark after, without activating it. With a numeric argument, it instead puts point after the text and the mark before.

10.3 Saving Rectangles in Registers

A register can contain a rectangle instead of linear text. See Section 9.5 [Rectangles], page 60, for basic information on how to specify a rectangle in the buffer.

`C-x r r r`   Copy the region-rectangle into register *r* (`copy-rectangle-to-register`). With numeric argument, delete it as well.

`C-x r i r`   Insert the rectangle stored in register *r* (if it contains a rectangle) (`insert-register`).

The `C-x r i r` (`insert-register`) command, previously documented in Section 10.2 [Text Registers], page 64, inserts a rectangle rather than a text string, if the register contains a rectangle.

10.4 Saving Window Configurations in Registers

You can save the window configuration of the selected frame in a register, or even the configuration of all windows in all frames, and restore the configuration later. See Chapter 17 [Windows], page 156, for information about window configurations.

C-x r w r   Save the state of the selected frame's windows in register r (`window-configuration-to-register`).

C-x r f r   Save the state of all frames, including all their windows, in register r (`frameset-to-register`).

Use C-x r j r to restore a window or frame configuration. This is the same command used to restore a cursor position. When you restore a frame configuration, any existing frames not included in the configuration become invisible. If you wish to delete these frames instead, use C-u C-x r j r.

10.5 Keeping Numbers in Registers

There are commands to store a number in a register, to insert the number in the buffer in decimal, and to increment it. These commands can be useful in keyboard macros (see Chapter 14 [Keyboard Macros], page 114).

C-u *number* C-x r n r

Store *number* into register r (`number-to-register`).

C-u *number* C-x r + r

If r contains a number, increment the number in that register by *number*. Note that command C-x r + (`increment-register`) behaves differently if r contains text. See Section 10.2 [Text Registers], page 64.

C-x r i r   Insert the number from register r into the buffer.

C-x r i is the same command used to insert any other sort of register contents into the buffer. C-x r + with no numeric argument increments the register value by 1; C-x r n with no numeric argument stores zero in the register.

10.6 Keeping File Names in Registers

If you visit certain file names frequently, you can visit them more conveniently if you put their names in registers. Here's the Lisp code used to put a file *name* into register r:

```
(set-register r '(file . name))
```

For example,

```
(set-register ?z '(file . "/gd/gnu/emacs/19.0/src/ChangeLog"))
```

puts the file name shown in register 'z'.

To visit the file whose name is in register *r*, type `C-x r j` *r*. (This is the same command used to jump to a position or restore a frame configuration.)

10.7 Keyboard Macro Registers

If you need to execute a keyboard macro (see Chapter 14 [Keyboard Macros], page 114) frequently, it is more convenient to put it in a register or save it (see Section 14.5 [Save Keyboard Macro], page 118). `C-x C-k x` *r* (`kmacro-to-register`) stores the last keyboard macro in register *r*.

To execute the keyboard macro in register *r*, type `C-x r j` *r*. (This is the same command used to jump to a position or restore a frameset.)

10.8 Bookmarks

Bookmarks are somewhat like registers in that they record positions you can jump to. Unlike registers, they have long names, and they persist automatically from one Emacs session to the next. The prototypical use of bookmarks is to record "where you were reading" in various files.

`C-x r m RET`
> Set the bookmark for the visited file, at point.

`C-x r m` *bookmark* `RET`
> Set the bookmark named *bookmark* at point (`bookmark-set`).

`C-x r b` *bookmark* `RET`
> Jump to the bookmark named *bookmark* (`bookmark-jump`).

`C-x r l`   List all bookmarks (`list-bookmarks`).

`M-x bookmark-save`
> Save all the current bookmark values in the default bookmark file.

The prototypical use for bookmarks is to record one current position in each of several files. So the command `C-x r m`, which sets a bookmark, uses the visited file name as the default for the bookmark name. If you name each bookmark after the file it points to, then you can conveniently revisit any of those files with `C-x r b`, and move to the position of the bookmark at the same time.

To display a list of all your bookmarks in a separate buffer, type `C-x r l` (`list-bookmarks`). If you switch to that buffer, you can use it to edit your bookmark definitions or annotate the bookmarks. Type `C-h m` in the bookmark buffer for more information about its special editing commands.

When you kill Emacs, Emacs saves your bookmarks, if you have changed any bookmark values. You can also save the bookmarks at any time with the `M-x bookmark-save` command. Bookmarks are saved to the file `~/.emacs.d/bookmarks` (for compatibility with older versions of Emacs, if you have a file named `~/.emacs.bmk`, that is used instead).

The bookmark commands load your default bookmark file automatically. This saving and loading is how bookmarks persist from one Emacs session to the next.

If you set the variable `bookmark-save-flag` to 1, each command that sets a bookmark will also save your bookmarks; this way, you don't lose any bookmark values even if Emacs crashes. The value, if a number, says how many bookmark modifications should go by between saving. If you set this variable to `nil`, Emacs only saves bookmarks if you explicitly use `M-x bookmark-save`.

The variable `bookmark-default-file` specifies the file in which to save bookmarks by default.

Bookmark position values are saved with surrounding context, so that `bookmark-jump` can find the proper position even if the file is modified slightly. The variable `bookmark-search-size` says how many characters of context to record on each side of the bookmark's position.

Here are some additional commands for working with bookmarks:

`M-x bookmark-load RET` *filename* `RET`

Load a file named *filename* that contains a list of bookmark values. You can use this command, as well as `bookmark-write`, to work with other files of bookmark values in addition to your default bookmark file.

`M-x bookmark-write RET` *filename* `RET`

Save all the current bookmark values in the file *filename*.

`M-x bookmark-delete RET` *bookmark* `RET`

Delete the bookmark named *bookmark*.

`M-x bookmark-insert-location RET` *bookmark* `RET`

Insert in the buffer the name of the file that bookmark *bookmark* points to.

`M-x bookmark-insert RET` *bookmark* `RET`

Insert in the buffer the *contents* of the file that bookmark *bookmark* points to.

11 Controlling the Display

Since only part of a large buffer fits in the window, Emacs has to show only a part of it. This chapter describes commands and variables that let you specify which part of the text you want to see, and how the text is displayed.

11.1 Scrolling

If a window is too small to display all the text in its buffer, it displays only a portion of it. *Scrolling* commands change which portion of the buffer is displayed.

Scrolling "forward" or "up" advances the portion of the buffer displayed in the window; equivalently, it moves the buffer text upwards relative to the window. Scrolling "backward" or "down" displays an earlier portion of the buffer, and moves the text downwards relative to the window.

In Emacs, scrolling "up" or "down" refers to the direction that the text moves in the window, *not* the direction that the window moves relative to the text. This terminology was adopted by Emacs before the modern meaning of "scrolling up" and "scrolling down" became widespread. Hence, the strange result that `PageDown` scrolls "up" in the Emacs sense.

The portion of a buffer displayed in a window always contains point. If you move point past the bottom or top of the window, scrolling occurs automatically to bring it back onscreen (see Section 11.3 [Auto Scrolling], page 71). You can also scroll explicitly with these commands:

C-v
next
PageDown   Scroll forward by nearly a full window (`scroll-up-command`).

M-v
prior
PageUp   Scroll backward (`scroll-down-command`).

C-v (`scroll-up-command`) scrolls forward by nearly the whole window height. The effect is to take the two lines at the bottom of the window and put them at the top, followed by lines that were not previously visible. If point was in the text that scrolled off the top, it ends up on the window's new topmost line. The `next` (or `PageDown`) key is equivalent to C-v.

M-v (`scroll-down-command`) scrolls backward in a similar way. The `prior` (or `PageUp`) key is equivalent to M-v.

The number of lines of overlap left by these scroll commands is controlled by the variable `next-screen-context-lines`, whose default value is 2. You can supply the commands with a numeric prefix argument, n, to scroll by n lines; Emacs attempts to leave point unchanged, so that the text and point move up or down together. C-v with a negative argument is like M-v and vice versa.

By default, these commands signal an error (by beeping or flashing the screen) if no more scrolling is possible, because the window has reached the beginning or end of the buffer. If you change the variable `scroll-error-top-bottom` to t, the command moves point to the farthest possible position. If point is already there, the command signals an error.

Some users like scroll commands to keep point at the same screen position, so that scrolling back to the same screen conveniently returns point to its original position. You can enable this behavior via the variable `scroll-preserve-screen-position`. If the value is `t`, Emacs adjusts point to keep the cursor at the same screen position whenever a scroll command moves it off-window, rather than moving it to the topmost or bottommost line. With any other non-`nil` value, Emacs adjusts point this way even if the scroll command leaves point in the window. This variable affects all the scroll commands documented in this section, as well as scrolling with the mouse wheel (see Section 18.1 [Mouse Commands], page 162); in general, it affects any command that has a non-`nil` `scroll-command` property. See Section "Property Lists" in *The Emacs Lisp Reference Manual*.

The commands M-x `scroll-up` and M-x `scroll-down` behave similarly to `scroll-up-command` and `scroll-down-command`, except they do not obey `scroll-error-top-bottom`. Prior to Emacs 24, these were the default commands for scrolling up and down. The commands M-x `scroll-up-line` and M-x `scroll-down-line` scroll the current window by one line at a time. If you intend to use any of these commands, you might want to give them key bindings (see Section 33.3.6 [Init Rebinding], page 432).

11.2 Recentering

C-l   Scroll the selected window so the current line is the center-most text line; on subsequent consecutive invocations, make the current line the top line, the bottom line, and so on in cyclic order. Possibly redisplay the screen too (`recenter-top-bottom`).

M-x recenter
           Scroll the selected window so the current line is the center-most text line. Possibly redisplay the screen too.

C-M-l   Scroll heuristically to bring useful information onto the screen (`reposition-window`).

The C-l (`recenter-top-bottom`) command *recenters* the selected window, scrolling it so that the current screen line is exactly in the center of the window, or as close to the center as possible.

Typing C-l twice in a row (C-l C-l) scrolls the window so that point is on the topmost screen line. Typing a third C-l scrolls the window so that point is on the bottom-most screen line. Each successive C-l cycles through these three positions.

You can change the cycling order by customizing the list variable `recenter-positions`. Each list element should be the symbol `top`, `middle`, or `bottom`, or a number; an integer means to move the line to the specified screen line, while a floating-point number between 0.0 and 1.0 specifies a percentage of the screen space from the top of the window. The default, (`middle top bottom`), is the cycling order described above. Furthermore, if you change the variable `scroll-margin` to a non-zero value n, C-l always leaves at least n screen lines between point and the top or bottom of the window (see Section 11.3 [Auto Scrolling], page 71).

You can also give C-l a prefix argument. A plain prefix argument, C-u C-l, simply recenters point. A positive argument n puts point n lines down from the top of the window. An argument of zero puts point on the topmost line. A negative argument $-n$ puts point *n* lines from the bottom of the window. When given an argument, `C-l` does not clear the screen or cycle through different screen positions.

If the variable `recenter-redisplay` has a non-`nil` value, each invocation of `C-l` also clears and redisplays the screen; the special value `tty` (the default) says to do this on text-terminal frames only. Redisplaying is useful in case the screen becomes garbled for any reason (see Section 34.2.3 [Screen Garbled], page 445).

The more primitive command `M-x recenter` behaves like `recenter-top-bottom`, but does not cycle among screen positions.

`C-M-l` (`reposition-window`) scrolls the current window heuristically in a way designed to get useful information onto the screen. For example, in a Lisp file, this command tries to get the entire current defun onto the screen if possible.

11.3 Automatic Scrolling

Emacs performs *automatic scrolling* when point moves out of the visible portion of the text. Normally, automatic scrolling centers point vertically in the window, but there are several ways to alter this behavior.

If you set `scroll-conservatively` to a small number *n*, then moving point just a little off the screen (no more than *n* lines) causes Emacs to scroll just enough to bring point back on screen; if doing so fails to make point visible, Emacs scrolls just far enough to center point in the window. If you set `scroll-conservatively` to a large number (larger than 100), automatic scrolling never centers point, no matter how far point moves; Emacs always scrolls text just enough to bring point into view, either at the top or bottom of the window depending on the scroll direction. By default, `scroll-conservatively` is 0, which means to always center point in the window.

Another way to control automatic scrolling is to customize the variable `scroll-step`. Its value determines the number of lines by which to automatically scroll, when point moves off the screen. If scrolling by that number of lines fails to bring point back into view, point is centered instead. The default value is zero, which (by default) causes point to always be centered after scrolling.

A third way to control automatic scrolling is to customize the variables `scroll-up-aggressively` and `scroll-down-aggressively`, which directly specify the vertical position of point after scrolling. The value of `scroll-up-aggressively` should be either `nil` (the default), or a floating point number *f* between 0 and 1. The latter means that when point goes below the bottom window edge (i.e., scrolling forward), Emacs scrolls the window so that point is *f* parts of the window height from the bottom window edge. Thus, larger *f* means more aggressive scrolling: more new text is brought into view. The default value, `nil`, is equivalent to 0.5.

Likewise, `scroll-down-aggressively` is used when point goes above the bottom window edge (i.e., scrolling backward). The value specifies how far point should be from the top margin of the window after scrolling. Thus, as with `scroll-up-aggressively`, a larger value is more aggressive.

Note that the variables `scroll-conservatively`, `scroll-step`, and `scroll-up-aggressively` / `scroll-down-aggressively` control automatic scrolling in contradictory ways. Therefore, you should pick no more than one of these methods to customize automatic scrolling. In case you customize multiple variables, the order of priority is: `scroll-conservatively`, then `scroll-step`, and finally `scroll-up-aggressively` / `scroll-down-aggressively`.

The variable `scroll-margin` restricts how close point can come to the top or bottom of a window (even if aggressive scrolling specifies a fraction *f* that is larger than the window portion between the top and the bottom margins). Its value is a number of screen lines; if point comes within that many lines of the top or bottom of the window, Emacs performs automatic scrolling. By default, `scroll-margin` is 0.

11.4 Horizontal Scrolling

Horizontal scrolling means shifting all the lines sideways within a window, so that some of the text near the left margin is not displayed. When the text in a window is scrolled horizontally, text lines are truncated rather than continued (see Section 11.21 [Line Truncation], page 87). If a window shows truncated lines, Emacs performs automatic horizontal scrolling whenever point moves off the left or right edge of the screen. To disable automatic horizontal scrolling, set the variable `auto-hscroll-mode` to `nil`. Note that when the automatic horizontal scrolling is turned off, if point moves off the edge of the screen, the cursor disappears to indicate that. (On text terminals, the cursor is left at the edge instead.)

The variable `hscroll-margin` controls how close point can get to the window's left and right edges before automatic scrolling occurs. It is measured in columns. For example, if the value is 5, then moving point within 5 columns of an edge causes horizontal scrolling away from that edge.

The variable `hscroll-step` determines how many columns to scroll the window when point gets too close to the edge. Zero, the default value, means to center point horizontally within the window. A positive integer value specifies the number of columns to scroll by. A floating-point number specifies the fraction of the window's width to scroll by.

You can also perform explicit horizontal scrolling with the following commands:

C-x <   Scroll text in current window to the left (`scroll-left`).

C-x >   Scroll to the right (`scroll-right`).

C-x < (`scroll-left`) scrolls text in the selected window to the left by the full width of the window, less two columns. (In other words, the text in the window moves left relative to the window.) With a numeric argument *n*, it scrolls by *n* columns.

If the text is scrolled to the left, and point moves off the left edge of the window, the cursor will freeze at the left edge of the window, until point moves back to the displayed portion of the text. This is independent of the current setting of `auto-hscroll-mode`, which, for text scrolled to the left, only affects the behavior at the right edge of the window.

C-x > (`scroll-right`) scrolls similarly to the right. The window cannot be scrolled any farther to the right once it is displayed normally, with each line starting at the window's left margin; attempting to do so has no effect. This means that you don't have to calculate the argument precisely for C-x >; any sufficiently large argument will restore the normal display.

If you use those commands to scroll a window horizontally, that sets a lower bound for automatic horizontal scrolling. Automatic scrolling will continue to scroll the window, but never farther to the right than the amount you previously set by `scroll-left`.

11.5 Narrowing

Narrowing means focusing in on some portion of the buffer, making the rest temporarily inaccessible. The portion which you can still get to is called the *accessible portion*. Canceling the narrowing, which makes the entire buffer once again accessible, is called *widening*. The bounds of narrowing in effect in a buffer are called the buffer's *restriction*.

Narrowing can make it easier to concentrate on a single subroutine or paragraph by eliminating clutter. It can also be used to limit the range of operation of a replace command or repeating keyboard macro.

C-x n n   Narrow down to between point and mark (`narrow-to-region`).

C-x n w   Widen to make the entire buffer accessible again (`widen`).

C-x n p   Narrow down to the current page (`narrow-to-page`).

C-x n d   Narrow down to the current defun (`narrow-to-defun`).

When you have narrowed down to a part of the buffer, that part appears to be all there is. You can't see the rest, you can't move into it (motion commands won't go outside the accessible part), you can't change it in any way. However, it is not gone, and if you save the file all the inaccessible text will be saved. The word '`Narrow`' appears in the mode line whenever narrowing is in effect.

The primary narrowing command is `C-x n n` (`narrow-to-region`). It sets the current buffer's restrictions so that the text in the current region remains accessible, but all text before the region or after the region is inaccessible. Point and mark do not change.

Alternatively, use `C-x n p` (`narrow-to-page`) to narrow down to the current page. See Section 22.4 [Pages], page 211, for the definition of a page. `C-x n d` (`narrow-to-defun`) narrows down to the defun containing point (see Section 23.2 [Defuns], page 241).

The way to cancel narrowing is to widen with `C-x n w` (`widen`). This makes all text in the buffer accessible again.

You can get information on what part of the buffer you are narrowed down to using the `C-x =` command. See Section 4.9 [Position Info], page 22.

Because narrowing can easily confuse users who do not understand it, `narrow-to-region` is normally a disabled command. Attempting to use this command asks for confirmation and gives you the option of enabling it; if you enable the command, confirmation will no longer be required for it. See Section 33.3.11 [Disabling], page 437.

11.6 View Mode

View mode is a minor mode that lets you scan a buffer by sequential screenfuls. It provides commands for scrolling through the buffer conveniently but not for changing it. Apart from the usual Emacs cursor motion commands, you can type SPC to scroll forward one windowful, S-SPC or DEL to scroll backward, and s to start an incremental search.

Typing q (`View-quit`) disables View mode, and switches back to the buffer and position before View mode was enabled. Typing e (`View-exit`) disables View mode, keeping the current buffer and position.

`M-x view-buffer` prompts for an existing Emacs buffer, switches to it, and enables View mode. `M-x view-file` prompts for a file and visits it with View mode enabled.

11.7 Follow Mode

Follow mode is a minor mode that makes two windows, both showing the same buffer, scroll as a single tall "virtual window". To use Follow mode, go to a frame with just one window, split it into two side-by-side windows using `C-x 3`, and then type `M-x follow-mode`. From then on, you can edit the buffer in either of the two windows, or scroll either one; the other window follows it.

In Follow mode, if you move point outside the portion visible in one window and into the portion visible in the other window, that selects the other window—again, treating the two as if they were parts of one large window.

To turn off Follow mode, type `M-x follow-mode` a second time.

11.8 Text Faces

Emacs can display text in several different styles, called *faces*. Each face can specify various *face attributes*, such as the font, height, weight, slant, foreground and background color, and underlining or overlining. Most major modes assign faces to the text automatically, via Font Lock mode. See Section 11.12 [Font Lock], page 78, for more information about how these faces are assigned.

To see what faces are currently defined, and what they look like, type `M-x list-faces-display`. With a prefix argument, this prompts for a regular expression, and displays only faces with names matching that regular expression (see Section 12.6 [Regexps], page 97).

It's possible for a given face to look different in different frames. For instance, some text terminals do not support all face attributes, particularly font, height, and width, and some support a limited range of colors. In addition, most Emacs faces are defined so that their attributes are different on light and dark frame backgrounds, for reasons of legibility. By default, Emacs automatically chooses which set of face attributes to display on each frame, based on the frame's current background color. However, you can override this by giving the variable `frame-background-mode` a non-`nil` value. A value of `dark` makes Emacs treat all frames as if they have a dark background, whereas a value of `light` makes it treat all frames as if they have a light background.

You can customize a face to alter its attributes, and save those customizations for future Emacs sessions. See Section 33.1.5 [Face Customization], page 416, for details.

The `default` face is the default for displaying text, and all of its attributes are specified. Its background color is also used as the frame's background color. See Section 11.9 [Colors], page 75.

Another special face is the `cursor` face. On graphical displays, the background color of this face is used to draw the text cursor. None of the other attributes of this face have any effect; the foreground color for text under the cursor is taken from the background color of the underlying text. On text terminals, the appearance of the text cursor is determined by the terminal, not by the `cursor` face.

You can also use X resources to specify attributes of any particular face. See Section D.1 [Resources], page 493.

Emacs can display variable-width fonts, but some Emacs commands, particularly indentation commands, do not account for variable character display widths. Therefore, we recommend not using variable width fonts for most faces, particularly those assigned by Font Lock mode.

11.9 Colors for Faces

Faces can have various foreground and background colors. When you specify a color for a face—for instance, when customizing the face (see Section 33.1.5 [Face Customization], page 416)—you can use either a *color name* or an *RGB triplet*.

A color name is a pre-defined name, such as 'dark orange' or 'medium sea green'. To view a list of color names, type M-x list-colors-display. To control the order in which colors are shown, customize list-colors-sort. If you run this command on a graphical display, it shows the full range of color names known to Emacs (these are the standard X11 color names, defined in X's rgb.txt file). If you run the command on a text terminal, it shows only a small subset of colors that can be safely displayed on such terminals. However, Emacs understands X11 color names even on text terminals; if a face is given a color specified by an X11 color name, it is displayed using the closest-matching terminal color.

An RGB triplet is a string of the form '#RRGGBB'. Each of the R, G, and B components is a hexadecimal number specifying the component's relative intensity, one to four digits long (usually two digits are used). The components must have the same number of digits. For hexadecimal values A to F, either upper or lower case are acceptable.

The M-x list-colors-display command also shows the equivalent RGB triplet for each named color. For instance, 'medium sea green' is equivalent to '#3CB371'.

You can change the foreground and background colors of a face with M-x set-face-foreground and M-x set-face-background. These commands prompt in the minibuffer for a face name and a color, with completion, and then set that face to use the specified color. They affect the face colors on all frames, but their effects do not persist for future Emacs sessions, unlike using the customization buffer or X resources. You can also use frame parameters to set foreground and background colors for a specific frame; See Section 18.11 [Frame Parameters], page 172.

11.10 Standard Faces

Here are the standard faces for specifying text appearance. You can apply them to specific text when you want the effects they produce.

default   This face is used for ordinary text that doesn't specify any face. Its background color is used as the frame's background color.

bold   This face uses a bold variant of the default font.

italic   This face uses an italic variant of the default font.

bold-italic
           This face uses a bold italic variant of the default font.

underline
           This face underlines text.

fixed-pitch
> This face forces use of a fixed-width font. It's reasonable to customize this face to use a different fixed-width font, if you like, but you should not make it a variable-width font.

variable-pitch
> This face forces use of a variable-width font.

shadow   This face is used for making the text less noticeable than the surrounding ordinary text. Usually this can be achieved by using shades of gray in contrast with either black or white default foreground color.

Here's an incomplete list of faces used to highlight parts of the text temporarily for specific purposes. (Many other modes define their own faces for this purpose.)

highlight
> This face is used for text highlighting in various contexts, such as when the mouse cursor is moved over a hyperlink.

isearch   This face is used to highlight the current Isearch match (see Section 12.1 [Incremental Search], page 90).

query-replace
> This face is used to highlight the current Query Replace match (see Section 12.10 [Replace], page 103).

lazy-highlight
> This face is used to highlight "lazy matches" for Isearch and Query Replace (matches other than the current one).

region   This face is used for displaying an active region (see Chapter 8 [Mark], page 45). When Emacs is built with GTK support, its colors are taken from the current GTK theme.

secondary-selection
> This face is used for displaying a secondary X selection (see Section 9.3.3 [Secondary Selection], page 58).

trailing-whitespace
> The face for highlighting excess spaces and tabs at the end of a line when **show-trailing-whitespace** is non-nil (see Section 11.16 [Useless Whitespace], page 82).

escape-glyph
> The face for displaying control characters and escape sequences (see Section 11.19 [Text Display], page 85).

nobreak-space
> The face for displaying "no-break" space characters (see Section 11.19 [Text Display], page 85).

The following faces control the appearance of parts of the Emacs frame:

mode-line

>This face is used for the mode line of the currently selected window, and for menu bars when toolkit menus are not used. By default, it's drawn with shadows for a "raised" effect on graphical displays, and drawn as the inverse of the default face on non-windowed terminals.

mode-line-inactive

>Like `mode-line`, but used for mode lines of the windows other than the selected one (if `mode-line-in-non-selected-windows` is non-nil). This face inherits from `mode-line`, so changes in that face affect mode lines in all windows.

mode-line-highlight

>Like `highlight`, but used for mouse-sensitive portions of text on mode lines. Such portions of text typically pop up tooltips (see Section 18.17 [Tooltips], page 174) when the mouse pointer hovers above them.

mode-line-buffer-id

>This face is used for buffer identification parts in the mode line.

header-line

>Similar to `mode-line` for a window's header line, which appears at the top of a window just as the mode line appears at the bottom. Most windows do not have a header line—only some special modes, such Info mode, create one.

vertical-border

>This face is used for the vertical divider between windows on text terminals.

minibuffer-prompt

>This face is used for the prompt strings displayed in the minibuffer. By default, Emacs automatically adds this face to the value of `minibuffer-prompt-properties`, which is a list of text properties used to display the prompt text. (This variable takes effect when you enter the minibuffer.)

fringe

>The face for the fringes to the left and right of windows on graphic displays. (The fringes are the narrow portions of the Emacs frame between the text area and the window's right and left borders.) See Section 11.14 [Fringes], page 81.

cursor

>The `:background` attribute of this face specifies the color of the text cursor. See Section 11.20 [Cursor Display], page 86.

tooltip

>This face is used for tooltip text. By default, if Emacs is built with GTK support, tooltips are drawn via GTK and this face has no effect. See Section 18.17 [Tooltips], page 174.

mouse

>This face determines the color of the mouse pointer.

The following faces likewise control the appearance of parts of the Emacs frame, but only on text terminals, or when Emacs is built on X with no toolkit support. (For all other cases, the appearance of the respective frame elements is determined by system-wide settings.)

scroll-bar

>This face determines the visual appearance of the scroll bar. See Section 18.12 [Scroll Bars], page 172.

tool-bar   This face determines the color of tool bar icons. See Section 18.15 [Tool Bars], page 173.

menu   This face determines the colors and font of Emacs's menus. See Section 18.14 [Menu Bars], page 173.

tty-menu-enabled-face

       This face is used to display enabled menu items on text-mode terminals.

tty-menu-disabled-face

       This face is used to display disabled menu items on text-mode terminals.

tty-menu-selected-face

       This face is used to display on text-mode terminals the menu item that would be selected if you click a mouse or press RET.

11.11 Text Scale

To increase the height of the default face in the current buffer, type C-x C-+ or C-x C-=. To decrease it, type C-x C--. To restore the default (global) face height, type C-x C-0. These keys are all bound to the same command, text-scale-adjust, which looks at the last key typed to determine which action to take.

The final key of these commands may be repeated without the leading C-x. For instance, C-x C-= C-= C-= increases the face height by three steps. Each step scales the text height by a factor of 1.2; to change this factor, customize the variable text-scale-mode-step. A numeric argument of 0 to the text-scale-adjust command restores the default height, the same as typing C-x C-0.

The commands text-scale-increase and text-scale-decrease increase or decrease the height of the default face, just like C-x C-+ and C-x C-- respectively. You may find it convenient to bind to these commands, rather than text-scale-adjust.

The command text-scale-set scales the height of the default face in the current buffer to an absolute level specified by its prefix argument.

The above commands automatically enable the minor mode text-scale-mode if the current font scaling is other than 1, and disable it otherwise.

11.12 Font Lock mode

Font Lock mode is a minor mode, always local to a particular buffer, which assigns faces to (or *fontifies*) the text in the buffer. Each buffer's major mode tells Font Lock mode which text to fontify; for instance, programming language modes fontify syntactically relevant constructs like comments, strings, and function names.

Font Lock mode is enabled by default. To toggle it in the current buffer, type M-x font-lock-mode. A positive numeric argument unconditionally enables Font Lock mode, and a negative or zero argument disables it.

Type M-x global-font-lock-mode to toggle Font Lock mode in all buffers. To impose this setting for future Emacs sessions, customize the variable global-font-lock-mode (see Section 33.1 [Easy Customization], page 412), or add the following line to your init file:

```
(global-font-lock-mode 0)
```

If you have disabled Global Font Lock mode, you can still enable Font Lock for specific major modes by adding the function `font-lock-mode` to the mode hooks (see Section 33.2.2 [Hooks], page 422). For example, to enable Font Lock mode for editing C files, you can do this:

```
(add-hook 'c-mode-hook 'font-lock-mode)
```

Font Lock mode uses several specifically named faces to do its job, including `font-lock-string-face`, `font-lock-comment-face`, and others. The easiest way to find them all is to use `M-x customize-group RET font-lock-faces RET`. You can then use that customization buffer to customize the appearance of these faces. See Section 33.1.5 [Face Customization], page 416.

You can customize the variable `font-lock-maximum-decoration` to alter the amount of fontification applied by Font Lock mode, for major modes that support this feature. The value should be a number (with 1 representing a minimal amount of fontification; some modes support levels as high as 3); or `t`, meaning "as high as possible" (the default). You can also specify different numbers for particular major modes; for example, to use level 1 for C/C++ modes, and the default level otherwise, use the value

```
'((c-mode . 1) (c++-mode . 1)))
```

Comment and string fontification (or "syntactic" fontification) relies on analysis of the syntactic structure of the buffer text. For the sake of speed, some modes, including Lisp mode, rely on a special convention: an open-parenthesis or open-brace in the leftmost column always defines the beginning of a defun, and is thus always outside any string or comment. Therefore, you should avoid placing an open-parenthesis or open-brace in the leftmost column, if it is inside a string or comment. See Section 23.2.1 [Left Margin Paren], page 241, for details.

The variable `font-lock-beginning-of-syntax-function`, which is always buffer-local, specifies how Font Lock mode can find a position guaranteed to be outside any comment or string. In modes which use the leftmost column parenthesis convention, the default value of the variable is `beginning-of-defun`—that tells Font Lock mode to use the convention. If you set this variable to `nil`, Font Lock no longer relies on the convention. This avoids incorrect results, but the price is that, in some cases, fontification for a changed text must rescan buffer text from the beginning of the buffer. This can considerably slow down redisplay while scrolling, particularly if you are close to the end of a large buffer.

Font Lock highlighting patterns already exist for most modes, but you may want to fontify additional patterns. You can use the function `font-lock-add-keywords`, to add your own highlighting patterns for a particular mode. For example, to highlight 'FIXME:' words in C comments, use this:

```
(add-hook 'c-mode-hook
          (lambda ()
           (font-lock-add-keywords nil
            '(("\\<\\(FIXME\\):" 1
               font-lock-warning-face t)))))
```

To remove keywords from the font-lock highlighting patterns, use the function `font-lock-remove-keywords`. See Section "Search-based Fontification" in *The Emacs Lisp Reference Manual*.

Fontifying large buffers can take a long time. To avoid large delays when a file is visited, Emacs initially fontifies only the visible portion of a buffer. As you scroll through the buffer, each portion that becomes visible is fontified as soon as it is displayed; this type of Font Lock is called *Just-In-Time* (or *JIT*) Lock. You can control how JIT Lock behaves, including telling it to perform fontification while idle, by customizing variables in the customization group 'jit-lock'. See Section 33.1.6 [Specific Customization], page 417.

11.13 Interactive Highlighting

Highlight Changes mode is a minor mode that *highlights* the parts of the buffer that were changed most recently, by giving that text a different face. To enable or disable Highlight Changes mode, use M-x highlight-changes-mode.

Hi Lock mode is a minor mode that highlights text that matches regular expressions you specify. For example, you can use it to highlight all the references to a certain variable in a program source file, highlight certain parts in a voluminous output of some program, or highlight certain names in an article. To enable or disable Hi Lock mode, use the command M-x hi-lock-mode. To enable Hi Lock mode for all buffers, use M-x global-hi-lock-mode or place (global-hi-lock-mode 1) in your .emacs file.

Hi Lock mode works like Font Lock mode (see Section 11.12 [Font Lock], page 78), except that you specify explicitly the regular expressions to highlight. You control them with these commands:

M-s h r *regexp* RET *face* RET
C-x w h *regexp* RET *face* RET

> Highlight text that matches *regexp* using face *face* (highlight-regexp). The highlighting will remain as long as the buffer is loaded. For example, to highlight all occurrences of the word "whim" using the default face (a yellow background) M-s h r whim RET RET. Any face can be used for highlighting, Hi Lock provides several of its own and these are pre-loaded into a list of default values. While being prompted for a face use M-n and M-p to cycle through them.
>
> Setting the option hi-lock-auto-select-face to a non-nil value causes this command (and other Hi Lock commands that read faces) to automatically choose the next face from the default list without prompting.
>
> You can use this command multiple times, specifying various regular expressions to highlight in different ways.

M-s h u *regexp* RET
C-x w r *regexp* RET

> Unhighlight *regexp* (unhighlight-regexp).
>
> If you invoke this from the menu, you select the expression to unhighlight from a list. If you invoke this from the keyboard, you use the minibuffer. It will show the most recently added regular expression; use M-n to show the next older expression and M-p to select the next newer expression. (You can also type the expression by hand, with completion.) When the expression you want to unhighlight appears in the minibuffer, press RET to exit the minibuffer and unhighlight it.

M-s h l *regexp* RET *face* RET
C-x w l *regexp* RET *face* RET

> Highlight entire lines containing a match for *regexp*, using face *face* (`highlight-lines-matching-regexp`).

M-s h p *phrase* RET *face* RET
C-x w p *phrase* RET *face* RET

> Highlight matches of *phrase*, using face *face* (`highlight-phrase`). *phrase* can be any regexp, but spaces will be replaced by matches to whitespace and initial lower-case letters will become case insensitive.

M-s h .
C-x w .

> Highlight the symbol found near point, using the next available face (`highlight-symbol-at-point`).

M-s h w
C-x w b

> Insert all the current highlighting regexp/face pairs into the buffer at point, with comment delimiters to prevent them from changing your program. (This key binding runs the `hi-lock-write-interactive-patterns` command.)
>
> These patterns are extracted from the comments, if appropriate, if you invoke M-x `hi-lock-find-patterns`, or if you visit the file while Hi Lock mode is enabled (since that runs `hi-lock-find-patterns`).

M-s h f
C-x w i

> Extract regexp/face pairs from comments in the current buffer (`hi-lock-find-patterns`). Thus, you can enter patterns interactively with `highlight-regexp`, store them into the file with `hi-lock-write-interactive-patterns`, edit them (perhaps including different faces for different parenthesized parts of the match), and finally use this command (`hi-lock-find-patterns`) to have Hi Lock highlight the edited patterns.
>
> The variable `hi-lock-file-patterns-policy` controls whether Hi Lock mode should automatically extract and highlight patterns found in a file when it is visited. Its value can be `nil` (never highlight), `ask` (query the user), or a function. If it is a function, `hi-lock-find-patterns` calls it with the patterns as argument; if the function returns non-`nil`, the patterns are used. The default is `ask`. Note that patterns are always highlighted if you call `hi-lock-find-patterns` directly, regardless of the value of this variable.
>
> Also, `hi-lock-find-patterns` does nothing if the current major mode's symbol is a member of the list `hi-lock-exclude-modes`.

11.14 Window Fringes

On graphical displays, each Emacs window normally has narrow *fringes* on the left and right edges. The fringes are used to display symbols that provide information about the text in the window. You can type M-x `fringe-mode` to disable the fringes, or modify their width. This command affects fringes in all frames; to modify fringes on the selected frame only, use M-x `set-fringe-style`. You can make your changes to the fringes permanent by customizing the variable `fringe-mode`.

The most common use of the fringes is to indicate a continuation line (see Section 4.8 [Continuation Lines], page 22). When one line of text is split into multiple screen lines, the left fringe shows a curving arrow for each screen line except the first, indicating that "this is not the real beginning". The right fringe shows a curving arrow for each screen line except the last, indicating that "this is not the real end". If the line's direction is right-to-left (see Section 19.19 [Bidirectional Editing], page 197), the meanings of the curving arrows in the fringes are swapped.

The fringes indicate line truncation with short horizontal arrows meaning "there's more text on this line which is scrolled horizontally out of view". Clicking the mouse on one of the arrows scrolls the display horizontally in the direction of the arrow.

The fringes can also indicate other things, such as buffer boundaries (see Section 11.15 [Displaying Boundaries], page 82), and where a program you are debugging is executing (see Section 24.6 [Debuggers], page 266).

The fringe is also used for drawing the cursor, if the current line is exactly as wide as the window and point is at the end of the line. To disable this, change the variable `overflow-newline-into-fringe` to `nil`; this causes Emacs to continue or truncate lines that are exactly as wide as the window.

11.15 Displaying Boundaries

On graphical displays, Emacs can indicate the buffer boundaries in the fringes. If you enable this feature, the first line and the last line are marked with angle images in the fringes. This can be combined with up and down arrow images which say whether it is possible to scroll the window.

The buffer-local variable `indicate-buffer-boundaries` controls how the buffer boundaries and window scrolling is indicated in the fringes. If the value is `left` or `right`, both angle and arrow bitmaps are displayed in the left or right fringe, respectively.

If value is an alist, each element (*indicator . position*) specifies the position of one of the indicators. The *indicator* must be one of `top`, `bottom`, `up`, `down`, or `t` which specifies the default position for the indicators not present in the alist. The *position* is one of `left`, `right`, or `nil` which specifies not to show this indicator.

For example, `((top . left) (t . right))` places the top angle bitmap in left fringe, the bottom angle bitmap in right fringe, and both arrow bitmaps in right fringe. To show just the angle bitmaps in the left fringe, but no arrow bitmaps, use `((top . left) (bottom . left))`.

11.16 Useless Whitespace

It is easy to leave unnecessary spaces at the end of a line, or empty lines at the end of a buffer, without realizing it. In most cases, this *trailing whitespace* has no effect, but sometimes it can be a nuisance.

You can make trailing whitespace at the end of a line visible by setting the buffer-local variable `show-trailing-whitespace` to `t`. Then Emacs displays trailing whitespace, using the face `trailing-whitespace`.

This feature does not apply when point is at the end of the line containing the whitespace. Strictly speaking, that is "trailing whitespace" nonetheless, but displaying it specially in that case looks ugly while you are typing in new text. In this special case, the location of point is enough to show you that the spaces are present.

Type M-x delete-trailing-whitespace to delete all trailing whitespace. This command deletes all extra spaces at the end of each line in the buffer, and all empty lines at the end of the buffer; to ignore the latter, change the variable delete-trailing-lines to nil. If the region is active, the command instead deletes extra spaces at the end of each line in the region.

On graphical displays, Emacs can indicate unused lines at the end of the window with a small image in the left fringe (see Section 11.14 [Fringes], page 81). The image appears for screen lines that do not correspond to any buffer text, so blank lines at the end of the buffer stand out because they lack this image. To enable this feature, set the buffer-local variable indicate-empty-lines to a non-nil value. You can enable or disable this feature for all new buffers by setting the default value of this variable, e.g., (setq-default indicate-empty-lines t).

Whitespace mode is a buffer-local minor mode that lets you "visualize" many kinds of whitespace in the buffer, by either drawing the whitespace characters with a special face or displaying them as special glyphs. To toggle this mode, type M-x whitespace-mode. The kinds of whitespace visualized are determined by the list variable whitespace-style. Here is a partial list of possible elements (see the variable's documentation for the full list):

face
: Enable all visualizations which use special faces. This element has a special meaning: if it is absent from the list, none of the other visualizations take effect except space-mark, tab-mark, and newline-mark.

trailing
: Highlight trailing whitespace.

tabs
: Highlight tab characters.

spaces
: Highlight space and non-breaking space characters.

lines
: Highlight lines longer than 80 columns. To change the column limit, customize the variable whitespace-line-column.

newline
: Highlight newlines.

empty
: Highlight empty lines.

space-mark
: Draw space and non-breaking characters with a special glyph.

tab-mark
: Draw tab characters with a special glyph.

newline-mark
: Draw newline characters with a special glyph.

11.17 Selective Display

Emacs has the ability to hide lines indented more than a given number of columns. You can use this to get an overview of a part of a program.

To hide lines in the current buffer, type C-x $ (set-selective-display) with a numeric argument n. Then lines with at least n columns of indentation disappear from the screen.

The only indication of their presence is that three dots ('...') appear at the end of each visible line that is followed by one or more hidden ones.

The commands C-n and C-p move across the hidden lines as if they were not there.

The hidden lines are still present in the buffer, and most editing commands see them as usual, so you may find point in the middle of the hidden text. When this happens, the cursor appears at the end of the previous line, after the three dots. If point is at the end of the visible line, before the newline that ends it, the cursor appears before the three dots.

To make all lines visible again, type C-x $ with no argument.

If you set the variable selective-display-ellipses to nil, the three dots do not appear at the end of a line that precedes hidden lines. Then there is no visible indication of the hidden lines. This variable becomes local automatically when set.

See also Section 22.8 [Outline Mode], page 217 for another way to hide part of the text in a buffer.

11.18 Optional Mode Line Features

The buffer percentage *pos* indicates the percentage of the buffer above the top of the window. You can additionally display the size of the buffer by typing M-x size-indication-mode to turn on Size Indication mode. The size will be displayed immediately following the buffer percentage like this:

> *pos* of *size*

Here *size* is the human readable representation of the number of characters in the buffer, which means that 'k' for 10^3, 'M' for 10^6, 'G' for 10^9, etc., are used to abbreviate.

The current line number of point appears in the mode line when Line Number mode is enabled. Use the command M-x line-number-mode to turn this mode on and off; normally it is on. The line number appears after the buffer percentage *pos*, with the letter 'L' to indicate what it is.

Similarly, you can display the current column number by turning on Column number mode with M-x column-number-mode. The column number is indicated by the letter 'C'. However, when both of these modes are enabled, the line and column numbers are displayed in parentheses, the line number first, rather than with 'L' and 'C'. For example: '(561,2)'. See Section 20.2 [Minor Modes], page 200, for more information about minor modes and about how to use these commands.

If you have narrowed the buffer (see Section 11.5 [Narrowing], page 73), the displayed line number is relative to the accessible portion of the buffer. Thus, it isn't suitable as an argument to goto-line. (Use what-line command to see the line number relative to the whole file.)

If the buffer is very large (larger than the value of line-number-display-limit), Emacs won't compute the line number, because that would be too slow; therefore, the line number won't appear on the mode-line. To remove this limit, set line-number-display-limit to nil.

Line-number computation can also be slow if the lines in the buffer are too long. For this reason, Emacs doesn't display line numbers if the average width, in characters, of lines near point is larger than the value of line-number-display-limit-width. The default value is 200 characters.

Emacs can optionally display the time and system load in all mode lines. To enable this feature, type M-x display-time or customize the option display-time-mode. The information added to the mode line looks like this:

hh:mmpm 1.11

Here *hh* and *mm* are the hour and minute, followed always by 'am' or 'pm'. *l.ll* is the average number, collected for the last few minutes, of processes in the whole system that were either running or ready to run (i.e., were waiting for an available processor). (Some fields may be missing if your operating system cannot support them.) If you prefer time display in 24-hour format, set the variable display-time-24hr-format to t.

The word 'Mail' appears after the load level if there is mail for you that you have not read yet. On graphical displays, you can use an icon instead of 'Mail' by customizing display-time-use-mail-icon; this may save some space on the mode line. You can customize display-time-mail-face to make the mail indicator prominent. Use display-time-mail-file to specify the mail file to check, or set display-time-mail-directory to specify the directory to check for incoming mail (any nonempty regular file in the directory is considered as "newly arrived mail").

When running Emacs on a laptop computer, you can display the battery charge on the mode-line, by using the command display-battery-mode or customizing the variable display-battery-mode. The variable battery-mode-line-format determines the way the battery charge is displayed; the exact mode-line message depends on the operating system, and it usually shows the current battery charge as a percentage of the total charge.

On graphical displays, the mode line is drawn as a 3D box. If you don't like this effect, you can disable it by customizing the mode-line face and setting its box attribute to nil. See Section 33.1.5 [Face Customization], page 416.

By default, the mode line of nonselected windows is displayed in a different face, called mode-line-inactive. Only the selected window is displayed in the mode-line face. This helps show which window is selected. When the minibuffer is selected, since it has no mode line, the window from which you activated the minibuffer has its mode line displayed using mode-line; as a result, ordinary entry to the minibuffer does not change any mode lines.

You can disable use of mode-line-inactive by setting variable mode-line-in-non-selected-windows to nil; then all mode lines are displayed in the mode-line face.

You can customize the mode line display for each of the end-of-line formats by setting each of the variables eol-mnemonic-unix, eol-mnemonic-dos, eol-mnemonic-mac, and eol-mnemonic-undecided to the strings you prefer.

11.19 How Text Is Displayed

Most characters are *printing characters*: when they appear in a buffer, they are displayed literally on the screen. Printing characters include ASCII numbers, letters, and punctuation characters, as well as many non-ASCII characters.

The ASCII character set contains non-printing *control characters*. Two of these are displayed specially: the newline character (Unicode code point U+000A) is displayed by starting a new line, while the tab character (U+0009) is displayed as a space that extends to the next tab stop column (normally every 8 columns). The number of spaces per tab is controlled by the buffer-local variable tab-width, which must have an integer value between

1 and 1000, inclusive. Note that how the tab character in the buffer is displayed has nothing to do with the definition of `TAB` as a command.

Other ASCII control characters, whose codes are below U+0020 (octal 40, decimal 32), are displayed as a caret ('^') followed by the non-control version of the character, with the `escape-glyph` face. For instance, the 'control-A' character, U+0001, is displayed as '^A'.

The raw bytes with codes U+0080 (octal 200) through U+009F (octal 237) are displayed as *octal escape sequences*, with the `escape-glyph` face. For instance, character code U+0098 (octal 230) is displayed as '\230'. If you change the buffer-local variable `ctl-arrow` to `nil`, the ASCII control characters are also displayed as octal escape sequences instead of caret escape sequences.

Some non-ASCII characters have the same appearance as an ASCII space or hyphen (minus) character. Such characters can cause problems if they are entered into a buffer without your realization, e.g., by yanking; for instance, source code compilers typically do not treat non-ASCII spaces as whitespace characters. To deal with this problem, Emacs displays such characters specially: it displays U+00A0 (no-break space) with the `nobreak-space` face, and it displays U+00AD (soft hyphen), U+2010 (hyphen), and U+2011 (non-breaking hyphen) with the `escape-glyph` face. To disable this, change the variable `nobreak-char-display` to `nil`. If you give this variable a non-`nil` and non-`t` value, Emacs instead displays such characters as a highlighted backslash followed by a space or hyphen.

You can customize the way any particular character code is displayed by means of a display table. See Section "Display Tables" in *The Emacs Lisp Reference Manual*.

On graphical displays, some characters may have no glyphs in any of the fonts available to Emacs. These *glyphless characters* are normally displayed as boxes containing the hexadecimal character code. Similarly, on text terminals, characters that cannot be displayed using the terminal encoding (see Section 19.12 [Terminal Coding], page 191) are normally displayed as question signs. You can control the display method by customizing the variable `glyphless-char-display-control`. See Section "Glyphless Character Display" in *The Emacs Lisp Reference Manual*, for details.

11.20 Displaying the Cursor

On a text terminal, the cursor's appearance is controlled by the terminal, largely out of the control of Emacs. Some terminals offer two different cursors: a "visible" static cursor, and a "very visible" blinking cursor. By default, Emacs uses the very visible cursor, and switches to it when you start or resume Emacs. If the variable `visible-cursor` is `nil` when Emacs starts or resumes, it uses the normal cursor.

On a graphical display, many more properties of the text cursor can be altered. To customize its color, change the `:background` attribute of the face named `cursor` (see Section 33.1.5 [Face Customization], page 416). (The other attributes of this face have no effect; the text shown under the cursor is drawn using the frame's background color.) To change its shape, customize the buffer-local variable `cursor-type`; possible values are `box` (the default), `hollow` (a hollow box), `bar` (a vertical bar), (`bar` . *n*) (a vertical bar *n* pixels wide), `hbar` (a horizontal bar), (`hbar` . *n*) (a horizontal bar *n* pixels tall), or `nil` (no cursor at all).

By default, the cursor stops blinking after 10 blinks, if Emacs does not get any input during that time; any input event restarts the count. You can customize the variable `blink-cursor-blinks` to control that: its value says how many times to blink without input before stopping. Setting that variable to a zero or negative value will make the cursor blink forever. To disable cursor blinking altogether, change the variable `blink-cursor-mode` to `nil` (see Section 33.1 [Easy Customization], page 412), or add the line

        (blink-cursor-mode 0)

to your init file. Alternatively, you can change how the cursor looks when it "blinks off" by customizing the list variable `blink-cursor-alist`. Each element in the list should have the form (*on-type . off-type*); this means that if the cursor is displayed as *on-type* when it blinks on (where *on-type* is one of the cursor types described above), then it is displayed as *off-type* when it blinks off.

Some characters, such as tab characters, are "extra wide". When the cursor is positioned over such a character, it is normally drawn with the default character width. You can make the cursor stretch to cover wide characters, by changing the variable `x-stretch-cursor` to a non-`nil` value.

The cursor normally appears in non-selected windows as a non-blinking hollow box. (For a bar cursor, it instead appears as a thinner bar.) To turn off cursors in non-selected windows, change the variable `cursor-in-non-selected-windows` to `nil`.

To make the cursor even more visible, you can use HL Line mode, a minor mode that highlights the line containing point. Use `M-x hl-line-mode` to enable or disable it in the current buffer. `M-x global-hl-line-mode` enables or disables the same mode globally.

11.21 Line Truncation

As an alternative to continuation (see Section 4.8 [Continuation Lines], page 22), Emacs can display long lines by *truncation*. This means that all the characters that do not fit in the width of the screen or window do not appear at all. On graphical displays, a small straight arrow in the fringe indicates truncation at either end of the line. On text terminals, this is indicated with '$' signs in the leftmost and/or rightmost columns.

Horizontal scrolling automatically causes line truncation (see Section 11.4 [Horizontal Scrolling], page 72). You can explicitly enable line truncation for a particular buffer with the command `M-x toggle-truncate-lines`. This works by locally changing the variable `truncate-lines`. If that variable is non-`nil`, long lines are truncated; if it is `nil`, they are continued onto multiple screen lines. Setting the variable `truncate-lines` in any way makes it local to the current buffer; until that time, the default value, which is normally `nil`, is in effect.

If a split window becomes too narrow, Emacs may automatically enable line truncation. See Section 17.2 [Split Window], page 156, for the variable `truncate-partial-width-windows` which controls this.

11.22 Visual Line Mode

Another alternative to ordinary line continuation is to use *word wrap*. Here, each long logical line is divided into two or more screen lines, like in ordinary line continuation. However, Emacs attempts to wrap the line at word boundaries near the right window edge. This makes the text easier to read, as wrapping does not occur in the middle of words.

Word wrap is enabled by Visual Line mode, an optional minor mode. To turn on Visual Line mode in the current buffer, type M-x visual-line-mode; repeating this command turns it off. You can also turn on Visual Line mode using the menu bar: in the Options menu, select the 'Line Wrapping in this Buffer' submenu, followed by the 'Word Wrap (Visual Line Mode)' menu item. While Visual Line mode is enabled, the mode-line shows the string 'wrap' in the mode display. The command M-x global-visual-line-mode toggles Visual Line mode in all buffers.

In Visual Line mode, some editing commands work on screen lines instead of logical lines: C-a (beginning-of-visual-line) moves to the beginning of the screen line, C-e (end-of-visual-line) moves to the end of the screen line, and C-k (kill-visual-line) kills text to the end of the screen line.

To move by logical lines, use the commands M-x next-logical-line and M-x previous-logical-line. These move point to the next logical line and the previous logical line respectively, regardless of whether Visual Line mode is enabled. If you use these commands frequently, it may be convenient to assign key bindings to them. See Section 33.3.6 [Init Rebinding], page 432.

By default, word-wrapped lines do not display fringe indicators. Visual Line mode is often used to edit files that contain many long logical lines, so having a fringe indicator for each wrapped line would be visually distracting. You can change this by customizing the variable visual-line-fringe-indicators.

11.23 Customization of Display

This section describes variables that control miscellaneous aspects of the appearance of the Emacs screen. Beginning users can skip it.

If the variable visible-bell is non-nil, Emacs attempts to make the whole screen blink when it would normally make an audible bell sound. This variable has no effect if your terminal does not have a way to make the screen blink.

The variable echo-keystrokes controls the echoing of multi-character keys; its value is the number of seconds of pause required to cause echoing to start, or zero, meaning don't echo at all. The value takes effect when there is something to echo. See Section 1.2 [Echo Area], page 7.

On graphical displays, Emacs displays the mouse pointer as an hourglass if Emacs is busy. To disable this feature, set the variable display-hourglass to nil. The variable hourglass-delay determines the number of seconds of "busy time" before the hourglass is shown; the default is 1.

If the mouse pointer lies inside an Emacs frame, Emacs makes it invisible each time you type a character to insert text, to prevent it from obscuring the text. (To be precise, the hiding occurs when you type a "self-inserting" character. See Section 4.1 [Inserting Text], page 16.) Moving the mouse pointer makes it visible again. To disable this feature, set the variable make-pointer-invisible to nil.

On graphical displays, the variable underline-minimum-offset determines the minimum distance between the baseline and underline, in pixels, for underlined text. By default, the value is 1; increasing it may improve the legibility of underlined text for certain fonts. (However, Emacs will never draw the underline below the current line area.) The variable `x-underline-at-descent-line` determines how to draw underlined text. The default is `nil`, which means to draw it at the baseline level of the font; if you change it to `nil`, Emacs draws the underline at the same height as the font's descent line.

The variable `overline-margin` specifies the vertical position of an overline above the text, including the height of the overline itself, in pixels; the default is 2.

On some text terminals, bold face and inverse video together result in text that is hard to read. Call the function `tty-suppress-bold-inverse-default-colors` with a non-`nil` argument to suppress the effect of bold-face in this case.

12 Searching and Replacement

Like other editors, Emacs has commands to search for occurrences of a string. Emacs also has commands to replace occurrences of a string with a different string. There are also commands that do the same thing, but search for patterns instead of fixed strings.

You can also search multiple files under the control of a tags table (see Section 25.3.6 [Tags Search], page 306) or through the Dired A command (see Section 27.7 [Operating on Files], page 320), or ask the grep program to do it (see Section 24.4 [Grep Searching], page 264).

12.1 Incremental Search

The principal search command in Emacs is *incremental*: it begins searching as soon as you type the first character of the search string. As you type in the search string, Emacs shows you where the string (as you have typed it so far) would be found. When you have typed enough characters to identify the place you want, you can stop. Depending on what you plan to do next, you may or may not need to terminate the search explicitly with RET.

C-s   Incremental search forward (isearch-forward).

C-r   Incremental search backward (isearch-backward).

12.1.1 Basics of Incremental Search

C-s   Begin incremental search (isearch-forward).

C-r   Begin reverse incremental search (isearch-backward).

C-s (isearch-forward) starts a forward incremental search. It reads characters from the keyboard, and moves point just past the end of the next occurrence of those characters in the buffer.

For instance, if you type C-s and then F, that puts the cursor after the first 'F' that occurs in the buffer after the starting point. Then if you then type O, the cursor moves to just after the first 'FO'; the 'F' in that 'FO' might not be the first 'F' previously found. After another O, the cursor moves to just after the first 'FOO'.

At each step, Emacs highlights the *current match*—the buffer text that matches the search string—using the isearch face (see Section 11.8 [Faces], page 74). The current search string is also displayed in the echo area.

If you make a mistake typing the search string, type DEL. Each DEL cancels the last character of the search string.

When you are satisfied with the place you have reached, type RET. This stops searching, leaving the cursor where the search brought it. Also, any command not specially meaningful in searches stops the searching and is then executed. Thus, typing C-a exits the search and then moves to the beginning of the line. RET is necessary only if the next command you want to type is a printing character, DEL, RET, or another character that is special within searches (C-q, C-w, C-r, C-s, C-y, M-y, M-r, M-c, M-e, and some others described below).

As a special exception, entering RET when the search string is empty launches nonincremental search (see Section 12.2 [Nonincremental Search], page 95).

When you exit the incremental search, it adds the original value of point to the mark ring, without activating the mark; you can thus use C-u C-SPC to return to where you were before beginning the search. See Section 8.4 [Mark Ring], page 48. It only does this if the mark was not already active.

To search backwards, use C-r (isearch-backward) instead of C-s to start the search. A backward search finds matches that end before the starting point, just as a forward search finds matches that begin after it.

12.1.2 Repeating Incremental Search

Suppose you search forward for 'FOO' and find a match, but not the one you expected to find: the 'FOO' you were aiming for occurs later in the buffer. In this event, type another C-s to move to the next occurrence of the search string. You can repeat this any number of times. If you overshoot, you can cancel some C-s characters with DEL. Similarly, each C-r in a backward incremental search repeats the backward search.

If you pause for a little while during incremental search, Emacs highlights all the other possible matches for the search string that are present on the screen. This helps you anticipate where you can get to by typing C-s or C-r to repeat the search. The other matches are highlighted differently from the current match, using the customizable face lazy-highlight (see Section 11.8 [Faces], page 74). If you don't like this feature, you can disable it by setting isearch-lazy-highlight to nil.

After exiting a search, you can search for the same string again by typing just C-s C-s. The first C-s is the key that invokes incremental search, and the second C-s means "search again". Similarly, C-r C-r searches backward for the last search string. In determining the last search string, it doesn't matter whether the string was searched for with C-s or C-r.

If you are searching forward but you realize you were looking for something before the starting point, type C-r to switch to a backward search, leaving the search string unchanged. Similarly, C-s in a backward search switches to a forward search.

If a search is failing and you ask to repeat it by typing another C-s, it starts again from the beginning of the buffer. Repeating a failing reverse search with C-r starts again from the end. This is called *wrapping around*, and 'Wrapped' appears in the search prompt once this has happened. If you keep on going past the original starting point of the search, it changes to 'Overwrapped', which means that you are revisiting matches that you have already seen.

To reuse earlier search strings, use the *search ring*. The commands M-p and M-n move through the ring to pick a search string to reuse. These commands leave the selected search ring element in the minibuffer, where you can edit it.

To edit the current search string in the minibuffer without replacing it with items from the search ring, type M-e. Type RET, C-s or C-r to finish editing the string and search for it.

12.1.3 Errors in Incremental Search

If your string is not found at all, the echo area says 'Failing I-Search', and the cursor moves past the place where Emacs found as much of your string as it could. Thus, if you search for 'FOOT', and there is no 'FOOT', you might see the cursor after the 'FOO' in 'FOOL'.

In the echo area, the part of the search string that failed to match is highlighted using the face `isearch-fail`.

At this point, there are several things you can do. If your string was mistyped, you can use DEL to erase some of it and correct it. If you like the place you have found, you can type RET to remain there. Or you can type C-g, which removes from the search string the characters that could not be found (the 'T' in 'FOOT'), leaving those that were found (the 'FOO' in 'FOOT'). A second C-g at that point cancels the search entirely, returning point to where it was when the search started.

The quit command, C-g, does special things during searches; just what it does depends on the status of the search. If the search has found what you specified and is waiting for input, C-g cancels the entire search, moving the cursor back to where you started the search. If C-g is typed when there are characters in the search string that have not been found—because Emacs is still searching for them, or because it has failed to find them—then the search string characters which have not been found are discarded from the search string. With them gone, the search is now successful and waiting for more input, so a second C-g will cancel the entire search.

12.1.4 Special Input for Incremental Search

Some of the characters you type during incremental search have special effects.

By default, incremental search performs *lax space matching*: each space, or sequence of spaces, matches any sequence of one or more spaces in the text. Hence, 'foo bar' matches 'foo bar', 'foo bar', 'foo bar', and so on (but not 'foobar'). More precisely, Emacs matches each sequence of space characters in the search string to a regular expression specified by the variable `search-whitespace-regexp`. For example, to make spaces match sequences of newlines as well as spaces, set it to '"[[:space:]\n]+"'.

To toggle lax space matching, type M-s SPC (`isearch-toggle-lax-whitespace`). To disable this feature entirely, change `search-whitespace-regexp` to `nil`; then each space in the search string matches exactly one space.

If the search string you entered contains only lower-case letters, the search is case-insensitive; as long as an upper-case letter exists in the search string, the search becomes case-sensitive. If you delete the upper-case character from the search string, it ceases to have this effect. See Section 12.9 [Search Case], page 102.

To toggle whether or not invisible text is searched, type M-s i (`isearch-toggle-invisible`). See [Outline Search], page 220.

To search for a newline character, type C-j.

To search for non-ASCII characters, use one of the following methods:

- Type C-q, followed by a non-graphic character or a sequence of octal digits. This adds a character to the search string, similar to inserting into a buffer using C-q (see Section 4.1 [Inserting Text], page 16). For example, C-q C-s during incremental search adds the 'control-S' character to the search string.

- Type C-x 8 RET, followed by a Unicode name or code-point. This adds the specified character into the search string, similar to the usual `insert-char` command (see Section 4.1 [Inserting Text], page 16).

- Use an input method (see Section 19.3 [Input Methods], page 181). If an input method is enabled in the current buffer when you start the search, you can use it in the search string also. While typing the search string, you can toggle the input method with `C-\` (`isearch-toggle-input-method`). You can also turn on a non-default input method with `C-^` (`isearch-toggle-specified-input-method`), which prompts for the name of the input method. When an input method is active during incremental search, the search prompt includes the input method mnemonic, like this:

>   `I-search [im]:`

where *im* is the mnemonic of the active input method. Any input method you enable during incremental search remains enabled in the current buffer afterwards.

Typing `M-%` in incremental search invokes `query-replace` or `query-replace-regexp` (depending on search mode) with the current search string used as the string to replace. A negative prefix argument means to replace backward. See Section 12.10.4 [Query Replace], page 105.

Typing `M-TAB` in incremental search invokes `isearch-complete`, which attempts to complete the search string using the search ring as a list of completion alternatives. See Section 5.4 [Completion], page 28. In many operating systems, the `M-TAB` key sequence is captured by the window manager; you then need to rebind `isearch-complete` to another key sequence if you want to use it (see Section 33.3.5 [Rebinding], page 431).

When incremental search is active, you can type `C-h C-h` to access interactive help options, including a list of special key bindings. These key bindings are part of the keymap `isearch-mode-map` (see Section 33.3.1 [Keymaps], page 429).

12.1.5 Isearch Yanking

Within incremental search, `C-y` (`isearch-yank-kill`) appends the current kill to the search string. `M-y` (`isearch-yank-pop`), if called after `C-y`, replaces that appended text with an earlier kill, similar to the usual `M-y` (`yank-pop`) command (see Section 9.2 [Yanking], page 55). `Mouse-2` appends the current X selection (see Section 9.3.2 [Primary Selection], page 58).

`C-w` (`isearch-yank-word-or-char`) appends the next character or word at point to the search string. This is an easy way to search for another occurrence of the text at point. (The decision of whether to copy a character or a word is heuristic.)

Similarly, `M-s C-e` (`isearch-yank-line`) appends the rest of the current line to the search string. If point is already at the end of a line, it appends the next line. With a prefix argument *n*, it appends the next *n* lines.

If the search is currently case-insensitive, both `C-w` and `M-s C-e` convert the text they copy to lower case, so that the search remains case-insensitive.

`C-M-w` (`isearch-del-char`) deletes the last character from the search string, and `C-M-y` (`isearch-yank-char`) appends the character after point to the search string. An alternative method to add the character after point is to enter the minibuffer with `M-e` (see Section 12.1.2 [Repeat Isearch], page 91) and type `C-f` at the end of the search string in the minibuffer.

12.1.6 Not Exiting Incremental Search

This subsection describes two categories of commands which you can type without exiting the current incremental search, even though they are not themselves part of incremental search.

Prefix Arguments

In incremental search, when you enter a prefix argument (see Section 4.10 [Arguments], page 23), by default it will apply either to the next action in the search or to the command that exits the search.

In previous versions of Emacs, entering a prefix argument always terminated the search. You can revert to this behavior by setting the variable `isearch-allow-prefix` to `nil`.

When `isearch-allow-scroll` is non-`nil` (see below), prefix arguments always have the default behavior described above.

Scrolling Commands

Normally, scrolling commands exit incremental search. If you change the variable `isearch-allow-scroll` to a non-`nil` value, that enables the use of the scroll-bar, as well as keyboard scrolling commands like `C-v`, `M-v`, and `C-l` (see Section 11.1 [Scrolling], page 69). This applies only to calling these commands via their bound key sequences—typing `M-x` will still exit the search. You can give prefix arguments to these commands in the usual way. This feature won't let you scroll the current match out of visibility, however.

The `isearch-allow-scroll` feature also affects some other commands, such as `C-x 2` (split-window-below) and `C-x ^` (enlarge-window), which don't exactly scroll but do affect where the text appears on the screen. It applies to any command whose name has a non-`nil` `isearch-scroll` property. So you can control which commands are affected by changing these properties.

For example, to make `C-h l` usable within an incremental search in all future Emacs sessions, use `C-h c` to find what command it runs (see Section 7.1 [Key Help], page 39), which is `view-lossage`. Then you can put the following line in your init file (see Section 33.4 [Init File], page 437):

```
(put 'view-lossage 'isearch-scroll t)
```

This feature can be applied to any command that doesn't permanently change point, the buffer contents, the match data, the current buffer, or the selected window and frame. The command must not itself attempt an incremental search.

12.1.7 Searching the Minibuffer

If you start an incremental search while the minibuffer is active, Emacs searches the contents of the minibuffer. Unlike searching an ordinary buffer, the search string is not shown in the echo area, because that is used to display the minibuffer.

If an incremental search fails in the minibuffer, it tries searching the minibuffer history. See Section 5.5 [Minibuffer History], page 32. You can visualize the minibuffer and its history as a series of "pages", with the earliest history element on the first page and the current minibuffer on the last page. A forward search, `C-s`, searches forward to later pages; a reverse search, `C-r`, searches backwards to earlier pages. Like in ordinary buffer search, a failing search can wrap around, going from the last page to the first page or vice versa.

When the current match is on a history element, that history element is pulled into the minibuffer. If you exit the incremental search normally (e.g., by typing `RET`), it remains in the minibuffer afterwards. Canceling the search, with `C-g`, restores the contents of the minibuffer when you began the search.

12.2 Nonincremental Search

Emacs also has conventional nonincremental search commands, which require you to type the entire search string before searching begins.

`C-s RET` *string* `RET`
>   Search for *string*.

`C-r RET` *string* `RET`
>   Search backward for *string*.

To start a nonincremental search, first type `C-s RET`. This enters the minibuffer to read the search string; terminate the string with `RET`, and then the search takes place. If the string is not found, the search command signals an error.

When you type `C-s RET`, the `C-s` invokes incremental search as usual. That command is specially programmed to invoke the command for nonincremental search, `search-forward`, if the string you specify is empty. (Such an empty argument would otherwise be useless.) `C-r RET` does likewise, invoking the command `search-backward`.

12.3 Word Search

A *word search* finds a sequence of words without regard to the type of punctuation between them. For instance, if you enter a search string that consists of two words separated by a single space, the search matches any sequence of those two words separated by one or more spaces, newlines, or other punctuation characters. This is particularly useful for searching text documents, because you don't have to worry whether the words you are looking for are separated by newlines or spaces.

`M-s w`   If incremental search is active, toggle word search mode (`isearch-toggle-word`); otherwise, begin an incremental forward word search (`isearch-forward-word`).

`M-s w RET` *words* `RET`
>   Search for *words*, using a forward nonincremental word search.

`M-s w C-r RET` *words* `RET`
>   Search backward for *words*, using a nonincremental word search.

To begin a forward incremental word search, type `M-s w`. If incremental search is not already active, this runs the command `isearch-forward-word`. If incremental search is already active (whether a forward or backward search), `M-s w` switches to a word search while keeping the direction of the search and the current search string unchanged. You can toggle word search back off by typing `M-s w` again.

To begin a nonincremental word search, type `M-s w RET` for a forward search, or `M-s w C-r RET` for a backward search. These run the commands `word-search-forward` and `word-search-backward` respectively.

Incremental and nonincremental word searches differ slightly in the way they find a match. In a nonincremental word search, each word in the search string must exactly match a whole word. In an incremental word search, the matching is more lax: while you are typing the search string, its first and last words need not match whole words. This is so that the matching can proceed incrementally as you type. This additional laxity does not apply to the lazy highlight, which always matches whole words.

12.4 Symbol Search

A *symbol search* is much like an ordinary search, except that the boundaries of the search must match the boundaries of a symbol. The meaning of *symbol* in this context depends on the major mode, and usually refers to a source code token, such as a Lisp symbol in Emacs Lisp mode. For instance, if you perform an incremental symbol search for the Lisp symbol `forward-word`, it would not match `isearch-forward-word`. This feature is thus mainly useful for searching source code.

M-s _   If incremental search is active, toggle symbol search mode (`isearch-toggle-symbol`); otherwise, begin an incremental forward symbol search (`isearch-forward-symbol`).

M-s .   Start a symbol incremental search forward with the symbol found near point added to the search string initially.

M-s _ RET *symbol* RET
              Search forward for *symbol*, nonincrementally.

M-s _ C-r RET *symbol* RET
              Search backward for *symbol*, nonincrementally.

To begin a forward incremental symbol search, type M-s _ (or M-s . if the symbol to search is near point). If incremental search is not already active, this runs the command `isearch-forward-symbol`. If incremental search is already active, M-s _ switches to a symbol search, preserving the direction of the search and the current search string; you can disable symbol search by typing M-s _ again. In incremental symbol search, only the beginning of the search string is required to match the beginning of a symbol.

To begin a nonincremental symbol search, type M-s _ RET for a forward search, or M-s _ C-r RET or a backward search. In nonincremental symbol searches, the beginning and end of the search string are required to match the beginning and end of a symbol, respectively.

12.5 Regular Expression Search

A *regular expression* (or *regexp* for short) is a pattern that denotes a class of alternative strings to match. Emacs provides both incremental and nonincremental ways to search for a match for a regexp. The syntax of regular expressions is explained in the next section.

C-M-s   Begin incremental regexp search (`isearch-forward-regexp`).

C-M-r   Begin reverse incremental regexp search (`isearch-backward-regexp`).

Incremental search for a regexp is done by typing C-M-s (`isearch-forward-regexp`), by invoking C-s with a prefix argument (whose value does not matter), or by typing M-r within a forward incremental search. This command reads a search string incrementally just like C-s, but it treats the search string as a regexp rather than looking for an exact match against the text in the buffer. Each time you add text to the search string, you make the regexp longer, and the new regexp is searched for. To search backward for a regexp, use `C-M-r` (`isearch-backward-regexp`), `C-r` with a prefix argument, or `M-r` within a backward incremental search.

All of the special key sequences in an ordinary incremental search do similar things in an incremental regexp search. For instance, typing `C-s` immediately after starting the search retrieves the last incremental search regexp used and searches forward for it. Incremental regexp and non-regexp searches have independent defaults. They also have separate search rings, which you can access with `M-p` and `M-n`.

Unlike ordinary incremental search, incremental regexp search do not use lax space matching by default. To toggle this feature use `M-s SPC` (`isearch-toggle-lax-whitespace`). Then any `SPC` typed in incremental regexp search will match any sequence of one or more whitespace characters. The variable `search-whitespace-regexp` specifies the regexp for the lax space matching. See Section 12.1.4 [Special Isearch], page 92.

In some cases, adding characters to the regexp in an incremental regexp search can make the cursor move back and start again. For example, if you have searched for 'foo' and you add '\|bar', the cursor backs up in case the first 'bar' precedes the first 'foo'. See Section 12.6 [Regexps], page 97.

Forward and backward regexp search are not symmetrical, because regexp matching in Emacs always operates forward, starting with the beginning of the regexp. Thus, forward regexp search scans forward, trying a forward match at each possible starting position. Backward regexp search scans backward, trying a forward match at each possible starting position. These search methods are not mirror images.

Nonincremental search for a regexp is done with the commands `re-search-forward` and `re-search-backward`. You can invoke these with `M-x`, or by way of incremental regexp search with `C-M-s RET` and `C-M-r RET`.

If you use the incremental regexp search commands with a prefix argument, they perform ordinary string search, like `isearch-forward` and `isearch-backward`. See Section 12.1 [Incremental Search], page 90.

12.6 Syntax of Regular Expressions

This manual describes regular expression features that users typically use. See Section "Regular Expressions" in *The Emacs Lisp Reference Manual*, for additional features used mainly in Lisp programs.

Regular expressions have a syntax in which a few characters are special constructs and the rest are *ordinary*. An ordinary character matches that same character and nothing else. The special characters are '$^.*+?[\'. The character ']' is special if it ends a character alternative (see later). The character '-' is special inside a character alternative. Any other character appearing in a regular expression is ordinary, unless a '\' precedes it. (When you use regular expressions in a Lisp program, each '\' must be doubled, see the example near the end of this section.)

For example, 'f' is not a special character, so it is ordinary, and therefore 'f' is a regular expression that matches the string 'f' and no other string. (It does *not* match the string 'ff'.) Likewise, 'o' is a regular expression that matches only 'o'. (When case distinctions are being ignored, these regexps also match 'F' and 'O', but we consider this a generalization of "the same string", rather than an exception.)

Any two regular expressions *a* and *b* can be concatenated. The result is a regular expression which matches a string if *a* matches some amount of the beginning of that string and *b* matches the rest of the string. For example, concatenating the regular expressions 'f' and 'o' gives the regular expression 'fo', which matches only the string 'fo'. Still trivial. To do something nontrivial, you need to use one of the special characters. Here is a list of them.

. (Period)   is a special character that matches any single character except a newline. For example, the regular expressions 'a.b' matches any three-character string that begins with 'a' and ends with 'b'.

*   is not a construct by itself; it is a postfix operator that means to match the preceding regular expression repetitively any number of times, as many times as possible. Thus, 'o*' matches any number of 'o's, including no 'o's.

'*' always applies to the *smallest* possible preceding expression. Thus, 'fo*' has a repeating 'o', not a repeating 'fo'. It matches 'f', 'fo', 'foo', and so on.

The matcher processes a '*' construct by matching, immediately, as many repetitions as can be found. Then it continues with the rest of the pattern. If that fails, backtracking occurs, discarding some of the matches of the '*'-modified construct in case that makes it possible to match the rest of the pattern. For example, in matching 'ca*ar' against the string 'caaar', the 'a*' first tries to match all three 'a's; but the rest of the pattern is 'ar' and there is only 'r' left to match, so this try fails. The next alternative is for 'a*' to match only two 'a's. With this choice, the rest of the regexp matches successfully.

+   is a postfix operator, similar to '*' except that it must match the preceding expression at least once. Thus, 'ca+r' matches the strings 'car' and 'caaaar' but not the string 'cr', whereas 'ca*r' matches all three strings.

?   is a postfix operator, similar to '*' except that it can match the preceding expression either once or not at all. Thus, 'ca?r' matches 'car' or 'cr', and nothing else.

*?, +?, ??   are non-*greedy* variants of the operators above. The normal operators '*', '+', '?' match as much as they can, as long as the overall regexp can still match. With a following '?', they will match as little as possible.

Thus, both 'ab*' and 'ab*?' can match the string 'a' and the string 'abbbb'; but if you try to match them both against the text 'abbb', 'ab*' will match it all (the longest valid match), while 'ab*?' will match just 'a' (the shortest valid match).

Non-greedy operators match the shortest possible string starting at a given starting point; in a forward search, though, the earliest possible starting point for match is always the one chosen. Thus, if you search for 'a.*?$' against the text 'abbab' followed by a newline, it matches the whole string. Since it *can* match starting at the first 'a', it does.

\{*n*\}   is a postfix operator specifying *n* repetitions—that is, the preceding regular expression must match exactly *n* times in a row. For example, 'x\{4\}' matches the string 'xxxx' and nothing else.

\{*n*,*m*\}   is a postfix operator specifying between *n* and *m* repetitions—that is, the preceding regular expression must match at least *n* times, but no more than *m* times. If *m* is omitted, then there is no upper limit, but the preceding regular expression must match at least *n* times.

‘\{0,1\}’ is equivalent to ‘?’.

‘\{0,\}’ is equivalent to ‘*’.

‘\{1,\}’ is equivalent to ‘+’.

[...]   is a *character set*, beginning with ‘[’ and terminated by ‘]’.

In the simplest case, the characters between the two brackets are what this set can match. Thus, ‘[ad]’ matches either one ‘a’ or one ‘d’, and ‘[ad]*’ matches any string composed of just ‘a’s and ‘d’s (including the empty string). It follows that ‘c[ad]*r’ matches ‘cr’, ‘car’, ‘cdr’, ‘caddaar’, etc.

You can also include character ranges in a character set, by writing the starting and ending characters with a ‘-’ between them. Thus, ‘[a-z]’ matches any lower-case ASCII letter. Ranges may be intermixed freely with individual characters, as in ‘[a-z$%.]’, which matches any lower-case ASCII letter or ‘$’, ‘%’ or period.

You can also include certain special *character classes* in a character set. A ‘[:’ and balancing ‘:]’ enclose a character class inside a character alternative. For instance, ‘[[:alnum:]]’ matches any letter or digit. See Section “Char Classes” in *The Emacs Lisp Reference Manual*, for a list of character classes.

To include a ‘]’ in a character set, you must make it the first character. For example, ‘[]a]’ matches ‘]’ or ‘a’. To include a ‘-’, write ‘-’ as the first or last character of the set, or put it after a range. Thus, ‘[]-]’ matches both ‘]’ and ‘-’.

To include ‘^’ in a set, put it anywhere but at the beginning of the set. (At the beginning, it complements the set—see below.)

When you use a range in case-insensitive search, you should write both ends of the range in upper case, or both in lower case, or both should be non-letters. The behavior of a mixed-case range such as ‘A-z’ is somewhat ill-defined, and it may change in future Emacs versions.

[^ ...]   ‘[^’ begins a *complemented character set*, which matches any character except the ones specified. Thus, ‘[^a-z0-9A-Z]’ matches all characters *except* ASCII letters and digits.

‘^’ is not special in a character set unless it is the first character. The character following the ‘^’ is treated as if it were first (in other words, ‘-’ and ‘]’ are not special there).

A complemented character set can match a newline, unless newline is mentioned as one of the characters not to match. This is in contrast to the handling of regexps in programs such as grep.

^   is a special character that matches the empty string, but only at the beginning of a line in the text being matched. Otherwise it fails to match anything. Thus, ‘^foo’ matches a ‘foo’ that occurs at the beginning of a line.

For historical compatibility reasons, '^' can be used with this meaning only at the beginning of the regular expression, or after '\(' or '\|'.

$ is similar to '^' but matches only at the end of a line. Thus, 'x+$' matches a string of one 'x' or more at the end of a line.

For historical compatibility reasons, '$' can be used with this meaning only at the end of the regular expression, or before '\)' or '\|'.

\   has two functions: it quotes the special characters (including '\'), and it introduces additional special constructs.

Because '\' quotes special characters, '\$' is a regular expression that matches only '$', and '\[' is a regular expression that matches only '[', and so on.

See the following section for the special constructs that begin with '\'.

Note: for historical compatibility, special characters are treated as ordinary ones if they are in contexts where their special meanings make no sense. For example, '*foo' treats '*' as ordinary since there is no preceding expression on which the '*' can act. It is poor practice to depend on this behavior; it is better to quote the special character anyway, regardless of where it appears.

As a '\' is not special inside a character alternative, it can never remove the special meaning of '-' or ']'. So you should not quote these characters when they have no special meaning either. This would not clarify anything, since backslashes can legitimately precede these characters where they *have* special meaning, as in '[^\]' ("[^\\]" for Lisp string syntax), which matches any single character except a backslash.

12.7 Backslash in Regular Expressions

For the most part, '\' followed by any character matches only that character. However, there are several exceptions: two-character sequences starting with '\' that have special meanings. The second character in the sequence is always an ordinary character when used on its own. Here is a table of '\' constructs.

\| specifies an alternative. Two regular expressions a and b with '\|' in between form an expression that matches some text if either a matches it or b matches it. It works by trying to match a, and if that fails, by trying to match b.

Thus, 'foo\|bar' matches either 'foo' or 'bar' but no other string.

'\|' applies to the largest possible surrounding expressions. Only a surrounding '\(... \)' grouping can limit the grouping power of '\|'.

Full backtracking capability exists to handle multiple uses of '\|'.

\(... \)   is a grouping construct that serves three purposes:

1. To enclose a set of '\|' alternatives for other operations. Thus, '\(foo\|bar\)x' matches either 'foox' or 'barx'.

2. To enclose a complicated expression for the postfix operators '*', '+' and '?' to operate on. Thus, 'ba\(na\)*' matches 'bananana', etc., with any (zero or more) number of 'na' strings.

3. To record a matched substring for future reference.

This last application is not a consequence of the idea of a parenthetical grouping; it is a separate feature that is assigned as a second meaning to the same '\(... \)' construct. In practice there is usually no conflict between the two meanings; when there is a conflict, you can use a "shy" group.

\(?: ... \)
> specifies a "shy" group that does not record the matched substring; you can't refer back to it with '\d'. This is useful in mechanically combining regular expressions, so that you can add groups for syntactic purposes without interfering with the numbering of the groups that are meant to be referred to.

\d
> matches the same text that matched the dth occurrence of a '\(... \)' construct. This is called a *back reference*.
>
> After the end of a '\(... \)' construct, the matcher remembers the beginning and end of the text matched by that construct. Then, later on in the regular expression, you can use '\' followed by the digit d to mean "match the same text matched the dth time by the '\(... \)' construct".
>
> The strings matching the first nine '\(... \)' constructs appearing in a regular expression are assigned numbers 1 through 9 in the order that the open-parentheses appear in the regular expression. So you can use '\1' through '\9' to refer to the text matched by the corresponding '\(... \)' constructs.
>
> For example, '\(.*\)\1' matches any newline-free string that is composed of two identical halves. The '\(.*\)' matches the first half, which may be anything, but the '\1' that follows must match the same exact text.
>
> If a particular '\(... \)' construct matches more than once (which can easily happen if it is followed by '*'), only the last match is recorded.

\'
> matches the empty string, but only at the beginning of the string or buffer (or its accessible portion) being matched against.

\'
> matches the empty string, but only at the end of the string or buffer (or its accessible portion) being matched against.

\=
> matches the empty string, but only at point.

\b
> matches the empty string, but only at the beginning or end of a word. Thus, '\bfoo\b' matches any occurrence of 'foo' as a separate word. '\bballs?\b' matches 'ball' or 'balls' as a separate word.
>
> '\b' matches at the beginning or end of the buffer regardless of what text appears next to it.

\B
> matches the empty string, but *not* at the beginning or end of a word.

\<
> matches the empty string, but only at the beginning of a word. '\<' matches at the beginning of the buffer only if a word-constituent character follows.

\>
> matches the empty string, but only at the end of a word. '\>' matches at the end of the buffer only if the contents end with a word-constituent character.

\w
> matches any word-constituent character. The syntax table determines which characters these are. See Section "Syntax Tables" in *The Emacs Lisp Reference Manual*.

\W   matches any character that is not a word-constituent.

_<   matches the empty string, but only at the beginning of a symbol. A symbol is a
            sequence of one or more symbol-constituent characters. A symbol-constituent
            character is a character whose syntax is either 'w' or '_'. '_<' matches at the
            beginning of the buffer only if a symbol-constituent character follows.

>   matches the empty string, but only at the end of a symbol. '>' matches at the
            end of the buffer only if the contents end with a symbol-constituent character.

\sc   matches any character whose syntax is c. Here c is a character that designates
            a particular syntax class: thus, 'w' for word constituent, '-' or ' ' for whitespace,
            '.' for ordinary punctuation, etc. See Section "Syntax Tables" in *The Emacs
            Lisp Reference Manual*.

\Sc   matches any character whose syntax is not c.

\cc   matches any character that belongs to the category c. For example, '\cc'
            matches Chinese characters, '\cg' matches Greek characters, etc. For the de-
            scription of the known categories, type M-x describe-categories RET.

\Cc   matches any character that does *not* belong to category c.

The constructs that pertain to words and syntax are controlled by the setting of the
syntax table. See Section "Syntax Tables" in *The Emacs Lisp Reference Manual*.

12.8 Regular Expression Example

Here is an example of a regexp—similar to the regexp that Emacs uses, by default, to
recognize the end of a sentence, not including the following space (i.e., the variable
sentence-end-base):

        [.?!][]\"')}]*

This contains two parts in succession: a character set matching period, '?', or '!', and a
character set matching close-brackets, quotes, or parentheses, repeated zero or more times.

12.9 Searching and Case

Searches in Emacs normally ignore the case of the text they are searching through, if you
specify the text in lower case. Thus, if you specify searching for 'foo', then 'Foo' and 'foo'
also match. Regexps, and in particular character sets, behave likewise: '[ab]' matches 'a'
or 'A' or 'b' or 'B'.

An upper-case letter anywhere in the incremental search string makes the search case-
sensitive. Thus, searching for 'Foo' does not find 'foo' or 'FOO'. This applies to regular
expression search as well as to string search. The effect ceases if you delete the upper-case
letter from the search string.

If you set the variable case-fold-search to nil, then all letters must match exactly,
including case. This is a per-buffer variable; altering the variable normally affects only the
current buffer, unless you change its default value. See Section 33.2.3 [Locals], page 423.
This variable applies to nonincremental searches also, including those performed by the replace commands (see Section 12.10 [Replace], page 103) and the minibuffer history matching
commands (see Section 5.5 [Minibuffer History], page 32).

Typing `M-c` within an incremental search toggles the case sensitivity of that search. The effect does not extend beyond the current incremental search to the next one, but it does override the effect of adding or removing an upper-case letter in the current search.

Several related variables control case-sensitivity of searching and matching for specific commands or activities. For instance, `tags-case-fold-search` controls case sensitivity for `find-tag`. To find these variables, do `M-x apropos-variable RET case-fold-search RET`.

12.10 Replacement Commands

Emacs provides several commands for performing search-and-replace operations. In addition to the simple `M-x replace-string` command, there is `M-%` (`query-replace`), which presents each occurrence of the pattern and asks you whether to replace it.

The replace commands normally operate on the text from point to the end of the buffer. When the region is active, they operate on it instead (see Chapter 8 [Mark], page 45). The basic replace commands replace one *search string* (or regexp) with one *replacement string*. It is possible to perform several replacements in parallel, using the command `expand-region-abbrevs` (see Section 26.3 [Expanding Abbrevs], page 310).

Unlike incremental search, the replacement commands do not use lax space matching (see Section 12.1.4 [Special Isearch], page 92) by default. To enable lax space matching for replacement, change the variable `replace-lax-whitespace` to `t`. (This only affects how Emacs finds the text to replace, not the replacement text.)

12.10.1 Unconditional Replacement

`M-x replace-string RET` *string* `RET` *newstring* `RET`
> Replace every occurrence of *string* with *newstring*.

To replace every instance of 'foo' after point with 'bar', use the command `M-x replace-string` with the two arguments 'foo' and 'bar'. Replacement happens only in the text after point, so if you want to cover the whole buffer you must go to the beginning first. All occurrences up to the end of the buffer are replaced; to limit replacement to part of the buffer, activate the region around that part. When the region is active, replacement is limited to the region (see Chapter 8 [Mark], page 45).

When `replace-string` exits, it leaves point at the last occurrence replaced. It adds the prior position of point (where the `replace-string` command was issued) to the mark ring, without activating the mark; use `C-u C-SPC` to move back there. See Section 8.4 [Mark Ring], page 48.

A prefix argument restricts replacement to matches that are surrounded by word boundaries.

See Section 12.10.3 [Replacement and Case], page 104, for details about case-sensitivity in replace commands.

12.10.2 Regexp Replacement

The `M-x replace-string` command replaces exact matches for a single string. The similar command `M-x replace-regexp` replaces any match for a specified pattern.

`M-x replace-regexp RET` *regexp* `RET` *newstring* `RET`
> Replace every match for *regexp* with *newstring*.

In `replace-regexp`, the *newstring* need not be constant: it can refer to all or part of what is matched by the *regexp*. '\&' in *newstring* stands for the entire match being replaced. '*d*' in *newstring*, where *d* is a digit, stands for whatever matched the *d*th parenthesized grouping in *regexp*. (This is called a "back reference".) '\#' refers to the count of replacements already made in this command, as a decimal number. In the first replacement, '\#' stands for '0'; in the second, for '1'; and so on. For example,

```
M-x replace-regexp RET c[ad]+r RET \&-safe RET
```

replaces (for example) 'cadr' with 'cadr-safe' and 'cddr' with 'cddr-safe'.

```
M-x replace-regexp RET \(c[ad]+r\)-safe RET \1 RET
```

performs the inverse transformation. To include a '\' in the text to replace with, you must enter '\\'.

If you want to enter part of the replacement string by hand each time, use '\?' in the replacement string. Each replacement will ask you to edit the replacement string in the minibuffer, putting point where the '\?' was.

The remainder of this subsection is intended for specialized tasks and requires knowledge of Lisp. Most readers can skip it.

You can use Lisp expressions to calculate parts of the replacement string. To do this, write '\,' followed by the expression in the replacement string. Each replacement calculates the value of the expression and converts it to text without quoting (if it's a string, this means using the string's contents), and uses it in the replacement string in place of the expression itself. If the expression is a symbol, one space in the replacement string after the symbol name goes with the symbol name, so the value replaces them both.

Inside such an expression, you can use some special sequences. '\&' and '*n*' refer here, as usual, to the entire match as a string, and to a submatch as a string. *n* may be multiple digits, and the value of '*n*' is `nil` if subexpression *n* did not match. You can also use '\#&' and '\#*n*' to refer to those matches as numbers (this is valid when the match or submatch has the form of a numeral). '\#' here too stands for the number of already-completed replacements.

Repeating our example to exchange 'x' and 'y', we can thus do it also this way:

```
M-x replace-regexp RET \(x\)\|y RET
\,(if \1 "y" "x") RET
```

For computing replacement strings for '\,', the `format` function is often useful (see Section "Formatting Strings" in *The Emacs Lisp Reference Manual*). For example, to add consecutively numbered strings like 'ABC00042' to columns 73 to 80 (unless they are already occupied), you can use

```
M-x replace-regexp RET ^.\{0,72\}$ RET
\,(format "%-72sABC%05d" \& \#) RET
```

12.10.3 Replace Commands and Case

If the first argument of a replace command is all lower case, the command ignores case while searching for occurrences to replace—provided `case-fold-search` is non-`nil`. If `case-fold-search` is set to `nil`, case is always significant in all searches.

In addition, when the *newstring* argument is all or partly lower case, replacement commands try to preserve the case pattern of each occurrence. Thus, the command

```
M-x replace-string RET foo RET bar RET
```

replaces a lower case 'foo' with a lower case 'bar', an all-caps 'FOO' with 'BAR', and a capitalized 'Foo' with 'Bar'. (These three alternatives—lower case, all caps, and capitalized, are the only ones that `replace-string` can distinguish.)

If upper-case letters are used in the replacement string, they remain upper case every time that text is inserted. If upper-case letters are used in the first argument, the second argument is always substituted exactly as given, with no case conversion. Likewise, if either `case-replace` or `case-fold-search` is set to `nil`, replacement is done without case conversion.

12.10.4 Query Replace

M-% *string* RET *newstring* RET

      Replace some occurrences of *string* with *newstring*.

C-M-% *regexp* RET *newstring* RET

      Replace some matches for *regexp* with *newstring*.

If you want to change only some of the occurrences of 'foo' to 'bar', not all of them, use M-% (`query-replace`). This command finds occurrences of 'foo' one by one, displays each occurrence and asks you whether to replace it. Aside from querying, `query-replace` works just like `replace-string` (see Section 12.10.1 [Unconditional Replace], page 103). In particular, it preserves case provided `case-replace` is non-`nil`, as it normally is (see Section 12.10.3 [Replacement and Case], page 104). A numeric argument means to consider only occurrences that are bounded by word-delimiter characters. A negative prefix argument replaces backward.

C-M-% performs regexp search and replace (`query-replace-regexp`). It works like `replace-regexp` except that it queries like `query-replace`.

These commands highlight the current match using the face `query-replace`. They highlight other matches using `lazy-highlight` just like incremental search (see Section 12.1 [Incremental Search], page 90). By default, `query-replace-regexp` will show the substituted replacement string for the current match in the minibuffer. If you want to keep special sequences '\&' and '\n' unexpanded, customize `query-replace-show-replacement` variable.

The characters you can type when you are shown a match for the string or regexp are:

SPC   to replace the occurrence with *newstring*.

DEL   to skip to the next occurrence without replacing this one.

, (Comma)

      to replace this occurrence and display the result. You are then asked for another input character to say what to do next. Since the replacement has already been made, DEL and SPC are equivalent in this situation; both move to the next occurrence.

      You can type C-r at this point (see below) to alter the replaced text. You can also type C-x u to undo the replacement; this exits the `query-replace`, so if you want to do further replacement you must use C-x ESC ESC RET to restart (see Section 5.6 [Repetition], page 34).

RET   to exit without doing any more replacements.

. (Period) to replace this occurrence and then exit without searching for more occurrences.

!   to replace all remaining occurrences without asking again.

Y (Upper-case)

to replace all remaining occurrences in all remaining buffers in multi-buffer replacements (like the Dired Q command that performs query replace on selected files). It answers this question and all subsequent questions in the series with "yes", without further user interaction.

N (Upper-case)

to skip to the next buffer in multi-buffer replacements without replacing remaining occurrences in the current buffer. It answers this question "no", gives up on the questions for the current buffer, and continues to the next buffer in the sequence.

^   to go back to the position of the previous occurrence (or what used to be an occurrence), in case you changed it by mistake or want to reexamine it.

C-r   to enter a recursive editing level, in case the occurrence needs to be edited rather than just replaced with *newstring*. When you are done, exit the recursive editing level with C-M-c to proceed to the next occurrence. See Section 31.10 [Recursive Edit], page 404.

C-w   to delete the occurrence, and then enter a recursive editing level as in C-r. Use the recursive edit to insert text to replace the deleted occurrence of *string*. When done, exit the recursive editing level with C-M-c to proceed to the next occurrence.

e   to edit the replacement string in the minibuffer. When you exit the minibuffer by typing RET, the minibuffer contents replace the current occurrence of the pattern. They also become the new replacement string for any further occurrences.

C-l   to redisplay the screen. Then you must type another character to specify what to do with this occurrence.

C-h   to display a message summarizing these options. Then you must type another character to specify what to do with this occurrence.

Some other characters are aliases for the ones listed above: y, n and q are equivalent to SPC, DEL and RET.

Aside from this, any other character exits the **query-replace**, and is then reread as part of a key sequence. Thus, if you type C-k, it exits the **query-replace** and then kills to end of line.

To restart a **query-replace** once it is exited, use C-x ESC ESC, which repeats the **query-replace** because it used the minibuffer to read its arguments. See Section 5.6 [Repetition], page 34.

The option **search-invisible** determines how **query-replace** treats invisible text. See [Outline Search], page 220.

See Section 27.7 [Operating on Files], page 320, for the Dired Q command which performs query replace on selected files. See also Section 27.9 [Transforming File Names], page 323, for Dired commands to rename, copy, or link files by replacing regexp matches in file names.

12.11 Other Search-and-Loop Commands

Here are some other commands that find matches for a regular expression. They all ignore case in matching, if the pattern contains no upper-case letters and `case-fold-search` is non-`nil`. Aside from `occur` and its variants, all operate on the text from point to the end of the buffer, or on the region if it is active.

`M-x multi-isearch-buffers`

> Prompt for one or more buffer names, ending with RET; then, begin a multi-buffer incremental search in those buffers. (If the search fails in one buffer, the next C-s tries searching the next specified buffer, and so forth.) With a prefix argument, prompt for a regexp and begin a multi-buffer incremental search in buffers matching that regexp.

`M-x multi-isearch-buffers-regexp`

> This command is just like `multi-isearch-buffers`, except it performs an incremental regexp search.

`M-x occur` Prompt for a regexp, and display a list showing each line in the buffer that contains a match for it. To limit the search to part of the buffer, narrow to that part (see Section 11.5 [Narrowing], page 73). A numeric argument n specifies that n lines of context are to be displayed before and after each matching line.

> In the *Occur* buffer, you can click on each entry, or move point there and type RET, to visit the corresponding position in the buffer that was searched. o and C-o display the match in another window; C-o does not select it. Alternatively, you can use the C-x ' (next-error) command to visit the occurrences one by one (see Section 24.2 [Compilation Mode], page 262).

> Typing e in the *Occur* buffer switches to Occur Edit mode, in which edits made to the entries are also applied to the text in the originating buffer. Type C-c C-c to return to Occur mode.

> The command M-x list-matching-lines is a synonym for M-x occur.

`M-s o` Run `occur` using the search string of the last incremental string search. You can also run M-s o when an incremental search is active; this uses the current search string.

`M-x multi-occur`

> This command is just like `occur`, except it is able to search through multiple buffers. It asks you to specify the buffer names one by one.

`M-x multi-occur-in-matching-buffers`

> This command is similar to `multi-occur`, except the buffers to search are specified by a regular expression that matches visited file names. With a prefix argument, it uses the regular expression to match buffer names instead.

`M-x how-many`

> Prompt for a regexp, and print the number of matches for it in the buffer after point. If the region is active, this operates on the region instead.

M-x flush-lines

> Prompt for a regexp, and delete each line that contains a match for it, operating on the text after point. This command deletes the current line if it contains a match starting after point. If the region is active, it operates on the region instead; if a line partially contained in the region contains a match entirely contained in the region, it is deleted.
>
> If a match is split across lines, **flush-lines** deletes all those lines. It deletes the lines before starting to look for the next match; hence, it ignores a match starting on the same line at which another match ended.

M-x keep-lines

> Prompt for a regexp, and delete each line that *does not* contain a match for it, operating on the text after point. If point is not at the beginning of a line, this command always keeps the current line. If the region is active, the command operates on the region instead; it never deletes lines that are only partially contained in the region (a newline that ends a line counts as part of that line).
>
> If a match is split across lines, this command keeps all those lines.

13 Commands for Fixing Typos

In this chapter we describe commands that are useful when you catch a mistake while editing. The most fundamental of these commands is the undo command `C-/` (also bound to `C-x u` and `C-_`). This undoes a single command, or a part of a command (as in the case of `query-replace`), or several consecutive character insertions. Consecutive repetitions of `C-/` undo earlier and earlier changes, back to the limit of the undo information available.

Aside from the commands described here, you can erase text using deletion commands such as `DEL` (`delete-backward-char`). These were described earlier in this manual. See Section 4.3 [Erasing], page 19.

13.1 Undo

The *undo* command reverses recent changes in the buffer's text. Each buffer records changes individually, and the undo command always applies to the current buffer. You can undo all the changes in a buffer for as far back as the buffer's records go. Usually, each editing command makes a separate entry in the undo records, but some commands such as `query-replace` divide their changes into multiple entries for flexibility in undoing. Consecutive character insertion commands are usually grouped together into a single undo record, to make undoing less tedious.

`C-/`
`C-x u`
`C-_`   Undo one entry in the current buffer's undo records (`undo`).

To begin to undo, type `C-/` (or its aliases, `C-_` or `C-x u`)[1]. This undoes the most recent change in the buffer, and moves point back to where it was before that change. Consecutive repetitions of `C-/` (or its aliases) undo earlier and earlier changes in the current buffer. If all the recorded changes have already been undone, the undo command signals an error.

Any command other than an undo command breaks the sequence of undo commands. Starting from that moment, the entire sequence of undo commands that you have just performed are themselves placed into the undo record, as a single set of changes. Therefore, to re-apply changes you have undone, type `C-f` or any other command that harmlessly breaks the sequence of undoing; then type `C-/` to undo the undo command.

Alternatively, if you want to resume undoing, without redoing previous undo commands, use `M-x undo-only`. This is like `undo`, but will not redo changes you have just undone.

If you notice that a buffer has been modified accidentally, the easiest way to recover is to type `C-/` repeatedly until the stars disappear from the front of the mode line (see Section 1.3 [Mode Line], page 8). Whenever an undo command makes the stars disappear from the mode line, it means that the buffer contents are the same as they were when the file was last read in or saved. If you do not remember whether you changed the buffer deliberately, type `C-/` once. When you see the last change you made undone, you will see whether it was an intentional change. If it was an accident, leave it undone. If it was deliberate, redo the change as described above.

---

[1] Aside from `C-/`, the `undo` command is also bound to `C-x u` because that is more straightforward for beginners to remember: 'u' stands for "undo". It is also bound to `C-_` because typing `C-/` on some text terminals actually enters `C-_`.

When there is an active region, any use of undo performs *selective undo*: it undoes the most recent change within the region, instead of the entire buffer. However, when Transient Mark mode is off (see Section 8.7 [Disabled Transient Mark], page 50), C-/ always operates on the entire buffer, ignoring the region. In this case, you can perform selective undo by supplying a prefix argument to the undo command: C-u C-/. To undo further changes in the same region, repeat the undo command (no prefix argument is needed).

Some specialized buffers do not make undo records. Buffers whose names start with spaces never do; these buffers are used internally by Emacs to hold text that users don't normally look at or edit.

When the undo information for a buffer becomes too large, Emacs discards the oldest records from time to time (during *garbage collection*). You can specify how much undo information to keep by setting the variables undo-limit, undo-strong-limit, and undo-outer-limit. Their values are expressed in bytes.

The variable undo-limit sets a soft limit: Emacs keeps undo data for enough commands to reach this size, and perhaps exceed it, but does not keep data for any earlier commands beyond that. Its default value is 80000. The variable undo-strong-limit sets a stricter limit: any previous command (though not the most recent one) that pushes the size past this amount is forgotten. The default value of undo-strong-limit is 120000.

Regardless of the values of those variables, the most recent change is never discarded unless it gets bigger than undo-outer-limit (normally 12,000,000). At that point, Emacs discards the undo data and warns you about it. This is the only situation in which you cannot undo the last command. If this happens, you can increase the value of undo-outer-limit to make it even less likely to happen in the future. But if you didn't expect the command to create such large undo data, then it is probably a bug and you should report it. See Section 34.3 [Reporting Bugs], page 448.

13.2 Transposing Text

C-t   Transpose two characters (transpose-chars).

M-t   Transpose two words (transpose-words).

C-M-t   Transpose two balanced expressions (transpose-sexps).

C-x C-t   Transpose two lines (transpose-lines).

The common error of transposing two characters can be fixed, when they are adjacent, with the C-t command (transpose-chars). Normally, C-t transposes the two characters on either side of point. When given at the end of a line, rather than transposing the last character of the line with the newline, which would be useless, C-t transposes the last two characters on the line. So, if you catch your transposition error right away, you can fix it with just a C-t. If you don't catch it so fast, you must move the cursor back between the two transposed characters before you type C-t. If you transposed a space with the last character of the word before it, the word motion commands are a good way of getting there. Otherwise, a reverse search (C-r) is often the best way. See Chapter 12 [Search], page 90.

M-t transposes the word before point with the word after point (transpose-words). It moves point forward over a word, dragging the word preceding or containing point forward as well. The punctuation characters between the words do not move. For example, 'FOO, BAR' transposes into 'BAR, FOO' rather than 'BAR FOO,'.

C-M-t (`transpose-sexps`) is a similar command for transposing two expressions (see Section 23.4.1 [Expressions], page 246), and C-x C-t (`transpose-lines`) exchanges lines. They work like M-t except as regards what units of text they transpose.

A numeric argument to a transpose command serves as a repeat count: it tells the transpose command to move the character (word, expression, line) before or containing point across several other characters (words, expressions, lines). For example, C-u 3 C-t moves the character before point forward across three other characters. It would change 'f⋆oobar' into 'oobf⋆ar'. This is equivalent to repeating C-t three times. C-u - 4 M-t moves the word before point backward across four words. C-u - C-M-t would cancel the effect of plain C-M-t.

A numeric argument of zero is assigned a special meaning (because otherwise a command with a repeat count of zero would do nothing): to transpose the character (word, expression, line) ending after point with the one ending after the mark.

13.3 Case Conversion

M-- M-l   Convert last word to lower case. Note `Meta--` is Meta-minus.

M-- M-u   Convert last word to all upper case.

M-- M-c   Convert last word to lower case with capital initial.

A very common error is to type words in the wrong case. Because of this, the word case-conversion commands M-l, M-u and M-c have a special feature when used with a negative argument: they do not move the cursor. As soon as you see you have mistyped the last word, you can simply case-convert it and go on typing. See Section 22.6 [Case], page 216.

13.4 Checking and Correcting Spelling

This section describes the commands to check the spelling of a single word or of a portion of a buffer. These commands only work if the spelling checker program Aspell, Ispell or Hunspell is installed. These programs are not part of Emacs, but one of them is usually installed in GNU/Linux and other free operating systems.

M-$ Check and correct spelling of the word at point (`ispell-word`). If the region is active, do it for all words in the region instead.

M-x ispell
           Check and correct spelling of all words in the buffer. If the region is active, do it for all words in the region instead.

M-x ispell-buffer
           Check and correct spelling in the buffer.

M-x ispell-region
           Check and correct spelling in the region.

M-x ispell-message
           Check and correct spelling in a draft mail message, excluding cited material.

M-x ispell-change-dictionary RET *dict* RET
           Restart the Aspell/Ispell/Hunspell process, using *dict* as the dictionary.

```
M-x ispell-kill-ispell
```
> Kill the Aspell/Ispell/Hunspell subprocess.

```
M-TAB
ESC TAB
```
> Complete the word before point based on the spelling dictionary (`ispell-complete-word`).

```
M-x flyspell-mode
```
> Enable Flyspell mode, which highlights all misspelled words.

```
M-x flyspell-prog-mode
```
> Enable Flyspell mode for comments and strings only.

To check the spelling of the word around or before point, and optionally correct it as well, type M-$ (`ispell-word`). If a region is active, M-$ checks the spelling of all words within the region. See Chapter 8 [Mark], page 45. (When Transient Mark mode is off, M-$ always acts on the word around or before point, ignoring the region; see Section 8.7 [Disabled Transient Mark], page 50.)

Similarly, the command M-x ispell performs spell-checking in the region if one is active, or in the entire buffer otherwise. The commands M-x ispell-buffer and M-x ispell-region explicitly perform spell-checking on the entire buffer or the region respectively. To check spelling in an email message you are writing, use M-x ispell-message; that command checks the whole buffer, except for material that is indented or appears to be cited from other messages. See Chapter 29 [Sending Mail], page 350.

When one of these commands encounters what appears to be an incorrect word, it asks you what to do. It usually displays a list of numbered "near-misses"—words that are close to the incorrect word. Then you must type a single-character response. Here are the valid responses:

digit
> Replace the word, just this time, with one of the displayed near-misses. Each near-miss is listed with a digit; type that digit to select it.

SPC
> Skip this word—continue to consider it incorrect, but don't change it here.

r *new* RET
> Replace the word, just this time, with *new*. (The replacement string will be rescanned for more spelling errors.)

R *new* RET
> Replace the word with *new*, and do a `query-replace` so you can replace it elsewhere in the buffer if you wish. (The replacements will be rescanned for more spelling errors.)

a
> Accept the incorrect word—treat it as correct, but only in this editing session.

A
> Accept the incorrect word—treat it as correct, but only in this editing session and for this buffer.

i
> Insert this word in your private dictionary file so that Aspell or Ispell or Hunspell will consider it correct from now on, even in future sessions.

m
> Like i, but you can also specify dictionary completion information.

u
> Insert the lower-case version of this word in your private dictionary file.

l *word* RET

> Look in the dictionary for words that match *word*. These words become the new list of "near-misses"; you can select one of them as the replacement by typing a digit. You can use '*' in *word* as a wildcard.

C-g

X

> Quit interactive spell checking, leaving point at the word that was being checked. You can restart checking again afterward with C-u M-$.

x

> Quit interactive spell checking and move point back to where it was when you started spell checking.

q

> Quit interactive spell checking and kill the spell-checker subprocess.

?

> Show the list of options.

In Text mode and related modes, M-TAB (ispell-complete-word) performs in-buffer completion based on spelling correction. Insert the beginning of a word, and then type M-TAB; this shows a list of completions. (If your window manager intercepts M-TAB, type ESC TAB or C-M-i.) Each completion is listed with a digit or character; type that digit or character to choose it.

Once started, the Aspell or Ispell or Hunspell subprocess continues to run, waiting for something to do, so that subsequent spell checking commands complete more quickly. If you want to get rid of the process, use M-x ispell-kill-ispell. This is not usually necessary, since the process uses no processor time except when you do spelling correction.

Ispell, Aspell and Hunspell look up spelling in two dictionaries: the standard dictionary and your personal dictionary. The standard dictionary is specified by the variable ispell-local-dictionary or, if that is nil, by the variable ispell-dictionary. If both are nil, the spelling program's default dictionary is used. The command M-x ispell-change-dictionary sets the standard dictionary for the buffer and then restarts the subprocess, so that it will use a different standard dictionary. Your personal dictionary is specified by the variable ispell-personal-dictionary. If that is nil, the spelling program looks for a personal dictionary in a default location.

A separate dictionary is used for word completion. The variable ispell-complete-word-dict specifies the file name of this dictionary. The completion dictionary must be different because it cannot use root and affix information. For some languages, there is a spell checking dictionary but no word completion dictionary.

Flyspell mode is a minor mode that performs automatic spell checking as you type. When it finds a word that it does not recognize, it highlights that word. Type M-x flyspell-mode to toggle Flyspell mode in the current buffer. To enable Flyspell mode in all text mode buffers, add flyspell-mode to text-mode-hook. See Section 33.2.2 [Hooks], page 422.

When Flyspell mode highlights a word as misspelled, you can click on it with Mouse-2 to display a menu of possible corrections and actions. You can also correct the word by editing it manually in any way you like.

Flyspell Prog mode works just like ordinary Flyspell mode, except that it only checks words in comments and string constants. This feature is useful for editing programs. Type M-x flyspell-prog-mode to enable or disable this mode in the current buffer. To enable this mode in all programming mode buffers, add flyspell-prog-mode to prog-mode-hook (see Section 33.2.2 [Hooks], page 422).

14 Keyboard Macros

In this chapter we describe how to record a sequence of editing commands so you can repeat it conveniently later.

A *keyboard macro* is a command defined by an Emacs user to stand for another sequence of keys. For example, if you discover that you are about to type C-n M-d C-d forty times, you can speed your work by defining a keyboard macro to do C-n M-d C-d, and then executing it 39 more times.

You define a keyboard macro by executing and recording the commands which are its definition. Put differently, as you define a keyboard macro, the definition is being executed for the first time. This way, you can see the effects of your commands, so that you don't have to figure them out in your head. When you close the definition, the keyboard macro is defined and also has been, in effect, executed once. You can then do the whole thing over again by invoking the macro.

Keyboard macros differ from ordinary Emacs commands in that they are written in the Emacs command language rather than in Lisp. This makes it easier for the novice to write them, and makes them more convenient as temporary hacks. However, the Emacs command language is not powerful enough as a programming language to be useful for writing anything intelligent or general. For such things, Lisp must be used.

14.1 Basic Use

F3   Start defining a keyboard macro (kmacro-start-macro-or-insert-counter).

F4   If a keyboard macro is being defined, end the definition; otherwise, execute the most recent keyboard macro (kmacro-end-or-call-macro).

C-u F3   Re-execute last keyboard macro, then append keys to its definition.

C-u C-u F3
            Append keys to the last keyboard macro without re-executing it.

C-x C-k r   Run the last keyboard macro on each line that begins in the region (apply-macro-to-region-lines).

To start defining a keyboard macro, type F3. From then on, your keys continue to be executed, but also become part of the definition of the macro. 'Def' appears in the mode line to remind you of what is going on. When you are finished, type F4 (kmacro-end-or-call-macro) to terminate the definition. For example,

        F3 M-f foo F4

defines a macro to move forward a word and then insert 'foo'. Note that F3 and F4 do not become part of the macro.

After defining the macro, you can call it with F4. For the above example, this has the same effect as typing M-f foo again. (Note the two roles of the F4 command: it ends the macro if you are in the process of defining one, or calls the last macro otherwise.) You can also supply F4 with a numeric prefix argument 'n', which means to invoke the macro 'n' times. An argument of zero repeats the macro indefinitely, until it gets an error or you type C-g (or, on MS-DOS, C-BREAK).

The above example demonstrates a handy trick that you can employ with keyboard macros: if you wish to repeat an operation at regularly spaced places in the text, include a motion command as part of the macro. In this case, repeating the macro inserts the string 'foo' after each successive word.

After terminating the definition of a keyboard macro, you can append more keystrokes to its definition by typing C-u F3. This is equivalent to plain F3 followed by retyping the whole definition so far. As a consequence, it re-executes the macro as previously defined. If you change the variable kmacro-execute-before-append to nil, the existing macro will not be re-executed before appending to it (the default is t). You can also add to the end of the definition of the last keyboard macro without re-executing it by typing C-u C-u F3.

When a command reads an argument with the minibuffer, your minibuffer input becomes part of the macro along with the command. So when you replay the macro, the command gets the same argument as when you entered the macro. For example,

        F3 C-a C-k C-x b foo RET C-y C-x b RET F4

defines a macro that kills the current line, yanks it into the buffer 'foo', then returns to the original buffer.

Most keyboard commands work as usual in a keyboard macro definition, with some exceptions. Typing C-g (keyboard-quit) quits the keyboard macro definition. Typing C-M-c (exit-recursive-edit) can be unreliable: it works as you'd expect if exiting a recursive edit that started within the macro, but if it exits a recursive edit that started before you invoked the keyboard macro, it also necessarily exits the keyboard macro too. Mouse events are also unreliable, even though you can use them in a keyboard macro: when the macro replays the mouse event, it uses the original mouse position of that event, the position that the mouse had while you were defining the macro. The effect of this may be hard to predict.

The command C-x C-k r (apply-macro-to-region-lines) repeats the last defined keyboard macro on each line that begins in the region. It does this line by line, by moving point to the beginning of the line and then executing the macro.

In addition to the F3 and F4 commands described above, Emacs also supports an older set of key bindings for defining and executing keyboard macros. To begin a macro definition, type C-x ((kmacro-start-macro); as with F3, a prefix argument appends this definition to the last keyboard macro. To end a macro definition, type C-x) (kmacro-end-macro). To execute the most recent macro, type C-x e (kmacro-end-and-call-macro). If you enter C-x e while defining a macro, the macro is terminated and executed immediately. Immediately after typing C-x e, you can type e repeatedly to immediately repeat the macro one or more times. You can also give C-x e a repeat argument, just like F4.

C-x) can be given a repeat count as an argument. This means to repeat the macro right after defining it. The macro definition itself counts as the first repetition, since it is executed as you define it, so C-u 4 C-x) executes the macro immediately 3 additional times.

14.2 The Keyboard Macro Ring

All defined keyboard macros are recorded in the *keyboard macro ring*. There is only one keyboard macro ring, shared by all buffers.

C-x C-k C-k

> Execute the keyboard macro at the head of the ring (`kmacro-end-or-call-macro-repeat`).

C-x C-k C-n

> Rotate the keyboard macro ring to the next macro (defined earlier) (`kmacro-cycle-ring-next`).

C-x C-k C-p

> Rotate the keyboard macro ring to the previous macro (defined later) (`kmacro-cycle-ring-previous`).

All commands which operate on the keyboard macro ring use the same C-x C-k prefix. Most of these commands can be executed and repeated immediately after each other without repeating the C-x C-k prefix. For example,

> C-x C-k C-p C-p C-k C-k C-k C-n C-n C-k C-p C-k C-d

will rotate the keyboard macro ring to the "second previous" macro, execute the resulting head macro three times, rotate back to the original head macro, execute that once, rotate to the "previous" macro, execute that, and finally delete it from the macro ring.

The command C-x C-k C-k (`kmacro-end-or-call-macro-repeat`) executes the keyboard macro at the head of the macro ring. You can repeat the macro immediately by typing another C-k, or you can rotate the macro ring immediately by typing C-n or C-p.

When a keyboard macro is being defined, C-x C-k C-k behaves like F4 except that, immediately afterward, you can use most key bindings of this section without the C-x C-k prefix. For instance, another C-k will re-execute the macro.

The commands C-x C-k C-n (`kmacro-cycle-ring-next`) and C-x C-k C-p (`kmacro-cycle-ring-previous`) rotate the macro ring, bringing the next or previous keyboard macro to the head of the macro ring. The definition of the new head macro is displayed in the echo area. You can continue to rotate the macro ring immediately by repeating just C-n and C-p until the desired macro is at the head of the ring. To execute the new macro ring head immediately, just type C-k.

Note that Emacs treats the head of the macro ring as the "last defined keyboard macro". For instance, F4 will execute that macro, and C-x C-k n will give it a name.

The maximum number of macros stored in the keyboard macro ring is determined by the customizable variable `kmacro-ring-max`.

14.3 The Keyboard Macro Counter

Each keyboard macro has an associated counter, which is initialized to 0 when you start defining the macro. This counter allows you to insert a number into the buffer that depends on the number of times the macro has been called. The counter is incremented each time its value is inserted into the buffer.

F3

> In a keyboard macro definition, insert the keyboard macro counter value in the buffer (`kmacro-start-macro-or-insert-counter`).

C-x C-k C-i

> Insert the keyboard macro counter value in the buffer (`kmacro-insert-counter`).

`C-x C-k C-c`

> Set the keyboard macro counter (`kmacro-set-counter`).

`C-x C-k C-a`

> Add the prefix arg to the keyboard macro counter (`kmacro-add-counter`).

`C-x C-k C-f`

> Specify the format for inserting the keyboard macro counter (`kmacro-set-format`).

When you are defining a keyboard macro, the command `F3` (`kmacro-start-macro-or-insert-counter`) inserts the current value of the keyboard macro's counter into the buffer, and increments the counter by 1. (If you are not defining a macro, `F3` begins a macro definition instead. See Section 14.1 [Basic Keyboard Macro], page 114.) You can use a numeric prefix argument to specify a different increment. If you just specify a `C-u` prefix, that is the same as an increment of zero: it inserts the current counter value without changing it.

As an example, let us show how the keyboard macro counter can be used to build a numbered list. Consider the following key sequence:

    F3 C-a F3 . SPC F4

As part of this keyboard macro definition, the string '0. ' was inserted into the beginning of the current line. If you now move somewhere else in the buffer and type `F4` to invoke the macro, the string '1. ' is inserted at the beginning of that line. Subsequent invocations insert '2. ', '3. ', and so forth.

The command `C-x C-k C-i` (`kmacro-insert-counter`) does the same thing as `F3`, but it can be used outside a keyboard macro definition. When no keyboard macro is being defined or executed, it inserts and increments the counter of the macro at the head of the keyboard macro ring.

The command `C-x C-k C-c` (`kmacro-set-counter`) sets the current macro counter to the value of the numeric argument. If you use it inside the macro, it operates on each repetition of the macro. If you specify just `C-u` as the prefix, while executing the macro, that resets the counter to the value it had at the beginning of the current repetition of the macro (undoing any increments so far in this repetition).

The command `C-x C-k C-a` (`kmacro-add-counter`) adds the prefix argument to the current macro counter. With just `C-u` as argument, it resets the counter to the last value inserted by any keyboard macro. (Normally, when you use this, the last insertion will be in the same macro and it will be the same counter.)

The command `C-x C-k C-f` (`kmacro-set-format`) prompts for the format to use when inserting the macro counter. The default format is '%d', which means to insert the number in decimal without any padding. You can exit with empty minibuffer to reset the format to this default. You can specify any format string that the `format` function accepts and that makes sense with a single integer extra argument (see Section "Formatting Strings" in *The Emacs Lisp Reference Manual*). Do not put the format string inside double quotes when you insert it in the minibuffer.

If you use this command while no keyboard macro is being defined or executed, the new format affects all subsequent macro definitions. Existing macros continue to use the format in effect when they were defined. If you set the format while defining a keyboard macro, this affects the macro being defined from that point on, but it does not affect subsequent macros. Execution of the macro will, at each step, use the format in effect at that step during its definition. Changes to the macro format during execution of a macro, like the corresponding changes during its definition, have no effect on subsequent macros.

The format set by `C-x C-k C-f` does not affect insertion of numbers stored in registers.

If you use a register as a counter, incrementing it on each repetition of the macro, that accomplishes the same thing as a keyboard macro counter. See Section 10.5 [Number Registers], page 66. For most purposes, it is simpler to use a keyboard macro counter.

14.4 Executing Macros with Variations

In a keyboard macro, you can create an effect similar to that of `query-replace`, in that the macro asks you each time around whether to make a change.

`C-x q`   When this point is reached during macro execution, ask for confirmation (`kbd-macro-query`).

While defining the macro, type `C-x q` at the point where you want the query to occur. During macro definition, the `C-x q` does nothing, but when you run the macro later, `C-x q` asks you interactively whether to continue.

The valid responses when `C-x q` asks are:

`SPC` (or `y`)   Continue executing the keyboard macro.

`DEL` (or `n`)   Skip the remainder of this repetition of the macro, and start right away with the next repetition.

`RET` (or `q`)   Skip the remainder of this repetition and cancel further repetitions.

`C-r`   Enter a recursive editing level, in which you can perform editing which is not part of the macro. When you exit the recursive edit using `C-M-c`, you are asked again how to continue with the keyboard macro. If you type a `SPC` at this time, the rest of the macro definition is executed. It is up to you to leave point and the text in a state such that the rest of the macro will do what you want.

`C-u C-x q`, which is `C-x q` with a numeric argument, performs a completely different function. It enters a recursive edit reading input from the keyboard, both when you type it during the definition of the macro, and when it is executed from the macro. During definition, the editing you do inside the recursive edit does not become part of the macro. During macro execution, the recursive edit gives you a chance to do some particularized editing on each repetition. See Section 31.10 [Recursive Edit], page 404.

14.5 Naming and Saving Keyboard Macros

`C-x C-k n`   Give a command name (for the duration of the Emacs session) to the most recently defined keyboard macro (`kmacro-name-last-macro`).

`C-x C-k b`   Bind the most recently defined keyboard macro to a key sequence (for the duration of the session) (`kmacro-bind-to-key`).

`M-x insert-kbd-macro`
            Insert in the buffer a keyboard macro's definition, as Lisp code.

If you wish to save a keyboard macro for later use, you can give it a name using `C-x C-k n` (`kmacro-name-last-macro`). This reads a name as an argument using the minibuffer and defines that name to execute the last keyboard macro, in its current form. (If you later add to the definition of this macro, that does not alter the name's definition as a macro.) The macro name is a Lisp symbol, and defining it in this way makes it a valid command name for calling with `M-x` or for binding a key to with `global-set-key` (see Section 33.3.1 [Keymaps], page 429). If you specify a name that has a prior definition other than a keyboard macro, an error message is shown and nothing is changed.

You can also bind the last keyboard macro (in its current form) to a key, using `C-x C-k b` (`kmacro-bind-to-key`) followed by the key sequence you want to bind. You can bind to any key sequence in the global keymap, but since most key sequences already have other bindings, you should select the key sequence carefully. If you try to bind to a key sequence with an existing binding (in any keymap), this command asks you for confirmation before replacing the existing binding.

To avoid problems caused by overriding existing bindings, the key sequences `C-x C-k 0` through `C-x C-k 9` and `C-x C-k A` through `C-x C-k Z` are reserved for your own keyboard macro bindings. In fact, to bind to one of these key sequences, you only need to type the digit or letter rather than the whole key sequences. For example,

     `C-x C-k b 4`

will bind the last keyboard macro to the key sequence `C-x C-k 4`.

Once a macro has a command name, you can save its definition in a file. Then it can be used in another editing session. First, visit the file you want to save the definition in. Then use this command:

     `M-x insert-kbd-macro RET` *macroname* `RET`

This inserts some Lisp code that, when executed later, will define the same macro with the same definition it has now. (You need not understand Lisp code to do this, because `insert-kbd-macro` writes the Lisp code for you.) Then save the file. You can load the file later with `load-file` (see Section 24.8 [Lisp Libraries], page 276). If the file you save in is your init file `~/.emacs` (see Section 33.4 [Init File], page 437) then the macro will be defined each time you run Emacs.

If you give `insert-kbd-macro` a numeric argument, it makes additional Lisp code to record the keys (if any) that you have bound to *macroname*, so that the macro will be reassigned the same keys when you load the file.

14.6 Editing a Keyboard Macro

`C-x C-k C-e`
> Edit the last defined keyboard macro (`kmacro-edit-macro`).

`C-x C-k e` *name* `RET`
> Edit a previously defined keyboard macro *name* (`edit-kbd-macro`).

`C-x C-k l`   Edit the last 300 keystrokes as a keyboard macro (`kmacro-edit-lossage`).

You can edit the last keyboard macro by typing `C-x C-k C-e` or `C-x C-k RET` (`kmacro-edit-macro`). This formats the macro definition in a buffer and enters a specialized major mode for editing it. Type C-h m once in that buffer to display details of how to edit the macro. When you are finished editing, type C-c C-c.

You can edit a named keyboard macro or a macro bound to a key by typing C-x C-k e (edit-kbd-macro). Follow that with the keyboard input that you would use to invoke the macro—C-x e or M-x *name* or some other key sequence.

You can edit the last 300 keystrokes as a macro by typing C-x C-k l (kmacro-edit-lossage).

14.7 Stepwise Editing a Keyboard Macro

You can interactively replay and edit the last keyboard macro, one command at a time, by typing C-x C-k SPC (kmacro-step-edit-macro). Unless you quit the macro using q or C-g, the edited macro replaces the last macro on the macro ring.

This macro editing feature shows the last macro in the minibuffer together with the first (or next) command to be executed, and prompts you for an action. You can enter ? to get a summary of your options. These actions are available:

- SPC and y execute the current command, and advance to the next command in the keyboard macro.

- n, d, and DEL skip and delete the current command.

- f skips the current command in this execution of the keyboard macro, but doesn't delete it from the macro.

- TAB executes the current command, as well as all similar commands immediately following the current command; for example, TAB may be used to insert a sequence of characters (corresponding to a sequence of self-insert-command commands).

- c continues execution (without further editing) until the end of the keyboard macro. If execution terminates normally, the edited macro replaces the original keyboard macro.

- C-k skips and deletes the rest of the keyboard macro, terminates step-editing, and replaces the original keyboard macro with the edited macro.

- q and C-g cancels the step-editing of the keyboard macro; discarding any changes made to the keyboard macro.

- i *key*... C-j reads and executes a series of key sequences (not including the final C-j), and inserts them before the current command in the keyboard macro, without advancing over the current command.

- I *key*... reads one key sequence, executes it, and inserts it before the current command in the keyboard macro, without advancing over the current command.

- r *key*... C-j reads and executes a series of key sequences (not including the final C-j), and replaces the current command in the keyboard macro with them, advancing over the inserted key sequences.

- R *key*... reads one key sequence, executes it, and replaces the current command in the keyboard macro with that key sequence, advancing over the inserted key sequence.

- a *key*... C-j executes the current command, then reads and executes a series of key sequences (not including the final C-j), and inserts them after the current command in the keyboard macro; it then advances over the current command and the inserted key sequences.

- A *key*... `C-j` executes the rest of the commands in the keyboard macro, then reads and executes a series of key sequences (not including the final `C-j`), and appends them at the end of the keyboard macro; it then terminates the step-editing and replaces the original keyboard macro with the edited macro.

15 File Handling

The operating system stores data permanently in named *files*, so most of the text you edit with Emacs comes from a file and is ultimately stored in a file.

To edit a file, you must tell Emacs to read the file and prepare a buffer containing a copy of the file's text. This is called *visiting* the file. Editing commands apply directly to text in the buffer; that is, to the copy inside Emacs. Your changes appear in the file itself only when you *save* the buffer back into the file.

In addition to visiting and saving files, Emacs can delete, copy, rename, and append to files, keep multiple versions of them, and operate on file directories.

15.1 File Names

Many Emacs commands that operate on a file require you to specify the file name, using the minibuffer (see Section 5.2 [Minibuffer File], page 26).

While in the minibuffer, you can use the usual completion and history commands (see Chapter 5 [Minibuffer], page 26). Note that file name completion ignores file names whose extensions appear in the variable `completion-ignored-extensions` (see Section 5.4.5 [Completion Options], page 32). Note also that most commands use "permissive completion with confirmation" for reading file names: you are allowed to submit a nonexistent file name, but if you type RET immediately after completing up to a nonexistent file name, Emacs prints '`[Confirm]`' and you must type a second RET to confirm. See Section 5.4.3 [Completion Exit], page 30, for details.

Each buffer has a *default directory*, stored in the buffer-local variable `default-directory`. Whenever Emacs reads a file name using the minibuffer, it usually inserts the default directory into the minibuffer as the initial contents. You can inhibit this insertion by changing the variable `insert-default-directory` to `nil` (see Section 5.2 [Minibuffer File], page 26). Regardless, Emacs always assumes that any relative file name is relative to the default directory, e.g., entering a file name without a directory specifies a file in the default directory.

When you visit a file, Emacs sets `default-directory` in the visiting buffer to the directory of its file. When you create a new buffer that is not visiting a file, via a command like `C-x b`, its default directory is usually copied from the buffer that was current at the time (see Section 16.1 [Select Buffer], page 147). You can use the command `M-x pwd` to see the value of `default-directory` in the current buffer. The command `M-x cd` prompts for a directory name, and sets the buffer's `default-directory` to that directory (doing this does not change the buffer's file name, if any).

As an example, when you visit the file `/u/rms/gnu/gnu.tasks`, the default directory is set to `/u/rms/gnu/`. If you invoke a command that reads a file name, entering just '`foo`' in the minibuffer, with a directory omitted, specifies the file `/u/rms/gnu/foo`; entering '`../.login`' specifies `/u/rms/.login`; and entering '`new/foo`' specifies `/u/rms/gnu/new/foo`.

When typing a file name into the minibuffer, you can make use of a couple of shortcuts: a double slash is interpreted as "ignore everything before the second slash in the pair", and '`~/`' is interpreted as your home directory. See Section 5.2 [Minibuffer File], page 26.

The character '$' is used to substitute an environment variable into a file name. The name of the environment variable consists of all the alphanumeric characters after the '$'; alternatively, it can be enclosed in braces after the '$'. For example, if you have used the shell command `export FOO=rms/hacks` to set up an environment variable named `FOO`, then both `/u/$FOO/test.c` and `/u/${FOO}/test.c` are abbreviations for `/u/rms/hacks/test.c`. If the environment variable is not defined, no substitution occurs, so that the character '$' stands for itself. Note that environment variables affect Emacs only if they are applied before Emacs is started.

To access a file with '$' in its name, if the '$' causes expansion, type '$$'. This pair is converted to a single '$' at the same time that variable substitution is performed for a single '$'. Alternatively, quote the whole file name with '/:' (see Section 15.14 [Quoted File Names], page 143). File names which begin with a literal '~' should also be quoted with '/:'.

You can include non-ASCII characters in file names. See Section 19.11 [File Name Coding], page 190.

15.2 Visiting Files

C-x C-f   Visit a file (`find-file`).

C-x C-r   Visit a file for viewing, without allowing changes to it (`find-file-read-only`).

C-x C-v   Visit a different file instead of the one visited last (`find-alternate-file`).

C-x 4 f   Visit a file, in another window (`find-file-other-window`). Don't alter what is displayed in the selected window.

C-x 5 f   Visit a file, in a new frame (`find-file-other-frame`). Don't alter what is displayed in the selected frame.

M-x find-file-literally
           Visit a file with no conversion of the contents.

Visiting a file means reading its contents into an Emacs buffer so you can edit them. Emacs makes a new buffer for each file that you visit.

To visit a file, type C-x C-f (`find-file`) and use the minibuffer to enter the name of the desired file. While in the minibuffer, you can abort the command by typing C-g. See Section 15.1 [File Names], page 122, for details about entering file names into minibuffers.

If the specified file exists but the system does not allow you to read it, an error message is displayed in the echo area. Otherwise, you can tell that C-x C-f has completed successfully by the appearance of new text on the screen, and by the buffer name shown in the mode line (see Section 1.3 [Mode Line], page 8). Emacs normally constructs the buffer name from the file name, omitting the directory name. For example, a file named `/usr/rms/emacs.tex` is visited in a buffer named '`emacs.tex`'. If there is already a buffer with that name, Emacs constructs a unique name; the normal method is to add a suffix based on the directory name (e.g., '`<rms>`', '`<tmp>`', and so on), but you can select other methods. See Section 16.7.1 [Uniquify], page 154.

To create a new file, just visit it using the same command, C-x C-f. Emacs displays '(`New file`)' in the echo area, but in other respects behaves as if you had visited an existing empty file.

After visiting a file, the changes you make with editing commands are made in the Emacs buffer. They do not take effect in the visited file, until you *save* the buffer (see Section 15.3 [Saving], page 126). If a buffer contains changes that have not been saved, we say the buffer is *modified*. This implies that some changes will be lost if the buffer is not saved. The mode line displays two stars near the left margin to indicate that the buffer is modified.

If you visit a file that is already in Emacs, C-x C-f switches to the existing buffer instead of making another copy. Before doing so, it checks whether the file has changed since you last visited or saved it. If the file has changed, Emacs offers to reread it.

If you try to visit a file larger than `large-file-warning-threshold` (the default is 10000000, which is about 10 megabytes), Emacs asks you for confirmation first. You can answer y to proceed with visiting the file. Note, however, that Emacs cannot visit files that are larger than the maximum Emacs buffer size, which is limited by the amount of memory Emacs can allocate and by the integers that Emacs can represent (see Chapter 16 [Buffers], page 147). If you try, Emacs displays an error message saying that the maximum buffer size has been exceeded.

If the file name you specify contains shell-style wildcard characters, Emacs visits all the files that match it. (On case-insensitive filesystems, Emacs matches the wildcards disregarding the letter case.) Wildcards include '?', '*', and '[...]' sequences. To enter the wild card '?' in a file name in the minibuffer, you need to type C-q ?. See Section 15.14 [Quoted File Names], page 143, for information on how to visit a file whose name actually contains wildcard characters. You can disable the wildcard feature by customizing `find-file-wildcards`.

If you visit the wrong file unintentionally by typing its name incorrectly, type C-x C-v (`find-alternate-file`) to visit the file you really wanted. C-x C-v is similar to C-x C-f, but it kills the current buffer (after first offering to save it if it is modified). When C-x C-v reads the file name to visit, it inserts the entire default file name in the buffer, with point just after the directory part; this is convenient if you made a slight error in typing the name.

If you "visit" a file that is actually a directory, Emacs invokes Dired, the Emacs directory browser. See Chapter 27 [Dired], page 315. You can disable this behavior by setting the variable `find-file-run-dired` to `nil`; in that case, it is an error to try to visit a directory.

Files which are actually collections of other files, or *file archives*, are visited in special modes which invoke a Dired-like environment to allow operations on archive members. See Section 15.12 [File Archives], page 141, for more about these features.

If you visit a file that the operating system won't let you modify, or that is marked read-only, Emacs makes the buffer read-only too, so that you won't go ahead and make changes that you'll have trouble saving afterward. You can make the buffer writable with C-x C-q (`read-only-mode`). See Section 16.3 [Misc Buffer], page 149.

If you want to visit a file as read-only in order to protect yourself from entering changes accidentally, visit it with the command C-x C-r (`find-file-read-only`) instead of C-x C-f.

C-x 4 f (`find-file-other-window`) is like C-x C-f except that the buffer containing the specified file is selected in another window. The window that was selected before C-x 4 f continues to show the same buffer it was already showing. If this command is used when only one window is being displayed, that window is split in two, with one window showing the same buffer as before, and the other one showing the newly requested file. See Chapter 17 [Windows], page 156.

`C-x 5 f` (`find-file-other-frame`) is similar, but opens a new frame, or selects any existing frame showing the specified file. See Chapter 18 [Frames], page 162.

On graphical displays, there are two additional methods for visiting files. Firstly, when Emacs is built with a suitable GUI toolkit, commands invoked with the mouse (by clicking on the menu bar or tool bar) use the toolkit's standard "File Selection" dialog instead of prompting for the file name in the minibuffer. On GNU/Linux and Unix platforms, Emacs does this when built with GTK, LessTif, and Motif toolkits; on MS-Windows and Mac, the GUI version does that by default. For information on how to customize this, see Section 18.16 [Dialog Boxes], page 174.

Secondly, Emacs supports "drag and drop": dropping a file into an ordinary Emacs window visits the file using that window. As an exception, dropping a file into a window displaying a Dired buffer moves or copies the file into the displayed directory. For details, see Section 18.13 [Drag and Drop], page 173, and Section 27.18 [Misc Dired Features], page 329.

On text-mode terminals and on graphical displays when Emacs was built without a GUI toolkit, you can visit files via the menu-bar "File" menu, which has a "Visit New File" item.

Each time you visit a file, Emacs automatically scans its contents to detect what character encoding and end-of-line convention it uses, and converts these to Emacs's internal encoding and end-of-line convention within the buffer. When you save the buffer, Emacs performs the inverse conversion, writing the file to disk with its original encoding and end-of-line convention. See Section 19.5 [Coding Systems], page 183.

If you wish to edit a file as a sequence of ASCII characters with no special encoding or conversion, use the `M-x find-file-literally` command. This visits a file, like `C-x C-f`, but does not do format conversion (see Section "Format Conversion" in *the Emacs Lisp Reference Manual*), character code conversion (see Section 19.5 [Coding Systems], page 183), or automatic uncompression (see Section 15.11 [Compressed Files], page 141), and does not add a final newline because of `require-final-newline` (see Section 15.3.3 [Customize Save], page 130). If you have already visited the same file in the usual (non-literal) manner, this command asks you whether to visit it literally instead.

Two special hook variables allow extensions to modify the operation of visiting files. Visiting a file that does not exist runs the functions in `find-file-not-found-functions`; this variable holds a list of functions, which are called one by one (with no arguments) until one of them returns non-`nil`. This is not a normal hook, and the name ends in '`-functions`' rather than '`-hook`' to indicate that fact.

Successful visiting of any file, whether existing or not, calls the functions in `find-file-hook`, with no arguments. This variable is a normal hook. In the case of a nonexistent file, the `find-file-not-found-functions` are run first. See Section 33.2.2 [Hooks], page 422.

There are several ways to specify automatically the major mode for editing the file (see Section 20.3 [Choosing Modes], page 202), and to specify local variables defined for that file (see Section 33.2.4 [File Variables], page 424).

15.3 Saving Files

Saving a buffer in Emacs means writing its contents back into the file that was visited in the buffer.

15.3.1 Commands for Saving Files

These are the commands that relate to saving and writing files.

C-x C-s   Save the current buffer to its file (`save-buffer`).

C-x s   Save any or all buffers to their files (`save-some-buffers`).

M-~   Forget that the current buffer has been changed (`not-modified`). With prefix argument (`C-u`), mark the current buffer as changed.

C-x C-w   Save the current buffer with a specified file name (`write-file`).

M-x set-visited-file-name
             Change the file name under which the current buffer will be saved.

When you wish to save the file and make your changes permanent, type C-x C-s (`save-buffer`). After saving is finished, C-x C-s displays a message like this:

        Wrote /u/rms/gnu/gnu.tasks

If the current buffer is not modified (no changes have been made in it since the buffer was created or last saved), saving is not really done, because it would have no effect. Instead, C-x C-s displays a message like this in the echo area:

        (No changes need to be saved)

With a prefix argument, C-u C-x C-s, Emacs also marks the buffer to be backed up when the next save is done. See Section 15.3.2 [Backup], page 127.

The command C-x s (`save-some-buffers`) offers to save any or all modified buffers. It asks you what to do with each buffer. The possible responses are analogous to those of `query-replace`:

y   Save this buffer and ask about the rest of the buffers.

n   Don't save this buffer, but ask about the rest of the buffers.

!   Save this buffer and all the rest with no more questions.

RET   Terminate `save-some-buffers` without any more saving.

.   Save this buffer, then exit `save-some-buffers` without even asking about other buffers.

C-r   View the buffer that you are currently being asked about. When you exit View mode, you get back to `save-some-buffers`, which asks the question again.

d   Diff the buffer against its corresponding file, so you can see what changes you would be saving. This calls the command `diff-buffer-with-file` (see Section 15.8 [Comparing Files], page 137).

C-h   Display a help message about these options.

C-x C-c, the key sequence to exit Emacs, invokes save-some-buffers and therefore asks the same questions.

If you have changed a buffer but do not wish to save the changes, you should take some action to prevent it. Otherwise, each time you use C-x s or C-x C-c, you are liable to save this buffer by mistake. One thing you can do is type M-~ (not-modified), which clears out the indication that the buffer is modified. If you do this, none of the save commands will believe that the buffer needs to be saved. ('~' is often used as a mathematical symbol for 'not'; thus M-~ is 'not', metafied.) Alternatively, you can cancel all the changes made since the file was visited or saved, by reading the text from the file again. This is called *reverting*. See Section 15.4 [Reverting], page 132. (You could also undo all the changes by repeating the undo command C-x u until you have undone all the changes; but reverting is easier.)

M-x set-visited-file-name alters the name of the file that the current buffer is visiting. It reads the new file name using the minibuffer. Then it marks the buffer as visiting that file name, and changes the buffer name correspondingly. set-visited-file-name does not save the buffer in the newly visited file; it just alters the records inside Emacs in case you do save later. It also marks the buffer as "modified" so that C-x C-s in that buffer *will* save.

If you wish to mark the buffer as visiting a different file and save it right away, use C-x C-w (write-file). This is equivalent to set-visited-file-name followed by C-x C-s, except that C-x C-w asks for confirmation if the file exists. C-x C-s used on a buffer that is not visiting a file has the same effect as C-x C-w; that is, it reads a file name, marks the buffer as visiting that file, and saves it there. The default file name in a buffer that is not visiting a file is made by combining the buffer name with the buffer's default directory (see Section 15.1 [File Names], page 122).

If the new file name implies a major mode, then C-x C-w switches to that major mode, in most cases. The command set-visited-file-name also does this. See Section 20.3 [Choosing Modes], page 202.

If Emacs is about to save a file and sees that the date of the latest version on disk does not match what Emacs last read or wrote, Emacs notifies you of this fact, because it probably indicates a problem caused by simultaneous editing and requires your immediate attention. See Section 15.3.4 [Simultaneous Editing], page 130.

15.3.2 Backup Files

On most operating systems, rewriting a file automatically destroys all record of what the file used to contain. Thus, saving a file from Emacs throws away the old contents of the file—or it would, except that Emacs carefully copies the old contents to another file, called the *backup* file, before actually saving.

Emacs makes a backup for a file only the first time the file is saved from a buffer. No matter how many times you subsequently save the file, its backup remains unchanged. However, if you kill the buffer and then visit the file again, a new backup file will be made.

For most files, the variable make-backup-files determines whether to make backup files. On most operating systems, its default value is t, so that Emacs does write backup files.

For files managed by a version control system (see Section 25.1 [Version Control], page 281), the variable vc-make-backup-files determines whether to make backup files.

By default it is `nil`, since backup files are redundant when you store all the previous versions in a version control system. See Section "General VC Options" in *Specialized Emacs Features*.

At your option, Emacs can keep either a single backup for each file, or make a series of numbered backup files for each file that you edit. See Section 15.3.2.1 [Backup Names], page 128.

The default value of the `backup-enable-predicate` variable prevents backup files being written for files in the directories used for temporary files, specified by `temporary-file-directory` or `small-temporary-file-directory`.

You can explicitly tell Emacs to make another backup file from a buffer, even though that buffer has been saved before. If you save the buffer with `C-u C-x C-s`, the version thus saved will be made into a backup file if you save the buffer again. `C-u C-u C-x C-s` saves the buffer, but first makes the previous file contents into a new backup file. `C-u C-u C-u C-x C-s` does both things: it makes a backup from the previous contents, and arranges to make another from the newly saved contents if you save again.

15.3.2.1 Single or Numbered Backups

When Emacs makes a backup file, its name is normally constructed by appending '~' to the file name being edited; thus, the backup file for `eval.c` would be `eval.c~`.

If access control stops Emacs from writing backup files under the usual names, it writes the backup file as `~/.emacs.d/%backup%~`. Only one such file can exist, so only the most recently made such backup is available.

Emacs can also make *numbered backup files*. Numbered backup file names contain '.~', the number, and another '~' after the original file name. Thus, the backup files of `eval.c` would be called `eval.c.~1~`, `eval.c.~2~`, and so on, all the way through names like `eval.c.~259~` and beyond.

The variable `version-control` determines whether to make single backup files or multiple numbered backup files. Its possible values are:

nil   Make numbered backups for files that have numbered backups already. Otherwise, make single backups. This is the default.

t   Make numbered backups.

never   Never make numbered backups; always make single backups.

The usual way to set this variable is globally, through your init file or the customization buffer. However, you can set `version-control` locally in an individual buffer to control the making of backups for that buffer's file (see Section 33.2.3 [Locals], page 423). You can have Emacs set `version-control` locally whenever you visit a given file (see Section 33.2.4 [File Variables], page 424). Some modes, such as Rmail mode, set this variable.

If you set the environment variable `VERSION_CONTROL`, to tell various GNU utilities what to do with backup files, Emacs also obeys the environment variable by setting the Lisp variable `version-control` accordingly at startup. If the environment variable's value is 't' or 'numbered', then `version-control` becomes t; if the value is 'nil' or 'existing', then `version-control` becomes nil; if it is 'never' or 'simple', then `version-control` becomes `never`.

You can customize the variable `backup-directory-alist` to specify that files matching certain patterns should be backed up in specific directories. This variable applies to both single and numbered backups. A typical use is to add an element (`"."` . *dir*) to make all backups in the directory with absolute name *dir*; Emacs modifies the backup file names to avoid clashes between files with the same names originating in different directories. Alternatively, adding, (`"."` . `".~"`) would make backups in the invisible subdirectory .~ of the original file's directory. Emacs creates the directory, if necessary, to make the backup.

If you set the variable `make-backup-file-name-function` to a suitable Lisp function, you can override the usual way Emacs constructs backup file names.

15.3.2.2 Automatic Deletion of Backups

To prevent excessive consumption of disk space, Emacs can delete numbered backup versions automatically. Generally Emacs keeps the first few backups and the latest few backups, deleting any in between. This happens every time a new backup is made.

The two variables `kept-old-versions` and `kept-new-versions` control this deletion. Their values are, respectively, the number of oldest (lowest-numbered) backups to keep and the number of newest (highest-numbered) ones to keep, each time a new backup is made. The backups in the middle (excluding those oldest and newest) are the excess middle versions—those backups are deleted. These variables' values are used when it is time to delete excess versions, just after a new backup version is made; the newly made backup is included in the count in `kept-new-versions`. By default, both variables are 2.

If `delete-old-versions` is t, Emacs deletes the excess backup files silently. If it is `nil`, the default, Emacs asks you whether it should delete the excess backup versions. If it has any other value, then Emacs never automatically deletes backups.

Dired's . (Period) command can also be used to delete old versions. See Section 27.3 [Dired Deletion], page 316.

15.3.2.3 Copying vs. Renaming

Backup files can be made by copying the old file or by renaming it. This makes a difference when the old file has multiple names (hard links). If the old file is renamed into the backup file, then the alternate names become names for the backup file. If the old file is copied instead, then the alternate names remain names for the file that you are editing, and the contents accessed by those names will be the new contents.

The method of making a backup file may also affect the file's owner and group. If copying is used, these do not change. If renaming is used, you become the file's owner, and the file's group becomes the default (different operating systems have different defaults for the group).

The choice of renaming or copying is made as follows:

- If the variable `backup-by-copying` is non-`nil` (the default is `nil`), use copying.

- Otherwise, if the variable `backup-by-copying-when-linked` is non-`nil` (the default is `nil`), and the file has multiple names, use copying.

- Otherwise, if the variable `backup-by-copying-when-mismatch` is non-`nil` (the default is t), and renaming would change the file's owner or group, use copying.

  If you change `backup-by-copying-when-mismatch` to nil, Emacs checks the numeric user-id of the file's owner. If this is higher than `backup-by-copying-`

when-privileged-mismatch, then it behaves as though backup-by-copying-when-mismatch is non-nil anyway.

- Otherwise, renaming is the default choice.

When a file is managed with a version control system (see Section 25.1 [Version Control], page 281), Emacs does not normally make backups in the usual way for that file. But check-in and check-out are similar in some ways to making backups. One unfortunate similarity is that these operations typically break hard links, disconnecting the file name you visited from any alternate names for the same file. This has nothing to do with Emacs—the version control system does it.

15.3.3 Customizing Saving of Files

If the value of the variable require-final-newline is t, saving or writing a file silently puts a newline at the end if there isn't already one there. If the value is visit, Emacs adds a newline at the end of any file that doesn't have one, just after it visits the file. (This marks the buffer as modified, and you can undo it.) If the value is visit-save, Emacs adds such newlines both on visiting and on saving. If the value is nil, Emacs leaves the end of the file unchanged; any other non-nil value means to asks you whether to add a newline. The default is nil.

Some major modes are designed for specific kinds of files that are always supposed to end in newlines. Such major modes set the variable require-final-newline to the value of mode-require-final-newline, which defaults to t. By setting the latter variable, you can control how these modes handle final newlines.

Normally, when a program writes a file, the operating system briefly caches the file's data in main memory before committing the data to disk. This can greatly improve performance; for example, when running on laptops, it can avoid a disk spin-up each time a file is written. However, it risks data loss if the operating system crashes before committing the cache to disk.

To lessen this risk, Emacs can invoke the fsync system call after saving a file. Using fsync does not eliminate the risk of data loss, partly because many systems do not implement fsync properly, and partly because Emacs's file-saving procedure typically relies also on directory updates that might not survive a crash even if fsync works properly.

The write-region-inhibit-fsync variable controls whether Emacs invokes fsync after saving a file. The variable's default value is nil when Emacs is interactive, and t when Emacs runs in batch mode.

Emacs never uses fsync when writing auto-save files, as these files might lose data anyway.

15.3.4 Protection against Simultaneous Editing

Simultaneous editing occurs when two users visit the same file, both make changes, and then both save them. If nobody is informed that this is happening, whichever user saves first would later find that his changes were lost.

On some systems, Emacs notices immediately when the second user starts to change the file, and issues an immediate warning. On all systems, Emacs checks when you save the file, and warns if you are about to overwrite another user's changes. You can prevent loss of the other user's work by taking the proper corrective action instead of saving the file.

When you make the first modification in an Emacs buffer that is visiting a file, Emacs records that the file is *locked* by you. (It does this by creating a specially-named symbolic link[1] with special contents in the same directory.) Emacs removes the lock when you save the changes. The idea is that the file is locked whenever an Emacs buffer visiting it has unsaved changes.

You can prevent the creation of lock files by setting the variable `create-lockfiles` to `nil`. **Caution:** by doing so you will lose the benefits that this feature provides.

If you begin to modify the buffer while the visited file is locked by someone else, this constitutes a *collision*. When Emacs detects a collision, it asks you what to do, by calling the Lisp function `ask-user-about-lock`. You can redefine this function for the sake of customization. The standard definition of this function asks you a question and accepts three possible answers:

s   Steal the lock. Whoever was already changing the file loses the lock, and you gain the lock.

p   Proceed. Go ahead and edit the file despite its being locked by someone else.

q   Quit. This causes an error (`file-locked`), and the buffer contents remain unchanged—the modification you were trying to make does not actually take place.

If Emacs or the operating system crashes, this may leave behind lock files which are stale, so you may occasionally get warnings about spurious collisions. When you determine that the collision is spurious, just use p to tell Emacs to go ahead anyway.

Note that locking works on the basis of a file name; if a file has multiple names, Emacs does not prevent two users from editing it simultaneously under different names.

A lock file cannot be written in some circumstances, e.g., if Emacs lacks the system permissions or cannot create lock files for some other reason. In these cases, Emacs can still detect the collision when you try to save a file, by checking the file's last-modification date. If the file has changed since the last time Emacs visited or saved it, that implies that changes have been made in some other way, and will be lost if Emacs proceeds with saving. Emacs then displays a warning message and asks for confirmation before saving; answer `yes` to save, and `no` or `C-g` cancel the save.

If you are notified that simultaneous editing has already taken place, one way to compare the buffer to its file is the `M-x diff-buffer-with-file` command. See Section 15.8 [Comparing Files], page 137.

15.3.5 Shadowing Files

`M-x shadow-initialize`
> Set up file shadowing.

`M-x shadow-define-literal-group`
> Declare a single file to be shared between sites.

`M-x shadow-define-regexp-group`
> Make all files that match each of a group of files be shared between hosts.

---

[1] If your file system does not support symbolic links, a regular file is used.

`M-x shadow-define-cluster RET` *name* `RET`
> Define a shadow file cluster *name*.

`M-x shadow-copy-files`
> Copy all pending shadow files.

`M-x shadow-cancel`
> Cancel the instruction to shadow some files.

You can arrange to keep identical *shadow* copies of certain files in more than one place—possibly on different machines. To do this, first you must set up a *shadow file group*, which is a set of identically-named files shared between a list of sites. The file group is permanent and applies to further Emacs sessions as well as the current one. Once the group is set up, every time you exit Emacs, it will copy the file you edited to the other files in its group. You can also do the copying without exiting Emacs, by typing `M-x shadow-copy-files`.

To set up a shadow file group, use `M-x shadow-define-literal-group` or `M-x shadow-define-regexp-group`. See their documentation strings for further information.

Before copying a file to its shadows, Emacs asks for confirmation. You can answer "no" to bypass copying of this file, this time. If you want to cancel the shadowing permanently for a certain file, use `M-x shadow-cancel` to eliminate or change the shadow file group.

A *shadow cluster* is a group of hosts that share directories, so that copying to or from one of them is sufficient to update the file on all of them. Each shadow cluster has a name, and specifies the network address of a primary host (the one we copy files to), and a regular expression that matches the host names of all the other hosts in the cluster. You can define a shadow cluster with `M-x shadow-define-cluster`.

15.3.6 Updating Time Stamps Automatically

You can arrange to put a time stamp in a file, so that it is updated automatically each time you edit and save the file. The time stamp must be in the first eight lines of the file, and you should insert it like this:

```
Time-stamp: <>
```

or like this:

```
Time-stamp: " "
```

Then add the function `time-stamp` to the hook `before-save-hook` (see Section 33.2.2 [Hooks], page 422). When you save the file, this function then automatically updates the time stamp with the current date and time. You can also use the command `M-x time-stamp` to update the time stamp manually. For other customizations, see the Custom group `time-stamp`. Note that the time stamp is formatted according to your locale setting (see Section C.4 [Environment], page 482).

15.4 Reverting a Buffer

If you have made extensive changes to a file-visiting buffer and then change your mind, you can *revert* the changes and go back to the saved version of the file. To do this, type `M-x revert-buffer`. Since reverting unintentionally could lose a lot of work, Emacs asks for confirmation first.

The `revert-buffer` command tries to position point in such a way that, if the file was edited only slightly, you will be at approximately the same part of the text as before. But if you have made major changes, point may end up in a totally different location.

Reverting marks the buffer as "not modified". It also clears the buffer's undo history (see Section 13.1 [Undo], page 109). Thus, the reversion cannot be undone—if you change your mind yet again, you can't use the undo commands to bring the reverted changes back.

Some kinds of buffers that are not associated with files, such as Dired buffers, can also be reverted. For them, reverting means recalculating their contents. Buffers created explicitly with `C-x b` cannot be reverted; `revert-buffer` reports an error if you try.

When you edit a file that changes automatically and frequently—for example, a log of output from a process that continues to run—it may be useful for Emacs to revert the file without querying you. To request this behavior, set the variable `revert-without-query` to a list of regular expressions. When a file name matches one of these regular expressions, `find-file` and `revert-buffer` will revert it automatically if it has changed—provided the buffer itself is not modified. (If you have edited the text, it would be wrong to discard your changes.)

You can also tell Emacs to revert buffers periodically. To do this for a specific buffer, enable the minor mode Auto-Revert mode by typing `M-x auto-revert-mode`. This automatically reverts the current buffer every five seconds; you can change the interval through the variable `auto-revert-interval`. To do the same for all file buffers, type `M-x global-auto-revert-mode` to enable Global Auto-Revert mode. These minor modes do not check or revert remote files, because that is usually too slow.

One use of Auto-Revert mode is to "tail" a file such as a system log, so that changes made to that file by other programs are continuously displayed. To do this, just move the point to the end of the buffer, and it will stay there as the file contents change. However, if you are sure that the file will only change by growing at the end, use Auto-Revert Tail mode instead (`auto-revert-tail-mode`). It is more efficient for this. Auto-Revert Tail mode works also for remote files.

See Section 25.1.8 [VC Undo], page 292, for commands to revert to earlier versions of files under version control. See Section 25.1.2 [VC Mode Line], page 284, for Auto Revert peculiarities when visiting files under version control.

15.5 Auto-Saving: Protection Against Disasters

From time to time, Emacs automatically saves each visited file in a separate file, without altering the file you actually use. This is called *auto-saving*. It prevents you from losing more than a limited amount of work if the system crashes.

When Emacs determines that it is time for auto-saving, it considers each buffer, and each is auto-saved if auto-saving is enabled for it and it has been changed since the last time it was auto-saved. The message 'Auto-saving...' is displayed in the echo area during auto-saving, if any files are actually auto-saved. Errors occurring during auto-saving are caught so that they do not interfere with the execution of commands you have been typing.

15.5.1 Auto-Save Files

Auto-saving does not normally save in the files that you visited, because it can be very undesirable to save a change that you did not want to make permanent. Instead, auto-saving is done in a different file called the *auto-save file*, and the visited file is changed only when you request saving explicitly (such as with C-x C-s).

Normally, the auto-save file name is made by appending '#' to the front and rear of the visited file name. Thus, a buffer visiting file foo.c is auto-saved in a file #foo.c#. Most buffers that are not visiting files are auto-saved only if you request it explicitly; when they are auto-saved, the auto-save file name is made by appending '#' to the front and rear of buffer name, then adding digits and letters at the end for uniqueness. For example, the *mail* buffer in which you compose messages to be sent might be auto-saved in a file named #*mail*#704juu. Auto-save file names are made this way unless you reprogram parts of Emacs to do something different (the functions make-auto-save-file-name and auto-save-file-name-p). The file name to be used for auto-saving in a buffer is calculated when auto-saving is turned on in that buffer.

The variable auto-save-file-name-transforms allows a degree of control over the auto-save file name. It lets you specify a series of regular expressions and replacements to transform the auto save file name. The default value puts the auto-save files for remote files (see Section 15.13 [Remote Files], page 142) into the temporary file directory on the local machine.

When you delete a substantial part of the text in a large buffer, auto save turns off temporarily in that buffer. This is because if you deleted the text unintentionally, you might find the auto-save file more useful if it contains the deleted text. To reenable auto-saving after this happens, save the buffer with C-x C-s, or use C-u 1 M-x auto-save-mode.

If you want auto-saving to be done in the visited file rather than in a separate auto-save file, set the variable auto-save-visited-file-name to a non-nil value. In this mode, there is no real difference between auto-saving and explicit saving.

A buffer's auto-save file is deleted when you save the buffer in its visited file. (You can inhibit this by setting the variable delete-auto-save-files to nil.) Changing the visited file name with C-x C-w or set-visited-file-name renames any auto-save file to go with the new visited name.

15.5.2 Controlling Auto-Saving

Each time you visit a file, auto-saving is turned on for that file's buffer if the variable auto-save-default is non-nil (but not in batch mode; see Section C.2 [Initial Options], page 480). The default for this variable is t, so auto-saving is the usual practice for file-visiting buffers. To toggle auto-saving in the current buffer, type M-x auto-save-mode. Auto Save mode acts as a buffer-local minor mode (see Section 20.2 [Minor Modes], page 200).

Emacs auto-saves periodically based on how many characters you have typed since the last auto-save. The variable auto-save-interval specifies how many characters there are between auto-saves. By default, it is 300. Emacs doesn't accept values that are too small: if you customize auto-save-interval to a value less than 20, Emacs will behave as if the value is 20.

Auto-saving also takes place when you stop typing for a while. By default, it does this after 30 seconds of idleness (at this time, Emacs may also perform garbage collection; see Section "Garbage Collection" in *The Emacs Lisp Reference Manual*). To change this interval, customize the variable auto-save-timeout. The actual time period is longer if the current buffer is long; this is a heuristic which aims to keep out of your way when you are editing long buffers, in which auto-save takes an appreciable amount of time. Auto-saving during idle periods accomplishes two things: first, it makes sure all your work is saved if you go away from the terminal for a while; second, it may avoid some auto-saving while you are actually typing.

Emacs also does auto-saving whenever it gets a fatal error. This includes killing the Emacs job with a shell command such as 'kill %emacs', or disconnecting a phone line or network connection.

You can perform an auto-save explicitly with the command M-x do-auto-save.

15.5.3 Recovering Data from Auto-Saves

You can use the contents of an auto-save file to recover from a loss of data with the command M-x recover-file RET *file* RET. This visits *file* and then (after your confirmation) restores the contents from its auto-save file #*file*#. You can then save with C-x C-s to put the recovered text into *file* itself. For example, to recover file foo.c from its auto-save file #foo.c#, do:

```
M-x recover-file RET foo.c RET
yes RET
C-x C-s
```

Before asking for confirmation, M-x recover-file displays a directory listing describing the specified file and the auto-save file, so you can compare their sizes and dates. If the auto-save file is older, M-x recover-file does not offer to read it.

If Emacs or the computer crashes, you can recover all the files you were editing from their auto save files with the command M-x recover-session. This first shows you a list of recorded interrupted sessions. Move point to the one you choose, and type C-c C-c.

Then recover-session asks about each of the files that were being edited during that session, asking whether to recover that file. If you answer y, it calls recover-file, which works in its normal fashion. It shows the dates of the original file and its auto-save file, and asks once again whether to recover that file.

When recover-session is done, the files you've chosen to recover are present in Emacs buffers. You should then save them. Only this—saving them—updates the files themselves.

Emacs records information about interrupted sessions in files named .saves-*pid-hostname* in the directory ~/.emacs.d/auto-save-list/. This directory is determined by the variable auto-save-list-file-prefix. If you set auto-save-list-file-prefix to nil, sessions are not recorded for recovery.

15.6 File Name Aliases

Symbolic links and hard links both make it possible for several file names to refer to the same file. Hard links are alternate names that refer directly to the file; all the names are equally valid, and no one of them is preferred. By contrast, a symbolic link is a kind of defined alias: when foo is a symbolic link to bar, you can use either name to refer to the file, but bar is the real name, while foo is just an alias. More complex cases occur when symbolic links point to directories.

Normally, if you visit a file which Emacs is already visiting under a different name, Emacs displays a message in the echo area and uses the existing buffer visiting that file. This can happen on systems that support hard or symbolic links, or if you use a long file name on a system that truncates long file names, or on a case-insensitive file system. You can suppress the message by setting the variable `find-file-suppress-same-file-warnings` to a non-`nil` value. You can disable this feature entirely by setting the variable `find-file-existing-other-name` to `nil`: then if you visit the same file under two different names, you get a separate buffer for each file name.

If the variable `find-file-visit-truename` is non-`nil`, then the file name recorded for a buffer is the file's *truename* (made by replacing all symbolic links with their target names), rather than the name you specify. Setting `find-file-visit-truename` also implies the effect of `find-file-existing-other-name`.

Sometimes, a directory is ordinarily accessed through a symbolic link, and you may want Emacs to preferentially show its "linked" name. To do this, customize `directory-abbrev-alist`. Each element in this list should have the form (*from . to*), which means to replace *from* with *to* whenever *from* appears in a directory name. The *from* string is a regular expression (see Section 12.6 [Regexps], page 97). It is matched against directory names anchored at the first character, and should start with '\'' (to support directory names with embedded newlines, which would defeat '^'). The *to* string should be an ordinary absolute directory name pointing to the same directory. Do not use '~' to stand for a home directory in the *to* string; Emacs performs these substitutions separately. Here's an example, from a system on which `/home/fsf` is normally accessed through a symbolic link named `/fsf`:

```
(("\\'/home/fsf" . "/fsf"))
```

15.7 File Directories

The file system groups files into *directories*. A *directory listing* is a list of all the files in a directory. Emacs provides commands to create and delete directories, and to make directory listings in brief format (file names only) and verbose format (sizes, dates, and authors included). Emacs also includes a directory browser feature called Dired; see Chapter 27 [Dired], page 315.

`C-x C-d` *dir-or-pattern* `RET`
> Display a brief directory listing (`list-directory`).

`C-u C-x C-d` *dir-or-pattern* `RET`
> Display a verbose directory listing.

`M-x make-directory RET` *dirname* `RET`
> Create a new directory named *dirname*.

`M-x delete-directory RET` *dirname* `RET`
> Delete the directory named *dirname*. If it isn't empty, you will be asked whether you want to delete it recursively.

The command to display a directory listing is `C-x C-d` (`list-directory`). It reads using the minibuffer a file name which is either a directory to be listed or a wildcard-containing pattern for the files to be listed. For example,

```
C-x C-d /u2/emacs/etc RET
```

lists all the files in directory `/u2/emacs/etc`. Here is an example of specifying a file name pattern:

```
C-x C-d /u2/emacs/src/*.c RET
```

Normally, `C-x C-d` displays a brief directory listing containing just file names. A numeric argument (regardless of value) tells it to make a verbose listing including sizes, dates, and owners (like '`ls -l`').

The text of a directory listing is mostly obtained by running `ls` in an inferior process. Two Emacs variables control the switches passed to `ls`: `list-directory-brief-switches` is a string giving the switches to use in brief listings (`"-CF"` by default), and `list-directory-verbose-switches` is a string giving the switches to use in a verbose listing (`"-l"` by default).

In verbose directory listings, Emacs adds information about the amount of free space on the disk that contains the directory. To do this, it runs the program specified by `directory-free-space-program` with arguments `directory-free-space-args`.

The command `M-x delete-directory` prompts for a directory name using the minibuffer, and deletes the directory if it is empty. If the directory is not empty, you will be asked whether you want to delete it recursively. On systems that have a "Trash" (or "Recycle Bin") feature, you can make this command move the specified directory to the Trash instead of deleting it outright, by changing the variable `delete-by-moving-to-trash` to `t`. See Section 15.10 [Misc File Ops], page 140, for more information about using the Trash.

15.8 Comparing Files

The command `M-x diff` prompts for two file names, using the minibuffer, and displays the differences between the two files in a buffer named `*diff*`. This works by running the `diff` program, using options taken from the variable `diff-switches`. The value of `diff-switches` should be a string; the default is `"-c"` to specify a context diff. See Section "Diff" in *Comparing and Merging Files*, for more information about the `diff` program.

The output of the `diff` command is shown using a major mode called Diff mode. See Section 15.9 [Diff Mode], page 138.

The command `M-x diff-backup` compares a specified file with its most recent backup. If you specify the name of a backup file, `diff-backup` compares it with the source file that it is a backup of. In all other respects, this behaves like `M-x diff`.

The command `M-x diff-buffer-with-file` compares a specified buffer with its corresponding file. This shows you what changes you would make to the file if you save the buffer.

The command `M-x compare-windows` compares the text in the current window with that in the next window. (For more information about windows in Emacs, Chapter 17 [Windows], page 156.) Comparison starts at point in each window, after pushing each initial point value on the mark ring in its respective buffer. Then it moves point forward in each window, one character at a time, until it reaches characters that don't match. Then the command exits.

If point in the two windows is followed by non-matching text when the command starts, `M-x compare-windows` tries heuristically to advance up to matching text in the two windows, and then exits. So if you use `M-x compare-windows` repeatedly, each time it either skips one matching range or finds the start of another.

With a numeric argument, `compare-windows` ignores changes in whitespace. If the variable `compare-ignore-case` is non-`nil`, the comparison ignores differences in case as well. If the variable `compare-ignore-whitespace` is non-`nil`, `compare-windows` normally ignores changes in whitespace, and a prefix argument turns that off.

You can use `M-x smerge-mode` to turn on Smerge mode, a minor mode for editing output from the `diff3` program. This is typically the result of a failed merge from a version control system "update" outside VC, due to conflicting changes to a file. Smerge mode provides commands to resolve conflicts by selecting specific changes.

See Section "Emerge" in *Specialized Emacs Features*, for the Emerge facility, which provides a powerful interface for merging files.

15.9 Diff Mode

Diff mode is a major mode used for the output of `M-x diff` and other similar commands. This kind of output is called a *patch*, because it can be passed to the `patch` command to automatically apply the specified changes. To select Diff mode manually, type `M-x diff-mode`.

The changes specified in a patch are grouped into *hunks*, which are contiguous chunks of text that contain one or more changed lines. Hunks can also include unchanged lines to provide context for the changes. Each hunk is preceded by a *hunk header*, which specifies the old and new line numbers at which the hunk occurs. Diff mode highlights each hunk header, to distinguish it from the actual contents of the hunk.

You can edit a Diff mode buffer like any other buffer. (If it is read-only, you need to make it writable first. See Section 16.3 [Misc Buffer], page 149.) Whenever you change a hunk, Diff mode attempts to automatically correct the line numbers in the hunk headers, to ensure that the patch remains "correct". To disable automatic line number correction, change the variable `diff-update-on-the-fly` to nil.

Diff mode treats each hunk as an "error message", similar to Compilation mode. Thus, you can use commands such as `C-x '` to visit the corresponding source locations. See Section 24.2 [Compilation Mode], page 262.

In addition, Diff mode provides the following commands to navigate, manipulate and apply parts of patches:

`M-n`   Move to the next hunk-start (`diff-hunk-next`).

This command has a side effect: it *refines* the hunk you move to, highlighting its changes with better granularity. To disable this feature, type `M-x diff-auto-refine-mode` to toggle off the minor mode Diff Auto-Refine mode. To disable Diff Auto Refine mode by default, add this to your init file (see Section 33.2.2 [Hooks], page 422):

```
(add-hook 'diff-mode-hook
          (lambda () (diff-auto-refine-mode -1)))
```

`M-p`   Move to the previous hunk-start (`diff-hunk-prev`). Like `M-n`, this has the side-effect of refining the hunk you move to, unless you disable Diff Auto-Refine mode.

`M-}`   Move to the next file-start, in a multi-file patch (`diff-file-next`).

M-{   Move to the previous file-start, in a multi-file patch (`diff-file-prev`).

M-k   Kill the hunk at point (`diff-hunk-kill`).

M-K   In a multi-file patch, kill the current file part. (`diff-file-kill`).

C-c C-a   Apply this hunk to its target file (`diff-apply-hunk`). With a prefix argument
            of C-u, revert this hunk.

C-c C-b   Highlight the changes of the hunk at point with a finer granularity
            (`diff-refine-hunk`). This allows you to see exactly which parts of each
            changed line were actually changed.

C-c C-c   Go to the source file and line corresponding to this hunk (`diff-goto-source`).

C-c C-e   Start an Ediff session with the patch (`diff-ediff-patch`). See Section "Ediff"
            in *The Ediff Manual*.

C-c C-n   Restrict the view to the current hunk (`diff-restrict-view`). See Section 11.5
            [Narrowing], page 73. With a prefix argument of C-u, restrict the view to the
            current file of a multiple-file patch. To widen again, use C-x n w (`widen`).

C-c C-r   Reverse the direction of comparison for the entire buffer (`diff-reverse-
            direction`).

C-c C-s   Split the hunk at point (`diff-split-hunk`). This is for manually editing
            patches, and only works with the *unified diff format* produced by the -u or
            --unified options to the `diff` program. If you need to split a hunk in the
            context diff format produced by the -c or --context options to `diff`, first
            convert the buffer to the unified diff format with C-c C-u.

C-c C-d   Convert the entire buffer to the *context diff format* (`diff-unified->context`).
            With a prefix argument, convert only the text within the region.

C-c C-u   Convert the entire buffer to unified diff format (`diff-context->unified`).
            With a prefix argument, convert unified format to context format. When the
            mark is active, convert only the text within the region.

C-c C-w   Refine the current hunk so that it disregards changes in whitespace
            (`diff-refine-hunk`).

C-x 4 A   Generate a ChangeLog entry, like C-x 4 a does (see Section 25.2 [Change Log],
            page 297), for each one of the hunks (`diff-add-change-log-entries-other-
            window`). This creates a skeleton of the log of changes that you can later fill
            with the actual descriptions of the changes. C-x 4 a itself in Diff mode operates
            on behalf of the current hunk's file, but gets the function name from the patch
            itself. This is useful for making log entries for functions that are deleted by the
            patch.

Patches sometimes include trailing whitespace on modified lines, as an unintentional
and undesired change. There are two ways to deal with this problem. Firstly, if you enable
Whitespace mode in a Diff buffer (see Section 11.16 [Useless Whitespace], page 82), it
automatically highlights trailing whitespace in modified lines. Secondly, you can use the
command M-x `diff-delete-trailing-whitespace`, which searches for trailing whitespace
in the lines modified by the patch, and removes that whitespace in both the patch and the

patched source file(s). This command does not save the modifications that it makes, so you can decide whether to save the changes (the list of modified files is displayed in the echo area). With a prefix argument, it tries to modify the original source files rather than the patched source files.

15.10 Miscellaneous File Operations

Emacs has commands for performing many other operations on files. All operate on one file; they do not accept wildcard file names.

M-x delete-file prompts for a file and deletes it. If you are deleting many files in one directory, it may be more convenient to use Dired rather than delete-file. See Section 27.3 [Dired Deletion], page 316.

M-x move-file-to-trash moves a file into the system *Trash* (or *Recycle Bin*). This is a facility available on most operating systems; files that are moved into the Trash can be brought back later if you change your mind.

By default, Emacs deletion commands do *not* use the Trash. To use the Trash (when it is available) for common deletion commands, change the variable delete-by-moving-to-trash to t. This affects the commands M-x delete-file and M-x delete-directory (see Section 15.7 [Directories], page 136), as well as the deletion commands in Dired (see Section 27.3 [Dired Deletion], page 316). Supplying a prefix argument to M-x delete-file or M-x delete-directory makes them delete outright, instead of using the Trash, regardless of delete-by-moving-to-trash.

M-x copy-file reads the file *old* and writes a new file named *new* with the same contents.

M-x copy-directory copies directories, similar to the cp -r shell command. It prompts for a directory *old* and a destination *new*. If *new* is an existing directory, it creates a copy of the *old* directory and puts it in *new*. If *new* is not an existing directory, it copies all the contents of *old* into a new directory named *new*.

M-x rename-file reads two file names *old* and *new* using the minibuffer, then renames file *old* as *new*. If the file name *new* already exists, you must confirm with yes or renaming is not done; this is because renaming causes the old meaning of the name *new* to be lost. If *old* and *new* are on different file systems, the file *old* is copied and deleted. If the argument *new* is just a directory name, the real new name is in that directory, with the same non-directory component as *old*. For example, M-x rename-file RET ~/foo RET /tmp RET renames ~/foo to /tmp/foo. The same rule applies to all the remaining commands in this section. All of them ask for confirmation when the new file name already exists, too.

M-x add-name-to-file adds an additional name to an existing file without removing its old name. The new name is created as a "hard link" to the existing file. The new name must belong on the same file system that the file is on. On MS-Windows, this command works only if the file resides in an NTFS file system. On MS-DOS, it works by copying the file.

M-x make-symbolic-link reads two file names *target* and *linkname*, then creates a symbolic link named *linkname*, which points at *target*. The effect is that future attempts to open file *linkname* will refer to whatever file is named *target* at the time the opening is done, or will get an error if the name *target* is nonexistent at that time. This command does not expand the argument *target*, so that it allows you to specify a relative name as the target of the link. On MS-Windows, this command works only on MS Windows Vista and later.

M-x insert-file (also C-x i) inserts a copy of the contents of the specified file into the current buffer at point, leaving point unchanged before the contents. The position after the inserted contents is added to the mark ring, without activating the mark (see Section 8.4 [Mark Ring], page 48).

M-x insert-file-literally is like M-x insert-file, except the file is inserted "literally": it is treated as a sequence of ASCII characters with no special encoding or conversion, similar to the M-x find-file-literally command (see Section 15.2 [Visiting], page 123).

M-x write-region is the inverse of M-x insert-file; it copies the contents of the region into the specified file. M-x append-to-file adds the text of the region to the end of the specified file. See Section 9.4 [Accumulating Text], page 59. The variable write-region-inhibit-fsync applies to these commands, as well as saving files; see Section 15.3.3 [Customize Save], page 130.

M-x set-file-modes reads a file name followed by a *file mode*, and applies that file mode to the specified file. File modes, also called *file permissions*, determine whether a file can be read, written to, or executed, and by whom. This command reads file modes using the same symbolic or octal format accepted by the chmod command; for instance, 'u+x' means to add execution permission for the user who owns the file. It has no effect on operating systems that do not support file modes. chmod is a convenience alias for this function.

15.11 Accessing Compressed Files

Emacs automatically uncompresses compressed files when you visit them, and automatically recompresses them if you alter them and save them. Emacs recognizes compressed files by their file names. File names ending in '.gz' indicate a file compressed with gzip. Other endings indicate other compression programs.

Automatic uncompression and compression apply to all the operations in which Emacs uses the contents of a file. This includes visiting it, saving it, inserting its contents into a buffer, loading it, and byte compiling it.

To disable this feature, type the command M-x auto-compression-mode. You can disable it permanently by customizing the variable auto-compression-mode.

15.12 File Archives

A file whose name ends in '.tar' is normally an *archive* made by the tar program. Emacs views these files in a special mode called Tar mode which provides a Dired-like list of the contents (see Chapter 27 [Dired], page 315). You can move around through the list just as you would in Dired, and visit the subfiles contained in the archive. However, not all Dired commands are available in Tar mode.

If Auto Compression mode is enabled (see Section 15.11 [Compressed Files], page 141), then Tar mode is used also for compressed archives—files with extensions '.tgz', .tar.Z and .tar.gz.

The keys e, f and RET all extract a component file into its own buffer. You can edit it there, and if you save the buffer, the edited version will replace the version in the Tar buffer. Clicking with the mouse on the file name in the Tar buffer does likewise. v extracts a file into a buffer in View mode (see Section 11.6 [View Mode], page 73). o extracts the file and displays it in another window, so you could edit the file and operate on the archive simultaneously.

d marks a file for deletion when you later use x, and u unmarks a file, as in Dired. C copies a file from the archive to disk and R renames a file within the archive. g reverts the buffer from the archive on disk. The keys M, G, and O change the file's permission bits, group, and owner, respectively.

Saving the Tar buffer writes a new version of the archive to disk with the changes you made to the components.

You don't need the `tar` program to use Tar mode—Emacs reads the archives directly. However, accessing compressed archives requires the appropriate uncompression program.

A separate but similar Archive mode is used for `arc`, `jar`, `lzh`, `zip`, `rar`, `7z`, and `zoo` archives, as well as `exe` files that are self-extracting executables.

The key bindings of Archive mode are similar to those in Tar mode, with the addition of the m key which marks a file for subsequent operations, and M-DEL which unmarks all the marked files. Also, the a key toggles the display of detailed file information, for those archive types where it won't fit in a single line. Operations such as renaming a subfile, or changing its mode or owner, are supported only for some of the archive formats.

Unlike Tar mode, Archive mode runs the archiving programs to unpack and repack archives. However, you don't need these programs to look at the archive table of contents, only to extract or manipulate the subfiles in the archive. Details of the program names and their options can be set in the 'Archive' Customize group.

15.13 Remote Files

You can refer to files on other machines using a special file name syntax:

>   /host:filename
>   /user@host:filename
>   /user@host#port:filename
>   /method:user@host:filename
>   /method:user@host#port:filename

To carry out this request, Emacs uses a remote-login program such as `ftp`, `ssh`, `rlogin`, or `telnet`. You can always specify in the file name which method to use—for example, `/ftp:user@host:filename` uses FTP, whereas `/ssh:user@host:filename` uses `ssh`. When you don't specify a method in the file name, Emacs chooses the method as follows:

1. If the host name starts with 'ftp.' (with dot), Emacs uses FTP.

2. If the user name is 'ftp' or 'anonymous', Emacs uses FTP.

3. If the variable `tramp-default-method` is set to 'ftp', Emacs uses FTP.

4. If `ssh-agent` is running, Emacs uses `scp`.

5. Otherwise, Emacs uses `ssh`.

You can entirely turn off the remote file name feature by setting the variable `tramp-mode` to `nil`. You can turn off the feature in individual cases by quoting the file name with '/:' (see Section 15.14 [Quoted File Names], page 143).

Remote file access through FTP is handled by the Ange-FTP package, which is documented in the following. Remote file access through the other methods is handled by the Tramp package, which has its own manual. See *The Tramp Manual*.

When the Ange-FTP package is used, Emacs logs in through FTP using the name *user*, if that is specified in the remote file name. If *user* is unspecified, Emacs logs in using your user name on the local system; but if you set the variable `ange-ftp-default-user` to a string, that string is used instead. When logging in, Emacs may also ask for a password.

For performance reasons, Emacs does not make backup files for files accessed via FTP by default. To make it do so, change the variable `ange-ftp-make-backup-files` to a non-`nil` value.

By default, auto-save files for remote files are made in the temporary file directory on the local machine, as specified by the variable `auto-save-file-name-transforms`. See Section 15.5.1 [Auto Save Files], page 133.

To visit files accessible by anonymous FTP, you use special user names 'anonymous' or 'ftp'. Passwords for these user names are handled specially. The variable `ange-ftp-generate-anonymous-password` controls what happens: if the value of this variable is a string, then that string is used as the password; if non-`nil` (the default), then the value of `user-mail-address` is used; if `nil`, then Emacs prompts you for a password as usual (see Section 5.7 [Passwords], page 34).

Sometimes you may be unable to access files on a remote machine because a *firewall* in between blocks the connection for security reasons. If you can log in on a *gateway* machine from which the target files *are* accessible, and whose FTP server supports gatewaying features, you can still use remote file names; all you have to do is specify the name of the gateway machine by setting the variable `ange-ftp-gateway-host`, and set `ange-ftp-smart-gateway` to `t`. Otherwise you may be able to make remote file names work, but the procedure is complex. You can read the instructions by typing `M-x finder-commentary RET ange-ftp RET`.

15.14 Quoted File Names

You can *quote* an absolute file name to prevent special characters and syntax in it from having their special effects. The way to do this is to add '/:' at the beginning.

For example, you can quote a local file name which appears remote, to prevent it from being treated as a remote file name. Thus, if you have a directory named `/foo:` and a file named `bar` in it, you can refer to that file in Emacs as '/:/foo:/bar'.

'/:' can also prevent '~' from being treated as a special character for a user's home directory. For example, /:/tmp/~hack refers to a file whose name is ~hack in directory /tmp.

Quoting with '/:' is also a way to enter in the minibuffer a file name that contains '$'. In order for this to work, the '/:' must be at the beginning of the minibuffer contents. (You can also double each '$'; see [File Names with $], page 122.)

You can also quote wildcard characters with '/:', for visiting. For example, /:/tmp/foo*bar visits the file /tmp/foo*bar.

Another method of getting the same result is to enter /tmp/foo[*]bar, which is a wildcard specification that matches only /tmp/foo*bar. However, in many cases there is no need to quote the wildcard characters because even unquoted they give the right result. For example, if the only file name in /tmp that starts with 'foo' and ends with 'bar' is foo*bar, then specifying /tmp/foo*bar will visit only /tmp/foo*bar.

15.15 File Name Cache

You can use the *file name cache* to make it easy to locate a file by name, without having to remember exactly where it is located. When typing a file name in the minibuffer, C-TAB (file-cache-minibuffer-complete) completes it using the file name cache. If you repeat C-TAB, that cycles through the possible completions of what you had originally typed. (However, note that the C-TAB character cannot be typed on most text terminals.)

The file name cache does not fill up automatically. Instead, you load file names into the cache using these commands:

M-x file-cache-add-directory RET *directory* RET
> Add each file name in *directory* to the file name cache.

M-x file-cache-add-directory-using-find RET *directory* RET
> Add each file name in *directory* and all of its nested subdirectories to the file name cache.

M-x file-cache-add-directory-using-locate RET *directory* RET
> Add each file name in *directory* and all of its nested subdirectories to the file name cache, using locate to find them all.

M-x file-cache-add-directory-list RET *variable* RET
> Add each file name in each directory listed in *variable* to the file name cache. *variable* should be a Lisp variable whose value is a list of directory names, like load-path.

M-x file-cache-clear-cache RET
> Clear the cache; that is, remove all file names from it.

The file name cache is not persistent: it is kept and maintained only for the duration of the Emacs session. You can view the contents of the cache with the file-cache-display command.

15.16 Convenience Features for Finding Files

In this section, we introduce some convenient facilities for finding recently-opened files, reading file names from a buffer, and viewing image files.

If you enable Recentf mode, with M-x recentf-mode, the 'File' menu includes a submenu containing a list of recently opened files. M-x recentf-save-list saves the current recent-file-list to a file, and M-x recentf-edit-list edits it.

The M-x ffap command generalizes find-file with more powerful heuristic defaults (see Section 31.11.3 [FFAP], page 405), often based on the text at point. Partial Completion mode offers other features extending find-file, which can be used with ffap. See Section 5.4.5 [Completion Options], page 32.

Visiting image files automatically selects Image mode. In this major mode, you can type C-c C-c (image-toggle-display) to toggle between displaying the file as an image in the

Emacs buffer, and displaying its underlying text (or raw byte) representation. Displaying the file as an image works only if Emacs is compiled with support for displaying such images. If the displayed image is wider or taller than the frame, the usual point motion keys (C-f, C-p, and so forth) cause different parts of the image to be displayed. You can press n (image-next-file) and p (image-previous-file) to visit the next image file and the previous image file in the same directory, respectively.

If the image can be animated, the command RET (image-toggle-animation) starts or stops the animation. Animation plays once, unless the option image-animate-loop is non-nil. With f (image-next-frame) and b (image-previous-frame) you can step through the individual frames. Both commands accept a numeric prefix to step through several frames at once. You can go to a specific frame with F (image-goto-frame). Typing a + (image-increase-speed) increases the speed of the animation, a - (image-decrease-speed) decreases it, and a r (image-reverse-speed) reverses it. The command a 0 (image-reset-speed) resets the speed to the original value.

If Emacs was compiled with support for the ImageMagick library, it can use ImageMagick to render a wide variety of images. The variable imagemagick-enabled-types lists the image types that Emacs may render using ImageMagick; each element in the list should be an internal ImageMagick name for an image type, as a symbol or an equivalent string (e.g., BMP for .bmp images). To enable ImageMagick for all possible image types, change imagemagick-enabled-types to t. The variable imagemagick-types-inhibit lists the image types which should never be rendered using ImageMagick, regardless of the value of imagemagick-enabled-types (the default list includes types like C and HTML, which ImageMagick can render as an "image" but Emacs should not). To disable ImageMagick entirely, change imagemagick-types-inhibit to t.

The Image-Dired package can also be used to view images as thumbnails. See Section 27.17 [Image-Dired], page 328.

15.17 Filesets

If you regularly edit a certain group of files, you can define them as a *fileset*. This lets you perform certain operations, such as visiting, query-replace, and shell commands on all the files at once. To make use of filesets, you must first add the expression (filesets-init) to your init file (see Section 33.4 [Init File], page 437). This adds a 'Filesets' menu to the menu bar.

The simplest way to define a fileset is by adding files to it one at a time. To add a file to fileset *name*, visit the file and type M-x filesets-add-buffer RET *name* RET. If there is no fileset *name*, this creates a new one, which initially contains only the current file. The command M-x filesets-remove-buffer removes the current file from a fileset.

You can also edit the list of filesets directly, with M-x filesets-edit (or by choosing 'Edit Filesets' from the 'Filesets' menu). The editing is performed in a Customize buffer (see Section 33.1 [Easy Customization], page 412). Normally, a fileset is a simple list of files, but you can also define a fileset as a regular expression matching file names. Some examples of these more complicated filesets are shown in the Customize buffer. Remember to select 'Save for future sessions' if you want to use the same filesets in future Emacs sessions.

You can use the command `M-x filesets-open` to visit all the files in a fileset, and `M-x filesets-close` to close them. Use `M-x filesets-run-cmd` to run a shell command on all the files in a fileset. These commands are also available from the '`Filesets`' menu, where each existing fileset is represented by a submenu.

See Section 25.1 [Version Control], page 281, for a different concept of "filesets": groups of files bundled together for version control operations. Filesets of that type are unnamed, and do not persist across Emacs sessions.

16 Using Multiple Buffers

The text you are editing in Emacs resides in an object called a *buffer*. Each time you visit a file, a buffer is used to hold the file's text. Each time you invoke Dired, a buffer is used to hold the directory listing. If you send a message with C-x m, a buffer is used to hold the text of the message. When you ask for a command's documentation, that appears in a buffer named *Help*.

Each buffer has a unique name, which can be of any length. When a buffer is displayed in a window, its name is shown in the mode line (see Section 1.3 [Mode Line], page 8). The distinction between upper and lower case matters in buffer names. Most buffers are made by visiting files, and their names are derived from the files' names; however, you can also create an empty buffer with any name you want. A newly started Emacs has several buffers, including one named *scratch*, which can be used for evaluating Lisp expressions and is not associated with any file (see Section 24.10 [Lisp Interaction], page 279).

At any time, one and only one buffer is *selected*; we call it the *current buffer*. We sometimes say that a command operates on "the buffer"; this really means that it operates on the current buffer. When there is only one Emacs window, the buffer displayed in that window is current. When there are multiple windows, the buffer displayed in the *selected window* is current. See Chapter 17 [Windows], page 156.

Aside from its textual contents, each buffer records several pieces of information, such as what file it is visiting (if any), whether it is modified, and what major mode and minor modes are in effect (see Chapter 20 [Modes], page 199). These are stored in *buffer-local variables*—variables that can have a different value in each buffer. See Section 33.2.3 [Locals], page 423.

A buffer's size cannot be larger than some maximum, which is defined by the largest buffer position representable by *Emacs integers*. This is because Emacs tracks buffer positions using that data type. For typical 64-bit machines, this maximum buffer size is $2^{61} - 2$ bytes, or about 2 EiB. For typical 32-bit machines, the maximum is usually $2^{29} - 2$ bytes, or about 512 MiB. Buffer sizes are also limited by the amount of memory in the system.

16.1 Creating and Selecting Buffers

C-x b *buffer* RET
> Select or create a buffer named *buffer* (switch-to-buffer).

C-x 4 b *buffer* RET
> Similar, but select *buffer* in another window (switch-to-buffer-other-window).

C-x 5 b *buffer* RET
> Similar, but select *buffer* in a separate frame (switch-to-buffer-other-frame).

C-x LEFT   Select the previous buffer in the buffer list (previous-buffer).

C-x RIGHT   Select the next buffer in the buffer list (next-buffer).

C-u M-g M-g
C-u M-g g   Read a number *n* and move to line *n* in the most recently selected buffer other than the current buffer.

The C-x b (switch-to-buffer) command reads a buffer name using the minibuffer. Then it makes that buffer current, and displays it in the currently-selected window. An empty input specifies the buffer that was current most recently among those not now displayed in any window.

While entering the buffer name, you can use the usual completion and history commands (see Chapter 5 [Minibuffer], page 26). Note that C-x b, and related commands, use "permissive completion with confirmation" for minibuffer completion: if you type RET immediately after completing up to a nonexistent buffer name, Emacs prints '[Confirm]' and you must type a second RET to submit that buffer name. See Section 5.4.3 [Completion Exit], page 30, for details.

If you specify a buffer that does not exist, C-x b creates a new, empty buffer that is not visiting any file, and selects it for editing. The default value of the variable major-mode determines the new buffer's major mode; the default value is Fundamental mode. See Section 20.1 [Major Modes], page 199. One reason to create a new buffer is to use it for making temporary notes. If you try to save it, Emacs asks for the file name to use, and the buffer's major mode is re-established taking that file name into account (see Section 20.3 [Choosing Modes], page 202).

For conveniently switching between a few buffers, use the commands C-x LEFT and C-x RIGHT. C-x LEFT (previous-buffer) selects the previous buffer (following the order of most recent selection in the current frame), while C-x RIGHT (next-buffer) moves through buffers in the reverse direction.

To select a buffer in a window other than the current one, type C-x 4 b (switch-to-buffer-other-window). This prompts for a buffer name using the minibuffer, displays that buffer in another window, and selects that window.

Similarly, C-x 5 b (switch-to-buffer-other-frame) prompts for a buffer name, displays that buffer in another frame, and selects that frame. If the buffer is already being shown in a window on another frame, Emacs selects that window and frame instead of creating a new frame.

See Section 17.6 [Displaying Buffers], page 160, for how the C-x 4 b and C-x 5 b commands get the window and/or frame to display in.

In addition, C-x C-f, and any other command for visiting a file, can also be used to switch to an existing file-visiting buffer. See Section 15.2 [Visiting], page 123.

C-u M-g M-g, that is goto-line with a plain prefix argument, reads a number n using the minibuffer, selects the most recently selected buffer other than the current buffer in another window, and then moves point to the beginning of line number n in that buffer. This is mainly useful in a buffer that refers to line numbers in another buffer: if point is on or just after a number, goto-line uses that number as the default for n. Note that prefix arguments other than just C-u behave differently. C-u 4 M-g M-g goes to line 4 in the *current* buffer, without reading a number from the minibuffer. (Remember that M-g M-g without prefix argument reads a number n and then moves to line number n in the current buffer. See Section 4.2 [Moving Point], page 17.)

Emacs uses buffer names that start with a space for internal purposes. It treats these buffers specially in minor ways—for example, by default they do not record undo information. It is best to avoid using such buffer names yourself.

16.2 Listing Existing Buffers

C-x C-b   List the existing buffers (`list-buffers`).

To display a list of existing buffers, type C-x C-b. Each line in the list shows one buffer's name, size, major mode and visited file. The buffers are listed in the order that they were current; the buffers that were current most recently come first.

'.' in the first field of a line indicates that the buffer is current. '%' indicates a read-only buffer. '*' indicates that the buffer is "modified". If several buffers are modified, it may be time to save some with C-x s (see Section 15.3.1 [Save Commands], page 126). Here is an example of a buffer list:

```
CRM Buffer              Size  Mode             File
.  * .emacs             3294  Emacs-Lisp       ~/.emacs
   % *Help*              101  Help
     search.c          86055  C                ~/cvs/emacs/src/search.c
   % src               20959  Dired by name    ~/cvs/emacs/src/
   * *mail*               42  Mail
   % HELLO              1607  Fundamental      ~/cvs/emacs/etc/HELLO
   % NEWS             481184  Outline          ~/cvs/emacs/etc/NEWS
     *scratch*           191  Lisp Interaction
   * *Messages*         1554  Messages
```

The buffer *Help* was made by a help request (see Chapter 7 [Help], page 37); it is not visiting any file. The buffer src was made by Dired on the directory ~/cvs/emacs/src/. You can list only buffers that are visiting files by giving the command a prefix argument, as in C-u C-x C-b.

`list-buffers` omits buffers whose names begin with a space, unless they visit files: such buffers are used internally by Emacs.

16.3 Miscellaneous Buffer Operations

C-x C-q   Toggle read-only status of buffer (`read-only-mode`).

M-x rename-buffer RET *name* RET
        Change the name of the current buffer.

M-x rename-uniquely
        Rename the current buffer by adding '*<number>*' to the end.

M-x view-buffer RET *buffer* RET
        Scroll through buffer *buffer*. See Section 11.6 [View Mode], page 73.

A buffer can be *read-only*, which means that commands to change its contents are not allowed. The mode line indicates read-only buffers with '%%' or '%*' near the left margin. Read-only buffers are usually made by subsystems such as Dired and Rmail that have special commands to operate on the text; also by visiting a file whose access control says you cannot write it.

The command C-x C-q (`read-only-mode`) makes a read-only buffer writable, and makes a writable buffer read-only. This works by setting the variable `buffer-read-only`, which has a local value in each buffer and makes the buffer read-only if its value is non-`nil`. If you change the option `view-read-only` to a non-`nil` value, making the buffer read-only with C-x C-q also enables View mode in the buffer (see Section 11.6 [View Mode], page 73).

M-x `rename-buffer` changes the name of the current buffer. You specify the new name as a minibuffer argument; there is no default. If you specify a name that is in use for some other buffer, an error happens and no renaming is done.

M-x `rename-uniquely` renames the current buffer to a similar name with a numeric suffix added to make it both different and unique. This command does not need an argument. It is useful for creating multiple shell buffers: if you rename the *shell* buffer, then do M-x `shell` again, it makes a new shell buffer named *shell*; meanwhile, the old shell buffer continues to exist under its new name. This method is also good for mail buffers, compilation buffers, and most Emacs features that create special buffers with particular names. (With some of these features, such as M-x `compile`, M-x `grep`, you need to switch to some other buffer before using the command again, otherwise it will reuse the current buffer despite the name change.)

The commands M-x `append-to-buffer` and M-x `insert-buffer` can also be used to copy text from one buffer to another. See Section 9.4 [Accumulating Text], page 59.

16.4 Killing Buffers

If you continue an Emacs session for a while, you may accumulate a large number of buffers. You may then find it convenient to *kill* the buffers you no longer need. (Some other editors call this operation *close*, and talk about "closing the buffer" or "closing the file" visited in the buffer.) On most operating systems, killing a buffer releases its space back to the operating system so that other programs can use it. Here are some commands for killing buffers:

C-x k *bufname* RET
> Kill buffer *bufname* (`kill-buffer`).

M-x `kill-some-buffers`
> Offer to kill each buffer, one by one.

M-x `kill-matching-buffers`
> Offer to kill all buffers matching a regular expression.

C-x k (`kill-buffer`) kills one buffer, whose name you specify in the minibuffer. The default, used if you type just RET in the minibuffer, is to kill the current buffer. If you kill the current buffer, another buffer becomes current: one that was current in the recent past but is not displayed in any window now. If you ask to kill a file-visiting buffer that is modified, then you must confirm with **yes** before the buffer is killed.

The command M-x `kill-some-buffers` asks about each buffer, one by one. An answer of y means to kill the buffer, just like `kill-buffer`. This command ignores buffers whose names begin with a space, which are used internally by Emacs.

The command M-x `kill-matching-buffers` prompts for a regular expression and kills all buffers whose names match that expression. See Section 12.6 [Regexps], page 97. Like `kill-some-buffers`, it asks for confirmation before each kill. This command normally ignores buffers whose names begin with a space, which are used internally by Emacs. To kill internal buffers as well, call `kill-matching-buffers` with a prefix argument.

The Buffer Menu feature is also convenient for killing various buffers. See Section 16.5 [Several Buffers], page 151.

If you want to do something special every time a buffer is killed, you can add hook functions to the hook `kill-buffer-hook` (see Section 33.2.2 [Hooks], page 422).

If you run one Emacs session for a period of days, as many people do, it can fill up with buffers that you used several days ago. The command `M-x clean-buffer-list` is a convenient way to purge them; it kills all the unmodified buffers that you have not used for a long time. An ordinary buffer is killed if it has not been displayed for three days; however, you can specify certain buffers that should never be killed automatically, and others that should be killed if they have been unused for a mere hour.

You can also have this buffer purging done for you, once a day, by enabling Midnight mode. Midnight mode operates each day at midnight; at that time, it runs `clean-buffer-list`, or whichever functions you have placed in the normal hook `midnight-hook` (see Section 33.2.2 [Hooks], page 422). To enable Midnight mode, use the Customization buffer to set the variable `midnight-mode` to `t`. See Section 33.1 [Easy Customization], page 412.

16.5 Operating on Several Buffers

`M-x buffer-menu`
> Begin editing a buffer listing all Emacs buffers.

`M-x buffer-menu-other-window.`
> Similar, but do it in another window.

The *Buffer Menu* opened by `C-x C-b` (see Section 16.2 [List Buffers], page 149) does not merely list buffers. It also allows you to perform various operations on buffers, through an interface similar to Dired (see Chapter 27 [Dired], page 315). You can save buffers, kill them (here called *deleting* them, for consistency with Dired), or display them.

To use the Buffer Menu, type `C-x C-b` and switch to the window displaying the `*Buffer List*` buffer. You can also type `M-x buffer-menu` to open the Buffer Menu in the selected window. Alternatively, the command `M-x buffer-menu-other-window` opens the Buffer Menu in another window, and selects that window.

The Buffer Menu is a read-only buffer, and can be changed only through the special commands described in this section. The usual cursor motion commands can be used in this buffer. The following commands apply to the buffer described on the current line:

d   Flag the buffer for deletion (killing), then move point to the next line (`Buffer-menu-delete`). The deletion flag is indicated by the character 'D' on the line, before the buffer name. The deletion occurs only when you type the x command (see below).

C-d   Like d, but move point up instead of down (`Buffer-menu-delete-backwards`).

s   Flag the buffer for saving (`Buffer-menu-save`). The save flag is indicated by the character 'S' on the line, before the buffer name. The saving occurs only when you type x. You may request both saving and deletion for the same buffer.

x   Perform all flagged deletions and saves (`Buffer-menu-execute`).

u   Remove all flags from the current line, and move down (`Buffer-menu-unmark`).

DEL   Move to the previous line and remove all flags on that line (`Buffer-menu-backup-unmark`).

The commands for adding or removing flags, d, C-d, s and u, all accept a numeric argument as a repeat count.

The following commands operate immediately on the buffer listed on the current line. They also accept a numeric argument as a repeat count.

~   Mark the buffer as unmodified (`Buffer-menu-not-modified`). See Section 15.3.1 [Save Commands], page 126.

%   Toggle the buffer's read-only status (`Buffer-menu-toggle-read-only`). See Section 16.3 [Misc Buffer], page 149.

t   Visit the buffer as a tags table (`Buffer-menu-visit-tags-table`). See Section 25.3.4 [Select Tags Table], page 304.

The following commands are used to select another buffer or buffers:

q   Quit the Buffer Menu (`quit-window`). The most recent formerly visible buffer is displayed in its place.

RET
f   Select this line's buffer, replacing the `*Buffer List*` buffer in its window (`Buffer-menu-this-window`).

o   Select this line's buffer in another window, as if by `C-x 4 b`, leaving `*Buffer List*` visible (`Buffer-menu-other-window`).

C-o   Display this line's buffer in another window, without selecting it (`Buffer-menu-switch-other-window`).

1   Select this line's buffer in a full-frame window (`Buffer-menu-1-window`).

2   Set up two windows on the current frame, with this line's buffer selected in one, and a previously current buffer (aside from `*Buffer List*`) in the other (`Buffer-menu-2-window`).

b   Bury this line's buffer (`Buffer-menu-bury`).

m   Mark this line's buffer to be displayed in another window if you exit with the v command (`Buffer-menu-mark`). The display flag is indicated by the character '>' at the beginning of the line. (A single buffer may not have both deletion and display flags.)

v   Select this line's buffer, and also display in other windows any buffers flagged with the m command (`Buffer-menu-select`). If you have not flagged any buffers, this command is equivalent to 1.

The following commands affect the entire buffer list:

S   Sort the Buffer Menu entries according to their values in the column at point. With a numeric prefix argument n, sort according to the n-th column (`tabulated-list-sort`).

T   Delete, or reinsert, lines for non-file buffers `Buffer-menu-toggle-files-only`). This command toggles the inclusion of such buffers in the buffer list.

Normally, the buffer *Buffer List* is not updated automatically when buffers are created and killed; its contents are just text. If you have created, deleted or renamed buffers, the way to update *Buffer List* to show what you have done is to type g (revert-buffer). You can make this happen regularly every auto-revert-interval seconds if you enable Auto Revert mode in this buffer, as long as it is not marked modified. Global Auto Revert mode applies to the *Buffer List* buffer only if global-auto-revert-non-file-buffers is non-nil. See Info file emacs-xtra, node 'Autorevert', for details.

16.6 Indirect Buffers

An *indirect buffer* shares the text of some other buffer, which is called the *base buffer* of the indirect buffer. In some ways it is a buffer analogue of a symbolic link between files.

M-x make-indirect-buffer RET *base-buffer* RET *indirect-name* RET
>   Create an indirect buffer named *indirect-name* with base buffer *base-buffer*.

M-x clone-indirect-buffer RET
>   Create an indirect buffer that is a twin copy of the current buffer.

C-x 4 c   Create an indirect buffer that is a twin copy of the current buffer, and select it in another window (clone-indirect-buffer-other-window).

The text of the indirect buffer is always identical to the text of its base buffer; changes made by editing either one are visible immediately in the other. But in all other respects, the indirect buffer and its base buffer are completely separate. They can have different names, different values of point, different narrowing, different markers, different major modes, and different local variables.

An indirect buffer cannot visit a file, but its base buffer can. If you try to save the indirect buffer, that actually works by saving the base buffer. Killing the base buffer effectively kills the indirect buffer, but killing an indirect buffer has no effect on its base buffer.

One way to use indirect buffers is to display multiple views of an outline. See Section 22.8.4 [Outline Views], page 221.

A quick and handy way to make an indirect buffer is with the command M-x clone-indirect-buffer. It creates and selects an indirect buffer whose base buffer is the current buffer. With a numeric argument, it prompts for the name of the indirect buffer; otherwise it uses the name of the current buffer, with a '<n>' suffix added. C-x 4 c (clone-indirect-buffer-other-window) works like M-x clone-indirect-buffer, but it selects the new buffer in another window. These functions run the hook clone-indirect-buffer-hook after creating the indirect buffer.

The more general way to make an indirect buffer is with the command M-x make-indirect-buffer. It creates an indirect buffer named *indirect-name* from a buffer *base-buffer*, prompting for both using the minibuffer.

16.7 Convenience Features and Customization of Buffer Handling

This section describes several modes and features that make it more convenient to switch between buffers.

16.7.1 Making Buffer Names Unique

When several buffers visit identically-named files, Emacs must give the buffers distinct names. The default method adds a suffix based on the names of the directories that contain the files. For example, if you visit files /foo/bar/mumble/name and /baz/quux/mumble/name at the same time, their buffers will be named 'name<bar/mumble>' and 'name<quux/mumble>', respectively. Emacs adds as many directory parts as are needed to make a unique name.

You can choose from several different styles for constructing unique buffer names, by customizing the option uniquify-buffer-name-style.

The forward naming method includes part of the file's directory name at the beginning of the buffer name; using this method, buffers visiting the files /u/rms/tmp/Makefile and /usr/projects/zaphod/Makefile would be named 'tmp/Makefile' and 'zaphod/Makefile'.

In contrast, the post-forward naming method would call the buffers 'Makefile|tmp' and 'Makefile|zaphod'. The default method post-forward-angle-brackets is like post-forward, except that it encloses the unique path in angle brackets. The reverse naming method would call them 'Makefile\tmp' and 'Makefile\zaphod'. The nontrivial difference between post-forward and reverse occurs when just one directory name is not enough to distinguish two files; then reverse puts the directory names in reverse order, so that /top/middle/file becomes 'file\middle\top', while post-forward puts them in forward order after the file name, as in 'file|top/middle'. If uniquify-buffer-name-style is set to nil, the buffer names simply get '<2>', '<3>', etc. appended.

Which rule to follow for putting the directory names in the buffer name is not very important if you are going to *look* at the buffer names before you type one. But as an experienced user, if you know the rule, you won't have to look. And then you may find that one rule or another is easier for you to remember and apply quickly.

16.7.2 Fast minibuffer selection

Icomplete global minor mode provides a convenient way to quickly select an element among the possible completions in a minibuffer. When enabled, typing in the minibuffer continuously displays a list of possible completions that match the string you have typed.

At any time, you can type C-j to select the first completion in the list. So the way to select a particular completion is to make it the first in the list. There are two ways to do this. You can type more of the completion name and thus narrow down the list, excluding unwanted completions above the desired one. Alternatively, you can use C-. and C-, to rotate the list until the desired buffer is first.

M-TAB will select the first completion in the list, like C-j but without exiting the minibuffer, so you can edit it further. This is typically used when entering a file name, where M-TAB can be used a few times to descend in the hierarchy of directories.

To enable Icomplete mode, type M-x icomplete-mode, or customize the variable icomplete-mode to t (see Section 33.1 [Easy Customization], page 412).

16.7.3 Customizing Buffer Menus

`M-x bs-show`

> Make a list of buffers similarly to `M-x list-buffers` but customizable.

`M-x bs-show` pops up a buffer list similar to the one normally displayed by `C-x C-b` but which you can customize. If you prefer this to the usual buffer list, you can bind this command to `C-x C-b`. To customize this buffer list, use the `bs` Custom group (see Section 33.1 [Easy Customization], page 412).

MSB global minor mode ("MSB" stands for "mouse select buffer") provides a different and customizable mouse buffer menu which you may prefer. It replaces the bindings of `mouse-buffer-menu`, normally on `C-Down-Mouse-1`, and the menu bar buffer menu. You can customize the menu in the `msb` Custom group.

17 Multiple Windows

Emacs can split a frame into two or many windows. Multiple windows can display parts of different buffers, or different parts of one buffer. Multiple frames always imply multiple windows, because each frame has its own set of windows. Each window belongs to one and only one frame.

17.1 Concepts of Emacs Windows

Each Emacs window displays one Emacs buffer at any time. A single buffer may appear in more than one window; if it does, any changes in its text are displayed in all the windows where it appears. But these windows can show different parts of the buffer, because each window has its own value of point.

At any time, one Emacs window is the *selected window*; the buffer this window is displaying is the current buffer. On graphical displays, the point is indicated by a solid blinking cursor in the selected window, and by a hollow box in non-selected windows. On text terminals, the cursor is drawn only in the selected window. See Section 11.20 [Cursor Display], page 86.

Commands to move point affect the value of point for the selected Emacs window only. They do not change the value of point in other Emacs windows, even those showing the same buffer. The same is true for buffer-switching commands such as C-x b; they do not affect other windows at all. However, there are other commands such as C-x 4 b that select a different window and switch buffers in it. Also, all commands that display information in a window, including (for example) C-h f (`describe-function`) and C-x C-b (`list-buffers`), work by switching buffers in a nonselected window without affecting the selected window.

When multiple windows show the same buffer, they can have different regions, because they can have different values of point. However, they all have the same value for the mark, because each buffer has only one mark position.

Each window has its own mode line, which displays the buffer name, modification status and major and minor modes of the buffer that is displayed in the window. The selected window's mode line appears in a different color. See Section 1.3 [Mode Line], page 8, for details.

17.2 Splitting Windows

C-x 2   Split the selected window into two windows, one above the other (`split-window-below`).

C-x 3   Split the selected window into two windows, positioned side by side (`split-window-right`).

C-Mouse-2
            In the mode line of a window, split that window.

C-x 2 (`split-window-below`) splits the selected window into two windows, one above the other. After splitting, the selected window is the upper one, and the newly split-off window is below. Both windows have the same value of point as before, and display the same portion of the buffer (or as close to it as possible). If necessary, the windows are scrolled to keep point on-screen. By default, the two windows each get half the height of the original window. A positive numeric argument specifies how many lines to give to the top window; a negative numeric argument specifies how many lines to give to the bottom window.

If you change the variable `split-window-keep-point` to `nil`, C-x 2 instead adjusts the portion of the buffer displayed by the two windows, as well as the value of point in each window, in order to keep the text on the screen as close as possible to what it was before; furthermore, if point was in the lower half of the original window, the bottom window is selected instead of the upper one.

C-x 3 (`split-window-right`) splits the selected window into two side-by-side windows. The left window is the selected one; the right window displays the same portion of the same buffer, and has the same value of point. A positive numeric argument specifies how many columns to give the left window; a negative numeric argument specifies how many columns to give the right window.

When you split a window with C-x 3, each resulting window occupies less than the full width of the frame. If it becomes too narrow, the buffer may be difficult to read if continuation lines are in use (see Section 4.8 [Continuation Lines], page 22). Therefore, Emacs automatically switches to line truncation if the window width becomes narrower than 50 columns. This truncation occurs regardless of the value of the variable `truncate-lines` (see Section 11.21 [Line Truncation], page 87); it is instead controlled by the variable `truncate-partial-width-windows`. If the value of this variable is a positive integer (the default is 50), that specifies the minimum width for a partial-width window before automatic line truncation occurs; if the value is `nil`, automatic line truncation is disabled; and for any other non-`nil` value, Emacs truncates lines in every partial-width window regardless of its width.

On text terminals, side-by-side windows are separated by a vertical divider which is drawn using the `vertical-border` face.

If you click C-Mouse-2 in the mode line of a window, that splits the window, putting a vertical divider where you click. Depending on how Emacs is compiled, you can also split a window by clicking C-Mouse-2 in the scroll bar, which puts a horizontal divider where you click (this feature does not work when Emacs uses GTK+ scroll bars).

By default, when you split a window, Emacs gives each of the resulting windows dimensions that are an integral multiple of the default font size of the frame. That might subdivide the screen estate unevenly between the resulting windows. If you set the variable `window-resize-pixelwise` to a non-`nil` value, Emacs will give each window the same number of pixels (give or take one pixel if the initial dimension was an odd number of pixels). Note that when a frame's pixel size is not a multiple of the frame's character size, at least one window may get resized pixelwise even if this option is `nil`.

17.3 Using Other Windows

C-x o   Select another window (`other-window`).

C-M-v   Scroll the next window (`scroll-other-window`).

Mouse-1   Mouse-1, in the text area of a window, selects the window and moves point
               to the position clicked. Clicking in the mode line selects the window without
               moving point in it.

With the keyboard, you can switch windows by typing C-x o (other-window). That is
an o, for "other", not a zero. When there are more than two windows, this command moves
through all the windows in a cyclic order, generally top to bottom and left to right. After
the rightmost and bottommost window, it goes back to the one at the upper left corner. A
numeric argument means to move several steps in the cyclic order of windows. A negative
argument moves around the cycle in the opposite order. When the minibuffer is active, the
minibuffer is the last window in the cycle; you can switch from the minibuffer window to one
of the other windows, and later switch back and finish supplying the minibuffer argument
that is requested. See Section 5.3 [Minibuffer Edit], page 27.

The usual scrolling commands (see Chapter 11 [Display], page 69) apply to the selected
window only, but there is one command to scroll the next window. C-M-v (scroll-other-
window) scrolls the window that C-x o would select. It takes arguments, positive and
negative, like C-v. (In the minibuffer, C-M-v scrolls the help window associated with the
minibuffer, if any, rather than the next window in the standard cyclic order; see Section 5.3
[Minibuffer Edit], page 27.)

If you set mouse-autoselect-window to a non-nil value, moving the mouse over a
different window selects that window. This feature is off by default.

17.4 Displaying in Another Window

C-x 4 is a prefix key for a variety of commands that switch to a buffer in a different window—
either another existing window, or a new window created by splitting the selected window.
See Section 17.6.1 [Window Choice], page 160, for how Emacs picks or creates the window
to use.

C-x 4 b *bufname* RET
               Select buffer *bufname* in another window (switch-to-buffer-other-window).

C-x 4 C-o *bufname* RET
               Display buffer *bufname* in some window, without trying to select it
               (display-buffer). See Section 17.6 [Displaying Buffers], page 160, for details
               about how the window is chosen.

C-x 4 f *filename* RET
               Visit file *filename* and select its buffer in another window (find-file-other-
               window). See Section 15.2 [Visiting], page 123.

C-x 4 d *directory* RET
               Select a Dired buffer for directory *directory* in another window (dired-other-
               window). See Chapter 27 [Dired], page 315.

C-x 4 m   Start composing a mail message, similar to C-x m (see Chapter 29 [Sending
               Mail], page 350), but in another window (mail-other-window).

C-x 4 .   Find a tag in the current tags table, similar to M-. (see Section 25.3 [Tags],
               page 299), but in another window (find-tag-other-window).

```
C-x 4 r filename RET
```
    Visit file *filename* read-only, and select its buffer in another window
    (`find-file-read-only-other-window`). See Section 15.2 [Visiting], page 123.

17.5 Deleting and Rearranging Windows

C-x 0   Delete the selected window (`delete-window`).

C-x 1   Delete all windows in the selected frame except the selected window
            (`delete-other-windows`).

C-x 4 0   Delete the selected window and kill the buffer that was showing in it
            (`kill-buffer-and-window`). The last character in this key sequence is a zero.

C-x ^   Make selected window taller (`enlarge-window`).

C-x }   Make selected window wider (`enlarge-window-horizontally`).

C-x {   Make selected window narrower (`shrink-window-horizontally`).

C-x -   Shrink this window if its buffer doesn't need so many lines (`shrink-window-if-larger-than-buffer`).

C-x +   Make all windows the same height (`balance-windows`).

To delete the selected window, type C-x 0 (`delete-window`). (That is a zero.) Once a window is deleted, the space that it occupied is given to an adjacent window (but not the minibuffer window, even if that is active at the time). Deleting the window has no effect on the buffer it used to display; the buffer continues to exist, and you can still switch to it with C-x b.

C-x 4 0 (`kill-buffer-and-window`) is a stronger command than C-x 0; it kills the current buffer and then deletes the selected window.

C-x 1 (`delete-other-windows`) deletes all the windows, *except* the selected one; the selected window expands to use the whole frame. (This command cannot be used while the minibuffer window is active; attempting to do so signals an error.)

The command C-x ^ (`enlarge-window`) makes the selected window one line taller, taking space from a vertically adjacent window without changing the height of the frame. With a positive numeric argument, this command increases the window height by that many lines; with a negative argument, it reduces the height by that many lines. If there are no vertically adjacent windows (i.e., the window is at the full frame height), that signals an error. The command also signals an error if you attempt to reduce the height of any window below a certain minimum number of lines, specified by the variable `window-min-height` (the default is 4).

Similarly, C-x } (`enlarge-window-horizontally`) makes the selected window wider, and C-x { (`shrink-window-horizontally`) makes it narrower. These commands signal an error if you attempt to reduce the width of any window below a certain minimum number of columns, specified by the variable `window-min-width` (the default is 10).

C-x - (`shrink-window-if-larger-than-buffer`) reduces the height of the selected window, if it is taller than necessary to show the whole text of the buffer it is displaying. It gives the extra lines to other windows in the frame.

You can also use `C-x +` (`balance-windows`) to even out the heights of all the windows in the selected frame.

Mouse clicks on the mode line provide another way to change window heights and to delete windows. See Section 18.5 [Mode Line Mouse], page 165.

17.6 Displaying a Buffer in a Window

It is a common Emacs operation to display or "pop up" some buffer in response to a user command. There are several different ways in which commands do this.

Many commands, like `C-x C-f` (`find-file`), display the buffer by "taking over" the selected window, expecting that the user's attention will be diverted to that buffer. These commands usually work by calling `switch-to-buffer` internally (see Section 16.1 [Select Buffer], page 147).

Some commands try to display "intelligently", trying not to take over the selected window, e.g., by splitting off a new window and displaying the desired buffer there. Such commands, which include the various help commands (see Chapter 7 [Help], page 37), work by calling `display-buffer` internally. See Section 17.6.1 [Window Choice], page 160, for details.

Other commands do the same as `display-buffer`, and additionally select the displaying window so that you can begin editing its buffer. The command `C-x '` (`next-error`) is one example (see Section 24.2 [Compilation Mode], page 262). Such commands work by calling the function `pop-to-buffer` internally. See Section "Switching to a Buffer in a Window" in *The Emacs Lisp Reference Manual*.

Commands with names ending in `-other-window` behave like `display-buffer`, except that they never display in the selected window. Several of these commands are bound in the `C-x 4` prefix key (see Section 17.4 [Pop Up Window], page 158).

Commands with names ending in `-other-frame` behave like `display-buffer`, except that they (i) never display in the selected window and (ii) prefer to create a new frame to display the desired buffer instead of splitting a window—as though the variable `pop-up-frames` is set to `t` (see Section 17.6.1 [Window Choice], page 160). Several of these commands are bound in the `C-x 5` prefix key.

17.6.1 How `display-buffer` works

The `display-buffer` command (as well as commands that call it internally) chooses a window to display by following the steps given below. See Section "Choosing a Window for Display" in *The Emacs Lisp Reference Manual*, for details about how to alter this sequence of steps.

- First, check if the buffer should be displayed in the selected window regardless of other considerations. You can tell Emacs to do this by adding the desired buffer's name to the list `same-window-buffer-names`, or adding a matching regular expression to the list `same-window-regexps`. By default, these variables are `nil`, so this step is skipped.

- Otherwise, if the buffer is already displayed in an existing window, "reuse" that window. Normally, only windows on the selected frame are considered, but windows on other frames are also reusable if you change `pop-up-frames` (see below) to `t`.

- Otherwise, optionally create a new frame and display the buffer there. By default, this step is skipped. To enable it, change the variable `pop-up-frames` to a non-`nil` value. The special value `graphic-only` means to do this only on graphical displays.

- Otherwise, try to create a new window by splitting the selected window, and display the buffer in that new window.

  The split can be either vertical or horizontal, depending on the variables `split-height-threshold` and `split-width-threshold`. These variables should have integer values. If `split-height-threshold` is smaller than the selected window's height, the split puts the new window below. Otherwise, if `split-width-threshold` is smaller than the window's width, the split puts the new window on the right. If neither condition holds, Emacs tries to split so that the new window is below—but only if the window was not split before (to avoid excessive splitting).

- Otherwise, display the buffer in an existing window on the selected frame.

- If all the above methods fail for whatever reason, create a new frame and display the buffer there.

17.7 Convenience Features for Window Handling

Winner mode is a global minor mode that records the changes in the window configuration (i.e., how the frames are partitioned into windows), so that you can "undo" them. You can toggle Winner mode with `M-x winner-mode`, or by customizing the variable `winner-mode`. When the mode is enabled, `C-c left` (`winner-undo`) undoes the last window configuration change. If you change your mind while undoing, you can redo the changes you had undone using `C-c right` (`M-x winner-redo`).

Follow mode (`M-x follow-mode`) synchronizes several windows on the same buffer so that they always display adjacent sections of that buffer. See Section 11.7 [Follow Mode], page 74.

The Windmove package defines commands for moving directionally between neighboring windows in a frame. `M-x windmove-right` selects the window immediately to the right of the currently selected one, and similarly for the "left", "up", and "down" counterparts. `M-x windmove-default-keybindings` binds these commands to `S-right` etc.; doing so disables shift selection for those keys (see Section 8.6 [Shift Selection], page 49).

The command `M-x compare-windows` lets you compare the text shown in different windows. See Section 15.8 [Comparing Files], page 137.

Scroll All mode (`M-x scroll-all-mode`) is a global minor mode that causes scrolling commands and point motion commands to apply to every single window.

18 Frames and Graphical Displays

When Emacs is started on a graphical display, e.g., on the X Window System, it occupies a graphical system-level "window". In this manual, we call this a *frame*, reserving the word "window" for the part of the frame used for displaying a buffer. A frame initially contains one window, but it can be subdivided into multiple windows (see Chapter 17 [Windows], page 156). A frame normally also contains a menu bar, tool bar, and echo area.

You can also create additional frames (see Section 18.6 [Creating Frames], page 166). All frames created in the same Emacs session have access to the same underlying buffers and other data. For instance, if a buffer is being shown in more than one frame, any changes made to it in one frame show up immediately in the other frames too.

Typing C-x C-c closes all the frames on the current display, and ends the Emacs session if it has no frames open on any other displays (see Section 3.2 [Exiting], page 15). To close just the selected frame, type C-x 5 0 (that is zero, not o).

This chapter describes Emacs features specific to graphical displays (particularly mouse commands), and features for managing multiple frames. On text terminals, many of these features are unavailable. However, it is still possible to create multiple "frames" on text terminals; such frames are displayed one at a time, filling the entire terminal screen (see Section 18.19 [Non-Window Terminals], page 175). It is also possible to use the mouse on some text terminals (see Section 18.20 [Text-Only Mouse], page 176, for doing so on GNU and Unix systems; and see Section "MS-DOS Mouse" in *Specialized Emacs Features*, for doing so on MS-DOS). Menus are supported on all text terminals.

18.1 Mouse Commands for Editing

Mouse-1   Move point to where you click (mouse-set-point).

Drag-Mouse-1
           Activate the region around the text selected by dragging, and put the text in the primary selection (mouse-set-region).

Mouse-2   Move point to where you click, and insert the contents of the primary selection there (mouse-yank-primary).

Mouse-3   If the region is active, move the nearer end of the region to the click position; otherwise, set mark at the current value of point and point at the click position. Save the resulting region in the kill ring; on a second click, kill it (mouse-save-then-kill).

The most basic mouse command is mouse-set-point, which is invoked by clicking with the left mouse button, Mouse-1, in the text area of a window. This moves point to the position where you clicked. If that window was not the selected window, it becomes the selected window.

Normally, if the frame you clicked in was not the selected frame, it is made the selected frame, in addition to selecting the window and setting the cursor. On the X Window System, you can change this by setting the variable x-mouse-click-focus-ignore-position to t. In that case, the initial click on an unselected frame just selects the frame, without doing anything else; clicking again selects the window and sets the cursor position.

Holding down `Mouse-1` and "dragging" the mouse over a stretch of text activates the region around that text (`mouse-set-region`), placing the mark where you started holding down the mouse button, and point where you release it (see Chapter 8 [Mark], page 45). In addition, the text in the region becomes the primary selection (see Section 9.3.2 [Primary Selection], page 58).

If you change the variable `mouse-drag-copy-region` to a non-`nil` value, dragging the mouse over a stretch of text also adds the text to the kill ring. The default is `nil`.

If you move the mouse off the top or bottom of the window while dragging, the window scrolls at a steady rate until you move the mouse back into the window. This way, you can select regions that don't fit entirely on the screen. The number of lines scrolled per step depends on how far away from the window edge the mouse has gone; the variable `mouse-scroll-min-lines` specifies a minimum step size.

Clicking with the middle mouse button, `Mouse-2`, moves point to the position where you clicked and inserts the contents of the primary selection (`mouse-yank-primary`). See Section 9.3.2 [Primary Selection], page 58. This behavior is consistent with other X applications. Alternatively, you can rebind `Mouse-2` to `mouse-yank-at-click`, which performs a yank at the position you click.

If you change the variable `mouse-yank-at-point` to a non-`nil` value, `Mouse-2` does not move point; it inserts the text at point, regardless of where you clicked or even which of the frame's windows you clicked on. This variable affects both `mouse-yank-primary` and `mouse-yank-at-click`.

Clicking with the right mouse button, `Mouse-3`, runs the command `mouse-save-then-kill`. This performs several actions depending on where you click and the status of the region:

- If no region is active, clicking `Mouse-3` activates the region, placing the mark where point was and point at the clicked position.

- If a region is active, clicking `Mouse-3` adjusts the nearer end of the region by moving it to the clicked position. The adjusted region's text is copied to the kill ring; if the text in the original region was already on the kill ring, it replaces it there.

- If you originally specified the region using a double or triple `Mouse-1`, so that the region is defined to consist of entire words or lines (see Section 18.2 [Word and Line Mouse], page 164), then adjusting the region with `Mouse-3` also proceeds by entire words or lines.

- If you use `Mouse-3` a second time consecutively, at the same place, that kills the region already selected. Thus, the simplest way to kill text with the mouse is to click `Mouse-1` at one end, then click `Mouse-3` twice at the other end. To copy the text into the kill ring without deleting it from the buffer, press `Mouse-3` just once—or just drag across the text with `Mouse-1`. Then you can copy it elsewhere by yanking it.

The `mouse-save-then-kill` command also obeys the variable `mouse-drag-copy-region` (described above). If the value is non-`nil`, then whenever the command sets or adjusts the active region, the text in the region is also added to the kill ring. If the latest kill ring entry had been added the same way, that entry is replaced rather than making a new entry.

Whenever you set the region using any of the mouse commands described above, the mark will be deactivated by any subsequent unshifted cursor motion command, in addition to the usual ways of deactivating the mark. See Section 8.6 [Shift Selection], page 49.

Some mice have a "wheel" which can be used for scrolling. Emacs supports scrolling windows with the mouse wheel, by default, on most graphical displays. To toggle this feature, use M-x mouse-wheel-mode. The variables mouse-wheel-follow-mouse and mouse-wheel-scroll-amount determine where and by how much buffers are scrolled. The variable mouse-wheel-progressive-speed determines whether the scroll speed is linked to how fast you move the wheel.

18.2 Mouse Commands for Words and Lines

These variants of Mouse-1 select entire words or lines at a time. Emacs activates the region around the selected text, which is also copied to the kill ring.

Double-Mouse-1
> Select the text around the word which you click on.
>
> Double-clicking on a character with "symbol" syntax (such as underscore, in C mode) selects the symbol surrounding that character. Double-clicking on a character with open- or close-parenthesis syntax selects the parenthetical grouping which that character starts or ends. Double-clicking on a character with string-delimiter syntax (such as a single-quote or double-quote in C) selects the string constant (Emacs uses heuristics to figure out whether that character is the beginning or the end of it).

Double-Drag-Mouse-1
> Select the text you drag across, in the form of whole words.

Triple-Mouse-1
> Select the line you click on.

Triple-Drag-Mouse-1
> Select the text you drag across, in the form of whole lines.

18.3 Following References with the Mouse

Some Emacs buffers include *buttons*, or *hyperlinks*: pieces of text that perform some action (e.g., following a reference) when activated (e.g., by clicking on them). Usually, a button's text is visually highlighted: it is underlined, or a box is drawn around it. If you move the mouse over a button, the shape of the mouse cursor changes and the button lights up. If you change the variable mouse-highlight to nil, Emacs disables this highlighting.

You can activate a button by moving point to it and typing RET, or by clicking either Mouse-1 or Mouse-2 on the button. For example, in a Dired buffer, each file name is a button; activating it causes Emacs to visit that file (see Chapter 27 [Dired], page 315). In a *Compilation* buffer, each error message is a button, and activating it visits the source code for that error (see Section 24.1 [Compilation], page 261).

Although clicking Mouse-1 on a button usually activates the button, if you hold the mouse button down for a period of time before releasing it (specifically, for more than 450 milliseconds), then Emacs moves point where you clicked, without activating the button.

In this way, you can use the mouse to move point over a button without activating it. Dragging the mouse over or onto a button has its usual behavior of setting the region, and does not activate the button.

You can change how Mouse-1 applies to buttons by customizing the variable mouse-1-click-follows-link. If the value is a positive integer, that determines how long you need to hold the mouse button down for, in milliseconds, to cancel button activation; the default is 450, as described in the previous paragraph. If the value is nil, Mouse-1 just sets point where you clicked, and does not activate buttons. If the value is double, double clicks activate buttons but single clicks just set point.

Normally, Mouse-1 on a button activates the button even if it is in a non-selected window. If you change the variable mouse-1-click-in-non-selected-windows to nil, Mouse-1 on a button in an unselected window moves point to the clicked position and selects that window, without activating the button.

18.4 Mouse Clicks for Menus

Several mouse clicks with the CTRL and SHIFT modifiers bring up menus.

C-Mouse-1

> This menu is for selecting a buffer.
>
> The MSB ("mouse select buffer") global minor mode makes this menu smarter and more customizable. See Section 16.7.3 [Buffer Menus], page 155.

C-Mouse-2

> This menu contains entries for examining faces and other text properties, and well as for setting them (the latter is mainly useful when editing enriched text; see Section 22.13 [Enriched Text], page 230).

C-Mouse-3

> This menu is mode-specific. For most modes if Menu-bar mode is on, this menu has the same items as all the mode-specific menu-bar menus put together. Some modes may specify a different menu for this button. If Menu Bar mode is off, this menu contains all the items which would be present in the menu bar—not just the mode-specific ones—so that you can access them without having to display the menu bar.

S-Mouse-1

> This menu is for changing the default face within the window's buffer. See Section 11.11 [Text Scale], page 78.

Some graphical applications use Mouse-3 for a mode-specific menu. If you prefer Mouse-3 in Emacs to bring up such a menu instead of running the mouse-save-then-kill command, rebind Mouse-3 by adding the following line to your init file (see Section 33.3.6 [Init Rebinding], page 432):

```
(global-set-key [mouse-3] 'mouse-popup-menubar-stuff)
```

18.5 Mode Line Mouse Commands

You can use mouse clicks on window mode lines to select and manipulate windows.

Some areas of the mode line, such as the buffer name, and major and minor mode names, have their own special mouse bindings. These areas are highlighted when you hold the mouse over them, and information about the special bindings will be displayed (see Section 18.17 [Tooltips], page 174). This section's commands do not apply in those areas.

Mouse-1   Mouse-1 on a mode line selects the window it belongs to. By dragging Mouse-1 on the mode line, you can move it, thus changing the height of the windows above and below. Changing heights with the mouse in this way never deletes windows, it just refuses to make any window smaller than the minimum height.

Mouse-2   Mouse-2 on a mode line expands that window to fill its frame.

Mouse-3   Mouse-3 on a mode line deletes the window it belongs to. If the frame has only one window, it does nothing.

C-Mouse-2

        C-Mouse-2 on a mode line splits that window, producing two side-by-side windows with the boundary running through the click position (see Section 17.2 [Split Window], page 156).

Furthermore, by clicking and dragging Mouse-1 on the divider between two side-by-side mode lines, you can move the vertical boundary to the left or right.

Note that resizing windows is affected by the value of window-resize-pixelwise, see Section 17.2 [Split Window], page 156.

18.6 Creating Frames

The prefix key C-x 5 is analogous to C-x 4. Whereas each C-x 4 command pops up a buffer in a different window in the selected frame (see Section 17.4 [Pop Up Window], page 158), the C-x 5 commands use a different frame. If an existing visible or iconified ("minimized") frame already displays the requested buffer, that frame is raised and deiconified ("unminimized"); otherwise, a new frame is created on the current display terminal.

The various C-x 5 commands differ in how they find or create the buffer to select:

C-x 5 2   Create a new frame (make-frame-command).

C-x 5 b *bufname* RET

        Select buffer *bufname* in another frame. This runs switch-to-buffer-other-frame.

C-x 5 f *filename* RET

        Visit file *filename* and select its buffer in another frame. This runs find-file-other-frame. See Section 15.2 [Visiting], page 123.

C-x 5 d *directory* RET

        Select a Dired buffer for directory *directory* in another frame. This runs dired-other-frame. See Chapter 27 [Dired], page 315.

C-x 5 m   Start composing a mail message in another frame. This runs mail-other-frame. It is the other-frame variant of C-x m. See Chapter 29 [Sending Mail], page 350.

C-x 5 .   Find a tag in the current tag table in another frame. This runs `find-tag-other-frame`, the multiple-frame variant of M-.. See Section 25.3 [Tags], page 299.

C-x 5 r *filename* RET

Visit file *filename* read-only, and select its buffer in another frame. This runs `find-file-read-only-other-frame`. See Section 15.2 [Visiting], page 123.

You can control the appearance and behavior of the newly-created frames by specifying *frame parameters*. See Section 18.11 [Frame Parameters], page 172.

18.7 Frame Commands

The following commands are used to delete and operate on frames:

C-x 5 0   Delete the selected frame (`delete-frame`). This signals an error if there is only one frame.

C-z   Minimize (or "iconify) the selected Emacs frame (`suspend-frame`). See Section 3.2 [Exiting], page 15.

C-x 5 o   Select another frame, and raise it. If you repeat this command, it cycles through all the frames on your terminal.

C-x 5 1   Delete all frames on the current terminal, except the selected one.

M-<F10>   Toggle the maximization state of the current frame. When a frame is maximized, it fills the screen.

<F11>   Toggle fullscreen mode for the current frame. (The difference between "fullscreen" and "maximized" is normally that the former hides window manager decorations, giving slightly more screen space to Emacs itself.)

Note that with some window managers you may have to customize the variable `frame-resize-pixelwise` to a non-`nil` value in order to make a frame truly "maximized" or "fullscreen". This variable, when set to a non-`nil` value, in general allows resizing frames at pixel resolution, rather than in integral multiples of lines and columns.

The C-x 5 0 (`delete-frame`) command deletes the selected frame. However, it will refuse to delete the last frame in an Emacs session, to prevent you from losing the ability to interact with the Emacs session. Note that when Emacs is run as a daemon (see Section 31.5 [Emacs Server], page 393), there is always a "virtual frame" that remains after all the ordinary, interactive frames are deleted. In this case, C-x 5 0 can delete the last interactive frame; you can use `emacsclient` to reconnect to the Emacs session.

The C-x 5 1 (`delete-other-frames`) command deletes all other frames on the current terminal (this terminal refers to either a graphical display, or a text terminal; see Section 18.19 [Non-Window Terminals], page 175). If the Emacs session has frames open on other graphical displays or text terminals, those are not deleted.

The C-x 5 o (`other-frame`) command selects the next frame on the current terminal. If you are using Emacs on the X Window System with a window manager that selects (or *gives focus to*) whatever frame the mouse cursor is over, you have to change the variable `focus-follows-mouse` to t in order for this command to work properly. Then invoking C-x 5 o will also warp the mouse cursor to the chosen frame.

18.8 Fonts

By default, Emacs displays text on graphical displays using a 10-point monospace font. There are several different ways to specify a different font:

- Click on 'Set Default Font' in the 'Options' menu. This makes the selected font the default on all existing graphical frames. To save this for future sessions, click on 'Save Options' in the 'Options' menu.

- Add a line to your init file, modifying the variable default-frame-alist to specify the font parameter (see Section 18.11 [Frame Parameters], page 172), like this:

  ```
  (add-to-list 'default-frame-alist
               '(font . "DejaVu Sans Mono-10"))
  ```

  This makes the font the default on all graphical frames created after restarting Emacs with that init file.

- Add an 'emacs.font' X resource setting to your X resource file, like this:

  ```
  emacs.font: DejaVu Sans Mono-12
  ```

  You must restart X, or use the xrdb command, for the X resources file to take effect. See Section D.1 [Resources], page 493. Do not quote font names in X resource files.

- If you are running Emacs on the GNOME desktop, you can tell Emacs to use the default system font by setting the variable font-use-system-font to t (the default is nil). For this to work, Emacs must have been compiled with Gconf support.

- Use the command line option '-fn' (or '--font'). See Section C.6 [Font X], page 487.

To check what font you're currently using, the C-u C-x = command can be helpful. It describes the character at point, and names the font that it's rendered in.

On X, there are four different ways to express a "font name". The first is to use a *Fontconfig pattern*. Fontconfig patterns have the following form:

```
fontname[-fontsize][:name1=values1][:name2=values2]...
```

Within this format, any of the elements in braces may be omitted. Here, *fontname* is the *family name* of the font, such as 'Monospace' or 'DejaVu Sans Mono'; *fontsize* is the *point size* of the font (one *printer's point* is about 1/72 of an inch); and the '*name=values*' entries specify settings such as the slant and weight of the font. Each *values* may be a single value, or a list of values separated by commas. In addition, some property values are valid with only one kind of property name, in which case the '*name=*' part may be omitted.

Here is a list of common font properties:

'slant'   One of 'italic', 'oblique', or 'roman'.

'weight'   One of 'light', 'medium', 'demibold', 'bold' or 'black'.

'style'   Some fonts define special styles which are a combination of slant and weight. For instance, 'Dejavu Sans' defines the 'book' style, which overrides the slant and weight properties.

'width'   One of 'condensed', 'normal', or 'expanded'.

'spacing'   One of 'monospace', 'proportional', 'dual-width', or 'charcell'.

Here are some examples of Fontconfig patterns:

```
Monospace
Monospace-12
Monospace-12:bold
DejaVu Sans Mono:bold:italic
Monospace-12:weight=bold:slant=italic
```

For a more detailed description of Fontconfig patterns, see the Fontconfig manual, which is distributed with Fontconfig and available online at `http://fontconfig.org/fontconfig-user.html`.

The second way to specify a font is to use a *GTK font pattern*. These have the syntax

> *fontname* [*properties*] [*fontsize*]

where *fontname* is the family name, *properties* is a list of property values separated by spaces, and *fontsize* is the point size. The properties that you may specify for GTK font patterns are as follows:

- Slant properties: 'Italic' or 'Oblique'. If omitted, the default (roman) slant is implied.

- Weight properties: 'Bold', 'Book', 'Light', 'Medium', 'Semi-bold', or 'Ultra-light'. If omitted, 'Medium' weight is implied.

- Width properties: 'Semi-Condensed' or 'Condensed'. If omitted, a default width is used.

Here are some examples of GTK font patterns:

```
Monospace 12
Monospace Bold Italic 12
```

The third way to specify a font is to use an *XLFD* (*X Logical Font Description*). This is the traditional method for specifying fonts under X. Each XLFD consists of fourteen words or numbers, separated by dashes, like this:

> `-misc-fixed-medium-r-semicondensed--13-*-*-*-c-60-iso8859-1`

A wildcard character ('*') in an XLFD matches any sequence of characters (including none), and '?' matches any single character. However, matching is implementation-dependent, and can be inaccurate when wildcards match dashes in a long name. For reliable results, supply all 14 dashes and use wildcards only within a field. Case is insignificant in an XLFD. The syntax for an XLFD is as follows:

> *-maker-family-weight-slant-widthtype-style...*
> *...-pixels-height-horiz-vert-spacing-width-registry-encoding*

The entries have the following meanings:

maker The name of the font manufacturer.

family The name of the font family (e.g., 'courier').

weight The font weight—normally either 'bold', 'medium' or 'light'. Some font names support other values.

slant The font slant—normally 'r' (roman), 'i' (italic), 'o' (oblique), 'ri' (reverse italic), or 'ot' (other). Some font names support other values.

widthtype The font width—normally 'normal', 'condensed', 'semicondensed', or 'extended'. Some font names support other values.

style   An optional additional style name. Usually it is empty—most XLFDs have two hyphens in a row at this point.

pixels   The font height, in pixels.

height   The font height on the screen, measured in tenths of a printer's point. This is the point size of the font, times ten. For a given vertical resolution, *height* and *pixels* are proportional; therefore, it is common to specify just one of them and use '*' for the other.

horiz   The horizontal resolution, in pixels per inch, of the screen for which the font is intended.

vert   The vertical resolution, in pixels per inch, of the screen for which the font is intended. Normally the resolution of the fonts on your system is the right value for your screen; therefore, you normally specify '*' for this and *horiz*.

spacing   This is 'm' (monospace), 'p' (proportional) or 'c' (character cell).

width   The average character width, in pixels, multiplied by ten.

registry
encoding   The X font character set that the font depicts. (X font character sets are not the same as Emacs character sets, but they are similar.) You can use the `xfontsel` program to check which choices you have. Normally you should use 'iso8859' for *registry* and '1' for *encoding*.

The fourth and final method of specifying a font is to use a "font nickname". Certain fonts have shorter nicknames, which you can use instead of a normal font specification. For instance, '6x13' is equivalent to

```
-misc-fixed-medium-r-semicondensed--13-*-*-*-c-60-iso8859-1
```

On X, Emacs recognizes two types of fonts: *client-side* fonts, which are provided by the Xft and Fontconfig libraries, and *server-side* fonts, which are provided by the X server itself. Most client-side fonts support advanced font features such as antialiasing and subpixel hinting, while server-side fonts do not. Fontconfig and GTK patterns match only client-side fonts.

You will probably want to use a fixed-width default font—that is, a font in which all characters have the same width. For Xft and Fontconfig fonts, you can use the `fc-list` command to list the available fixed-width fonts, like this:

```
fc-list :spacing=mono fc-list :spacing=charcell
```

For server-side X fonts, you can use the `xlsfonts` program to list the available fixed-width fonts, like this:

```
xlsfonts -fn '*x*' | egrep "^[0-9]+x[0-9]+"
xlsfonts -fn '*-*-*-*-*-*-*-*-*-*-*-m*'
xlsfonts -fn '*-*-*-*-*-*-*-*-*-*-*-c*'
```

Any font with 'm' or 'c' in the *spacing* field of the XLFD is a fixed-width font. To see what a particular font looks like, use the `xfd` command. For example:

```
xfd -fn 6x13
```

displays the entire font '6x13'.

While running Emacs, you can also set the font of a specific kind of text (see Section 11.8 [Faces], page 74), or a particular frame (see Section 18.11 [Frame Parameters], page 172).

18.9 Speedbar Frames

The *speedbar* is a special frame for conveniently navigating in or operating on another frame. The speedbar, when it exists, is always associated with a specific frame, called its *attached frame*; all speedbar operations act on that frame.

Type `M-x speedbar` to create the speedbar and associate it with the current frame. To dismiss the speedbar, type `M-x speedbar` again, or select the speedbar and type `q`. (You can also delete the speedbar frame like any other Emacs frame.) If you wish to associate the speedbar with a different frame, dismiss it and call `M-x speedbar` from that frame.

The speedbar can operate in various modes. Its default mode is *File Display* mode, which shows the files in the current directory of the selected window of the attached frame, one file per line. Clicking on a file name visits that file in the selected window of the attached frame, and clicking on a directory name shows that directory in the speedbar (see Section 18.3 [Mouse References], page 164). Each line also has a box, '[+]' or '<+>', that you can click on to *expand* the contents of that item. Expanding a directory adds the contents of that directory to the speedbar display, underneath the directory's own line. Expanding an ordinary file adds a list of the tags in that file to the speedbar display; you can click on a tag name to jump to that tag in the selected window of the attached frame. When a file or directory is expanded, the '[+]' changes to '[-]'; you can click on that box to *contract* the item, hiding its contents.

You navigate through the speedbar using the keyboard, too. Typing `RET` while point is on a line in the speedbar is equivalent to clicking the item on the current line, and `SPC` expands or contracts the item. `U` displays the parent directory of the current directory. To copy, delete, or rename the file on the current line, type `C`, `D`, and `R` respectively. To create a new directory, type `M`.

Another general-purpose speedbar mode is *Buffer Display* mode; in this mode, the speedbar displays a list of Emacs buffers. To switch to this mode, type `b` in the speedbar. To return to File Display mode, type `f`. You can also change the display mode by clicking `mouse-3` anywhere in the speedbar window (or `mouse-1` on the mode-line) and selecting 'Displays' in the pop-up menu.

Some major modes, including Rmail mode, Info, and GUD, have specialized ways of putting useful items into the speedbar for you to select. For example, in Rmail mode, the speedbar shows a list of Rmail files, and lets you move the current message to another Rmail file by clicking on its '<M>' box.

For more details on using and programming the speedbar, See *Speedbar Manual*.

18.10 Multiple Displays

A single Emacs can talk to more than one X display. Initially, Emacs uses just one display—the one specified with the `DISPLAY` environment variable or with the '`--display`' option (see Section C.2 [Initial Options], page 480). To connect to another display, use the command `make-frame-on-display`:

`M-x make-frame-on-display RET` *display* `RET`
> Create a new frame on display *display*.

A single X server can handle more than one screen. When you open frames on two screens belonging to one server, Emacs knows they share a single keyboard, and it treats all the commands arriving from these screens as a single stream of input.

When you open frames on different X servers, Emacs makes a separate input stream for each server. Each server also has its own selected frame. The commands you enter with a particular X server apply to that server's selected frame.

18.11 Frame Parameters

You can control the default appearance and behavior of all frames by specifying a default list of *frame parameters* in the variable `default-frame-alist`. Its value should be a list of entries, each specifying a parameter name and a value for that parameter. These entries take effect whenever Emacs creates a new frame, including the initial frame.

For example, you can add the following lines to your init file (see Section 33.4 [Init File], page 437) to set the default frame width to 90 character columns, the default frame height to 40 character rows, and the default font to 'Monospace-10':

```
(add-to-list 'default-frame-alist '(width  . 90))
(add-to-list 'default-frame-alist '(height . 40))
(add-to-list 'default-frame-alist '(font . "Monospace-10"))
```

For a list of frame parameters and their effects, see Section "Frame Parameters" in *The Emacs Lisp Reference Manual*.

You can also specify a list of frame parameters which apply to just the initial frame, by customizing the variable `initial-frame-alist`.

If Emacs is compiled to use an X toolkit, frame parameters that specify colors and fonts don't affect menus and the menu bar, since those are drawn by the toolkit and not directly by Emacs.

18.12 Scroll Bars

On graphical displays, there is a *scroll bar* on the side of each Emacs window. Clicking `Mouse-1` on the scroll bar's up and down buttons scrolls the window by one line at a time. Clicking `Mouse-1` above or below the scroll bar's inner box scrolls the window by nearly the entire height of the window, like `M-v` and `C-v` respectively (see Section 4.2 [Moving Point], page 17). Dragging the inner box scrolls continuously.

If Emacs is compiled on the X Window System without X toolkit support, the scroll bar behaves differently. Clicking `Mouse-1` anywhere on the scroll bar scrolls forward like `C-v`, while `Mouse-3` scrolls backward like `M-v`. Clicking `Mouse-2` in the scroll bar lets you drag the inner box up and down.

To toggle the use of scroll bars, type `M-x scroll-bar-mode`. This command applies to all frames, including frames yet to be created. To toggle scroll bars for just the selected frame, use the command `M-x toggle-scroll-bar`.

To control the use of scroll bars at startup, customize the variable `scroll-bar-mode`. Its value should be either `right` (put scroll bars on the right side of windows), `left` (put them on the left), or `nil` (disable scroll bars). By default, Emacs puts scroll bars on the right if it was compiled with GTK+ support on the X Window System, and on MS-Windows or

Mac OS; Emacs puts scroll bars on the left if compiled on the X Window System without GTK+ support (following the old convention for X applications).

You can also use the X resource 'verticalScrollBars' to enable or disable the scroll bars (see Section D.1 [Resources], page 493). To control the scroll bar width, change the `scroll-bar-width` frame parameter (see Section "Frame Parameters" in *The Emacs Lisp Reference Manual*).

If you're using Emacs on X (with GTK+ or Motif), you can customize the variable `scroll-bar-adjust-thumb-portion` to control *overscrolling* of the scroll bar, i.e. dragging the thumb down even when the end of the buffer is visible. If its value is non-`nil`, the scroll bar can be dragged downwards even if the end of the buffer is shown; if `nil`, the thumb will be at the bottom when the end of the buffer is shown. You can not over-scroll when the entire buffer is visible.

The visual appearance of the scroll bars is controlled by the `scroll-bar` face.

18.13 Drag and Drop

In most graphical desktop environments, Emacs has basic support for *drag and drop* operations. For instance, dropping text onto an Emacs frame inserts the text where it is dropped. Dropping a file onto an Emacs frame visits that file. As a special case, dropping the file on a Dired buffer moves or copies the file (according to the conventions of the application it came from) into the directory displayed in that buffer.

Dropping a file normally visits it in the window you drop it on. If you prefer to visit the file in a new window in such cases, customize the variable `dnd-open-file-other-window`.

The XDND and Motif drag and drop protocols, and the old KDE 1.x protocol, are currently supported.

18.14 Menu Bars

You can toggle the use of menu bars with `M-x menu-bar-mode`. With no argument, this command toggles Menu Bar mode, a global minor mode. With an argument, the command turns Menu Bar mode on if the argument is positive, off if the argument is not positive. To control the use of menu bars at startup, customize the variable `menu-bar-mode`.

Expert users often turn off the menu bar, especially on text terminals, where this makes one additional line available for text. If the menu bar is off, you can still pop up a menu of its contents with `C-Mouse-3` on a display which supports pop-up menus. See Section 18.4 [Menu Mouse Clicks], page 165.

See Section 1.4 [Menu Bar], page 9, for information on how to invoke commands with the menu bar. See Appendix D [X Resources], page 493, for how to customize the menu bar menus' visual appearance.

18.15 Tool Bars

On graphical displays, Emacs puts a *tool bar* at the top of each frame, just below the menu bar. This is a row of icons which you can click on with the mouse to invoke various commands.

The global (default) tool bar contains general commands. Some major modes define their own tool bars; whenever a buffer with such a major mode is current, the mode's tool bar replaces the global tool bar.

To toggle the use of tool bars, type `M-x tool-bar-mode`. This command applies to all frames, including frames yet to be created. To control the use of tool bars at startup, customize the variable `tool-bar-mode`.

When Emacs is compiled with GTK+ support, each tool bar item can consist of an image, or a text label, or both. By default, Emacs follows the Gnome desktop's tool bar style setting; if none is defined, it displays tool bar items as just images. To impose a specific tool bar style, customize the variable `tool-bar-style`.

You can also control the placement of the tool bar for the GTK+ tool bar with the frame parameter `tool-bar-position`. See Section "Frame Parameters" in *The Emacs Lisp Reference Manual*.

18.16 Using Dialog Boxes

A dialog box is a special kind of menu for asking you a yes-or-no question or some other special question. Many Emacs commands use a dialog box to ask a yes-or-no question, if you used the mouse to invoke the command that led to the question.

To disable the use of dialog boxes, change the variable `use-dialog-box` to `nil`. In that case, Emacs always performs yes-or-no prompts using the echo area and keyboard input. This variable also controls whether to use file selection windows (but those are not supported on all platforms).

A file selection window is a special kind of dialog box for asking for file names. You can customize the variable `use-file-dialog` to suppress the use of file selection windows, even if you still want other kinds of dialogs. This variable has no effect if you have suppressed all dialog boxes with the variable `use-dialog-box`.

When Emacs is compiled with GTK+ support, it uses the GTK+ "file chooser" dialog. Emacs adds an additional toggle button to this dialog, which you can use to enable or disable the display of hidden files (files starting with a dot) in that dialog. If you want this toggle to be activated by default, change the variable `x-gtk-show-hidden-files` to `t`. In addition, Emacs adds help text to the GTK+ file chooser dialog; to disable this help text, change the variable `x-gtk-file-dialog-help-text` to `nil`.

18.17 Tooltips

Tooltips are small windows that display text information at the current mouse position. They activate when there is a pause in mouse movement over some significant piece of text in a window, or the mode line, or some other part of the Emacs frame such as a tool bar button or menu item.

You can toggle the use of tooltips with the command `M-x tooltip-mode`. When Tooltip mode is disabled, the help text is displayed in the echo area instead. To control the use of tooltips at startup, customize the variable `tooltip-mode`.

The variables `tooltip-delay` specifies how long Emacs should wait before displaying a tooltip. For additional customization options for displaying tooltips, use `M-x customize-group RET tooltip RET`.

If Emacs is built with GTK+ support, it displays tooltips via GTK+, using the default appearance of GTK+ tooltips. To disable this, change the variable `x-gtk-use-system-tooltips` to `nil`. If you do this, or if Emacs is built without GTK+ support, most attributes of the tooltip text are specified by the `tooltip` face, and by X resources (see Appendix D [X Resources], page 493).

GUD tooltips are special tooltips that show the values of variables when debugging a program with GUD. See Section 24.6.2 [Debugger Operation], page 267.

18.18 Mouse Avoidance

On graphical terminals, the mouse pointer may obscure the text in the Emacs frame. Emacs provides two methods to avoid this problem.

Firstly, Emacs hides the mouse pointer each time you type a self-inserting character, if the pointer lies inside an Emacs frame; moving the mouse pointer makes it visible again. To disable this feature, set the variable `make-pointer-invisible` to `nil`.

Secondly, you can use Mouse Avoidance mode, a minor mode, to keep the mouse pointer away from point. To use Mouse Avoidance mode, customize the variable `mouse-avoidance-mode`. You can set this to various values to move the mouse in several ways:

banish   Move the pointer to a corner of the frame on any key-press. You can customize the variable `mouse-avoidance-banish-position` to specify where the pointer goes when it is banished.

exile   Banish the pointer only if the cursor gets too close, and allow it to return once the cursor is out of the way.

jump   If the cursor gets too close to the pointer, displace the pointer by a random distance and direction.

animate   As `jump`, but shows steps along the way for illusion of motion.

cat-and-mouse
            The same as `animate`.

proteus   As `animate`, but changes the shape of the mouse pointer too.

You can also use the command `M-x mouse-avoidance-mode` to enable the mode. Whenever Mouse Avoidance mode moves the mouse, it also raises the frame.

18.19 Non-Window Terminals

On a text terminal, Emacs can display only one Emacs frame at a time. However, you can still create multiple Emacs frames, and switch between them. Switching frames on these terminals is much like switching between different window configurations.

Use `C-x 5 2` to create a new frame and switch to it; use `C-x 5 o` to cycle through the existing frames; use `C-x 5 0` to delete the current frame.

Each frame has a number to distinguish it. If your terminal can display only one frame at a time, the selected frame's number *n* appears near the beginning of the mode line, in the form 'F*n*'.

'F*n*' is in fact the frame's initial name. You can give frames more meaningful names if you wish, and you can select a frame by its name. Use the command `M-x set-frame-name RET` *name* RET to specify a new name for the selected frame, and use M-x select-frame-by-name RET *name* RET to select a frame according to its name. The name you specify appears in the mode line when the frame is selected.

18.20 Using a Mouse in Text Terminals

Some text terminals support mouse clicks in the terminal window.

In a terminal emulator which is compatible with xterm, you can use M-x xterm-mouse-mode to give Emacs control over simple uses of the mouse—basically, only non-modified single clicks are supported. The normal xterm mouse functionality for such clicks is still available by holding down the SHIFT key when you press the mouse button. Xterm Mouse mode is a global minor mode (see Section 20.2 [Minor Modes], page 200). Repeating the command turns the mode off again.

In the console on GNU/Linux, you can use M-x gpm-mouse-mode to enable mouse support. You must have the gpm server installed and running on your system in order for this to work.

See Section "MS-DOS Mouse" in *Specialized Emacs Features*, for information about mouse support on MS-DOS.

19 International Character Set Support

Emacs supports a wide variety of international character sets, including European and Vietnamese variants of the Latin alphabet, as well as Arabic scripts, Brahmic scripts (for languages such as Bengali, Hindi, and Thai), Cyrillic, Ethiopic, Georgian, Greek, Han (for Chinese and Japanese), Hangul (for Korean), Hebrew and IPA. Emacs also supports various encodings of these characters that are used by other internationalized software, such as word processors and mailers.

Emacs allows editing text with international characters by supporting all the related activities:

- You can visit files with non-ASCII characters, save non-ASCII text, and pass non-ASCII text between Emacs and programs it invokes (such as compilers, spell-checkers, and mailers). Setting your language environment (see Section 19.2 [Language Environments], page 179) takes care of setting up the coding systems and other options for a specific language or culture. Alternatively, you can specify how Emacs should encode or decode text for each command; see Section 19.9 [Text Coding], page 188.

- You can display non-ASCII characters encoded by the various scripts. This works by using appropriate fonts on graphics displays (see Section 19.14 [Defining Fontsets], page 192), and by sending special codes to text displays (see Section 19.12 [Terminal Coding], page 191). If some characters are displayed incorrectly, refer to Section 19.16 [Undisplayable Characters], page 195, which describes possible problems and explains how to solve them.

- Characters from scripts whose natural ordering of text is from right to left are reordered for display (see Section 19.19 [Bidirectional Editing], page 197). These scripts include Arabic, Hebrew, Syriac, Thaana, and a few others.

- You can insert non-ASCII characters or search for them. To do that, you can specify an input method (see Section 19.4 [Select Input Method], page 182) suitable for your language, or use the default input method set up when you chose your language environment. If your keyboard can produce non-ASCII characters, you can select an appropriate keyboard coding system (see Section 19.12 [Terminal Coding], page 191), and Emacs will accept those characters. Latin-1 characters can also be input by using the `C-x 8` prefix, see Section 19.17 [Unibyte Mode], page 195.

  With the X Window System, your locale should be set to an appropriate value to make sure Emacs interprets keyboard input correctly; see Section 19.2 [Language Environments], page 179.

The rest of this chapter describes these issues in detail.

19.1 Introduction to International Character Sets

The users of international character sets and scripts have established many more-or-less standard coding systems for storing files. These coding systems are typically *multibyte*, meaning that sequences of two or more bytes are used to represent individual non-ASCII characters.

Internally, Emacs uses its own multibyte character encoding, which is a superset of the *Unicode* standard. This internal encoding allows characters from almost every known script to be intermixed in a single buffer or string. Emacs translates between the multibyte character encoding and various other coding systems when reading and writing files, and when exchanging data with subprocesses.

The command C-h h (view-hello-file) displays the file etc/HELLO, which illustrates various scripts by showing how to say "hello" in many languages. If some characters can't be displayed on your terminal, they appear as '?' or as hollow boxes (see Section 19.16 [Undisplayable Characters], page 195).

Keyboards, even in the countries where these character sets are used, generally don't have keys for all the characters in them. You can insert characters that your keyboard does not support, using C-q (quoted-insert) or C-x 8 RET (insert-char). See Section 4.1 [Inserting Text], page 16. Emacs also supports various *input methods*, typically one for each script or language, which make it easier to type characters in the script. See Section 19.3 [Input Methods], page 181.

The prefix key C-x RET is used for commands that pertain to multibyte characters, coding systems, and input methods.

The command C-x = (what-cursor-position) shows information about the character at point. In addition to the character position, which was described in Section 4.9 [Position Info], page 22, this command displays how the character is encoded. For instance, it displays the following line in the echo area for the character 'c':

```
Char: c (99, #o143, #x63) point=28062 of 36168 (78%) column=53
```

The four values after 'Char:' describe the character that follows point, first by showing it and then by giving its character code in decimal, octal and hex. For a non-ASCII multibyte character, these are followed by 'file' and the character's representation, in hex, in the buffer's coding system, if that coding system encodes the character safely and with a single byte (see Section 19.5 [Coding Systems], page 183). If the character's encoding is longer than one byte, Emacs shows 'file ...'.

As a special case, if the character lies in the range 128 (0200 octal) through 159 (0237 octal), it stands for a "raw" byte that does not correspond to any specific displayable character. Such a "character" lies within the eight-bit-control character set, and is displayed as an escaped octal character code. In this case, C-x = shows 'part of display ...' instead of 'file'.

With a prefix argument (C-u C-x =), this command displays a detailed description of the character in a window:

- The character set name, and the codes that identify the character within that character set; ASCII characters are identified as belonging to the ascii character set.

- The character's script, syntax and categories.

- What keys to type to input the character in the current input method (if it supports the character).

- The character's encodings, both internally in the buffer, and externally if you were to save the file.

- If you are running Emacs on a graphical display, the font name and glyph code for the character. If you are running Emacs on a text terminal, the code(s) sent to the terminal.

- The character's text properties (see Section "Text Properties" in *the Emacs Lisp Reference Manual*), including any non-default faces used to display the character, and any overlays containing it (see Section "Overlays" in *the same manual*).

Here's an example, with some lines folded to fit into this manual:

```
            position: 1 of 1 (0%), column: 0
           character: ê (displayed as ê) (codepoint 234, #o352, #xea)
   preferred charset: unicode (Unicode (ISO10646))
code point in charset: 0xEA
              script: latin
              syntax: w        which means: word
            category: .:Base, L:Left-to-right (strong), c:Chinese,
                      j:Japanese, l:Latin, v:Viet
            to input: type "C-x 8 RET HEX-CODEPOINT" or "C-x 8 RET NAME"
         buffer code: #xC3 #xAA
           file code: #xC3 #xAA (encoded by coding system utf-8-unix)
             display: by this font (glyph code)
    xft:-unknown-DejaVu Sans Mono-normal-normal-
        normal-*-15-*-*-*-m-0-iso10646-1 (#xAC)


Character code properties: customize what to show
  name: LATIN SMALL LETTER E WITH CIRCUMFLEX
  old-name: LATIN SMALL LETTER E CIRCUMFLEX
  general-category: Ll (Letter, Lowercase)
  decomposition: (101 770) ('e' '^')
```

19.2 Language Environments

All supported character sets are supported in Emacs buffers whenever multibyte characters are enabled; there is no need to select a particular language in order to display its characters. However, it is important to select a *language environment* in order to set various defaults. Roughly speaking, the language environment represents a choice of preferred script rather than a choice of language.

The language environment controls which coding systems to recognize when reading text (see Section 19.6 [Recognize Coding], page 185). This applies to files, incoming mail, and any other text you read into Emacs. It may also specify the default coding system to use when you create a file. Each language environment also specifies a default input method.

To select a language environment, customize `current-language-environment` or use the command `M-x set-language-environment`. It makes no difference which buffer is current when you use this command, because the effects apply globally to the Emacs session. See the variable `language-info-alist` for the list of supported language environments, and use the command `C-h L` *lang-env* `RET` (`describe-language-environment`) for more information about the language environment *lang-env*. Supported language environments include:

ASCII, Arabic, Belarusian, Bengali, Brazilian Portuguese, Bulgarian, Burmese, Cham, Chinese-BIG5, Chinese-CNS, Chinese-EUC-TW, Chinese-GB, Chinese-GB18030, Chinese-GBK, Croatian, Cyrillic-ALT, Cyrillic-ISO, Cyrillic-KOI8, Czech, Devanagari, Dutch, English, Esperanto, Ethiopic, French, Georgian, German, Greek, Gujarati, Hebrew, IPA, Italian, Japanese, Kannada, Khmer, Korean, Lao, Latin-1, Latin-2, Latin-3, Latin-4, Latin-5, Latin-6, Latin-7, Latin-8, Latin-9, Latvian, Lithuanian, Malayalam, Oriya, Persian, Polish, Punjabi, Romanian, Russian, Sinhala, Slovak, Slovenian, Spanish, Swedish, TaiViet, Tajik, Tamil, Telugu, Thai, Tibetan, Turkish, UTF-8, Ukrainian, Vietnamese, Welsh, and Windows-1255.

To display the script(s) used by your language environment on a graphical display, you need to have suitable fonts. See Section 19.13 [Fontsets], page 192, for more details about setting up your fonts.

Some operating systems let you specify the character-set locale you are using by setting the locale environment variables `LC_ALL`, `LC_CTYPE`, or `LANG`. (If more than one of these is set, the first one that is nonempty specifies your locale for this purpose.) During startup, Emacs looks up your character-set locale's name in the system locale alias table, matches its canonical name against entries in the value of the variables `locale-charset-language-names` and `locale-language-names` (the former overrides the latter), and selects the corresponding language environment if a match is found. It also adjusts the display table and terminal coding system, the locale coding system, the preferred coding system as needed for the locale, and—last but not least—the way Emacs decodes non-ASCII characters sent by your keyboard.

If you modify the `LC_ALL`, `LC_CTYPE`, or `LANG` environment variables while running Emacs (by using `M-x setenv`), you may want to invoke the `set-locale-environment` function afterwards to readjust the language environment from the new locale.

The `set-locale-environment` function normally uses the preferred coding system established by the language environment to decode system messages. But if your locale matches an entry in the variable `locale-preferred-coding-systems`, Emacs uses the corresponding coding system instead. For example, if the locale 'ja_JP.PCK' matches `japanese-shift-jis` in `locale-preferred-coding-systems`, Emacs uses that encoding even though it might normally use `japanese-iso-8bit`.

You can override the language environment chosen at startup with explicit use of the command `set-language-environment`, or with customization of `current-language-environment` in your init file.

To display information about the effects of a certain language environment *lang-env*, use the command `C-h L` *lang-env* `RET` (`describe-language-environment`). This tells you which languages this language environment is useful for, and lists the character sets, coding systems, and input methods that go with it. It also shows some sample text to illustrate scripts used in this language environment. If you give an empty input for *lang-env*, this command describes the chosen language environment.

You can customize any language environment with the normal hook `set-language-environment-hook`. The command `set-language-environment` runs that hook after setting up the new language environment. The hook functions can test for a specific language environment by checking the variable `current-language-environment`. This hook is where you should put non-default settings for specific language environments, such as coding systems for keyboard input and terminal output, the default input method, etc.

Before it starts to set up the new language environment, `set-language-environment` first runs the hook `exit-language-environment-hook`. This hook is useful for undoing customizations that were made with `set-language-environment-hook`. For instance, if you set up a special key binding in a specific language environment using `set-language-`

environment-hook, you should set up `exit-language-environment-hook` to restore the normal binding for that key.

19.3 Input Methods

An *input method* is a kind of character conversion designed specifically for interactive input. In Emacs, typically each language has its own input method; sometimes several languages that use the same characters can share one input method. A few languages support several input methods.

The simplest kind of input method works by mapping ASCII letters into another alphabet; this allows you to use one other alphabet instead of ASCII. The Greek and Russian input methods work this way.

A more powerful technique is composition: converting sequences of characters into one letter. Many European input methods use composition to produce a single non-ASCII letter from a sequence that consists of a letter followed by accent characters (or vice versa). For example, some methods convert the sequence o ^ into a single accented letter. These input methods have no special commands of their own; all they do is compose sequences of printing characters.

The input methods for syllabic scripts typically use mapping followed by composition. The input methods for Thai and Korean work this way. First, letters are mapped into symbols for particular sounds or tone marks; then, sequences of these that make up a whole syllable are mapped into one syllable sign.

Chinese and Japanese require more complex methods. In Chinese input methods, first you enter the phonetic spelling of a Chinese word (in input method `chinese-py`, among others), or a sequence of portions of the character (input methods `chinese-4corner` and `chinese-sw`, and others). One input sequence typically corresponds to many possible Chinese characters. You select the one you mean using keys such as `C-f`, `C-b`, `C-n`, `C-p` (or the arrow keys), and digits, which have special meanings in this situation.

The possible characters are conceptually arranged in several rows, with each row holding up to 10 alternatives. Normally, Emacs displays just one row at a time, in the echo area; (*i/j*) appears at the beginning, to indicate that this is the *i*th row out of a total of *j* rows. Type `C-n` or `C-p` to display the next row or the previous row.

Type `C-f` and `C-b` to move forward and backward among the alternatives in the current row. As you do this, Emacs highlights the current alternative with a special color; type `C-SPC` to select the current alternative and use it as input. The alternatives in the row are also numbered; the number appears before the alternative. Typing a number selects the associated alternative of the current row and uses it as input.

`TAB` in these Chinese input methods displays a buffer showing all the possible characters at once; then clicking `Mouse-2` on one of them selects that alternative. The keys `C-f`, `C-b`, `C-n`, `C-p`, and digits continue to work as usual, but they do the highlighting in the buffer showing the possible characters, rather than in the echo area.

In Japanese input methods, first you input a whole word using phonetic spelling; then, after the word is in the buffer, Emacs converts it into one or more characters using a large dictionary. One phonetic spelling corresponds to a number of different Japanese words; to select one of them, use `C-n` and `C-p` to cycle through the alternatives.

Sometimes it is useful to cut off input method processing so that the characters you have just entered will not combine with subsequent characters. For example, in input method `latin-1-postfix`, the sequence o ^ combines to form an 'o' with an accent. What if you want to enter them as separate characters?

One way is to type the accent twice; this is a special feature for entering the separate letter and accent. For example, o ^ ^ gives you the two characters 'o^'. Another way is to type another letter after the o—something that won't combine with that—and immediately delete it. For example, you could type o o DEL ^ to get separate 'o' and '^'.

Another method, more general but not quite as easy to type, is to use C-\ C-\ between two characters to stop them from combining. This is the command C-\ (`toggle-input-method`) used twice.

C-\ C-\ is especially useful inside an incremental search, because it stops waiting for more characters to combine, and starts searching for what you have already entered.

To find out how to input the character after point using the current input method, type C-u C-x =. See Section 4.9 [Position Info], page 22.

The variables `input-method-highlight-flag` and `input-method-verbose-flag` control how input methods explain what is happening. If `input-method-highlight-flag` is non-`nil`, the partial sequence is highlighted in the buffer (for most input methods—some disable this feature). If `input-method-verbose-flag` is non-`nil`, the list of possible characters to type next is displayed in the echo area (but not when you are in the minibuffer).

Another facility for typing characters not on your keyboard is by using C-x 8 RET (`insert-char`) to insert a single character based on its Unicode name or code-point; see Section 4.1 [Inserting Text], page 16.

19.4 Selecting an Input Method

C-\   Enable or disable use of the selected input method (`toggle-input-method`).

C-x RET C-\ *method* RET
                   Select a new input method for the current buffer (`set-input-method`).

C-h I *method* RET
C-h C-\ *method* RET
                   Describe the input method *method* (`describe-input-method`). By default, it describes the current input method (if any). This description should give you the full details of how to use any particular input method.

M-x list-input-methods
                   Display a list of all the supported input methods.

To choose an input method for the current buffer, use C-x RET C-\ (`set-input-method`). This command reads the input method name from the minibuffer; the name normally starts with the language environment that it is meant to be used with. The variable `current-input-method` records which input method is selected.

Input methods use various sequences of ASCII characters to stand for non-ASCII characters. Sometimes it is useful to turn off the input method temporarily. To do this, type C-\ (`toggle-input-method`). To reenable the input method, type C-\ again.

If you type C-\ and you have not yet selected an input method, it prompts you to specify one. This has the same effect as using C-x RET C-\ to specify an input method.

When invoked with a numeric argument, as in C-u C-\, toggle-input-method always prompts you for an input method, suggesting the most recently selected one as the default.

Selecting a language environment specifies a default input method for use in various buffers. When you have a default input method, you can select it in the current buffer by typing C-\. The variable default-input-method specifies the default input method (nil means there is none).

In some language environments, which support several different input methods, you might want to use an input method different from the default chosen by set-language-environment. You can instruct Emacs to select a different default input method for a certain language environment, if you wish, by using set-language-environment-hook (see Section 19.2 [Language Environments], page 179). For example:

```
(defun my-chinese-setup ()
  "Set up my private Chinese environment."
  (if (equal current-language-environment "Chinese-GB")
      (setq default-input-method "chinese-tonepy")))
(add-hook 'set-language-environment-hook 'my-chinese-setup)
```

This sets the default input method to be chinese-tonepy whenever you choose a Chinese-GB language environment.

You can instruct Emacs to activate a certain input method automatically. For example:

```
(add-hook 'text-mode-hook
  (lambda () (set-input-method "german-prefix")))
```

This automatically activates the input method "german-prefix" in Text mode.

Some input methods for alphabetic scripts work by (in effect) remapping the keyboard to emulate various keyboard layouts commonly used for those scripts. How to do this remapping properly depends on your actual keyboard layout. To specify which layout your keyboard has, use the command M-x quail-set-keyboard-layout.

You can use the command M-x quail-show-key to show what key (or key sequence) to type in order to input the character following point, using the selected keyboard layout. The command C-u C-x = also shows that information, in addition to other information about the character.

M-x list-input-methods displays a list of all the supported input methods. The list gives information about each input method, including the string that stands for it in the mode line.

19.5 Coding Systems

Users of various languages have established many more-or-less standard coding systems for representing them. Emacs does not use these coding systems internally; instead, it converts from various coding systems to its own system when reading data, and converts the internal coding system to other coding systems when writing data. Conversion is possible in reading or writing files, in sending or receiving from the terminal, and in exchanging data with subprocesses.

Emacs assigns a name to each coding system. Most coding systems are used for one language, and the name of the coding system starts with the language name. Some coding systems are used for several languages; their names usually start with 'iso'. There are also special coding systems, such as `no-conversion`, `raw-text`, and `emacs-internal`.

A special class of coding systems, collectively known as *codepages*, is designed to support text encoded by MS-Windows and MS-DOS software. The names of these coding systems are `cpnnnn`, where *nnnn* is a 3- or 4-digit number of the codepage. You can use these encodings just like any other coding system; for example, to visit a file encoded in codepage 850, type `C-x RET c cp850 RET C-x C-f` *filename* `RET`.

In addition to converting various representations of non-ASCII characters, a coding system can perform end-of-line conversion. Emacs handles three different conventions for how to separate lines in a file: newline ("unix"), carriage-return linefeed ("dos"), and just carriage-return ("mac").

`C-h C` *coding* `RET`
>	Describe coding system *coding* (`describe-coding-system`).

`C-h C RET`	Describe the coding systems currently in use.

`M-x list-coding-systems`
>	Display a list of all the supported coding systems.

The command `C-h C` (`describe-coding-system`) displays information about particular coding systems, including the end-of-line conversion specified by those coding systems. You can specify a coding system name as the argument; alternatively, with an empty argument, it describes the coding systems currently selected for various purposes, both in the current buffer and as the defaults, and the priority list for recognizing coding systems (see Section 19.6 [Recognize Coding], page 185).

To display a list of all the supported coding systems, type `M-x list-coding-systems`. The list gives information about each coding system, including the letter that stands for it in the mode line (see Section 1.3 [Mode Line], page 8).

Each of the coding systems that appear in this list—except for `no-conversion`, which means no conversion of any kind—specifies how and whether to convert printing characters, but leaves the choice of end-of-line conversion to be decided based on the contents of each file. For example, if the file appears to use the sequence carriage-return linefeed to separate lines, DOS end-of-line conversion will be used.

Each of the listed coding systems has three variants, which specify exactly what to do for end-of-line conversion:

`...-unix`	Don't do any end-of-line conversion; assume the file uses newline to separate lines. (This is the convention normally used on Unix and GNU systems, and Mac OS X.)

`...-dos`	Assume the file uses carriage-return linefeed to separate lines, and do the appropriate conversion. (This is the convention normally used on Microsoft systems.[1])

---

[1] It is also specified for MIME 'text/*' bodies and in other network transport contexts. It is different from the SGML reference syntax record-start/record-end format, which Emacs doesn't support directly.

`...-mac`   Assume the file uses carriage-return to separate lines, and do the appropriate conversion. (This was the convention used on the Macintosh system prior to OS X.)

These variant coding systems are omitted from the `list-coding-systems` display for brevity, since they are entirely predictable. For example, the coding system `iso-latin-1` has variants `iso-latin-1-unix`, `iso-latin-1-dos` and `iso-latin-1-mac`.

The coding systems `unix`, `dos`, and `mac` are aliases for `undecided-unix`, `undecided-dos`, and `undecided-mac`, respectively. These coding systems specify only the end-of-line conversion, and leave the character code conversion to be deduced from the text itself.

The coding system `raw-text` is good for a file which is mainly ASCII text, but may contain byte values above 127 that are not meant to encode non-ASCII characters. With `raw-text`, Emacs copies those byte values unchanged, and sets `enable-multibyte-characters` to `nil` in the current buffer so that they will be interpreted properly. `raw-text` handles end-of-line conversion in the usual way, based on the data encountered, and has the usual three variants to specify the kind of end-of-line conversion to use.

In contrast, the coding system `no-conversion` specifies no character code conversion at all—none for non-ASCII byte values and none for end of line. This is useful for reading or writing binary files, tar files, and other files that must be examined verbatim. It, too, sets `enable-multibyte-characters` to `nil`.

The easiest way to edit a file with no conversion of any kind is with the `M-x find-file-literally` command. This uses `no-conversion`, and also suppresses other Emacs features that might convert the file contents before you see them. See Section 15.2 [Visiting], page 123.

The coding system `emacs-internal` (or `utf-8-emacs`, which is equivalent) means that the file contains non-ASCII characters stored with the internal Emacs encoding. This coding system handles end-of-line conversion based on the data encountered, and has the usual three variants to specify the kind of end-of-line conversion.

19.6 Recognizing Coding Systems

Whenever Emacs reads a given piece of text, it tries to recognize which coding system to use. This applies to files being read, output from subprocesses, text from X selections, etc. Emacs can select the right coding system automatically most of the time—once you have specified your preferences.

Some coding systems can be recognized or distinguished by which byte sequences appear in the data. However, there are coding systems that cannot be distinguished, not even potentially. For example, there is no way to distinguish between Latin-1 and Latin-2; they use the same byte values with different meanings.

Emacs handles this situation by means of a priority list of coding systems. Whenever Emacs reads a file, if you do not specify the coding system to use, Emacs checks the data against each coding system, starting with the first in priority and working down the list, until it finds a coding system that fits the data. Then it converts the file contents assuming that they are represented in this coding system.

The priority list of coding systems depends on the selected language environment (see Section 19.2 [Language Environments], page 179). For example, if you use French, you probably want Emacs to prefer Latin-1 to Latin-2; if you use Czech, you probably want Latin-2 to be preferred. This is one of the reasons to specify a language environment.

However, you can alter the coding system priority list in detail with the command M-x prefer-coding-system. This command reads the name of a coding system from the minibuffer, and adds it to the front of the priority list, so that it is preferred to all others. If you use this command several times, each use adds one element to the front of the priority list.

If you use a coding system that specifies the end-of-line conversion type, such as iso-8859-1-dos, what this means is that Emacs should attempt to recognize iso-8859-1 with priority, and should use DOS end-of-line conversion when it does recognize iso-8859-1.

Sometimes a file name indicates which coding system to use for the file. The variable file-coding-system-alist specifies this correspondence. There is a special function modify-coding-system-alist for adding elements to this list. For example, to read and write all '.txt' files using the coding system chinese-iso-8bit, you can execute this Lisp expression:

```
(modify-coding-system-alist 'file "\\.txt\\'" 'chinese-iso-8bit)
```

The first argument should be file, the second argument should be a regular expression that determines which files this applies to, and the third argument says which coding system to use for these files.

Emacs recognizes which kind of end-of-line conversion to use based on the contents of the file: if it sees only carriage-returns, or only carriage-return linefeed sequences, then it chooses the end-of-line conversion accordingly. You can inhibit the automatic use of end-of-line conversion by setting the variable inhibit-eol-conversion to non-nil. If you do that, DOS-style files will be displayed with the '^M' characters visible in the buffer; some people prefer this to the more subtle '(DOS)' end-of-line type indication near the left edge of the mode line (see Section 1.3 [Mode Line], page 8).

By default, the automatic detection of coding system is sensitive to escape sequences. If Emacs sees a sequence of characters that begin with an escape character, and the sequence is valid as an ISO-2022 code, that tells Emacs to use one of the ISO-2022 encodings to decode the file.

However, there may be cases that you want to read escape sequences in a file as is. In such a case, you can set the variable inhibit-iso-escape-detection to non-nil. Then the code detection ignores any escape sequences, and never uses an ISO-2022 encoding. The result is that all escape sequences become visible in the buffer.

The default value of inhibit-iso-escape-detection is nil. We recommend that you not change it permanently, only for one specific operation. That's because some Emacs Lisp source files in the Emacs distribution contain non-ASCII characters encoded in the coding system iso-2022-7bit, and they won't be decoded correctly when you visit those files if you suppress the escape sequence detection.

The variables auto-coding-alist and auto-coding-regexp-alist are the strongest way to specify the coding system for certain patterns of file names, or for files containing certain patterns, respectively. These variables even override '-*-coding:-*-' tags in the file itself (see Section 19.7 [Specify Coding], page 187). For example, Emacs uses auto-coding-alist for tar and archive files, to prevent it from being confused by a '-*-coding:-*-' tag in a member of the archive and thinking it applies to the archive file as a whole.

Another way to specify a coding system is with the variable `auto-coding-functions`. For example, one of the builtin `auto-coding-functions` detects the encoding for XML files. Unlike the previous two, this variable does not override any '-*-coding:-*-' tag.

19.7 Specifying a File's Coding System

If Emacs recognizes the encoding of a file incorrectly, you can reread the file using the correct coding system with `C-x RET r` (`revert-buffer-with-coding-system`). This command prompts for the coding system to use. To see what coding system Emacs actually used to decode the file, look at the coding system mnemonic letter near the left edge of the mode line (see Section 1.3 [Mode Line], page 8), or type `C-h C` (`describe-coding-system`).

You can specify the coding system for a particular file in the file itself, using the '-*-...-*-' construct at the beginning, or a local variables list at the end (see Section 33.2.4 [File Variables], page 424). You do this by defining a value for the "variable" named `coding`. Emacs does not really have a variable `coding`; instead of setting a variable, this uses the specified coding system for the file. For example, '-*-mode: C; coding: latin-1;-*-' specifies use of the Latin-1 coding system, as well as C mode. When you specify the coding explicitly in the file, that overrides `file-coding-system-alist`.

19.8 Choosing Coding Systems for Output

Once Emacs has chosen a coding system for a buffer, it stores that coding system in `buffer-file-coding-system`. That makes it the default for operations that write from this buffer into a file, such as `save-buffer` and `write-region`. You can specify a different coding system for further file output from the buffer using `set-buffer-file-coding-system` (see Section 19.9 [Text Coding], page 188).

You can insert any character Emacs supports into any Emacs buffer, but most coding systems can only handle a subset of these characters. Therefore, it's possible that the characters you insert cannot be encoded with the coding system that will be used to save the buffer. For example, you could visit a text file in Polish, encoded in `iso-8859-2`, and add some Russian words to it. When you save that buffer, Emacs cannot use the current value of `buffer-file-coding-system`, because the characters you added cannot be encoded by that coding system.

When that happens, Emacs tries the most-preferred coding system (set by `M-x prefer-coding-system` or `M-x set-language-environment`). If that coding system can safely encode all of the characters in the buffer, Emacs uses it, and stores its value in `buffer-file-coding-system`. Otherwise, Emacs displays a list of coding systems suitable for encoding the buffer's contents, and asks you to choose one of those coding systems.

If you insert the unsuitable characters in a mail message, Emacs behaves a bit differently. It additionally checks whether the most-preferred coding system is recommended for use in MIME messages; if not, it informs you of this fact and prompts you for another coding system. This is so you won't inadvertently send a message encoded in a way that your recipient's mail software will have difficulty decoding. (You can still use an unsuitable coding system if you enter its name at the prompt.)

When you send a mail message (see Chapter 29 [Sending Mail], page 350), Emacs has four different ways to determine the coding system to use for encoding the message text. It tries the buffer's own value of `buffer-file-coding-system`, if that is non-`nil`. Otherwise, it uses the value of `sendmail-coding-system`, if that is non-`nil`. The third way is to use the default coding system for new files, which is controlled by your choice of language environment, if that is non-`nil`. If all of these three values are `nil`, Emacs encodes outgoing mail using the Latin-1 coding system.

19.9 Specifying a Coding System for File Text

In cases where Emacs does not automatically choose the right coding system for a file's contents, you can use these commands to specify one:

C-x RET f *coding* RET

> Use coding system *coding* to save or revisit the file in the current buffer (`set-buffer-file-coding-system`).

C-x RET c *coding* RET

> Specify coding system *coding* for the immediately following command (`universal-coding-system-argument`).

C-x RET r *coding* RET

> Revisit the current file using the coding system *coding* (`revert-buffer-with-coding-system`).

M-x recode-region RET *right* RET *wrong* RET

> Convert a region that was decoded using coding system *wrong*, decoding it using coding system *right* instead.

The command C-x RET f (`set-buffer-file-coding-system`) sets the file coding system for the current buffer (i.e., the coding system to use when saving or reverting the file). You specify which coding system using the minibuffer. You can also invoke this command by clicking with `Mouse-3` on the coding system indicator in the mode line (see Section 1.3 [Mode Line], page 8).

If you specify a coding system that cannot handle all the characters in the buffer, Emacs will warn you about the troublesome characters, and ask you to choose another coding system, when you try to save the buffer (see Section 19.8 [Output Coding], page 187).

You can also use this command to specify the end-of-line conversion (see Section 19.5 [Coding Systems], page 183) for encoding the current buffer. For example, C-x RET f dos RET will cause Emacs to save the current buffer's text with DOS-style carriage-return linefeed line endings.

Another way to specify the coding system for a file is when you visit the file. First use the command C-x RET c (`universal-coding-system-argument`); this command uses the minibuffer to read a coding system name. After you exit the minibuffer, the specified coding system is used for *the immediately following command.*

So if the immediately following command is C-x C-f, for example, it reads the file using that coding system (and records the coding system for when you later save the file). Or if the immediately following command is C-x C-w, it writes the file using that coding system. When you specify the coding system for saving in this way, instead of with C-x RET f, there is no warning if the buffer contains characters that the coding system cannot handle.

Other file commands affected by a specified coding system include C-x i and C-x C-v, as well as the other-window variants of C-x C-f. C-x RET c also affects commands that start subprocesses, including M-x shell (see Section 31.4 [Shell], page 383). If the immediately following command does not use the coding system, then C-x RET c ultimately has no effect.

An easy way to visit a file with no conversion is with the M-x find-file-literally command. See Section 15.2 [Visiting], page 123.

The default value of the variable buffer-file-coding-system specifies the choice of coding system to use when you create a new file. It applies when you find a new file, and when you create a buffer and then save it in a file. Selecting a language environment typically sets this variable to a good choice of default coding system for that language environment.

If you visit a file with a wrong coding system, you can correct this with C-x RET r (revert-buffer-with-coding-system). This visits the current file again, using a coding system you specify.

If a piece of text has already been inserted into a buffer using the wrong coding system, you can redo the decoding of it using M-x recode-region. This prompts you for the proper coding system, then for the wrong coding system that was actually used, and does the conversion. It first encodes the region using the wrong coding system, then decodes it again using the proper coding system.

19.10 Coding Systems for Interprocess Communication

This section explains how to specify coding systems for use in communication with other processes.

C-x RET x *coding* RET

> Use coding system *coding* for transferring selections to and from other graphical applications (set-selection-coding-system).

C-x RET X *coding* RET

> Use coding system *coding* for transferring *one* selection—the next one—to or from another graphical application (set-next-selection-coding-system).

C-x RET p *input-coding* RET *output-coding* RET

> Use coding systems *input-coding* and *output-coding* for subprocess input and output in the current buffer (set-buffer-process-coding-system).

The command C-x RET x (set-selection-coding-system) specifies the coding system for sending selected text to other windowing applications, and for receiving the text of selections made in other applications. This command applies to all subsequent selections, until you override it by using the command again. The command C-x RET X (set-next-selection-coding-system) specifies the coding system for the next selection made in Emacs or read by Emacs.

The variable x-select-request-type specifies the data type to request from the X Window System for receiving text selections from other applications. If the value is nil (the default), Emacs tries UTF8_STRING and COMPOUND_TEXT, in this order, and uses various heuristics to choose the more appropriate of the two results; if none of these succeed, Emacs falls back on STRING. If the value of x-select-request-type is one of the symbols

`COMPOUND_TEXT`, `UTF8_STRING`, `STRING`, or `TEXT`, Emacs uses only that request type. If the value is a list of some of these symbols, Emacs tries only the request types in the list, in order, until one of them succeeds, or until the list is exhausted.

The command `C-x RET p` (`set-buffer-process-coding-system`) specifies the coding system for input and output to a subprocess. This command applies to the current buffer; normally, each subprocess has its own buffer, and thus you can use this command to specify translation to and from a particular subprocess by giving the command in the corresponding buffer.

You can also use `C-x RET c` (`universal-coding-system-argument`) just before the command that runs or starts a subprocess, to specify the coding system for communicating with that subprocess. See Section 19.9 [Text Coding], page 188.

The default for translation of process input and output depends on the current language environment.

The variable `locale-coding-system` specifies a coding system to use when encoding and decoding system strings such as system error messages and `format-time-string` formats and time stamps. That coding system is also used for decoding non-ASCII keyboard input on the X Window System. You should choose a coding system that is compatible with the underlying system's text representation, which is normally specified by one of the environment variables `LC_ALL`, `LC_CTYPE`, and `LANG`. (The first one, in the order specified above, whose value is nonempty is the one that determines the text representation.)

19.11 Coding Systems for File Names

`C-x RET F` *coding* `RET`
> Use coding system *coding* for encoding and decoding file names (`set-file-name-coding-system`).

The command `C-x RET F` (`set-file-name-coding-system`) specifies a coding system to use for encoding file *names*. It has no effect on reading and writing the *contents* of files.

In fact, all this command does is set the value of the variable `file-name-coding-system`. If you set the variable to a coding system name (as a Lisp symbol or a string), Emacs encodes file names using that coding system for all file operations. This makes it possible to use non-ASCII characters in file names—or, at least, those non-ASCII characters that the specified coding system can encode.

If `file-name-coding-system` is `nil`, Emacs uses a default coding system determined by the selected language environment, and stored in the `default-file-name-coding-system` variable. In the default language environment, non-ASCII characters in file names are not encoded specially; they appear in the file system using the internal Emacs representation.

When Emacs runs on MS-Windows versions that are descendants of the NT family (Windows 2000, XP, Vista, Windows 7, and Windows 8), the value of `file-name-coding-system` is largely ignored, as Emacs by default uses APIs that allow to pass Unicode file names directly. By contrast, on Windows 9X, file names are encoded using `file-name-coding-system`, which should be set to the codepage (see Section 19.5 [Coding Systems], page 183) pertinent for the current system locale. The value of the variable `w32-unicode-filenames` controls whether Emacs uses the Unicode APIs when it calls OS functions that accept file names. This variable is set by the startup code to `nil` on Windows 9X, and to `t` on newer versions of MS-Windows.

Warning: if you change `file-name-coding-system` (or the language environment) in the middle of an Emacs session, problems can result if you have already visited files whose names were encoded using the earlier coding system and cannot be encoded (or are encoded differently) under the new coding system. If you try to save one of these buffers under the visited file name, saving may use the wrong file name, or it may encounter an error. If such a problem happens, use `C-x C-w` to specify a new file name for that buffer.

If a mistake occurs when encoding a file name, use the command `M-x recode-file-name` to change the file name's coding system. This prompts for an existing file name, its old coding system, and the coding system to which you wish to convert.

19.12 Coding Systems for Terminal I/O

`C-x RET t` *coding* `RET`

> Use coding system *coding* for terminal output (`set-terminal-coding-system`).

`C-x RET k` *coding* `RET`

> Use coding system *coding* for keyboard input (`set-keyboard-coding-system`).

The command `C-x RET t` (`set-terminal-coding-system`) specifies the coding system for terminal output. If you specify a character code for terminal output, all characters output to the terminal are translated into that coding system.

This feature is useful for certain character-only terminals built to support specific languages or character sets—for example, European terminals that support one of the ISO Latin character sets. You need to specify the terminal coding system when using multibyte text, so that Emacs knows which characters the terminal can actually handle.

By default, output to the terminal is not translated at all, unless Emacs can deduce the proper coding system from your terminal type or your locale specification (see Section 19.2 [Language Environments], page 179).

The command `C-x RET k` (`set-keyboard-coding-system`), or the variable `keyboard-coding-system`, specifies the coding system for keyboard input. Character-code translation of keyboard input is useful for terminals with keys that send non-ASCII graphic characters—for example, some terminals designed for ISO Latin-1 or subsets of it.

By default, keyboard input is translated based on your system locale setting. If your terminal does not really support the encoding implied by your locale (for example, if you find it inserts a non-ASCII character if you type `M-i`), you will need to set `keyboard-coding-system` to `nil` to turn off encoding. You can do this by putting

```
(set-keyboard-coding-system nil)
```

in your init file.

There is a similarity between using a coding system translation for keyboard input, and using an input method: both define sequences of keyboard input that translate into single characters. However, input methods are designed to be convenient for interactive use by humans, and the sequences that are translated are typically sequences of ASCII printing characters. Coding systems typically translate sequences of non-graphic characters.

19.13 Fontsets

A font typically defines shapes for a single alphabet or script. Therefore, displaying the entire range of scripts that Emacs supports requires a collection of many fonts. In Emacs, such a collection is called a *fontset*. A fontset is defined by a list of font specifications, each assigned to handle a range of character codes, and may fall back on another fontset for characters that are not covered by the fonts it specifies.

Each fontset has a name, like a font. However, while fonts are stored in the system and the available font names are defined by the system, fontsets are defined within Emacs itself. Once you have defined a fontset, you can use it within Emacs by specifying its name, anywhere that you could use a single font. Of course, Emacs fontsets can use only the fonts that the system supports. If some characters appear on the screen as empty boxes or hex codes, this means that the fontset in use for them has no font for those characters. In this case, or if the characters are shown, but not as well as you would like, you may need to install extra fonts. Your operating system may have optional fonts that you can install; or you can install the GNU Intlfonts package, which includes fonts for most supported scripts.[2]

Emacs creates three fontsets automatically: the *standard fontset*, the *startup fontset* and the *default fontset*. The default fontset is most likely to have fonts for a wide variety of non-ASCII characters, and is the default fallback for the other two fontsets, and if you set a default font rather than fontset. However, it does not specify font family names, so results can be somewhat random if you use it directly. You can specify use of a particular fontset by starting Emacs with the '-fn' option. For example,

```
emacs -fn fontset-standard
```

You can also specify a fontset with the 'Font' resource (see Appendix D [X Resources], page 493).

If no fontset is specified for use, then Emacs uses an ASCII font, with 'fontset-default' as a fallback for characters the font does not cover. The standard fontset is only used if explicitly requested, despite its name.

A fontset does not necessarily specify a font for every character code. If a fontset specifies no font for a certain character, or if it specifies a font that does not exist on your system, then it cannot display that character properly. It will display that character as a hex code or thin space or an empty box instead. (See Section 11.19 [glyphless characters], page 85, for details.)

19.14 Defining fontsets

When running on X, Emacs creates a standard fontset automatically according to the value of `standard-fontset-spec`. This fontset's name is

```
-*-fixed-medium-r-normal-*-16-*-*-*-*-*-fontset-standard
```

or just 'fontset-standard' for short.

---

[2] If you run Emacs on X, you may need to inform the X server about the location of the newly installed fonts with commands such as:

```
xset fp+ /usr/local/share/emacs/fonts
xset fp rehash
```

On GNUstep and Mac OS X, the standard fontset is created using the value of `ns-standard-fontset-spec`, and on MS Windows it is created using the value of `w32-standard-fontset-spec`.

Bold, italic, and bold-italic variants of the standard fontset are created automatically. Their names have 'bold' instead of 'medium', or 'i' instead of 'r', or both.

Emacs generates a fontset automatically, based on any default ASCII font that you specify with the 'Font' resource or the '-fn' argument, or the default font that Emacs found when it started. This is the *startup fontset* and its name is `fontset-startup`. It does this by replacing the *charset_registry* field with 'fontset', and replacing *charset_encoding* field with 'startup', then using the resulting string to specify a fontset.

For instance, if you start Emacs with a font of this form,

```
emacs -fn "*courier-medium-r-normal--14-140-*-iso8859-1"
```

Emacs generates the following fontset and uses it for the initial X window frame:

```
-*-courier-medium-r-normal-*-14-140-*-*-*-*-fontset-startup
```

The startup fontset will use the font that you specify, or a variant with a different registry and encoding, for all the characters that are supported by that font, and fallback on 'fontset-default' for other characters.

With the X resource 'Emacs.Font', you can specify a fontset name just like an actual font name. But be careful not to specify a fontset name in a wildcard resource like 'Emacs*Font'—that wildcard specification matches various other resources, such as for menus, and menus cannot handle fontsets. See Appendix D [X Resources], page 493.

You can specify additional fontsets using X resources named 'Fontset-*n*', where *n* is an integer starting from 0. The resource value should have this form:

```
fontpattern, [charset:font]...
```

fontpattern should have the form of a standard X font name (see the previous fontset-startup example), except for the last two fields. They should have the form 'fontset-*alias*'.

The fontset has two names, one long and one short. The long name is *fontpattern*. The short name is 'fontset-*alias*'. You can refer to the fontset by either name.

The construct '*charset:font*' specifies which font to use (in this fontset) for one particular character set. Here, *charset* is the name of a character set, and *font* is the font to use for that character set. You can use this construct any number of times in defining one fontset.

For the other character sets, Emacs chooses a font based on *fontpattern*. It replaces 'fontset-*alias*' with values that describe the character set. For the ASCII character font, 'fontset-*alias*' is replaced with 'ISO8859-1'.

In addition, when several consecutive fields are wildcards, Emacs collapses them into a single wildcard. This is to prevent use of auto-scaled fonts. Fonts made by scaling larger fonts are not usable for editing, and scaling a smaller font is not also useful, because it is better to use the smaller font in its own size, which is what Emacs does.

Thus if *fontpattern* is this,

```
-*-fixed-medium-r-normal-*-24-*-*-*-*-*-fontset-24
```

the font specification for ASCII characters would be this:

```
-*-fixed-medium-r-normal-*-24-*-ISO8859-1
```

and the font specification for Chinese GB2312 characters would be this:

```
-*-fixed-medium-r-normal-*-24-*-gb2312*-*
```

You may not have any Chinese font matching the above font specification. Most X distributions include only Chinese fonts that have 'song ti' or 'fangsong ti' in the *family* field. In such a case, 'Fontset-*n*' can be specified as:

```
Emacs.Fontset-0: -*-fixed-medium-r-normal-*-24-*-*-*-*-*-fontset-24,\
        chinese-gb2312:-*-*-medium-r-normal-*-24-*-gb2312*-*
```

Then, the font specifications for all but Chinese GB2312 characters have 'fixed' in the *family* field, and the font specification for Chinese GB2312 characters has a wild card '*' in the *family* field.

The function that processes the fontset resource value to create the fontset is called create-fontset-from-fontset-spec. You can also call this function explicitly to create a fontset.

See Section 18.8 [Fonts], page 168, for more information about font naming.

19.15 Modifying Fontsets

Fontsets do not always have to be created from scratch. If only minor changes are required it may be easier to modify an existing fontset. Modifying 'fontset-default' will also affect other fontsets that use it as a fallback, so can be an effective way of fixing problems with the fonts that Emacs chooses for a particular script.

Fontsets can be modified using the function set-fontset-font, specifying a character, a charset, a script, or a range of characters to modify the font for, and a font specification for the font to be used. Some examples are:

```
;; Use Liberation Mono for latin-3 charset.
(set-fontset-font "fontset-default" 'iso-8859-3
                  "Liberation Mono")

;; Prefer a big5 font for han characters
(set-fontset-font "fontset-default"
                  'han (font-spec :registry "big5")
                  nil 'prepend)

;; Use DejaVu Sans Mono as a fallback in fontset-startup
;; before resorting to fontset-default.
(set-fontset-font "fontset-startup" nil "DejaVu Sans Mono"
                  nil 'append)

;; Use MyPrivateFont for the Unicode private use area.
(set-fontset-font "fontset-default" '(#xe000 . #xf8ff)
                  "MyPrivateFont")
```

19.16 Undisplayable Characters

There may be some non-ASCII characters that your terminal cannot display. Most text terminals support just a single character set (use the variable `default-terminal-coding-system` to tell Emacs which one, Section 19.12 [Terminal Coding], page 191); characters that can't be encoded in that coding system are displayed as '?' by default.

Graphical displays can display a broader range of characters, but you may not have fonts installed for all of them; characters that have no font appear as a hollow box.

If you use Latin-1 characters but your terminal can't display Latin-1, you can arrange to display mnemonic ASCII sequences instead, e.g., '"o' for o-umlaut. Load the library `iso-ascii` to do this.

If your terminal can display Latin-1, you can display characters from other European character sets using a mixture of equivalent Latin-1 characters and ASCII mnemonics. Customize the variable `latin1-display` to enable this. The mnemonic ASCII sequences mostly correspond to those of the prefix input methods.

19.17 Unibyte Editing Mode

The ISO 8859 Latin-n character sets define character codes in the range 0240 to 0377 octal (160 to 255 decimal) to handle the accented letters and punctuation needed by various European languages (and some non-European ones). Note that Emacs considers bytes with codes in this range as raw bytes, not as characters, even in a unibyte buffer, i.e., if you disable multibyte characters. However, Emacs can still handle these character codes as if they belonged to *one* of the single-byte character sets at a time. To specify *which* of these codes to use, invoke `M-x set-language-environment` and specify a suitable language environment such as 'Latin-n'. See Section "Disabling Multibyte Characters" in *GNU Emacs Lisp Reference Manual*.

Emacs can also display bytes in the range 160 to 255 as readable characters, provided the terminal or font in use supports them. This works automatically. On a graphical display, Emacs can also display single-byte characters through fontsets, in effect by displaying the equivalent multibyte characters according to the current language environment. To request this, set the variable `unibyte-display-via-language-environment` to a non-`nil` value. Note that setting this only affects how these bytes are displayed, but does not change the fundamental fact that Emacs treats them as raw bytes, not as characters.

If your terminal does not support display of the Latin-1 character set, Emacs can display these characters as ASCII sequences which at least give you a clear idea of what the characters are. To do this, load the library `iso-ascii`. Similar libraries for other Latin-n character sets could be implemented, but have not been so far.

Normally non-ISO-8859 characters (decimal codes between 128 and 159 inclusive) are displayed as octal escapes. You can change this for non-standard "extended" versions of ISO-8859 character sets by using the function `standard-display-8bit` in the `disp-table` library.

There are two ways to input single-byte non-ASCII characters:

- You can use an input method for the selected language environment. See Section 19.3 [Input Methods], page 181. When you use an input method in a unibyte buffer, the non-ASCII character you specify with it is converted to unibyte.

- If your keyboard can generate character codes 128 (decimal) and up, representing non-ASCII characters, you can type those character codes directly.

  On a graphical display, you should not need to do anything special to use these keys; they should simply work. On a text terminal, you should use the command `M-x set-keyboard-coding-system` or customize the variable `keyboard-coding-system` to specify which coding system your keyboard uses (see Section 19.12 [Terminal Coding], page 191). Enabling this feature will probably require you to use `ESC` to type Meta characters; however, on a console terminal or in `xterm`, you can arrange for Meta to be converted to `ESC` and still be able type 8-bit characters present directly on the keyboard or using `Compose` or `AltGr` keys. See Section 2.1 [User Input], page 11.

- For Latin-1 only, you can use the key `C-x 8` as a "compose character" prefix for entry of non-ASCII Latin-1 printing characters. `C-x 8` is good for insertion (in the minibuffer as well as other buffers), for searching, and in any other context where a key sequence is allowed.

  `C-x 8` works by loading the `iso-transl` library. Once that library is loaded, the `Alt` modifier key, if the keyboard has one, serves the same purpose as `C-x 8`: use `Alt` together with an accent character to modify the following letter. In addition, if the keyboard has keys for the Latin-1 "dead accent characters", they too are defined to compose with the following character, once `iso-transl` is loaded.

  Use `C-x 8 C-h` to list all the available `C-x 8` translations.

19.18 Charsets

In Emacs, *charset* is short for "character set". Emacs supports most popular charsets (such as `ascii`, `iso-8859-1`, `cp1250`, `big5`, and `unicode`), in addition to some charsets of its own (such as `emacs`, `unicode-bmp`, and `eight-bit`). All supported characters belong to one or more charsets.

Emacs normally "does the right thing" with respect to charsets, so that you don't have to worry about them. However, it is sometimes helpful to know some of the underlying details about charsets.

One example is font selection (see Section 18.8 [Fonts], page 168). Each language environment (see Section 19.2 [Language Environments], page 179) defines a "priority list" for the various charsets. When searching for a font, Emacs initially attempts to find one that can display the highest-priority charsets. For instance, in the Japanese language environment, the charset `japanese-jisx0208` has the highest priority, so Emacs tries to use a font whose `registry` property is 'JISX0208.1983-0'.

There are two commands that can be used to obtain information about charsets. The command `M-x list-charset-chars` prompts for a charset name, and displays all the characters in that character set. The command `M-x describe-character-set` prompts for a charset name, and displays information about that charset, including its internal representation within Emacs.

`M-x list-character-sets` displays a list of all supported charsets. The list gives the names of charsets and additional information to identity each charset; see the International Register of Coded Character Sets (`http://www.itscj.ipsj.or.jp/ISO-IR/`) for more details. In this list, charsets are divided into two categories: *normal charsets* are listed first, followed by *supplementary charsets*. A supplementary charset is one that is used to define another charset (as a parent or a subset), or to provide backward-compatibility for older Emacs versions.

To find out which charset a character in the buffer belongs to, put point before it and type C-u C-x = (see Section 19.1 [International Chars], page 177).

19.19 Bidirectional Editing

Emacs supports editing text written in scripts, such as Arabic and Hebrew, whose natural ordering of horizontal text for display is from right to left. However, digits and Latin text embedded in these scripts are still displayed left to right. It is also not uncommon to have small portions of text in Arabic or Hebrew embedded in an otherwise Latin document; e.g., as comments and strings in a program source file. For these reasons, text that uses these scripts is actually *bidirectional*: a mixture of runs of left-to-right and right-to-left characters.

This section describes the facilities and options provided by Emacs for editing bidirectional text.

Emacs stores right-to-left and bidirectional text in the so-called *logical* (or *reading*) order: the buffer or string position of the first character you read precedes that of the next character. Reordering of bidirectional text into the *visual* order happens at display time. As result, character positions no longer increase monotonically with their positions on display. Emacs implements the Unicode Bidirectional Algorithm described in the Unicode Standard Annex #9, for reordering of bidirectional text for display.

The buffer-local variable `bidi-display-reordering` controls whether text in the buffer is reordered for display. If its value is non-`nil`, Emacs reorders characters that have right-to-left directionality when they are displayed. The default value is `t`.

Each paragraph of bidirectional text can have its own *base direction*, either right-to-left or left-to-right. (Paragraph boundaries are empty lines, i.e., lines consisting entirely of whitespace characters.) Text in left-to-right paragraphs begins on the screen at the left margin of the window and is truncated or continued when it reaches the right margin. By contrast, text in right-to-left paragraphs is displayed starting at the right margin and is continued or truncated at the left margin.

Emacs determines the base direction of each paragraph dynamically, based on the text at the beginning of the paragraph. However, sometimes a buffer may need to force a certain base direction for its paragraphs. The variable `bidi-paragraph-direction`, if non-`nil`, disables the dynamic determination of the base direction, and instead forces all paragraphs in the buffer to have the direction specified by its buffer-local value. The value can be either `right-to-left` or `left-to-right`. Any other value is interpreted as `nil`.

Alternatively, you can control the base direction of a paragraph by inserting special formatting characters in front of the paragraph. The special character RIGHT-TO-LEFT MARK, or RLM, forces the right-to-left direction on the following paragraph, while LEFT-TO-RIGHT MARK, or LRM forces the left-to-right direction. (You can use C-x 8 RET to insert these characters.) In a GUI session, the LRM and RLM characters display as very thin blank characters; on text terminals they display as blanks.

Because characters are reordered for display, Emacs commands that operate in the logical order or on stretches of buffer positions may produce unusual effects. For example, C-f and

`C-b` commands move point in the logical order, so the cursor will sometimes jump when point traverses reordered bidirectional text. Similarly, a highlighted region covering a contiguous range of character positions may look discontinuous if the region spans reordered text. This is normal and similar to the behavior of other programs that support bidirectional text. If you set `visual-order-cursor-movement` to a non-`nil` value, cursor motion by the arrow keys follows the visual order on screen (see Section 4.2 [Moving Point], page 17).

20 Major and Minor Modes

Emacs contains many *editing modes* that alter its basic behavior in useful ways. These are divided into *major modes* and *minor modes*.

Major modes provide specialized facilities for working on a particular file type, such as a C source file (see Chapter 23 [Programs], page 240), or a particular type of non-file buffer, such as a shell buffer (see Section 31.4 [Shell], page 383). Major modes are mutually exclusive; each buffer has one and only one major mode at any time.

Minor modes are optional features which you can turn on or off, not necessarily specific to a type of file or buffer. For example, Auto Fill mode is a minor mode in which SPC breaks lines between words as you type (see Section 22.5.1 [Auto Fill], page 212). Minor modes are independent of one another, and of the selected major mode.

20.1 Major Modes

Every buffer possesses a major mode, which determines the editing behavior of Emacs while that buffer is current. The mode line normally shows the name of the current major mode, in parentheses (see Section 1.3 [Mode Line], page 8).

The least specialized major mode is called *Fundamental mode*. This mode has no mode-specific redefinitions or variable settings, so that each Emacs command behaves in its most general manner, and each user option variable is in its default state.

For editing text of a specific type that Emacs knows about, such as Lisp code or English text, you typically use a more specialized major mode, such as Lisp mode or Text mode. Most major modes fall into three major groups. The first group contains modes for normal text, either plain or with mark-up. It includes Text mode, HTML mode, SGML mode, TEX mode and Outline mode. The second group contains modes for specific programming languages. These include Lisp mode (which has several variants), C mode, Fortran mode, and others. The third group consists of major modes that are not associated directly with files; they are used in buffers created for specific purposes by Emacs, such as Dired mode for buffers made by Dired (see Chapter 27 [Dired], page 315), Message mode for buffers made by C-x m (see Chapter 29 [Sending Mail], page 350), and Shell mode for buffers used to communicate with an inferior shell process (see Section 31.4.2 [Interactive Shell], page 384).

Usually, the major mode is automatically set by Emacs, when you first visit a file or create a buffer (see Section 20.3 [Choosing Modes], page 202). You can explicitly select a new major mode by using an M-x command. Take the name of the mode and add -mode to get the name of the command to select that mode (e.g., M-x lisp-mode enters Lisp mode).

The value of the buffer-local variable major-mode is a symbol with the same name as the major mode command (e.g., lisp-mode). This variable is set automatically; you should not change it yourself.

The default value of major-mode determines the major mode to use for files that do not specify a major mode, and for new buffers created with C-x b. Normally, this default value is the symbol fundamental-mode, which specifies Fundamental mode. You can change this default value via the Customization interface (see Section 33.1 [Easy Customization], page 412), or by adding a line like this to your init file (see Section 33.4 [Init File], page 437):

```
(setq-default major-mode 'text-mode)
```

If the default value of `major-mode` is `nil`, the major mode is taken from the previously current buffer.

Specialized major modes often change the meanings of certain keys to do something more suitable for the mode. For instance, programming language modes bind `TAB` to indent the current line according to the rules of the language (see Chapter 21 [Indentation], page 205). The keys that are commonly changed are `TAB`, `DEL`, and `C-j`. Many modes also define special commands of their own, usually bound in the prefix key `C-c`. Major modes can also alter user options and variables; for instance, programming language modes typically set a buffer-local value for the variable `comment-start`, which determines how source code comments are delimited (see Section 23.5 [Comments], page 249).

To view the documentation for the current major mode, including a list of its key bindings, type `C-h m` (`describe-mode`).

Every major mode, apart from Fundamental mode, defines a *mode hook*, a customizable list of Lisp functions to run each time the mode is enabled in a buffer. See Section 33.2.2 [Hooks], page 422, for more information about hooks. Each mode hook is named after its major mode, e.g., Fortran mode has `fortran-mode-hook`. Furthermore, all text-based major modes run `text-mode-hook`, and all programming language modes run `prog-mode-hook`, prior to running their own mode hooks. Hook functions can look at the value of the variable `major-mode` to see which mode is actually being entered.

Mode hooks are commonly used to enable minor modes (see Section 20.2 [Minor Modes], page 200). For example, you can put the following lines in your init file to enable Flyspell minor mode in all text-based major modes (see Section 13.4 [Spelling], page 111), and Eldoc minor mode in Emacs Lisp mode (see Section 23.6.3 [Lisp Doc], page 253):

```
(add-hook 'text-mode-hook 'flyspell-mode)
(add-hook 'emacs-lisp-mode-hook 'eldoc-mode)
```

20.2 Minor Modes

A minor mode is an optional editing mode that alters the behavior of Emacs in some well-defined way. Unlike major modes, any number of minor modes can be in effect at any time. Some minor modes are *buffer-local*, and can be turned on (enabled) in certain buffers and off (disabled) in others. Other minor modes are *global*: while enabled, they affect everything you do in the Emacs session, in all buffers. Most minor modes are disabled by default, but a few are enabled by default.

Most buffer-local minor modes say in the mode line when they are enabled, just after the major mode indicator. For example, 'Fill' in the mode line means that Auto Fill mode is enabled. See Section 1.3 [Mode Line], page 8.

Like major modes, each minor mode is associated with a *mode command*, whose name consists of the mode name followed by '`-mode`'. For instance, the mode command for Auto Fill mode is `auto-fill-mode`. But unlike a major mode command, which simply enables the mode, the mode command for a minor mode can either enable or disable it:

- If you invoke the mode command directly with no prefix argument (either via `M-x`, or by binding it to a key and typing that key; see Section 33.3 [Key Bindings], page 428), that *toggles* the minor mode. The minor mode is turned on if it was off, and turned off if it was on.

- If you invoke the mode command with a prefix argument, the minor mode is unconditionally turned off if that argument is zero or negative; otherwise, it is unconditionally turned on.

- If the mode command is called via Lisp, the minor mode is unconditionally turned on if the argument is omitted or `nil`. This makes it easy to turn on a minor mode from a major mode's mode hook (see Section 20.1 [Major Modes], page 199). A non-`nil` argument is handled like an interactive prefix argument, as described above.

Most minor modes also have a *mode variable*, with the same name as the mode command. Its value is non-`nil` if the mode is enabled, and `nil` if it is disabled. In general, you should not try to enable or disable the mode by changing the value of the mode variable directly in Lisp; you should run the mode command instead. However, setting the mode variable through the Customize interface (see Section 33.1 [Easy Customization], page 412) will always properly enable or disable the mode, since Customize automatically runs the mode command for you.

The following is a list of some buffer-local minor modes:

- Abbrev mode automatically expands text based on pre-defined abbreviation definitions. See Chapter 26 [Abbrevs], page 309.

- Auto Fill mode inserts newlines as you type to prevent lines from becoming too long. See Section 22.5 [Filling], page 212.

- Auto Save mode saves the buffer contents periodically to reduce the amount of work you can lose in case of a crash. See Section 15.5 [Auto Save], page 133.

- Enriched mode enables editing and saving of formatted text. See Section 22.13 [Enriched Text], page 230.

- Flyspell mode automatically highlights misspelled words. See Section 13.4 [Spelling], page 111.

- Font-Lock mode automatically highlights certain textual units found in programs. It is enabled globally by default, but you can disable it in individual buffers. See Section 11.8 [Faces], page 74.

- Linum mode displays each line's line number in the window's left margin.

- Outline minor mode provides similar facilities to the major mode called Outline mode. See Section 22.8 [Outline Mode], page 217.

- Overwrite mode causes ordinary printing characters to replace existing text instead of shoving it to the right. For example, if point is in front of the 'B' in 'FOOBAR', then in Overwrite mode typing a G changes it to 'FOOGAR', instead of producing 'FOOGBAR' as usual. In Overwrite mode, the command C-q inserts the next character whatever it may be, even if it is a digit—this gives you a way to insert a character instead of replacing an existing character. The mode command, `overwrite-mode`, is bound to the Insert key.

- Binary Overwrite mode is a variant of Overwrite mode for editing binary files; it treats newlines and tabs like other characters, so that they overwrite other characters and can be overwritten by them. In Binary Overwrite mode, digits after C-q specify an octal character code, as usual.

- Visual Line mode performs "word wrapping", causing long lines to be wrapped at word boundaries. See Section 11.22 [Visual Line Mode], page 87.

And here are some useful global minor modes:

- Column Number mode enables display of the current column number in the mode line. See Section 1.3 [Mode Line], page 8.

- Delete Selection mode causes text insertion to first delete the text in the region, if the region is active. See Section 8.3 [Using Region], page 47.

- Icomplete mode displays an indication of available completions when you are in the minibuffer and completion is active. See Section 16.7.2 [Icomplete], page 154.

- Line Number mode enables display of the current line number in the mode line. It is enabled by default. See Section 1.3 [Mode Line], page 8.

- Menu Bar mode gives each frame a menu bar. It is enabled by default. See Section 18.14 [Menu Bars], page 173.

- Scroll Bar mode gives each window a scroll bar. It is enabled by default, but the scroll bar is only displayed on graphical terminals. See Section 18.12 [Scroll Bars], page 172.

- Tool Bar mode gives each frame a tool bar. It is enabled by default, but the tool bar is only displayed on graphical terminals. See Section 18.15 [Tool Bars], page 173.

- Transient Mark mode highlights the region, and makes many Emacs commands operate on the region when the mark is active. It is enabled by default. See Chapter 8 [Mark], page 45.

20.3 Choosing File Modes

When you visit a file, Emacs chooses a major mode automatically. Normally, it makes the choice based on the file name—for example, files whose names end in '.c' are normally edited in C mode—but sometimes it chooses the major mode based on special text in the file. This special text can also be used to enable buffer-local minor modes.

Here is the exact procedure:

First, Emacs checks whether the file contains file-local mode variables. See Section 33.2.4 [File Variables], page 424. If there is a file-local variable that specifies a major mode, then Emacs uses that major mode, ignoring all other criteria. There are several methods to specify a major mode using a file-local variable; the simplest is to put the mode name in the first nonblank line, preceded and followed by '-*-'. Other text may appear on the line as well. For example,

```
; -*-Lisp-*-
```

tells Emacs to use Lisp mode. Note how the semicolon is used to make Lisp treat this line as a comment. You could equivalently write

```
; -*- mode: Lisp;-*-
```

You can also use file-local variables to specify buffer-local minor modes, by using `eval` specifications. For example, this first nonblank line puts the buffer in Lisp mode and enables Auto-Fill mode:

```
; -*- mode: Lisp; eval: (auto-fill-mode 1); -*-
```

Note, however, that it is usually inappropriate to enable minor modes this way, since most minor modes represent individual user preferences. If you personally want to use a minor mode for a particular file type, it is better to enable the minor mode via a major mode hook (see Section 20.1 [Major Modes], page 199).

Second, if there is no file variable specifying a major mode, Emacs checks whether the file's contents begin with '#!'. If so, that indicates that the file can serve as an executable shell command, which works by running an interpreter named on the file's first line (the rest of the file is used as input to the interpreter). Therefore, Emacs tries to use the interpreter name to choose a mode. For instance, a file that begins with '#!/usr/bin/perl' is opened in Perl mode. The variable `interpreter-mode-alist` specifies the correspondence between interpreter program names and major modes.

When the first line starts with '#!', you usually cannot use the '-*-' feature on the first line, because the system would get confused when running the interpreter. So Emacs looks for '-*-' on the second line in such files as well as on the first line. The same is true for man pages which start with the magic string ''\"' to specify a list of troff preprocessors.

Third, Emacs tries to determine the major mode by looking at the text at the start of the buffer, based on the variable `magic-mode-alist`. By default, this variable is `nil` (an empty list), so Emacs skips this step; however, you can customize it in your init file (see Section 33.4 [Init File], page 437). The value should be a list of elements of the form

    (*regexp* . *mode-function*)

where *regexp* is a regular expression (see Section 12.6 [Regexps], page 97), and *mode-function* is a major mode command. If the text at the beginning of the file matches *regexp*, Emacs chooses the major mode specified by *mode-function*.

Alternatively, an element of `magic-mode-alist` may have the form

    (*match-function* . *mode-function*)

where *match-function* is a Lisp function that is called at the beginning of the buffer; if the function returns non-`nil`, Emacs set the major mode with *mode-function*.

Fourth—if Emacs still hasn't found a suitable major mode—it looks at the file's name. The correspondence between file names and major modes is controlled by the variable `auto-mode-alist`. Its value is a list in which each element has this form,

    (*regexp* . *mode-function*)

or this form,

    (*regexp* *mode-function* *flag*)

For example, one element normally found in the list has the form (`"\\.c\\'"` . `c-mode`), and it is responsible for selecting C mode for files whose names end in .c. (Note that '\\' is needed in Lisp syntax to include a '\' in the string, which must be used to suppress the special meaning of '.' in regexps.) If the element has the form (*regexp* *mode-function* *flag*) and *flag* is non-`nil`, then after calling *mode-function*, Emacs discards the suffix that matched *regexp* and searches the list again for another match.

On GNU/Linux and other systems with case-sensitive file names, Emacs performs a case-sensitive search through `auto-mode-alist`; if this search fails, it performs a second case-insensitive search through the alist. To suppress the second search, change the variable `auto-mode-case-fold` to nil. On systems with case-insensitive file names, such as Microsoft Windows, Emacs performs a single case-insensitive search through `auto-mode-alist`.

Finally, if Emacs *still* hasn't found a major mode to use, it compares the text at the start of the buffer to the variable `magic-fallback-mode-alist`. This variable works like `magic-mode-alist`, described above, except that is consulted only after `auto-mode-alist`. By default, `magic-fallback-mode-alist` contains forms that check for image files, HTML/XML/SGML files, and PostScript files.

If you have changed the major mode of a buffer, you can return to the major mode Emacs would have chosen automatically, by typing `M-x normal-mode`. This is the same function that `find-file` calls to choose the major mode. It also processes the file's '-*-' line or local variables list (if any). See Section 33.2.4 [File Variables], page 424.

The commands `C-x C-w` and `set-visited-file-name` change to a new major mode if the new file name implies a mode (see Section 15.3 [Saving], page 126). (`C-x C-s` does this too, if the buffer wasn't visiting a file.) However, this does not happen if the buffer contents specify a major mode, and certain "special" major modes do not allow the mode to change. You can turn off this mode-changing feature by setting `change-major-mode-with-file-name` to `nil`.

21 Indentation

Indentation refers to inserting or adjusting *whitespace characters* (space and/or tab characters) at the beginning of a line of text. This chapter documents indentation commands and options which are common to Text mode and related modes, as well as programming language modes. See Section 23.3 [Program Indent], page 243, for additional documentation about indenting in programming modes.

The simplest way to perform indentation is the TAB key. In most major modes, this runs the command `indent-for-tab-command`. (In C and related modes, TAB runs the command `c-indent-line-or-region`, which behaves similarly).

TAB   Insert whitespace, or indent the current line, in a mode-appropriate way (`indent-for-tab-command`). If the region is active, indent all the lines within it.

The exact behavior of TAB depends on the major mode. In Text mode and related major modes, TAB normally inserts some combination of space and tab characters to advance point to the next tab stop (see Section 21.2 [Tab Stops], page 206). For this purpose, the position of the first non-whitespace character on the preceding line is treated as an additional tab stop, so you can use TAB to "align" point with the preceding line. If the region is active (see Section 8.3 [Using Region], page 47), TAB acts specially: it indents each line in the region so that its first non-whitespace character is aligned with the preceding line.

In programming modes, TAB indents the current line of code in a way that makes sense given the code in the preceding lines. If the region is active, all the lines in the region are indented this way. If point was initially within the current line's indentation, it is repositioned to the first non-whitespace character on the line.

If you just want to insert a tab character in the buffer, type C-q TAB (see Section 4.1 [Inserting Text], page 16).

21.1 Indentation Commands

Apart from the TAB (`indent-for-tab-command`) command, Emacs provides a variety of commands to perform indentation in other ways.

C-M-o   Split the current line at point (`split-line`). The text on the line after point becomes a new line, indented to the same column where point is located. This command first moves point forward over any spaces and tabs. Afterward, point is positioned before the inserted newline.

M-m   Move (forward or back) to the first non-whitespace character on the current line (`back-to-indentation`). If there are no non-whitespace characters on the line, move to the end of the line.

M-i   Indent whitespace at point, up to the next tab stop (`tab-to-tab-stop`). See Section 21.2 [Tab Stops], page 206.

M-x indent-relative
           Insert whitespace at point, until point is aligned with the first non-whitespace character on the previous line (actually, the last non-blank line). If point is already farther right than that, run `tab-to-tab-stop` instead—unless called with a numeric argument, in which case do nothing.

M-^   Merge the previous and the current line (`delete-indentation`). This "joins" the two lines cleanly, by replacing any indentation at the front of the current line, together with the line boundary, with a single space.

As a special case (useful for Lisp code), the single space is omitted if the characters to be joined are consecutive opening and closing parentheses, or if the junction follows another newline.

If there is a fill prefix, M-^ deletes the fill prefix if it appears after the newline that is deleted. See Section 22.5.3 [Fill Prefix], page 214.

C-M-\   Indent all the lines in the region, as though you had typed `TAB` at the beginning of each line (`indent-region`).

If a numeric argument is supplied, indent every line in the region to that column number.

C-x TAB   This command is used to change the indentation of all lines that begin in the region, moving the affected lines as a "rigid" unit.

If called with no argument, the command activates a transient mode for adjusting the indentation of the affected lines interactively. While this transient mode is active, typing `LEFT` or `RIGHT` indents leftward and rightward, respectively, by one space. You can also type `S-LEFT` or `S-RIGHT` to indent leftward or rightward to the next tab stop (see Section 21.2 [Tab Stops], page 206). Typing any other key disables the transient mode, and resumes normal editing.

If called with a prefix argument n, this command indents the lines forward by n spaces (without enabling the transient mode). Negative values of n indent backward, so you can remove all indentation from the lines in the region using a large negative argument, like this:

```
C-u -999 C-x TAB
```

21.2 Tab Stops

Emacs defines certain column numbers to be *tab stops*. These are used as stopping points by `TAB` when inserting whitespace in Text mode and related modes (see Chapter 21 [Indentation], page 205), and by commands like M-i (see Section 21.1 [Indentation Commands], page 205). The variable `tab-stop-list` controls these positions. The default value is `nil`, which means a tab stop every 8 columns. The value can also be a list of zero-based column numbers (in increasing order) at which to place tab stops. Emacs extends the list forever by repeating the difference between the last and next-to-last elements.

Instead of customizing the variable `tab-stop-list` directly, a convenient way to view and set tab stops is via the command M-x edit-tab-stops. This switches to a buffer containing a description of the tab stop settings, which looks like this:

```
        :       :       :       :       :       :
0       1       2       3       4
0123456789012345678901234567890123456789012345678
To install changes, type C-c C-c
```

The first line contains a colon at each tab stop. The numbers on the next two lines are present just to indicate where the colons are. If the value of `tab-stop-list` is `nil`, as it is by default, no colons are displayed initially.

You can edit this buffer to specify different tab stops by placing colons on the desired columns. The buffer uses Overwrite mode (see Section 20.2 [Minor Modes], page 200). Remember that Emacs will extend the list of tab stops forever by repeating the difference between the last two explicit stops that you place. When you are done, type C-c C-c to make the new tab stops take effect. Normally, the new tab stop settings apply to all buffers. However, if you have made the `tab-stop-list` variable local to the buffer where you called M-x `edit-tab-stops` (see Section 33.2.3 [Locals], page 423), then the new tab stop settings apply only to that buffer. To save the tab stop settings for future Emacs sessions, use the Customize interface to save the value of `tab-stop-list` (see Section 33.1 [Easy Customization], page 412).

Note that the tab stops discussed in this section have nothing to do with how tab characters are displayed in the buffer. Tab characters are always displayed as empty spaces extending to the next *display tab stop*. See Section 11.19 [Text Display], page 85.

21.3 Tabs vs. Spaces

Normally, indentation commands insert (or remove) an optimal mix of space characters and tab characters to align to the desired column. Tab characters are displayed as a stretch of empty space extending to the next *display tab stop*. By default, there is one display tab stop every `tab-width` columns (the default is 8). See Section 11.19 [Text Display], page 85.

If you prefer, all indentation can be made from spaces only. To request this, set the buffer-local variable `indent-tabs-mode` to `nil`. See Section 33.2.3 [Locals], page 423, for information about setting buffer-local variables. Note, however, that C-q TAB always inserts a tab character, regardless of the value of `indent-tabs-mode`.

One reason to set `indent-tabs-mode` to `nil` is that not all editors display tab characters in the same way. Emacs users, too, may have different customized values of `tab-width`. By using spaces only, you can make sure that your file always looks the same. If you only care about how it looks within Emacs, another way to tackle this problem is to set the `tab-width` variable in a file-local variable (see Section 33.2.4 [File Variables], page 424).

There are also commands to convert tabs to spaces or vice versa, always preserving the columns of all non-whitespace text. M-x `tabify` scans the region for sequences of spaces, and converts sequences of at least two spaces to tabs if that can be done without changing indentation. M-x `untabify` changes all tabs in the region to appropriate numbers of spaces.

21.4 Convenience Features for Indentation

The variable `tab-always-indent` tweaks the behavior of the TAB (`indent-for-tab-command`) command. The default value, `t`, gives the behavior described in Chapter 21 [Indentation], page 205. If you change the value to the symbol `complete`, then TAB first tries to indent the current line, and if the line was already indented, it tries to complete the text at point (see Section 23.8 [Symbol Completion], page 254). If the value is `nil`, then TAB indents the current line only if point is at the left margin or in the line's indentation; otherwise, it inserts a tab character.

Electric Indent mode is a global minor mode that automatically indents the line after every RET you type. This mode is enabled by default. To toggle this minor mode, type M-x `electric-indent-mode`. To toggle the mode in a single buffer, use M-x `electric-indent-local-mode`.

22 Commands for Human Languages

This chapter describes Emacs commands that act on *text*, by which we mean sequences of characters in a human language (as opposed to, say, a computer programming language). These commands act in ways that take into account the syntactic and stylistic conventions of human languages: conventions involving words, sentences, paragraphs, and capital letters. There are also commands for *filling*, which means rearranging the lines of a paragraph to be approximately equal in length. These commands, while intended primarily for editing text, are also often useful for editing programs.

Emacs has several major modes for editing human-language text. If the file contains ordinary text, use Text mode, which customizes Emacs in small ways for the syntactic conventions of text. Outline mode provides special commands for operating on text with an outline structure. Org mode extends Outline mode and turn Emacs into a full-fledged organizer: you can manage TODO lists, store notes and publish them in many formats.

See Section 22.8 [Outline Mode], page 217.

Emacs has other major modes for text which contains "embedded" commands, such as TeX and LaTeX (see Section 22.10 [TeX Mode], page 224); HTML and SGML (see Section 22.11 [HTML Mode], page 228); XML (see the nXML mode Info manual, which is distributed with Emacs); and Groff and Nroff (see Section 22.12 [Nroff Mode], page 229).

If you need to edit pictures made out of text characters (commonly referred to as "ASCII art"), use Picture mode, a special major mode for editing such pictures. See Section "Picture Mode" in *Specialized Emacs Features*.

22.1 Words

Emacs defines several commands for moving over or operating on words:

M-f   Move forward over a word (`forward-word`).

M-b   Move backward over a word (`backward-word`).

M-d   Kill up to the end of a word (`kill-word`).

M-DEL   Kill back to the beginning of a word (`backward-kill-word`).

M-@   Mark the end of the next word (`mark-word`).

M-t   Transpose two words or drag a word across others (`transpose-words`).

Notice how these keys form a series that parallels the character-based C-f, C-b, C-d, DEL and C-t. M-@ is cognate to C-@, which is an alias for C-SPC.

The commands M-f (`forward-word`) and M-b (`backward-word`) move forward and backward over words. These META-based key sequences are analogous to the key sequences C-f and C-b, which move over single characters. The analogy extends to numeric arguments, which serve as repeat counts. M-f with a negative argument moves backward, and M-b with a negative argument moves forward. Forward motion stops right after the last letter of the word, while backward motion stops right before the first letter.

M-d (`kill-word`) kills the word after point. To be precise, it kills everything from point to the place M-f would move to. Thus, if point is in the middle of a word, M-d kills just the part after point. If some punctuation comes between point and the next word, it is killed along with the word. (If you wish to kill only the next word but not the punctuation before it, simply do M-f to get the end, and kill the word backwards with M-DEL.) M-d takes arguments just like M-f.

M-DEL (backward-kill-word) kills the word before point. It kills everything from point back to where M-b would move to. For instance, if point is after the space in 'FOO, BAR', it kills 'FOO, '. If you wish to kill just 'FOO', and not the comma and the space, use M-b M-d instead of M-DEL.

M-t (transpose-words) exchanges the word before or containing point with the following word. The delimiter characters between the words do not move. For example, 'FOO, BAR' transposes into 'BAR, FOO' rather than 'BAR FOO,'. See Section 13.2 [Transpose], page 110, for more on transposition.

To operate on words with an operation which acts on the region, use the command M-@ (mark-word). This command sets the mark where M-f would move to. See Section 8.2 [Marking Objects], page 47, for more information about this command.

The word commands' understanding of word boundaries is controlled by the syntax table. Any character can, for example, be declared to be a word delimiter. See Section "Syntax Tables" in *The Emacs Lisp Reference Manual*.

In addition, see Section 4.9 [Position Info], page 22 for the M-= (count-words-region) and M-x count-words commands, which count and report the number of words in the region or buffer.

22.2 Sentences

The Emacs commands for manipulating sentences and paragraphs are mostly on Meta keys, like the word-handling commands.

M-a   Move back to the beginning of the sentence (backward-sentence).

M-e   Move forward to the end of the sentence (forward-sentence).

M-k   Kill forward to the end of the sentence (kill-sentence).

C-x DEL   Kill back to the beginning of the sentence (backward-kill-sentence).

The commands M-a (backward-sentence) and M-e (forward-sentence) move to the beginning and end of the current sentence, respectively. Their bindings were chosen to resemble C-a and C-e, which move to the beginning and end of a line. Unlike them, M-a and M-e move over successive sentences if repeated.

Moving backward over a sentence places point just before the first character of the sentence; moving forward places point right after the punctuation that ends the sentence. Neither one moves over the whitespace at the sentence boundary.

Just as C-a and C-e have a kill command, C-k, to go with them, M-a and M-e have a corresponding kill command: M-k (kill-sentence) kills from point to the end of the sentence. With a positive numeric argument n, it kills the next n sentences; with a negative argument $-n$, it kills back to the beginning of the nth preceding sentence.

The C-x DEL (backward-kill-sentence) kills back to the beginning of a sentence.

The sentence commands assume that you follow the American typist's convention of putting two spaces at the end of a sentence. That is, a sentence ends wherever there is a

'.', '?' or '!' followed by the end of a line or two spaces, with any number of ')', ']', ''',
or '"' characters allowed in between. A sentence also begins or ends wherever a paragraph
begins or ends. It is useful to follow this convention, because it allows the Emacs sentence
commands to distinguish between periods that end a sentence and periods that indicate
abbreviations.

If you want to use just one space between sentences, you can set the variable
`sentence-end-double-space` to `nil` to make the sentence commands stop for single
spaces. However, this has a drawback: there is no way to distinguish between periods
that end sentences and those that indicate abbreviations. For convenient and reliable
editing, we therefore recommend you follow the two-space convention. The variable
`sentence-end-double-space` also affects filling (see Section 22.5.2 [Fill Commands],
page 213).

The variable `sentence-end` controls how to recognize the end of a sentence. If non-`nil`,
its value should be a regular expression, which is used to match the last few characters of a
sentence, together with the whitespace following the sentence (see Section 12.6 [Regexps],
page 97). If the value is `nil`, the default, then Emacs computes sentence ends according to
various criteria such as the value of `sentence-end-double-space`.

Some languages, such as Thai, do not use periods to indicate the end of a sentence. Set
the variable `sentence-end-without-period` to `t` in such cases.

22.3 Paragraphs

The Emacs commands for manipulating paragraphs are also on Meta keys.

M-{   Move back to previous paragraph beginning (`backward-paragraph`).

M-}   Move forward to next paragraph end (`forward-paragraph`).

M-h   Put point and mark around this or next paragraph (`mark-paragraph`).

M-{ (`backward-paragraph`) moves to the beginning of the current or previous paragraph
(see below for the definition of a paragraph). M-} (`forward-paragraph`) moves to the end
of the current or next paragraph. If there is a blank line before the paragraph, M-{ moves
to the blank line.

When you wish to operate on a paragraph, type M-h (`mark-paragraph`) to set the region
around it. For example, M-h C-w kills the paragraph around or after point. M-h puts point
at the beginning and mark at the end of the paragraph point was in. If point is between
paragraphs (in a run of blank lines, or at a boundary), M-h sets the region around the
paragraph following point. If there are blank lines preceding the first line of the paragraph,
one of these blank lines is included in the region. If the region is already active, the command
sets the mark without changing point, and each subsequent M-h further advances the mark
by one paragraph.

The definition of a paragraph depends on the major mode. In Fundamental mode, as
well as Text mode and related modes, a paragraph is separated each neighboring paragraph
another by one or more *blank lines*—lines that are either empty, or consist solely of space,
tab and/or formfeed characters. In programming language modes, paragraphs are usually
defined in a similar way, so that you can use the paragraph commands even though there
are no paragraphs as such in a program.

Note that an indented line is *not* itself a paragraph break in Text mode. If you want indented lines to separate paragraphs, use Paragraph-Indent Text mode instead. See Section 22.7 [Text Mode], page 217.

If you set a fill prefix, then paragraphs are delimited by all lines which don't start with the fill prefix. See Section 22.5 [Filling], page 212.

The precise definition of a paragraph boundary is controlled by the variables `paragraph-separate` and `paragraph-start`. The value of `paragraph-start` is a regular expression that should match lines that either start or separate paragraphs (see Section 12.6 [Regexps], page 97). The value of `paragraph-separate` is another regular expression that should match lines that separate paragraphs without being part of any paragraph (for example, blank lines). Lines that start a new paragraph and are contained in it must match only `paragraph-start`, not `paragraph-separate`. For example, in Fundamental mode, `paragraph-start` is `"\f\\|[ \t]*$"`, and `paragraph-separate` is `"[ \t\f]*$"`.

22.4 Pages

Within some text files, text is divided into *pages* delimited by the *formfeed character* (ASCII code 12, also denoted as 'control-L'), which is displayed in Emacs as the escape sequence '^L' (see Section 11.19 [Text Display], page 85). Traditionally, when such text files are printed to hardcopy, each formfeed character forces a page break. Most Emacs commands treat it just like any other character, so you can insert it with C-q C-l, delete it with DEL, etc. In addition, Emacs provides commands to move over pages and operate on them.

M-x what-page
> Display the page number of point, and the line number within that page.

C-x [Move point to previous page boundary (`backward-page`).

C-x]   Move point to next page boundary (`forward-page`).

C-x C-p   Put point and mark around this page (or another page) (`mark-page`).

C-x l   Count the lines in this page (`count-lines-page`).

M-x what-page counts pages from the beginning of the file, and counts lines within the page, showing both numbers in the echo area.

The C-x [(`backward-page`) command moves point to immediately after the previous page delimiter. If point is already right after a page delimiter, it skips that one and stops at the previous one. A numeric argument serves as a repeat count. The C-x] (`forward-page`) command moves forward past the next page delimiter.

The C-x C-p command (`mark-page`) puts point at the beginning of the current page (after that page delimiter at the front), and the mark at the end of the page (after the page delimiter at the end).

C-x C-p C-w is a handy way to kill a page to move it elsewhere. If you move to another page delimiter with C-x [and C-x], then yank the killed page, all the pages will be properly delimited once again. The reason C-x C-p includes only the following page delimiter in the region is to ensure that.

A numeric argument to C-x C-p specifies which page to go to, relative to the current one. Zero means the current page, one the next page, and −1 the previous one.

The `C-x l` command (`count-lines-page`) is good for deciding where to break a page in two. It displays in the echo area the total number of lines in the current page, and then divides it up into those preceding the current line and those following, as in

    Page has 96 (72+25) lines

Notice that the sum is off by one; this is correct if point is not at the beginning of a line.

The variable `page-delimiter` controls where pages begin. Its value is a regular expression that matches the beginning of a line that separates pages (see Section 12.6 [Regexps], page 97). The normal value of this variable is `"^\f"`, which matches a formfeed character at the beginning of a line.

22.5 Filling Text

Filling text means breaking it up into lines that fit a specified width. Emacs does filling in two ways. In Auto Fill mode, inserting text with self-inserting characters also automatically fills it. There are also explicit fill commands that you can use when editing text.

22.5.1 Auto Fill Mode

Auto Fill mode is a buffer-local minor mode (see Section 20.2 [Minor Modes], page 200) in which lines are broken automatically when they become too wide. Breaking happens only when you type a SPC or RET.

`M-x auto-fill-mode`
> Enable or disable Auto Fill mode.

`SPC`
`RET`   In Auto Fill mode, break lines when appropriate.

The mode command `M-x auto-fill-mode` toggles Auto Fill mode in the current buffer. With a positive numeric argument, it enables Auto Fill mode, and with a negative argument it disables it. If `auto-fill-mode` is called from Lisp with an omitted or `nil` argument, it enables Auto Fill mode. To enable Auto Fill mode automatically in certain major modes, add `auto-fill-mode` to the mode hooks (see Section 20.1 [Major Modes], page 199). When Auto Fill mode is enabled, the mode indicator 'Fill' appears in the mode line (see Section 1.3 [Mode Line], page 8).

Auto Fill mode breaks lines automatically at spaces whenever they get longer than the desired width. This line breaking occurs only when you type SPC or RET. If you wish to insert a space or newline without permitting line-breaking, type `C-q SPC` or `C-q C-j` respectively. Also, `C-o` inserts a newline without line breaking.

When Auto Fill mode breaks a line, it tries to obey the *adaptive fill prefix*: if a fill prefix can be deduced from the first and/or second line of the current paragraph, it is inserted into the new line (see Section 22.5.4 [Adaptive Fill], page 215). Otherwise the new line is indented, as though you had typed TAB on it (see Chapter 21 [Indentation], page 205). In a programming language mode, if a line is broken in the middle of a comment, the comment is split by inserting new comment delimiters as appropriate.

Auto Fill mode does not refill entire paragraphs; it breaks lines but does not merge lines. Therefore, editing in the middle of a paragraph can result in a paragraph that is not correctly filled. To fill it, call the explicit fill commands described in the next section.

22.5.2 Explicit Fill Commands

M-q   Fill current paragraph (`fill-paragraph`).

C-x f   Set the fill column (`set-fill-column`).

M-x fill-region
                Fill each paragraph in the region (`fill-region`).

M-x fill-region-as-paragraph
                Fill the region, considering it as one paragraph.

M-o M-s   Center a line.

The command `M-q` (`fill-paragraph`) *fills* the current paragraph. It redistributes the line breaks within the paragraph, and deletes any excess space and tab characters occurring within the paragraph, in such a way that the lines end up fitting within a certain maximum width.

Normally, `M-q` acts on the paragraph where point is, but if point is between paragraphs, it acts on the paragraph after point. If the region is active, it acts instead on the text in the region. You can also call `M-x fill-region` to specifically fill the text in the region.

`M-q` and `fill-region` use the usual Emacs criteria for finding paragraph boundaries (see Section 22.3 [Paragraphs], page 210). For more control, you can use `M-x fill-region-as-paragraph`, which refills everything between point and mark as a single paragraph. This command deletes any blank lines within the region, so separate blocks of text end up combined into one block.

A numeric argument to `M-q` tells it to *justify* the text as well as filling it. This means that extra spaces are inserted to make the right margin line up exactly at the fill column. To remove the extra spaces, use `M-q` with no argument. (Likewise for `fill-region`.)

The maximum line width for filling is specified by the buffer-local variable `fill-column`. The default value (see Section 33.2.3 [Locals], page 423) is 70. The easiest way to set `fill-column` in the current buffer is to use the command C-x f (`set-fill-column`). With a numeric argument, it uses that as the new fill column. With just `C-u` as argument, it sets `fill-column` to the current horizontal position of point.

The command `M-o M-s` (`center-line`) centers the current line within the current fill column. With an argument n, it centers n lines individually and moves past them. This binding is made by Text mode and is available only in that and related modes (see Section 22.7 [Text Mode], page 217).

By default, Emacs considers a period followed by two spaces or by a newline as the end of a sentence; a period followed by just one space indicates an abbreviation, not the end of a sentence. Accordingly, the fill commands will not break a line after a period followed by just one space. If you set the variable `sentence-end-double-space` to `nil`, the fill commands will break a line after a period followed by one space, and put just one space after each period. See Section 22.2 [Sentences], page 209, for other effects and possible drawbacks of this.

If the variable `colon-double-space` is non-`nil`, the fill commands put two spaces after a colon.

To specify additional conditions where line-breaking is not allowed, customize the abnormal hook variable `fill-nobreak-predicate` (see Section 33.2.2 [Hooks], page 422). Each function in this hook is called with no arguments, with point positioned where Emacs is considering breaking a line. If a function returns a non-`nil` value, Emacs will not break the line there. Functions you can use there include: `fill-single-word-nobreak-p` (don't break after the first word of a sentence or before the last); `fill-single-char-nobreak-p` (don't break after a one-letter word); and `fill-french-nobreak-p` (don't break after '(' or before ')', ':' or '?').

22.5.3 The Fill Prefix

The *fill prefix* feature allows paragraphs to be filled so that each line starts with a special string of characters (such as a sequence of spaces, giving an indented paragraph). You can specify a fill prefix explicitly; otherwise, Emacs tries to deduce one automatically (see Section 22.5.4 [Adaptive Fill], page 215).

C-x .   Set the fill prefix (`set-fill-prefix`).

M-q   Fill a paragraph using current fill prefix (`fill-paragraph`).

M-x fill-individual-paragraphs
             Fill the region, considering each change of indentation as starting a new paragraph.

M-x fill-nonuniform-paragraphs
             Fill the region, considering only paragraph-separator lines as starting a new paragraph.

To specify a fill prefix for the current buffer, move to a line that starts with the desired prefix, put point at the end of the prefix, and type `C-x .` (`set-fill-prefix`). (That's a period after the `C-x`.) To turn off the fill prefix, specify an empty prefix: type `C-x .` with point at the beginning of a line.

When a fill prefix is in effect, the fill commands remove the fill prefix from each line of the paragraph before filling, and insert it on each line after filling. (The beginning of the first line of the paragraph is left unchanged, since often that is intentionally different.) Auto Fill mode also inserts the fill prefix automatically when it makes a new line (see Section 22.5.1 [Auto Fill], page 212). The `C-o` command inserts the fill prefix on new lines it creates, when you use it at the beginning of a line (see Section 4.7 [Blank Lines], page 21). Conversely, the command `M-^` deletes the prefix (if it occurs) after the newline that it deletes (see Chapter 21 [Indentation], page 205).

For example, if `fill-column` is 40 and you set the fill prefix to ';; ', then `M-q` in the following text

```
;; This is an
;; example of a paragraph
;; inside a Lisp-style comment.
```
produces this:
```
;; This is an example of a paragraph
;; inside a Lisp-style comment.
```

Lines that do not start with the fill prefix are considered to start paragraphs, both in `M-q` and the paragraph commands; this gives good results for paragraphs with hanging indentation (every line indented except the first one). Lines which are blank or indented once the prefix is removed also separate or start paragraphs; this is what you want if you are writing multi-paragraph comments with a comment delimiter on each line.

You can use M-x fill-individual-paragraphs to set the fill prefix for each paragraph automatically. This command divides the region into paragraphs, treating every change in the amount of indentation as the start of a new paragraph, and fills each of these paragraphs. Thus, all the lines in one "paragraph" have the same amount of indentation. That indentation serves as the fill prefix for that paragraph.

M-x fill-nonuniform-paragraphs is a similar command that divides the region into paragraphs in a different way. It considers only paragraph-separating lines (as defined by paragraph-separate) as starting a new paragraph. Since this means that the lines of one paragraph may have different amounts of indentation, the fill prefix used is the smallest amount of indentation of any of the lines of the paragraph. This gives good results with styles that indent a paragraph's first line more or less that the rest of the paragraph.

The fill prefix is stored in the variable fill-prefix. Its value is a string, or nil when there is no fill prefix. This is a per-buffer variable; altering the variable affects only the current buffer, but there is a default value which you can change as well. See Section 33.2.3 [Locals], page 423.

The indentation text property provides another way to control the amount of indentation paragraphs receive. See Section 22.13.5 [Enriched Indentation], page 232.

22.5.4 Adaptive Filling

The fill commands can deduce the proper fill prefix for a paragraph automatically in certain cases: either whitespace or certain punctuation characters at the beginning of a line are propagated to all lines of the paragraph.

If the paragraph has two or more lines, the fill prefix is taken from the paragraph's second line, but only if it appears on the first line as well.

If a paragraph has just one line, fill commands *may* take a prefix from that line. The decision is complicated because there are three reasonable things to do in such a case:

- Use the first line's prefix on all the lines of the paragraph.

- Indent subsequent lines with whitespace, so that they line up under the text that follows the prefix on the first line, but don't actually copy the prefix from the first line.

- Don't do anything special with the second and following lines.

All three of these styles of formatting are commonly used. So the fill commands try to determine what you would like, based on the prefix that appears and on the major mode. Here is how.

If the prefix found on the first line matches adaptive-fill-first-line-regexp, or if it appears to be a comment-starting sequence (this depends on the major mode), then the prefix found is used for filling the paragraph, provided it would not act as a paragraph starter on subsequent lines.

Otherwise, the prefix found is converted to an equivalent number of spaces, and those spaces are used as the fill prefix for the rest of the lines, provided they would not act as a paragraph starter on subsequent lines.

In Text mode, and other modes where only blank lines and page delimiters separate paragraphs, the prefix chosen by adaptive filling never acts as a paragraph starter, so it can always be used for filling.

The variable `adaptive-fill-regexp` determines what kinds of line beginnings can serve as a fill prefix: any characters at the start of the line that match this regular expression are used. If you set the variable `adaptive-fill-mode` to `nil`, the fill prefix is never chosen automatically.

You can specify more complex ways of choosing a fill prefix automatically by setting the variable `adaptive-fill-function` to a function. This function is called with point after the left margin of a line, and it should return the appropriate fill prefix based on that line. If it returns `nil`, `adaptive-fill-regexp` gets a chance to find a prefix.

22.6 Case Conversion Commands

Emacs has commands for converting either a single word or any arbitrary range of text to upper case or to lower case.

M-l   Convert following word to lower case (`downcase-word`).

M-u   Convert following word to upper case (`upcase-word`).

M-c   Capitalize the following word (`capitalize-word`).

C-x C-l   Convert region to lower case (`downcase-region`).

C-x C-u   Convert region to upper case (`upcase-region`).

`M-l` (`downcase-word`) converts the word after point to lower case, moving past it. Thus, repeating `M-l` converts successive words. `M-u` (`upcase-word`) converts to all capitals instead, while `M-c` (`capitalize-word`) puts the first letter of the word into upper case and the rest into lower case. All these commands convert several words at once if given an argument. They are especially convenient for converting a large amount of text from all upper case to mixed case, because you can move through the text using `M-l`, `M-u` or `M-c` on each word as appropriate, occasionally using `M-f` instead to skip a word.

When given a negative argument, the word case conversion commands apply to the appropriate number of words before point, but do not move point. This is convenient when you have just typed a word in the wrong case: you can give the case conversion command and continue typing.

If a word case conversion command is given in the middle of a word, it applies only to the part of the word which follows point. (This is comparable to what `M-d` (`kill-word`) does.) With a negative argument, case conversion applies only to the part of the word before point.

The other case conversion commands are `C-x C-u` (`upcase-region`) and `C-x C-l` (`downcase-region`), which convert everything between point and mark to the specified case. Point and mark do not move.

The region case conversion commands `upcase-region` and `downcase-region` are normally disabled. This means that they ask for confirmation if you try to use them. When you confirm, you may enable the command, which means it will not ask for confirmation again. See Section 33.3.11 [Disabling], page 437.

22.7 Text Mode

Text mode is a major mode for editing files of text in a human language. Files which have names ending in the extension `.txt` are usually opened in Text mode (see Section 20.3 [Choosing Modes], page 202). To explicitly switch to Text mode, type `M-x text-mode`.

In Text mode, only blank lines and page delimiters separate paragraphs. As a result, paragraphs can be indented, and adaptive filling determines what indentation to use when filling a paragraph. See Section 22.5.4 [Adaptive Fill], page 215.

In Text mode, the `TAB` (`indent-for-tab-command`) command usually inserts whitespace up to the next tab stop, instead of indenting the current line. See Chapter 21 [Indentation], page 205, for details.

Text mode turns off the features concerned with comments except when you explicitly invoke them. It changes the syntax table so that single-quotes are considered part of words (e.g., 'don't' is considered one word). However, if a word starts with a single-quote, it is treated as a prefix for the purposes of capitalization (e.g., `M-c` converts `''hello''` into `''Hello''`, as expected).

If you indent the first lines of paragraphs, then you should use Paragraph-Indent Text mode (`M-x paragraph-indent-text-mode`) rather than Text mode. In that mode, you do not need to have blank lines between paragraphs, because the first-line indentation is sufficient to start a paragraph; however paragraphs in which every line is indented are not supported. Use `M-x paragraph-indent-minor-mode` to enable an equivalent minor mode for situations where you shouldn't change the major mode—in mail composition, for instance.

Text mode binds `M-TAB` to `ispell-complete-word`. This command performs completion of the partial word in the buffer before point, using the spelling dictionary as the space of possible words. See Section 13.4 [Spelling], page 111. If your window manager defines `M-TAB` to switch windows, you can type `ESC TAB` or `C-M-i` instead.

Entering Text mode runs the mode hook `text-mode-hook` (see Section 20.1 [Major Modes], page 199).

The following sections describe several major modes that are *derived* from Text mode. These derivatives share most of the features of Text mode described above. In particular, derivatives of Text mode run `text-mode-hook` prior to running their own mode hooks.

22.8 Outline Mode

Outline mode is a major mode derived from Text mode, which is specialized for editing outlines. It provides commands to navigate between entries in the outline structure, and commands to make parts of a buffer temporarily invisible, so that the outline structure may be more easily viewed. Type `M-x outline-mode` to switch to Outline mode. Entering Outline mode runs the hook `text-mode-hook` followed by the hook `outline-mode-hook` (see Section 33.2.2 [Hooks], page 422).

When you use an Outline mode command to make a line invisible (see Section 22.8.3 [Outline Visibility], page 219), the line disappears from the screen. An ellipsis (three periods in a row) is displayed at the end of the previous visible line, to indicate the hidden text. Multiple consecutive invisible lines produce just one ellipsis.

Editing commands that operate on lines, such as C-n and C-p, treat the text of the invisible line as part of the previous visible line. Killing the ellipsis at the end of a visible line really kills all the following invisible text associated with the ellipsis.

Outline minor mode is a buffer-local minor mode which provides the same commands as the major mode, Outline mode, but can be used in conjunction with other major modes. You can type M-x outline-minor-mode to toggle Outline minor mode in the current buffer, or use a file-local variable setting to enable it in a specific file (see Section 33.2.4 [File Variables], page 424).

The major mode, Outline mode, provides special key bindings on the C-c prefix. Outline minor mode provides similar bindings with C-c @ as the prefix; this is to reduce the conflicts with the major mode's special commands. (The variable outline-minor-mode-prefix controls the prefix used.)

22.8.1 Format of Outlines

Outline mode assumes that the lines in the buffer are of two types: *heading lines* and *body lines*. A heading line represents a topic in the outline. Heading lines start with one or more asterisk ('*') characters; the number of asterisks determines the depth of the heading in the outline structure. Thus, a heading line with one '*' is a major topic; all the heading lines with two '*'s between it and the next one-'*' heading are its subtopics; and so on. Any line that is not a heading line is a body line. Body lines belong with the preceding heading line. Here is an example:

```
* Food
This is the body,
which says something about the topic of food.

** Delicious Food
This is the body of the second-level header.

** Distasteful Food
This could have
a body too, with
several lines.

*** Dormitory Food

* Shelter
Another first-level topic with its header line.
```

A heading line together with all following body lines is called collectively an *entry*. A heading line together with all following deeper heading lines and their body lines is called a *subtree*.

You can customize the criterion for distinguishing heading lines by setting the variable outline-regexp. (The recommended ways to do this are in a major mode function or with a file local variable.) Any line whose beginning has a match for this regexp is considered a heading line. Matches that start within a line (not at the left margin) do not count.

The length of the matching text determines the level of the heading; longer matches make a more deeply nested level. Thus, for example, if a text formatter has commands

'@chapter', '@section' and '@subsection' to divide the document into chapters and sections, you could make those lines count as heading lines by setting `outline-regexp` to '"@chap\\|@\\(sub\\)*section"'. Note the trick: the two words 'chapter' and 'section' are equally long, but by defining the regexp to match only 'chap' we ensure that the length of the text matched on a chapter heading is shorter, so that Outline mode will know that sections are contained in chapters. This works as long as no other command starts with '@chap'.

You can explicitly specify a rule for calculating the level of a heading line by setting the variable `outline-level`. The value of `outline-level` should be a function that takes no arguments and returns the level of the current heading. The recommended ways to set this variable are in a major mode command or with a file local variable.

22.8.2 Outline Motion Commands

Outline mode provides special motion commands that move backward and forward to heading lines.

C-c C-n   Move point to the next visible heading line (`outline-next-visible-heading`).

C-c C-p   Move point to the previous visible heading line (`outline-previous-visible-heading`).

C-c C-f   Move point to the next visible heading line at the same level as the one point is on (`outline-forward-same-level`).

C-c C-b   Move point to the previous visible heading line at the same level (`outline-backward-same-level`).

C-c C-u   Move point up to a lower-level (more inclusive) visible heading line (`outline-up-heading`).

C-c C-n (`outline-next-visible-heading`) moves down to the next heading line. C-c C-p (`outline-previous-visible-heading`) moves similarly backward. Both accept numeric arguments as repeat counts.

C-c C-f (`outline-forward-same-level`) and C-c C-b (`outline-backward-same-level`) move from one heading line to another visible heading at the same depth in the outline. C-c C-u (`outline-up-heading`) moves backward to another heading that is less deeply nested.

22.8.3 Outline Visibility Commands

Outline mode provides several commands for temporarily hiding or revealing parts of the buffer, based on the outline structure. These commands are not undoable; their effects are simply not recorded by the undo mechanism, so you can undo right past them (see Section 13.1 [Undo], page 109).

Many of these commands act on the "current" heading line. If point is on a heading line, that is the current heading line; if point is on a body line, the current heading line is the nearest preceding header line.

C-c C-c   Make the current heading line's body invisible (`hide-entry`).

C-c C-e   Make the current heading line's body visible (`show-entry`).

`C-c C-d`	Make everything under the current heading invisible, not including the heading itself (`hide-subtree`).
`C-c C-s`	Make everything under the current heading visible, including body, subheadings, and their bodies (`show-subtree`).
`C-c C-l`	Make the body of the current heading line, and of all its subheadings, invisible (`hide-leaves`).
`C-c C-k`	Make all subheadings of the current heading line, at all levels, visible (`show-branches`).
`C-c C-i`	Make immediate subheadings (one level down) of the current heading line visible (`show-children`).
`C-c C-t`	Make all body lines in the buffer invisible (`hide-body`).
`C-c C-a`	Make all lines in the buffer visible (`show-all`).
`C-c C-q`	Hide everything except the top n levels of heading lines (`hide-sublevels`).
`C-c C-o`	Hide everything except for the heading or body that point is in, plus the headings leading up from there to the top level of the outline (`hide-other`).

The simplest of these commands are `C-c C-c` (`hide-entry`), which hides the body lines directly following the current heading line, and `C-c C-e` (`show-entry`), which reveals them. Subheadings and their bodies are not affected.

The commands `C-c C-d` (`hide-subtree`) and `C-c C-s` (`show-subtree`) are more powerful. They apply to the current heading line's *subtree*: its body, all of its subheadings, both direct and indirect, and all of their bodies.

The command `C-c C-l` (`hide-leaves`) hides the body of the current heading line as well as all the bodies in its subtree; the subheadings themselves are left visible. The command `C-c C-k` (`show-branches`) reveals the subheadings, if they had previously been hidden (e.g., by `C-c C-d`). The command `C-c C-i` (`show-children`) is a weaker version of this; it reveals just the direct subheadings, i.e., those one level down.

The command `C-c C-o` (`hide-other`) hides everything except the entry that point is in, plus its parents (the headers leading up from there to top level in the outline) and the top level headings.

The remaining commands affect the whole buffer. `C-c C-t` (`hide-body`) makes all body lines invisible, so that you see just the outline structure (as a special exception, it will not hide lines at the top of the file, preceding the first header line, even though these are technically body lines). `C-c C-a` (`show-all`) makes all lines visible. `C-c C-q` (`hide-sublevels`) hides all but the top level headings; with a numeric argument n, it hides everything except the top n levels of heading lines.

When incremental search finds text that is hidden by Outline mode, it makes that part of the buffer visible. If you exit the search at that position, the text remains visible. To toggle whether or not an active incremental search can match hidden text, type `M-s i`. To change the default for future searches, customize the option `search-invisible`. (This option also affects how `query-replace` and related functions treat hidden text, see Section 12.10.4 [Query Replace], page 105.) You can also automatically make text visible as you navigate in it by using Reveal mode (`M-x reveal-mode`), a buffer-local minor mode.

22.8.4 Viewing One Outline in Multiple Views

You can display two views of a single outline at the same time, in different windows. To do this, you must create an indirect buffer using M-x make-indirect-buffer. The first argument of this command is the existing outline buffer name, and its second argument is the name to use for the new indirect buffer. See Section 16.6 [Indirect Buffers], page 153.

Once the indirect buffer exists, you can display it in a window in the normal fashion, with C-x 4 b or other Emacs commands. The Outline mode commands to show and hide parts of the text operate on each buffer independently; as a result, each buffer can have its own view. If you want more than two views on the same outline, create additional indirect buffers.

22.8.5 Folding Editing

The Foldout package extends Outline mode and Outline minor mode with "folding" commands. The idea of folding is that you zoom in on a nested portion of the outline, while hiding its relatives at higher levels.

Consider an Outline mode buffer with all the text and subheadings under level-1 headings hidden. To look at what is hidden under one of these headings, you could use C-c C-e (M-x show-entry) to expose the body, or C-c C-i to expose the child (level-2) headings.

With Foldout, you use C-c C-z (M-x foldout-zoom-subtree). This exposes the body and child subheadings, and narrows the buffer so that only the level-1 heading, the body and the level-2 headings are visible. Now to look under one of the level-2 headings, position the cursor on it and use C-c C-z again. This exposes the level-2 body and its level-3 child subheadings and narrows the buffer again. Zooming in on successive subheadings can be done as much as you like. A string in the mode line shows how deep you've gone.

When zooming in on a heading, to see only the child subheadings specify a numeric argument: C-u C-c C-z. The number of levels of children can be specified too (compare M-x show-children), e.g., M-2 C-c C-z exposes two levels of child subheadings. Alternatively, the body can be specified with a negative argument: M-- C-c C-z. The whole subtree can be expanded, similarly to C-c C-s (M-x show-subtree), by specifying a zero argument: M-0 C-c C-z.

While you're zoomed in, you can still use Outline mode's exposure and hiding functions without disturbing Foldout. Also, since the buffer is narrowed, "global" editing actions will only affect text under the zoomed-in heading. This is useful for restricting changes to a particular chapter or section of your document.

To unzoom (exit) a fold, use C-c C-x (M-x foldout-exit-fold). This hides all the text and subheadings under the top-level heading and returns you to the previous view of the buffer. Specifying a numeric argument exits that many levels of folds. Specifying a zero argument exits all folds.

To cancel the narrowing of a fold without hiding the text and subheadings, specify a negative argument. For example, M--2 C-c C-x exits two folds and leaves the text and subheadings exposed.

Foldout mode also provides mouse commands for entering and exiting folds, and for showing and hiding text:

C-M-Mouse-1 zooms in on the heading clicked on
        single click: expose body.

> double click: expose subheadings.
>
> triple click: expose body and subheadings.
>
> quad click: expose entire subtree.

C-M-Mouse-2 exposes text under the heading clicked on

> single click: expose body.
>
> double click: expose subheadings.
>
> triple click: expose body and subheadings.
>
> quad click: expose entire subtree.

C-M-Mouse-3 hides text under the heading clicked on or exits fold

> single click: hide subtree.
>
> double click: exit fold and hide text.
>
> triple click: exit fold without hiding text.
>
> quad click: exit all folds and hide text.

You can specify different modifier keys (instead of Ctrl-META-) by setting foldout-mouse-modifiers; but if you have already loaded the foldout.el library, you must reload it in order for this to take effect.

To use the Foldout package, you can type M-x load-library RET foldout RET; or you can arrange for to do that automatically by putting the following in your init file:

```
(eval-after-load "outline" '(require 'foldout))
```

22.9 Org Mode

Org mode is a variant of Outline mode for using Emacs as an organizer and/or authoring system. Files with names ending in the extension .org are opened in Org mode (see Section 20.3 [Choosing Modes], page 202). To explicitly switch to Org mode, type M-x org-mode.

In Org mode, as in Outline mode, each entry has a heading line that starts with one or more '*' characters. See Section 22.8.1 [Outline Format], page 218. In addition, any line that begins with the '#' character is treated as a comment.

Org mode provides commands for easily viewing and manipulating the outline structure. The simplest of these commands is TAB (org-cycle). If invoked on a heading line, it cycles through the different visibility states of the subtree: (i) showing only that heading line, (ii) showing only the heading line and the heading lines of its direct children, if any, and (iii) showing the entire subtree. If invoked in a body line, the global binding for TAB is executed.

Typing S-TAB (org-shifttab) anywhere in an Org mode buffer cycles the visibility of the entire outline structure, between (i) showing only top-level heading lines, (ii) showing all heading lines but no body lines, and (iii) showing everything.

You can move an entire entry up or down in the buffer, including its body lines and subtree (if any), by typing M-<up> (org-metaup) or M-<down> (org-metadown) on the heading line. Similarly, you can promote or demote a heading line with M-<left> (org-metaleft) and M-<right> (org-metaright). These commands execute their global bindings if invoked on a body line.

The following subsections give basic instructions for using Org mode as an organizer and as an authoring system. For details, see Section "Introduction" in *The Org Manual*.

22.9.1 Org as an organizer

You can tag an Org entry as a *TODO* item by typing `C-c C-t` (`org-todo`) anywhere in the entry. This adds the keyword 'TODO' to the heading line. Typing `C-c C-t` again switches the keyword to 'DONE'; another `C-c C-t` removes the keyword entirely, and so forth. You can customize the keywords used by `C-c C-t` via the variable `org-todo-keywords`.

Apart from marking an entry as TODO, you can attach a date to it, by typing `C-c C-s` (`org-schedule`) in the entry. This prompts for a date by popping up the Emacs Calendar (see Chapter 28 [Calendar/Diary], page 331), and then adds the tag 'SCHEDULED', together with the selected date, beneath the heading line. The command `C-c C-d` (`org-deadline`) has the same effect, except that it uses the tag DEADLINE.

Once you have some TODO items planned in an Org file, you can add that file to the list of *agenda files* by typing `C-c [` (`org-agenda-file-to-front`). Org mode is designed to let you easily maintain multiple agenda files, e.g., for organizing different aspects of your life. The list of agenda files is stored in the variable `org-agenda-files`.

To view items coming from your agenda files, type `M-x org-agenda`. This command prompts for what you want to see: a list of things to do this week, a list of TODO items with specific keywords, etc.

22.9.2 Org as an authoring system

You may want to format your Org notes nicely and to prepare them for export and publication. To export the current buffer, type `C-c C-e` (`org-export`) anywhere in an Org buffer. This command prompts for an export format; currently supported formats include HTML, LaTeX, OpenDocument (`.odt`), and PDF. Some formats, such as PDF, require certain system tools to be installed.

To export several files at once to a specific directory, either locally or over the network, you must define a list of projects through the variable `org-publish-project-alist`. See its documentation for details.

Org supports a simple markup scheme for applying text formatting to exported documents:

```
- This text is /emphasized/
- This text is *in bold*
- This text is _underlined_
- This text uses =a teletype font=

#+begin_quote
''This is a quote.''
#+end_quote

#+begin_example
This is an example.
#+end_example
```

For further details, Section "Exporting" in *The Org Manual*, and Section "Publishing" in *The Org Manual*.

22.10 TeX Mode

Emacs provides special major modes for editing files written in TeX and its related formats. TeX is a powerful text formatter written by Donald Knuth; like GNU Emacs, it is free software. LaTeX is a simplified input format for TeX, implemented using TeX macros. DocTeX is a special file format in which the LaTeX sources are written, combining sources with documentation. SliTeX is an obsolete special form of LaTeX.[1]

TeX mode has four variants: Plain TeX mode, LaTeX mode, DocTeX mode, and SliTeX mode. These distinct major modes differ only slightly, and are designed for editing the four different formats. Emacs selects the appropriate mode by looking at the contents of the buffer. (This is done by the `tex-mode` command, which is normally called automatically when you visit a TeX-like file. See Section 20.3 [Choosing Modes], page 202.) If the contents are insufficient to determine this, Emacs chooses the mode specified by the variable `tex-default-mode`; its default value is `latex-mode`. If Emacs does not guess right, you can select the correct variant of TeX mode using the command M-x `plain-tex-mode`, M-x `latex-mode`, M-x `slitex-mode`, or `doctex-mode`.

The following sections document the features of TeX mode and its variants. There are several other TeX-related Emacs packages, which are not documented in this manual:

- BibTeX mode is a major mode for BibTeX files, which are commonly used for keeping bibliographic references for LaTeX documents. For more information, see the documentation string for the command `bibtex-mode`.

- The RefTeX package provides a minor mode which can be used with LaTeX mode to manage bibliographic references. For more information, see the RefTeX Info manual, which is distributed with Emacs.

- The AUCTeX package provides more advanced features for editing TeX and its related formats, including the ability to preview TeX equations within Emacs buffers. Unlike BibTeX mode and the RefTeX package, AUCTeX is not distributed with Emacs by default. It can be downloaded via the Package Menu (see Chapter 32 [Packages], page 408); once installed, see the AUCTeX manual, which is included with the package.

22.10.1 TeX Editing Commands

"   Insert, according to context, either ' " ' or ' " ' or ' " ' (`tex-insert-quote`).

C-j   Insert a paragraph break (two newlines) and check the previous paragraph for unbalanced braces or dollar signs (`tex-terminate-paragraph`).

M-x tex-validate-region
             Check each paragraph in the region for unbalanced braces or dollar signs.

C-c {   Insert '{}' and position point between them (`tex-insert-braces`).

C-c }   Move forward past the next unmatched close brace (`up-list`).

In TeX, the character ' " ' is not normally used; instead, quotations begin with ' " ' and end with ' " '. TeX mode therefore binds the " key to the `tex-insert-quote` command. This inserts ' " ' after whitespace or an open brace, ' " ' after a backslash, and ' " ' after any other character.

---

[1] It has been replaced by the '`slides`' document class, which comes with LaTeX.

As a special exception, if you type " when the text before point is either '' ' ' ' or '' ' ' '', Emacs replaces that preceding text with a single '"' character. You can therefore type "" to insert '"', should you ever need to do so. (You can also use C-q " to insert this character.)

In TEX mode, '$' has a special syntax code which attempts to understand the way TEX math mode delimiters match. When you insert a '$' that is meant to exit math mode, the position of the matching '$' that entered math mode is displayed for a second. This is the same feature that displays the open brace that matches a close brace that is inserted. However, there is no way to tell whether a '$' enters math mode or leaves it; so when you insert a '$' that enters math mode, the previous '$' position is shown as if it were a match, even though they are actually unrelated.

TEX uses braces as delimiters that must match. Some users prefer to keep braces balanced at all times, rather than inserting them singly. Use C-c { (tex-insert-braces) to insert a pair of braces. It leaves point between the two braces so you can insert the text that belongs inside. Afterward, use the command C-c } (up-list) to move forward past the close brace.

There are two commands for checking the matching of braces. C-j (tex-terminate-paragraph) checks the paragraph before point, and inserts two newlines to start a new paragraph. It outputs a message in the echo area if any mismatch is found. M-x tex-validate-region checks a region, paragraph by paragraph. The errors are listed in an *Occur* buffer; you can use the usual Occur mode commands in that buffer, such as C-c C-c, to visit a particular mismatch (see Section 12.11 [Other Repeating Search], page 107).

Note that Emacs commands count square brackets and parentheses in TEX mode, not just braces. This is not strictly correct for the purpose of checking TEX syntax. However, parentheses and square brackets are likely to be used in text as matching delimiters, and it is useful for the various motion commands and automatic match display to work with them.

22.10.2 LaTEX Editing Commands

LaTEX mode provides a few extra features not applicable to plain TEX:

C-c C-o   Insert '\begin' and '\end' for LaTEX block and position point on a line between them (tex-latex-block).

C-c C-e   Close the innermost LaTEX block not yet closed (tex-close-latex-block).

In LaTEX input, '\begin' and '\end' tags are used to group blocks of text. To insert a block, type C-c C-o (tex-latex-block). This prompts for a block type, and inserts the appropriate matching '\begin' and '\end' tags, leaving a blank line between the two and moving point there.

When entering the block type argument to C-c C-o, you can use the usual completion commands (see Section 5.4 [Completion], page 28). The default completion list contains the standard LaTEX block types. If you want additional block types for completion, customize the list variable latex-block-names.

In LaTEX input, '\begin' and '\end' tags must balance. You can use C-c C-e (tex-close-latex-block) to insert an '\end' tag which matches the last unmatched '\begin'. It also indents the '\end' to match the corresponding '\begin', and inserts a newline after the '\end' tag if point is at the beginning of a line. The minor mode `latex-electric-env-pair-mode` automatically inserts an '\end' or '\begin' tag for you when you type the corresponding one.

22.10.3 TeX Printing Commands

You can invoke TeX as an subprocess of Emacs, supplying either the entire contents of the buffer or just part of it (e.g., one chapter of a larger document).

C-c C-b   Invoke TeX on the entire current buffer (`tex-buffer`).

C-c C-r   Invoke TeX on the current region, together with the buffer's header (`tex-region`).

C-c C-f   Invoke TeX on the current file (`tex-file`).

C-c C-v   Preview the output from the last C-c C-r, C-c C-b, or C-c C-f command (`tex-view`).

C-c C-p   Print the output from the last C-c C-b, C-c C-r, or C-c C-f command (`tex-print`).

C-c TAB   Invoke BibTeX on the current file (`tex-bibtex-file`).

C-c C-l   Recenter the window showing output from TeX so that the last line can be seen (`tex-recenter-output-buffer`).

C-c C-k   Kill the TeX subprocess (`tex-kill-job`).

C-c C-c   Invoke some other compilation command on the entire current buffer (`tex-compile`).

To pass the current buffer through TeX, type C-c C-b (`tex-buffer`). The formatted output goes in a temporary file, normally a `.dvi` file. Afterwards, you can type C-c C-v (`tex-view`) to launch an external program, such as `xdvi`, to view this output file. You can also type C-c C-p (`tex-print`) to print a hardcopy of the output file.

By default, C-c C-b runs TeX in the current directory. The output of TeX also goes in this directory. To run TeX in a different directory, change the variable `tex-directory` to the desired directory name. If your environment variable `TEXINPUTS` contains relative directory names, or if your files contains '\input' commands with relative file names, then `tex-directory` *must* be "." or you will get the wrong results. Otherwise, it is safe to specify some other directory, such as "/tmp".

The buffer's TeX variant determines what shell command C-c C-b actually runs. In Plain TeX mode, it is specified by the variable `tex-run-command`, which defaults to "tex". In LaTeX mode, it is specified by `latex-run-command`, which defaults to "latex". The shell command that C-c C-v runs to view the `.dvi` output is determined by the variable `tex-dvi-view-command`, regardless of the TeX variant. The shell command that C-c C-p runs to print the output is determined by the variable `tex-dvi-print-command`.

Normally, Emacs automatically appends the output file name to the shell command strings described in the preceding paragraph. For example, if `tex-dvi-view-command` is "xdvi", C-c C-v runs `xdvi output-file-name`. In some cases, however, the file name needs to be embedded in the command, e.g., if you need to provide the file name as an argument to one command whose output is piped to another. You can specify where to put the file name with '*' in the command string. For example,

```
(setq tex-dvi-print-command "dvips -f * | lpr")
```

The terminal output from TEX, including any error messages, appears in a buffer called `*tex-shell*`. If TEX gets an error, you can switch to this buffer and feed it input (this works as in Shell mode; see Section 31.4.2 [Interactive Shell], page 384). Without switching to this buffer you can scroll it so that its last line is visible by typing `C-c C-l`.

Type `C-c C-k` (`tex-kill-job`) to kill the TEX process if you see that its output is no longer useful. Using `C-c C-b` or `C-c C-r` also kills any TEX process still running.

You can also pass an arbitrary region through TEX by typing `C-c C-r` (`tex-region`). This is tricky, however, because most files of TEX input contain commands at the beginning to set parameters and define macros, without which no later part of the file will format correctly. To solve this problem, `C-c C-r` allows you to designate a part of the file as containing essential commands; it is included before the specified region as part of the input to TEX. The designated part of the file is called the *header*.

To indicate the bounds of the header in Plain TEX mode, you insert two special strings in the file. Insert '`%**start of header`' before the header, and '`%**end of header`' after it. Each string must appear entirely on one line, but there may be other text on the line before or after. The lines containing the two strings are included in the header. If '`%**start of header`' does not appear within the first 100 lines of the buffer, `C-c C-r` assumes that there is no header.

In LATEX mode, the header begins with '`\documentclass`' or '`\documentstyle`' and ends with '`\begin{document}`'. These are commands that LATEX requires you to use in any case, so nothing special needs to be done to identify the header.

The commands (`tex-buffer`) and (`tex-region`) do all of their work in a temporary directory, and do not have available any of the auxiliary files needed by TEX for cross-references; these commands are generally not suitable for running the final copy in which all of the cross-references need to be correct.

When you want the auxiliary files for cross references, use `C-c C-f` (`tex-file`) which runs TEX on the current buffer's file, in that file's directory. Before running TEX, it offers to save any modified buffers. Generally, you need to use (`tex-file`) twice to get the cross-references right.

The value of the variable `tex-start-options` specifies options for the TEX run.

The value of the variable `tex-start-commands` specifies TEX commands for starting TEX. The default value causes TEX to run in nonstop mode. To run TEX interactively, set the variable to `""`.

Large TEX documents are often split into several files—one main file, plus subfiles. Running TEX on a subfile typically does not work; you have to run it on the main file. In order to make `tex-file` useful when you are editing a subfile, you can set the variable `tex-main-file` to the name of the main file. Then `tex-file` runs TEX on that file.

The most convenient way to use `tex-main-file` is to specify it in a local variable list in each of the subfiles. See Section 33.2.4 [File Variables], page 424.

For LATEX files, you can use BibTEX to process the auxiliary file for the current buffer's file. BibTEX looks up bibliographic citations in a data base and prepares the cited references for the bibliography section. The command `C-c TAB` (`tex-bibtex-file`) runs the shell command (`tex-bibtex-command`) to produce a '`.bbl`' file for the current buffer's file.

Generally, you need to do C-c C-f (tex-file) once to generate the '.aux' file, then do C-c TAB (tex-bibtex-file), and then repeat C-c C-f (tex-file) twice more to get the cross-references correct.

To invoke some other compilation program on the current TEX buffer, type C-c C-c (tex-compile). This command knows how to pass arguments to many common programs, including pdflatex, yap, xdvi, and dvips. You can select your desired compilation program using the standard completion keys (see Section 5.4 [Completion], page 28).

22.10.4 TEX Mode Miscellany

Entering any variant of TEX mode runs the hooks text-mode-hook and tex-mode-hook. Then it runs either plain-tex-mode-hook, latex-mode-hook, or slitex-mode-hook, whichever is appropriate. Starting the TEX shell runs the hook tex-shell-hook. See Section 33.2.2 [Hooks], page 422.

The commands M-x iso-iso2tex, M-x iso-tex2iso, M-x iso-iso2gtex and M-x iso-gtex2iso can be used to convert between Latin-1 encoded files and TEX-encoded equivalents.

22.11 SGML and HTML Modes

The major modes for SGML and HTML provide indentation support and commands for operating on tags. HTML mode is a slightly customized variant of SGML mode.

C-c C-n   Interactively specify a special character and insert the SGML '&'-command for that character (sgml-name-char).

C-c C-t   Interactively specify a tag and its attributes (sgml-tag). This command asks you for a tag name and for the attribute values, then inserts both the opening tag and the closing tag, leaving point between them.

With a prefix argument n, the command puts the tag around the n words already present in the buffer after point. Whenever a region is active, it puts the tag around the region (when Transient Mark mode is off, it does this when a numeric argument of -1 is supplied.)

C-c C-a   Interactively insert attribute values for the current tag (sgml-attributes).

C-c C-f   Skip across a balanced tag group (which extends from an opening tag through its corresponding closing tag) (sgml-skip-tag-forward). A numeric argument acts as a repeat count.

C-c C-b   Skip backward across a balanced tag group (which extends from an opening tag through its corresponding closing tag) (sgml-skip-tag-backward). A numeric argument acts as a repeat count.

C-c C-d   Delete the tag at or after point, and delete the matching tag too (sgml-delete-tag). If the tag at or after point is an opening tag, delete the closing tag too; if it is a closing tag, delete the opening tag too.

C-c ? *tag* RET

     Display a description of the meaning of tag *tag* (sgml-tag-help). If the argument *tag* is empty, describe the tag at point.

C-c /   Insert a close tag for the innermost unterminated tag (`sgml-close-tag`). If
           called within a tag or a comment, close it instead of inserting a close tag.

C-c 8   Toggle a minor mode in which Latin-1 characters insert the corresponding
           SGML commands that stand for them, instead of the characters themselves
           (`sgml-name-8bit-mode`).

C-c C-v   Run a shell command (which you must specify) to validate the current buffer
           as SGML (`sgml-validate`).

C-c TAB   Toggle the visibility of existing tags in the buffer. This can be used as a cheap
           preview (`sgml-tags-invisible`).

The major mode for editing XML documents is called nXML mode. This is a powerful major mode that can recognize many existing XML schema and use them to provide completion of XML elements via `M-TAB`, as well as "on-the-fly" XML validation with error highlighting. To enable nXML mode in an existing buffer, type `M-x nxml-mode`, or, equivalently, `M-x xml-mode`. Emacs uses nXML mode for files which have the extension `.xml`. For XHTML files, which have the extension `.xhtml`, Emacs uses HTML mode by default; you can make it use nXML mode by customizing the variable `auto-mode-alist` (see Section 20.3 [Choosing Modes], page 202). nXML mode is described in an Info manual, which is distributed with Emacs.

You may choose to use the less powerful SGML mode for editing XML, since XML is a strict subset of SGML. To enable SGML mode in an existing buffer, type `M-x sgml-mode`. On enabling SGML mode, Emacs examines the buffer to determine whether it is XML; if so, it sets the variable `sgml-xml-mode` to a non-`nil` value. This causes SGML mode's tag insertion commands, described above, to always insert explicit closing tags as well.

22.12 Nroff Mode

Nroff mode, a major mode derived from Text mode, is specialized for editing nroff files (e.g., Unix man pages). Type `M-x nroff-mode` to enter this mode. Entering Nroff mode runs the hook `text-mode-hook`, then `nroff-mode-hook` (see Section 33.2.2 [Hooks], page 422).

In Nroff mode, nroff command lines are treated as paragraph separators, pages are separated by '`.bp`' commands, and comments start with backslash-doublequote. It also defines these commands:

M-n   Move to the beginning of the next line that isn't an nroff command
           (`forward-text-line`). An argument is a repeat count.

M-p   Like `M-n` but move up (`backward-text-line`).

M-?   Displays in the echo area the number of text lines (lines that are not nroff
           commands) in the region (`count-text-lines`).

Electric Nroff mode is a buffer-local minor mode that can be used with Nroff mode. To toggle this minor mode, type `M-x electric-nroff-mode` (see Section 20.2 [Minor Modes], page 200). When the mode is on, each time you type `RET` to end a line containing an nroff command that opens a kind of grouping, the nroff command to close that grouping is automatically inserted on the following line.

If you use Outline minor mode with Nroff mode (see Section 22.8 [Outline Mode], page 217), heading lines are lines of the form '`.H`' followed by a number (the header level).

22.13 Enriched Text

Enriched mode is a minor mode for editing formatted text files in a WYSIWYG ("what you see is what you get") fashion. When Enriched mode is enabled, you can apply various formatting properties to the text in the buffer, such as fonts and colors; upon saving the buffer, those properties are saved together with the text, using the MIME 'text/enriched' file format.

Enriched mode is typically used with Text mode (see Section 22.7 [Text Mode], page 217). It is *not* compatible with Font Lock mode, which is used by many major modes, including most programming language modes, for syntax highlighting (see Section 11.12 [Font Lock], page 78). Unlike Enriched mode, Font Lock mode assigns text properties automatically, based on the current buffer contents; those properties are not saved to disk.

The file enriched.txt in Emacs's data-directory serves as an example of the features of Enriched mode.

22.13.1 Enriched Mode

Enriched mode is a buffer-local minor mode (see Section 20.2 [Minor Modes], page 200). When you visit a file that has been saved in the 'text/enriched' format, Emacs automatically enables Enriched mode, and applies the formatting information in the file to the buffer text. When you save a buffer with Enriched mode enabled, it is saved using the 'text/enriched' format, including the formatting information.

To create a new file of formatted text, visit the nonexistent file and type M-x enriched-mode. This command actually toggles Enriched mode. With a prefix argument, it enables Enriched mode if the argument is positive, and disables Enriched mode otherwise. If you disable Enriched mode, Emacs no longer saves the buffer using the 'text/enriched' format; any formatting properties that have been added to the buffer remain in the buffer, but they are not saved to disk.

Enriched mode does not save all Emacs text properties, only those specified in the variable enriched-translations. These include properties for fonts, colors, indentation, and justification.

If you visit a file and Emacs fails to recognize that it is in the 'text/enriched' format, type M-x format-decode-buffer. This command prompts for a file format, and re-reads the file in that format. Specifying the 'text/enriched' format automatically enables Enriched mode.

To view a 'text/enriched' file in raw form (as plain text with markup tags rather than formatted text), use M-x find-file-literally (see Section 15.2 [Visiting], page 123).

See Section "Format Conversion" in *the Emacs Lisp Reference Manual*, for details of how Emacs recognizes and converts file formats like 'text/enriched'. See Section "Text Properties" in *the Emacs Lisp Reference Manual*, for more information about text properties.

22.13.2 Hard and Soft Newlines

In Enriched mode, Emacs distinguishes between two different kinds of newlines, *hard* newlines and *soft* newlines. You can also enable or disable this feature in other buffers, by typing M-x use-hard-newlines.

Hard newlines are used to separate paragraphs, or anywhere there needs to be a line break regardless of how the text is filled; soft newlines are used for filling. The RET (newline) and C-o (open-line) commands insert hard newlines. The fill commands, including Auto Fill (see Section 22.5.1 [Auto Fill], page 212), insert only soft newlines and delete only soft newlines, leaving hard newlines alone.

Thus, when editing with Enriched mode, you should not use RET or C-o to break lines in the middle of filled paragraphs. Use Auto Fill mode or explicit fill commands (see Section 22.5.2 [Fill Commands], page 213) instead. Use RET or C-o where line breaks should always remain, such as in tables and lists. For such lines, you may also want to set the justification style to unfilled (see Section 22.13.6 [Enriched Justification], page 233).

22.13.3 Editing Format Information

The easiest way to alter properties is with the 'Text Properties' menu. You can get to this menu from the 'Edit' menu in the menu bar (see Section 1.4 [Menu Bar], page 9), or with C-Mouse-2 (see Section 18.4 [Menu Mouse Clicks], page 165). Some of the commands in the 'Text Properties' menu are listed below (you can also invoke them with M-x):

Remove Face Properties
> Remove face properties from the region (facemenu-remove-face-props).

Remove Text Properties
> Remove all text properties from the region, including face properties (facemenu-remove-all).

Describe Properties
> List all text properties and other information about the character following point (describe-text-properties).

Display Faces
> Display a list of defined faces (list-faces-display). See Section 11.8 [Faces], page 74.

Display Colors
> Display a list of defined colors (list-colors-display). See Section 11.9 [Colors], page 75.

The other menu entries are described in the following sections.

22.13.4 Faces in Enriched Text

The following commands can be used to add or remove faces (see Section 11.8 [Faces], page 74). Each applies to the text in the region if the mark is active, and to the next self-inserting character if the mark is inactive. With a prefix argument, each command applies to the next self-inserting character even if the region is active.

M-o d   Remove all face properties (facemenu-set-default).

M-o b   Apply the bold face (facemenu-set-bold).

M-o i   Apply the italic face (facemenu-set-italic).

M-o l   Apply the bold-italic face (facemenu-set-bold-italic).

M-o u   Apply the underline face (facemenu-set-underline).

M-o o *face* RET

>Apply the face *face* (`facemenu-set-face`).

M-x facemenu-set-foreground

>Prompt for a color (see Section 11.9 [Colors], page 75), and apply it as a foreground color.

M-x facemenu-set-background

>Prompt for a color, and apply it as a background color.

These command are also available via the Text Properties menu.

A self-inserting character normally inherits the face properties (and most other text properties) from the preceding character in the buffer. If you use one of the above commands to specify the face for the next self-inserting character, that character will not inherit the faces properties from the preceding character, but it will still inherit other text properties.

Enriched mode defines two additional faces: `excerpt` and `fixed`. These correspond to codes used in the text/enriched file format. The `excerpt` face is intended for quotations; by default, it appears the same as `italic`. The `fixed` face specifies fixed-width text; by default, it appears the same as `bold`.

22.13.5 Indentation in Enriched Text

In Enriched mode, you can specify different amounts of indentation for the right or left margin of a paragraph or a part of a paragraph. These margins also affect fill commands such as M-q (see Section 22.5 [Filling], page 212).

The Indentation submenu of Text Properties offers commands for specifying indentation:

Indent More

>Indent the region by 4 columns (`increase-left-margin`). In Enriched mode, this command is also available on C-x TAB; if you supply a numeric argument, that says how many columns to add to the margin (a negative argument reduces the number of columns).

Indent Less

>Remove 4 columns of indentation from the region.

Indent Right More

>Make the text narrower by indenting 4 columns at the right margin.

Indent Right Less

>Remove 4 columns of indentation from the right margin.

The variable `standard-indent` specifies how many columns these commands should add to or subtract from the indentation. The default value is 4. The default right margin for Enriched mode is controlled by the variable `fill-column`, as usual.

You can also type C-c [(`set-left-margin`) and C-c] (`set-right-margin`) to set the left and right margins. You can specify the margin width with a numeric argument; otherwise these commands prompt for a value via the minibuffer.

The fill prefix, if any, works in addition to the specified paragraph indentation: C-x . does not include the specified indentation's whitespace in the new value for the fill prefix, and the fill commands look for the fill prefix after the indentation on each line. See Section 22.5.3 [Fill Prefix], page 214.

22.13.6 Justification in Enriched Text

In Enriched mode, you can use the following commands to specify various *justification styles* for filling. These commands apply to the paragraph containing point, or, if the region is active, to all paragraphs overlapping the region.

M-j l   Align lines to the left margin (`set-justification-left`).

M-j r   Align lines to the right margin (`set-justification-right`).

M-j b   Align lines to both margins, inserting spaces in the middle of the line to achieve this (`set-justification-full`).

M-j c
M-S   Center lines between the margins (`set-justification-center`).

M-j u   Turn off filling entirely (`set-justification-none`). The fill commands do nothing on text with this setting. You can, however, still indent the left margin.

You can also specify justification styles using the Justification submenu in the Text Properties menu. The default justification style is specified by the per-buffer variable `default-justification`. Its value should be one of the symbols `left`, `right`, `full`, `center`, or `none`; their meanings correspond to the commands above.

22.13.7 Setting Other Text Properties

The Special Properties submenu of Text Properties has entries for adding or removing three other text properties: `read-only`, (which disallows alteration of the text), `invisible` (which hides text), and `intangible` (which disallows moving point within the text). The 'Remove Special' menu item removes all of these special properties from the text in the region.

The `invisible` and `intangible` properties are not saved.

22.14 Editing Text-based Tables

The `table` package provides commands to easily edit text-based tables. Here is an example of what such a table looks like:

```
+----------------+-------------------------------+-----------------+
|    Command     |          Description          |   Key Binding   |
+----------------+-------------------------------+-----------------+
|  forward-char  |Move point right N characters  |      C-f        |
|                |(left if N is negative).       |                 |
|                |                               |                 |
+----------------+-------------------------------+-----------------+
|  backward-char |Move point left N characters   |      C-b        |
|                |(right if N is negative).      |                 |
|                |                               |                 |
+----------------+-------------------------------+-----------------+
```

When Emacs recognizes such a stretch of text as a table (see Section 22.14.3 [Table Recognition], page 234), editing the contents of each table cell will automatically resize the table, whenever the contents become too large to fit in the cell. You can use the commands defined in the following sections for navigating and editing the table layout.

Type `M-x table-fixed-width-mode` to toggle the automatic table resizing feature.

22.14.1 What is a Text-based Table?

A *table* consists of a rectangular text area which is divided into *cells*. Each cell must be at least one character wide and one character high, not counting its border lines. A cell can be subdivided into more cells, but they cannot overlap.

Cell border lines are drawn with three special characters, specified by the following variables:

`table-cell-vertical-char`
>   The character used for vertical lines. The default is '|'.

`table-cell-horizontal-chars`
>   The characters used for horizontal lines. The default is '"-="'.

`table-cell-intersection-char`
>   The character used for the intersection of horizontal and vertical lines. The default is '+'.

The following are examples of *invalid* tables:

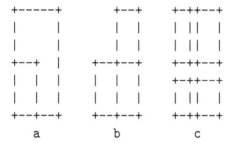

From left to right:

a. Overlapped cells or non-rectangular cells are not allowed.

b. The border must be rectangular.

c. Cells must have a minimum width/height of one character.

22.14.2 Creating a Table

To create a text-based table from scratch, type M-x `table-insert`. This command prompts for the number of table columns, the number of table rows, cell width and cell height. The cell width and cell height do not include the cell borders; each can be specified as a single integer (which means each cell is given the same width/height), or as a sequence of integers separated by spaces or commas (which specify the width/height of the individual table columns/rows, counting from left to right for table columns and from top to bottom for table rows). The specified table is then inserted at point.

The table inserted by M-x `table-insert` contains special text properties, which tell Emacs to treat it specially as a text-based table. If you save the buffer to a file and visit it again later, those properties are lost, and the table appears to Emacs as an ordinary piece of text. See the next section, for how to convert it back into a table.

22.14.3 Table Recognition

Existing text-based tables in a buffer, which lack the special text properties applied by M-x `table-insert`, are not treated specially as tables. To apply those text properties, type `M-x table-recognize`. This command scans the current buffer, *recognizes* valid table cells, and applies the relevant text properties. Conversely, type `M-x table-unrecognize` to *unrecognize* all tables in the current buffer, removing the special text properties and converting tables back to plain text.

You can also use the following commands to selectively recognize or unrecognize tables:

`M-x table-recognize-region`
> Recognize tables within the current region.

`M-x table-unrecognize-region`
> Unrecognize tables within the current region.

`M-x table-recognize-table`
> Recognize the table at point and activate it.

`M-x table-unrecognize-table`
> Deactivate the table at point.

`M-x table-recognize-cell`
> Recognize the cell at point and activate it.

`M-x table-unrecognize-cell`
> Deactivate the cell at point.

See Section 22.14.7 [Table Conversion], page 236, for another way to recognize a table.

22.14.4 Commands for Table Cells

The commands `M-x table-forward-cell` and `M-x table-backward-cell` move point from the current cell to an adjacent cell. The order is cyclic: when point is in the last cell of a table, `M-x table-forward-cell` moves to the first cell. Likewise, when point is on the first cell, `M-x table-backward-cell` moves to the last cell.

`M-x table-span-cell` prompts for a direction—right, left, above, or below—and merges the current cell with the adjacent cell in that direction. This command signals an error if the merge would result in an illegitimate cell layout.

`M-x table-split-cell` splits the current cell vertically or horizontally, prompting for the direction with the minibuffer. To split in a specific direction, use `M-x table-split-cell-vertically` and `M-x table-split-cell-horizontally`. When splitting vertically, the old cell contents are automatically split between the two new cells. When splitting horizontally, you are prompted for how to divide the cell contents, if the cell is non-empty; the options are '`split`' (divide the contents at point), '`left`' (put all the contents in the left cell), and '`right`' (put all the contents in the right cell).

The following commands enlarge or shrink a cell. By default, they resize by one row or column; if a numeric argument is supplied, that specifies the number of rows or columns to resize by.

`M-x table-heighten-cell`
> Enlarge the current cell vertically.

`M-x table-shorten-cell`
> Shrink the current cell vertically.

`M-x table-widen-cell`
>   Enlarge the current cell horizontally.

`M-x table-narrow-cell`
>   Shrink the current cell horizontally.

22.14.5 Cell Justification

The command `M-x table-justify` imposes *justification* on one or more cells in a text-based table. Justification determines how the text in the cell is aligned, relative to the edges of the cell. Each cell in a table can be separately justified.

`M-x table-justify` first prompts for what to justify; the options are 'cell' (just the current cell), 'column' (all cells in the current table column) and 'row' (all cells in the current table row). The command then prompts for the justification style; the options are `left`, `center`, `right`, `top`, `middle`, `bottom`, or `none` (meaning no vertical justification).

Horizontal and vertical justification styles are specified independently, and both types can be in effect simultaneously; for instance, you can call `M-x table-justify` twice, once to specify `right` justification and once to specify `bottom` justification, to align the contents of a cell to the bottom right.

The justification style is stored in the buffer as a text property, and is lost when you kill the buffer or exit Emacs. However, the table recognition commands, such as `M-x table-recognize` (see Section 22.14.3 [Table Recognition], page 234), attempt to determine and re-apply each cell's justification style, by examining its contents. To disable this feature, change the variable `table-detect-cell-alignment` to `nil`.

22.14.6 Table Rows and Columns

`M-x table-insert-row` inserts a row of cells before the current table row. The current row, together with point, is pushed down past the new row. To insert a row after the last row at the bottom of a table, invoke this command with point below the table, just below the bottom edge. You can insert more than one row at a time by using a numeric prefix argument.

Similarly, `M-x table-insert-column` inserts a column of cells to the left of the current table column. To insert a column to the right side of the rightmost column, invoke this command with point to the right of the rightmost column, outside the table. A numeric prefix argument specifies the number of columns to insert.

`M-x table-delete-column` deletes the column of cells at point. Similarly, `M-x table-delete-row` deletes the row of cells at point. A numeric prefix argument to either command specifies the number of columns or rows to delete.

22.14.7 Converting Between Plain Text and Tables

The command `M-x table-capture` captures plain text in a region and turns it into a table. Unlike `M-x table-recognize` (see Section 22.14.3 [Table Recognition], page 234), the original text does not need to have a table appearance; it only needs to have a logical table-like structure.

For example, suppose we have the following numbers, which are divided into three lines and separated horizontally by commas:

```
1, 2, 3, 4
5, 6, 7, 8
, 9, 10
```

Invoking `M-x table-capture` on that text produces this table:

```
+-----+-----+-----+-----+
|1    |2    |3    |4    |
+-----+-----+-----+-----+
|5    |6    |7    |8    |
+-----+-----+-----+-----+
|     |9    |10   |     |
+-----+-----+-----+-----+
```

`M-x table-release` does the opposite: it converts a table back to plain text, removing its cell borders.

One application of this pair of commands is to edit a text in layout. Look at the following three paragraphs (the latter two are indented with header lines):

```
table-capture is a powerful command.
Here are some things it can do:

Parse Cell Items    Using row and column delimiter regexps,
                    it parses the specified text area and
                    extracts cell items into a table.
```

Applying `table-capture` to a region containing the above text, with empty strings for the column and row delimiter regexps, creates a table with a single cell like the following one.

```
+---------------------------------------------------------+
|table-capture is a powerful command.                     |
|Here are some things it can do:                          |
|                                                         |
|Parse Cell Items    Using row and column delimiter regexps,|
|                    it parses the specified text area and |
|                    extracts cell items into a table.     |
+---------------------------------------------------------+
```

We can then use the cell splitting commands (see Section 22.14.4 [Cell Commands], page 235) to subdivide the table so that each paragraph occupies a cell:

```
+---------------------------------------------------------+
|table-capture is a powerful command.                     |
|Here are some things it can do:                          |
+----------------+----------------------------------------+
|Parse Cell Items | Using row and column delimiter regexps,|
|                 | it parses the specified text area and  |
|                 | extracts cell items into a table.      |
+----------------+----------------------------------------+
```

Each cell can now be edited independently without affecting the layout of other cells. When finished, we can invoke `M-x table-release` to convert the table back to plain text.

22.14.8 Table Miscellany

The command `table-query-dimension` reports the layout of the table and table cell at point. Here is an example of its output:

```
     Cell: (21w, 6h), Table: (67w, 16h), Dim: (2c, 3r), Total Cells: 5
```

This indicates that the current cell is 21 characters wide and 6 lines high, the table is 67 characters wide and 16 lines high with 2 columns and 3 rows, and a total of 5 cells.

`M-x table-insert-sequence` inserts a string into each cell. Each string is a part of a sequence i.e., a series of increasing integer numbers.

`M-x table-generate-source` generates a table formatted for a specific markup language. It asks for a language (which must be one of `html`, `latex`, or `cals`), a destination buffer in which to put the result, and a table caption, and then inserts the generated table into the specified buffer. The default destination buffer is `table.`*lang*, where *lang* is the language you specified.

22.15 Two-Column Editing

Two-column mode lets you conveniently edit two side-by-side columns of text. It uses two side-by-side windows, each showing its own buffer. There are three ways to enter two-column mode:

F2 2 or C-x 6 2

> Enter two-column mode with the current buffer on the left, and on the right, a buffer whose name is based on the current buffer's name (`2C-two-columns`). If the right-hand buffer doesn't already exist, it starts out empty; the current buffer's contents are not changed.
>
> This command is appropriate when the current buffer is empty or contains just one column and you want to add another column.

F2 s or C-x 6 s

> Split the current buffer, which contains two-column text, into two buffers, and display them side by side (`2C-split`). The current buffer becomes the left-hand buffer, but the text in the right-hand column is moved into the right-hand buffer. The current column specifies the split point. Splitting starts with the current line and continues to the end of the buffer.
>
> This command is appropriate when you have a buffer that already contains two-column text, and you wish to separate the columns temporarily.

F2 b *buffer* RET
C-x 6 b *buffer* RET

> Enter two-column mode using the current buffer as the left-hand buffer, and using buffer *buffer* as the right-hand buffer (`2C-associate-buffer`).

`F2 s` or `C-x 6 s` looks for a column separator, which is a string that appears on each line between the two columns. You can specify the width of the separator with a numeric argument to `F2 s`; that many characters, before point, constitute the separator string. By default, the width is 1, so the column separator is the character before point.

When a line has the separator at the proper place, `F2 s` puts the text after the separator into the right-hand buffer, and deletes the separator. Lines that don't have the column separator at the proper place remain unsplit; they stay in the left-hand buffer, and the right-hand buffer gets an empty line to correspond. (This is the way to write a line that "spans both columns while in two-column mode": write it in the left-hand buffer, and put an empty line in the right-hand buffer.)

The command `C-x 6 RET` or `F2 RET` (`2C-newline`) inserts a newline in each of the two buffers at corresponding positions. This is the easiest way to add a new line to the two-column text while editing it in split buffers.

When you have edited both buffers as you wish, merge them with `F2 1` or `C-x 6 1` (`2C-merge`). This copies the text from the right-hand buffer as a second column in the other buffer. To go back to two-column editing, use `F2 s`.

Use `F2 d` or `C-x 6 d` to dissociate the two buffers, leaving each as it stands (`2C-dissociate`). If the other buffer, the one not current when you type `F2 d`, is empty, `F2 d` kills it.

23 Editing Programs

This chapter describes Emacs features for facilitating editing programs. Some of the things these features can do are:

- Find or move over top-level definitions (see Section 23.2 [Defuns], page 241).

- Apply the usual indentation conventions of the language (see Section 23.3 [Program Indent], page 243).

- Balance parentheses (see Section 23.4 [Parentheses], page 246).

- Insert, kill or align comments (see Section 23.5 [Comments], page 249).

- Highlight program syntax (see Section 11.12 [Font Lock], page 78).

23.1 Major Modes for Programming Languages

Emacs has specialized major modes (see Section 20.1 [Major Modes], page 199) for many programming languages. A programming language mode typically specifies the syntax of expressions, the customary rules for indentation, how to do syntax highlighting for the language, and how to find the beginning or end of a function definition. It often has features for compiling and debugging programs as well. The major mode for each language is named after the language; for instance, the major mode for the C programming language is c-mode.

Emacs has programming language modes for Lisp, Scheme, the Scheme-based DSSSL expression language, Ada, ASM, AWK, C, C++, Fortran, Icon, IDL (CORBA), IDLWAVE, Java, Javascript, Metafont (TeX's companion for font creation), Modula2, Object Pascal, Objective-C, Octave, Pascal, Perl, Pike, PostScript, Prolog, Python, Ruby, Simula, Tcl, and VHDL. An alternative mode for Perl is called CPerl mode. Modes are also available for the scripting languages of the common GNU and Unix shells, VMS DCL, and MS-DOS/MS-Windows 'BAT' files, and for makefiles, DNS master files, and various sorts of configuration files.

Ideally, Emacs should have a major mode for each programming language that you might want to edit. If it doesn't have a mode for your favorite language, the mode might be implemented in a package not distributed with Emacs (see Chapter 32 [Packages], page 408); or you can contribute one.

In most programming languages, indentation should vary from line to line to illustrate the structure of the program. Therefore, in most programming language modes, typing TAB updates the indentation of the current line (see Section 23.3 [Program Indent], page 243). Furthermore, DEL is usually bound to backward-delete-char-untabify, which deletes backward treating each tab as if it were the equivalent number of spaces, so that you can delete one column of indentation without worrying whether the whitespace consists of spaces or tabs.

Entering a programming language mode runs the custom Lisp functions specified in the hook variable prog-mode-hook, followed by those specified in the mode's own mode hook (see Section 20.1 [Major Modes], page 199). For instance, entering C mode runs the hooks prog-mode-hook and c-mode-hook. See Section 33.2.2 [Hooks], page 422, for information about hooks.

The Emacs distribution contains Info manuals for the major modes for Ada, C/C++/Objective C/Java/Corba IDL/Pike/AWK, and IDLWAVE. For Fortran mode, see Section "Fortran" in *Specialized Emacs Features*.

23.2 Top-Level Definitions, or Defuns

In Emacs, a major definition at the top level in the buffer, such as a function, is called a *defun*. The name comes from Lisp, but in Emacs we use it for all languages.

23.2.1 Left Margin Convention

Many programming-language modes assume by default that any opening delimiter found at the left margin is the start of a top-level definition, or defun. Therefore, **don't put an opening delimiter at the left margin unless it should have that significance**. For instance, never put an open-parenthesis at the left margin in a Lisp file unless it is the start of a top-level list.

The convention speeds up many Emacs operations, which would otherwise have to scan back to the beginning of the buffer to analyze the syntax of the code.

If you don't follow this convention, not only will you have trouble when you explicitly use the commands for motion by defuns; other features that use them will also give you trouble. This includes the indentation commands (see Section 23.3 [Program Indent], page 243) and Font Lock mode (see Section 11.12 [Font Lock], page 78).

The most likely problem case is when you want an opening delimiter at the start of a line inside a string. To avoid trouble, put an escape character ('\', in C and Emacs Lisp, '/' in some other Lisp dialects) before the opening delimiter. This will not affect the contents of the string, but will prevent that opening delimiter from starting a defun. Here's an example:

```
    (insert "Foo:
  \(bar)
  ")
```

To help you catch violations of this convention, Font Lock mode highlights confusing opening delimiters (those that ought to be quoted) in bold red.

If you need to override this convention, you can do so by setting the variable `open-paren-in-column-0-is-defun-start`. If this user option is set to `t` (the default), opening parentheses or braces at column zero always start defuns. When it is `nil`, defuns are found by searching for parens or braces at the outermost level.

Usually, you should leave this option at its default value of `t`. If your buffer contains parentheses or braces in column zero which don't start defuns, and it is somehow impractical to remove these parentheses or braces, it might be helpful to set the option to `nil`. Be aware that this might make scrolling and display in large buffers quite sluggish. Furthermore, the parentheses and braces must be correctly matched throughout the buffer for it to work properly.

23.2.2 Moving by Defuns

These commands move point or set up the region based on top-level major definitions, also called *defuns*.

C-M-a   Move to beginning of current or preceding defun (`beginning-of-defun`).

C-M-e   Move to end of current or following defun (`end-of-defun`).

C-M-h   Put region around whole current or following defun (`mark-defun`).

The commands to move to the beginning and end of the current defun are `C-M-a` (`beginning-of-defun`) and `C-M-e` (`end-of-defun`). If you repeat one of these commands, or use a positive numeric argument, each repetition moves to the next defun in the direction of motion.

`C-M-a` with a negative argument $-n$ moves forward n times to the next beginning of a defun. This is not exactly the same place that `C-M-e` with argument n would move to; the end of this defun is not usually exactly the same place as the beginning of the following defun. (Whitespace, comments, and perhaps declarations can separate them.) Likewise, `C-M-e` with a negative argument moves back to an end of a defun, which is not quite the same as `C-M-a` with a positive argument.

To operate on the current defun, use `C-M-h` (`mark-defun`), which sets the mark at the end of the current defun and puts point at its beginning. See Section 8.2 [Marking Objects], page 47. This is the easiest way to get ready to kill the defun in order to move it to a different place in the file. If you use the command while point is between defuns, it uses the following defun. If you use the command while the mark is already active, it sets the mark but does not move point; furthermore, each successive use of `C-M-h` extends the end of the region to include one more defun.

In C mode, `C-M-h` runs the function `c-mark-function`, which is almost the same as `mark-defun`; the difference is that it backs up over the argument declarations, function name and returned data type so that the entire C function is inside the region. This is an example of how major modes adjust the standard key bindings so that they do their standard jobs in a way better fitting a particular language. Other major modes may replace any or all of these key bindings for that purpose.

23.2.3 Imenu

The Imenu facility offers a way to find the major definitions in a file by name. It is also useful in text formatter major modes, where it treats each chapter, section, etc., as a definition. (See Section 25.3 [Tags], page 299, for a more powerful feature that handles multiple files together.)

If you type `M-x imenu`, it reads the name of a definition using the minibuffer, then moves point to that definition. You can use completion to specify the name; the command always displays the whole list of valid names.

Alternatively, you can bind the command `imenu` to a mouse click. Then it displays mouse menus for you to select a definition name. You can also add the buffer's index to the menu bar by calling `imenu-add-menubar-index`. If you want to have this menu bar item available for all buffers in a certain major mode, you can do this by adding `imenu-add-menubar-index` to its mode hook. But if you have done that, you will have to wait a little while each time you visit a file in that mode, while Emacs finds all the definitions in that buffer.

When you change the contents of a buffer, if you add or delete definitions, you can update the buffer's index based on the new contents by invoking the '`*Rescan*`' item in the menu. Rescanning happens automatically if you set `imenu-auto-rescan` to a non-`nil` value. There is no need to rescan because of small changes in the text.

You can customize the way the menus are sorted by setting the variable `imenu-sort-function`. By default, names are ordered as they occur in the buffer; if you want alphabetic sorting, use the symbol `imenu--sort-by-name` as the value. You can also define your own comparison function by writing Lisp code.

Imenu provides the information to guide Which Function mode (see below). The Speedbar can also use it (see Section 18.9 [Speedbar], page 171).

23.2.4 Which Function Mode

Which Function mode is a global minor mode (see Section 20.2 [Minor Modes], page 200) which displays the current function name in the mode line, updating it as you move around in a buffer.

To either enable or disable Which Function mode, use the command `M-x which-function-mode`. Which Function mode is a global minor mode. By default, it takes effect in all major modes major modes that know how to support it (i.e., all the major modes that support Imenu). You can restrict it to a specific list of major modes by changing the value of the variable `which-func-modes` from `t` (which means to support all available major modes) to a list of major mode names.

23.3 Indentation for Programs

The best way to keep a program properly indented is to use Emacs to reindent it as you change it. Emacs has commands to indent either a single line, a specified number of lines, or all of the lines inside a single parenthetical grouping.

See Chapter 21 [Indentation], page 205, for general information about indentation. This section describes indentation features specific to programming language modes.

Emacs also provides a Lisp pretty-printer in the `pp` package, which reformats Lisp objects with nice-looking indentation.

23.3.1 Basic Program Indentation Commands

TAB   Adjust indentation of current line (`indent-for-tab-command`).

RET   Insert a newline, then adjust indentation of following line (`newline`).

The basic indentation command is `TAB` (`indent-for-tab-command`), which was documented in Chapter 21 [Indentation], page 205. In programming language modes, `TAB` indents the current line, based on the indentation and syntactic content of the preceding lines; if the region is active, `TAB` indents each line within the region, not just the current line.

The command `RET` (`newline`), which was documented in Section 4.1 [Inserting Text], page 16, does the same as `C-j` followed by `TAB`: it inserts a new line, then adjusts the line's indentation.

When indenting a line that starts within a parenthetical grouping, Emacs usually places the start of the line under the preceding line within the group, or under the text after the parenthesis. If you manually give one of these lines a nonstandard indentation (e.g., for aesthetic purposes), the lines below will follow it.

The indentation commands for most programming language modes assume that a open-parenthesis, open-brace or other opening delimiter at the left margin is the start of a function. If the code you are editing violates this assumption—even if the delimiters occur in strings or comments—you must set `open-paren-in-column-0-is-defun-start` to `nil` for indentation to work properly. See Section 23.2.1 [Left Margin Paren], page 241.

23.3.2 Indenting Several Lines

Sometimes, you may want to reindent several lines of code at a time. One way to do this is to use the mark; when the mark is active and the region is non-empty, TAB indents every line in the region. Alternatively, the command C-M-\ (`indent-region`) indents every line in the region, whether or not the mark is active (see Section 21.1 [Indentation Commands], page 205).

In addition, Emacs provides the following commands for indenting large chunks of code:

C-M-q   Reindent all the lines within one parenthetical grouping.

C-u TAB   Shift an entire parenthetical grouping rigidly sideways so that its first line is
           properly indented.

M-x indent-code-rigidly
           Shift all the lines in the region rigidly sideways, but do not alter lines that start
           inside comments and strings.

To reindent the contents of a single parenthetical grouping, position point before the beginning of the grouping and type C-M-q. This changes the relative indentation within the grouping, without affecting its overall indentation (i.e., the indentation of the line where the grouping starts). The function that C-M-q runs depends on the major mode; it is `indent-pp-sexp` in Lisp mode, `c-indent-exp` in C mode, etc. To correct the overall indentation as well, type TAB first.

If you like the relative indentation within a grouping but not the indentation of its first line, move point to that first line and type C-u TAB. In Lisp, C, and some other major modes, TAB with a numeric argument reindents the current line as usual, then reindents by the same amount all the lines in the parenthetical grouping starting on the current line. It is clever, though, and does not alter lines that start inside strings. Neither does it alter C preprocessor lines when in C mode, but it does reindent any continuation lines that may be attached to them.

The command M-x indent-code-rigidly rigidly shifts all the lines in the region sideways, like `indent-rigidly` does (see Section 21.1 [Indentation Commands], page 205). It doesn't alter the indentation of lines that start inside a string, unless the region also starts inside that string. The prefix arg specifies the number of columns to indent.

23.3.3 Customizing Lisp Indentation

The indentation pattern for a Lisp expression can depend on the function called by the expression. For each Lisp function, you can choose among several predefined patterns of indentation, or define an arbitrary one with a Lisp program.

The standard pattern of indentation is as follows: the second line of the expression is indented under the first argument, if that is on the same line as the beginning of the expression; otherwise, the second line is indented underneath the function name. Each following line is indented under the previous line whose nesting depth is the same.

If the variable `lisp-indent-offset` is non-`nil`, it overrides the usual indentation pattern for the second line of an expression, so that such lines are always indented `lisp-indent-offset` more columns than the containing list.

Certain functions override the standard pattern. Functions whose names start with `def` treat the second lines as the start of a *body*, by indenting the second line `lisp-body-indent` additional columns beyond the open-parenthesis that starts the expression.

You can override the standard pattern in various ways for individual functions, according to the `lisp-indent-function` property of the function name. This is normally done for macro definitions, using the `declare` construct. See Section "Defining Macros" in *the Emacs Lisp Reference Manual*.

23.3.4 Commands for C Indentation

Here are special features for indentation in C mode and related modes:

C-c C-q   Reindent the current top-level function definition or aggregate type declaration (`c-indent-defun`).

C-M-q   Reindent each line in the balanced expression that follows point (`c-indent-exp`). A prefix argument inhibits warning messages about invalid syntax.

TAB   Reindent the current line, and/or in some cases insert a tab character (`c-indent-command`).

            If `c-tab-always-indent` is `t`, this command always reindents the current line and does nothing else. This is the default.

            If that variable is `nil`, this command reindents the current line only if point is at the left margin or in the line's indentation; otherwise, it inserts a tab (or the equivalent number of spaces, if `indent-tabs-mode` is `nil`).

            Any other value (not `nil` or `t`) means always reindent the line, and also insert a tab if within a comment or a string.

To reindent the whole current buffer, type C-x h C-M-\. This first selects the whole buffer as the region, then reindents that region.

To reindent the current block, use C-M-u C-M-q. This moves to the front of the block and then reindents it all.

23.3.5 Customizing C Indentation

C mode and related modes use a flexible mechanism for customizing indentation. C mode indents a source line in two steps: first it classifies the line syntactically according to its contents and context; second, it determines the indentation offset associated by your selected *style* with the syntactic construct and adds this onto the indentation of the *anchor statement*.

C-c . *style* RET

            Select a predefined style *style* (`c-set-style`).

A *style* is a named collection of customizations that can be used in C mode and the related modes. Section "Styles" in *The CC Mode Manual*, for a complete description. Emacs comes with several predefined styles, including **gnu**, **k&r**, **bsd**, **stroustrup**, **linux**, **python**, **java**, **whitesmith**, **ellemtel**, and **awk**. Some of these styles are primarily intended for one language, but any of them can be used with any of the languages supported by these modes. To find out what a style looks like, select it and reindent some code, e.g., by typing C-M-q at the start of a function definition.

To choose a style for the current buffer, use the command C-c .. Specify a style name as an argument (case is not significant). This command affects the current buffer only, and it affects only future invocations of the indentation commands; it does not reindent the code already in the buffer. To reindent the whole buffer in the new style, you can type C-x h C-M-\.

You can also set the variable c-default-style to specify the default style for various major modes. Its value should be either the style's name (a string) or an alist, in which each element specifies one major mode and which indentation style to use for it. For example,

```
(setq c-default-style
      '((java-mode . "java")
        (awk-mode . "awk")
        (other . "gnu")))
```

specifies explicit choices for Java and AWK modes, and the default 'gnu' style for the other C-like modes. (These settings are actually the defaults.) This variable takes effect when you select one of the C-like major modes; thus, if you specify a new default style for Java mode, you can make it take effect in an existing Java mode buffer by typing M-x java-mode there.

The gnu style specifies the formatting recommended by the GNU Project for C; it is the default, so as to encourage use of our recommended style.

See Section "Indentation Engine Basics" in *the CC Mode Manual*, and Section "Customizing Indentation" in *the CC Mode Manual*, for more information on customizing indentation for C and related modes, including how to override parts of an existing style and how to define your own styles.

As an alternative to specifying a style, you can tell Emacs to guess a style by typing M-x c-guess in a sample code buffer. You can then apply the guessed style to other buffers with M-x c-guess-install. See Section "Guessing the Style" in *the CC Mode Manual*, for details.

23.4 Commands for Editing with Parentheses

This section describes the commands and features that take advantage of the parenthesis structure in a program, or help you keep it balanced.

When talking about these facilities, the term "parenthesis" also includes braces, brackets, or whatever delimiters are defined to match in pairs. The major mode controls which delimiters are significant, through the syntax table (see Section "Syntax Tables" in *The Emacs Lisp Reference Manual*). In Lisp, only parentheses count; in C, these commands apply to braces and brackets too.

You can use M-x check-parens to find any unbalanced parentheses and unbalanced string quotes in the buffer.

23.4.1 Expressions with Balanced Parentheses

Each programming language mode has its own definition of a *balanced expression*. Balanced expressions typically include individual symbols, numbers, and string constants, as well as pieces of code enclosed in a matching pair of delimiters. The following commands deal with balanced expressions (in Emacs, such expressions are referred to internally as *sexps*[1]).

C-M-f   Move forward over a balanced expression (`forward-sexp`).

C-M-b   Move backward over a balanced expression (`backward-sexp`).

C-M-k   Kill balanced expression forward (`kill-sexp`).

C-M-t   Transpose expressions (`transpose-sexps`).

C-M-@
C-M-SPC Put mark after following expression (`mark-sexp`).

To move forward over a balanced expression, use C-M-f (`forward-sexp`). If the first significant character after point is an opening delimiter (e.g., '(', '[' or '{' in C), this command moves past the matching closing delimiter. If the character begins a symbol, string, or number, the command moves over that.

The command C-M-b (`backward-sexp`) moves backward over a balanced expression—like C-M-f, but in the reverse direction. If the expression is preceded by any prefix characters (single-quote, backquote and comma, in Lisp), the command moves back over them as well.

C-M-f or C-M-b with an argument repeats that operation the specified number of times; with a negative argument means to move in the opposite direction. In most modes, these two commands move across comments as if they were whitespace. Note that their keys, C-M-f and C-M-b, are analogous to C-f and C-b, which move by characters (see Section 4.2 [Moving Point], page 17), and M-f and M-b, which move by words (see Section 22.1 [Words], page 208).

To kill a whole balanced expression, type C-M-k (`kill-sexp`). This kills the text that C-M-f would move over.

C-M-t (`transpose-sexps`) switches the positions of the previous balanced expression and the next one. It is analogous to the C-t command, which transposes characters (see Section 13.2 [Transpose], page 110). An argument to C-M-t serves as a repeat count, moving the previous expression over that many following ones. A negative argument moves the previous balanced expression backwards across those before it. An argument of zero, rather than doing nothing, transposes the balanced expressions ending at or after point and the mark.

To operate on balanced expressions with a command which acts on the region, type C-M-SPC (`mark-sexp`). This sets the mark where C-M-f would move to. While the mark is active, each successive call to this command extends the region by shifting the mark by one expression. Positive or negative numeric arguments move the mark forward or backward by the specified number of expressions. The alias C-M-@ is equivalent to C-M-SPC. See Section 8.2 [Marking Objects], page 47, for more information about this and related commands.

In languages that use infix operators, such as C, it is not possible to recognize all balanced expressions because there can be multiple possibilities at a given position. For example, C mode does not treat '`foo + bar`' as a single expression, even though it *is* one C expression;

---

[1] The word "sexp" is used to refer to an expression in Lisp.

instead, it recognizes 'foo' as one expression and 'bar' as another, with the '+' as punctuation between them. However, C mode recognizes '(foo + bar)' as a single expression, because of the parentheses.

23.4.2 Moving in the Parenthesis Structure

The following commands move over groupings delimited by parentheses (or whatever else serves as delimiters in the language you are working with). They ignore strings and comments, including any parentheses within them, and also ignore parentheses that are "quoted" with an escape character. These commands are mainly intended for editing programs, but can be useful for editing any text containing parentheses. They are referred to internally as "list" commands because in Lisp these groupings are lists.

These commands assume that the starting point is not inside a string or a comment. If you invoke them from inside a string or comment, the results are unreliable.

C-M-n   Move forward over a parenthetical group (`forward-list`).

C-M-p   Move backward over a parenthetical group (`backward-list`).

C-M-u   Move up in parenthesis structure (`backward-up-list`).

C-M-d   Move down in parenthesis structure (`down-list`).

The "list" commands C-M-n (`forward-list`) and C-M-p (`backward-list`) move forward or backward over one (or *n*) parenthetical groupings.

C-M-n and C-M-p try to stay at the same level in the parenthesis structure. To move *up* one (or *n*) levels, use C-M-u (`backward-up-list`). C-M-u moves backward up past one unmatched opening delimiter. A positive argument serves as a repeat count; a negative argument reverses the direction of motion, so that the command moves forward and up one or more levels.

To move *down* in the parenthesis structure, use C-M-d (`down-list`). In Lisp mode, where '(' is the only opening delimiter, this is nearly the same as searching for a '('. An argument specifies the number of levels to go down.

23.4.3 Matching Parentheses

Emacs has a number of *parenthesis matching* features, which make it easy to see how and whether parentheses (or other delimiters) match up.

Whenever you type a self-inserting character that is a closing delimiter, Emacs briefly indicates the location of the matching opening delimiter, provided that is on the screen. If it is not on the screen, Emacs displays some of the text near it in the echo area. Either way, you can tell which grouping you are closing off. If the opening delimiter and closing delimiter are mismatched—such as in '[x)'—a warning message is displayed in the echo area.

Three variables control the display of matching parentheses:

- `blink-matching-paren` turns the feature on or off: `nil` disables it, but the default is `t` to enable it. Set it to `jump` to make indication work by momentarily moving the cursor to the matching opening delimiter.

- `blink-matching-delay` says how many seconds to keep indicating the matching opening delimiter. This may be an integer or floating-point number; the default is 1.

- `blink-matching-paren-distance` specifies how many characters back to search to find the matching opening delimiter. If the match is not found in that distance, Emacs stops scanning and nothing is displayed. The default is 102400.

Show Paren mode, a global minor mode, provides a more powerful kind of automatic matching. Whenever point is before an opening delimiter or after a closing delimiter, both that delimiter and its opposite delimiter are highlighted. To toggle Show Paren mode, type `M-x show-paren-mode`.

Electric Pair mode, a global minor mode, provides a way to easily insert matching delimiters. Whenever you insert an opening delimiter, the matching closing delimiter is automatically inserted as well, leaving point between the two. Conversely, when you insert a closing delimiter over an existing one, no inserting takes places and that position is simply skipped over. These variables control additional features of Electric Pair mode:

- `electric-pair-preserve-balance`, when non-`nil`, makes the default pairing logic balance out the number of opening and closing delimiters.

- `electric-pair-delete-adjacent-pairs`, when non-`nil`, makes backspacing between two adjacent delimiters also automatically delete the closing delimiter.

- `electric-pair-open-newline-between-pairs`, when non-`nil`, makes inserting inserting a newline between two adjacent pairs also automatically open and extra newline after point.

- `electric-pair-skip-whitespace`, when non-`nil`, causes the minor mode to skip whitespace forward before deciding whether to skip over the closing delimiter.

To toggle Electric Pair mode, type `M-x electric-pair-mode`.

23.5 Manipulating Comments

Because comments are such an important part of programming, Emacs provides special commands for editing and inserting comments. It can also do spell checking on comments with Flyspell Prog mode (see Section 13.4 [Spelling], page 111).

Some major modes have special rules for indenting different kinds of comments. For example, in Lisp code, comments starting with two semicolons are indented as if they were lines of code, while those starting with three semicolons are supposed to be aligned to the left margin and are often used for sectioning purposes. Emacs understand these conventions; for instance, typing `TAB` on a comment line will indent the comment to the appropriate position.

```
;; This function is just an example.
;;; Here either two or three semicolons are appropriate.
(defun foo (x)
;;;  And now, the first part of the function:
  ;; The following line adds one.
  (1+ x))            ; This line adds one.
```

23.5.1 Comment Commands

The following commands operate on comments:

`M-;`   Insert or realign comment on current line; if the region is active, comment or uncomment the region instead (`comment-dwim`).

C-u M-;   Kill comment on current line (`comment-kill`).

C-x ;   Set comment column (`comment-set-column`).

C-M-j
M-j   Like `RET` followed by inserting and aligning a comment (`comment-indent-new-line`). See Section 23.5.2 [Multi-Line Comments], page 251.

M-x comment-region
C-c C-c (in C-like modes)
             Add comment delimiters to all the lines in the region.

The command to create or align a comment is M-; (`comment-dwim`). The word "dwim" is an acronym for "Do What I Mean"; it indicates that this command can be used for many different jobs relating to comments, depending on the situation where you use it.

When a region is active (see Chapter 8 [Mark], page 45), M-; either adds comment delimiters to the region, or removes them. If every line in the region is already a comment, it "uncomments" each of those lines by removing their comment delimiters. Otherwise, it adds comment delimiters to enclose the text in the region.

If you supply a prefix argument to M-; when a region is active, that specifies the number of comment delimiters to add or delete. A positive argument n adds n delimiters, while a negative argument $-n$ removes n delimiters.

If the region is not active, and there is no existing comment on the current line, M-; adds a new comment to the current line. If the line is blank (i.e., empty or containing only whitespace characters), the comment is indented to the same position where `TAB` would indent to (see Section 23.3.1 [Basic Indent], page 243). If the line is non-blank, the comment is placed after the last non-whitespace character on the line; normally, Emacs tries putting it at the column specified by the variable `comment-column` (see Section 23.5.3 [Options for Comments], page 251), but if the line already extends past that column, it puts the comment at some suitable position, usually separated from the non-comment text by at least one space. In each case, Emacs places point after the comment's starting delimiter, so that you can start typing the comment text right away.

You can also use M-; to align an existing comment. If a line already contains the comment-start string, M-; realigns it to the conventional alignment and moves point after the comment's starting delimiter. As an exception, comments starting in column 0 are not moved. Even when an existing comment is properly aligned, M-; is still useful for moving directly to the start of the comment text.

C-u M-; (`comment-dwim` with a prefix argument) kills any comment on the current line, along with the whitespace before it. Since the comment is saved to the kill ring, you can reinsert it on another line by moving to the end of that line, doing C-y, and then M-; to realign the comment. You can achieve the same effect as C-u M-; by typing M-x `comment-kill` (`comment-dwim` actually calls `comment-kill` as a subroutine when it is given a prefix argument).

The command M-x `comment-region` is equivalent to calling M-; on an active region, except that it always acts on the region, even if the mark is inactive. In C mode and related modes, this command is bound to C-c C-c. The command M-x `uncomment-region` uncomments each line in the region; a numeric prefix argument specifies the number of comment delimiters to remove (negative arguments specify the number of comment to delimiters to add).

For C-like modes, you can configure the exact effect of M-; by setting the variables `c-indent-comment-alist` and `c-indent-comments-syntactically-p`. For example, on a line ending in a closing brace, M-; puts the comment one space after the brace rather than at `comment-column`. For full details see Section "Comment Commands" in *The CC Mode Manual*.

23.5.2 Multiple Lines of Comments

If you are typing a comment and wish to continue it to another line, type M-j or C-M-j (`comment-indent-new-line`). This breaks the current line, and inserts the necessary comment delimiters and indentation to continue the comment.

For languages with closing comment delimiters (e.g., '*/' in C), the exact behavior of M-j depends on the value of the variable `comment-multi-line`. If the value is `nil`, the command closes the comment on the old line and starts a new comment on the new line. Otherwise, it opens a new line within the current comment delimiters.

When Auto Fill mode is on, going past the fill column while typing a comment also continues the comment, in the same way as an explicit invocation of M-j.

To turn existing lines into comment lines, use M-; with the region active, or use M-x `comment-region` as described in the preceding section.

You can configure C Mode such that when you type a '/' at the start of a line in a multi-line block comment, this closes the comment. Enable the `comment-close-slash` clean-up for this. See Section "Clean-ups" in *The CC Mode Manual*.

23.5.3 Options Controlling Comments

As mentioned in Section 23.5.1 [Comment Commands], page 249, when the M-j command adds a comment to a line, it tries to place the comment at the column specified by the buffer-local variable `comment-column`. You can set either the local value or the default value of this buffer-local variable in the usual way (see Section 33.2.3 [Locals], page 423). Alternatively, you can type C-x ; (`comment-set-column`) to set the value of `comment-column` in the current buffer to the column where point is currently located. C-u C-x ; sets the comment column to match the last comment before point in the buffer, and then does a M-; to align the current line's comment under the previous one.

The comment commands recognize comments based on the regular expression that is the value of the variable `comment-start-skip`. Make sure this regexp does not match the null string. It may match more than the comment starting delimiter in the strictest sense of the word; for example, in C mode the value of the variable is `"\\(//+\\|/\\*+\\)\\s *"`, which matches extra stars and spaces after the '/*' itself, and accepts C++ style comments also. (Note that '\\' is needed in Lisp syntax to include a '\' in the string, which is needed to deny the first star its special meaning in regexp syntax. See Section 12.7 [Regexp Backslash], page 100.)

When a comment command makes a new comment, it inserts the value of `comment-start` as an opening comment delimiter. It also inserts the value of `comment-end` after point, as a closing comment delimiter. For example, in Lisp mode, `comment-start` is '";"'

and `comment-end` is `""` (the empty string). In C mode, `comment-start` is `"/* "` and `comment-end` is `" */"`.

The variable `comment-padding` specifies a string that the commenting commands should insert between the comment delimiter(s) and the comment text. The default, '`" "`', specifies a single space. Alternatively, the value can be a number, which specifies that number of spaces, or `nil`, which means no spaces at all.

The variable `comment-multi-line` controls how `M-j` and Auto Fill mode continue comments over multiple lines. See Section 23.5.2 [Multi-Line Comments], page 251.

The variable `comment-indent-function` should contain a function that will be called to compute the alignment for a newly inserted comment or for aligning an existing comment. It is set differently by various major modes. The function is called with no arguments, but with point at the beginning of the comment, or at the end of a line if a new comment is to be inserted. It should return the column in which the comment ought to start. For example, in Lisp mode, the indent hook function bases its decision on how many semicolons begin an existing comment, and on the code in the preceding lines.

23.6 Documentation Lookup

Emacs provides several features you can use to look up the documentation of functions, variables and commands that you plan to use in your program.

23.6.1 Info Documentation Lookup

For major modes that apply to languages which have documentation in Info, you can use `C-h S` (`info-lookup-symbol`) to view the Info documentation for a symbol used in the program. You specify the symbol with the minibuffer; the default is the symbol appearing in the buffer at point. For example, in C mode this looks for the symbol in the C Library Manual. The command only works if the appropriate manual's Info files are installed.

The major mode determines where to look for documentation for the symbol—which Info files to look in, and which indices to search. You can also use `M-x info-lookup-file` to look for documentation for a file name.

If you use `C-h S` in a major mode that does not support it, it asks you to specify the "symbol help mode". You should enter a command such as `c-mode` that would select a major mode which `C-h S` does support.

23.6.2 Man Page Lookup

On Unix, the main form of on-line documentation was the *manual page* or *man page*. In the GNU operating system, we aim to replace man pages with better-organized manuals that you can browse with Info (see Section 7.7 [Misc Help], page 43). This process is not finished, so it is still useful to read manual pages.

You can read the man page for an operating system command, library function, or system call, with the `M-x man` command. This prompts for a topic, with completion (see Section 5.4 [Completion], page 28), and runs the `man` program to format the corresponding man page. If the system permits, it runs `man` asynchronously, so that you can keep on editing while the page is being formatted. The result goes in a buffer named `*Man topic*`. These buffers use a special major mode, Man mode, that facilitates scrolling and jumping to other manual pages. For details, type `C-h m` while in a Man mode buffer.

Each man page belongs to one of ten or more *sections*, each named by a digit or by a digit and a letter. Sometimes there are man pages with the same name in different sections. To read a man page from a specific section, type '*topic(section)*' or '*section topic*' when M-x manual-entry prompts for the topic. For example, the man page for the C library function chmod is in section 2, but there is a shell command of the same name, whose man page is in section 1; to view the former, type M-x manual-entry RET chmod(2) RET.

If you do not specify a section, M-x man normally displays only the first man page found. On some systems, the man program accepts a '-a' command-line option, which tells it to display all the man pages for the specified topic. To make use of this, change the value of the variable Man-switches to '"-a"'. Then, in the Man mode buffer, you can type M-n and M-p to switch between man pages in different sections. The mode line shows how many manual pages are available.

An alternative way of reading manual pages is the M-x woman command. Unlike M-x man, it does not run any external programs to format and display the man pages; the formatting is done by Emacs, so it works on systems such as MS-Windows where the man program may be unavailable. It prompts for a man page, and displays it in a buffer named *WoMan *section topic*.

M-x woman computes the completion list for manpages the first time you invoke the command. With a numeric argument, it recomputes this list; this is useful if you add or delete manual pages.

If you type a name of a manual page and M-x woman finds that several manual pages by the same name exist in different sections, it pops up a window with possible candidates asking you to choose one of them.

For more information about setting up and using M-x woman, see the WoMan Info manual, which is distributed with Emacs.

23.6.3 Emacs Lisp Documentation Lookup

When editing Emacs Lisp code, you can use the commands C-h f (describe-function) and C-h v (describe-variable) to view the built-in documentation for the Lisp functions and variables that you want to use. See Section 7.2 [Name Help], page 39.

Eldoc is a buffer-local minor mode that helps with looking up Lisp documentation. When it is enabled, the echo area displays some useful information whenever there is a Lisp function or variable at point; for a function, it shows the argument list, and for a variable it shows the first line of the variable's documentation string. To toggle Eldoc mode, type M-x eldoc-mode. Eldoc mode can be used with the Emacs Lisp and Lisp Interaction major modes.

23.7 Hideshow minor mode

Hideshow mode is a buffer-local minor mode that allows you to selectively display portions of a program, which are referred to as *blocks*. Type M-x hs-minor-mode to toggle this minor mode (see Section 20.2 [Minor Modes], page 200).

When you use Hideshow mode to hide a block, the block disappears from the screen, to be replaced by an ellipsis (three periods in a row). Just what constitutes a block depends on the major mode. In C mode and related modes, blocks are delimited by braces, while in Lisp mode they are delimited by parentheses. Multi-line comments also count as blocks.

Hideshow mode provides the following commands:

C-c @ C-h   Hide the current block (`hs-hide-block`).

C-c @ C-s   Show the current block (`hs-show-block`).

C-c @ C-c   Either hide or show the current block (`hs-toggle-hiding`).

S-Mouse-2
        Toggle hiding for the block you click on (`hs-mouse-toggle-hiding`).

C-c @ C-M-h
        Hide all top-level blocks (`hs-hide-all`).

C-c @ C-M-s
        Show all blocks in the buffer (`hs-show-all`).

C-c @ C-l   Hide all blocks n levels below this block (`hs-hide-level`).

These variables can be used to customize Hideshow mode:

`hs-hide-comments-when-hiding-all`
        If non-`nil`, C-c @ C-M-h (`hs-hide-all`) hides comments too.

`hs-isearch-open`
        This variable specifies the conditions under which incremental search should unhide a hidden block when matching text occurs within the block. Its value should be either `code` (unhide only code blocks), `comment` (unhide only comments), `t` (unhide both code blocks and comments), or `nil` (unhide neither code blocks nor comments). The default value is `code`.

23.8 Completion for Symbol Names

Completion is normally done in the minibuffer (see Section 5.4 [Completion], page 28), but you can also complete symbol names in ordinary Emacs buffers.

In programming language modes, type C-M-i or M-TAB to complete the partial symbol before point. On graphical displays, the M-TAB key is usually reserved by the window manager for switching graphical windows, so you should type C-M-i or ESC TAB instead.

In most programming language modes, C-M-i (or M-TAB) invokes the command `completion-at-point`, which generates its completion list in a flexible way. If Semantic mode is enabled, it tries to use the Semantic parser data for completion (see Section 23.10 [Semantic], page 255). If Semantic mode is not enabled or fails at performing completion, it tries to complete using the selected tags table (see Section 25.3 [Tags], page 299). If in Emacs Lisp mode, it performs completion using the function, variable, or property names defined in the current Emacs session.

In all other respects, in-buffer symbol completion behaves like minibuffer completion. For instance, if Emacs cannot complete to a unique symbol, it displays a list of completion alternatives in another window. See Section 5.4 [Completion], page 28.

In Text mode and related modes, M-TAB completes words based on the spell-checker's dictionary. See Section 13.4 [Spelling], page 111.

23.9 MixedCase Words

Some programming styles make use of mixed-case (or "CamelCase") symbols like 'unReadableSymbol'. (In the GNU project, we recommend using underscores to separate words within an identifier, rather than using case distinctions.) Emacs has various features to make it easier to deal with such symbols.

Glasses mode is a buffer-local minor mode that makes it easier to read such symbols, by altering how they are displayed. By default, it displays extra underscores between each lower-case letter and the following capital letter. This does not alter the buffer text, only how it is displayed.

To toggle Glasses mode, type M-x glasses-mode (see Section 20.2 [Minor Modes], page 200). When Glasses mode is enabled, the minor mode indicator 'o^o' appears in the mode line. For more information about Glasses mode, type C-h P glasses RET.

Subword mode is another buffer-local minor mode. In subword mode, Emacs's word commands recognize upper case letters in 'StudlyCapsIdentifiers' as word boundaries. When Subword mode is enabled, the minor mode indicator ',' appears in the mode line. See also the similar superword-mode (see Section 23.11 [Misc for Programs], page 256).

23.10 Semantic

Semantic is a package that provides language-aware editing commands based on source code parsers. This section provides a brief description of Semantic; for full details, see the Semantic Info manual, which is distributed with Emacs.

Most of the "language aware" features in Emacs, such as Font Lock mode (see Section 11.12 [Font Lock], page 78), rely on "rules of thumb"[2] that usually give good results but are never completely exact. In contrast, the parsers used by Semantic have an exact understanding of programming language syntax. This allows Semantic to provide search, navigation, and completion commands that are powerful and precise.

To begin using Semantic, type M-x semantic-mode or click on the menu item named 'Source Code Parsers (Semantic)' in the 'Tools' menu. This enables Semantic mode, a global minor mode.

When Semantic mode is enabled, Emacs automatically attempts to parse each file you visit. Currently, Semantic understands C, C++, Scheme, Javascript, Java, HTML, and Make. Within each parsed buffer, the following commands are available:

C-c , j   Prompt for the name of a function defined in the current file, and move point there (semantic-complete-jump-local).

C-c , J   Prompt for the name of a function defined in any file Emacs has parsed, and move point there (semantic-complete-jump).

C-c , SPC   Display a list of possible completions for the symbol at point (semantic-complete-analyze-inline). This also activates a set of special key bindings for choosing a completion: RET accepts the current completion, M-n and M-p cycle through possible completions, TAB completes as far as possible and then cycles, and C-g or any other key aborts completion.

---

[2] Regular expressions and syntax tables.

C-c , l   Display a list of the possible completions of the symbol at point, in another window (`semantic-analyze-possible-completions`).

In addition to the above commands, the Semantic package provides a variety of other ways to make use of parser information. For instance, you can use it to display a list of completions when Emacs is idle.

23.11 Other Features Useful for Editing Programs

Some Emacs commands that aren't designed specifically for editing programs are useful for that nonetheless.

The Emacs commands that operate on words, sentences and paragraphs are useful for editing code. Most symbols names contain words (see Section 22.1 [Words], page 208), while sentences can be found in strings and comments (see Section 22.2 [Sentences], page 209). As for paragraphs, they are defined in most programming language modes to begin and end at blank lines (see Section 22.3 [Paragraphs], page 210). Therefore, judicious use of blank lines to make the program clearer will also provide useful chunks of text for the paragraph commands to work on. Auto Fill mode, if enabled in a programming language major mode, indents the new lines which it creates.

Superword mode is a buffer-local minor mode that causes editing and motion commands to treat symbols (e.g., '`this_is_a_symbol`') as words. When Superword mode is enabled, the minor mode indicator '2' appears in the mode line. See also the similar **subword-mode** (see Section 23.9 [MixedCase Words], page 255).

Electric Layout mode (M-x `electric-layout-mode`) is a global minor mode that automatically inserts newlines when you type certain characters; for example, '{', '}' and ';' in Javascript mode.

Apart from Hideshow mode (see Section 23.7 [Hideshow], page 253), another way to selectively display parts of a program is to use the selective display feature (see Section 11.17 [Selective Display], page 83). Programming modes often also support Outline minor mode (see Section 22.8 [Outline Mode], page 217), which can be used with the Foldout package (see Section 22.8.5 [Foldout], page 221).

Prettify Symbols mode is a buffer-local minor mode that replaces certain strings with more "attractive" versions for display purposes. For example, in Emacs Lisp mode, it replaces the string "lambda" with the Greek lambda character. You may wish to use this in non-programming modes as well. You can customize the mode by adding more entries to **prettify-symbols-alist**. There is also a global version, **global-prettify-symbols-mode**, which enables the mode in all buffers that support it.

23.12 C and Related Modes

This section gives a brief description of the special features available in C, C++, Objective-C, Java, CORBA IDL, Pike and AWK modes. (These are called "C mode and related modes".) For more details, see the CC mode Info manual, which is distributed with Emacs.

23.12.1 C Mode Motion Commands

This section describes commands for moving point, in C mode and related modes.

C-M-a

C-M-e   Move point to the beginning or end of the current function or top-level defi-
               nition. In languages with enclosing scopes (such as C++'s classes) the *current
               function* is the immediate one, possibly inside a scope. Otherwise it is the one
               defined by the least enclosing braces. (By contrast, `beginning-of-defun` and
               `end-of-defun` search for braces in column zero.) See Section 23.2.2 [Moving
               by Defuns], page 241.

C-c C-u   Move point back to the containing preprocessor conditional, leaving the mark
               behind. A prefix argument acts as a repeat count. With a negative argument,
               move point forward to the end of the containing preprocessor conditional.

               '`#elif`' is equivalent to '`#else`' followed by '`#if`', so the function will stop at a
               '`#elif`' when going backward, but not when going forward.

C-c C-p   Move point back over a preprocessor conditional, leaving the mark behind.
               A prefix argument acts as a repeat count. With a negative argument, move
               forward.

C-c C-n   Move point forward across a preprocessor conditional, leaving the mark behind.
               A prefix argument acts as a repeat count. With a negative argument, move
               backward.

M-a   Move point to the beginning of the innermost C statement (`c-beginning-of-`
               `statement`). If point is already at the beginning of a statement, move to the
               beginning of the preceding statement. With prefix argument n, move back $n -$
               1 statements.

               In comments or in strings which span more than one line, this command moves
               by sentences instead of statements.

M-e   Move point to the end of the innermost C statement or sentence; like M-a except
               that it moves in the other direction (`c-end-of-statement`).

23.12.2 Electric C Characters

In C mode and related modes, certain printing characters are *electric*—in addition to inserting themselves, they also reindent the current line, and optionally also insert newlines.
The "electric" characters are {, }, :, #, ;, ,, <, >, /, *, (, and).

   You might find electric indentation inconvenient if you are editing chaotically indented
code. If you are new to CC Mode, you might find it disconcerting. You can toggle electric
action with the command C-c C-l; when it is enabled, '/l' appears in the mode line after
the mode name:

C-c C-l   Toggle electric action (`c-toggle-electric-state`). With a positive prefix ar-
               gument, this command enables electric action, with a negative one it disables
               it.

   Electric characters insert newlines only when, in addition to the electric state, the *auto-
newline* feature is enabled (indicated by '/la' in the mode line after the mode name). You
can turn this feature on or off with the command C-c C-a:

C-c C-a   Toggle the auto-newline feature (`c-toggle-auto-newline`). With a prefix ar-
               gument, this command turns the auto-newline feature on if the argument is
               positive, and off if it is negative.

Usually the CC Mode style configures the exact circumstances in which Emacs inserts auto-newlines. You can also configure this directly. See Section "Custom Auto-newlines" in *The CC Mode Manual*.

23.12.3 Hungry Delete Feature in C

If you want to delete an entire block of whitespace at point, you can use *hungry deletion*. This deletes all the contiguous whitespace either before point or after point in a single operation. *Whitespace* here includes tabs and newlines, but not comments or preprocessor commands.

`C-c C-DEL`

`C-c DEL` Delete the entire block of whitespace preceding point (`c-hungry-delete-backwards`).

`C-c C-d`

`C-c C-Delete`

`C-c Delete`

  Delete the entire block of whitespace after point (`c-hungry-delete-forward`).

As an alternative to the above commands, you can enable *hungry delete mode*. When this feature is enabled (indicated by '/h' in the mode line after the mode name), a single `DEL` deletes all preceding whitespace, not just one space, and a single `C-d` (but *not* plain `Delete`) deletes all following whitespace.

`M-x c-toggle-hungry-state`

  Toggle the hungry-delete feature (`c-toggle-hungry-state`). With a prefix argument, this command turns the hungry-delete feature on if the argument is positive, and off if it is negative.

The variable `c-hungry-delete-key` controls whether the hungry-delete feature is enabled.

23.12.4 Other Commands for C Mode

`M-x c-context-line-break`

  This command inserts a line break and indents the new line in a manner appropriate to the context. In normal code, it does the work of `RET` (`newline`), in a C preprocessor line it additionally inserts a '\' at the line break, and within comments it's like `M-j` (`c-indent-new-comment-line`).

  `c-context-line-break` isn't bound to a key by default, but it needs a binding to be useful. The following code will bind it to `RET`. We use `c-initialization-hook` here to make sure the keymap is loaded before we try to change it.

```
(defun my-bind-clb ()
  (define-key c-mode-base-map "\C-m"
              'c-context-line-break))
(add-hook 'c-initialization-hook 'my-bind-clb)
```

`C-M-h` Put mark at the end of a function definition, and put point at the beginning (`c-mark-function`).

M-q   Fill a paragraph, handling C and C++ comments (`c-fill-paragraph`). If any part of the current line is a comment or within a comment, this command fills the comment or the paragraph of it that point is in, preserving the comment indentation and comment delimiters.

C-c C-e   Run the C preprocessor on the text in the region, and show the result, which includes the expansion of all the macro calls (`c-macro-expand`). The buffer text before the region is also included in preprocessing, for the sake of macros defined there, but the output from this part isn't shown.

             When you are debugging C code that uses macros, sometimes it is hard to figure out precisely how the macros expand. With this command, you don't have to figure it out; you can see the expansions.

C-c C-\   Insert or align '\' characters at the ends of the lines of the region (`c-backslash-region`). This is useful after writing or editing a C macro definition.

             If a line already ends in '\', this command adjusts the amount of whitespace before it. Otherwise, it inserts a new '\'. However, the last line in the region is treated specially; no '\' is inserted on that line, and any '\' there is deleted.

M-x cpp-highlight-buffer
             Highlight parts of the text according to its preprocessor conditionals. This command displays another buffer named *CPP Edit*, which serves as a graphic menu for selecting how to display particular kinds of conditionals and their contents. After changing various settings, click on '[A]pply these settings' (or go to that buffer and type a) to rehighlight the C mode buffer accordingly.

C-c C-s   Display the syntactic information about the current source line (`c-show-syntactic-information`). This information directs how the line is indented.

M-x cwarn-mode
M-x global-cwarn-mode
             CWarn minor mode highlights certain suspicious C and C++ constructions:

             • Assignments inside expressions.

             • Semicolon following immediately after 'if', 'for', and 'while' (except after a 'do ... while' statement);

             • C++ functions with reference parameters.

             You can enable the mode for one buffer with the command M-x cwarn-mode, or for all suitable buffers with the command M-x global-cwarn-mode or by customizing the variable `global-cwarn-mode`. You must also enable Font Lock mode to make it work.

M-x hide-ifdef-mode
             Hide-ifdef minor mode hides selected code within '#if' and '#ifdef' preprocessor blocks. If you change the variable `hide-ifdef-shadow` to t, Hide-ifdef minor mode "shadows" preprocessor blocks by displaying them with a less prominent face, instead of hiding them entirely. See the documentation string of `hide-ifdef-mode` for more information.

`M-x ff-find-related-file`

> Find a file "related" in a special way to the file visited by the current buffer. Typically this will be the header file corresponding to a C/C++ source file, or vice versa. The variable `ff-related-file-alist` specifies how to compute related file names.

23.13 Asm Mode

Asm mode is a major mode for editing files of assembler code. It defines these commands:

TAB   `tab-to-tab-stop`.

C-j   Insert a newline and then indent using `tab-to-tab-stop`.

:   Insert a colon and then remove the indentation from before the label preceding colon. Then do `tab-to-tab-stop`.

;   Insert or align a comment.

The variable `asm-comment-char` specifies which character starts comments in assembler syntax.

24 Compiling and Testing Programs

The previous chapter discusses the Emacs commands that are useful for making changes in programs. This chapter deals with commands that assist in the process of compiling and testing programs.

24.1 Running Compilations under Emacs

Emacs can run compilers for languages such as C and Fortran, feeding the compilation log into an Emacs buffer. It can also parse the error messages and show you where the errors occurred.

`M-x compile`

> Run a compiler asynchronously under Emacs, with error messages going to the `*compilation*` buffer.

`M-x recompile`

> Invoke a compiler with the same command as in the last invocation of `M-x compile`.

`M-x kill-compilation`

> Kill the running compilation subprocess.

To run `make` or another compilation command, type `M-x compile`. This reads a shell command line using the minibuffer, and then executes the command by running a shell as a subprocess (or *inferior process*) of Emacs. The output is inserted in a buffer named `*compilation*`. The current buffer's default directory is used as the working directory for the execution of the command; normally, therefore, compilation takes place in this directory.

The default compilation command is '`make -k`', which is usually correct for programs compiled using the `make` utility (the '`-k`' flag tells `make` to continue compiling as much as possible after an error). See Section "Make" in *GNU Make Manual*. If you have done `M-x compile` before, the command that you specified is automatically stored in the variable `compile-command`; this is used as the default the next time you type `M-x compile`. A file can also specify a file-local value for `compile-command` (see Section 33.2.4 [File Variables], page 424).

Starting a compilation displays the `*compilation*` buffer in another window but does not select it. While the compilation is running, the word '`run`' is shown in the major mode indicator for the `*compilation*` buffer, and the word '`Compiling`' appears in all mode lines. You do not have to keep the `*compilation*` buffer visible while compilation is running; it continues in any case. When the compilation ends, for whatever reason, the mode line of the `*compilation*` buffer changes to say '`exit`' (followed by the exit code: '`[0]`' for a normal exit), or '`signal`' (if a signal terminated the process).

If you want to watch the compilation transcript as it appears, switch to the `*compilation*` buffer and move point to the end of the buffer. When point is at the end, new compilation output is inserted above point, which remains at the end. Otherwise, point remains fixed while compilation output is added at the end of the buffer.

If you change the variable `compilation-scroll-output` to a non-`nil` value, the `*compilation*` buffer scrolls automatically to follow the output. If the value is `first-error`, scrolling stops when the first error appears, leaving point at that error. For any other non-`nil` value, scrolling continues until there is no more output.

To rerun the last compilation with the same command, type `M-x recompile`. This reuses the compilation command from the last invocation of `M-x compile`. It also reuses the `*compilation*` buffer and starts the compilation in its default directory, which is the directory in which the previous compilation was started.

Starting a new compilation also kills any compilation already running in `*compilation*`, as the buffer can only handle one compilation at any time. However, `M-x compile` asks for confirmation before actually killing a compilation that is running; to always automatically kill the compilation without asking, change the variable `compilation-always-kill` to `t`. You can also kill a compilation process with the command `M-x kill-compilation`.

To run two compilations at once, start the first one, then rename the `*compilation*` buffer (perhaps using `rename-uniquely`; see Section 16.3 [Misc Buffer], page 149), then switch buffers and start the other compilation. This will create a new `*compilation*` buffer.

You can control the environment passed to the compilation command with the variable `compilation-environment`. Its value is a list of environment variable settings; each element should be a string of the form `"envvarname=value"`. These environment variable settings override the usual ones.

24.2 Compilation Mode

The `*compilation*` buffer uses a major mode called Compilation mode. Compilation mode turns each error message in the buffer into a hyperlink; you can move point to it and type RET, or click on it with the mouse (see Section 18.3 [Mouse References], page 164), to visit the *locus* of the error message in a separate window. The locus is the specific position in a file where that error occurred.

If you change the variable `compilation-auto-jump-to-first-error` to a non-nil value, Emacs automatically visits the locus of the first error message that appears in the `*compilation*` buffer.

Compilation mode provides the following additional commands. These commands can also be used in `*grep*` buffers, where the hyperlinks are search matches rather than error messages (see Section 24.4 [Grep Searching], page 264).

M-g M-n
M-g n
C-x `          Visit the locus of the next error message or match (`next-error`).

M-g M-p
M-g p   Visit the locus of the previous error message or match (`previous-error`).

M-n   Move point to the next error message or match, without visiting its locus (`compilation-next-error`).

M-p   Move point to the previous error message or match, without visiting its locus (`compilation-previous-error`).

M-}   Move point to the next error message or match occurring in a different file (`compilation-next-file`).

M-{   Move point to the previous error message or match occurring in a different file
(`compilation-previous-file`).

C-c C-f   Toggle Next Error Follow minor mode, which makes cursor motion in the compilation buffer produce automatic source display.

To visit errors sequentially, type C-x ' (`next-error`), or equivalently M-g M-n or M-g n. This command can be invoked from any buffer, not just a Compilation mode buffer. The first time you invoke it after a compilation, it visits the locus of the first error message. Each subsequent C-x ' visits the next error, in a similar fashion. If you visit a specific error with RET or a mouse click in the *compilation* buffer, subsequent C-x ' commands advance from there. When C-x ' finds no more error messages to visit, it signals an error. C-u C-x ' starts again from the beginning of the compilation buffer, and visits the first locus.

M-g M-p or M-g p (`previous-error`) iterates through errors in the opposite direction.

The `next-error` and `previous-error` commands don't just act on the errors or matches listed in *compilation* and *grep* buffers; they also know how to iterate through error or match lists produced by other commands, such as M-x occur (see Section 12.11 [Other Repeating Search], page 107). If you are already in a buffer containing error messages or matches, those are the ones that are iterated through; otherwise, Emacs looks for a buffer containing error messages or matches amongst the windows of the selected frame, then for one that `next-error` or `previous-error` previously iterated through, and finally amongst all other buffers. If the buffer chosen for iterating through is not currently displayed in a window, it will be displayed.

By default, the `next-error` and `previous-error` commands skip less important messages. The variable `compilation-skip-threshold` controls this. The default value, 1, means to skip anything less important than a warning. A value of 2 means to skip anything less important than an error, while 0 means not to skip any messages.

When Emacs visits the locus of an error message, it momentarily highlights the relevant source line. The duration of this highlight is determined by the variable `next-error-highlight`.

If the *compilation* buffer is shown in a window with a left fringe (see Section 11.14 [Fringes], page 81), the locus-visiting commands put an arrow in the fringe, pointing to the current error message. If the window has no left fringe, such as on a text terminal, these commands scroll the window so that the current message is at the top of the window. If you change the variable `compilation-context-lines` to an integer value n, these commands scroll the window so that the current error message is n lines from the top, whether or not there is a fringe; the default value, `nil`, gives the behavior described above.

To parse messages from the compiler, Compilation mode uses the variable `compilation-error-regexp-alist` which lists various error message formats and tells Emacs how to extract the locus from each. A similar variable, `grep-regexp-alist`, tells Emacs how to parse output from a `grep` command (see Section 24.4 [Grep Searching], page 264).

Compilation mode also defines the keys SPC and DEL to scroll by screenfuls; M-n (`compilation-next-error`) and M-p (`compilation-previous-error`) to move to the next or previous error message; and M-{ (`compilation-next-file`) and M-}

(`compilation-previous-file`) to move to the next or previous error message for a different source file.

You can type C-c C-f to toggle Next Error Follow mode. In this minor mode, ordinary cursor motion in the compilation buffer automatically updates the source buffer, i.e., moving the cursor over an error message causes the locus of that error to be displayed.

The features of Compilation mode are also available in a minor mode called Compilation Minor mode. This lets you parse error messages in any buffer, not just a normal compilation output buffer. Type M-x compilation-minor-mode to enable the minor mode. For instance, in an Rlogin buffer (see Section 31.4.10 [Remote Host], page 393), Compilation minor mode automatically accesses remote source files by FTP (see Section 15.1 [File Names], page 122).

24.3 Subshells for Compilation

The M-x compile command uses a shell to run the compilation command, but specifies the option for a noninteractive shell. This means, in particular, that the shell should start with no prompt. If you find your usual shell prompt making an unsightly appearance in the *compilation* buffer, it means you have made a mistake in your shell's init file by setting the prompt unconditionally. (This init file may be named .bashrc, .profile, .cshrc, .shrc, etc., depending on what shell you use.) The shell init file should set the prompt only if there already is a prompt. Here's how to do it in bash:

```
if [ "${PS1+set}" = set ]
then PS1=...
fi
```

And here's how to do it in csh:

```
if ($?prompt) set prompt = ...
```

Emacs does not expect a compiler process to launch asynchronous subprocesses; if it does, and they keep running after the main compiler process has terminated, Emacs may kill them or their output may not arrive in Emacs. To avoid this problem, make the main compilation process wait for its subprocesses to finish. In a shell script, you can do this using '$!' and 'wait', like this:

```
(sleep 10; echo 2nd)& pid=$!   # Record pid of subprocess
echo first message
wait $pid                      # Wait for subprocess
```

If the background process does not output to the compilation buffer, so you only need to prevent it from being killed when the main compilation process terminates, this is sufficient:

```
nohup command; sleep 1
```

24.4 Searching with Grep under Emacs

Just as you can run a compiler from Emacs and then visit the lines with compilation errors, you can also run grep and then visit the lines on which matches were found. This works by treating the matches reported by grep as if they were "errors". The output buffer uses Grep mode, which is a variant of Compilation mode (see Section 24.2 [Compilation Mode], page 262).

```
M-x grep
M-x lgrep  Run grep asynchronously under Emacs, listing matching lines in the buffer
           named *grep*.

M-x grep-find
M-x find-grep
M-x rgrep  Run grep via find, and collect output in the *grep* buffer.

M-x zrgrep
           Run zgrep and collect output in the *grep* buffer.

M-x kill-grep
           Kill the running grep subprocess.
```

To run grep, type M-x grep, then enter a command line that specifies how to run grep. Use the same arguments you would give grep when running it normally: a grep-style regexp (usually in single-quotes to quote the shell's special characters) followed by file names, which may use wildcards. If you specify a prefix argument for M-x grep, it finds the tag (see Section 25.3 [Tags], page 299) in the buffer around point, and puts that into the default grep command.

Your command need not simply run grep; you can use any shell command that produces output in the same format. For instance, you can chain grep commands, like this:

```
grep -nH -e foo *.el | grep bar | grep toto
```

The output from grep goes in the *grep* buffer. You can find the corresponding lines in the original files using C-x ', RET, and so forth, just like compilation errors.

Some grep programs accept a '--color' option to output special markers around matches for the purpose of highlighting. You can make use of this feature by setting grep-highlight-matches to t. When displaying a match in the source buffer, the exact match will be highlighted, instead of the entire source line.

The command M-x grep-find (also available as M-x find-grep) is similar to M-x grep, but it supplies a different initial default for the command—one that runs both find and grep, so as to search every file in a directory tree. See also the find-grep-dired command, in Section 27.15 [Dired and Find], page 327.

The commands M-x lgrep (local grep) and M-x rgrep (recursive grep) are more user-friendly versions of grep and grep-find, which prompt separately for the regular expression to match, the files to search, and the base directory for the search. Case sensitivity of the search is controlled by the current value of case-fold-search. The command M-x zrgrep is similar to M-x rgrep, but it calls zgrep instead of grep to search the contents of gzipped files.

These commands build the shell commands based on the variables grep-template (for lgrep) and grep-find-template (for rgrep). The files to search can use aliases defined in the variable grep-files-aliases.

Directories listed in the variable grep-find-ignored-directories are automatically skipped by M-x rgrep. The default value includes the data directories used by various version control systems.

24.5 Finding Syntax Errors On The Fly

Flymake mode is a minor mode that performs on-the-fly syntax checking for many programming and markup languages, including C, C++, Perl, HTML, and TeX/LaTeX. It is somewhat analogous to Flyspell mode, which performs spell checking for ordinary human languages in a similar fashion (see Section 13.4 [Spelling], page 111). As you edit a file, Flymake mode runs an appropriate syntax checking tool in the background, using a temporary copy of the buffer. It then parses the error and warning messages, and highlights the erroneous lines in the buffer. The syntax checking tool used depends on the language; for example, for C/C++ files this is usually the C compiler. Flymake can also use build tools such as `make` for checking complicated projects.

To enable Flymake mode, type `M-x flymake-mode`. You can jump to the errors that it finds by using `M-x flymake-goto-next-error` and `M-x flymake-goto-prev-error`. To display any error messages associated with the current line, type `M-x flymake-display-err-menu-for-current-line`.

For more details about using Flymake, see the Flymake Info manual, which is distributed with Emacs.

24.6 Running Debuggers Under Emacs

The GUD (Grand Unified Debugger) library provides an Emacs interface to a wide variety of symbolic debuggers. It can run the GNU Debugger (GDB), as well as DBX, SDB, XDB, Perl's debugging mode, the Python debugger PDB, and the Java Debugger JDB.

Emacs provides a special interface to GDB, which uses extra Emacs windows to display the state of the debugged program. See Section 24.6.5 [GDB Graphical Interface], page 270.

Emacs also has a built-in debugger for Emacs Lisp programs. See Section "The Lisp Debugger" in *the Emacs Lisp Reference Manual*.

24.6.1 Starting GUD

There are several commands for starting a debugger subprocess, each corresponding to a particular debugger program.

`M-x gdb`   Run GDB as a subprocess, and interact with it via an IDE-like Emacs interface. See Section 24.6.5 [GDB Graphical Interface], page 270, for more information about this command.

`M-x gud-gdb`

Run GDB, using a GUD interaction buffer for input and output to the GDB subprocess (see Section 24.6.2 [Debugger Operation], page 267). If such a buffer already exists, switch to it; otherwise, create the buffer and switch to it.

The other commands in this list do the same, for other debugger programs.

`M-x perldb`

Run the Perl interpreter in debug mode.

`M-x jdb`   Run the Java debugger.

`M-x pdb`   Run the Python debugger.

`M-x dbx`   Run the DBX debugger.

M-x xdb   Run the XDB debugger.

M-x sdb   Run the SDB debugger.

Each of these commands reads a command line to invoke the debugger, using the mini-buffer. The minibuffer's initial contents contain the standard executable name and options for the debugger, and sometimes also a guess for the name of the executable file you want to debug. Shell wildcards and variables are not allowed in this command line. Emacs assumes that the first command argument which does not start with a '-' is the executable file name.

Tramp provides a facility for remote debugging, whereby both the debugger and the program being debugged are on the same remote host. See Section "Running a debugger on a remote host" in *The Tramp Manual*, for details. This is separate from GDB's remote debugging feature, where the program and the debugger run on different machines (see Section "Debugging Remote Programs" in *The GNU debugger*).

24.6.2 Debugger Operation

The *GUD interaction buffer* is an Emacs buffer which is used to send text commands to a debugger subprocess, and record its output. This is the basic interface for interacting with a debugger, used by M-x gud-gdb and other commands listed in the preceding section. The M-x gdb command extends this interface with additional specialized buffers for controlling breakpoints, stack frames, and other aspects of the debugger state (see Section 24.6.5 [GDB Graphical Interface], page 270).

The GUD interaction buffer uses a variant of Shell mode, so the Emacs commands defined by Shell mode are available (see Section 31.4.3 [Shell Mode], page 385). Completion is available for most debugger commands (see Section 5.4 [Completion], page 28), and you can use the usual Shell mode history commands to repeat them. See the next section for special commands that can be used in the GUD interaction buffer.

As you debug a program, Emacs displays the relevant source files by visiting them in Emacs buffers, with an arrow in the left fringe indicating the current execution line. (On a text terminal, the arrow appears as '=>', overlaid on the first two text columns.) Moving point in such a buffer does not move the arrow. You are free to edit these source files, but note that inserting or deleting lines will throw off the arrow's positioning, as Emacs has no way to figure out which edited source line corresponds to the line reported by the debugger subprocess. To update this information, you typically have to recompile and restart the program.

GUD Tooltip mode is a global minor mode that adds tooltip support to GUD. To toggle this mode, type M-x gud-tooltip-mode. It is disabled by default. If enabled, you can move the mouse cursor over a variable, a function, or a macro (collectively called *identifiers*) to show their values in tooltips (see Section 18.17 [Tooltips], page 174). Alternatively, mark an identifier or an expression by dragging the mouse over it, then leave the mouse in the marked area to have the value of the expression displayed in a tooltip. The GUD Tooltip mode takes effect in the GUD interaction buffer, and in all source buffers with major modes listed in the variable gud-tooltip-modes. If the variable gud-tooltip-echo-area is non-nil, or if you turned off the tooltip mode, values are shown in the echo area instead of a tooltip.

When using GUD Tooltip mode with M-x gud-gdb, displaying an expression's value in GDB can sometimes expand a macro, potentially causing side effects in the debugged program. For that reason, using tooltips in `gud-gdb` is disabled. If you use the `M-x gdb` interface, this problem does not occur, as there is special code to avoid side-effects; furthermore, you can display macro definitions associated with an identifier when the program is not executing.

24.6.3 Commands of GUD

GUD provides commands for setting and clearing breakpoints, selecting stack frames, and stepping through the program.

C-x C-a C-b

> Set a breakpoint on the source line that point is on.

`C-x C-a C-b` (`gud-break`), when called in a source buffer, sets a debugger breakpoint on the current source line. This command is available only after starting GUD. If you call it in a buffer that is not associated with any debugger subprocess, it signals a error.

The following commands are available both in the GUD interaction buffer and globally, but with different key bindings. The keys starting with `C-c` are available only in the GUD interaction buffer, while those starting with `C-x C-a` are available globally. Some of these commands are also available via the tool bar; some are not supported by certain debuggers.

C-c C-l
C-x C-a C-l

> Display, in another window, the last source line referred to in the GUD interaction buffer (`gud-refresh`).

C-c C-s
C-x C-a C-s

> Execute the next single line of code (`gud-step`). If the line contains a function call, execution stops after entering the called function.

C-c C-n
C-x C-a C-n

> Execute the next single line of code, stepping across function calls without stopping inside the functions (`gud-next`).

C-c C-i
C-x C-a C-i

> Execute a single machine instruction (`gud-stepi`).

C-c C-p
C-x C-a C-p

> Evaluate the expression at point (`gud-print`). If Emacs does not print the exact expression that you want, mark it as a region first.

C-c C-r
C-x C-a C-r

> Continue execution without specifying any stopping point. The program will run until it hits a breakpoint, terminates, or gets a signal that the debugger is checking for (gud-cont).

C-c C-d
C-x C-a C-d

> Delete the breakpoint(s) on the current source line, if any (gud-remove). If you use this command in the GUD interaction buffer, it applies to the line where the program last stopped.

C-c C-t
C-x C-a C-t

> Set a temporary breakpoint on the current source line, if any (gud-tbreak). If you use this command in the GUD interaction buffer, it applies to the line where the program last stopped.

C-c <
C-x C-a <   Select the next enclosing stack frame (gud-up). This is equivalent to the GDB command 'up'.

C-c >
C-x C-a >   Select the next inner stack frame (gud-down). This is equivalent to the GDB command 'down'.

C-c C-u
C-x C-a C-u

> Continue execution to the current line (gud-until). The program will run until it hits a breakpoint, terminates, gets a signal that the debugger is checking for, or reaches the line on which the cursor currently sits.

C-c C-f
C-x C-a C-f

> Run the program until the selected stack frame returns or stops for some other reason (gud-finish).

If you are using GDB, these additional key bindings are available:

C-x C-a C-j

> Only useful in a source buffer, gud-jump transfers the program's execution point to the current line. In other words, the next line that the program executes will be the one where you gave the command. If the new execution line is in a different function from the previously one, GDB prompts for confirmation since the results may be bizarre. See the GDB manual entry regarding jump for details.

TAB   With GDB, complete a symbol name (gud-gdb-complete-command). This key is available only in the GUD interaction buffer.

These commands interpret a numeric argument as a repeat count, when that makes sense.

Because TAB serves as a completion command, you can't use it to enter a tab as input to the program you are debugging with GDB. Instead, type C-q TAB to enter a tab.

24.6.4 GUD Customization

On startup, GUD runs one of the following hooks: `gdb-mode-hook`, if you are using GDB; `dbx-mode-hook`, if you are using DBX; `sdb-mode-hook`, if you are using SDB; `xdb-mode-hook`, if you are using XDB; `perldb-mode-hook`, for Perl debugging mode; `pdb-mode-hook`, for PDB; `jdb-mode-hook`, for JDB. See Section 33.2.2 [Hooks], page 422.

The `gud-def` Lisp macro (see Section "Defining Macros" in *the Emacs Lisp Reference Manual*) provides a convenient way to define an Emacs command that sends a particular command string to the debugger, and set up a key binding for in the GUD interaction buffer:

   `(gud-def` *function* `cmdstring` `binding` `docstring)`

This defines a command named *function* which sends *cmdstring* to the debugger process, and gives it the documentation string *docstring*. You can then use the command *function* in any buffer. If *binding* is non-`nil`, `gud-def` also binds the command to `C-c` *binding* in the GUD buffer's mode and to `C-x C-a` *binding* generally.

The command string *cmdstring* may contain certain '%'-sequences that stand for data to be filled in at the time *function* is called:

'%f'   The name of the current source file. If the current buffer is the GUD buffer, then the "current source file" is the file that the program stopped in.

'%l'   The number of the current source line. If the current buffer is the GUD buffer, then the "current source line" is the line that the program stopped in.

'%e'   In transient-mark-mode the text in the region, if it is active. Otherwise the text of the C lvalue or function-call expression at or adjacent to point.

'%a'   The text of the hexadecimal address at or adjacent to point.

'%p'   The numeric argument of the called function, as a decimal number. If the command is used without a numeric argument, '%p' stands for the empty string.

            If you don't use '%p' in the command string, the command you define ignores any numeric argument.

'%d'   The name of the directory of the current source file.

'%c'   Fully qualified class name derived from the expression surrounding point (jdb only).

24.6.5 GDB Graphical Interface

The command `M-x gdb` starts GDB in an IDE-like interface, with specialized buffers for controlling breakpoints, stack frames, and other aspects of the debugger state. It also provides additional ways to control the debugging session with the mouse, such as clicking in the fringe of a source buffer to set a breakpoint there.

To run GDB using just the GUD interaction buffer interface, without these additional features, use `M-x gud-gdb` (see Section 24.6.1 [Starting GUD], page 266). You must use this if you want to debug multiple programs within one Emacs session, as that is currently unsupported by `M-x gdb`.

Internally, `M-x gdb` informs GDB that its "screen size" is unlimited; for correct operation, you must not change GDB's screen height and width values during the debugging session.

24.6.5.1 GDB User Interface Layout

If the variable `gdb-many-windows` is `nil` (the default), `M-x gdb` normally displays only the GUD interaction buffer. However, if the variable `gdb-show-main` is also non-`nil`, it starts with two windows: one displaying the GUD interaction buffer, and the other showing the source for the `main` function of the program you are debugging.

If `gdb-many-windows` is non-`nil`, then `M-x gdb` displays the following frame layout:

```
+--------------------------------+--------------------------------+
|   GUD interaction buffer       |    Locals/Registers buffer     |
|--------------------------------+--------------------------------|
|   Primary Source buffer        |    I/O buffer for debugged pgm  |
|--------------------------------+--------------------------------|
|   Stack buffer                 |    Breakpoints/Threads buffer   |
+--------------------------------+--------------------------------+
```

If you ever change the window layout, you can restore the "many windows" layout by typing `M-x gdb-restore-windows`. To toggle between the many windows layout and a simple layout with just the GUD interaction buffer and a source file, type `M-x gdb-many-windows`.

You may also specify additional GDB-related buffers to display, either in the same frame or a different one. Select the buffers you want by typing `M-x gdb-display-`*buffertype*`-buffer` or `M-x gdb-frame-`*buffertype*`-buffer`, where *buffertype* is the relevant buffer type, such as '`breakpoints`'. You can do the same with the menu bar, with the '`GDB-Windows`' and '`GDB-Frames`' sub-menus of the '`GUD`' menu.

When you finish debugging, kill the GUD interaction buffer with `C-x k`, which will also kill all the buffers associated with the session. However you need not do this if, after editing and re-compiling your source code within Emacs, you wish to continue debugging. When you restart execution, GDB automatically finds the new executable. Keeping the GUD interaction buffer has the advantage of keeping the shell history as well as GDB's breakpoints. You do need to check that the breakpoints in recently edited source files are still in the right places.

24.6.5.2 Source Buffers

`Mouse-1` (in fringe)
> Set or clear a breakpoint on that line.

`C-Mouse-1` (in fringe)
> Enable or disable a breakpoint on that line.

`Mouse-3` (in fringe)
> Continue execution to that line.

`C-Mouse-3` (in fringe)
> Jump to that line.

On a graphical display, you can click `Mouse-1` in the fringe of a source buffer, to set a breakpoint on that line (see Section 11.14 [Fringes], page 81). A red dot appears in the fringe, where you clicked. If a breakpoint already exists there, the click removes it. A `C-Mouse-1` click enables or disables an existing breakpoint; a breakpoint that is disabled, but not unset, is indicated by a gray dot.

On a text terminal, or when fringes are disabled, enabled breakpoints are indicated with a 'B' character in the left margin of the window. Disabled breakpoints are indicated with 'b'. (The margin is only displayed if a breakpoint is present.)

A solid arrow in the left fringe of a source buffer indicates the line of the innermost frame where the debugged program has stopped. A hollow arrow indicates the current execution line of a higher-level frame. If you drag the arrow in the fringe with Mouse-1, that causes execution to advance to the line where you release the button. Alternatively, you can click Mouse-3 in the fringe to advance to that line. You can click C-Mouse-3 in the fringe to jump to that line without executing the intermediate lines. This command allows you to go backwards, which can be useful for running through code that has already executed, in order to examine its execution in more detail.

24.6.5.3 Breakpoints Buffer

The GDB Breakpoints buffer shows the breakpoints, watchpoints and catchpoints in the debugger session. See Section "Breakpoints" in *The GNU debugger*. It provides the following commands, which mostly apply to the *current breakpoint* (the breakpoint which point is on):

SPC   Enable/disable current breakpoint (gdb-toggle-breakpoint). On a graphical display, this changes the color of the dot in the fringe of the source buffer at that line. The dot is red when the breakpoint is enabled, and gray when it is disabled.

D   Delete the current breakpoint (gdb-delete-breakpoint).

RET   Visit the source line for the current breakpoint (gdb-goto-breakpoint).

Mouse-2   Visit the source line for the breakpoint you click on.

When gdb-many-windows is non-nil, the GDB Breakpoints buffer shares its window with the GDB Threads buffer. To switch from one to the other click with Mouse-1 on the relevant button in the header line. If gdb-show-threads-by-default is non-nil, the GDB Threads buffer is the one shown by default.

24.6.5.4 Threads Buffer

The GDB Threads buffer displays a summary of the threads in the debugged program. See Section "Debugging programs with multiple threads" in *The GNU debugger*. To select a thread, move point there and press RET (gdb-select-thread), or click on it with Mouse-2. This also displays the associated source buffer, and updates the contents of the other GDB buffers.

You can customize variables under gdb-buffers group to select fields included in GDB Threads buffer.

gdb-thread-buffer-verbose-names
            Show long thread names like 'Thread 0x4e2ab70 (LWP 1983)'.

gdb-thread-buffer-arguments
            Show arguments of thread top frames.

gdb-thread-buffer-locations
            Show file information or library names.

`gdb-thread-buffer-addresses`
> Show addresses for thread frames in threads buffer.

To view information for several threads simultaneously, use the following commands from the GDB Threads buffer.

d
> Display disassembly buffer for the thread at current line (`gdb-display-disassembly-for-thread`).

f
> Display the GDB Stack buffer for the thread at current line (`gdb-display-stack-for-thread`).

l
> Display the GDB Locals buffer for the thread at current line (`gdb-display-locals-for-thread`).

r
> Display the GDB Registers buffer for the thread at current line (`gdb-display-registers-for-thread`).

Their upper-case counterparts, `D`, `F` ,`L` and `R`, display the corresponding buffer in a new frame.

When you create a buffer showing information about some specific thread, it becomes bound to that thread and keeps showing actual information while you debug your program. The mode indicator for each GDB buffer shows the number of thread it is showing information about. The thread number is also included in the buffer name of bound buffers.

Further commands are available in the GDB Threads buffer which depend on the mode of GDB that is used for controlling execution of your program. See Section 24.6.5.8 [Multithreaded Debugging], page 275.

24.6.5.5 Stack Buffer

The GDB Stack buffer displays a *call stack*, with one line for each of the nested subroutine calls (*stack frames*) in the debugger session. See Section "Backtraces" in *The GNU debugger*.

On graphical displays, the selected stack frame is indicated by an arrow in the fringe. On text terminals, or when fringes are disabled, the selected stack frame is displayed in reverse contrast. To select a stack frame, move point in its line and type `RET` (`gdb-frames-select`), or click `Mouse-2` on it. Doing so also updates the Locals buffer (described in the next section).

24.6.5.6 Other GDB Buffers

Locals Buffer
> This buffer displays the values of local variables of the current frame for simple data types (see Section "Information on a frame" in *The GNU debugger*). Press `RET` or click `Mouse-2` on the value if you want to edit it.

> Arrays and structures display their type only. With GDB 6.4 or later, you can examine the value of the local variable at point by typing `RET`, or with a `Mouse-2` click. With earlier versions of GDB, use `RET` or `Mouse-2` on the type description ('`[struct/union]`' or '`[array]`'). See Section 24.6.5.7 [Watch Expressions], page 274.

Registers Buffer

      This buffer displays the values held by the registers (see Section "Registers" in *The GNU debugger*). Press `RET` or click `Mouse-2` on a register if you want to edit its value. With GDB 6.4 or later, recently changed register values display with `font-lock-warning-face`.

Assembler Buffer

      The assembler buffer displays the current frame as machine code. An arrow points to the current instruction, and you can set and remove breakpoints as in a source buffer. Breakpoint icons also appear in the fringe or margin.

Memory Buffer

      The memory buffer lets you examine sections of program memory (see Section "Examining memory" in *The GNU debugger*). Click `Mouse-1` on the appropriate part of the header line to change the starting address or number of data items that the buffer displays. Alternatively, use `S` or `N` respectively. Click `Mouse-3` on the header line to select the display format or unit size for these data items.

When `gdb-many-windows` is non-`nil`, the locals buffer shares its window with the registers buffer, just like breakpoints and threads buffers. To switch from one to the other, click with `Mouse-1` on the relevant button in the header line.

24.6.5.7 Watch Expressions

If you want to see how a variable changes each time your program stops, move point into the variable name and click on the watch icon in the tool bar (`gud-watch`) or type `C-x C-a C-w`. If you specify a prefix argument, you can enter the variable name in the minibuffer.

Each watch expression is displayed in the speedbar (see Section 18.9 [Speedbar], page 171). Complex data types, such as arrays, structures and unions are represented in a tree format. Leaves and simple data types show the name of the expression and its value and, when the speedbar frame is selected, display the type as a tooltip. Higher levels show the name, type and address value for pointers and just the name and type otherwise. Root expressions also display the frame address as a tooltip to help identify the frame in which they were defined.

To expand or contract a complex data type, click `Mouse-2` or press `SPC` on the tag to the left of the expression. Emacs asks for confirmation before expanding the expression if its number of immediate children exceeds the value of the variable `gdb-max-children`.

To delete a complex watch expression, move point to the root expression in the speedbar and type `D` (`gdb-var-delete`).

To edit a variable with a simple data type, or a simple element of a complex data type, move point there in the speedbar and type `RET` (`gdb-edit-value`). Or you can click `Mouse-2` on a value to edit it. Either way, this reads the new value using the minibuffer.

If you set the variable `gdb-show-changed-values` to non-`nil` (the default value), Emacs uses `font-lock-warning-face` to highlight values that have recently changed and `shadow` face to make variables which have gone out of scope less noticeable. When a variable goes out of scope you can't edit its value.

If the variable `gdb-delete-out-of-scope` is non-`nil` (the default value), Emacs automatically deletes watch expressions which go out of scope. Sometimes, when re-entering the same function, it may be useful to set this value to `nil` so that you don't need to recreate the watch expression.

If the variable `gdb-use-colon-colon-notation` is non-nil, Emacs uses the '*function*::*variable*' format. This allows the user to display watch expressions which share the same variable name. The default value is `nil`.

To automatically raise the speedbar every time the display of watch expressions updates, set `gdb-speedbar-auto-raise` to non-nil. This can be useful if you are debugging with a full screen Emacs frame.

24.6.5.8 Multithreaded Debugging

In GDB's *all-stop mode*, whenever your program stops, all execution threads stop. Likewise, whenever you restart the program, all threads start executing. See Section "All-Stop Mode" in *The GNU debugger*. For some multi-threaded targets, GDB supports a further mode of operation, called *non-stop mode*, in which you can examine stopped program threads in the debugger while other threads continue to execute freely. See Section "Non-Stop Mode" in *The GNU debugger*. Versions of GDB prior to 7.0 do not support non-stop mode, and it does not work on all targets.

The variable `gdb-non-stop-setting` determines whether Emacs runs GDB in all-stop mode or non-stop mode. The default is `t`, which means it tries to use non-stop mode if that is available. If you change the value to `nil`, or if non-stop mode is unavailable, Emacs runs GDB in all-stop mode. The variable takes effect when Emacs begins a debugging session; if you change its value, you should restart any active debugging session.

When a thread stops in non-stop mode, Emacs usually switches to that thread. If you don't want Emacs to do this switch if another stopped thread is already selected, change the variable `gdb-switch-when-another-stopped` to `nil`.

Emacs can decide whether or not to switch to the stopped thread depending on the reason which caused the stop. Customize the variable `gdb-switch-reasons` to select the stop reasons which will cause a thread switch.

The variable `gdb-stopped-functions` allows you to execute your functions whenever some thread stops.

In non-stop mode, you can switch between different modes for GUD execution control commands.

Non-stop/A

When `gdb-gud-control-all-threads` is `t` (the default value), interruption and continuation commands apply to all threads, so you can halt or continue all your threads with one command using `gud-stop-subjob` and `gud-cont`, respectively. The 'Go' button is shown on the toolbar when at least one thread is stopped, whereas 'Stop' button is shown when at least one thread is running.

Non-stop/T

When `gdb-gud-control-all-threads` is `nil`, only the current thread is stopped/continued. 'Go' and 'Stop' buttons on the GUD toolbar are shown depending on the state of current thread.

You can change the current value of `gdb-gud-control-all-threads` from the tool bar or from 'GUD->GDB-MI' menu.

Stepping commands always apply to the current thread.

In non-stop mode, you can interrupt/continue your threads without selecting them. Hitting `i` in threads buffer interrupts thread under point, `c` continues it, `s` steps through. More such commands may be added in the future.

Note that when you interrupt a thread, it stops with the 'signal received' reason. If that reason is included in your `gdb-switch-reasons` (it is by default), Emacs will switch to that thread.

24.7 Executing Lisp Expressions

Emacs has major modes for several variants of Lisp. They use the same editing commands as other programming language modes (see Chapter 23 [Programs], page 240). In addition, they provide special commands for executing Lisp expressions.

Emacs Lisp mode

> The mode for editing Emacs Lisp source files. It defines `C-M-x` to evaluate the current top-level Lisp expression. See Section 24.9 [Lisp Eval], page 278.

Lisp Interaction mode

> The mode for an interactive Emacs Lisp session. It defines `C-j` to evaluate the expression before point and insert its value in the buffer. See Section 24.10 [Lisp Interaction], page 279.

Lisp mode The mode for editing source files of programs that run in Lisps other than Emacs Lisp. It defines `C-M-x` to evaluate the current top-level expression in an external Lisp. See Section 24.11 [External Lisp], page 279.

Inferior Lisp mode

> The mode for an interactive session with an external Lisp which is being run as a subprocess (or *inferior process*) of Emacs.

Scheme mode

> Like Lisp mode, but for Scheme programs.

Inferior Scheme mode

> Like Inferior Lisp mode, but for Scheme.

24.8 Libraries of Lisp Code for Emacs

Emacs Lisp code is stored in files whose names conventionally end in `.el`. Such files are automatically visited in Emacs Lisp mode.

Emacs Lisp code can be compiled into byte-code, which loads faster, takes up less space, and executes faster. By convention, compiled Emacs Lisp code goes in a separate file whose name ends in '.elc'. For example, the compiled code for `foo.el` goes in `foo.elc`. See Section "Byte Compilation" in *the Emacs Lisp Reference Manual*.

To *load* an Emacs Lisp file, type `M-x load-file`. This command reads a file name using the minibuffer, and executes the contents of that file as Emacs Lisp code. It is not necessary to visit the file first; this command reads the file directly from disk, not from an existing Emacs buffer.

If an Emacs Lisp file is installed in the Emacs Lisp *load path* (defined below), you can load it by typing M-x load-library, instead of using M-x load-file. The M-x load-library command prompts for a *library name* rather than a file name; it searches through each directory in the Emacs Lisp load path, trying to find a file matching that library name. If the library name is '*foo*', it tries looking for files named *foo*.elc, *foo*.el, and *foo*. The default behavior is to load the first file found. This command prefers .elc files over .el files because compiled files load and run faster. If it finds that *lib*.el is newer than *lib*.elc, it issues a warning, in case someone made changes to the .el file and forgot to recompile it, but loads the .elc file anyway. (Due to this behavior, you can save unfinished edits to Emacs Lisp source files, and not recompile until your changes are ready for use.) If you set the option load-prefer-newer to a non-nil value, however, then rather than the procedure described above, Emacs loads whichever version of the file is newest.

Emacs Lisp programs usually load Emacs Lisp files using the load function. This is similar to load-library, but is lower-level and accepts additional arguments. See Section "How Programs Do Loading" in *the Emacs Lisp Reference Manual*.

The Emacs Lisp load path is specified by the variable load-path. Its value should be a list of directory names (strings). These directories are searched, in the specified order, by the M-x load-library command, the lower-level load function, and other Emacs functions that find Emacs Lisp libraries. A list entry in load-path can also have the special value nil, which stands for the current default directory, but it is almost always a bad idea to use this. (If you find yourself wishing that nil were in the list, most likely what you really want is to use M-x load-file.)

The default value of load-path is a list of directories where the Lisp code for Emacs itself is stored. If you have libraries of your own in another directory, you can add that directory to the load path. Unlike most other variables described in this manual, load-path cannot be changed via the Customize interface (see Section 33.1 [Easy Customization], page 412), but you can add a directory to it by putting a line like this in your init file (see Section 33.4 [Init File], page 437):

```
(add-to-list 'load-path "/path/to/my/lisp/library")
```

Some commands are *autoloaded*; when you run them, Emacs automatically loads the associated library first. For instance, the M-x compile command (see Section 24.1 [Compilation], page 261) is autoloaded; if you call it, Emacs automatically loads the compile library first. In contrast, the command M-x recompile is not autoloaded, so it is unavailable until you load the compile library.

Automatic loading can also occur when you look up the documentation of an autoloaded command (see Section 7.2 [Name Help], page 39), if the documentation refers to other functions and variables in its library (loading the library lets Emacs properly set up the hyperlinks in the *Help* buffer). To disable this feature, change the variable help-enable-auto-load to nil.

By default, Emacs refuses to load compiled Lisp files which were compiled with XEmacs, a modified versions of Emacs—they can cause Emacs to crash. Set the variable load-dangerous-libraries to t if you want to try loading them.

24.9 Evaluating Emacs Lisp Expressions

Emacs Lisp mode is the major mode for editing Emacs Lisp. Its mode command is `M-x emacs-lisp-mode`.

Emacs provides several commands for evaluating Emacs Lisp expressions. You can use these commands in Emacs Lisp mode, to test your Emacs Lisp code as it is being written. For example, after re-writing a function, you can evaluate the function definition to make it take effect for subsequent function calls. These commands are also available globally, and can be used outside Emacs Lisp mode.

`M-:`   Read a single Emacs Lisp expression in the minibuffer, evaluate it, and print the value in the echo area (`eval-expression`).

`C-x C-e`   Evaluate the Emacs Lisp expression before point, and print the value in the echo area (`eval-last-sexp`).

`C-M-x` (in Emacs Lisp mode)
`M-x eval-defun`
              Evaluate the defun containing or after point, and print the value in the echo area (`eval-defun`).

`M-x eval-region`
              Evaluate all the Emacs Lisp expressions in the region.

`M-x eval-buffer`
              Evaluate all the Emacs Lisp expressions in the buffer.

`M-:` (`eval-expression`) reads an expression using the minibuffer, and evaluates it. (Before evaluating the expression, the current buffer switches back to the buffer that was current when you typed `M-:`, not the minibuffer into which you typed the expression.)

The command `C-x C-e` (`eval-last-sexp`) evaluates the Emacs Lisp expression preceding point in the buffer, and displays the value in the echo area. When the result of an evaluation is an integer, it is displayed together with the value in other formats (octal, hexadecimal, and character).

If `M-:` or `C-x C-e` is given a prefix argument, it inserts the value into the current buffer at point, rather than displaying it in the echo area. If the prefix argument is zero, any integer output is inserted together with its value in other formats (octal, hexadecimal, and character). Such a prefix argument also prevents abbreviation of the output according to the variables `eval-expression-print-level` and `eval-expression-print-length` (see below).

The `eval-defun` command is bound to `C-M-x` in Emacs Lisp mode. It evaluates the top-level Lisp expression containing or following point, and prints the value in the echo area. In this context, a top-level expression is referred to as a "defun", but it need not be an actual `defun` (function definition). In particular, this command treats `defvar` expressions specially. Normally, evaluating a `defvar` expression does nothing if the variable it defines already has a value. But this command unconditionally resets the variable to the initial value specified by the `defvar`; this is convenient for debugging Emacs Lisp programs. `defcustom` and `defface` expressions are treated similarly. Note that the other commands documented in this section do not have this special feature.

With a prefix argument, `C-M-x` instruments the function definition for Edebug, the Emacs Lisp Debugger. See Section "Instrumenting" in *the Emacs Lisp Reference Manual*.

The command `M-x eval-region` parses the text of the region as one or more Lisp expressions, evaluating them one by one. `M-x eval-buffer` is similar but evaluates the entire buffer.

The options `eval-expression-print-level` and `eval-expression-print-length` control the maximum depth and length of lists to print in the result of the evaluation commands before abbreviating them. Supplying a zero prefix argument to `eval-expression` or `eval-last-sexp` causes lists to be printed in full. `eval-expression-debug-on-error` controls whether evaluation errors invoke the debugger when these commands are used; its default is `t`.

24.10 Lisp Interaction Buffers

When Emacs starts up, it contains a buffer named `*scratch*`, which is provided for evaluating Emacs Lisp expressions interactively. Its major mode is Lisp Interaction mode. You can also enable Lisp Interaction mode by typing `M-x lisp-interaction-mode`.

In the `*scratch*` buffer, and other Lisp Interaction mode buffers, `C-j` (`eval-print-last-sexp`) evaluates the Lisp expression before point, and inserts the value at point. Thus, as you type expressions into the buffer followed by `C-j` after each expression, the buffer records a transcript of the evaluated expressions and their values. All other commands in Lisp Interaction mode are the same as in Emacs Lisp mode.

At startup, the `*scratch*` buffer contains a short message, in the form of a Lisp comment, that explains what it is for. This message is controlled by the variable `initial-scratch-message`, which should be either a string, or `nil` (which means to suppress the message).

An alternative way of evaluating Emacs Lisp expressions interactively is to use Inferior Emacs Lisp mode, which provides an interface rather like Shell mode (see Section 31.4.3 [Shell Mode], page 385) for evaluating Emacs Lisp expressions. Type `M-x ielm` to create an `*ielm*` buffer which uses this mode. For more information, see that command's documentation.

24.11 Running an External Lisp

Lisp mode is the major mode for editing programs written in general-purpose Lisp dialects, such as Common Lisp. Its mode command is `M-x lisp-mode`. Emacs uses Lisp mode automatically for files whose names end in `.l`, `.lsp`, or `.lisp`.

You can run an external Lisp session as a subprocess or *inferior process* of Emacs, and pass expressions to it to be evaluated. To begin an external Lisp session, type `M-x run-lisp`. This runs the program named `lisp`, and sets it up so that both input and output go through an Emacs buffer named `*inferior-lisp*`. To change the name of the Lisp program run by `M-x run-lisp`, change the variable `inferior-lisp-program`.

The major mode for the `*lisp*` buffer is Inferior Lisp mode, which combines the characteristics of Lisp mode and Shell mode (see Section 31.4.3 [Shell Mode], page 385). To send input to the Lisp session, go to the end of the `*lisp*` buffer and type the input, followed by `RET`. Terminal output from the Lisp session is automatically inserted in the buffer.

When you edit a Lisp program in Lisp mode, you can type C-M-x (`lisp-eval-defun`) to send an expression from the Lisp mode buffer to a Lisp session that you had started with M-x `run-lisp`. The expression sent is the top-level Lisp expression at or following point. The resulting value goes as usual into the `*inferior-lisp*` buffer. Note that the effect of C-M-x in Lisp mode is thus very similar to its effect in Emacs Lisp mode (see Section 24.9 [Lisp Eval], page 278), except that the expression is sent to a different Lisp environment instead of being evaluated in Emacs.

The facilities for editing Scheme code, and for sending expressions to a Scheme subprocess, are very similar. Scheme source files are edited in Scheme mode, which can be explicitly enabled with M-x `scheme-mode`. You can initiate a Scheme session by typing M-x `run-scheme` (the buffer for interacting with Scheme is named `*scheme*`), and send expressions to it by typing C-M-x.

25 Maintaining Large Programs

This chapter describes Emacs features for maintaining large programs. If you are maintaining a large Lisp program, then in addition to the features described here, you may find the ERT ("Emacs Lisp Regression Testing") library useful (see Section "ERT" in *Emacs Lisp Regression Testing*).

25.1 Version Control

A *version control system* is a program that can record multiple versions of a source file, storing information such as the creation time of each version, who made it, and a description of what was changed.

The Emacs version control interface is called *VC*. VC commands work with several different version control systems; currently, it supports GNU Arch, Bazaar, CVS, Git, Mercurial, Monotone, RCS, SCCS/CSSC, and Subversion. Of these, the GNU project distributes CVS, Arch, RCS, and Bazaar.

VC is enabled automatically whenever you visit a file governed by a version control system. To disable VC entirely, set the customizable variable `vc-handled-backends` to `nil` (see Section "Customizing VC" in *Specialized Emacs Features*).

25.1.1 Introduction to Version Control

VC allows you to use a version control system from within Emacs, integrating the version control operations smoothly with editing. It provides a uniform interface for common operations in many version control operations.

Some uncommon or intricate version control operations, such as altering repository settings, are not supported in VC. You should perform such tasks outside Emacs, e.g., via the command line.

This section provides a general overview of version control, and describes the version control systems that VC supports. You can skip this section if you are already familiar with the version control system you want to use.

25.1.1.1 Understanding the problems it addresses

Version control systems provide you with three important capabilities:

- *Reversibility*: the ability to back up to a previous state if you discover that some modification you did was a mistake or a bad idea.

- *Concurrency*: the ability to have many people modifying the same collection of files knowing that conflicting modifications can be detected and resolved.

- *History*: the ability to attach historical data to your data, such as explanatory comments about the intention behind each change to it. Even for a programmer working solo, change histories are an important aid to memory; for a multi-person project, they are a vitally important form of communication among developers.

25.1.1.2 Supported Version Control Systems

VC currently works with many different version control systems, which it refers to as *back ends*:

- SCCS was the first version control system ever built, and was long ago superseded by more advanced ones. VC compensates for certain features missing in SCCS (e.g., tag names for releases) by implementing them itself. Other VC features, such as multiple branches, are simply unavailable. Since SCCS is non-free, we recommend avoiding it.

- CSSC is a free replacement for SCCS. You should use CSSC only if, for some reason, you cannot use a more recent and better-designed version control system.

- RCS is the free version control system around which VC was initially built. It is relatively primitive: it cannot be used over the network, and works at the level of individual files. Almost everything you can do with RCS can be done through VC.

- CVS is the free version control system that was, until recently (circa 2008), used by the majority of free software projects. Nowadays, it is slowly being superseded by newer systems. CVS allows concurrent multi-user development either locally or over the network. Unlike newer systems, it lacks support for atomic commits and file moving/renaming. VC supports all basic editing operations under CVS.

- Subversion (svn) is a free version control system designed to be similar to CVS but without its problems (e.g., it supports atomic commits of filesets, and versioning of directories, symbolic links, meta-data, renames, copies, and deletes).

- GNU Arch is one of the earliest *decentralized* version control systems (the other being Monotone). See Section 25.1.1.3 [VCS Concepts], page 282, for a description of decentralized version control systems. It is no longer under active development, and has been deprecated in favor of Bazaar.

- Git is a decentralized version control system originally invented by Linus Torvalds to support development of Linux (his kernel). VC supports many common Git operations, but others, such as repository syncing, must be done from the command line.

- Mercurial (hg) is a decentralized version control system broadly resembling Git. VC supports most Mercurial commands, with the exception of repository sync operations.

- Bazaar (bzr) is a decentralized version control system that supports both repository-based and decentralized versioning. VC supports most basic editing operations under Bazaar.

25.1.1.3 Concepts of Version Control

When a file is under version control, we say that it is *registered* in the version control system. The system has a *repository* which stores both the file's present state and its change history—enough to reconstruct the current version or any earlier version. The repository also contains other information, such as *log entries* that describe the changes made to each file.

The copy of a version-controlled file that you actually edit is called the *work file*. You can change each work file as you would an ordinary file. After you are done with a set of changes, you may *commit* (or *check in*) the changes; this records the changes in the repository, along with a descriptive log entry.

A directory tree of work files is called a *working tree*.

Each commit creates a new *revision* in the repository. The version control system keeps track of all past revisions and the changes that were made in each revision. Each revision is named by a *revision ID*, whose format depends on the version control system; in the simplest case, it is just an integer.

To go beyond these basic concepts, you will need to understand three aspects in which version control systems differ. As explained in the next three sections, they can be lock-based or merge-based; file-based or changeset-based; and centralized or decentralized. VC handles all these modes of operation, but it cannot hide the differences.

25.1.1.4 Merge-based vs lock-based Version Control

A version control system typically has some mechanism to coordinate between users who want to change the same file. There are two ways to do this: merging and locking.

In a version control system that uses merging, each user may modify a work file at any time. The system lets you *merge* your work file, which may contain changes that have not been committed, with the latest changes that others have committed.

Older version control systems use a *locking* scheme instead. Here, work files are normally read-only. To edit a file, you ask the version control system to make it writable for you by *locking* it; only one user can lock a given file at any given time. This procedure is analogous to, but different from, the locking that Emacs uses to detect simultaneous editing of ordinary files (see Section 15.3.4 [Interlocking], page 130). When you commit your changes, that unlocks the file, and the work file becomes read-only again. Other users may then lock the file to make their own changes.

Both locking and merging systems can have problems when multiple users try to modify the same file at the same time. Locking systems have *lock conflicts*; a user may try to check a file out and be unable to because it is locked. In merging systems, *merge conflicts* happen when you commit a change to a file that conflicts with a change committed by someone else after your checkout. Both kinds of conflict have to be resolved by human judgment and communication. Experience has shown that merging is superior to locking, both in convenience to developers and in minimizing the number and severity of conflicts that actually occur.

SCCS always uses locking. RCS is lock-based by default but can be told to operate in a merging style. CVS and Subversion are merge-based by default but can be told to operate in a locking mode. Decentralized version control systems, such as GNU Arch, Git, and Mercurial, are exclusively merging-based.

VC mode supports both locking and merging version control. The terms "commit" and "update" are used in newer version control systems; older lock-based systems use the terms "check in" and "check out". VC hides the differences between them as much as possible.

25.1.1.5 Changeset-based vs File-based Version Control

On SCCS, RCS, CVS, and other early version control systems, version control operations are *file-based*: each file has its own comment and revision history separate from that of all other files. Newer systems, beginning with Subversion, are *changeset-based*: a commit may include changes to several files, and the entire set of changes is handled as a unit. Any comment associated with the change does not belong to a single file, but to the changeset itself.

Changeset-based version control is more flexible and powerful than file-based version control; usually, when a change to multiple files has to be reversed, it's good to be able to easily identify and remove all of it.

25.1.1.6 Decentralized vs Centralized Repositories

Early version control systems were designed around a *centralized* model in which each project has only one repository used by all developers. SCCS, RCS, CVS, and Subversion share this kind of model. One of its drawbacks is that the repository is a choke point for reliability and efficiency.

GNU Arch pioneered the concept of *distributed* or *decentralized* version control, later implemented in Git, Mercurial, and Bazaar. A project may have several different repositories, and these systems support a sort of super-merge between repositories that tries to reconcile their change histories. In effect, there is one repository for each developer, and repository merges take the place of commit operations.

VC helps you manage the traffic between your personal workfiles and a repository. Whether the repository is a single master, or one of a network of peer repositories, is not something VC has to care about.

25.1.1.7 Types of Log File

Projects that use a version control system can have two types of log for changes. One is the log maintained by the version control system: each time you commit a change, you fill out a *log entry* for the change (see Section 25.1.4 [Log Buffer], page 287). This is called the *version control log*.

The other kind of log is the file `ChangeLog` (see Section 25.2 [Change Log], page 297). It provides a chronological record of all changes to a large portion of a program—typically one directory and its subdirectories. A small program would use one `ChangeLog` file; a large program may have a `ChangeLog` file in each major directory. See Section 25.2 [Change Log], page 297. Programmers have used change logs since long before version control systems.

Changeset-based version systems typically maintain a changeset-based modification log for the entire system, which makes change log files somewhat redundant. One advantage that they retain is that it is sometimes useful to be able to view the transaction history of a single directory separately from those of other directories. Another advantage is that commit logs can't be fixed in many version control systems.

A project maintained with version control can use just the version control log, or it can use both kinds of logs. It can handle some files one way and some files the other way. Each project has its policy, which you should follow.

When the policy is to use both, you typically want to write an entry for each change just once, then put it into both logs. You can write the entry in `ChangeLog`, then copy it to the log buffer with `C-c C-a` when committing the change (see Section 25.1.4 [Log Buffer], page 287). Or you can write the entry in the log buffer while committing the change, and later use the `C-x v a` command to copy it to `ChangeLog` (see Section "Change Logs and VC" in *Specialized Emacs Features*).

25.1.2 Version Control and the Mode Line

When you visit a file that is under version control, Emacs indicates this on the mode line. For example, 'Bzr-1223' says that Bazaar is used for that file, and the current revision ID is 1223.

The character between the back-end name and the revision ID indicates the *version control status* of the work file. In a merge-based version control system, a '-' character indicates that the work file is unmodified, and ':' indicates that it has been modified. '!' indicates that the file contains conflicts as result of a recent merge operation (see Section 25.1.11.3 [Merging], page 296), or that the file was removed from the version control. Finally, '?' means that the file is under version control, but is missing from the working tree.

In a lock-based system, '-' indicates an unlocked file, and ':' a locked file; if the file is locked by another user (for instance, 'jim'), that is displayed as 'RCS:jim:1.3'. '@' means that the file was locally added, but not yet committed to the master repository.

On a graphical display, you can move the mouse over this mode line indicator to pop up a "tool-tip", which displays a more verbose description of the version control status. Pressing Mouse-1 over the indicator pops up a menu of VC commands, identical to 'Tools / Version Control' on the menu bar.

When Auto Revert mode (see Section 15.4 [Reverting], page 132) reverts a buffer that is under version control, it updates the version control information in the mode line. However, Auto Revert mode may not properly update this information if the version control status changes without changes to the work file, from outside the current Emacs session. If you set auto-revert-check-vc-info to t, Auto Revert mode updates the version control status information every auto-revert-interval seconds, even if the work file itself is unchanged. The resulting CPU usage depends on the version control system, but is usually not excessive.

25.1.3 Basic Editing under Version Control

Most VC commands operate on *VC filesets*. A VC fileset is a collection of one or more files that a VC operation acts on. When you type VC commands in a buffer visiting a version-controlled file, the VC fileset is simply that one file. When you type them in a VC Directory buffer, and some files in it are marked, the VC fileset consists of the marked files (see Section 25.1.10 [VC Directory Mode], page 292).

On modern changeset-based version control systems (see Section 25.1.1.5 [VCS Changesets], page 283), VC commands handle multi-file VC filesets as a group. For example, committing a multi-file VC fileset generates a single revision, containing the changes to all those files. On older file-based version control systems like CVS, each file in a multi-file VC fileset is handled individually; for example, a commit generates one revision for each changed file.

C-x v v   Perform the next appropriate version control operation on the current VC fileset.

The principal VC command is a multi-purpose command, C-x v v (vc-next-action), which performs the "most appropriate" action on the current VC fileset: either registering it with a version control system, or committing it, or unlocking it, or merging changes into it. The precise actions are described in detail in the following subsections. You can use C-x v v either in a file-visiting buffer or in a VC Directory buffer.

Note that VC filesets are distinct from the "named filesets" used for viewing and visiting files in functional groups (see Section 15.17 [Filesets], page 145). Unlike named filesets, VC filesets are not named and don't persist across sessions.

25.1.3.1 Basic Version Control with Merging

On a merging-based version control system (i.e., most modern ones; see Section 25.1.1.4 [VCS Merging], page 283), C-x v v does the following:

- If there is more than one file in the VC fileset and the files have inconsistent version control statuses, signal an error. (Note, however, that a fileset is allowed to include both "newly-added" files and "modified" files; see Section 25.1.5 [Registering], page 288.)

- If none of the files in the VC fileset are registered with a version control system, register the VC fileset, i.e., place it under version control. See Section 25.1.5 [Registering], page 288. If Emacs cannot find a system to register under, it prompts for a repository type, creates a new repository, and registers the VC fileset with it.

- If every work file in the VC fileset is unchanged, do nothing.

- If every work file in the VC fileset has been modified, commit the changes. To do this, Emacs pops up a *vc-log* buffer; type the desired log entry for the new revision, followed by C-c C-c to commit. See Section 25.1.4 [Log Buffer], page 287.

  If committing to a shared repository, the commit may fail if the repository that has been changed since your last update. In that case, you must perform an update before trying again. On a decentralized version control system, use C-x v + (see Section 25.1.11.2 [VC Pull], page 296) or C-x v m (see Section 25.1.11.3 [Merging], page 296). On a centralized version control system, type C-x v v again to merge in the repository changes.

- Finally, if you are using a centralized version control system, check if each work file in the VC fileset is up-to-date. If any file has been changed in the repository, offer to update it.

These rules also apply when you use RCS in its "non-locking" mode, except that changes are not automatically merged from the repository. Nothing informs you if another user has committed changes in the same file since you began editing it; when you commit your revision, his changes are removed (however, they remain in the repository and are thus not irrevocably lost). Therefore, you must verify that the current revision is unchanged before committing your changes. In addition, locking is possible with RCS even in this mode: C-x v v with an unmodified file locks the file, just as it does with RCS in its normal locking mode (see Section 25.1.3.2 [VC With A Locking VCS], page 286).

25.1.3.2 Basic Version Control with Locking

On a locking-based version control system (such as SCCS, and RCS in its default mode), C-x v v does the following:

- If there is more than one file in the VC fileset and the files have inconsistent version control statuses, signal an error.

- If each file in the VC fileset is not registered with a version control system, register the VC fileset. See Section 25.1.5 [Registering], page 288. If Emacs cannot find a system to register under, it prompts for a repository type, creates a new repository, and registers the VC fileset with it.

- If each file is registered and unlocked, lock it and make it writable, so that you can begin to edit it.

- If each file is locked by you and contains changes, commit the changes. To do this, Emacs pops up a *vc-log* buffer; type the desired log entry for the new revision, followed by C-c C-c to commit (see Section 25.1.4 [Log Buffer], page 287).

- If each file is locked by you, but you have not changed it, release the lock and make the file read-only again.

- If each file is locked by another user, ask whether you want to "steal the lock". If you say yes, the file becomes locked by you, and a warning message is sent to the user who had formerly locked the file.

These rules also apply when you use CVS in locking mode, except that CVS does not support stealing locks.

25.1.3.3 Advanced Control in C-x v v

When you give a prefix argument to vc-next-action (C-u C-x v v), it still performs the next logical version control operation, but accepts additional arguments to specify precisely how to do the operation.

- You can specify the name of a version control system. This is useful if the fileset can be managed by more than one version control system, and Emacs fails to detect the correct one.

- Otherwise, if using CVS or RCS, you can specify a revision ID.

  If the fileset is modified (or locked), this makes Emacs commit with that revision ID. You can create a new branch by supplying an appropriate revision ID (see Section 25.1.11 [Branches], page 295).

  If the fileset is unmodified (and unlocked), this checks the specified revision into the working tree. You can also specify a revision on another branch by giving its revision or branch ID (see Section 25.1.11.1 [Switching Branches], page 295). An empty argument (i.e., C-u C-x v v RET) checks out the latest ("head") revision on the current branch.

  This signals an error on a decentralized version control system. Those systems do not let you specify your own revision IDs, nor do they use the concept of "checking out" individual files.

25.1.4 Features of the Log Entry Buffer

When you tell VC to commit a change, it pops up a buffer named *vc-log*. In this buffer, you should write a *log entry* describing the changes you have made (see Section 25.1.1.1 [Why Version Control?], page 281). After you are done, type C-c C-c (log-edit-done) to exit the buffer and commit the change, together with your log entry.

The major mode for the *vc-log* buffer is Log Edit mode, a variant of Text mode (see Section 22.7 [Text Mode], page 217). On entering Log Edit mode, Emacs runs the hooks text-mode-hook and vc-log-mode-hook (see Section 33.2.2 [Hooks], page 422).

In the *vc-log* buffer, you can write one or more *header lines*, specifying additional information to be supplied to the version control system. Each header line must occupy a single line at the top of the buffer; the first line that is not a header line is treated as the start of the log entry. For example, the following header line states that the present change was not written by you, but by another developer:

        Author: J. R. Hacker <jrh@example.com>

Apart from the 'Author' header, Emacs recognizes the headers 'Date' (a manually-specified commit time) and 'Fixes' (a reference to a bug fixed by the change). Not all version control systems recognize all headers: Bazaar recognizes all three headers, while Git, Mercurial, and Monotone recognize only 'Author' and 'Date'. If you specify a header for a system that does not support it, the header is treated as part of the log entry.

While in the *vc-log* buffer, the "current VC fileset" is considered to be the fileset that will be committed if you type C-c C-c. To view a list of the files in the VC fileset, type C-c C-f (log-edit-show-files). To view a diff of changes between the VC fileset and the version from which you started editing (see Section 25.1.6 [Old Revisions], page 289), type C-c C-d (log-edit-show-diff).

If the VC fileset includes one or more ChangeLog files (see Section 25.2 [Change Log], page 297), type C-c C-a (log-edit-insert-changelog) to pull the relevant entries into the *vc-log* buffer. If the topmost item in each ChangeLog was made under your user name on the current date, this command searches that item for entries matching the file(s) to be committed, and inserts them.

To abort a commit, just *don't* type C-c C-c in that buffer. You can switch buffers and do other editing. As long as you don't try to make another commit, the entry you were editing remains in the *vc-log* buffer, and you can go back to that buffer at any time to complete the commit.

You can also browse the history of previous log entries to duplicate a commit comment. This can be useful when you want to make several commits with similar comments. The commands M-n, M-p, M-s and M-r for doing this work just like the minibuffer history commands (see Section 5.5 [Minibuffer History], page 32), except that they are used outside the minibuffer.

25.1.5 Registering a File for Version Control

C-x v i   Register the visited file for version control.

The command C-x v i (vc-register) *registers* each file in the current VC fileset, placing it under version control. This is essentially equivalent to the action of C-x v v on an unregistered VC fileset (see Section 25.1.3 [Basic VC Editing], page 285), except that if the VC fileset is already registered, C-x v i signals an error whereas C-x v v performs some other action.

To register a file, Emacs must choose a version control system. For a multi-file VC fileset, the VC Directory buffer specifies the system to use (see Section 25.1.10 [VC Directory Mode], page 292). For a single-file VC fileset, if the file's directory already contains files registered in a version control system, or if the directory is part of a directory tree controlled by a version control system, Emacs chooses that system. In the event that more than one version control system is applicable, Emacs uses the one that appears first in the variable vc-handled-backends. If Emacs cannot find a version control system to register the file under, it prompts for a repository type, creates a new repository, and registers the file into that repository.

On most version control systems, registering a file with C-x v i or C-x v v adds it to the "working tree" but not to the repository. Such files are labeled as 'added' in the VC Directory buffer, and show a revision ID of '@@' in the mode line. To make the registration take effect in the repository, you must perform a commit (see Section 25.1.3 [Basic VC Editing], page 285). Note that a single commit can include both file additions and edits to existing files.

On a locking-based version control system (see Section 25.1.1.4 [VCS Merging], page 283), registering a file leaves it unlocked and read-only. Type C-x v v to start editing it.

25.1.6 Examining And Comparing Old Revisions

C-x v =   Compare the work files in the current VC fileset with the versions you started
            from (`vc-diff`). With a prefix argument, prompt for two revisions of the
            current VC fileset and compare them. You can also call this command from a
            Dired buffer (see Chapter 27 [Dired], page 315).

C-x v D   Compare the entire working tree to the revision you started from (`vc-root-
            diff`). With a prefix argument, prompt for two revisions and compare their
            trees.

C-x v ~   Prompt for a revision of the current file, and visit it in a separate buffer
            (`vc-revision-other-window`).

C-x v g   Display an annotated version of the current file: for each line, show the latest
            revision in which it was modified (`vc-annotate`).

`C-x v =` (`vc-diff`) displays a *diff* which compares each work file in the current VC fileset
to the version(s) from which you started editing. The diff is displayed in another window,
in a Diff mode buffer (see Section 15.9 [Diff Mode], page 138) named `*vc-diff*`. The usual
Diff mode commands are available in this buffer. In particular, the `g` (`revert-buffer`)
command performs the file comparison again, generating a new diff.

To compare two arbitrary revisions of the current VC fileset, call `vc-diff` with a prefix
argument: `C-u C-x v =`. This prompts for two revision IDs (see Section 25.1.1.3 [VCS
Concepts], page 282), and displays a diff between those versions of the fileset. This will not
work reliably for multi-file VC filesets, if the version control system is file-based rather than
changeset-based (e.g., CVS), since then revision IDs for different files would not be related
in any meaningful way.

Instead of the revision ID, some version control systems let you specify revisions in other
formats. For instance, under Bazaar you can enter '`date:yesterday`' for the argument to
`C-u C-x v =` (and related commands) to specify the first revision committed after yesterday.
See the documentation of the version control system for details.

If you invoke `C-x v =` or `C-u C-x v =` from a Dired buffer (see Chapter 27 [Dired],
page 315), the file listed on the current line is treated as the current VC fileset.

`C-x v D` (`vc-root-diff`) is similar to `C-x v =`, but it displays the changes in the entire
current working tree (i.e., the working tree containing the current VC fileset). If you invoke
this command from a Dired buffer, it applies to the working tree containing the directory.

You can customize the `diff` options that `C-x v =` and `C-x v D` use for generating diffs.
The options used are taken from the first non-`nil` value amongst the variables *vc-backend-
diff-switches*, *vc-diff-switches*, and **diff-switches** (see Section 15.8 [Comparing
Files], page 137), in that order. Here, *backend* stands for the relevant version control system, e.g., `bzr` for Bazaar. Since `nil` means to check the next variable in the sequence, either
of the first two may use the value `t` to mean no switches at all. Most of the *vc-backend-
diff-switches* variables default to `nil`, but some default to `t`; these are for version control
systems whose `diff` implementations do not accept common diff options, such as Subversion.

To directly examine an older version of a file, visit the work file and type `C-x v ~` *revision* RET (`vc-revision-other-window`). This retrieves the file version corresponding to
revision, saves it to `filename.~revision~`, and visits it in a separate window.

Many version control systems allow you to view files *annotated* with per-line revision information, by typing `C-x v g` (`vc-annotate`). This creates a new buffer (the "annotate buffer") displaying the file's text, with each line colored to show how old it is. Red text is new, blue is old, and intermediate colors indicate intermediate ages. By default, the color is scaled over the full range of ages, such that the oldest changes are blue, and the newest changes are red.

When you give a prefix argument to this command, Emacs reads two arguments using the minibuffer: the revision to display and annotate (instead of the current file contents), and the time span in days the color range should cover.

From the annotate buffer, these and other color scaling options are available from the 'VC-Annotate' menu. In this buffer, you can also use the following keys to browse the annotations of past revisions, view diffs, or view log entries:

p   Annotate the previous revision, i.e., the revision before the one currently annotated. A numeric prefix argument is a repeat count, so `C-u 10 p` would take you back 10 revisions.

n   Annotate the next revision, i.e., the revision after the one currently annotated. A numeric prefix argument is a repeat count.

j   Annotate the revision indicated by the current line.

a   Annotate the revision before the one indicated by the current line. This is useful to see the state the file was in before the change on the current line was made.

f   Show in a buffer the file revision indicated by the current line.

d   Display the diff between the current line's revision and the previous revision. This is useful to see what the current line's revision actually changed in the file.

D   Display the diff between the current line's revision and the previous revision for all files in the changeset (for VC systems that support changesets). This is useful to see what the current line's revision actually changed in the tree.

l   Show the log of the current line's revision. This is useful to see the author's description of the changes in the revision on the current line.

w   Annotate the working revision–the one you are editing. If you used p and n to browse to other revisions, use this key to return to your working revision.

v   Toggle the annotation visibility. This is useful for looking just at the file contents without distraction from the annotations.

25.1.7 VC Change Log

C-x v l   Display the change history for the current fileset (`vc-print-log`).

C-x v L   Display the change history for the current repository (`vc-print-root-log`).

C-x v I   Display the changes that a pull operation will retrieve (`vc-log-incoming`).

C-x v O   Display the changes that will be sent by the next push operation (`vc-log-outgoing`).

C-x v l (vc-print-log) displays a buffer named *vc-change-log*, showing the history of changes made to the current file, including who made the changes, the dates, and the log entry for each change (these are the same log entries you would enter via the *vc-log* buffer; see Section 25.1.4 [Log Buffer], page 287). Point is centered at the revision of the file currently being visited. With a prefix argument, the command prompts for the revision to center on, and the maximum number of revisions to display.

If you call C-x v l from a VC Directory buffer (see Section 25.1.10 [VC Directory Mode], page 292) or a Dired buffer (see Chapter 27 [Dired], page 315), it applies to the file listed on the current line.

C-x v L (vc-print-root-log) displays a *vc-change-log* buffer showing the history of the entire version-controlled directory tree (RCS, SCCS, and CVS do not support this feature). With a prefix argument, the command prompts for the maximum number of revisions to display.

The C-x v L history is shown in a compact form, usually showing only the first line of each log entry. However, you can type RET (log-view-toggle-entry-display) in the *vc-change-log* buffer to reveal the entire log entry for the revision at point. A second RET hides it again.

On a decentralized version control system, the C-x v I (vc-log-incoming) command displays a log buffer showing the changes that will be applied, the next time you run the version control system's "pull" command to get new revisions from another repository (see Section 25.1.11.2 [VC Pull], page 296). This other repository is the default one from which changes are pulled, as defined by the version control system; with a prefix argument, vc-log-incoming prompts for a specific repository. Similarly, C-x v O (vc-log-outgoing) shows the changes that will be sent to another repository, the next time you run the "push" command; with a prefix argument, it prompts for a specific destination repository.

In the *vc-change-log* buffer, you can use the following keys to move between the logs of revisions and of files, and to examine and compare past revisions (see Section 25.1.6 [Old Revisions], page 289):

p	Move to the previous revision entry. (Revision entries in the log buffer are usually in reverse-chronological order, so the previous revision-item usually corresponds to a newer revision.) A numeric prefix argument is a repeat count.
n	Move to the next revision entry. A numeric prefix argument is a repeat count.
P	Move to the log of the previous file, if showing logs for a multi-file VC fileset. Otherwise, just move to the beginning of the log. A numeric prefix argument is a repeat count.
N	Move to the log of the next file, if showing logs for a multi-file VC fileset. A numeric prefix argument is a repeat count.
a	Annotate the revision on the current line (see Section 25.1.6 [Old Revisions], page 289).
e	Modify the change comment displayed at point. Note that not all VC systems support modifying change comments.
f	Visit the revision indicated at the current line.

d   Display a diff between the revision at point and the next earlier revision, for
            the specific file.

D   Display the changeset diff between the revision at point and the next earlier
            revision. This shows the changes to all files made in that revision.

RET   In a compact-style log buffer (e.g., the one created by C-x v L), toggle between
            showing and hiding the full log entry for the revision at point.

Because fetching many log entries can be slow, the *vc-change-log* buffer displays no
more than 2000 revisions by default. The variable vc-log-show-limit specifies this limit;
if you set the value to zero, that removes the limit. You can also increase the number of
revisions shown in an existing *vc-change-log* buffer by clicking on the 'Show 2X entries'
or 'Show unlimited entries' buttons at the end of the buffer. However, RCS, SCCS, and
CVS do not support this feature.

25.1.8 Undoing Version Control Actions

C-x v u   Revert the work file(s) in the current VC fileset to the last revision (vc-revert).

If you want to discard all the changes you have made to the current VC fileset, type C-x v
u (vc-revert-buffer). This shows you a diff between the work file(s) and the revision from
which you started editing, and asks for confirmation for discarding the changes. If you agree,
the fileset is reverted. If you don't want C-x v u to show a diff, set the variable vc-revert-
show-diff to nil (you can still view the diff directly with C-x v =; see Section 25.1.6 [Old
Revisions], page 289). Note that C-x v u cannot be reversed with the usual undo commands
(see Section 13.1 [Undo], page 109), so use it with care.

On locking-based version control systems, C-x v u leaves files unlocked; you must lock
again to resume editing. You can also use C-x v u to unlock a file if you lock it and then
decide not to change it.

25.1.9 Ignore Version Control Files

C-x v G   Ignore a file under current version control system. (vc-ignore).

Many source trees contain some files that do not need to be versioned, such as editor
backups, object or bytecode files, and built programs. You can simply not add them, but
then they'll always crop up as unknown files. You can also tell the version control system
to ignore these files by adding them to the ignore file at the top of the tree. C-x v G
(vc-ignore) can help you do this. When called with a prefix argument, you can remove a
file from the ignored file list.

25.1.10 VC Directory Mode

The *VC Directory buffer* is a specialized buffer for viewing the version control statuses of
the files in a directory tree, and performing version control operations on those files. In
particular, it is used to specify multi-file VC filesets for commands like C-x v v to act on
(see Section 25.1.10.2 [VC Directory Commands], page 293).

To use the VC Directory buffer, type C-x v d (vc-dir). This reads a directory name
using the minibuffer, and switches to a VC Directory buffer for that directory. By default,
the buffer is named *vc-dir*. Its contents are described below.

The `vc-dir` command automatically detects the version control system to be used in the specified directory. In the event that more than one system is being used in the directory, you should invoke the command with a prefix argument, `C-u C-x v d`; this prompts for the version control system which the VC Directory buffer should use.

25.1.10.1 The VC Directory Buffer

The VC Directory buffer contains a list of version-controlled files and their version control statuses. It lists files in the current directory (the one specified when you called `C-x v d`) and its subdirectories, but only those with a "noteworthy" status. Files that are up-to-date (i.e., the same as in the repository) are omitted. If all the files in a subdirectory are up-to-date, the subdirectory is not listed either. As an exception, if a file has become up-to-date as a direct result of a VC command, it is listed.

Here is an example of a VC Directory buffer listing:

```
                        ./
        edited          configure.ac
   *    added           README
        unregistered    temp.txt
                        src/
   *    edited          src/main.c
```

Two work files have been modified but not committed: `configure.ac` in the current directory, and `foo.c` in the `src/` subdirectory. The file named `README` has been added but is not yet committed, while `temp.txt` is not under version control (see Section 25.1.5 [Registering], page 288).

The '`*`' characters next to the entries for `README` and `src/main.c` indicate that the user has marked out these files as the current VC fileset (see below).

The above example is typical for a decentralized version control system like Bazaar, Git, or Mercurial. Other systems can show other statuses. For instance, CVS shows the '`needs-update`' status if the repository has changes that have not been applied to the work file. RCS and SCCS show the name of the user locking a file as its status.

The VC Directory buffer omits subdirectories listed in the variable `vc-directory-exclusion-list`. Its default value contains directories that are used internally by version control systems.

25.1.10.2 VC Directory Commands

Emacs provides several commands for navigating the VC Directory buffer, and for "marking" files as belonging to the current VC fileset.

`n`
`SPC`   Move point to the next entry (`vc-dir-next-line`).

`p`   Move point to the previous entry (`vc-dir-previous-line`).

`TAB`   Move to the next directory entry (`vc-dir-next-directory`).

`S-TAB`   Move to the previous directory entry (`vc-dir-previous-directory`).

`RET`
`f`   Visit the file or directory listed on the current line (`vc-dir-find-file`).

o   Visit the file or directory on the current line, in a separate window (`vc-dir-find-file-other-window`).

m   Mark the file or directory on the current line (`vc-dir-mark`), putting it in the current VC fileset. If the region is active, mark all files in the region.

            A file cannot be marked with this command if it is already in a marked directory, or one of its subdirectories. Similarly, a directory cannot be marked with this command if any file in its tree is marked.

M   If point is on a file entry, mark all files with the same status; if point is on a directory entry, mark all files in that directory tree (`vc-dir-mark-all-files`). With a prefix argument, mark all listed files and directories.

q   Quit the VC Directory buffer, and bury it (`quit-window`).

u   Unmark the file or directory on the current line. If the region is active, unmark all the files in the region (`vc-dir-unmark`).

U   If point is on a file entry, unmark all files with the same status; if point is on a directory entry, unmark all files in that directory tree (`vc-dir-unmark-all-files`). With a prefix argument, unmark all files and directories.

x   Hide files with 'up-to-date' status (`vc-dir-hide-up-to-date`). With a prefix argument, hide items whose state is that of the item at point.

While in the VC Directory buffer, all the files that you mark with m (`vc-dir-mark`) or M (`vc-dir-mark`) are in the current VC fileset. If you mark a directory entry with m, all the listed files in that directory tree are in the current VC fileset. The files and directories that belong to the current VC fileset are indicated with a '*' character in the VC Directory buffer, next to their VC status. In this way, you can set up a multi-file VC fileset to be acted on by VC commands like C-x v v (see Section 25.1.3 [Basic VC Editing], page 285), C-x v = (see Section 25.1.6 [Old Revisions], page 289), and C-x v u (see Section 25.1.8 [VC Undo], page 292).

The VC Directory buffer also defines some single-key shortcuts for VC commands with the C-x v prefix: =, +, l, i, D, L, G, I and v.

For example, you can commit a set of edited files by opening a VC Directory buffer, where the files are listed with the 'edited' status; marking the files; and typing v or C-x v v (`vc-next-action`). If the version control system is changeset-based, Emacs will commit the files in a single revision.

While in the VC Directory buffer, you can also perform search and replace on the current VC fileset, with the following commands:

S   Search the fileset (`vc-dir-search`).

Q   Do a regular expression query replace on the fileset (`vc-dir-query-replace-regexp`).

M-s a C-s   Do an incremental search on the fileset (`vc-dir-isearch`).

M-s a C-M-s
            Do an incremental regular expression search on the fileset (`vc-dir-isearch-regexp`).

Apart from acting on multiple files, these commands behave much like their single-buffer counterparts (see Chapter 12 [Search], page 90).

The above commands are also available via the menu bar, and via a context menu invoked by Mouse-2. Furthermore, some VC backends use the menu to provide extra backend-specific commands. For example, Git and Bazaar allow you to manipulate *stashes* and *shelves* (where are a way to temporarily put aside uncommitted changes, and bring them back at a later time).

25.1.11 Version Control Branches

One use of version control is to support multiple independent lines of development, which are called *branches*. Amongst other things, branches can be used for maintaining separate "stable" and "development" versions of a program, and for developing unrelated features in isolation from one another.

VC's support for branch operations is currently fairly limited. For decentralized version control systems, it provides commands for *updating* one branch with the contents of another, and for *merging* the changes made to two different branches (see Section 25.1.11.3 [Merging], page 296). For centralized version control systems, it supports checking out different branches and committing into new or different branches.

25.1.11.1 Switching between Branches

The various version control systems differ in how branches are implemented, and these differences cannot be entirely concealed by VC.

On some decentralized version control systems, including Bazaar and Mercurial in its normal mode of operation, each branch has its own working directory tree, so switching between branches just involves switching directories. On Git, branches are normally *co-located* in the same directory, and switching between branches is done using the `git checkout` command, which changes the contents of the working tree to match the branch you switch to. Bazaar also supports co-located branches, in which case the `bzr switch` command will switch branches in the current directory. With Subversion, you switch to another branch using the `svn switch` command.

The VC command to switch to another branch in the current directory is C-x v r *branch-name* RET (`vc-retrieve-tag`).

On centralized version control systems, you can also switch between branches by typing C-u C-x v v in an up-to-date work file (see Section 25.1.3.3 [Advanced C-x v v], page 287), and entering the revision ID for a revision on another branch. On CVS, for instance, revisions on the *trunk* (the main line of development) normally have IDs of the form 1.1, 1.2, 1.3, . . ., while the first branch created from (say) revision 1.2 has revision IDs 1.2.1.1, 1.2.1.2, . . ., the second branch created from revision 1.2 has revision IDs 1.2.2.1, 1.2.2.2, . . ., and so forth. You can also specify the *branch ID*, which is a branch revision ID omitting its final component (e.g., 1.2.1), to switch to the latest revision on that branch.

On a locking-based system, switching to a different branch also unlocks (write-protects) the working tree.

Once you have switched to a branch, VC commands will apply to that branch until you switch away; for instance, any VC filesets that you commit will be committed to that specific branch.

25.1.11.2 Pulling Changes into a Branch

C-x v +   On a decentralized version control system, update the current branch by
            "pulling in" changes from another location.

            On a centralized version control system, update the current VC fileset.

On a decentralized version control system, the command C-x v + (vc-pull) updates the current branch and working tree. It is typically used to update a copy of a remote branch. If you supply a prefix argument, the command prompts for the exact version control command to use, which lets you specify where to pull changes from. Otherwise, it pulls from a default location determined by the version control system.

Amongst decentralized version control systems, C-x v + is currently supported only by Bazaar, Git, and Mercurial. On Bazaar, it calls bzr pull for ordinary branches (to pull from a master branch into a mirroring branch), and bzr update for a bound branch (to pull from a central repository). On Git, it calls git pull to fetch changes from a remote repository and merge it into the current branch. On Mercurial, it calls hg pull -u to fetch changesets from the default remote repository and update the working directory.

Prior to pulling, you can use C-x v I (vc-log-incoming) to view a log buffer of the changes to be applied. See Section 25.1.7 [VC Change Log], page 290.

On a centralized version control system like CVS, C-x v + updates the current VC fileset from the repository.

25.1.11.3 Merging Branches

C-x v m   On a decentralized version control system, merge changes from another branch
            into the current one.

            On a centralized version control system, merge changes from another branch
            into the current VC fileset.

While developing a branch, you may sometimes need to *merge* in changes that have already been made in another branch. This is not a trivial operation, as overlapping changes may have been made to the two branches.

On a decentralized version control system, merging is done with the command C-x v m (vc-merge). On Bazaar, this prompts for the exact arguments to pass to bzr merge, offering a sensible default if possible. On Git, this prompts for the name of a branch to merge from, with completion (based on the branch names known to the current repository). The output from running the merge command is shown in a separate buffer.

On a centralized version control system like CVS, C-x v m prompts for a branch ID, or a pair of revision IDs (see Section 25.1.11.1 [Switching Branches], page 295); then it finds the changes from that branch, or the changes between the two revisions you specified, and merges those changes into the current VC fileset. If you just type RET, Emacs simply merges any changes that were made on the same branch since you checked the file out.

Immediately after performing a merge, only the working tree is modified, and you can review the changes produced by the merge with C-x v D and related commands (see Section 25.1.6 [Old Revisions], page 289). If the two branches contained overlapping changes, merging produces a *conflict*; a warning appears in the output of the merge command, and *conflict markers* are inserted into each affected work file, surrounding the two sets of conflicting changes. You must then resolve the conflict by editing the conflicted files. Once you are done, the modified files must be committed in the usual way for the merge to take effect (see Section 25.1.3 [Basic VC Editing], page 285).

25.1.11.4 Creating New Branches

On centralized version control systems like CVS, Emacs supports creating new branches as part of a commit operation. When committing a modified VC fileset, type `C-u C-x v v` (`vc-next-action` with a prefix argument; see Section 25.1.3.3 [Advanced C-x v v], page 287). Then Emacs prompts for a revision ID for the new revision. You should specify a suitable branch ID for a branch starting at the current revision. For example, if the current revision is 2.5, the branch ID should be 2.5.1, 2.5.2, and so on, depending on the number of existing branches at that point.

To create a new branch at an older revision (one that is no longer the head of a branch), first select that revision (see Section 25.1.11.1 [Switching Branches], page 295). Your procedure will then differ depending on whether you are using a locking or merging-based VCS.

On a locking VCS, you will need to lock the old revision branch with `C-x v v`. You'll be asked to confirm, when you lock the old revision, that you really mean to create a new branch—if you say no, you'll be offered a chance to lock the latest revision instead. On a merging-based VCS you will skip this step.

Then make your changes and type `C-x v v` again to commit a new revision. This creates a new branch starting from the selected revision.

After the branch is created, subsequent commits create new revisions on that branch. To leave the branch, you must explicitly select a different revision with `C-u C-x v v`.

25.2 Change Logs

Many software projects keep a *change log*. This is a file, normally named `ChangeLog`, containing a chronological record of when and how the program was changed. Sometimes, these files are automatically generated from the change log entries stored in version control systems, or are used to generate these change log entries. Sometimes, there are several change log files, each recording the changes in one directory or directory tree.

25.2.1 Change Log Commands

The Emacs command `C-x 4 a` adds a new entry to the change log file for the file you are editing (`add-change-log-entry-other-window`). If that file is actually a backup file, it makes an entry appropriate for the file's parent—that is useful for making log entries for functions that have been deleted in the current version.

`C-x 4 a` visits the change log file and creates a new entry unless the most recent entry is for today's date and your name. It also creates a new item for the current file. For many languages, it can even guess the name of the function or other object that was changed.

When the variable `add-log-keep-changes-together` is non-`nil`, `C-x 4 a` adds to any existing item for the file rather than starting a new item.

You can combine multiple changes of the same nature. If you don't enter any text after the initial `C-x 4 a`, any subsequent `C-x 4 a` adds another symbol to the change log entry.

If `add-log-always-start-new-record` is non-nil, C-x 4 a always makes a new entry, even if the last entry was made by you and on the same date.

If the value of the variable `change-log-version-info-enabled` is non-nil, C-x 4 a adds the file's version number to the change log entry. It finds the version number by searching the first ten percent of the file, using regular expressions from the variable `change-log-version-number-regexp-list`.

The change log file is visited in Change Log mode. In this major mode, each bunch of grouped items counts as one paragraph, and each entry is considered a page. This facilitates editing the entries. C-j and auto-fill indent each new line like the previous line; this is convenient for entering the contents of an entry.

You can use the `next-error` command (by default bound to C-x ') to move between entries in the Change Log, when Change Log mode is on. You will jump to the actual site in the file that was changed, not just to the next Change Log entry. You can also use `previous-error` to move back in the same list.

You can use the command M-x `change-log-merge` to merge other log files into a buffer in Change Log Mode, preserving the date ordering of entries.

Version control systems are another way to keep track of changes in your program and keep a change log. In the VC log buffer, typing C-c C-a (`log-edit-insert-changelog`) inserts the relevant Change Log entry, if one exists. See Section 25.1.4 [Log Buffer], page 287.

25.2.2 Format of ChangeLog

A change log entry starts with a header line that contains the current date, your name (taken from the variable `add-log-full-name`), and your email address (taken from the variable `add-log-mailing-address`). Aside from these header lines, every line in the change log starts with a space or a tab. The bulk of the entry consists of *items*, each of which starts with a line starting with whitespace and a star. Here are two entries, both dated in May 1993, with two items and one item respectively.

```
1993-05-25  Richard Stallman  <rms@gnu.org>

        * man.el: Rename symbols 'man-*' to 'Man-*'.
        (manual-entry): Make prompt string clearer.

        * simple.el (blink-matching-paren-distance):
        Change default to 12,000.

1993-05-24  Richard Stallman  <rms@gnu.org>

        * vc.el (minor-mode-map-alist): Don't use it if it's void.
        (vc-cancel-version): Doc fix.
```

One entry can describe several changes; each change should have its own item, or its own line in an item. Normally there should be a blank line between items. When items are related (parts of the same change, in different places), group them by leaving no blank line between them.

You should put a copyright notice and permission notice at the end of the change log file. Here is an example:

```
Copyright 1997, 1998 Free Software Foundation, Inc.
Copying and distribution of this file, with or without modification, are
```

```
        permitted provided the copyright notice and this notice are preserved.
```
Of course, you should substitute the proper years and copyright holder.

25.3 Tags Tables

A *tag* is a reference to a subunit in a program or in a document. In source code, tags reference syntactic elements of the program: functions, subroutines, data types, macros, etc. In a document, tags reference chapters, sections, appendices, etc. Each tag specifies the name of the file where the corresponding subunit is defined, and the position of the subunit's definition in that file.

A *tags table* records the tags extracted by scanning the source code of a certain program or a certain document. Tags extracted from generated files reference the original files, rather than the generated files that were scanned during tag extraction. Examples of generated files include C files generated from Cweb source files, from a Yacc parser, or from Lex scanner definitions; `.i` preprocessed C files; and Fortran files produced by preprocessing `.fpp` source files.

To produce a tags table, you run the `etags` shell command on a document or the source code file. The 'etags' program writes the tags to a *tags table file*, or *tags file* in short. The conventional name for a tags file is `TAGS`. See Section 25.3.2 [Create Tags Table], page 301.

Emacs provides many commands for searching and replacing using the information recorded in tags tables. For instance, the `M-.` (`find-tag`) jumps to the location of a specified function definition in its source file. See Section 25.3.5 [Find Tag], page 304.

The Ebrowse facility is similar to `etags` but specifically tailored for C++. See Section "Ebrowse" in *Ebrowse User's Manual*. The Semantic package provides another way to generate and use tags, separate from the `etags` facility. See Section 23.10 [Semantic], page 255.

25.3.1 Source File Tag Syntax

Here is how tag syntax is defined for the most popular languages:

- In C code, any C function or typedef is a tag, and so are definitions of `struct`, `union` and `enum`. `#define` macro definitions, `#undef` and `enum` constants are also tags, unless you specify '`--no-defines`' when making the tags table. Similarly, global variables are tags, unless you specify '`--no-globals`', and so are struct members, unless you specify '`--no-members`'. Use of '`--no-globals`', '`--no-defines`' and '`--no-members`' can make the tags table file much smaller.

  You can tag function declarations and external variables in addition to function definitions by giving the '`--declarations`' option to `etags`.

- In C++ code, in addition to all the tag constructs of C code, member functions are also recognized; member variables are also recognized, unless you use the '`--no-members`' option. Tags for variables and functions in classes are named '`class::variable`' and '`class::function`'. `operator` definitions have tag names like '`operator+`'.

- In Java code, tags include all the constructs recognized in C++, plus the `interface`, `extends` and `implements` constructs. Tags for variables and functions in classes are named '`class.variable`' and '`class.function`'.

- In LaTeX documents, the arguments for \chapter, \section, \subsection, \subsubsection, \eqno, \label, \ref, \cite, \bibitem, \part, \appendix, \entry, \index, \def, \newcommand, \renewcommand, \newenvironment and \renewenvironment are tags.

  Other commands can make tags as well, if you specify them in the environment variable TEXTAGS before invoking etags. The value of this environment variable should be a colon-separated list of command names. For example,

  ```
  TEXTAGS="mycommand:myothercommand"
  export TEXTAGS
  ```

  specifies (using Bourne shell syntax) that the commands '\mycommand' and '\myothercommand' also define tags.

- In Lisp code, any function defined with defun, any variable defined with defvar or defconst, and in general the first argument of any expression that starts with '(def' in column zero is a tag. As an exception, expressions of the form (defvar *foo*) are treated as declarations, and are only tagged if the '--declarations' option is given.

- In Scheme code, tags include anything defined with def or with a construct whose name starts with 'def'. They also include variables set with set! at top level in the file.

Several other languages are also supported:

- In Ada code, functions, procedures, packages, tasks and types are tags. Use the '--packages-only' option to create tags for packages only.

  In Ada, the same name can be used for different kinds of entity (e.g., for a procedure and for a function). Also, for things like packages, procedures and functions, there is the spec (i.e., the interface) and the body (i.e., the implementation). To make it easier to pick the definition you want, Ada tag name have suffixes indicating the type of entity:

  '/b'   package body.

  '/f'   function.

  '/k'   task.

  '/p'   procedure.

  '/s'   package spec.

  '/t'   type.

  Thus, M-x find-tag RET bidule/b RET will go directly to the body of the package bidule, while M-x find-tag RET bidule RET will just search for any tag bidule.

- In assembler code, labels appearing at the start of a line, followed by a colon, are tags.

- In Bison or Yacc input files, each rule defines as a tag the nonterminal it constructs. The portions of the file that contain C code are parsed as C code.

- In Cobol code, tags are paragraph names; that is, any word starting in column 8 and followed by a period.

- In Erlang code, the tags are the functions, records and macros defined in the file.

- In Fortran code, functions, subroutines and block data are tags.

- In HTML input files, the tags are the `title` and the `h1`, `h2`, `h3` headers. Also, tags are `name=` in anchors and all occurrences of `id=`.

- In Lua input files, all functions are tags.

- In makefiles, targets are tags; additionally, variables are tags unless you specify '`--no-globals`'.

- In Objective C code, tags include Objective C definitions for classes, class categories, methods and protocols. Tags for variables and functions in classes are named '`class::variable`' and '`class::function`'.

- In Pascal code, the tags are the functions and procedures defined in the file.

- In Perl code, the tags are the packages, subroutines and variables defined by the `package`, `sub`, `use constant`, `my`, and `local` keywords. Use '`--globals`' if you want to tag global variables. Tags for subroutines are named '`package::sub`'. The name for subroutines defined in the default package is '`main::sub`'.

- In PHP code, tags are functions, classes and defines. Vars are tags too, unless you use the '`--no-members`' option.

- In PostScript code, the tags are the functions.

- In Prolog code, tags are predicates and rules at the beginning of line.

- In Python code, `def` or `class` at the beginning of a line generate a tag.

You can also generate tags based on regexp matching (see Section 25.3.3 [Etags Regexps], page 302) to handle other formats and languages.

25.3.2 Creating Tags Tables

The `etags` program is used to create a tags table file. It knows the syntax of several languages, as described in the previous section. Here is how to run `etags`:

```
etags inputfiles...
```

The `etags` program reads the specified files, and writes a tags table named `TAGS` in the current working directory. You can optionally specify a different file name for the tags table by using the '`--output=file`' option; specifying – as a file name prints the tags table to standard output.

If the specified files don't exist, `etags` looks for compressed versions of them and uncompresses them to read them. Under MS-DOS, `etags` also looks for file names like `mycode.cgz` if it is given '`mycode.c`' on the command line and `mycode.c` does not exist.

If the tags table becomes outdated due to changes in the files described in it, you can update it by running the `etags` program again. If the tags table does not record a tag, or records it for the wrong file, then Emacs will not be able to find that definition until you update the tags table. But if the position recorded in the tags table becomes a little bit wrong (due to other editing), Emacs will still be able to find the right position, with a slight delay.

Thus, there is no need to update the tags table after each edit. You should update a tags table when you define new tags that you want to have listed, or when you move tag definitions from one file to another, or when changes become substantial.

You can make a tags table *include* another tags table, by passing the '`--include=file`' option to `etags`. It then covers all the files covered by the included tags file, as well as its own.

If you specify the source files with relative file names when you run **etags**, the tags file will contain file names relative to the directory where the tags file was initially written. This way, you can move an entire directory tree containing both the tags file and the source files, and the tags file will still refer correctly to the source files. If the tags file is - or is in the **/dev** directory, however, the file names are made relative to the current working directory. This is useful, for example, when writing the tags to **/dev/stdout**.

When using a relative file name, it should not be a symbolic link pointing to a tags file in a different directory, because this would generally render the file names invalid.

If you specify absolute file names as arguments to **etags**, then the tags file will contain absolute file names. This way, the tags file will still refer to the same files even if you move it, as long as the source files remain in the same place. Absolute file names start with '/', or with '*device:/*' on MS-DOS and MS-Windows.

When you want to make a tags table from a great number of files, you may have problems listing them on the command line, because some systems have a limit on its length. You can circumvent this limit by telling **etags** to read the file names from its standard input, by typing a dash in place of the file names, like this:

```
find . -name "*.[chCH]" -print | etags -
```

etags recognizes the language used in an input file based on its file name and contents. You can specify the language explicitly with the '**--language=***name*' option. You can intermix these options with file names; each one applies to the file names that follow it. Specify '**--language=auto**' to tell **etags** to resume guessing the language from the file names and file contents. Specify '**--language=none**' to turn off language-specific processing entirely; then **etags** recognizes tags by regexp matching alone (see Section 25.3.3 [Etags Regexps], page 302).

The option '**--parse-stdin=***file*' is mostly useful when calling **etags** from programs. It can be used (only once) in place of a file name on the command line. **etags** will read from standard input and mark the produced tags as belonging to the file *file*.

'**etags --help**' outputs the list of the languages **etags** knows, and the file name rules for guessing the language. It also prints a list of all the available **etags** options, together with a short explanation. If followed by one or more '**--language=***lang*' options, it outputs detailed information about how tags are generated for *lang*.

25.3.3 Etags Regexps

The '**--regex**' option to **etags** allows tags to be recognized by regular expression matching. You can intermix this option with file names; each one applies to the source files that follow it. If you specify multiple '**--regex**' options, all of them are used in parallel. The syntax is:

```
--regex=[{language}]/tagregexp/[nameregexp/]modifiers
```

The essential part of the option value is *tagregexp*, the regexp for matching tags. It is always used anchored, that is, it only matches at the beginning of a line. If you want to allow indented tags, use a regexp that matches initial whitespace; start it with '**[\t]***'.

In these regular expressions, '\' quotes the next character, and all the GCC character escape sequences are supported ('\a' for bell, '\b' for back space, '\d' for delete, '\e' for escape, '\f' for formfeed, '\n' for newline, '\r' for carriage return, '\t' for tab, and '\v' for vertical tab).

Ideally, *tagregexp* should not match more characters than are needed to recognize what you want to tag. If the syntax requires you to write *tagregexp* so it matches more characters beyond the tag itself, you should add a *nameregexp*, to pick out just the tag. This will enable Emacs to find tags more accurately and to do completion on tag names more reliably. You can find some examples below.

The *modifiers* are a sequence of zero or more characters that modify the way `etags` does the matching. A regexp with no modifiers is applied sequentially to each line of the input file, in a case-sensitive way. The modifiers and their meanings are:

'i'   Ignore case when matching this regexp.

'm'   Match this regular expression against the whole file, so that multi-line matches are possible.

's'   Match this regular expression against the whole file, and allow '.' in *tagregexp* to match newlines.

The '-R' option cancels all the regexps defined by preceding '--regex' options. It too applies to the file names following it. Here's an example:

```
etags --regex=/reg1/i voo.doo --regex=/reg2/m \
    bar.ber -R --lang=lisp los.er
```

Here `etags` chooses the parsing language for `voo.doo` and `bar.ber` according to their contents. `etags` also uses *reg1* to recognize additional tags in `voo.doo`, and both *reg1* and *reg2* to recognize additional tags in `bar.ber`. *reg1* is checked against each line of `voo.doo` and `bar.ber`, in a case-insensitive way, while *reg2* is checked against the whole `bar.ber` file, permitting multi-line matches, in a case-sensitive way. `etags` uses only the Lisp tags rules, with no user-specified regexp matching, to recognize tags in `los.er`.

You can restrict a '--regex' option to match only files of a given language by using the optional prefix *{language}*. ('etags --help' prints the list of languages recognized by `etags`.) This is particularly useful when storing many predefined regular expressions for `etags` in a file. The following example tags the `DEFVAR` macros in the Emacs source files, for the C language only:

```
--regex='{c}/[ \t]*DEFVAR_[A-Z_ \t(]+"\([^"]+\)"/'
```

When you have complex regular expressions, you can store the list of them in a file. The following option syntax instructs `etags` to read two files of regular expressions. The regular expressions contained in the second file are matched without regard to case.

```
--regex=@case-sensitive-file --ignore-case-regex=@ignore-case-file
```

A regex file for `etags` contains one regular expression per line. Empty lines, and lines beginning with space or tab are ignored. When the first character in a line is '@', `etags` assumes that the rest of the line is the name of another file of regular expressions; thus, one such file can include another file. All the other lines are taken to be regular expressions. If the first non-whitespace text on the line is '--', that line is a comment.

For example, we can create a file called 'emacs.tags' with the following contents:

```
        -- This is for GNU Emacs C source files
{c}/[ \t]*DEFVAR_[A-Z_ \t(]+"\([^"]+\)"/\1/
```

and then use it like this:

```
etags --regex=@emacs.tags *.[ch] */*.[ch]
```

Here are some more examples. The regexps are quoted to protect them from shell interpretation.

- Tag Octave files:

```
etags --language=none \
      --regex='/[ \t]*function.*=[ \t]*\([^ \t]*\)[ \t]*(/\1/' \
      --regex='/###key \(.*\)/\1/' \
      --regex='/[ \t]*global[ \t].*/' \
      *.m
```

Note that tags are not generated for scripts, so that you have to add a line by yourself of the form '###key *scriptname*' if you want to jump to it.

- Tag Tcl files:

```
etags --language=none --regex='/proc[ \t]+\([^ \t]+\)/\1/' *.tcl
```

- Tag VHDL files:

```
etags --language=none \
    --regex='/[ \t]*\(ARCHITECTURE\|CONFIGURATION\) +[^ ]* +OF/' \
    --regex='/[ \t]*\(ATTRIBUTE\|ENTITY\|FUNCTION\|PACKAGE\
    \( BODY\)?\|PROCEDURE\|PROCESS\|TYPE\)[ \t]+\([^ \t(]+\)/\3/'
```

25.3.4 Selecting a Tags Table

Emacs has at any time one *selected* tags table. All the commands for working with tags tables use the selected one. To select a tags table, type M-x `visit-tags-table`, which reads the tags table file name as an argument, with `TAGS` in the default directory as the default.

Emacs does not actually read in the tags table contents until you try to use them; all `visit-tags-table` does is store the file name in the variable `tags-file-name`, and setting the variable yourself is just as good. The variable's initial value is `nil`; that value tells all the commands for working with tags tables that they must ask for a tags table file name to use.

Using `visit-tags-table` when a tags table is already loaded gives you a choice: you can add the new tags table to the current list of tags tables, or start a new list. The tags commands use all the tags tables in the current list. If you start a new list, the new tags table is used *instead* of others. If you add the new table to the current list, it is used *as well as* the others.

You can specify a precise list of tags tables by setting the variable `tags-table-list` to a list of strings, like this:

```
(setq tags-table-list
      '("~/emacs" "/usr/local/lib/emacs/src"))
```

This tells the tags commands to look at the `TAGS` files in your `~/emacs` directory and in the `/usr/local/lib/emacs/src` directory. The order depends on which file you are in and which tags table mentions that file, as explained above.

Do not set both `tags-file-name` and `tags-table-list`.

25.3.5 Finding a Tag

The most important thing that a tags table enables you to do is to find the definition of a specific tag.

M-. *tag* RET

> Find first definition of *tag* (find-tag).

C-u M-.   Find next alternate definition of last tag specified.

C-u - M-.   Go back to previous tag found.

C-M-. *pattern* RET

> Find a tag whose name matches *pattern* (find-tag-regexp).

C-u C-M-.   Find the next tag whose name matches the last pattern used.

C-x 4 . *tag* RET

> Find first definition of *tag*, but display it in another window (find-tag-other-window).

C-x 5 . *tag* RET

> Find first definition of *tag*, and create a new frame to select the buffer (find-tag-other-frame).

M-*   Pop back to where you previously invoked M-. and friends.

M-. (find-tag) prompts for a tag name and jumps to its source definition. It works by searching through the tags table for that tag's file and approximate character position, visiting that file, and searching for the tag definition at ever-increasing distances away from the recorded approximate position.

When entering the tag argument to M-., the usual minibuffer completion commands can be used (see Section 5.4 [Completion], page 28), with the tag names in the selected tags table as completion candidates. If you specify an empty argument, the balanced expression in the buffer before or around point is the default argument. See Section 23.4.1 [Expressions], page 246.

You don't need to give M-. the full name of the tag; a part will do. M-. finds tags which contain that argument as a substring. However, it prefers an exact match to a substring match. To find other tags that match the same substring, give find-tag a numeric argument, as in C-u M-. or M-0 M-.; this does not read a tag name, but continues searching the tags table's text for another tag containing the same substring last used.

Like most commands that can switch buffers, find-tag has a variant that displays the new buffer in another window, and one that makes a new frame for it. The former is C-x 4 . (find-tag-other-window), and the latter is C-x 5 . (find-tag-other-frame).

To move back to previous tag definitions, use C-u - M-.; more generally, M-. with a negative numeric argument. Similarly, C-x 4 . with a negative argument finds the previous tag location in another window.

As well as going back to places you've found tags recently, you can go back to places *from where* you found them, using M-* (pop-tag-mark). Thus you can find and examine the definition of something with M-. and then return to where you were with M-*.

Both C-u - M-. and M-* allow you to retrace your steps to a depth determined by the variable find-tag-marker-ring-length.

The command C-M-. (find-tag-regexp) visits the tags that match a specified regular expression. It is just like M-. except that it does regexp matching instead of substring matching.

25.3.6 Searching and Replacing with Tags Tables

The commands in this section visit and search all the files listed in the selected tags table, one by one. For these commands, the tags table serves only to specify a sequence of files to search. These commands scan the list of tags tables starting with the first tags table (if any) that describes the current file, proceed from there to the end of the list, and then scan from the beginning of the list until they have covered all the tables in the list.

M-x tags-search RET *regexp* RET

> Search for *regexp* through the files in the selected tags table.

M-x tags-query-replace RET *regexp* RET *replacement* RET

> Perform a `query-replace-regexp` on each file in the selected tags table.

M-,   Restart one of the commands above, from the current location of point (`tags-loop-continue`).

M-x `tags-search` reads a regexp using the minibuffer, then searches for matches in all the files in the selected tags table, one file at a time. It displays the name of the file being searched so you can follow its progress. As soon as it finds an occurrence, `tags-search` returns.

Having found one match, you probably want to find all the rest. Type M-, (`tags-loop-continue`) to resume the `tags-search`, finding one more match. This searches the rest of the current buffer, followed by the remaining files of the tags table.

M-x `tags-query-replace` performs a single `query-replace-regexp` through all the files in the tags table. It reads a regexp to search for and a string to replace with, just like ordinary M-x `query-replace-regexp`. It searches much like M-x `tags-search`, but repeatedly, processing matches according to your input. See Section 12.10.4 [Query Replace], page 105, for more information on query replace.

You can control the case-sensitivity of tags search commands by customizing the value of the variable `tags-case-fold-search`. The default is to use the same setting as the value of `case-fold-search` (see Section 12.9 [Search Case], page 102).

It is possible to get through all the files in the tags table with a single invocation of M-x `tags-query-replace`. But often it is useful to exit temporarily, which you can do with any input event that has no special query replace meaning. You can resume the query replace subsequently by typing M-,; this command resumes the last tags search or replace command that you did. For instance, to skip the rest of the current file, you can type M-> M-,.

The commands in this section carry out much broader searches than the `find-tag` family. The `find-tag` commands search only for definitions of tags that match your substring or regexp. The commands `tags-search` and `tags-query-replace` find every occurrence of the regexp, as ordinary search commands and replace commands do in the current buffer.

These commands create buffers only temporarily for the files that they have to search (those which are not already visited in Emacs buffers). Buffers in which no match is found are quickly killed; the others continue to exist.

As an alternative to `tags-search`, you can run `grep` as a subprocess and have Emacs show you the matching lines one by one. See Section 24.4 [Grep Searching], page 264.

25.3.7 Tags Table Inquiries

C-M-i
M-TAB   Perform completion on the text around point, using the selected tags table if
               one is loaded (`completion-at-point`).

M-x list-tags RET *file* RET
               Display a list of the tags defined in the program file *file*.

M-x tags-apropos RET *regexp* RET
               Display a list of all tags matching *regexp*.

In most programming language modes, you can type `C-M-i` or `M-TAB` (`completion-at-point`) to complete the symbol at point. If there is a selected tags table, this command can use it to generate completion candidates. See Section 23.8 [Symbol Completion], page 254.

`M-x list-tags` reads the name of one of the files covered by the selected tags table, and displays a list of tags defined in that file. Do not include a directory as part of the file name unless the file name recorded in the tags table includes a directory.

`M-x tags-apropos` is like `apropos` for tags (see Section 7.3 [Apropos], page 40). It displays a list of tags in the selected tags table whose entries match *regexp*. If the variable `tags-apropos-verbose` is non-`nil`, it displays the names of the tags files together with the tag names. You can customize the appearance of the output by setting the variable `tags-tag-face` to a face. You can display additional output by customizing the variable `tags-apropos-additional-actions`; see its documentation for details.

`M-x next-file` visits files covered by the selected tags table. The first time it is called, it visits the first file covered by the table. Each subsequent call visits the next covered file, unless a prefix argument is supplied, in which case it returns to the first file.

25.4 Emacs Development Environment

EDE (*Emacs Development Environment*) is a package that simplifies the task of creating, building, and debugging large programs with Emacs. It provides some of the features of an IDE, or *Integrated Development Environment*, in Emacs.

This section provides a brief description of EDE usage. For full details on Ede, type `C-h i` and then select the EDE manual.

EDE is implemented as a global minor mode (see Section 20.2 [Minor Modes], page 200). To enable it, type `M-x global-ede-mode` or click on the 'Project Support (EDE)' item in the 'Tools' menu. You can also enable EDE each time you start Emacs, by adding the following line to your initialization file:

```
(global-ede-mode t)
```

Activating EDE adds a menu named 'Development' to the menu bar. Many EDE commands, including the ones described below, can be invoked from this menu.

EDE organizes files into *projects*, which correspond to directory trees. The *project root* is the topmost directory of a project. To define a new project, visit a file in the desired project root and type `M-x ede-new`. This command prompts for a *project type*, which refers to the underlying method that EDE will use to manage the project (see Section "Creating a project" in *Emacs Development Environment*). The most common project types are 'Make', which uses Makefiles, and 'Automake', which uses GNU Automake (see *Automake*).

In both cases, EDE also creates a file named `Project.ede`, which stores information about the project.

A project may contain one or more *targets*. A target can be an object file, executable program, or some other type of file, which is "built" from one or more of the files in the project.

To add a new *target* to a project, type `C-c . t` (`M-x ede-new-target`). This command also asks if you wish to "add" the current file to that target, which means that the target is to be built from that file. After you have defined a target, you can add more files to it by typing `C-c . a` (`ede-add-file`).

To build a target, type `C-c . c` (`ede-compile-target`). To build all the targets in the project, type `C-c . C` (`ede-compile-project`). EDE uses the file types to guess how the target should be built.

26 Abbrevs

A defined *abbrev* is a word which *expands*, if you insert it, into some different text. Abbrevs are defined by the user to expand in specific ways. For example, you might define 'foo' as an abbrev expanding to 'find outer otter'. Then you could insert 'find outer otter ' into the buffer by typing f o o SPC.

A second kind of abbreviation facility is called *dynamic abbrev expansion*. You use dynamic abbrev expansion with an explicit command to expand the letters in the buffer before point by looking for other words in the buffer that start with those letters. See Section 26.6 [Dynamic Abbrevs], page 313.

"Hippie" expansion generalizes abbreviation expansion. See Section "Hippie Expansion" in *Features for Automatic Typing*.

26.1 Abbrev Concepts

An *abbrev* is a word that has been defined to *expand* into a specified *expansion*. When you insert a word-separator character following the abbrev, that expands the abbrev—replacing the abbrev with its expansion. For example, if 'foo' is defined as an abbrev expanding to 'find outer otter', then typing f o o . will insert 'find outer otter.'.

Abbrevs expand only when Abbrev mode, a buffer-local minor mode, is enabled. Disabling Abbrev mode does not cause abbrev definitions to be forgotten, but they do not expand until Abbrev mode is enabled again. The command M-x abbrev-mode toggles Abbrev mode; with a numeric argument, it turns Abbrev mode on if the argument is positive, off otherwise. See Section 20.2 [Minor Modes], page 200.

Abbrevs can have *mode-specific* definitions, active only in one major mode. Abbrevs can also have *global* definitions that are active in all major modes. The same abbrev can have a global definition and various mode-specific definitions for different major modes. A mode-specific definition for the current major mode overrides a global definition.

You can define abbrevs interactively during the editing session, irrespective of whether Abbrev mode is enabled. You can also save lists of abbrev definitions in files, which you can the reload for use in later sessions.

26.2 Defining Abbrevs

C-x a g Define an abbrev, using one or more words before point as its expansion (add-global-abbrev).

C-x a l Similar, but define an abbrev specific to the current major mode (add-mode-abbrev).

C-x a i g Define a word in the buffer as an abbrev (inverse-add-global-abbrev).

C-x a i l Define a word in the buffer as a mode-specific abbrev (inverse-add-mode-abbrev).

M-x define-global-abbrev RET *abbrev* RET *exp* RET
        Define *abbrev* as an abbrev expanding into *exp*.

M-x define-mode-abbrev RET *abbrev* RET *exp* RET
        Define *abbrev* as a mode-specific abbrev expanding into *exp*.

```
M-x kill-all-abbrevs
```
        Discard all abbrev definitions, leaving a blank slate.

The usual way to define an abbrev is to enter the text you want the abbrev to expand to, position point after it, and type `C-x a g` (`add-global-abbrev`). This reads the abbrev itself using the minibuffer, and then defines it as an abbrev for one or more words before point. Use a numeric argument to say how many words before point should be taken as the expansion. For example, to define the abbrev 'foo' as mentioned above, insert the text 'find outer otter' and then type `C-u 3 C-x a g f o o RET`.

An argument of zero to `C-x a g` means to use the contents of the region as the expansion of the abbrev being defined.

The command `C-x a l` (`add-mode-abbrev`) is similar, but defines a mode-specific abbrev for the current major mode. The arguments work the same as for `C-x a g`.

`C-x a i g` (`inverse-add-global-abbrev`) and `C-x a i l` (`inverse-add-mode-abbrev`) perform the opposite task: if the abbrev text is already in the buffer, you use these commands to define an abbrev by specifying the expansion in the minibuffer. These commands will expand the abbrev text used for the definition.

You can define an abbrev without inserting either the abbrev or its expansion in the buffer using the command `define-global-abbrev`. It reads two arguments—the abbrev, and its expansion. The command `define-mode-abbrev` does likewise for a mode-specific abbrev.

To change the definition of an abbrev, just make a new definition. When an abbrev has a prior definition, the abbrev definition commands ask for confirmation before replacing it.

To remove an abbrev definition, give a negative argument to the abbrev definition command: `C-u - C-x a g` or `C-u - C-x a l`. The former removes a global definition, while the latter removes a mode-specific definition. `M-x kill-all-abbrevs` removes all abbrev definitions, both global and local.

26.3 Controlling Abbrev Expansion

When Abbrev mode is enabled, an abbrev expands whenever it is present in the buffer just before point and you type a self-inserting whitespace or punctuation character (SPC, comma, etc.). More precisely, any character that is not a word constituent expands an abbrev, and any word-constituent character can be part of an abbrev. The most common way to use an abbrev is to insert it and then insert a punctuation or whitespace character to expand it.

Abbrev expansion preserves case: 'foo' expands to 'find outer otter', and 'Foo' to 'Find outer otter'. 'FOO' expands to 'Find Outer Otter' by default, but if you change the variable `abbrev-all-caps` to a non-`nil` value, it expands to 'FIND OUTER OTTER'.

These commands are used to control abbrev expansion:

`M-'`   Separate a prefix from a following abbrev to be expanded (`abbrev-prefix-mark`).

`C-x a e`   Expand the abbrev before point (`expand-abbrev`). This is effective even when Abbrev mode is not enabled.

`M-x expand-region-abbrevs`
> Expand some or all abbrevs found in the region.

You may wish to expand an abbrev and attach a prefix to the expansion; for example, if 'cnst' expands into 'construction', you might want to use it to enter 'reconstruction'. It does not work to type `recnst`, because that is not necessarily a defined abbrev. What you can do is use the command M-' (`abbrev-prefix-mark`) in between the prefix 're' and the abbrev 'cnst'. First, insert 're'. Then type M-'; this inserts a hyphen in the buffer to indicate that it has done its work. Then insert the abbrev 'cnst'; the buffer now contains 're-cnst'. Now insert a non-word character to expand the abbrev 'cnst' into 'construction'. This expansion step also deletes the hyphen that indicated M-' had been used. The result is the desired 'reconstruction'.

If you actually want the text of the abbrev in the buffer, rather than its expansion, you can accomplish this by inserting the following punctuation with C-q. Thus, foo C-q , leaves 'foo,' in the buffer, not expanding it.

If you expand an abbrev by mistake, you can undo the expansion by typing C-/ (`undo`). See Section 13.1 [Undo], page 109. This undoes the insertion of the abbrev expansion and brings back the abbrev text. If the result you want is the terminating non-word character plus the unexpanded abbrev, you must reinsert the terminating character, quoting it with C-q. You can also use the command M-x `unexpand-abbrev` to cancel the last expansion without deleting the terminating character.

M-x `expand-region-abbrevs` searches through the region for defined abbrevs, and for each one found offers to replace it with its expansion. This command is useful if you have typed in text using abbrevs but forgot to turn on Abbrev mode first. It may also be useful together with a special set of abbrev definitions for making several global replacements at once. This command is effective even if Abbrev mode is not enabled.

The function `expand-abbrev` performs the expansion by calling the function that `abbrev-expand-function` specifies. By changing this function you can make arbitrary changes to the abbrev expansion. See Section "Abbrev Expansion" in *The Emacs Lisp Reference Manual*.

26.4 Examining and Editing Abbrevs

`M-x list-abbrevs`
> Display a list of all abbrev definitions. With a numeric argument, list only local abbrevs.

`M-x edit-abbrevs`
> Edit a list of abbrevs; you can add, alter or remove definitions.

The output from M-x `list-abbrevs` looks like this:

```
various other tables...
(lisp-mode-abbrev-table)
"dk"          0    "define-key"
(global-abbrev-table)
"dfn"         0    "definition"
```

(Some blank lines of no semantic significance, and some other abbrev tables, have been omitted.)

A line containing a name in parentheses is the header for abbrevs in a particular abbrev table; `global-abbrev-table` contains all the global abbrevs, and the other abbrev tables that are named after major modes contain the mode-specific abbrevs.

Within each abbrev table, each nonblank line defines one abbrev. The word at the beginning of the line is the abbrev. The number that follows is the number of times the abbrev has been expanded. Emacs keeps track of this to help you see which abbrevs you actually use, so that you can eliminate those that you don't use often. The string at the end of the line is the expansion.

Some abbrevs are marked with '`(sys)`'. These "system" abbrevs (see Section "Abbrevs" in *The Emacs Lisp Reference Manual*) are pre-defined by various modes, and are not saved to your abbrev file. To disable a "system" abbrev, define an abbrev of the same name that expands to itself, and save it to your abbrev file.

`M-x edit-abbrevs` allows you to add, change or kill abbrev definitions by editing a list of them in an Emacs buffer. The list has the same format described above. The buffer of abbrevs is called `*Abbrevs*`, and is in Edit-Abbrevs mode. Type `C-c C-c` in this buffer to install the abbrev definitions as specified in the buffer—and delete any abbrev definitions not listed.

The command `edit-abbrevs` is actually the same as `list-abbrevs` except that it selects the buffer `*Abbrevs*` whereas `list-abbrevs` merely displays it in another window.

26.5 Saving Abbrevs

These commands allow you to keep abbrev definitions between editing sessions.

`M-x write-abbrev-file RET` *file* `RET`

> Write a file *file* describing all defined abbrevs.

`M-x read-abbrev-file RET` *file* `RET`

> Read the file *file* and define abbrevs as specified therein.

`M-x define-abbrevs`

> Define abbrevs from definitions in current buffer.

`M-x insert-abbrevs`

> Insert all abbrevs and their expansions into current buffer.

`M-x write-abbrev-file` reads a file name using the minibuffer and then writes a description of all current abbrev definitions into that file. This is used to save abbrev definitions for use in a later session. The text stored in the file is a series of Lisp expressions that, when executed, define the same abbrevs that you currently have.

`M-x read-abbrev-file` reads a file name using the minibuffer and then reads the file, defining abbrevs according to the contents of the file. The function `quietly-read-abbrev-file` is similar except that it does not display a message in the echo area; you cannot invoke it interactively, and it is used primarily in your init file (see Section 33.4 [Init File], page 437). If either of these functions is called with `nil` as the argument, it uses the file given by the variable `abbrev-file-name`, which is `~/.emacs.d/abbrev_defs` by default. This is your standard abbrev definition file, and Emacs loads abbrevs from it automatically when it starts up. (As an exception, Emacs does not load the abbrev file when it is started in batch mode. See Section C.2 [Initial Options], page 480, for a description of batch mode.)

Emacs will offer to save abbrevs automatically if you have changed any of them, whenever it offers to save all files (for C-x s or C-x C-c). It saves them in the file specified by `abbrev-file-name`. This feature can be inhibited by setting the variable `save-abbrevs` to `nil`.

The commands M-x `insert-abbrevs` and M-x `define-abbrevs` are similar to the previous commands but work on text in an Emacs buffer. M-x `insert-abbrevs` inserts text into the current buffer after point, describing all current abbrev definitions; M-x `define-abbrevs` parses the entire current buffer and defines abbrevs accordingly.

26.6 Dynamic Abbrev Expansion

The abbrev facility described above operates automatically as you insert text, but all abbrevs must be defined explicitly. By contrast, *dynamic abbrevs* allow the meanings of abbreviations to be determined automatically from the contents of the buffer, but dynamic abbrev expansion happens only when you request it explicitly.

M-/   Expand the word in the buffer before point as a *dynamic abbrev*, by searching in the buffer for words starting with that abbreviation (`dabbrev-expand`).

C-M-/   Complete the word before point as a dynamic abbrev (`dabbrev-completion`).

For example, if the buffer contains 'does this follow ' and you type f o M-/, the effect is to insert 'follow' because that is the last word in the buffer that starts with 'fo'. A numeric argument to M-/ says to take the second, third, etc. distinct expansion found looking backward from point. Repeating M-/ searches for an alternative expansion by looking farther back. After scanning all the text before point, it searches the text after point. The variable `dabbrev-limit`, if non-`nil`, specifies how far away in the buffer to search for an expansion.

After scanning the current buffer, M-/ normally searches other buffers, unless you have set `dabbrev-check-all-buffers` to `nil`.

For finer control over which buffers to scan, customize the variable `dabbrev-ignored-buffer-regexps`. Its value is a list of regular expressions. If a buffer's name matches any of these regular expressions, dynamic abbrev expansion skips that buffer.

A negative argument to M-/, as in C-u - M-/, says to search first for expansions after point, then other buffers, and consider expansions before point only as a last resort. If you repeat the M-/ to look for another expansion, do not specify an argument. Repeating M-/ cycles through all the expansions after point and then the expansions before point.

After you have expanded a dynamic abbrev, you can copy additional words that follow the expansion in its original context. Simply type SPC M-/ for each additional word you want to copy. The spacing and punctuation between words is copied along with the words.

The command C-M-/ (`dabbrev-completion`) performs completion of a dynamic abbrev. Instead of trying the possible expansions one by one, it finds all of them, then inserts the text that they have in common. If they have nothing in common, C-M-/ displays a list of completions, from which you can select a choice in the usual manner. See Section 5.4 [Completion], page 28.

Dynamic abbrev expansion is completely independent of Abbrev mode; the expansion of a word with M-/ is completely independent of whether it has a definition as an ordinary abbrev.

26.7 Customizing Dynamic Abbreviation

Normally, dynamic abbrev expansion ignores case when searching for expansions. That is, the expansion need not agree in case with the word you are expanding.

This feature is controlled by the variable `dabbrev-case-fold-search`. If it is `t`, case is ignored in this search; if it is `nil`, the word and the expansion must match in case. If the value is `case-fold-search` (the default), then the variable `case-fold-search` controls whether to ignore case while searching for expansions (see Section 12.9 [Search Case], page 102).

Normally, dynamic abbrev expansion preserves the case pattern *of the dynamic abbrev you are expanding*, by converting the expansion to that case pattern.

The variable `dabbrev-case-replace` controls whether to preserve the case pattern of the dynamic abbrev. If it is `t`, the dynamic abbrev's case pattern is preserved in most cases; if it is `nil`, the expansion is always copied verbatim. If the value is `case-replace` (the default), then the variable `case-replace` controls whether to copy the expansion verbatim (see Section 12.10.3 [Replacement and Case], page 104).

However, if the expansion contains a complex mixed case pattern, and the dynamic abbrev matches this pattern as far as it goes, then the expansion is always copied verbatim, regardless of those variables. Thus, for example, if the buffer contains `variableWithSillyCasePattern`, and you type `v a M-/`, it copies the expansion verbatim including its case pattern.

The variable `dabbrev-abbrev-char-regexp`, if non-`nil`, controls which characters are considered part of a word, for dynamic expansion purposes. The regular expression must match just one character, never two or more. The same regular expression also determines which characters are part of an expansion. The value `nil` has a special meaning: dynamic abbrevs are made of word characters, but expansions are made of word and symbol characters.

In shell scripts and makefiles, a variable name is sometimes prefixed with '$' and sometimes not. Major modes for this kind of text can customize dynamic abbrev expansion to handle optional prefixes by setting the variable `dabbrev-abbrev-skip-leading-regexp`. Its value should be a regular expression that matches the optional prefix that dynamic abbrev expression should ignore.

27 Dired, the Directory Editor

Dired makes an Emacs buffer containing a listing of a directory, and optionally some of its subdirectories as well. You can use the normal Emacs commands to move around in this buffer, and special Dired commands to operate on the listed files.

The Dired buffer is "read-only", and inserting text in it is not allowed. Ordinary printing characters such as d and x are redefined for special Dired commands. Some Dired commands *mark* or *flag* the *current file* (that is, the file on the current line); other commands operate on the marked files or on the flagged files. You first mark certain files in order to operate on all of them with one command.

The Dired-X package provides various extra features for Dired mode. See *Dired Extra User's Manual*.

You can also view a list of files in a directory with C-x C-d (list-directory). Unlike Dired, this command does not allow you to operate on the listed files. See Section 15.7 [Directories], page 136.

27.1 Entering Dired

To invoke Dired, type C-x d (dired). This reads a directory name using the minibuffer, and opens a *Dired buffer* listing the files in that directory. You can also supply a wildcard file name pattern as the minibuffer argument, in which case the Dired buffer lists all files matching that pattern. The usual history and completion commands can be used in the minibuffer; in particular, M-n puts the name of the visited file (if any) in the minibuffer (see Section 5.5 [Minibuffer History], page 32).

You can also invoke Dired by giving C-x C-f (find-file) a directory name.

The variable dired-listing-switches specifies the options to give to ls for listing the directory; this string *must* contain '-l'. If you use a prefix argument with the dired command, you can specify the ls switches with the minibuffer before you enter the directory specification. No matter how they are specified, the ls switches can include short options (that is, single characters) requiring no arguments, and long options (starting with '--') whose arguments are specified with '='.

If your ls program supports the '--dired' option, Dired automatically passes it that option; this causes ls to emit special escape sequences for certain unusual file names, without which Dired will not be able to parse those names. The first time you run Dired in an Emacs session, it checks whether ls supports the '--dired' option by calling it once with that option. If the exit code is 0, Dired will subsequently use the '--dired' option; otherwise it will not. You can inhibit this check by customizing the variable dired-use-ls-dired. The value unspecified (the default) means to perform the check; any other non-nil value means to use the '--dired' option; and nil means not to use the '--dired' option.

On MS-Windows and MS-DOS systems, Emacs emulates ls. See Section G.4 [ls in Lisp], page 508, for options and peculiarities of this emulation.

To display the Dired buffer in another window, use C-x 4 d (dired-other-window). C-x 5 d (dired-other-frame) displays the Dired buffer in a separate frame.

Typing q (quit-window) buries the Dired buffer, and deletes its window if the window was created just for that buffer.

27.2 Navigation in the Dired Buffer

All the usual Emacs cursor motion commands are available in Dired buffers. The keys `C-n` and `C-p` are redefined to put the cursor at the beginning of the file name on the line, rather than at the beginning of the line.

For extra convenience, `SPC` and `n` in Dired are equivalent to `C-n`. `p` is equivalent to `C-p`. (Moving by lines is so common in Dired that it deserves to be easy to type.) `DEL` (move up and unflag) is also often useful simply for moving up (see Section 27.3 [Dired Deletion], page 316).

`j` (`dired-goto-file`) prompts for a file name using the minibuffer, and moves point to the line in the Dired buffer describing that file.

`M-s f C-s` (`dired-isearch-filenames`) performs a forward incremental search in the Dired buffer, looking for matches only amongst the file names and ignoring the rest of the text in the buffer. `M-s f M-C-s` (`dired-isearch-filenames-regexp`) does the same, using a regular expression search. If you change the variable `dired-isearch-filenames` to `t`, then the usual search commands also limit themselves to the file names; for instance, `C-s` behaves like `M-s f C-s`. If the value is `dwim`, then search commands match the file names only when point was on a file name initially. See Chapter 12 [Search], page 90, for information about incremental search.

Some additional navigation commands are available when the Dired buffer includes several directories. See Section 27.12 [Subdirectory Motion], page 325.

27.3 Deleting Files with Dired

One of the most frequent uses of Dired is to first *flag* files for deletion, then delete the files that were flagged.

d   Flag this file for deletion (`dired-flag-file-deletion`).

u   Remove the deletion flag (`dired-unmark`).

DEL   Move point to previous line and remove the deletion flag on that line (`dired-unmark-backward`).

x   Delete files flagged for deletion (`dired-do-flagged-delete`).

You can flag a file for deletion by moving to the line describing the file and typing `d` (`dired-flag-file-deletion`). The deletion flag is visible as a 'D' at the beginning of the line. This command moves point to the next line, so that repeated `d` commands flag successive files. A numeric prefix argument serves as a repeat count; a negative count means to flag preceding files.

If the region is active, the `d` command flags all files in the region for deletion; in this case, the command does not move point, and ignores any prefix argument.

The reason for flagging files for deletion, rather than deleting files immediately, is to reduce the danger of deleting a file accidentally. Until you direct Dired to delete the flagged files, you can remove deletion flags using the commands `u` and `DEL`. `u` (`dired-unmark`) works just like `d`, but removes flags rather than making flags. `DEL` (`dired-unmark-backward`) moves upward, removing flags; it is like `u` with argument −1. A numeric prefix argument to either command serves as a repeat count, with a negative count meaning to unflag in the opposite direction. If the region is active, these commands instead unflag all files in the region, without moving point.

To delete flagged files, type x (`dired-do-flagged-delete`). This command displays a list of all the file names flagged for deletion, and requests confirmation with **yes**. If you confirm, Dired deletes the flagged files, then deletes their lines from the text of the Dired buffer. The Dired buffer, with somewhat fewer lines, remains selected.

If you answer **no** or quit with **C-g** when asked to confirm, you return immediately to Dired, with the deletion flags still present in the buffer, and no files actually deleted.

You can delete empty directories just like other files, but normally Dired cannot delete directories that are nonempty. If the variable `dired-recursive-deletes` is non-**nil**, then Dired can delete nonempty directories including all their contents. That can be somewhat risky.

If you change the variable `delete-by-moving-to-trash` to **t**, the above deletion commands will move the affected files or directories into the operating system's Trash, instead of deleting them outright. See Section 15.10 [Misc File Ops], page 140.

27.4 Flagging Many Files at Once

The #, ~, ., % &, and % d commands flag many files for deletion, based on their file names:

Flag all auto-save files (files whose names start and end with '#') for deletion (see Section 15.5 [Auto Save], page 133).

~   Flag all backup files (files whose names end with '~') for deletion (see Section 15.3.2 [Backup], page 127).

. (Period) Flag excess numeric backup files for deletion. The oldest and newest few backup files of any one file are exempt; the middle ones are flagged.

% &   Flag for deletion all files with certain kinds of names which suggest you could easily create those files again.

% d *regexp* RET
            Flag for deletion all files whose names match the regular expression *regexp*.

   # (`dired-flag-auto-save-files`) flags all files whose names look like auto-save files—that is, files whose names begin and end with '#'. See Section 15.5 [Auto Save], page 133.

   ~ (`dired-flag-backup-files`) flags all files whose names say they are backup files—that is, files whose names end in '~'. See Section 15.3.2 [Backup], page 127.

   . (period, `dired-clean-directory`) flags just some of the backup files for deletion: all but the oldest few and newest few backups of any one file. Normally, the number of newest versions kept for each file is given by the variable `dired-kept-versions` (*not* kept-new-versions; that applies only when saving). The number of oldest versions to keep is given by the variable `kept-old-versions`.

   Period with a positive numeric argument, as in **C-u 3 .**, specifies the number of newest versions to keep, overriding `dired-kept-versions`. A negative numeric argument overrides `kept-old-versions`, using minus the value of the argument to specify the number of oldest versions of each file to keep.

% & (dired-flag-garbage-files) flags files whose names match the regular expression specified by the variable dired-garbage-files-regexp. By default, this matches certain files produced by TEX, '.bak' files, and the '.orig' and '.rej' files produced by patch.

% d flags all files whose names match a specified regular expression (dired-flag-files-regexp). Only the non-directory part of the file name is used in matching. You can use '^' and '$' to anchor matches. You can exclude certain subdirectories from marking by hiding them while you use % d. See Section 27.13 [Hiding Subdirectories], page 326.

27.5 Visiting Files in Dired

There are several Dired commands for visiting or examining the files listed in the Dired buffer. All of them apply to the current line's file; if that file is really a directory, these commands invoke Dired on that subdirectory (making a separate Dired buffer).

f	Visit the file described on the current line, like typing C-x C-f and supplying that file name (dired-find-file). See Section 15.2 [Visiting], page 123.
RET e	Equivalent to f.
o	Like f, but uses another window to display the file's buffer (dired-find-file-other-window). The Dired buffer remains visible in the first window. This is like using C-x 4 C-f to visit the file. See Chapter 17 [Windows], page 156.
C-o	Visit the file described on the current line, and display the buffer in another window, but do not select that window (dired-display-file).
Mouse-1 Mouse-2	Visit the file whose name you clicked on (dired-mouse-find-file-other-window). This uses another window to display the file, like the o command.
v	View the file described on the current line, with View mode (dired-view-file). View mode provides convenient commands to navigate the buffer but forbids changing it; See Section 11.6 [View Mode], page 73.
^	Visit the parent directory of the current directory (dired-up-directory). This is equivalent to moving to the line for .. and typing f there.

27.6 Dired Marks vs. Flags

Instead of flagging a file with 'D', you can *mark* the file with some other character (usually '*'). Most Dired commands to operate on files use the files marked with '*'. The only command that operates on flagged files is x, which deletes them.

Here are some commands for marking with '*', for unmarking, and for operating on marks. (See Section 27.3 [Dired Deletion], page 316, for commands to flag and unflag files.)

m * m	Mark the current file with '*' (dired-mark). If the region is active, mark all files in the region instead; otherwise, if a numeric argument n is supplied, mark the next n files instead, starting with the current file (if n is negative, mark the previous −n files).

* *   Mark all executable files with '*' (dired-mark-executables). With a numeric argument, unmark all those files.

* @   Mark all symbolic links with '*' (dired-mark-symlinks). With a numeric argument, unmark all those files.

* /   Mark with '*' all files which are directories, except for . and .. (dired-mark-directories). With a numeric argument, unmark all those files.

* s   Mark all the files in the current subdirectory, aside from . and .. (dired-mark-subdir-files).

u
* u   Remove any mark on this line (dired-unmark). If the region is active, unmark all files in the region instead; otherwise, if a numeric argument n is supplied, unmark the next n files instead, starting with the current file (if n is negative, unmark the previous −n files).

DEL
* DEL   Move point to previous line and remove any mark on that line (dired-unmark-backward). If the region is active, unmark all files in the region instead; otherwise, if a numeric argument n is supplied, unmark the n preceding files instead, starting with the current file (if n is negative, unmark the next −n files).

* !
U   Remove all marks from all the files in this Dired buffer (dired-unmark-all-marks).

* ? markchar
M-DEL   Remove all marks that use the character markchar (dired-unmark-all-files). The argument is a single character—do not use RET to terminate it. See the description of the * c command below, which lets you replace one mark character with another.

             With a numeric argument, this command queries about each marked file, asking whether to remove its mark. You can answer y meaning yes, n meaning no, or ! to remove the marks from the remaining files without asking about them.

* C-n
M-}   Move down to the next marked file (dired-next-marked-file) A file is "marked" if it has any kind of mark.

* C-p
M-{   Move up to the previous marked file (dired-prev-marked-file)

t
* t   Toggle all marks (dired-toggle-marks): files marked with '*' become unmarked, and unmarked files are marked with '*'. Files marked in any other way are not affected.

* c old-markchar new-markchar
             Replace all marks that use the character old-markchar with marks that use the character new-markchar (dired-change-marks). This command is the

primary way to create or use marks other than '*' or 'D'. The arguments are single characters—do not use RET to terminate them.

You can use almost any character as a mark character by means of this command, to distinguish various classes of files. If *old-markchar* is a space (' '), then the command operates on all unmarked files; if *new-markchar* is a space, then the command unmarks the files it acts on.

To illustrate the power of this command, here is how to put 'D' flags on all the files that have no marks, while unflagging all those that already have 'D' flags:

* c D t   * c SPC D   * c t SPC

This assumes that no files were already marked with 't'.

% m *regexp* RET

* % *regexp* RET

> Mark (with '*') all files whose names match the regular expression *regexp* (`dired-mark-files-regexp`). This command is like % d, except that it marks files with '*' instead of flagging with 'D'.
>
> Only the non-directory part of the file name is used in matching. Use '^' and '$' to anchor matches. You can exclude subdirectories by temporarily hiding them (see Section 27.13 [Hiding Subdirectories], page 326).

% g *regexp* RET

> Mark (with '*') all files whose *contents* contain a match for the regular expression *regexp* (`dired-mark-files-containing-regexp`). This command is like % m, except that it searches the file contents instead of the file name.

C-/

C-x u

C-_

> Undo changes in the Dired buffer, such as adding or removing marks (`dired-undo`). *This command does not revert the actual file operations, nor recover lost files!* It just undoes changes in the buffer itself.
>
> In some cases, using this after commands that operate on files can cause trouble. For example, after renaming one or more files, `dired-undo` restores the original names in the Dired buffer, which gets the Dired buffer out of sync with the actual contents of the directory.

27.7 Operating on Files

This section describes the basic Dired commands to operate on one file or several files. All of these commands are capital letters; all of them use the minibuffer, either to read an argument or to ask for confirmation, before they act. All of them let you specify the files to manipulate in these ways:

- If you give the command a numeric prefix argument *n*, it operates on the next *n* files, starting with the current file. (If *n* is negative, the command operates on the −*n* files preceding the current line.)
- Otherwise, if some files are marked with '*', the command operates on all those files.
- Otherwise, the command operates on the current file only.

Certain other Dired commands, such as ! and the '%' commands, use the same conventions to decide which files to work on.

Commands which ask for a destination directory, such as those which copy and rename files or create links for them, try to guess the default target directory for the operation. Normally, they suggest the Dired buffer's default directory, but if the variable `dired-dwim-target` is non-`nil`, and if there is another Dired buffer displayed in the next window, that other buffer's directory is suggested instead.

Here are the file-manipulating Dired commands that operate on files.

C *new* RET   Copy the specified files (`dired-do-copy`). The argument *new* is the directory to copy into, or (if copying a single file) the new name. This is like the shell command `cp`.

              If `dired-copy-preserve-time` is non-`nil`, then copying with this command preserves the modification time of the old file in the copy, like 'cp -p'.

              The variable `dired-recursive-copies` controls whether to copy directories recursively (like 'cp -r'). The default is `top`, which means to ask before recursively copying a directory.

D   Delete the specified files (`dired-do-delete`). This is like the shell command `rm`.

              Like the other commands in this section, this command operates on the *marked* files, or the next *n* files. By contrast, x (`dired-do-flagged-delete`) deletes all *flagged* files.

R *new* RET   Rename the specified files (`dired-do-rename`). If you rename a single file, the argument *new* is the new name of the file. If you rename several files, the argument *new* is the directory into which to move the files (this is like the shell command `mv`).

              Dired automatically changes the visited file name of buffers associated with renamed files so that they refer to the new names.

H *new* RET   Make hard links to the specified files (`dired-do-hardlink`). This is like the shell command `ln`. The argument *new* is the directory to make the links in, or (if making just one link) the name to give the link.

S *new* RET   Make symbolic links to the specified files (`dired-do-symlink`). This is like 'ln -s'. The argument *new* is the directory to make the links in, or (if making just one link) the name to give the link.

M *modespec* RET

              Change the mode (also called *permission bits*) of the specified files (`dired-do-chmod`). *modespec* can be in octal or symbolic notation, like arguments handled by the `chmod` program.

G *newgroup* RET

              Change the group of the specified files to *newgroup* (`dired-do-chgrp`).

O *newowner* RET

              Change the owner of the specified files to *newowner* (`dired-do-chown`). (On most systems, only the superuser can do this.)

The variable `dired-chown-program` specifies the name of the program to use to do the work (different systems put `chown` in different places).

T *timestamp* RET

Touch the specified files (`dired-do-touch`). This means updating their modification times to the present time. This is like the shell command `touch`.

P *command* RET

Print the specified files (`dired-do-print`). You must specify the command to print them with, but the minibuffer starts out with a suitable guess made using the variables `lpr-command` and `lpr-switches` (the same variables that `lpr-buffer` uses; see Section 31.6 [Printing], page 397).

Z   Compress the specified files (`dired-do-compress`). If the file appears to be a compressed file already, uncompress it instead.

:d   Decrypt the specified files (`epa-dired-do-decrypt`). See Section "Dired integration" in *EasyPG Assistant User's Manual*.

:v   Verify digital signatures on the specified files (`epa-dired-do-verify`). See Section "Dired integration" in *EasyPG Assistant User's Manual*.

:s   Digitally sign the specified files (`epa-dired-do-sign`). See Section "Dired integration" in *EasyPG Assistant User's Manual*.

:e   Encrypt the specified files (`epa-dired-do-encrypt`). See Section "Dired integration" in *EasyPG Assistant User's Manual*.

L   Load the specified Emacs Lisp files (`dired-do-load`). See Section 24.8 [Lisp Libraries], page 276.

B   Byte compile the specified Emacs Lisp files (`dired-do-byte-compile`). See Section "Byte Compilation" in *The Emacs Lisp Reference Manual*.

A *regexp* RET

Search all the specified files for the regular expression *regexp* (`dired-do-search`).

This command is a variant of `tags-search`. The search stops at the first match it finds; use M-, to resume the search and find the next match. See Section 25.3.6 [Tags Search], page 306.

Q *regexp* RET *to* RET

Perform `query-replace-regexp` on each of the specified files, replacing matches for *regexp* with the string *to* (`dired-do-query-replace-regexp`).

This command is a variant of `tags-query-replace`. If you exit the query replace loop, you can use M-, to resume the scan and replace more matches. See Section 25.3.6 [Tags Search], page 306.

27.8 Shell Commands in Dired

The Dired command ! (`dired-do-shell-command`) reads a shell command string in the minibuffer, and runs that shell command on one or more files. The files that the shell command operates on are determined in the usual way for Dired commands (see Section 27.7 [Operating on Files], page 320). The command X is a synonym for !.

The command & (`dired-do-async-shell-command`) does the same, except that it runs the shell command asynchronously. (You can also do this with !, by appending a '&' character to the end of the shell command.) When the command operates on more than one file, it runs multiple parallel copies of the specified shell command, one for each file. As an exception, if the specified shell command ends in ';' or ';&', the shell command is run in the background on each file sequentially; Emacs waits for each invoked shell command to terminate before running the next one.

For both ! and &, the working directory for the shell command is the top-level directory of the Dired buffer.

If you tell ! or & to operate on more than one file, the shell command string determines how those files are passed to the shell command:

- If you use '*' surrounded by whitespace in the command string, then the command runs just once, with the list of file names substituted for the '*'. The order of file names is the order of appearance in the Dired buffer.

  Thus, ! `tar cf foo.tar *` RET runs `tar` on the entire list of file names, putting them into one tar file `foo.tar`.

  If you want to use '*' as a shell wildcard with whitespace around it, write '*""'. In the shell, this is equivalent to '*'; but since the '*' is not surrounded by whitespace, Dired does not treat it specially.

- Otherwise, if the command string contains '?' surrounded by whitespace, Emacs runs the shell command once *for each file*, substituting the current file name for '?' each time. You can use '?' more than once in the command; the same file name replaces each occurrence.

- If the command string contains neither '*' nor '?', Emacs runs the shell command once for each file, adding the file name at the end. For example, ! `uudecode` RET runs `uudecode` on each file.

To iterate over the file names in a more complicated fashion, use an explicit shell loop. For example, here is how to uuencode each file, making the output file name by appending '.uu' to the input file name:

```
for file in * ; do uuencode "$file" "$file" >"$file".uu; done
```

The ! and & commands do not attempt to update the Dired buffer to show new or modified files, because they don't know what files will be changed. Use the g command to update the Dired buffer (see Section 27.14 [Dired Updating], page 326).

See Section 31.4.1 [Single Shell], page 383, for information about running shell commands outside Dired.

27.9 Transforming File Names in Dired

This section describes Dired commands which alter file names in a systematic way. Each command operates on some or all of the marked files, using a new name made by transforming the existing name.

Like the basic Dired file-manipulation commands (see Section 27.7 [Operating on Files], page 320), the commands described here operate either on the next *n* files, or on all files marked with '*', or on the current file. (To mark files, use the commands described in Section 27.6 [Marks vs Flags], page 318.)

All of the commands described in this section work *interactively*: they ask you to confirm the operation for each candidate file. Thus, you can select more files than you actually need to operate on (e.g., with a regexp that matches many files), and then filter the selected names by typing y or n when the command prompts for confirmation.

% u   Rename each of the selected files to an upper-case name (`dired-upcase`). If the old file names are `Foo` and `bar`, the new names are `FOO` and `BAR`.

% l   Rename each of the selected files to a lower-case name (`dired-downcase`). If the old file names are `Foo` and `bar`, the new names are `foo` and `bar`.

% R *from* RET *to* RET
% C *from* RET *to* RET
% H *from* RET *to* RET
% S *from* RET *to* RET

These four commands rename, copy, make hard links and make soft links, in each case computing the new name by regular-expression substitution from the name of the old file.

The four regular-expression substitution commands effectively perform a search-and-replace on the selected file names. They read two arguments: a regular expression *from*, and a substitution pattern *to*; they match each "old" file name against *from*, and then replace the matching part with *to*. You can use '\&' and '*digit*' in *to* to refer to all or part of what the pattern matched in the old file name, as in `replace-regexp` (see Section 12.10.2 [Regexp Replace], page 103). If the regular expression matches more than once in a file name, only the first match is replaced.

For example, % R ^.*$ RET x-\& RET renames each selected file by prepending 'x-' to its name. The inverse of this, removing 'x-' from the front of each file name, is also possible: one method is % R ^x-\(.*\)$ RET \1 RET; another is % R ^x- RET RET. (Use '^' and '$' to anchor matches that should span the whole file name.)

Normally, the replacement process does not consider the files' directory names; it operates on the file name within the directory. If you specify a numeric argument of zero, then replacement affects the entire absolute file name including directory name. (A non-zero argument specifies the number of files to operate on.)

You may want to select the set of files to operate on using the same regexp *from* that you will use to operate on them. To do this, mark those files with % m *from* RET, then use the same regular expression in the command to operate on the files. To make this more convenient, the % commands to operate on files use the last regular expression specified in any % command as a default.

27.10 File Comparison with Dired

The = (`dired-diff`) command compares the current file (the file at point) with another file (read using the minibuffer) using the `diff` program. The file specified with the minibuffer is the first argument of `diff`, and file at point is the second argument. The output of the `diff` program is shown in a buffer using Diff mode (see Section 15.8 [Comparing Files], page 137).

If the region is active, the default for the file read using the minibuffer is the file at the mark (i.e., the ordinary Emacs mark, not a Dired mark; see Section 8.1 [Setting Mark], page 45). Otherwise, if the file at point has a backup file (see Section 15.3.2 [Backup], page 127), that is the default.

27.11 Subdirectories in Dired

A Dired buffer usually displays just one directory, but you can optionally include its subdirectories as well.

The simplest way to include multiple directories in one Dired buffer is to specify the options '-lR' for running ls. (If you give a numeric argument when you run Dired, then you can specify these options in the minibuffer.) That produces a recursive directory listing showing all subdirectories at all levels.

More often, you will want to show only specific subdirectories. You can do this with i (dired-maybe-insert-subdir):

i   Insert the contents of a subdirectory later in the buffer.

If you use this command on a line that describes a file which is a directory, it inserts the contents of that directory into the same Dired buffer, and moves there. Inserted subdirectory contents follow the top-level directory of the Dired buffer, just as they do in 'ls -lR' output.

If the subdirectory's contents are already present in the buffer, the i command just moves to it.

In either case, i sets the Emacs mark before moving, so C-u C-SPC returns to your previous position in the Dired buffer (see Section 8.1 [Setting Mark], page 45). You can also use '^' to return to the parent directory in the same Dired buffer (see Section 27.5 [Dired Visiting], page 318).

Use the l command (dired-do-redisplay) to update the subdirectory's contents, and use C-u k on the subdirectory header line to remove the subdirectory listing (see Section 27.14 [Dired Updating], page 326). You can also hide and show inserted subdirectories (see Section 27.13 [Hiding Subdirectories], page 326).

27.12 Moving Over Subdirectories

When a Dired buffer lists subdirectories, you can use the page motion commands C-x [and C-x] to move by entire directories (see Section 22.4 [Pages], page 211).

The following commands move across, up and down in the tree of directories within one Dired buffer. They move to *directory header lines*, which are the lines that give a directory's name, at the beginning of the directory's contents.

C-M-n   Go to next subdirectory header line, regardless of level (dired-next-subdir).

C-M-p   Go to previous subdirectory header line, regardless of level (dired-prev-subdir).

C-M-u   Go up to the parent directory's header line (dired-tree-up).

C-M-d   Go down in the directory tree, to the first subdirectory's header line (dired-tree-down).

<   Move up to the previous directory-file line (`dired-prev-dirline`). These lines are the ones that describe a directory as a file in its parent directory.

>   Move down to the next directory-file line (`dired-prev-dirline`).

27.13 Hiding Subdirectories

Hiding a subdirectory means to make it invisible, except for its header line.

$ Hide or show the subdirectory that point is in, and move point to the next subdirectory (`dired-hide-subdir`). This is a toggle. A numeric argument serves as a repeat count.

M-$ Hide all subdirectories in this Dired buffer, leaving only their header lines (`dired-hide-all`). Or, if any subdirectory is currently hidden, make all subdirectories visible again. You can use this command to get an overview in very deep directory trees or to move quickly to subdirectories far away.

Ordinary Dired commands never consider files inside a hidden subdirectory. For example, the commands to operate on marked files ignore files in hidden directories even if they are marked. Thus you can use hiding to temporarily exclude subdirectories from operations without having to remove the Dired marks on files in those subdirectories.

See Section 27.11 [Subdirectories in Dired], page 325, for how to insert a subdirectory listing, and see Section 27.14 [Dired Updating], page 326 for how delete it.

27.14 Updating the Dired Buffer

This section describes commands to update the Dired buffer to reflect outside (non-Dired) changes in the directories and files, and to delete part of the Dired buffer.

g   Update the entire contents of the Dired buffer (`revert-buffer`).

l   Update the specified files (`dired-do-redisplay`). You specify the files for `l` in the same way as for file operations.

k   Delete the specified *file lines*—not the files, just the lines (`dired-do-kill-lines`).

s   Toggle between alphabetical order and date/time order (`dired-sort-toggle-or-edit`).

C-u s *switches* RET
       Refresh the Dired buffer using *switches* as `dired-listing-switches`.

Type g (`revert-buffer`) to update the contents of the Dired buffer, based on changes in the files and directories listed. This preserves all marks except for those on files that have vanished. Hidden subdirectories are updated but remain hidden.

To update only some of the files, type l (`dired-do-redisplay`). Like the Dired file-operating commands, this command operates on the next *n* files (or previous −*n* files), or on the marked files if any, or on the current file. Updating the files means reading their current status, then updating their lines in the buffer to indicate that status.

If you use l on a subdirectory header line, it updates the contents of the corresponding subdirectory.

If you use C-x d or some other Dired command to visit a directory that is already being shown in a Dired buffer, Dired switches to that buffer but does not update it. If the buffer is not up-to-date, Dired displays a warning telling you to type g to update it. You can also tell Emacs to revert each Dired buffer automatically when you revisit it, by setting the variable dired-auto-revert-buffer to a non-nil value.

To delete *file lines* from the buffer—without actually deleting the files—type k (dired-do-kill-lines). Like the file-operating commands, this command operates on the next *n* files, or on the marked files if any. However, it does not operate on the current file, since otherwise mistyping k could be annoying.

If you use k to kill the line for a directory file which you had inserted in the Dired buffer as a subdirectory (see Section 27.11 [Subdirectories in Dired], page 325), it removes the subdirectory listing as well. Typing C-u k on the header line for a subdirectory also removes the subdirectory line from the Dired buffer.

The g command brings back any individual lines that you have killed in this way, but not subdirectories—you must use i to reinsert a subdirectory.

The files in a Dired buffers are normally listed in alphabetical order by file names. Alternatively Dired can sort them by date/time. The Dired command s (dired-sort-toggle-or-edit) switches between these two sorting modes. The mode line in a Dired buffer indicates which way it is currently sorted—by name, or by date.

C-u s *switches* RET lets you specify a new value for dired-listing-switches.

27.15 Dired and find

You can select a set of files for display in a Dired buffer more flexibly by using the find utility to choose the files.

To search for files with names matching a wildcard pattern use M-x find-name-dired. It reads arguments *directory* and *pattern*, and chooses all the files in *directory* or its subdirectories whose individual names match *pattern*.

The files thus chosen are displayed in a Dired buffer, in which the ordinary Dired commands are available.

If you want to test the contents of files, rather than their names, use M-x find-grep-dired. This command reads two minibuffer arguments, *directory* and *regexp*; it chooses all the files in *directory* or its subdirectories that contain a match for *regexp*. It works by running the programs find and grep. See also M-x grep-find, in Section 24.4 [Grep Searching], page 264. Remember to write the regular expression for grep, not for Emacs. (An alternative method of showing files whose contents match a given regexp is the % g *regexp* command, see Section 27.6 [Marks vs Flags], page 318.)

The most general command in this series is M-x find-dired, which lets you specify any condition that find can test. It takes two minibuffer arguments, *directory* and *find-args*; it runs find in *directory*, passing *find-args* to tell find what condition to test. To use this command, you need to know how to use find.

The format of listing produced by these commands is controlled by the variable find-ls-option. This is a pair of options; the first specifying how to call find to produce the file listing, and the second telling Dired to parse the output.

The command M-x locate provides a similar interface to the locate program. M-x locate-with-filter is similar, but keeps only files whose names match a given regular expression.

These buffers don't work entirely like ordinary Dired buffers: file operations work, but do not always automatically update the buffer. Reverting the buffer with g deletes all inserted subdirectories, and erases all flags and marks.

27.16 Editing the Dired Buffer

Wdired is a special mode that allows you to perform file operations by editing the Dired buffer directly (the "W" in "Wdired" stands for "writable".) To enter Wdired mode, type C-x C-q (dired-toggle-read-only) while in a Dired buffer. Alternatively, use the 'Immediate / Edit File Names' menu item.

While in Wdired mode, you can rename files by editing the file names displayed in the Dired buffer. All the ordinary Emacs editing commands, including rectangle operations and query-replace, are available for this. Once you are done editing, type C-c C-c (wdired-finish-edit). This applies your changes and switches back to ordinary Dired mode.

Apart from simply renaming files, you can move a file to another directory by typing in the new file name (either absolute or relative). To mark a file for deletion, delete the entire file name. To change the target of a symbolic link, edit the link target name which appears next to the link name.

The rest of the text in the buffer, such as the file sizes and modification dates, is marked read-only, so you can't edit it. However, if you set wdired-allow-to-change-permissions to t, you can edit the file permissions. For example, you can change '-rw-r--r--' to '-rw-rw-rw-' to make a file world-writable. These changes also take effect when you type C-c C-c.

27.17 Viewing Image Thumbnails in Dired

Image-Dired is a facility for browsing image files. It provides viewing the images either as thumbnails or in full size, either inside Emacs or through an external viewer.

To enter Image-Dired, mark the image files you want to look at in the Dired buffer, using m as usual. Then type C-t d (image-dired-display-thumbs). This creates and switches to a buffer containing image-dired, corresponding to the marked files.

You can also enter Image-Dired directly by typing M-x image-dired. This prompts for a directory; specify one that has image files. This creates thumbnails for all the images in that directory, and displays them all in the "thumbnail buffer". This takes a long time if the directory contains many image files, and it asks for confirmation if the number of image files exceeds image-dired-show-all-from-dir-max-files.

With point in the thumbnail buffer, you can type RET (image-dired-display-thumbnail-original-image) to display a sized version of it in another window. This sizes the image to fit the window. Use the arrow keys to move around in the buffer. For easy browsing, use SPC (image-dired-display-next-thumbnail-original) to advance and display the next image. Typing DEL (image-dired-display-previous-thumbnail-original) backs up to the previous thumbnail and displays that instead.

To view and the image in its original size, either provide a prefix argument (C-u) before pressing RET, or type C-RET (`image-dired-thumbnail-display-external`) to display the image in an external viewer. You must first configure `image-dired-external-viewer`.

You can delete images through Image-Dired also. Type d (`image-dired-flag-thumb-original-file`) to flag the image file for deletion in the Dired buffer. You can also delete the thumbnail image from the thumbnail buffer with C-d (`image-dired-delete-char`).

More advanced features include *image tags*, which are metadata used to categorize image files. The tags are stored in a plain text file configured by `image-dired-db-file`.

To tag image files, mark them in the dired buffer (you can also mark files in Dired from the thumbnail buffer by typing m) and type C-t t (`image-dired-tag-files`). This reads the tag name in the minibuffer. To mark files having a certain tag, type C-t f (`image-dired-mark-tagged-files`). After marking image files with a certain tag, you can use C-t d to view them.

You can also tag a file directly from the thumbnail buffer by typing t t and you can remove a tag by typing t r. There is also a special "tag" called "comment" for each file (it is not a tag in the exact same sense as the other tags, it is handled slightly different). That is used to enter a comment or description about the image. You comment a file from the thumbnail buffer by typing c. You will be prompted for a comment. Type C-t c to add a comment from Dired (`image-dired-dired-comment-files`).

Image-Dired also provides simple image manipulation. In the thumbnail buffer, type L to rotate the original image 90 degrees anti clockwise, and R to rotate it 90 degrees clockwise. This rotation is lossless, and uses an external utility called JpegTRAN.

27.18 Other Dired Features

The command + (`dired-create-directory`) reads a directory name, and creates that directory. It signals an error if the directory already exists.

The command M-s a C-s (`dired-do-isearch`) begins a "multi-file" incremental search on the marked files. If a search fails at the end of a file, typing C-s advances to the next marked file and repeats the search; at the end of the last marked file, the search wraps around to the first marked file. The command M-s a M-C-s (`dired-do-isearch-regexp`) does the same with a regular expression search. See Section 12.1.2 [Repeat Isearch], page 91, for information about search repetition.

The command w (`dired-copy-filename-as-kill`) puts the names of the marked (or next *n*) files into the kill ring, as if you had killed them with C-w. The names are separated by a space.

With a zero prefix argument, this uses the absolute file name of each marked file. With just C-u as the prefix argument, it uses file names relative to the Dired buffer's default directory. (This can still contain slashes if in a subdirectory.) As a special case, if point is on a directory headerline, w gives you the absolute name of that directory. Any prefix argument or marked files are ignored in this case.

The main purpose of this command is so that you can yank the file names into arguments for other Emacs commands. It also displays what it added to the kill ring, so you can use it to display the list of currently marked files in the echo area.

The command ((`dired-hide-details-mode`) toggles whether details, such as ownership or file permissions, are visible in the current Dired buffer. By default, it also hides the targets of symbolic links, and all lines other than the header line and file/directory listings. To change this, customize the options `dired-hide-details-hide-symlink-targets` and `dired-hide-details-hide-information-lines`, respectively.

If the directory you are visiting is under version control (see Section 25.1 [Version Control], page 281), then the normal VC diff and log commands will operate on the selected files.

The command `M-x dired-compare-directories` is used to compare the current Dired buffer with another directory. It marks all the files that are "different" between the two directories. It puts these marks in all Dired buffers where these files are listed, which of course includes the current buffer.

The default comparison method (used if you type `RET` at the prompt) is to compare just the file names—each file name that does not appear in the other directory is "different". You can specify more stringent comparisons by entering a Lisp expression, which can refer to the variables `size1` and `size2`, the respective file sizes; `mtime1` and `mtime2`, the last modification times in seconds, as floating point numbers; and `fa1` and `fa2`, the respective file attribute lists (as returned by the function `file-attributes`). This expression is evaluated for each pair of like-named files, and if the expression's value is non-`nil`, those files are considered "different".

For instance, the sequence `M-x dired-compare-directories RET (> mtime1 mtime2)` `RET` marks files newer in this directory than in the other, and marks files older in the other directory than in this one. It also marks files with no counterpart, in both directories, as always.

On the X Window System, Emacs supports the "drag and drop" protocol. You can drag a file object from another program, and drop it onto a Dired buffer; this either moves, copies, or creates a link to the file in that directory. Precisely which action is taken is determined by the originating program. Dragging files out of a Dired buffer is currently not supported.

28 The Calendar and the Diary

Emacs provides the functions of a desk calendar, with a diary of planned or past events. It also has facilities for managing your appointments, and keeping track of how much time you spend working on certain projects.

To enter the calendar, type `M-x calendar`; this displays a three-month calendar centered on the current month, with point on the current date. With a numeric argument, as in `C-u M-x calendar`, it prompts you for the month and year to be the center of the three-month calendar. The calendar uses its own buffer, whose major mode is Calendar mode.

`Mouse-3` in the calendar brings up a menu of operations on a particular date; `Mouse-2` brings up a menu of commonly used calendar features that are independent of any particular date. To exit the calendar, type `q`.

This chapter describes the basic calendar features. For more advanced topics, see Section "Advanced Calendar/Diary Usage" in *Specialized Emacs Features*.

28.1 Movement in the Calendar

Calendar mode provides commands to move through the calendar in logical units of time such as days, weeks, months, and years. If you move outside the three months originally displayed, the calendar display "scrolls" automatically through time to make the selected date visible. Moving to a date lets you view its holidays or diary entries, or convert it to other calendars; moving by long time periods is also useful simply to scroll the calendar.

28.1.1 Motion by Standard Lengths of Time

The commands for movement in the calendar buffer parallel the commands for movement in text. You can move forward and backward by days, weeks, months, and years.

`C-f`	Move point one day forward (`calendar-forward-day`).
`C-b`	Move point one day backward (`calendar-backward-day`).
`C-n`	Move point one week forward (`calendar-forward-week`).
`C-p`	Move point one week backward (`calendar-backward-week`).
`M-}`	Move point one month forward (`calendar-forward-month`).
`M-{`	Move point one month backward (`calendar-backward-month`).
`C-x ]`	Move point one year forward (`calendar-forward-year`).
`C-x [`	Move point one year backward (`calendar-backward-year`).

The day and week commands are natural analogues of the usual Emacs commands for moving by characters and by lines. Just as `C-n` usually moves to the same column in the following line, in Calendar mode it moves to the same day in the following week. And `C-p` moves to the same day in the previous week.

The arrow keys are equivalent to `C-f`, `C-b`, `C-n` and `C-p`, just as they normally are in other modes.

The commands for motion by months and years work like those for weeks, but move a larger distance. The month commands `M-}` and `M-{` move forward or backward by an entire month. The year commands `C-x ]` and `C-x [` move forward or backward a whole year.

The easiest way to remember these commands is to consider months and years analogous to paragraphs and pages of text, respectively. But the commands themselves are not quite analogous. The ordinary Emacs paragraph commands move to the beginning or end of a paragraph, whereas these month and year commands move by an entire month or an entire year, keeping the same date within the month or year.

All these commands accept a numeric argument as a repeat count. For convenience, the digit keys and the minus sign specify numeric arguments in Calendar mode even without the Meta modifier. For example, 100 C-f moves point 100 days forward from its present location.

28.1.2 Beginning or End of Week, Month or Year

A week (or month, or year) is not just a quantity of days; we think of weeks (months, years) as starting on particular dates. So Calendar mode provides commands to move to the start or end of a week, month or year:

C-a   Move point to start of week (`calendar-beginning-of-week`).

C-e   Move point to end of week (`calendar-end-of-week`).

M-a   Move point to start of month (`calendar-beginning-of-month`).

M-e   Move point to end of month (`calendar-end-of-month`).

M-<   Move point to start of year (`calendar-beginning-of-year`).

M->   Move point to end of year (`calendar-end-of-year`).

These commands also take numeric arguments as repeat counts, with the repeat count indicating how many weeks, months, or years to move backward or forward.

By default, weeks begin on Sunday. To make them begin on Monday instead, set the variable `calendar-week-start-day` to 1.

28.1.3 Specified Dates

Calendar mode provides commands for moving to a particular date specified in various ways.

g d   Move point to specified date (`calendar-goto-date`).

g D   Move point to specified day of year (`calendar-goto-day-of-year`).

g w   Move point to specified week of year (`calendar-iso-goto-week`).

o   Center calendar around specified month (`calendar-other-month`).

.   Move point to today's date (`calendar-goto-today`).

g d (`calendar-goto-date`) prompts for a year, a month, and a day of the month, and then moves to that date. Because the calendar includes all dates from the beginning of the current era, you must type the year in its entirety; that is, type '1990', not '90'.

g D (`calendar-goto-day-of-year`) prompts for a year and day number, and moves to that date. Negative day numbers count backward from the end of the year. g w (`calendar-iso-goto-week`) prompts for a year and week number, and moves to that week.

o (`calendar-other-month`) prompts for a month and year, then centers the three-month calendar around that month.

You can return to today's date with . (`calendar-goto-today`).

28.2 Scrolling in the Calendar

The calendar display scrolls automatically through time when you move out of the visible portion. You can also scroll it manually. Imagine that the calendar window contains a long strip of paper with the months on it. Scrolling the calendar means moving the strip horizontally, so that new months become visible in the window.

> `>`   Scroll calendar one month forward (`calendar-scroll-left`).

> `<`   Scroll calendar one month backward (`calendar-scroll-right`).

`C-v`
`next`   Scroll forward by three months (`calendar-scroll-left-three-months`).

`M-v`
`prior`   Scroll backward by three months (`calendar-scroll-right-three-months`).

The most basic calendar scroll commands scroll by one month at a time. This means that there are two months of overlap between the display before the command and the display after. `>` scrolls the calendar contents one month forward in time. `<` scrolls the contents one month backwards in time.

The commands `C-v` and `M-v` scroll the calendar by an entire "screenful"—three months— in analogy with the usual meaning of these commands. `C-v` makes later dates visible and `M-v` makes earlier dates visible. These commands take a numeric argument as a repeat count; in particular, since `C-u` multiplies the next command by four, typing `C-u C-v` scrolls the calendar forward by a year and typing `C-u M-v` scrolls the calendar backward by a year.

The function keys `next` and `prior` are equivalent to `C-v` and `M-v`, just as they are in other modes.

28.3 Counting Days

`M-=`   Display the number of days in the current region (`calendar-count-days-`
                   `region`).

To determine the number of days in a range, set the mark on one date using `C-SPC`, move point to another date, and type `M-=` (`calendar-count-days-region`). The numbers of days shown is *inclusive*; that is, it includes the days specified by mark and point.

28.4 Miscellaneous Calendar Commands

`p d`   Display day-in-year (`calendar-print-day-of-year`).

`C-c C-l`   Regenerate the calendar window (`calendar-redraw`).

`SPC`   Scroll the next window up (`scroll-other-window`).

`DEL`
`S-SPC`   Scroll the next window down (`scroll-other-window-down`).

`q`   Exit from calendar (`calendar-exit`).

To display the number of days elapsed since the start of the year, or the number of days remaining in the year, type the `p d` command (`calendar-print-day-of-year`). This displays both of those numbers in the echo area. The count of days elapsed includes the selected date. The count of days remaining does not include that date.

If the calendar window text gets corrupted, type C-c C-l (`calendar-redraw`) to redraw it. (This can only happen if you use non-Calendar-mode editing commands.)

In Calendar mode, you can use SPC (`scroll-other-window`) and DEL (`scroll-other-window-down`) to scroll the other window (if there is one) up or down, respectively. This is handy when you display a list of holidays or diary entries in another window.

To exit from the calendar, type q (`calendar-exit`). This buries all buffers related to the calendar, selecting other buffers. (If a frame contains a dedicated calendar window, exiting from the calendar deletes or iconifies that frame depending on the value of `calendar-remove-frame-by-deleting`.)

28.5 Writing Calendar Files

You can write calendars and diary entries to HTML and LaTeX files.

The Calendar HTML commands produce files of HTML code that contain calendar, holiday, and diary entries. Each file applies to one month, and has a name of the format *yyyy-mm*.`html`, where *yyyy* and *mm* are the four-digit year and two-digit month, respectively. The variable `cal-html-directory` specifies the default output directory for the HTML files. To prevent holidays from being shown, customize `cal-html-holidays`.

Diary entries enclosed by < and > are interpreted as HTML tags (for example: this is a diary entry with <font color="red">some red text</font>). You can change the overall appearance of the displayed HTML pages (for example, the color of various page elements, header styles) via a stylesheet `cal.css` in the directory containing the HTML files (see the value of the variable `cal-html-css-default` for relevant style settings).

H m   Generate a one-month calendar (`cal-html-cursor-month`).

H y   Generate a calendar file for each month of a year, as well as an index page (`cal-html-cursor-year`). By default, this command writes files to a *yyyy* subdirectory—if this is altered some hyperlinks between years will not work.

If the variable `cal-html-print-day-number-flag` is non-`nil`, then the monthly calendars show the day-of-the-year number. The variable `cal-html-year-index-cols` specifies the number of columns in the yearly index page.

The Calendar LaTeX commands produce a buffer of LaTeX code that prints as a calendar. Depending on the command you use, the printed calendar covers the day, week, month or year that point is in.

t m   Generate a one-month calendar (`cal-tex-cursor-month`).

t M   Generate a sideways-printing one-month calendar (`cal-tex-cursor-month-landscape`).

t d   Generate a one-day calendar (`cal-tex-cursor-day`).

t w 1   Generate a one-page calendar for one week, with hours (`cal-tex-cursor-week`).

t w 2   Generate a two-page calendar for one week, with hours (`cal-tex-cursor-week2`).

t w 3   Generate an ISO-style calendar for one week, without hours (`cal-tex-cursor-week-iso`).

t w 4   Generate a calendar for one Monday-starting week, with hours (`cal-tex-cursor-week-monday`).

t w W   Generate a two-page calendar for one week, without hours (`cal-tex-cursor-week2-summary`).

t f w   Generate a Filofax-style two-weeks-at-a-glance calendar (`cal-tex-cursor-filofax-2week`).

t f W   Generate a Filofax-style one-week-at-a-glance calendar (`cal-tex-cursor-filofax-week`).

t y   Generate a calendar for one year (`cal-tex-cursor-year`).

t Y   Generate a sideways-printing calendar for one year (`cal-tex-cursor-year-landscape`).

t f y   Generate a Filofax-style calendar for one year (`cal-tex-cursor-filofax-year`).

Some of these commands print the calendar sideways (in "landscape mode"), so it can be wider than it is long. Some of them use Filofax paper size (3.75in x 6.75in). All of these commands accept a prefix argument, which specifies how many days, weeks, months or years to print (starting always with the selected one).

If the variable `cal-tex-holidays` is non-`nil` (the default), then the printed calendars show the holidays in `calendar-holidays`. If the variable `cal-tex-diary` is non-`nil` (the default is `nil`), diary entries are included also (in monthly, filofax, and iso-week calendars only). If the variable `cal-tex-rules` is non-`nil` (the default is `nil`), the calendar displays ruled pages in styles that have sufficient room. Consult the documentation of the individual cal-tex functions to see which calendars support which features.

You can use the variable `cal-tex-preamble-extra` to insert extra LaTeX commands in the preamble of the generated document if you need to.

28.6 Holidays

The Emacs calendar knows about many major and minor holidays, and can display them. You can add your own holidays to the default list.

Mouse-3 Holidays

h   Display holidays for the selected date (`calendar-cursor-holidays`).

x   Mark holidays in the calendar window (`calendar-mark-holidays`).

u   Unmark calendar window (`calendar-unmark`).

a   List all holidays for the displayed three months in another window (`calendar-list-holidays`).

M-x holidays
      List all holidays for three months around today's date in another window.

`M-x list-holidays`
> List holidays in another window for a specified range of years.

To see if any holidays fall on a given date, position point on that date in the calendar window and use the `h` command. Alternatively, click on that date with `Mouse-3` and then choose `Holidays` from the menu that appears. Either way, this displays the holidays for that date, in the echo area if they fit there, otherwise in a separate window.

To view the distribution of holidays for all the dates shown in the calendar, use the `x` command. This displays the dates that are holidays in a different face. See Section "Calendar Customizing" in *Specialized Emacs Features*. The command applies both to the currently visible months and to other months that subsequently become visible by scrolling. To turn marking off and erase the current marks, type `u`, which also erases any diary marks (see Section 28.10 [Diary], page 341). If the variable `calendar-mark-holidays-flag` is non-`nil`, creating or updating the calendar marks holidays automatically.

To get even more detailed information, use the `a` command, which displays a separate buffer containing a list of all holidays in the current three-month range. You can use `SPC` and `DEL` in the calendar window to scroll that list up and down, respectively.

The command `M-x holidays` displays the list of holidays for the current month and the preceding and succeeding months; this works even if you don't have a calendar window. If the variable `calendar-view-holidays-initially-flag` is non-`nil`, creating the calendar displays holidays in this way. If you want the list of holidays centered around a different month, use `C-u M-x holidays`, which prompts for the month and year.

The holidays known to Emacs include United States holidays and the major Bahá'í, Chinese, Christian, Islamic, and Jewish holidays; also the solstices and equinoxes.

The command `M-x holiday-list` displays the list of holidays for a range of years. This function asks you for the starting and stopping years, and allows you to choose all the holidays or one of several categories of holidays. You can use this command even if you don't have a calendar window.

The dates used by Emacs for holidays are based on *current practice*, not historical fact. For example Veteran's Day began in 1919, but is shown in earlier years.

28.7 Times of Sunrise and Sunset

Special calendar commands can tell you, to within a minute or two, the times of sunrise and sunset for any date.

`Mouse-3 Sunrise/sunset`
`S`
> Display times of sunrise and sunset for the selected date (`calendar-sunrise-sunset`).

`M-x sunrise-sunset`
> Display times of sunrise and sunset for today's date.

`C-u M-x sunrise-sunset`
> Display times of sunrise and sunset for a specified date.

`M-x calendar-sunrise-sunset-month`
> Display times of sunrise and sunset for the selected month.

Within the calendar, to display the *local times* of sunrise and sunset in the echo area, move point to the date you want, and type S. Alternatively, click Mouse-3 on the date, then choose 'Sunrise/sunset' from the menu that appears. The command M-x sunrise-sunset is available outside the calendar to display this information for today's date or a specified date. To specify a date other than today, use C-u M-x sunrise-sunset, which prompts for the year, month, and day.

You can display the times of sunrise and sunset for any location and any date with C-u C-u M-x sunrise-sunset. This asks you for a longitude, latitude, number of minutes difference from Coordinated Universal Time, and date, and then tells you the times of sunrise and sunset for that location on that date.

Because the times of sunrise and sunset depend on the location on earth, you need to tell Emacs your latitude, longitude, and location name before using these commands. Here is an example of what to set:

```
(setq calendar-latitude 40.1)
(setq calendar-longitude -88.2)
(setq calendar-location-name "Urbana, IL")
```

Use one decimal place in the values of calendar-latitude and calendar-longitude.

Your time zone also affects the local time of sunrise and sunset. Emacs usually gets time zone information from the operating system, but if these values are not what you want (or if the operating system does not supply them), you must set them yourself. Here is an example:

```
(setq calendar-time-zone -360)
(setq calendar-standard-time-zone-name "CST")
(setq calendar-daylight-time-zone-name "CDT")
```

The value of calendar-time-zone is the number of minutes difference between your local standard time and Coordinated Universal Time (Greenwich time). The values of calendar-standard-time-zone-name and calendar-daylight-time-zone-name are the abbreviations used in your time zone. Emacs displays the times of sunrise and sunset *corrected for daylight saving time*. See Section 28.13 [Daylight Saving], page 347, for how daylight saving time is determined.

As a user, you might find it convenient to set the calendar location variables for your usual physical location in your .emacs file. If you are a system administrator, you may want to set these variables for all users in a default.el file. See Section 33.4 [Init File], page 437.

28.8 Phases of the Moon

These calendar commands display the dates and times of the phases of the moon (new moon, first quarter, full moon, last quarter). This feature is useful for debugging problems that "depend on the phase of the moon".

M   Display the dates and times for all the quarters of the moon for the three-month period shown (calendar-lunar-phases).

M-x lunar-phases
             Display dates and times of the quarters of the moon for three months around today's date.

Within the calendar, use the M command to display a separate buffer of the phases of the moon for the current three-month range. The dates and times listed are accurate to within a few minutes.

Outside the calendar, use the command M-x lunar-phases to display the list of the phases of the moon for the current month and the preceding and succeeding months. For information about a different month, use C-u M-x lunar-phases, which prompts for the month and year.

The dates and times given for the phases of the moon are given in local time (corrected for daylight saving, when appropriate). See the discussion in the previous section. See Section 28.7 [Sunrise/Sunset], page 336.

28.9 Conversion To and From Other Calendars

The Emacs calendar displayed is *always* the Gregorian calendar, sometimes called the "new style" calendar, which is used in most of the world today. However, this calendar did not exist before the sixteenth century and was not widely used before the eighteenth century; it did not fully displace the Julian calendar and gain universal acceptance until the early twentieth century. The Emacs calendar can display any month since January, year 1 of the current era, but the calendar displayed is always the Gregorian, even for a date at which the Gregorian calendar did not exist.

While Emacs cannot display other calendars, it can convert dates to and from several other calendars.

28.9.1 Supported Calendar Systems

The ISO commercial calendar is often used in business.

The Julian calendar, named after Julius Caesar, was the one used in Europe throughout medieval times, and in many countries up until the nineteenth century.

Astronomers use a simple counting of days elapsed since noon, Monday, January 1, 4713 B.C. on the Julian calendar. The number of days elapsed is called the *Julian day number* or the *Astronomical day number*.

The Hebrew calendar is used by tradition in the Jewish religion. The Emacs calendar program uses the Hebrew calendar to determine the dates of Jewish holidays. Hebrew calendar dates begin and end at sunset.

The Islamic calendar is used in many predominantly Islamic countries. Emacs uses it to determine the dates of Islamic holidays. There is no universal agreement in the Islamic world about the calendar; Emacs uses a widely accepted version, but the precise dates of Islamic holidays often depend on proclamation by religious authorities, not on calculations. As a consequence, the actual dates of observance can vary slightly from the dates computed by Emacs. Islamic calendar dates begin and end at sunset.

The French Revolutionary calendar was created by the Jacobins after the 1789 revolution, to represent a more secular and nature-based view of the annual cycle, and to install a 10-day week in a rationalization measure similar to the metric system. The French government officially abandoned this calendar at the end of 1805.

The Maya of Central America used three separate, overlapping calendar systems, the *long count*, the *tzolkin*, and the *haab*. Emacs knows about all three of these calendars. Experts dispute the exact correlation between the Mayan calendar and our calendar; Emacs uses the Goodman-Martinez-Thompson correlation in its calculations.

The Copts use a calendar based on the ancient Egyptian solar calendar. Their calendar consists of twelve 30-day months followed by an extra five-day period. Once every fourth year they add a leap day to this extra period to make it six days. The Ethiopic calendar is identical in structure, but has different year numbers and month names.

The Persians use a solar calendar based on a design of Omar Khayyam. Their calendar consists of twelve months of which the first six have 31 days, the next five have 30 days, and the last has 29 in ordinary years and 30 in leap years. Leap years occur in a complicated pattern every four or five years. The calendar implemented here is the arithmetical Persian calendar championed by Birashk, based on a 2,820-year cycle. It differs from the astronomical Persian calendar, which is based on astronomical events. As of this writing the first future discrepancy is projected to occur on March 20, 2025. It is currently not clear what the official calendar of Iran will be at that time.

The Chinese calendar is a complicated system of lunar months arranged into solar years. The years go in cycles of sixty, each year containing either twelve months in an ordinary year or thirteen months in a leap year; each month has either 29 or 30 days. Years, ordinary months, and days are named by combining one of ten "celestial stems" with one of twelve "terrestrial branches" for a total of sixty names that are repeated in a cycle of sixty.

The Bahá'í calendar system is based on a solar cycle of 19 months with 19 days each. The four remaining "intercalary" days are placed between the 18th and 19th months.

28.9.2 Converting To Other Calendars

The following commands describe the selected date (the date at point) in various other calendar systems:

Mouse-3 Other calendars

p o	Display the selected date in various other calendars. (`calendar-print-other-dates`).
p c	Display ISO commercial calendar equivalent for selected day (`calendar-iso-print-date`).
p j	Display Julian date for selected day (`calendar-julian-print-date`).
p a	Display astronomical (Julian) day number for selected day (`calendar-astro-print-day-number`).
p h	Display Hebrew date for selected day (`calendar-hebrew-print-date`).
p i	Display Islamic date for selected day (`calendar-islamic-print-date`).
p f	Display French Revolutionary date for selected day (`calendar-french-print-date`).
p b	Display Bahá'í date for selected day (`calendar-bahai-print-date`).
p C	Display Chinese date for selected day (`calendar-chinese-print-date`).
p k	Display Coptic date for selected day (`calendar-coptic-print-date`).
p e	Display Ethiopic date for selected day (`calendar-ethiopic-print-date`).

p p   Display Persian date for selected day (`calendar-persian-print-date`).

p m   Display Mayan date for selected day (`calendar-mayan-print-date`).

Otherwise, move point to the date you want to convert, then type the appropriate command starting with p from the table above. The prefix p is a mnemonic for "print", since Emacs "prints" the equivalent date in the echo area. p o displays the date in all forms known to Emacs. You can also use **Mouse-3** and then choose **Other calendars** from the menu that appears. This displays the equivalent forms of the date in all the calendars Emacs understands, in the form of a menu. (Choosing an alternative from this menu doesn't actually do anything—the menu is used only for display.)

28.9.3 Converting From Other Calendars

You can use the other supported calendars to specify a date to move to. This section describes the commands for doing this using calendars other than Mayan; for the Mayan calendar, see the following section.

g c   Move to a date specified in the ISO commercial calendar (`calendar-iso-goto-date`).

g w   Move to a week specified in the ISO commercial calendar (`calendar-iso-goto-week`).

g j   Move to a date specified in the Julian calendar (`calendar-julian-goto-date`).

g a   Move to a date specified with an astronomical (Julian) day number (`calendar-astro-goto-day-number`).

g b   Move to a date specified in the Bahá'í calendar (`calendar-bahai-goto-date`).

g h   Move to a date specified in the Hebrew calendar (`calendar-hebrew-goto-date`).

g i   Move to a date specified in the Islamic calendar (`calendar-islamic-goto-date`).

g f   Move to a date specified in the French Revolutionary calendar (`calendar-french-goto-date`).

g C   Move to a date specified in the Chinese calendar (`calendar-chinese-goto-date`).

g p   Move to a date specified in the Persian calendar (`calendar-persian-goto-date`).

g k   Move to a date specified in the Coptic calendar (`calendar-coptic-goto-date`).

g e   Move to a date specified in the Ethiopic calendar (`calendar-ethiopic-goto-date`).

These commands ask you for a date on the other calendar, move point to the Gregorian calendar date equivalent to that date, and display the other calendar's date in the echo area. Emacs uses strict completion (see Section 5.4.3 [Completion Exit], page 30) whenever it asks you to type a month name, so you don't have to worry about the spelling of Hebrew, Islamic, or French names.

One common issue concerning the Hebrew calendar is the computation of the anniversary of a date of death, called a "yahrzeit". The Emacs calendar includes a facility for such calculations. If you are in the calendar, the command `M-x calendar-hebrew-list-yahrzeits` asks you for a range of years and then displays a list of the yahrzeit dates for those years for the date given by point. If you are not in the calendar, this command first asks you for the date of death and the range of years, and then displays the list of yahrzeit dates.

28.10 The Diary

The Emacs diary keeps track of appointments or other events on a daily basis, in conjunction with the calendar. To use the diary feature, you must first create a *diary file* containing a list of events and their dates. Then Emacs can automatically pick out and display the events for today, for the immediate future, or for any specified date.

The name of the diary file is specified by the variable `diary-file`; `~/diary` is the default. Here's an example showing what that file looks like:

```
12/22/2012  Twentieth wedding anniversary!!
&1/1.       Happy New Year!
10/22       Ruth's birthday.
* 21, *:    Payday
Tuesday--weekly meeting with grad students at 10am
         Supowit, Shen, Bitner, and Kapoor to attend.
1/13/89     Friday the thirteenth!!
&thu 4pm    squash game with Lloyd.
mar 16      Dad's birthday
April 15, 2013 Income tax due.
&* 15       time cards due.
```

This format is essentially the same as the one used by the separate `calendar` utility that is present on some Unix systems. This example uses extra spaces to align the event descriptions of most of the entries. Such formatting is purely a matter of taste.

Although you probably will start by creating a diary manually, Emacs provides a number of commands to let you view, add, and change diary entries.

28.10.1 Displaying the Diary

Once you have created a diary file, you can use the calendar to view it. You can also view today's events outside of Calendar mode. In the following, key bindings refer to the Calendar buffer.

Mouse-3 Diary

d   Display all diary entries for the selected date (`diary-view-entries`).

s   Display the entire diary file (`diary-show-all-entries`).

m   Mark all visible dates that have diary entries (`diary-mark-entries`).

u   Unmark the calendar window (`calendar-unmark`).

M-x diary-print-entries
             Print hard copy of the diary display as it appears.

M-x diary Display all diary entries for today's date.

```
M-x diary-mail-entries
```
> Mail yourself email reminders about upcoming diary entries.

Displaying the diary entries with d shows in a separate window the diary entries for the selected date in the calendar. The mode line of the new window shows the date of the diary entries. Holidays are shown either in the buffer or in the mode line, depending on the display method you choose (see Section "Diary Display" in *Specialized Emacs Features*). If you specify a numeric argument with d, it shows all the diary entries for that many successive days. Thus, 2 d displays all the entries for the selected date and for the following day.

Another way to display the diary entries for a date is to click Mouse-3 on the date, and then choose Diary entries from the menu that appears. If the variable calendar-view-diary-initially-flag is non-nil, creating the calendar lists the diary entries for the current date (provided the current date is visible).

To get a broader view of which days are mentioned in the diary, use the m command. This marks the dates that have diary entries in a different face. See Section "Calendar Customizing" in *Specialized Emacs Features*.

This command applies both to the months that are currently visible and to those that subsequently become visible after scrolling. To turn marking off and erase the current marks, type u, which also turns off holiday marks (see Section 28.6 [Holidays], page 335). If the variable calendar-mark-diary-entries-flag is non-nil, creating or updating the calendar marks diary dates automatically.

To see the full diary file, rather than just some of the entries, use the s command.

The command M-x diary displays the diary entries for the current date, independently of the calendar display, and optionally for the next few days as well; the variable diary-number-of-entries specifies how many days to include. See Section "Diary Customizing" in *Specialized Emacs Features*.

If you put (diary) in your .emacs file, this automatically displays a window with the day's diary entries when you start Emacs.

Some people like to receive email notifications of events in their diary. To send such mail to yourself, use the command M-x diary-mail-entries. A prefix argument specifies how many days (starting with today) to check; otherwise, the variable diary-mail-days says how many days.

28.10.2 The Diary File

Your *diary file* is a file that records events associated with particular dates. The name of the diary file is specified by the variable diary-file; ~/diary is the default. The calendar utility program supports a subset of the format allowed by the Emacs diary facilities, so you can use that utility to view the diary file, with reasonable results aside from the entries it cannot understand.

Each entry in the diary file describes one event and consists of one or more lines. An entry always begins with a date specification at the left margin. The rest of the entry is simply text to describe the event. If the entry has more than one line, then the lines after the first must begin with whitespace to indicate they continue a previous entry. Lines that do not begin with valid dates and do not continue a preceding entry are ignored.

You can also use a format where the first line of a diary entry consists only of the date or day name (with no following blanks or punctuation). For example:

```
02/11/2012
        Bill B. visits Princeton today
        2pm Cognitive Studies Committee meeting
        2:30-5:30 Liz at Lawrenceville
        4:00pm Dentist appt
        7:30pm Dinner at George's
        8:00-10:00pm concert
```

This entry will have a different appearance if you use the simple diary display (see Section "Diary Display" in *Specialized Emacs Features*). The simple diary display omits the date line at the beginning; only the continuation lines appear. This style of entry looks neater when you display just a single day's entries, but can cause confusion if you ask for more than one day's entries.

You can inhibit the marking of certain diary entries in the calendar window; to do this, insert the string that `diary-nonmarking-symbol` specifies (default '&') at the beginning of the entry, before the date. This has no effect on display of the entry in the diary window; it only affects marks on dates in the calendar window. Nonmarking entries are especially useful for generic entries that would otherwise mark many different dates.

28.10.3 Date Formats

Here are some sample diary entries, illustrating different ways of formatting a date. The examples all show dates in American order (month, day, year), but Calendar mode supports European order (day, month, year) and ISO order (year, month, day) as options.

```
4/20/12  Switch-over to new tabulation system
apr. 25  Start tabulating annual results
4/30  Results for April are due
*/25  Monthly cycle finishes
Friday  Don't leave without backing up files
```

The first entry appears only once, on April 20, 2012. The second and third appear every year on the specified dates, and the fourth uses a wildcard (asterisk) for the month, so it appears on the 25th of every month. The final entry appears every week on Friday.

You can use just numbers to express a date, as in '*month/day*' or '*month/day/year*'. This must be followed by a nondigit. In the date itself, *month* and *day* are numbers of one or two digits. The optional *year* is also a number, and may be abbreviated to the last two digits; that is, you can use '11/12/2012' or '11/12/12'.

Dates can also have the form '*monthname day*' or '*monthname day, year*', where the month's name can be spelled in full or abbreviated (with or without a period). The preferred abbreviations for month and day names can be set using the variables `calendar-abbrev-length`, `calendar-month-abbrev-array`, and `calendar-day-abbrev-array`. The default is to use the first three letters of a name as its abbreviation. Case is not significant.

A date may be *generic*; that is, partially unspecified. Then the entry applies to all dates that match the specification. If the date does not contain a year, it is generic and applies to any year. Alternatively, *month*, *day*, or *year* can be '*'; this matches any month, day, or year, respectively. Thus, a diary entry '3/*/*' matches any day in March of any year; so does 'march *'.

If you prefer the European style of writing dates (in which the day comes before the month), or the ISO style (in which the order is year, month, day), type `M-x calendar-set-date-style` while in the calendar, or customize the variable `calendar-date-style`. This affects how diary dates are interpreted, date display, and the order in which some commands expect their arguments to be given.

You can use the name of a day of the week as a generic date which applies to any date falling on that day of the week. You can abbreviate the day of the week as described above, or spell it in full; case is not significant.

28.10.4 Commands to Add to the Diary

While in the calendar, there are several commands to create diary entries. The basic commands are listed here; more sophisticated commands are in the next section (see Section 28.10.5 [Special Diary Entries], page 344). Entries can also be based on non-Gregorian calendars. See Section "Non-Gregorian Diary" in *Specialized Emacs Features*.

i d   Add a diary entry for the selected date (`diary-insert-entry`).

i w   Add a diary entry for the selected day of the week (`diary-insert-weekly-entry`).

i m   Add a diary entry for the selected day of the month (`diary-insert-monthly-entry`).

i y   Add a diary entry for the selected day of the year (`diary-insert-yearly-entry`).

You can make a diary entry for a specific date by selecting that date in the calendar window and typing the i d command. This command displays the end of your diary file in another window and inserts the date; you can then type the rest of the diary entry.

If you want to make a diary entry that applies to a specific day of the week, select that day of the week (any occurrence will do) and type i w. This inserts the day-of-week as a generic date; you can then type the rest of the diary entry. You can make a monthly diary entry in the same fashion: select the day of the month, use the i m command, and type the rest of the entry. Similarly, you can insert a yearly diary entry with the i y command.

All of the above commands make marking diary entries by default. To make a nonmarking diary entry, give a prefix argument to the command. For example, C-u i w makes a nonmarking weekly diary entry.

When you modify the diary file, be sure to save the file before exiting Emacs. Saving the diary file after using any of the above insertion commands will automatically update the diary marks in the calendar window, if appropriate. You can use the command `calendar-redraw` to force an update at any time.

28.10.5 Special Diary Entries

In addition to entries based on calendar dates, the diary file can contain *sexp entries* for regular events such as anniversaries. These entries are based on Lisp expressions (sexps) that Emacs evaluates as it scans the diary file. Instead of a date, a sexp entry contains '%%' followed by a Lisp expression which must begin and end with parentheses. The Lisp expression determines which dates the entry applies to.

Calendar mode provides commands to insert certain commonly used sexp entries:

i a   Add an anniversary diary entry for the selected date (`diary-insert-anniversary-entry`).

i b   Add a block diary entry for the current region (`diary-insert-block-entry`).

i c   Add a cyclic diary entry starting at the date (`diary-insert-cyclic-entry`).

If you want to make a diary entry that applies to the anniversary of a specific date, move point to that date and use the `i a` command. This displays the end of your diary file in another window and inserts the anniversary description; you can then type the rest of the diary entry. The entry looks like this:

    %%(diary-anniversary 10 31 1948) Arthur's birthday

This entry applies to October 31 in any year after 1948; '10 31 1948' specifies the date. (If you are using the European or ISO calendar style, the input order of month, day and year is different.) The reason this expression requires a beginning year is that advanced diary functions can use it to calculate the number of elapsed years.

A *block* diary entry applies to a specified range of consecutive dates. Here is a block diary entry that applies to all dates from June 24, 2012 through July 10, 2012:

    %%(diary-block 6 24 2012 7 10 2012) Vacation

The '6 24 2012' indicates the starting date and the '7 10 2012' indicates the stopping date. (Again, if you are using the European or ISO calendar style, the input order of month, day and year is different.)

To insert a block entry, place point and the mark on the two dates that begin and end the range, and type `i b`. This command displays the end of your diary file in another window and inserts the block description; you can then type the diary entry.

Cyclic diary entries repeat after a fixed interval of days. To create one, select the starting date and use the `i c` command. The command prompts for the length of interval, then inserts the entry, which looks like this:

    %%(diary-cyclic 50 3 1 2012) Renew medication

This entry applies to March 1, 2012 and every 50th day following; '3 1 2012' specifies the starting date. (If you are using the European or ISO calendar style, the input order of month, day and year is different.)

All three of these commands make marking diary entries. To insert a nonmarking entry, give a prefix argument to the command. For example, `C-u i a` makes a nonmarking anniversary diary entry.

Marking sexp diary entries in the calendar can be time-consuming, since every date visible in the calendar window must be individually checked. So it's a good idea to make sexp diary entries nonmarking (with '&') when possible.

Another sophisticated kind of sexp entry, a *floating* diary entry, specifies a regularly occurring event by offsets specified in days, weeks, and months. It is comparable to a crontab entry interpreted by the `cron` utility. Here is a nonmarking, floating diary entry that applies to the fourth Thursday in November:

    &%%(diary-float 11 4 4) American Thanksgiving

The 11 specifies November (the eleventh month), the 4 specifies Thursday (the fourth day of the week, where Sunday is numbered zero), and the second 4 specifies the fourth Thursday

(1 would mean "first", 2 would mean "second", −2 would mean "second-to-last", and so on). The month can be a single month or a list of months. Thus you could change the 11 above to ''(1 2 3)' and have the entry apply to the last Thursday of January, February, and March. If the month is t, the entry applies to all months of the year.

Each of the standard sexp diary entries takes an optional parameter specifying the name of a face or a single-character string to use when marking the entry in the calendar. Most generally, sexp diary entries can perform arbitrary computations to determine when they apply. See Section "Sexp Diary Entries" in *Specialized Emacs Features*.

28.11 Appointments

If you have a diary entry for an appointment, and that diary entry begins with a recognizable time of day, Emacs can warn you in advance that an appointment is pending. Emacs alerts you to the appointment by displaying a message in your chosen format, as specified by the variable `appt-display-format`. If the value of `appt-audible` is non-nil, the warning includes an audible reminder. In addition, if `appt-display-mode-line` is non-nil, Emacs displays the number of minutes to the appointment on the mode line.

If `appt-display-format` has the value `window`, then the variable `appt-display-duration` controls how long the reminder window is visible for; and the variables `appt-disp-window-function` and `appt-delete-window-function` give the names of functions used to create and destroy the window, respectively.

To enable appointment notification, type M-x appt-activate. With a positive argument, it enables notification; with a negative argument, it disables notification; with no argument, it toggles. Enabling notification also sets up an appointment list for today from the diary file, giving all diary entries found with recognizable times of day, and reminds you just before each of them.

For example, suppose the diary file contains these lines:

```
Monday
   9:30am Coffee break
  12:00pm Lunch
```

Then on Mondays, you will be reminded at around 9:20am about your coffee break and at around 11:50am about lunch. The variable `appt-message-warning-time` specifies how many minutes (default 12) in advance to warn you. This is a default warning time. Each appointment can specify a different warning time by adding a piece matching `appt-warning-time-regexp` (see that variable's documentation for details).

You can write times in am/pm style (with '12:00am' standing for midnight and '12:00pm' standing for noon), or 24-hour European/military style. You need not be consistent; your diary file can have a mixture of the two styles. Times must be at the beginning of diary entries if they are to be recognized.

Emacs updates the appointments list from the diary file automatically just after midnight. You can force an update at any time by re-enabling appointment notification. Both these actions also display the day's diary buffer, unless you set `appt-display-diary` to nil. The appointments list is also updated whenever the diary file (or a file it includes; see Section "Fancy Diary Display" in *Specialized Emacs Features*) is saved.

You can also use the appointment notification facility like an alarm clock. The command M-x appt-add adds entries to the appointment list without affecting your diary file. You delete entries from the appointment list with M-x appt-delete.

28.12 Importing and Exporting Diary Entries

You can transfer diary entries between Emacs diary files and a variety of other formats.

You can import diary entries from Outlook-generated appointment messages. While viewing such a message in Rmail or Gnus, do M-x diary-from-outlook to import the entry. You can make this command recognize additional appointment message formats by customizing the variable `diary-outlook-formats`. Other mail clients can set `diary-from-outlook-function` to an appropriate value.

The icalendar package allows you to transfer data between your Emacs diary file and iCalendar files, which are defined in "RFC 2445—Internet Calendaring and Scheduling Core Object Specification (iCalendar)" (as well as the earlier vCalendar format).

The command `icalendar-import-buffer` extracts iCalendar data from the current buffer and adds it to your diary file. This function is also suitable for automatic extraction of iCalendar data; for example with the Rmail mail client one could use:

```
(add-hook 'rmail-show-message-hook 'icalendar-import-buffer)
```

The command `icalendar-import-file` imports an iCalendar file and adds the results to an Emacs diary file. For example:

```
(icalendar-import-file "/here/is/calendar.ics"
                       "/there/goes/ical-diary")
```

You can use an `#include` directive to add the import file contents to the main diary file, if these are different files. See Section "Fancy Diary Display" in *Specialized Emacs Features*.

Use `icalendar-export-file` to interactively export an entire Emacs diary file to iCalendar format. To export only a part of a diary file, mark the relevant area, and call `icalendar-export-region`. In both cases, Emacs appends the result to the target file.

28.13 Daylight Saving Time

Emacs understands the difference between standard time and daylight saving time—the times given for sunrise, sunset, solstices, equinoxes, and the phases of the moon take that into account. The rules for daylight saving time vary from place to place and have also varied historically from year to year. To do the job properly, Emacs needs to know which rules to use.

Some operating systems keep track of the rules that apply to the place where you are; on these systems, Emacs gets the information it needs from the system automatically. If some or all of this information is missing, Emacs fills in the gaps with the rules currently used in Cambridge, Massachusetts. If the resulting rules are not what you want, you can tell Emacs the rules to use by setting certain variables: `calendar-daylight-savings-starts` and `calendar-daylight-savings-ends`.

These values should be Lisp expressions that refer to the variable `year`, and evaluate to the Gregorian date on which daylight saving time starts or (respectively) ends, in the form of a list (*month day year*). The values should be `nil` if your area does not use daylight saving time.

Emacs uses these expressions to determine the starting date of daylight saving time for the holiday list and for correcting times of day in the solar and lunar calculations.

The values for Cambridge, Massachusetts are as follows:

```
(calendar-nth-named-day 2 0 3 year)
(calendar-nth-named-day 1 0 11 year)
```

That is, the second 0th day (Sunday) of the third month (March) in the year specified by year, and the first Sunday of the eleventh month (November) of that year. If daylight saving time were changed to start on October 1, you would set calendar-daylight-savings-starts to this:

```
(list 10 1 year)
```

If there is no daylight saving time at your location, or if you want all times in standard time, set calendar-daylight-savings-starts and calendar-daylight-savings-ends to nil.

The variable calendar-daylight-time-offset specifies the difference between daylight saving time and standard time, measured in minutes. The value for Cambridge, Massachusetts is 60.

Finally, the two variables calendar-daylight-savings-starts-time and calendar-daylight-savings-ends-time specify the number of minutes after midnight local time when the transition to and from daylight saving time should occur. For Cambridge, Massachusetts both variables' values are 120.

28.14 Summing Time Intervals

The timeclock package adds up time intervals, so you can (for instance) keep track of how much time you spend working on particular projects.

Use the M-x timeclock-in command when you start working on a project, and M-x timeclock-out command when you're done. Each time you do this, it adds one time interval to the record of the project. You can change to working on a different project with M-x timeclock-change.

Once you've collected data from a number of time intervals, you can use M-x timeclock-workday-remaining to see how much time is left to work today (assuming a typical average of 8 hours a day), and M-x timeclock-when-to-leave which will calculate when you're "done".

If you want Emacs to display the amount of time "left" of your workday in the mode line, either customize the timeclock-modeline-display variable and set its value to t, or invoke the M-x timeclock-modeline-display command.

Terminating the current Emacs session might or might not mean that you have stopped working on the project and, by default, Emacs asks you. You can, however, customize the value of the variable timeclock-ask-before-exiting to nil to avoid the question; then, only an explicit M-x timeclock-out or M-x timeclock-change will tell Emacs that the current interval is over.

The timeclock functions work by accumulating the data in a file called ~/.emacs.d/timelog. You can specify a different name for this file by customizing the variable timeclock-file. If you edit the timeclock file manually, or if you change the value of any of timeclock's customizable variables, you should run the command `M-x timeclock-reread-log` to update the data in Emacs from the file.

29 Sending Mail

To send an email message from Emacs, type `C-x m`. This switches to a buffer named `*unsent mail*`, where you can edit the text and headers of the message. When done, type `C-c C-s` or `C-c C-c` to send it.

`C-x m`   Begin composing mail (`compose-mail`).

`C-x 4 m`   Likewise, in another window (`compose-mail-other-window`).

`C-x 5 m`   Likewise, but in a new frame (`compose-mail-other-frame`).

`C-c C-s`   In the mail buffer, send the message (`message-send`).

`C-c C-c`   In the mail buffer, send the message and bury the buffer (`message-send-and-exit`).

The mail buffer is an ordinary Emacs buffer, so you can switch to other buffers while composing the mail. If you want to send another mail before finishing the current one, type `C-x m` again to open a new mail buffer whose name has a different numeric suffix (see Section 16.3 [Misc Buffer], page 149). If you invoke the command with a prefix argument, `C-u C-x m`, Emacs switches back to the last mail buffer, and asks if you want to erase the message in that buffer; if you answer no, this lets you pick up editing the message where you left off.

The command `C-x 4 m` (`compose-mail-other-window`) does the same as `C-x m`, except it displays the mail buffer in a different window. The command `C-x 5 m` (`compose-mail-other-frame`) does it in a new frame.

When you type `C-c C-c` or `C-c C-s` to send the mail, Emacs may ask you how it should deliver the mail—either directly via SMTP, or using some other method. See Section 29.4.1 [Mail Sending], page 353, for details.

29.1 The Format of the Mail Buffer

Here is an example of the contents of a mail buffer:

```
To: subotai@example.org
CC: mongol.soldier@example.net, rms@gnu.org
Subject: Re: What is best in life?
From: conan@example.org
--text follows this line--
To crush your enemies, see them driven before you, and to
hear the lamentation of their women.
```

At the top of the mail buffer is a set of *header fields*, which are used for specifying information about the email's recipient(s), subject, and so on. The above buffer contains header fields for 'To', 'Cc', 'Subject', and 'From'. Some header fields are automatically pre-initialized in the mail buffer, when appropriate.

The line that says '`--text follows this line--`' separates the header fields from the *body* (or *text*) of the message. Everything above that line is treated as part of the headers; everything below it is treated as the body. The delimiter line itself does not appear in the message actually sent.

You can insert and edit header fields using ordinary editing commands. See Section 29.4.2 [Header Editing], page 354, for commands specific to editing header fields. Certain headers, such as 'Date' and 'Message-Id', are normally omitted from the mail buffer and are created automatically when the message is sent.

29.2 Mail Header Fields

A header field in the mail buffer starts with a field name at the beginning of a line, terminated by a colon. Upper and lower case are equivalent in field names. After the colon and optional whitespace comes the contents of the field.

You can use any name you like for a header field, but normally people use only standard field names with accepted meanings.

The 'From' header field identifies the person sending the email (i.e., you). This should be a valid mailing address, as replies are normally sent there. The default contents of this header field are computed from the variables user-full-name (which specifies your full name) and user-mail-address (your email address). On some operating systems, Emacs initializes these two variables using environment variables (see Section C.4.1 [General Variables], page 483). If this information is unavailable or wrong, you should customize the variables yourself (see Section 33.1 [Easy Customization], page 412).

The value of the variable mail-from-style specifies how to format the contents of the 'From' field:

nil   Use just the address, as in 'king@grassland.com'.

parens   Use both address and full name, as in:
             'king@grassland.com (Elvis Parsley)'.

angles   Use both address and full name, as in:
             'Elvis Parsley <king@grassland.com>'.

any other value
             Use angles normally. But if the address must be "quoted" to remain syntactically valid under the angles format but not under the parens format, use parens instead. This is the default.

Apart from 'From', here is a table of commonly-used fields:

'To'   The mailing address(es) to which the message is addressed. To list more than one address, use commas to separate them.

'Subject'   The subject of the message.

'CC'   Additional mailing address(es) to send the message to. This is like 'To', except that these readers should not regard the message as directed at them.

'BCC'   Additional mailing address(es) to send the message to, which should not appear in the header of the message actually sent. "BCC" stands for *blind carbon copies*.

'FCC'   The name of a file, to which a copy of the sent message should be appended. Emacs writes the message in mbox format, unless the file is in Babyl format (used by Rmail before Emacs 23), in which case Emacs writes in Babyl format.

If an Rmail buffer is visiting the file, Emacs updates it accordingly. To specify more than one file, use several 'FCC' fields, with one file name in each field.

'Reply-to'
>An address to which replies should be sent, instead of 'From'. This is used if, for some reason, your 'From' address cannot receive replies.

'Mail-reply-to'
>This field takes precedence over 'Reply-to'. It is used because some mailing lists set the 'Reply-to' field for their own purposes (a somewhat controversial practice).

'Mail-followup-to'
>One of more address(es) to use as default recipient(s) for follow-up messages. This is typically used when you reply to a message from a mailing list that you are subscribed to, and want replies to go to the list without sending an extra copy to you.

'In-reply-to'
>An identifier for the message you are replying to. Most mail readers use this information to group related messages together. Normally, this header is filled in automatically when you reply to a message in any mail program built into Emacs.

'References'
>Identifiers for previous related messages. Like 'In-reply-to', this is normally filled in automatically for you.

The 'To', 'CC', and 'BCC' fields can appear any number of times, and each such header field can contain multiple addresses, separated by commas. This way, you can specify any number of places to send the message. These fields can also have continuation lines: one or more lines starting with whitespace, following the starting line of the field, are considered part of the field. Here's an example of a 'To' field with a continuation line:

```
To: foo@example.net, this@example.net,
    bob@example.com
```

You can direct Emacs to insert certain default headers into the mail buffer by setting the variable `mail-default-headers` to a string. Then C-x m inserts this string into the message headers. For example, here is how to add a 'Reply-to' and 'FCC' header to each message:

```
(setq mail-default-headers
      "Reply-to: foo@example.com\nFCC: ~/Mail/sent")
```

If the default header fields are not appropriate for a particular message, edit them as necessary before sending the message.

29.3 Mail Aliases

You can define *mail aliases*, which are short mnemonic names that stand for one or more mailing addresses. By default, mail aliases are defined in the file `~/.mailrc`. You can specify a different file name to use, by setting the variable `mail-personal-alias-file`.

To define an alias in `.mailrc`, write a line like this:

```
alias nick fulladdresses
```

This means that *nick* should expand into *fulladdresses*, where *fulladdresses* can be either a single address, or multiple addresses separated with spaces. For instance, to make `maingnu` stand for gnu@gnu.org plus a local address of your own, put in this line:

```
alias maingnu gnu@gnu.org local-gnu
```

If an address contains a space, quote the whole address with a pair of double quotes, like this:

```
alias jsmith "John Q. Smith <none@example.com>"
```

Note that you need not include double quotes around individual parts of the address, such as the person's full name. Emacs puts them in if they are needed. For instance, it inserts the above address as '"John Q. Smith" <none@example.com>'.

Emacs also recognizes "include" commands in .mailrc. They look like this:

```
source filename
```

The .mailrc file is not unique to Emacs; many other mail-reading programs use it for mail aliases, and it can contain various other commands. However, Emacs ignores everything except alias definitions and include commands.

Mail aliases expand as abbrevs—that is to say, as soon as you type a word-separator character after an alias (see Chapter 26 [Abbrevs], page 309). This expansion takes place only within the 'To', 'From', 'CC', 'BCC', and 'Reply-to' header fields (plus their 'Resent-' variants); it does not take place in other header fields, such as 'Subject'.

You can also insert an aliased address directly, using the command `M-x mail-abbrev-insert-alias`. This reads an alias name, with completion, and inserts its definition at point.

29.4 Mail Commands

The default major mode for the `*mail*` buffer is called Message mode. It behaves like Text mode in many ways, but provides several additional commands on the `C-c` prefix, which make editing a message more convenient.

In this section, we will describe some of the most commonly-used commands available in Message mode.

29.4.1 Mail Sending

`C-c C-c`   Send the message, and bury the mail buffer (`message-send-and-exit`).

`C-c C-s`   Send the message, and leave the mail buffer selected (`message-send`).

The usual command to send a message is `C-c C-c` (`mail-send-and-exit`). This sends the message and then "buries" the mail buffer, putting it at the lowest priority for reselection. If you want it to kill the mail buffer instead, change the variable `message-kill-buffer-on-exit` to t.

The command `C-c C-s` (`message-send`) sends the message and leaves the buffer selected. Use this command if you want to modify the message (perhaps with new recipients) and send it again.

Sending a message runs the hook `message-send-hook`. It also marks the mail buffer as unmodified, except if the mail buffer is also a file-visiting buffer (in that case, only saving the file does that, and you don't get a warning if you try to send the same message twice).

The variable `send-mail-function` controls how the message is delivered. Its value should be one of the following functions:

`sendmail-query-once`

> Query for a delivery method (one of the other entries in this list), and use that method for this message; then save the method to `send-mail-function`, so that it is used for future deliveries. This is the default, unless you have already set the variables for sending mail via `smtpmail-send-it` (see below).

`smtpmail-send-it`

> Send mail through an external mail host, such as your Internet service provider's outgoing SMTP mail server. If you have not told Emacs how to contact the SMTP server, it prompts for this information, which is saved in the `smtpmail-smtp-server` variable and the file `~/.authinfo`. See Section "Emacs SMTP Library" in *Sending mail via SMTP*.

`sendmail-send-it`

> Send mail using the system's default `sendmail` program, or equivalent. This requires the system to be set up for delivering mail directly via SMTP.

`mailclient-send-it`

> Pass the mail buffer on to the system's designated mail client. See the commentary section in the file `mailclient.el` for details.

`feedmail-send-it`

> This is similar to `sendmail-send-it`, but allows you to queue messages for later sending. See the commentary section in the file `feedmail.el` for details.

When you send a message containing non-ASCII characters, they need to be encoded with a coding system (see Section 19.5 [Coding Systems], page 183). Usually the coding system is specified automatically by your chosen language environment (see Section 19.2 [Language Environments], page 179). You can explicitly specify the coding system for outgoing mail by setting the variable `sendmail-coding-system` (see Section 19.6 [Recognize Coding], page 185). If the coding system thus determined does not handle the characters in a particular message, Emacs asks you to select the coding system to use, showing a list of possible coding systems.

29.4.2 Mail Header Editing

Message mode provides the following special commands to move to particular header fields and to complete addresses in headers.

`C-c C-f C-t`

> Move to the 'To' header (`message-goto-to`).

`C-c C-f C-s`

> Move to the 'Subject' header (`message-goto-subject`).

`C-c C-f C-c`

> Move to the 'CC' header (`message-goto-cc`).

`C-c C-f C-b`
> Move to the 'BCC' header (`message-goto-bcc`).

`C-c C-f C-r`
> Move to the 'Reply-To' header (`message-goto-reply-to`).

`C-c C-f C-f`
> Move to the 'Mail-Followup-To' header field (`message-goto-followup-to`).

`C-c C-f C-w`
> Add a new 'FCC' header field, with file-name completion (`message-goto-fcc`).

`C-c C-b`   Move to the start of the message body (`message-goto-body`).

`TAB`   Complete a mailing address (`message-tab`).

The commands to move point to particular header fields are all based on the prefix C-c C-f ('C-f' is for "field"). If the field in question does not exist, the command creates one (the exception is `mail-fcc`, which creates a new field each time).

The command C-c C-b (`message-goto-body`) moves point to just after the header separator line—that is, to the beginning of the body.

While editing a header field that contains addresses, such as 'To:', 'CC:' and 'BCC:', you can complete an address by typing TAB (`message-tab`). This attempts to insert the full name corresponding to the address based on a couple of methods, including EUDC, a library that recognizes a number of directory server protocols (see Section "EUDC" in *The Emacs Unified Directory Client*). Failing that, it attempts to expand the address as a mail alias (see Section 29.3 [Mail Aliases], page 352). If point is on a header field that does not take addresses, or if it is in the message body, then TAB just inserts a tab character.

29.4.3 Citing Mail

`C-c C-y`   Yank the selected message from the mail reader, as a citation (`message-yank-original`).

`C-c C-q`   Fill each paragraph cited from another message (`message-fill-yanked-message`).

You can use the command C-c C-y (`message-yank-original`) to *cite* a message that you are replying to. This inserts the text of that message into the mail buffer. This command works only if the mail buffer is invoked from a mail reader running in Emacs, such as Rmail.

By default, Emacs inserts the string '>' in front of each line of the cited text; this prefix string is specified by the variable `message-yank-prefix`. If you call `message-yank-original` with a prefix argument, the citation prefix is not inserted.

After using C-c C-y, you can type C-c C-q (`message-fill-yanked-message`) to fill the paragraphs of the cited message. One use of C-c C-q fills all such paragraphs, each one individually. To fill a single paragraph of the quoted message, use M-q. If filling does not automatically handle the type of citation prefix you use, try setting the fill prefix explicitly. See Section 22.5 [Filling], page 212.

You can customize mail citation through the hook `mail-citation-hook`. For example, you can use the Supercite package, which provides more flexible citation (see Section "Introduction" in *Supercite*).

29.4.4 Mail Miscellany

You can *attach* a file to an outgoing message by typing C-c C-a (mml-attach-file) in the mail buffer. Attaching is done using the Multipurpose Internet Mail Extensions (MIME) standard.

The mml-attach-file command prompts for the name of the file, and for the attachment's *content type*, *description*, and *disposition*. The content type is normally detected automatically; just type RET to accept the default. The description is a single line of text that the recipient will see next to the attachment; you may also choose to leave this empty. The disposition is either 'inline' (the default), which means the recipient will see a link to the attachment within the message body, or 'attachment', which means the link will be separate from the body.

The mml-attach-file command is specific to Message mode; in Mail mode use mail-add-attachment instead. It will prompt only for the name of the file, and will determine the content type and the disposition automatically. If you want to include some description of the attached file, type that in the message body.

The actual contents of the attached file are not inserted into the mail buffer. Instead, some placeholder text is inserted into the mail buffer, like this:

```
<#part type="text/plain" filename="~/foo.txt" disposition=inline>
<#/part>
```

When you type C-c C-c or C-c C-s to send the message, the attached file will be delivered with it.

While composing a message, you can do spelling correction on the message text by typing M-x ispell-message. If you have yanked an incoming message into the outgoing draft, this command skips what was yanked, but it checks the text that you yourself inserted (it looks for indentation or mail-yank-prefix to distinguish the cited lines from your input). See Section 13.4 [Spelling], page 111.

Turning on Message mode (which C-x m does automatically) runs the normal hooks text-mode-hook and message-mode-hook. Initializing a new outgoing message runs the normal hook message-setup-hook; you can use this hook if you want to make changes to the appearance of the mail buffer. See Section 33.2.2 [Hooks], page 422.

The main difference between these hooks is just when they are invoked. Whenever you type C-x m, message-mode-hook runs as soon as the mail buffer is created. Then the message-setup function inserts the default contents of the buffer. After these default contents are inserted, message-setup-hook runs.

If you use C-x m to continue an existing composition, message-mode-hook runs immediately after switching to the mail buffer. If the buffer is unmodified, or if you decide to erase it and start again, message-setup-hook runs after the default contents are inserted.

29.5 Mail Signature

You can add a standard piece of text—your *mail signature*—to the end of every message. This signature may contain information such as your telephone number or your physical location. The variable message-signature determines how Emacs handles the mail signature.

The default value of `message-signature` is `t`; this means to look for your mail signature in the file `~/.signature`. If this file exists, its contents are automatically inserted into the end of the mail buffer. You can change the signature file via the variable `message-signature-file`.

If you change `message-signature` to a string, that specifies the text of the signature directly.

If you change `message-signature` to `nil`, Emacs will not insert your mail signature automatically. You can insert your mail signature by typing `C-c C-w` (`message-insert-signature`) in the mail buffer. Emacs will look for your signature in the signature file.

If you use Mail mode rather than Message mode for composing your mail, the corresponding variables that determine how your signature is sent are `mail-signature` and `mail-signature-file` instead.

By convention, a mail signature should be marked by a line whose contents are '-- '. If your signature lacks this prefix, it is added for you. The remainder of your signature should be no more than four lines.

29.6 Mail Amusements

`M-x spook` adds a line of randomly chosen keywords to an outgoing mail message. The keywords are chosen from a list of words that suggest you are discussing something subversive.

The idea behind this feature is the suspicion that the NSA[1] and other intelligence agencies snoop on all electronic mail messages that contain keywords suggesting they might find them interesting. (The agencies say that they don't, but that's what they *would* say.) The idea is that if lots of people add suspicious words to their messages, the agencies will get so busy with spurious input that they will have to give up reading it all. Whether or not this is true, it at least amuses some people.

You can use the `fortune` program to put a "fortune cookie" message into outgoing mail. To do this, add `fortune-to-signature` to `mail-setup-hook`:

```
(add-hook 'mail-setup-hook 'fortune-to-signature)
```

You will probably need to set the variable `fortune-file` before using this.

29.7 Mail-Composition Methods

In this chapter we have described the usual Emacs mode for editing and sending mail—Message mode. This is only one of several available modes. Prior to Emacs 23.2, the default mode was Mail mode, which is similar to Message mode in many respects but lacks features such as MIME support. Another available mode is MH-E (see Section "MH-E" in *The Emacs Interface to MH*).

You can choose any of these *mail user agents* as your preferred method for editing and sending mail. The commands `C-x m`, `C-x 4 m` and `C-x 5 m` use whichever agent you have specified; so do various other parts of Emacs that send mail, such as the bug reporter (see Section 34.3 [Bugs], page 448). To specify a mail user agent, customize the variable `mail-user-agent`. Currently, legitimate values include `message-user-agent` (Message mode) `sendmail-user-agent` (Mail mode), `gnus-user-agent`, and `mh-e-user-agent`.

---

[1] The US National Security Agency.

If you select a different mail-composition method, the information in this chapter about the mail buffer and Message mode does not apply; the other methods use a different format of text in a different buffer, and their commands are different as well.

Similarly, to specify your preferred method for reading mail, customize the variable `read-mail-command`. The default is `rmail` (see Chapter 30 [Rmail], page 359).

30 Reading Mail with Rmail

Rmail is an Emacs subsystem for reading and disposing of mail that you receive. Rmail stores mail messages in files called Rmail files. Reading the messages in an Rmail file is done in a special major mode, Rmail mode, which redefines most letters to run commands for managing mail.

30.1 Basic Concepts of Rmail

Using Rmail in the simplest fashion, you have one Rmail file `~/RMAIL` in which all of your mail is saved. It is called your *primary Rmail file*. The command `M-x rmail` reads your primary Rmail file, merges new mail in from your inboxes, displays the first message you haven't read yet, and lets you begin reading. The variable `rmail-file-name` specifies the name of the primary Rmail file.

Rmail displays only one message in the Rmail file at a time. The message that is shown is called the *current message*. Rmail mode's special commands can do such things as delete the current message, copy it into another file, send a reply, or move to another message. You can also create multiple Rmail files and use Rmail to move messages between them.

Within the Rmail file, messages are normally arranged sequentially in order of receipt; you can specify other ways to sort them (see Section 30.12 [Rmail Sorting], page 372). Messages are identified by consecutive integers which are their *message numbers*. The number of the current message is displayed in Rmail's mode line, followed by the total number of messages in the file. You can move to a message by specifying its message number with the `j` key (see Section 30.3 [Rmail Motion], page 360).

Following the usual conventions of Emacs, changes in an Rmail file become permanent only when you save the file. You can save it with `s` (`rmail-expunge-and-save`), which also expunges deleted messages from the file first (see Section 30.4 [Rmail Deletion], page 361). To save the file without expunging, use `C-x C-s`. Rmail also saves the Rmail file after merging new mail from an inbox file (see Section 30.5 [Rmail Inbox], page 362).

You can exit Rmail with `q` (`rmail-quit`); this expunges and saves the Rmail file, then buries the Rmail buffer as well as its summary buffer, if present (see Section 30.11 [Rmail Summary], page 369). But there is no need to "exit" formally. If you switch from Rmail to editing in other buffers, and never switch back, you have exited. Just make sure to save the Rmail file eventually (like any other file you have changed). `C-x s` is a suitable way to do this (see Section 15.3.1 [Save Commands], page 126). The Rmail command `b`, `rmail-bury`, buries the Rmail buffer and its summary without expunging and saving the Rmail file.

30.2 Scrolling Within a Message

When Rmail displays a message that does not fit on the screen, you must scroll through it to read the rest. You could do this with `C-v`, `M-v` and `M-<`, but in Rmail scrolling is so frequent that it deserves to be easier.

SPC	Scroll forward (`scroll-up-command`).
DEL S-SPC	Scroll backward (`scroll-down-command`).
.	Scroll to start of message (`rmail-beginning-of-message`).

/   Scroll to end of message (`rmail-end-of-message`).

Since the most common thing to do while reading a message is to scroll through it by screenfuls, Rmail makes SPC and DEL (or S-SPC) do the same as C-v (`scroll-up-command`) and M-v (`scroll-down-command`) respectively.

The command . (`rmail-beginning-of-message`) scrolls back to the beginning of the selected message. This is not quite the same as M-<: for one thing, it does not set the mark; for another, it resets the buffer boundaries of the current message if you have changed them. Similarly, the command / (`rmail-end-of-message`) scrolls forward to the end of the selected message.

30.3 Moving Among Messages

The most basic thing to do with a message is to read it. The way to do this in Rmail is to make the message current. The usual practice is to move sequentially through the file, since this is the order of receipt of messages. When you enter Rmail, you are positioned at the first message that you have not yet made current (that is, the first one that has the 'unseen' attribute; see Section 30.9 [Rmail Attributes], page 366). Move forward to see the other new messages; move backward to re-examine old messages.

n   Move to the next nondeleted message, skipping any intervening deleted messages (`rmail-next-undeleted-message`).

p   Move to the previous nondeleted message (`rmail-previous-undeleted-message`).

M-n   Move to the next message, including deleted messages (`rmail-next-message`).

M-p   Move to the previous message, including deleted messages (`rmail-previous-message`).

C-c C-n   Move to the next message with the same subject as the current one (`rmail-next-same-subject`).

C-c C-p   Move to the previous message with the same subject as the current one (`rmail-previous-same-subject`).

j   Move to the first message. With argument n, move to message number n (`rmail-show-message`).

>   Move to the last message (`rmail-last-message`).

<   Move to the first message (`rmail-first-message`).

M-s regexp RET
            Move to the next message containing a match for regexp (`rmail-search`).

- M-s regexp RET
            Move to the previous message containing a match for regexp.

n and p are the usual way of moving among messages in Rmail. They move through the messages sequentially, but skip over deleted messages, which is usually what you want to do. Their command definitions are named **rmail-next-undeleted-message** and **rmail-previous-undeleted-message**. If you do not want to skip deleted messages—for example, if you want to move to a message to undelete it—use the variants M-n and M-p (`rmail-next-message` and `rmail-previous-message`). A numeric argument to any of these commands serves as a repeat count.

In Rmail, you can specify a numeric argument by typing just the digits. You don't need to type C-u first.

The M-s (`rmail-search`) command is Rmail's version of search. The usual incremental search command C-s works in Rmail, but it searches only within the current message. The purpose of M-s is to search for another message. It reads a regular expression (see Section 12.6 [Regexps], page 97) nonincrementally, then searches starting at the beginning of the following message for a match. It then selects that message. If *regexp* is empty, M-s reuses the regexp used the previous time.

To search backward in the file for another message, give M-s a negative argument. In Rmail you can do this with - M-s. This begins searching from the end of the previous message.

It is also possible to search for a message based on labels. See Section 30.8 [Rmail Labels], page 365.

The C-c C-n (`rmail-next-same-subject`) command moves to the next message with the same subject as the current one. A prefix argument serves as a repeat count. With a negative argument, this command moves backward, acting like C-c C-p (`rmail-previous-same-subject`). When comparing subjects, these commands ignore the prefixes typically added to the subjects of replies.

To move to a message specified by absolute message number, use j (`rmail-show-message`) with the message number as argument. With no argument, j selects the first message. < (`rmail-first-message`) also selects the first message. > (`rmail-last-message`) selects the last message.

30.4 Deleting Messages

When you no longer need to keep a message, you can *delete* it. This flags it as ignorable, and some Rmail commands pretend it is no longer present; but it still has its place in the Rmail file, and still has its message number.

Expunging the Rmail file actually removes the deleted messages. The remaining messages are renumbered consecutively.

d   Delete the current message, and move to the next nondeleted message (`rmail-delete-forward`).

C-d   Delete the current message, and move to the previous nondeleted message (`rmail-delete-backward`).

u   Undelete the current message, or move back to the previous deleted message and undelete it (`rmail-undelete-previous-message`).

x   Expunge the Rmail file (`rmail-expunge`).

There are two Rmail commands for deleting messages. Both delete the current message and select another. d (`rmail-delete-forward`) moves to the following message, skipping messages already deleted, while C-d (`rmail-delete-backward`) moves to the previous nondeleted message. If there is no nondeleted message to move to in the specified direction, the message that was just deleted remains current. d with a prefix argument is equivalent to C-d. Note that the Rmail summary versions of these commands behave slightly differently (see Section 30.11.2 [Rmail Summary Edit], page 370).

Whenever Rmail deletes a message, it runs the hook `rmail-delete-message-hook`. When the hook functions are invoked, the message has been marked deleted, but it is still the current message in the Rmail buffer.

To make all the deleted messages finally vanish from the Rmail file, type x (`rmail-expunge`). Until you do this, you can still *undelete* the deleted messages. The undeletion command, u (`rmail-undelete-previous-message`), is designed to cancel the effect of a d command in most cases. It undeletes the current message if the current message is deleted. Otherwise it moves backward to previous messages until a deleted message is found, and undeletes that message.

You can usually undo a d with a u because the u moves back to and undeletes the message that the d deleted. But this does not work when the d skips a few already-deleted messages that follow the message being deleted; then the u command undeletes the last of the messages that were skipped. There is no clean way to avoid this problem. However, by repeating the u command, you can eventually get back to the message that you intend to undelete. You can also select a particular deleted message with the M-p command, then type u to undelete it.

A deleted message has the '`deleted`' attribute, and as a result '`deleted`' appears in the mode line when the current message is deleted. In fact, deleting or undeleting a message is nothing more than adding or removing this attribute. See Section 30.9 [Rmail Attributes], page 366.

30.5 Rmail Files and Inboxes

When you receive mail locally, the operating system places incoming mail for you in a file that we call your *inbox*. When you start up Rmail, it runs a C program called `movemail` to copy the new messages from your local inbox into your primary Rmail file, which also contains other messages saved from previous Rmail sessions. It is in this file that you actually read the mail with Rmail. This operation is called *getting new mail*. You can get new mail at any time in Rmail by typing g.

The variable `rmail-primary-inbox-list` contains a list of the files that are inboxes for your primary Rmail file. If you don't set this variable explicitly, Rmail uses the MAIL environment variable, or, as a last resort, a default inbox based on `rmail-spool-directory`. The default inbox file depends on your operating system; often it is /var/mail/*username*, /var/spool/mail/*username*, or /usr/spool/mail/*username*.

You can specify the inbox file(s) for any Rmail file for the current session with the command `set-rmail-inbox-list`; see Section 30.6 [Rmail Files], page 363.

There are two reasons for having separate Rmail files and inboxes.

1. The inbox file format varies between operating systems and according to the other mail software in use. Only one part of Rmail needs to know about the alternatives, and it need only understand how to convert all of them to Rmail's own format.

2. It is very cumbersome to access an inbox file without danger of losing mail, because it is necessary to interlock with mail delivery. Moreover, different operating systems use

different interlocking techniques. The strategy of moving mail out of the inbox once and for all into a separate Rmail file avoids the need for interlocking in all the rest of Rmail, since only Rmail operates on the Rmail file.

Rmail was originally written to use the Babyl format as its internal format. Since then, we have recognized that the usual inbox format ('mbox') on Unix and GNU systems is adequate for the job, and so since Emacs 23 Rmail uses that as its internal format. The Rmail file is still separate from the inbox file, even though their format is the same. (In fact, there are a few slightly different mbox formats. The differences are not very important, but you can set the variable `rmail-mbox-format` to tell Rmail which form your system uses. See that variable's documentation for more details.)

When getting new mail, Rmail first copies the new mail from the inbox file to the Rmail file; then it saves the Rmail file; then it clears out the inbox file. This way, a system crash may cause duplication of mail between the inbox and the Rmail file, but cannot lose mail. If `rmail-preserve-inbox` is non-`nil`, then Rmail does not clear out the inbox file when it gets new mail. You may wish to set this, for example, on a portable computer you use to check your mail via POP while traveling, so that your mail will remain on the server and you can save it later on your workstation.

In some cases, Rmail copies the new mail from the inbox file indirectly. First it runs the `movemail` program to move the mail from the inbox to an intermediate file called `.newmail-inboxname`, in the same directory as the Rmail file. Then Rmail merges the new mail from that file, saves the Rmail file, and only then deletes the intermediate file. If there is a crash at the wrong time, this file continues to exist, and Rmail will use it again the next time it gets new mail from that inbox.

If Rmail is unable to convert the data in `.newmail-inboxname` into mbox format, it renames the file to `RMAILOSE.n` (*n* is an integer chosen to make the name unique) so that Rmail will not have trouble with the data again. You should look at the file, find whatever message confuses Rmail (probably one that includes the control-underscore character, octal code 037), and delete it. Then you can use `1 g` to get new mail from the corrected file.

30.6 Multiple Rmail Files

Rmail operates by default on your *primary Rmail file*, which is named `~/RMAIL` and receives your incoming mail from your system inbox file. But you can also have other Rmail files and edit them with Rmail. These files can receive mail through their own inboxes, or you can move messages into them with explicit Rmail commands (see Section 30.7 [Rmail Output], page 364).

`i file RET`
> Read *file* into Emacs and run Rmail on it (`rmail-input`).

`M-x set-rmail-inbox-list RET files RET`
> Specify inbox file names for current Rmail file to get mail from.

`g`   Merge new mail from current Rmail file's inboxes (`rmail-get-new-mail`).

`C-u g file RET`
> Merge new mail from inbox file *file*.

To run Rmail on a file other than your primary Rmail file, you can use the i (`rmail-input`) command in Rmail. This visits the file in Rmail mode. You can use M-x `rmail-input` even when not in Rmail, but it is easier to type `C-u M-x rmail`, which does the same thing.

The file you read with i should normally be a valid mbox file. If it is not, Rmail tries to convert its text to mbox format, and visits the converted text in the buffer. If you save the buffer, that converts the file.

If you specify a file name that doesn't exist, i initializes a new buffer for creating a new Rmail file.

You can also select an Rmail file from a menu. In the Classify menu, choose the Input Rmail File item; then choose the Rmail file you want. The variables `rmail-secondary-file-directory` and `rmail-secondary-file-regexp` specify which files to offer in the menu: the first variable says which directory to find them in; the second says which files in that directory to offer (all those that match the regular expression). If no files match, you cannot select this menu item. These variables also apply to choosing a file for output (see Section 30.7 [Rmail Output], page 364).

The inbox files to use are specified by the variable `rmail-inbox-list`, which is buffer-local in Rmail mode. As a special exception, if you have specified no inbox files for your primary Rmail file, it uses the `MAIL` environment variable, or your standard system inbox.

The g command (`rmail-get-new-mail`) merges mail into the current Rmail file from its inboxes. If the Rmail file has no inboxes, g does nothing. The command M-x rmail also merges new mail into your primary Rmail file.

To merge mail from a file that is not the usual inbox, give the g key a numeric argument, as in `C-u g`. Then it reads a file name and merges mail from that file. The inbox file is not deleted or changed in any way when g with an argument is used. This is, therefore, a general way of merging one file of messages into another.

30.7 Copying Messages Out to Files

These commands copy messages from an Rmail file into another file.

o *file* RET

> Append a full copy of the current message to the file *file* (`rmail-output`).

C-o *file* RET

> Append a copy of the current message, as displayed, to the file *file* (`rmail-output-as-seen`).

w *file* RET

> Output just the message body to the file *file*, taking the default file name from the message 'Subject' header.

The commands o and C-o copy the current message into a specified file, adding it at the end. The two commands differ mainly in how much to copy: o copies the full message headers, even if they are not all visible, while C-o copies exactly the headers currently displayed and no more. See Section 30.13 [Rmail Display], page 373. In addition, o converts the message to Babyl format (used by Rmail in Emacs version 22 and before) if the file is in Babyl format; C-o cannot output to Babyl files at all.

If the output file is currently visited in an Emacs buffer, the output commands append the message to that buffer. It is up to you to save the buffer eventually in its file.

Sometimes you may receive a message whose body holds the contents of a file. You can save the body to a file (excluding the message header) with the w command (`rmail-output-body-to-file`). Often these messages contain the intended file name in the 'Subject' field, so the w command uses the 'Subject' field as the default for the output file name. However, the file name is read using the minibuffer, so you can specify a different name if you wish.

You can also output a message to an Rmail file chosen with a menu. In the Classify menu, choose the Output Rmail File menu item; then choose the Rmail file you want. This outputs the current message to that file, like the o command. The variables `rmail-secondary-file-directory` and `rmail-secondary-file-regexp` specify which files to offer in the menu: the first variable says which directory to find them in; the second says which files in that directory to offer (all those that match the regular expression). If no files match, you cannot select this menu item.

Copying a message with o or C-o gives the original copy of the message the 'filed' attribute, so that 'filed' appears in the mode line when such a message is current.

If you like to keep just a single copy of every mail message, set the variable `rmail-delete-after-output` to t; then the o, C-o and w commands delete the original message after copying it. (You can undelete it afterward if you wish.)

The variable `rmail-output-file-alist` lets you specify intelligent defaults for the output file, based on the contents of the current message. The value should be a list whose elements have this form:

> (*regexp* . *name-exp*)

If there's a match for *regexp* in the current message, then the default file name for output is *name-exp*. If multiple elements match the message, the first matching element decides the default file name. The subexpression *name-exp* may be a string constant giving the file name to use, or more generally it may be any Lisp expression that returns a file name as a string. `rmail-output-file-alist` applies to both o and C-o.

Rmail can automatically save messages from your primary Rmail file (the one that `rmail-file-name` specifies) to other files, based on the value of the variable `rmail-automatic-folder-directives`. This variable is a list of elements ('directives') that say which messages to save where. Each directive is a list consisting of an output file, followed by one or more pairs of a header name and a regular expression. If a message has a header matching the specified regular expression, that message is saved to the given file. If the directive has more than one header entry, all must match. Rmail checks directives when it shows a message from the file `rmail-file-name`, and applies the first that matches (if any). If the output file is `nil`, the message is deleted, not saved. For example, you can use this feature to save messages from a particular address, or with a particular subject, to a dedicated file.

30.8 Labels

Each message can have various *labels* assigned to it as a means of classification. Each label has a name; different names are different labels. Any given label is either present or absent on a particular message. A few label names have standard meanings and are given to messages automatically by Rmail when appropriate; these special labels are called *attributes*. All other labels are assigned only by users.

a *label* RET

> Assign the label *label* to the current message (`rmail-add-label`).

k *label* RET

> Remove the label *label* from the current message (`rmail-kill-label`).

C-M-n *labels* RET

> Move to the next message that has one of the labels *labels* (`rmail-next-labeled-message`).

C-M-p *labels* RET

> Move to the previous message that has one of the labels *labels* (`rmail-previous-labeled-message`).

l *labels* RET
C-M-l *labels* RET

> Make a summary of all messages containing any of the labels *labels* (`rmail-summary-by-labels`).

The a (`rmail-add-label`) and k (`rmail-kill-label`) commands allow you to assign or remove any label on the current message. If the *label* argument is empty, it means to assign or remove the same label most recently assigned or removed.

Once you have given messages labels to classify them as you wish, there are three ways to use the labels: in moving, in summaries, and in sorting.

C-M-n *labels* RET (`rmail-next-labeled-message`) moves to the next message that has one of the labels *labels*. The argument *labels* specifies one or more label names, separated by commas. **C-M-p** (`rmail-previous-labeled-message`) is similar, but moves backwards to previous messages. A numeric argument to either command serves as a repeat count.

The command **C-M-l *labels* RET** (`rmail-summary-by-labels`) displays a summary containing only the messages that have at least one of a specified set of labels. The argument *labels* is one or more label names, separated by commas. See Section 30.11 [Rmail Summary], page 369, for information on summaries.

If the *labels* argument to **C-M-n**, **C-M-p** or **C-M-l** is empty, it means to use the last set of labels specified for any of these commands.

See Section 30.12 [Rmail Sorting], page 372, for information on sorting messages with labels.

30.9 Rmail Attributes

Some labels such as '`deleted`' and '`filed`' have built-in meanings, and Rmail assigns them to messages automatically at appropriate times; these labels are called *attributes*. Here is a list of Rmail attributes:

'`unseen`'   Means the message has never been current. Assigned to messages when they come from an inbox file, and removed when a message is made current. When you start Rmail, it initially shows the first message that has this attribute.

'deleted'   Means the message is deleted. Assigned by deletion commands and removed by undeletion commands (see Section 30.4 [Rmail Deletion], page 361).

'filed'   Means the message has been copied to some other file. Assigned by the o and C-o file output commands (see Section 30.7 [Rmail Output], page 364).

'answered'
             Means you have mailed an answer to the message. Assigned by the r command (rmail-reply). See Section 30.10 [Rmail Reply], page 367.

'forwarded'
             Means you have forwarded the message. Assigned by the f command (rmail-forward). See Section 30.10 [Rmail Reply], page 367.

'edited'   Means you have edited the text of the message within Rmail. See Section 30.15 [Rmail Editing], page 374.

'resent'   Means you have resent the message. Assigned by the command M-x rmail-resend. See Section 30.10 [Rmail Reply], page 367.

'retried'   Means you have retried a failed outgoing message. Assigned by the command M-x rmail-retry-failure. See Section 30.10 [Rmail Reply], page 367.

All other labels are assigned or removed only by users, and have no standard meaning.

30.10 Sending Replies

Rmail has several commands to send outgoing mail. See Chapter 29 [Sending Mail], page 350, for information on using Message mode, including certain features meant to work with Rmail. What this section documents are the special commands of Rmail for entering the mail buffer. Note that the usual keys for sending mail—C-x m, C-x 4 m, and C-x 5 m—also work normally in Rmail mode.

m   Send a message (rmail-mail).

c   Continue editing the already started outgoing message (rmail-continue).

r   Send a reply to the current Rmail message (rmail-reply).

f   Forward the current message to other users (rmail-forward).

C-u f   Resend the current message to other users (rmail-resend).

M-m   Try sending a bounced message a second time (rmail-retry-failure).

The most common reason to send a message while in Rmail is to reply to the message you are reading. To do this, type r (rmail-reply). This displays a mail composition buffer in another window, much like C-x 4 m, but preinitializes the 'Subject', 'To', 'CC', 'In-reply-to' and 'References' header fields based on the message you are replying to. The 'To' field starts out as the address of the person who sent the message you received, and the 'CC' field starts out with all the other recipients of that message.

You can exclude certain recipients from being included automatically in replies, using the variable mail-dont-reply-to-names. Its value should be a regular expression; any recipients that match are excluded from the 'CC' field. They are also excluded from the 'To' field, unless this would leave the field empty. If this variable is `nil`, then the first time you compose a reply it is initialized to a default value that matches your own address.

To omit the 'CC' field completely for a particular reply, enter the reply command with a numeric argument: `C-u r` or `1 r`. This means to reply only to the sender of the original message.

Once the mail composition buffer has been initialized, editing and sending the mail goes as usual (see Chapter 29 [Sending Mail], page 350). You can edit the presupplied header fields if they are not what you want. You can also use commands such as `C-c C-y`, which yanks in the message that you are replying to (see Section 29.4 [Mail Commands], page 353). You can also switch to the Rmail buffer, select a different message there, switch back, and yank the new current message.

Sometimes a message does not reach its destination. Mailers usually send the failed message back to you, enclosed in a *failure message*. The Rmail command `M-m` (`rmail-retry-failure`) prepares to send the same message a second time: it sets up a mail composition buffer with the same text and header fields as before. If you type `C-c C-c` right away, you send the message again exactly the same as the first time. Alternatively, you can edit the text or headers and then send it. The variable `rmail-retry-ignored-headers`, in the same format as `rmail-ignored-headers` (see Section 30.13 [Rmail Display], page 373), controls which headers are stripped from the failed message when retrying it.

Another frequent reason to send mail in Rmail is to *forward* the current message to other users. `f` (`rmail-forward`) makes this easy by preinitializing the mail composition buffer with the current message as the text, and a subject of the form `[from: subject]`, where *from* and *subject* are the sender and subject of the original message. All you have to do is fill in the recipients and send. When you forward a message, recipients get a message which is "from" you, and which has the original message in its contents.

Rmail offers two formats for forwarded messages. The default is to use MIME (see Section 30.13 [Rmail Display], page 373) format. This includes the original message as a separate part. You can use a simpler format if you prefer, by setting the variable `rmail-enable-mime-composing` to `nil`. In this case, Rmail just includes the original message enclosed between two delimiter lines. It also modifies every line that starts with a dash, by inserting '- ' at the start of the line. When you receive a forwarded message in this format, if it contains something besides ordinary text—for example, program source code—you might find it useful to undo that transformation. You can do this by selecting the forwarded message and typing `M-x unforward-rmail-message`. This command extracts the original forwarded message, deleting the inserted '- ' strings, and inserts it into the Rmail file as a separate message immediately following the current one.

Resending is an alternative similar to forwarding; the difference is that resending sends a message that is "from" the original sender, just as it reached you—with a few added header fields ('Resent-From' and 'Resent-To') to indicate that it came via you. To resend a message in Rmail, use `C-u f`. (`f` runs `rmail-forward`, which invokes `rmail-resend` if you provide a numeric argument.)

Use the `m` (`rmail-mail`) command to start editing an outgoing message that is not a reply. It leaves the header fields empty. Its only difference from `C-x 4 m` is that it makes the Rmail buffer accessible for `C-c C-y`, just as `r` does.

The c (`rmail-continue`) command resumes editing the mail composition buffer, to finish editing an outgoing message you were already composing, or to alter a message you have sent.

If you set the variable `rmail-mail-new-frame` to a non-`nil` value, then all the Rmail commands to start sending a message create a new frame to edit it in. This frame is deleted when you send the message.

All the Rmail commands to send a message use the mail-composition method that you have chosen (see Section 29.7 [Mail Methods], page 357).

30.11 Summaries

A *summary* is a buffer containing one line per message to give you an overview of the mail in an Rmail file. Each line shows the message number and date, the sender, the line count, the labels, and the subject. Moving point in the summary buffer selects messages as you move to their summary lines. Almost all Rmail commands are valid in the summary buffer also; when used there, they apply to the message described by the current line of the summary.

A summary buffer applies to a single Rmail file only; if you are editing multiple Rmail files, each one can have its own summary buffer. The summary buffer name is made by appending '`-summary`' to the Rmail buffer's name. Normally only one summary buffer is displayed at a time.

30.11.1 Making Summaries

Here are the commands to create a summary for the current Rmail buffer. Once the Rmail buffer has a summary, changes in the Rmail buffer (such as deleting or expunging messages, and getting new mail) automatically update the summary.

h
C-M-h   Summarize all messages (`rmail-summary`).

l *labels* RET
C-M-l *labels* RET
            Summarize messages that have one or more of the specified labels
            (`rmail-summary-by-labels`).

C-M-r *rcpts* RET
            Summarize messages that match the specified recipients (`rmail-summary-by-recipients`).

C-M-t *topic* RET
            Summarize messages that have a match for the specified regexp *topic* in their
            subjects (`rmail-summary-by-topic`).

C-M-s *regexp* RET
            Summarize messages whose headers match the specified regular expression *regexp* (`rmail-summary-by-regexp`).

C-M-f *senders* RET
            Summarize messages that match the specified senders. (`rmail-summary-by-senders`).

The h or C-M-h (rmail-summary) command fills the summary buffer for the current Rmail buffer with a summary of all the messages in the buffer. It then displays and selects the summary buffer in another window.

C-M-l *labels* RET (rmail-summary-by-labels) makes a partial summary mentioning only the messages that have one or more of the labels *labels*. *labels* should contain label names separated by commas.

C-M-r *rcpts* RET (rmail-summary-by-recipients) makes a partial summary mentioning only the messages that have one or more recipients matching the regular expression *rcpts*. You can use commas to separate multiple regular expressions. These are matched against the 'To', 'From', and 'CC' headers (supply a prefix argument to exclude this header).

C-M-t *topic* RET (rmail-summary-by-topic) makes a partial summary mentioning only the messages whose subjects have a match for the regular expression *topic*. You can use commas to separate multiple regular expressions. With a prefix argument, the match is against the whole message, not just the subject.

C-M-s *regexp* RET (rmail-summary-by-regexp) makes a partial summary that mentions only the messages whose headers (including the date and the subject lines) match the regular expression *regexp*.

C-M-f *senders* RET (rmail-summary-by-senders) makes a partial summary that mentions only the messages whose 'From' fields match the regular expression *senders*. You can use commas to separate multiple regular expressions.

Note that there is only one summary buffer for any Rmail buffer; making any kind of summary discards any previous summary.

The variable rmail-summary-window-size says how many lines to use for the summary window. The variable rmail-summary-line-count-flag controls whether the summary line for a message should include the line count of the message. Setting this option to nil might speed up the generation of summaries.

30.11.2 Editing in Summaries

You can use the Rmail summary buffer to do almost anything you can do in the Rmail buffer itself. In fact, once you have a summary buffer, there's no need to switch back to the Rmail buffer.

You can select and display various messages in the Rmail buffer, from the summary buffer, just by moving point in the summary buffer to different lines. It doesn't matter what Emacs command you use to move point; whichever line point is on at the end of the command, that message is selected in the Rmail buffer.

Almost all Rmail commands work in the summary buffer as well as in the Rmail buffer. Thus, d in the summary buffer deletes the current message, u undeletes, and x expunges. (However, in the summary buffer, a numeric argument to d, C-d and u serves as a repeat count. A negative argument reverses the meaning of d and C-d. Also, if there are no more undeleted messages in the relevant direction, the delete commands go to the first or last message, rather than staying on the current message.) o and C-o output the current message to a FILE; r starts a reply to it; etc. You can scroll the current message while remaining in the summary buffer using SPC and DEL.

M-u (rmail-summary-undelete-many) undeletes all deleted messages in the summary. A prefix argument means to undelete that many of the previous deleted messages.

The Rmail commands to move between messages also work in the summary buffer, but with a twist: they move through the set of messages included in the summary. They also ensure the Rmail buffer appears on the screen (unlike cursor motion commands, which update the contents of the Rmail buffer but don't display it in a window unless it already appears). Here is a list of these commands:

n   Move to next line, skipping lines saying 'deleted', and select its message (`rmail-summary-next-msg`).

p   Move to previous line, skipping lines saying 'deleted', and select its message (`rmail-summary-previous-msg`).

M-n   Move to next line and select its message (`rmail-summary-next-all`).

M-p   Move to previous line and select its message (`rmail-summary-previous-all`).

>   Move to the last line, and select its message (`rmail-summary-last-message`).

<   Move to the first line, and select its message (`rmail-summary-first-message`).

j
RET   Select the message on the current line (ensuring that the Rmail buffer appears on the screen; `rmail-summary-goto-msg`). With argument *n*, select message number *n* and move to its line in the summary buffer; this signals an error if the message is not listed in the summary buffer.

M-s *pattern* RET
            Search through messages for *pattern* starting with the current message; select the message found, and move point in the summary buffer to that message's line (`rmail-summary-search`). A prefix argument acts as a repeat count; a negative argument means search backward (equivalent to `rmail-summary-search-backward`.)

C-M-n *labels* RET
            Move to the next message with at least one of the specified labels (`rmail-summary-next-labeled-message`). *labels* is a comma-separated list of labels. A prefix argument acts as a repeat count.

C-M-p *labels* RET
            Move to the previous message with at least one of the specified labels (`rmail-summary-previous-labeled-message`).

C-c C-n RET
            Move to the next message with the same subject as the current message (`rmail-summary-next-same-subject`). A prefix argument acts as a repeat count.

C-c C-p RET
            Move to the previous message with the same subject as the current message (`rmail-summary-previous-same-subject`).

Deletion, undeletion, and getting new mail, and even selection of a different message all update the summary buffer when you do them in the Rmail buffer. If the variable `rmail-redisplay-summary` is non-`nil`, these actions also bring the summary buffer back onto the screen.

When you are finished using the summary, type Q (`rmail-summary-wipe`) to delete the summary buffer's window. You can also exit Rmail while in the summary: q (`rmail-summary-quit`) deletes the summary window, then exits from Rmail by saving the Rmail file and switching to another buffer. Alternatively, b (`rmail-summary-bury`) simply buries the Rmail summary and buffer.

30.12 Sorting the Rmail File

`C-c C-s C-d`
`M-x rmail-sort-by-date`
> Sort messages of current Rmail buffer by date.

`C-c C-s C-s`
`M-x rmail-sort-by-subject`
> Sort messages of current Rmail buffer by subject.

`C-c C-s C-a`
`M-x rmail-sort-by-author`
> Sort messages of current Rmail buffer by author's name.

`C-c C-s C-r`
`M-x rmail-sort-by-recipient`
> Sort messages of current Rmail buffer by recipient's names.

`C-c C-s C-c`
`M-x rmail-sort-by-correspondent`
> Sort messages of current Rmail buffer by the name of the other correspondent.

`C-c C-s C-l`
`M-x rmail-sort-by-lines`
> Sort messages of current Rmail buffer by number of lines.

`C-c C-s C-k RET labels RET`
`M-x rmail-sort-by-labels RET labels RET`
> Sort messages of current Rmail buffer by labels. The argument *labels* should be a comma-separated list of labels. The order of these labels specifies the order of messages; messages with the first label come first, messages with the second label come second, and so on. Messages that have none of these labels come last.

The Rmail sort commands perform a *stable sort*: if there is no reason to prefer either one of two messages, their order remains unchanged. You can use this to sort by more than one criterion. For example, if you use `rmail-sort-by-date` and then `rmail-sort-by-author`, messages from the same author appear in order by date.

With a prefix argument, all these commands reverse the order of comparison. This means they sort messages from newest to oldest, from biggest to smallest, or in reverse alphabetical order.

The same keys in the summary buffer run similar functions; for example, `C-c C-s C-l` runs `rmail-summary-sort-by-lines`. Note that these commands always sort the whole Rmail buffer, even if the summary is only showing a subset of messages.

Note that you cannot undo a sort, so you may wish to save the Rmail buffer before sorting it.

30.13 Display of Messages

This section describes how Rmail displays mail headers, MIME sections and attachments, URLs, and encrypted messages.

t   Toggle display of complete header (`rmail-toggle-header`).

Before displaying each message for the first time, Rmail reformats its header, hiding uninteresting header fields to reduce clutter. The `t` (`rmail-toggle-header`) command toggles this, switching between showing the reformatted header fields and showing the complete, original header. With a positive prefix argument, the command shows the reformatted header; with a zero or negative prefix argument, it shows the full header. Selecting the message again also reformats it if necessary.

The variable `rmail-ignored-headers` holds a regular expression specifying the header fields to hide; any matching header line will be hidden. The variable `rmail-nonignored-headers` overrides this: any header field matching that regular expression is shown even if it matches `rmail-ignored-headers` too. The variable `rmail-displayed-headers` is an alternative to these two variables; if non-`nil`, this should be a regular expression specifying which headers to display (the default is `nil`).

Rmail highlights certain header fields that are especially interesting—by default, the 'From' and 'Subject' fields. This highlighting uses the `rmail-highlight` face. The variable `rmail-highlighted-headers` holds a regular expression specifying the header fields to highlight; if it matches the beginning of a header field, that whole field is highlighted. To disable this feature, set `rmail-highlighted-headers` to `nil`.

If a message is in MIME (Multipurpose Internet Mail Extensions) format and contains multiple parts (MIME entities), Rmail displays each part with a *tagline*. The tagline summarizes the part's index, size, and content type. Depending on the content type, it may also contain one or more buttons; these perform actions such as saving the part into a file.

RET   Hide or show the MIME part at point (`rmail-mime-toggle-hidden`).

TAB   Move point to the next MIME tagline button. (`rmail-mime-next-item`).

S-TAB   Move point to the previous MIME part (`rmail-mime-previous-item`).

v   Toggle between MIME display and raw message (`rmail-mime`).

Each plain-text MIME part is initially displayed immediately after its tagline, as part of the Rmail buffer, while MIME parts of other types are represented only by their taglines, with their actual contents hidden. In either case, you can toggle a MIME part between its "displayed" and "hidden" states by typing RET anywhere in the part—or anywhere in its tagline (except for buttons for other actions, if there are any). Type RET (or click with the mouse) to activate a tagline button, and TAB to cycle point between tagline buttons.

The `v` (`rmail-mime`) command toggles between the default MIME display described above, and a "raw" display showing the undecoded MIME data. With a prefix argument, this command toggles the display of only an entity at point.

To prevent Rmail from handling MIME decoded messages, change the variable `rmail-enable-mime` to `nil`. When this is the case, the `v` (`rmail-mime`) command instead creates a temporary buffer to display the current MIME message.

If the current message is an encrypted one, use the command `M-x rmail-epa-decrypt` to decrypt it, using the EasyPG library (see Section "EasyPG" in *EasyPG Assistant User's Manual*).

You can highlight and activate URLs in the Rmail buffer using Goto Address mode:

```
(add-hook 'rmail-show-message-hook 'goto-address-mode)
```

Then you can browse these URLs by clicking on them with `Mouse-2` (or `Mouse-1` quickly) or by moving to one and typing `C-c RET`. See Section 31.11.2 [Activating URLs], page 405.

30.14 Rmail and Coding Systems

Rmail automatically decodes messages which contain non-ASCII characters, just as Emacs does with files you visit and with subprocess output. Rmail uses the standard '`charset=charset`' header in the message, if any, to determine how the message was encoded by the sender. It maps *charset* into the corresponding Emacs coding system (see Section 19.5 [Coding Systems], page 183), and uses that coding system to decode message text. If the message header doesn't have the '`charset`' specification, or if *charset* is not recognized, Rmail chooses the coding system with the usual Emacs heuristics and defaults (see Section 19.6 [Recognize Coding], page 185).

Occasionally, a message is decoded incorrectly, either because Emacs guessed the wrong coding system in the absence of the '`charset`' specification, or because the specification was inaccurate. For example, a misconfigured mailer could send a message with a '`charset=iso-8859-1`' header when the message is actually encoded in `koi8-r`. When you see the message text garbled, or some of its characters displayed as hex codes or empty boxes, this may have happened.

You can correct the problem by decoding the message again using the right coding system, if you can figure out or guess which one is right. To do this, invoke the `M-x rmail-redecode-body` command. It reads the name of a coding system, and then redecodes the message using the coding system you specified. If you specified the right coding system, the result should be readable.

When you get new mail in Rmail, each message is translated automatically from the coding system it is written in, as if it were a separate file. This uses the priority list of coding systems that you have specified. If a MIME message specifies a character set, Rmail obeys that specification. For reading and saving Rmail files themselves, Emacs uses the coding system specified by the variable `rmail-file-coding-system`. The default value is `nil`, which means that Rmail files are not translated (they are read and written in the Emacs internal character code).

30.15 Editing Within a Message

Most of the usual Emacs key bindings are available in Rmail mode, though a few, such as `C-M-n` and `C-M-h`, are redefined by Rmail for other purposes. However, the Rmail buffer is normally read only, and most of the letters are redefined as Rmail commands. If you want to edit the text of a message, you must use the Rmail command `e`.

e   Edit the current message as ordinary text.

The `e` command (`rmail-edit-current-message`) switches from Rmail mode into Rmail Edit mode, another major mode which is nearly the same as Text mode. The mode line indicates this change.

In Rmail Edit mode, letters insert themselves as usual and the Rmail commands are not available. You can edit the message body and header fields. When you are finished editing the message, type `C-c C-c` to switch back to Rmail mode. Alternatively, you can return to Rmail mode but cancel any editing that you have done, by typing `C-c C-]`.

Entering Rmail Edit mode runs the hook `text-mode-hook`; then it runs the hook `rmail-edit-mode-hook` (see Section 33.2.2 [Hooks], page 422). Returning to ordinary Rmail mode adds the attribute 'edited' to the message, if you have made any changes in it.

30.16 Digest Messages

A *digest message* is a message which exists to contain and carry several other messages. Digests are used on some mailing lists; all the messages that arrive for the list during a period of time such as one day are put inside a single digest which is then sent to the subscribers. Transmitting the single digest uses less computer time than transmitting the individual messages even though the total size is the same, because of the per-message overhead in network mail transmission.

When you receive a digest message, the most convenient way to read it is to *undigestify* it: to turn it back into many individual messages. Then you can read and delete the individual messages as it suits you. To do this, select the digest message and type the command `M-x undigestify-rmail-message`. This extracts the submessages as separate Rmail messages, and inserts them following the digest. The digest message itself is flagged as deleted.

30.17 Reading Rot13 Messages

Mailing list messages that might offend or annoy some readers are sometimes encoded in a simple code called *rot13*—so named because it rotates the alphabet by 13 letters. This code is not for secrecy, as it provides none; rather, it enables those who wish to to avoid seeing the real text of the message. For example, a review of a film might use rot13 to hide important plot points.

To view a buffer that uses the rot13 code, use the command `M-x rot13-other-window`. This displays the current buffer in another window which applies the code when displaying the text.

30.18 `movemail` program

Rmail uses the `movemail` program to move mail from your inbox to your Rmail file (see Section 30.5 [Rmail Inbox], page 362). When loaded for the first time, Rmail attempts to locate the `movemail` program and determine its version. There are two versions of the `movemail` program: the native one, shipped with GNU Emacs (the "emacs version") and the one included in GNU mailutils (the "mailutils version", see Section "movemail" in

GNU mailutils). They support the same command line syntax and the same basic subset of options. However, the Mailutils version offers additional features.

The Emacs version of `movemail` is able to retrieve mail from the usual Unix mailbox formats and from remote mailboxes using the POP3 protocol.

The Mailutils version is able to handle a wide set of mailbox formats, such as plain Unix mailboxes, `maildir` and `MH` mailboxes, etc. It is able to access remote mailboxes using the POP3 or IMAP4 protocol, and can retrieve mail from them using a TLS encrypted channel. It also accepts mailbox arguments in URL form. The detailed description of mailbox URLs can be found in Section "URL" in *Mailbox URL Formats*. In short, a URL is:

        `proto://[user[:password]@]host-or-file-name`

where square brackets denote optional elements.

proto   Specifies the *mailbox protocol*, or *format* to use. The exact semantics of the
            rest of URL elements depends on the actual value of *proto* (see below).

user   User name to access the remote mailbox.

password   User password to access the remote mailbox.

host-or-file-name
            Hostname of the remote server for remote mailboxes or file name of a local
            mailbox.

Proto can be one of:

mbox   Usual Unix mailbox format. In this case, neither *user* nor *pass* are used,
            and *host-or-file-name* denotes the file name of the mailbox file, e.g.,
            `mbox://var/spool/mail/smith`.

mh   A local mailbox in the MH format. *User* and *pass* are not used. *Host-or-file-
            name* denotes the name of MH folder, e.g., `mh://Mail/inbox`.

maildir   A local mailbox in the maildir format. *User* and *pass* are not used, and *host-or-
            file-name* denotes the name of `maildir` mailbox, e.g., `maildir://mail/inbox`.

file   Any local mailbox format. Its actual format is detected automatically by
            `movemail`.

pop   A remote mailbox to be accessed via POP3 protocol. *User* specifies the remote
            user name to use, *pass* may be used to specify the user password, *host-or-file-
            name* is the name or IP address of the remote mail server to connect to; e.g.,
            `pop://smith:guessme@remote.server.net`.

imap   A remote mailbox to be accessed via IMAP4 protocol. *User* specifies the remote
            user name to use, *pass* may be used to specify the user password, *host-or-file-
            name* is the name or IP address of the remote mail server to connect to; e.g.,
            `imap://smith:guessme@remote.server.net`.

Alternatively, you can specify the file name of the mailbox to use. This is equivalent to specifying the 'file' protocol:

        `/var/spool/mail/user` ≡ `file://var/spool/mail/user`

The variable `rmail-movemail-program` controls which version of `movemail` to use. If that is a string, it specifies the absolute file name of the `movemail` executable. If it is `nil`,

Rmail searches for `movemail` in the directories listed in `rmail-movemail-search-path`, then in `exec-path` (see Section 31.4 [Shell], page 383), then in `exec-directory`.

30.19 Retrieving Mail from Remote Mailboxes

Some sites use a method called POP for accessing users' inbox data instead of storing the data in inbox files. By default, the Emacs `movemail` can work with POP (unless the Emacs `configure` script was run with the option '`--without-pop`').

Similarly, the Mailutils `movemail` by default supports POP, unless it was configured with the '`--disable-pop`' option.

Both versions of `movemail` only work with POP3, not with older versions of POP.

No matter which flavor of `movemail` you use, you can specify a POP inbox by using a POP *URL* (see Section 30.18 [Movemail], page 375). A POP URL is a "file name" of the form '`pop://username@hostname`', where *hostname* is the host name or IP address of the remote mail server and *username* is the user name on that server. Additionally, you may specify the password in the mailbox URL: '`pop://username:password@hostname`'. In this case, *password* takes preference over the one set by `rmail-remote-password` (see below). This is especially useful if you have several remote mailboxes with different passwords.

For backward compatibility, Rmail also supports an alternative way of specifying remote POP mailboxes. Specifying an inbox name in the form '`po:username:hostname`' is equivalent to '`pop://username@hostname`'. If you omit the *:hostname* part, the `MAILHOST` environment variable specifies the machine on which to look for the POP server.

Another method for accessing remote mailboxes is IMAP. This method is supported only by the Mailutils `movemail`. To specify an IMAP mailbox in the inbox list, use the following mailbox URL: '`imap://username[:password]@hostname`'. The *password* part is optional, as described above.

Accessing a remote mailbox may require a password. Rmail uses the following algorithm to retrieve it:

1. If a *password* is present in the mailbox URL (see above), it is used.

2. If the variable `rmail-remote-password-required` is `nil`, Rmail assumes no password is required.

3. If the variable `rmail-remote-password` is non-`nil`, its value is used.

4. Otherwise, Rmail will ask you for the password to use.

If you need to pass additional command-line flags to `movemail`, set the variable `rmail-movemail-flags` a list of the flags you wish to use. Do not use this variable to pass the '`-p`' flag to preserve your inbox contents; use `rmail-preserve-inbox` instead.

The `movemail` program installed at your site may support Kerberos authentication (the Emacs `movemail` does so if Emacs was configured with the option `--with-kerberos` or `--with-kerberos5`). If it is supported, it is used by default whenever you attempt to retrieve POP mail when `rmail-remote-password` and `rmail-remote-password-required` are unset.

Some POP servers store messages in reverse order. If your server does this, and you would rather read your mail in the order in which it was received, you can tell `movemail` to reverse the order of downloaded messages by adding the '`-r`' flag to `rmail-movemail-flags`.

Mailutils `movemail` supports TLS encryption. If you wish to use it, add the '`--tls`' flag to `rmail-movemail-flags`.

30.20 Retrieving Mail from Local Mailboxes in Various Formats

If your incoming mail is stored on a local machine in a format other than Unix mailbox, you will need the Mailutils `movemail` to retrieve it. See Section 30.18 [Movemail], page 375, for the detailed description of `movemail` versions. For example, to access mail from a inbox in `maildir` format located in `/var/spool/mail/in`, you would include the following in the Rmail inbox list:

```
maildir://var/spool/mail/in
```

31 Miscellaneous Commands

This chapter contains several brief topics that do not fit anywhere else: viewing "document files", reading Usenet news, running shell commands and shell subprocesses, using a single shared Emacs for utilities that expect to run an editor as a subprocess, printing hardcopy, sorting text, editing binary files, saving an Emacs session for later resumption, following hyperlinks, emulating other editors, and various diversions and amusements.

31.1 Gnus

Gnus is an Emacs package primarily designed for reading and posting Usenet news. It can also be used to read and respond to messages from a number of other sources—email, remote directories, digests, and so on. Here we introduce Gnus and describe several basic features. For full details on Gnus, type `C-h i` and then select the Gnus manual.

31.1.1 Gnus Buffers

Gnus uses several buffers to display information and to receive commands. The three most commonly-used Gnus buffers are the *group buffer*, the *summary buffer* and the *article buffer*.

The *group buffer* contains a list of article sources (e.g., newsgroups and email inboxes), which are collectively referred to as *groups*. This is the first buffer Gnus displays when it starts up. It normally displays only the groups to which you subscribe and that contain unread articles. From this buffer, you can select a group to read.

The *summary buffer* lists the articles in a single group, showing one article per line. By default, it displays each article's author, subject, and line number. The summary buffer is created when you select a group in the group buffer, and is killed when you exit the group.

From the summary buffer, you can choose an article to view. The article is displayed in the *article buffer*. In normal Gnus usage, you view this buffer but do not select it—all useful Gnus commands can be invoked from the summary buffer. But you can select the article buffer, and execute Gnus commands from it, if you wish.

31.1.2 When Gnus Starts Up

If your system has been set up for reading Usenet news, getting started with Gnus is easy—just type `M-x gnus`.

On starting up, Gnus reads your *news initialization file*: a file named `.newsrc` in your home directory which lists your Usenet newsgroups and subscriptions (this file is not unique to Gnus; it is used by many other newsreader programs). It then tries to contact the system's default news server, which is typically specified by the `NNTPSERVER` environment variable.

If your system does not have a default news server, or if you wish to use Gnus for reading email, then before invoking `M-x gnus` you need to tell Gnus where to get news and/or mail. To do this, customize the variables `gnus-select-method` and/or `gnus-secondary-select-methods`. See the Gnus manual for details.

Once Gnus has started up, it displays the group buffer. By default, the group buffer shows only a small number of *subscribed groups*. Groups with other statuses—*unsubscribed*, *killed*, or *zombie*—are hidden. The first time you start Gnus, any group to which you are not subscribed is made into a killed group; any group that subsequently appears on the news server becomes a zombie group.

To proceed, you must select a group in the group buffer to open the summary buffer for that group; then, select an article in the summary buffer to view its article buffer in a separate window. The following sections explain how to use the group and summary buffers to do this.

To quit Gnus, type `q` in the group buffer. This automatically records your group statuses in the files `.newsrc` and `.newsrc.eld`, so that they take effect in subsequent Gnus sessions.

31.1.3 Using the Gnus Group Buffer

The following commands are available in the Gnus group buffer:

SPC   Switch to the summary buffer for the group on the current line.

l

A s   In the group buffer, list only the groups to which you subscribe and which contain unread articles (this is the default listing).

L

A u   List all subscribed and unsubscribed groups, but not killed or zombie groups.

A k   List killed groups.

A z   List zombie groups.

u   Toggle the subscription status of the group on the current line (i.e., turn a subscribed group into an unsubscribed group, or vice versa). Invoking this on a killed or zombie group turns it into an unsubscribed group.

C-k   Kill the group on the current line. Killed groups are not recorded in the `.newsrc` file, and they are not shown in the `l` or `L` listings.

DEL   Move point to the previous group containing unread articles.

n   Move point to the next unread group.

p   Move point to the previous unread group.

q   Update your Gnus settings, and quit Gnus.

31.1.4 Using the Gnus Summary Buffer

The following commands are available in the Gnus summary buffer:

SPC   If there is no article selected, select the article on the current line and display its article buffer. Otherwise, try scrolling the selected article buffer in its window; on reaching the end of the buffer, select the next unread article.

            Thus, you can read through all articles by repeatedly typing SPC.

DEL   Scroll the text of the article backwards.

n   Select the next unread article.

p   Select the previous unread article.

s   Do an incremental search on the selected article buffer, as if you switched to the buffer and typed `C-s` (see Section 12.1 [Incremental Search], page 90).

M-s *regexp* RET
            Search forward for articles containing a match for *regexp*.

q   Exit the summary buffer and return to the group buffer.

31.2 Document Viewing

DocView mode is a major mode for viewing DVI, PostScript (PS), PDF, OpenDocument, and Microsoft Office documents. It provides features such as slicing, zooming, and searching inside documents. It works by converting the document to a set of images using the gs (GhostScript) or mudraw/pdfdraw (MuPDF) commands and other external tools[1], and displaying those images.

When you visit a document file that can be displayed with DocView mode, Emacs automatically uses DocView mode[2]. As an exception, when you visit a PostScript file, Emacs switches to PS mode, a major mode for editing PostScript files as text; however, it also enables DocView minor mode, so you can type C-c C-c to view the document with DocView. In either DocView mode or DocView minor mode, repeating C-c C-c (doc-view-toggle-display) toggles between DocView and the underlying file contents.

When you visit a file which would normally be handled by DocView mode but some requirement is not met (e.g., you operate in a terminal frame or emacs has no PNG support), you are queried if you want to view the document's contents as plain text. If you confirm, the buffer is put in text mode and DocView minor mode is activated. Thus, by typing C-c C-c you switch to the fallback mode. With another C-c C-c you return to DocView mode. The plain text contents can also be displayed from within DocView mode by typing C-c C-t (doc-view-open-text).

You can explicitly enable DocView mode with the command M-x doc-view-mode. You can toggle DocView minor mode with M-x doc-view-minor-mode.

When DocView mode starts, it displays a welcome screen and begins formatting the file, page by page. It displays the first page once that has been formatted.

To kill the DocView buffer, type k (doc-view-kill-proc-and-buffer). To bury it, type q (quit-window).

31.2.1 DocView Navigation

In DocView mode, you can scroll the current page using the usual Emacs movement keys: C-p, C-n, C-b, C-f, and the arrow keys.

By default, the line-motion keys C-p and C-n stop scrolling at the beginning and end of the current page, respectively. However, if you change the variable doc-view-continuous to a non-nil value, then C-p displays the previous page if you are already at the beginning of the current page, and C-n displays the next page if you are at the end of the current page.

You can also display the next page by typing n, next or C-x] (doc-view-next-page). To display the previous page, type p, prior or C-x [(doc-view-previous-page).

SPC (doc-view-scroll-up-or-next-page) is a convenient way to advance through the document. It scrolls within the current page or advances to the next. DEL moves backwards in a similar way (doc-view-scroll-down-or-previous-page).

---

[1] For PostScript files, GhostScript is a hard requirement. For DVI files, dvipdf or dvipdfm is needed. For OpenDocument and Microsoft Office documents, the unoconv tool is needed.

[2] The needed external tools for the document type must be available, and Emacs must be running in a graphical frame and have PNG image support. If any of these requirements is not fulfilled, Emacs falls back to another major mode.

To go to the first page, type M-< (doc-view-first-page); to go to the last one, type M-> (doc-view-last-page). To jump to a page by its number, type M-g M-g or M-g g (doc-view-goto-page).

You can enlarge or shrink the document with + (doc-view-enlarge) and - (doc-view-shrink). These commands work by reconverting the document at the new size. To specify the default size for DocView, customize the variable doc-view-resolution.

31.2.2 DocView Searching

In DocView mode, you can search the file's text for a regular expression (see Section 12.6 [Regexps], page 97). The interface for searching is inspired by isearch (see Section 12.1 [Incremental Search], page 90).

To begin a search, type C-s (doc-view-search) or C-r (doc-view-search-backward). This reads a regular expression using a minibuffer, then echoes the number of matches found within the document. You can move forward and back among the matches by typing C-s and C-r. DocView mode has no way to show the match inside the page image; instead, it displays a tooltip (at the mouse position) listing all matching lines in the current page. To force display of this tooltip, type C-t (doc-view-show-tooltip).

To start a new search, use the search command with a prefix argument; i.e., C-u C-s for a forward search or C-u C-r for a backward search.

31.2.3 DocView Slicing

Documents often have wide margins for printing. They are annoying when reading the document on the screen, because they use up screen space and can cause inconvenient scrolling.

With DocView you can hide these margins by selecting a *slice* of pages to display. A slice is a rectangle within the page area; once you specify a slice in DocView, it applies to whichever page you look at.

To specify the slice numerically, type s s (doc-view-set-slice); then enter the top left pixel position and the slice's width and height.

A more convenient graphical way to specify the slice is with s m (doc-view-set-slice-using-mouse), where you use the mouse to select the slice. Simply press and hold the left mouse button at the upper-left corner of the region you want to have in the slice, then move the mouse pointer to the lower-right corner and release the button.

The most convenient way is to set the optimal slice by using BoundingBox information automatically determined from the document by typing s b (doc-view-set-slice-from-bounding-box).

To cancel the selected slice, type s r (doc-view-reset-slice). Then DocView shows the entire page including its entire margins.

31.2.4 DocView Conversion

For efficiency, DocView caches the images produced by gs. The name of this directory is given by the variable doc-view-cache-directory. You can clear the cache directory by typing M-x doc-view-clear-cache.

To force reconversion of the currently viewed document, type r or g (revert-buffer). To kill the converter process associated with the current buffer, type K (doc-view-kill-proc). The command k (doc-view-kill-proc-and-buffer) kills the converter process and the DocView buffer.

31.3 Web Browsing with EWW

EWW, the Emacs Web Wowser, is a web browser package for Emacs. It allows browsing URLs within an Emacs buffer. The command M-x eww will open a URL or search the web. You can open a file using the command M-x eww-open-file. You can use EWW as the web browser for browse-url, see Section 31.11.1 [Browse-URL], page 405. For full details, see *The Emacs Web Wowser Manual*.

31.4 Running Shell Commands from Emacs

Emacs has commands for passing single command lines to shell subprocesses, and for running a shell interactively with input and output to an Emacs buffer, and for running a shell in a terminal emulator window.

M-! *cmd* RET

> Run the shell command *cmd* and display the output (shell-command).

M-| *cmd* RET

> Run the shell command *cmd* with region contents as input; optionally replace the region with the output (shell-command-on-region).

M-& *cmd* RET

> Run the shell command *cmd* asynchronously, and display the output (async-shell-command).

M-x shell   Run a subshell with input and output through an Emacs buffer. You can then give commands interactively.

M-x term   Run a subshell with input and output through an Emacs buffer. You can then give commands interactively. Full terminal emulation is available.

Whenever you specify a relative file name for an executable program (either in the *cmd* argument to one of the above commands, or in other contexts), Emacs searches for the program in the directories specified by the variable exec-path. The value of this variable must be a list of directory names; the default value is initialized from the environment variable PATH when Emacs is started (see Section C.4.1 [General Variables], page 483).

M-x eshell invokes a shell implemented entirely in Emacs. It is documented in its own manual. See the Eshell Info manual, which is distributed with Emacs.

31.4.1 Single Shell Commands

M-! (shell-command) reads a line of text using the minibuffer and executes it as a shell command, in a subshell made just for that command. Standard input for the command comes from the null device. If the shell command produces any output, the output appears either in the echo area (if it is short), or in an Emacs buffer named *Shell Command Output*, displayed in another window (if the output is long).

For instance, one way to decompress a file named `foo.gz` is to type `M-!` `gunzip foo.gz` `RET`. That shell command normally creates the file `foo` and produces no terminal output.

A numeric argument to `shell-command`, e.g., `M-1 M-!`, causes it to insert terminal output into the current buffer instead of a separate buffer. It puts point before the output, and sets the mark after the output. For instance, `M-1 M-!` `gunzip < foo.gz` `RET` would insert the uncompressed form of the file `foo.gz` into the current buffer.

Provided the specified shell command does not end with '&', it runs *synchronously*, and you must wait for it to exit before continuing to use Emacs. To stop waiting, type `C-g` to quit; this sends a `SIGINT` signal to terminate the shell command (this is the same signal that `C-c` normally generates in the shell). Emacs then waits until the command actually terminates. If the shell command doesn't stop (because it ignores the `SIGINT` signal), type `C-g` again; this sends the command a `SIGKILL` signal, which is impossible to ignore.

A shell command that ends in '&' is executed *asynchronously*, and you can continue to use Emacs as it runs. You can also type `M-&` (`async-shell-command`) to execute a shell command asynchronously; this is exactly like calling `M-!` with a trailing '&', except that you do not need the '&'. The default output buffer for asynchronous shell commands is named '`*Async Shell Command*`'. Emacs inserts the output into this buffer as it comes in, whether or not the buffer is visible in a window.

If you want to run more than one asynchronous shell command at the same time, they could end up competing for the output buffer. The option `async-shell-command-buffer` specifies what to do about this; e.g., whether to rename the pre-existing output buffer, or to use a different buffer for the new command. Consult the variable's documentation for more possibilities.

`M-|` (`shell-command-on-region`) is like `M-!`, but passes the contents of the region as the standard input to the shell command, instead of no input. With a numeric argument, it deletes the old region and replaces it with the output from the shell command.

For example, you can use `M-|` with the `gpg` program to see what keys are in the buffer. If the buffer contains a GnuPG key, type `C-x h M-|` `gpg` `RET` to feed the entire buffer contents to `gpg`. This will output the list of keys to the `*Shell Command Output*` buffer.

The above commands use the shell specified by the variable `shell-file-name`. Its default value is determined by the `SHELL` environment variable when Emacs is started. If the file name is relative, Emacs searches the directories listed in `exec-path` (see Section 31.4 [Shell], page 383).

To specify a coding system for `M-!` or `M-|`, use the command `C-x RET c` immediately beforehand. See Section 19.10 [Communication Coding], page 189.

By default, error output is intermixed with the regular output in the output buffer. But if you change the value of the variable `shell-command-default-error-buffer` to a string, error output is inserted into a buffer of that name.

31.4.2 Interactive Subshell

To run a subshell interactively, type `M-x shell`. This creates (or reuses) a buffer named `*shell*`, and runs a shell subprocess with input coming from and output going to that buffer. That is to say, any terminal output from the subshell goes into the buffer, advancing point, and any terminal input for the subshell comes from text in the buffer. To give input to the subshell, go to the end of the buffer and type the input, terminated by `RET`.

While the subshell is waiting or running a command, you can switch windows or buffers and perform other editing in Emacs. Emacs inserts the output from the subshell into the Shell buffer whenever it has time to process it (e.g., while waiting for keyboard input).

In the Shell buffer, prompts are displayed with the face `comint-highlight-prompt`, and submitted input lines are displayed with the face `comint-highlight-input`. This makes it easier to distinguish input lines from the shell output. See Section 11.8 [Faces], page 74.

To make multiple subshells, invoke `M-x shell` with a prefix argument (e.g., `C-u M-x shell`). Then the command will read a buffer name, and create (or reuse) a subshell in that buffer. You can also rename the `*shell*` buffer using `M-x rename-uniquely`, then create a new `*shell*` buffer using plain `M-x shell`. Subshells in different buffers run independently and in parallel.

To specify the shell file name used by `M-x shell`, customize the variable `explicit-shell-file-name`. If this is `nil` (the default), Emacs uses the environment variable `ESHELL` if it exists. Otherwise, it usually uses the variable `shell-file-name` (see Section 31.4.1 [Single Shell], page 383); but if the default directory is remote (see Section 15.13 [Remote Files], page 142), it prompts you for the shell file name.

Emacs sends the new shell the contents of the file `~/.emacs_shellname` as input, if it exists, where *shellname* is the name of the file that the shell was loaded from. For example, if you use bash, the file sent to it is `~/.emacs_bash`. If this file is not found, Emacs tries with `~/.emacs.d/init_shellname.sh`.

To specify a coding system for the shell, you can use the command `C-x RET c` immediately before `M-x shell`. You can also change the coding system for a running subshell by typing `C-x RET p` in the shell buffer. See Section 19.10 [Communication Coding], page 189.

Emacs sets the environment variable `INSIDE_EMACS` in the subshell to '*version*,comint', where *version* is the Emacs version (e.g., '24.1'). Programs can check this variable to determine whether they are running inside an Emacs subshell. (It also sets the `EMACS` environment variable to `t`, if that environment variable is not already defined. However, this environment variable is deprecated; programs that use it should switch to using `INSIDE_EMACS` instead.)

31.4.3 Shell Mode

The major mode for Shell buffers is Shell mode. Many of its special commands are bound to the `C-c` prefix, and resemble the usual editing and job control characters present in ordinary shells, except that you must type `C-c` first. Here is a list of Shell mode commands:

RET   Send the current line as input to the subshell (`comint-send-input`). Any shell prompt at the beginning of the line is omitted (see Section 31.4.4 [Shell Prompts], page 387). If point is at the end of buffer, this is like submitting the command line in an ordinary interactive shell. However, you can also invoke RET elsewhere in the shell buffer to submit the current line as input.

TAB   Complete the command name or file name before point in the shell buffer (`completion-at-point`). This uses the usual Emacs completion rules (see Section 5.4 [Completion], page 28), with the completion alternatives being file names, environment variable names, the shell command history, and history references (see Section 31.4.5.3 [History References], page 390). For options controlling the completion, see Section 31.4.7 [Shell Options], page 390.

`M-?`	Display temporarily a list of the possible completions of the file name before point (`comint-dynamic-list-filename-completions`).
`C-d`	Either delete a character or send EOF (`comint-delchar-or-maybe-eof`). Typed at the end of the shell buffer, this sends EOF to the subshell. Typed at any other position in the buffer, this deletes a character as usual.
`C-c C-a`	Move to the beginning of the line, but after the prompt if any (`comint-bol-or-process-mark`). If you repeat this command twice in a row, the second time it moves back to the process mark, which is the beginning of the input that you have not yet sent to the subshell. (Normally that is the same place—the end of the prompt on this line—but after `C-c SPC` the process mark may be in a previous line.)
`C-c SPC`	Accumulate multiple lines of input, then send them together. This command inserts a newline before point, but does not send the preceding text as input to the subshell—at least, not yet. Both lines, the one before this newline and the one after, will be sent together (along with the newline that separates them), when you type `RET`.
`C-c C-u`	Kill all text pending at end of buffer to be sent as input (`comint-kill-input`). If point is not at end of buffer, this only kills the part of this text that precedes point.
`C-c C-w`	Kill a word before point (`backward-kill-word`).
`C-c C-c`	Interrupt the shell or its current subjob if any (`comint-interrupt-subjob`). This command also kills any shell input pending in the shell buffer and not yet sent.
`C-c C-z`	Stop the shell or its current subjob if any (`comint-stop-subjob`). This command also kills any shell input pending in the shell buffer and not yet sent.
`C-c C-\`	Send quit signal to the shell or its current subjob if any (`comint-quit-subjob`). This command also kills any shell input pending in the shell buffer and not yet sent.
`C-c C-o`	Delete the last batch of output from a shell command (`comint-delete-output`). This is useful if a shell command spews out lots of output that just gets in the way.
`C-c C-s`	Write the last batch of output from a shell command to a file (`comint-write-output`). With a prefix argument, the file is appended to instead. Any prompt at the end of the output is not written.
`C-c C-r` `C-M-l`	Scroll to display the beginning of the last batch of output at the top of the window; also move the cursor there (`comint-show-output`).
`C-c C-e`	Scroll to put the end of the buffer at the bottom of the window (`comint-show-maximum-output`).
`C-c C-f`	Move forward across one shell command, but not beyond the current line (`shell-forward-command`). The variable `shell-command-regexp` specifies how to recognize the end of a command.

C-c C-b   Move backward across one shell command, but not beyond the current line (`shell-backward-command`).

M-x dirs   Ask the shell for its working directory, and update the Shell buffer's default directory. See Section 31.4.6 [Directory Tracking], page 390.

M-x send-invisible RET *text* RET

Send *text* as input to the shell, after reading it without echoing. This is useful when a shell command runs a program that asks for a password.

Please note that Emacs will not echo passwords by default. If you really want them to be echoed, evaluate (see Section 24.9 [Lisp Eval], page 278) the following Lisp expression:

```
(remove-hook 'comint-output-filter-functions
             'comint-watch-for-password-prompt)
```

M-x comint-continue-subjob

Continue the shell process. This is useful if you accidentally suspend the shell process.[3]

M-x comint-strip-ctrl-m

Discard all control-M characters from the current group of shell output. The most convenient way to use this command is to make it run automatically when you get output from the subshell. To do that, evaluate this Lisp expression:

```
(add-hook 'comint-output-filter-functions
          'comint-strip-ctrl-m)
```

M-x comint-truncate-buffer

This command truncates the shell buffer to a certain maximum number of lines, specified by the variable `comint-buffer-maximum-size`. Here's how to do this automatically each time you get output from the subshell:

```
(add-hook 'comint-output-filter-functions
          'comint-truncate-buffer)
```

Shell mode is a derivative of Comint mode, a general-purpose mode for communicating with interactive subprocesses. Most of the features of Shell mode actually come from Comint mode, as you can see from the command names listed above. The special features of Shell mode include the directory tracking feature, and a few user commands.

Other Emacs features that use variants of Comint mode include GUD (see Section 24.6 [Debuggers], page 266) and M-x run-lisp (see Section 24.11 [External Lisp], page 279).

You can use M-x comint-run to execute any program of your choice in a subprocess using unmodified Comint mode—without the specializations of Shell mode.

31.4.4 Shell Prompts

A prompt is text output by a program to show that it is ready to accept new user input. Normally, Comint mode (and thus Shell mode) automatically figures out part of the buffer is

---

[3] You should not suspend the shell process. Suspending a subjob of the shell is a completely different matter—that is normal practice, but you must use the shell to continue the subjob; this command won't do it.

a prompt, based on the output of the subprocess. (Specifically, it assumes that any received output line which doesn't end with a newline is a prompt.)

Comint mode divides the buffer into two types of *fields*: input fields (where user input is typed) and output fields (everywhere else). Prompts are part of the output fields. Most Emacs motion commands do not cross field boundaries, unless they move over multiple lines. For instance, when point is in the input field on a shell command line, C-a puts point at the beginning of the input field, after the prompt. Internally, the fields are implemented using the `field` text property (see Section "Text Properties" in *the Emacs Lisp Reference Manual*).

If you change the variable `comint-use-prompt-regexp` to a non-`nil` value, then Comint mode recognize prompts using a regular expression (see Section 12.6 [Regexps], page 97). In Shell mode, the regular expression is specified by the variable `shell-prompt-pattern`. The default value of `comint-use-prompt-regexp` is `nil`, because this method for recognizing prompts is unreliable, but you may want to set it to a non-`nil` value in unusual circumstances. In that case, Emacs does not divide the Comint buffer into fields, so the general motion commands behave as they normally do in buffers without special text properties. However, you can use the paragraph motion commands to conveniently navigate the buffer (see Section 22.3 [Paragraphs], page 210); in Shell mode, Emacs uses `shell-prompt-pattern` as paragraph boundaries.

31.4.5 Shell Command History

Shell buffers support three ways of repeating earlier commands. You can use keys like those used for the minibuffer history; these work much as they do in the minibuffer, inserting text from prior commands while point remains always at the end of the buffer. You can move through the buffer to previous inputs in their original place, then resubmit them or copy them to the end. Or you can use a '!'-style history reference.

31.4.5.1 Shell History Ring

M-p
C-UP   Fetch the next earlier old shell command.

M-n
C-DOWN   Fetch the next later old shell command.

M-r   Begin an incremental regexp search of old shell commands.

C-c C-x   Fetch the next subsequent command from the history.

C-c .   Fetch one argument from an old shell command.

C-c C-l   Display the buffer's history of shell commands in another window (`comint-dynamic-list-input-ring`).

Shell buffers provide a history of previously entered shell commands. To reuse shell commands from the history, use the editing commands M-p, M-n, M-r and M-s. These work just like the minibuffer history commands (see Section 5.5 [Minibuffer History], page 32), except that they operate within the Shell buffer rather than the minibuffer.

M-p fetches an earlier shell command to the end of the shell buffer. Successive use of M-p fetches successively earlier shell commands, each replacing any text that was already present as potential shell input. M-n does likewise except that it finds successively more recent shell commands from the buffer. C-UP works like M-p, and C-DOWN like M-n.

The history search command M-r begins an incremental regular expression search of previous shell commands. After typing M-r, start typing the desired string or regular expression; the last matching shell command will be displayed in the current line. Incremental search commands have their usual effects—for instance, C-s and C-r search forward and backward for the next match (see Section 12.1 [Incremental Search], page 90). When you find the desired input, type RET to terminate the search. This puts the input in the command line. Any partial input you were composing before navigating the history list is restored when you go to the beginning or end of the history ring.

Often it is useful to reexecute several successive shell commands that were previously executed in sequence. To do this, first find and reexecute the first command of the sequence. Then type C-c C-x; that will fetch the following command—the one that follows the command you just repeated. Then type RET to reexecute this command. You can reexecute several successive commands by typing C-c C-x RET over and over.

The command C-c . (comint-input-previous-argument) copies an individual argument from a previous command, like ESC . in Bash. The simplest use copies the last argument from the previous shell command. With a prefix argument n, it copies the nth argument instead. Repeating C-c . copies from an earlier shell command instead, always using the same value of n (don't give a prefix argument when you repeat the C-c . command).

These commands get the text of previous shell commands from a special history list, not from the shell buffer itself. Thus, editing the shell buffer, or even killing large parts of it, does not affect the history that these commands access.

Some shells store their command histories in files so that you can refer to commands from previous shell sessions. Emacs reads the command history file for your chosen shell, to initialize its own command history. The file name is ~/.bash_history for bash, ~/.sh_history for ksh, and ~/.history for other shells.

31.4.5.2 Shell History Copying

C-c C-p   Move point to the previous prompt (comint-previous-prompt).

C-c C-n   Move point to the following prompt (comint-next-prompt).

C-c RET   Copy the input command at point, inserting the copy at the end of the buffer (comint-copy-old-input). This is useful if you move point back to a previous command. After you copy the command, you can submit the copy as input with RET. If you wish, you can edit the copy before resubmitting it. If you use this command on an output line, it copies that line to the end of the buffer.

Mouse-2   If comint-use-prompt-regexp is nil (the default), copy the old input command that you click on, inserting the copy at the end of the buffer (comint-insert-input). If comint-use-prompt-regexp is non-nil, or if the click is not over old input, just yank as usual.

Moving to a previous input and then copying it with C-c RET or Mouse-2 produces the same results—the same buffer contents—that you would get by using M-p enough times to fetch that previous input from the history list. However, C-c RET copies the text from the buffer, which can be different from what is in the history list if you edit the input text in the buffer after it has been sent.

31.4.5.3 Shell History References

Various shells including csh and bash support *history references* that begin with '!' and '^'. Shell mode recognizes these constructs, and can perform the history substitution for you.

If you insert a history reference and type TAB, this searches the input history for a matching command, performs substitution if necessary, and places the result in the buffer in place of the history reference. For example, you can fetch the most recent command beginning with 'mv' with ! m v TAB. You can edit the command if you wish, and then resubmit the command to the shell by typing RET.

Shell mode can optionally expand history references in the buffer when you send them to the shell. To request this, set the variable comint-input-autoexpand to input. You can make SPC perform history expansion by binding SPC to the command comint-magic-space.

Shell mode recognizes history references when they follow a prompt. See Section 31.4.4 [Shell Prompts], page 387, for how Shell mode recognizes prompts.

31.4.6 Directory Tracking

Shell mode keeps track of 'cd', 'pushd' and 'popd' commands given to the subshell, in order to keep the Shell buffer's default directory (see Section 15.1 [File Names], page 122) the same as the shell's working directory. It recognizes these commands by examining lines of input that you send.

If you use aliases for these commands, you can tell Emacs to recognize them also, by setting the variables shell-pushd-regexp, shell-popd-regexp, and shell-cd-regexp to the appropriate regular expressions (see Section 12.6 [Regexps], page 97). For example, if shell-pushd-regexp matches the beginning of a shell command line, that line is regarded as a pushd command. These commands are recognized only at the beginning of a shell command line.

If Emacs gets confused about changes in the working directory of the subshell, type M-x dirs. This command asks the shell for its working directory and updates the default directory accordingly. It works for shells that support the most common command syntax, but may not work for unusual shells.

You can also use Dirtrack mode, a buffer-local minor mode that implements an alternative method of tracking the shell's working directory. To use this method, your shell prompt must contain the working directory at all times, and you must supply a regular expression for recognizing which part of the prompt contains the working directory; see the documentation of the variable dirtrack-list for details. To use Dirtrack mode, type M-x dirtrack-mode in the Shell buffer, or add dirtrack-mode to shell-mode-hook (see Section 33.2.2 [Hooks], page 422).

31.4.7 Shell Mode Options

If the variable comint-scroll-to-bottom-on-input is non-nil, insertion and yank commands scroll the selected window to the bottom before inserting. The default is nil.

If comint-scroll-show-maximum-output is non-nil, then arrival of output when point is at the end tries to scroll the last line of text to the bottom line of the window, showing as much useful text as possible. (This mimics the scrolling behavior of most terminals.) The default is `t`.

By setting `comint-move-point-for-output`, you can opt for having point jump to the end of the buffer whenever output arrives—no matter where in the buffer point was before. If the value is `this`, point jumps in the selected window. If the value is `all`, point jumps in each window that shows the Comint buffer. If the value is `other`, point jumps in all nonselected windows that show the current buffer. The default value is `nil`, which means point does not jump to the end.

If you set `comint-prompt-read-only`, the prompts in the Comint buffer are read-only.

The variable `comint-input-ignoredups` controls whether successive identical inputs are stored in the input history. A non-`nil` value means to omit an input that is the same as the previous input. The default is `nil`, which means to store each input even if it is equal to the previous input.

Three variables customize file name completion. The variable `comint-completion-addsuffix` controls whether completion inserts a space or a slash to indicate a fully completed file or directory name (non-`nil` means do insert a space or slash). `comint-completion-recexact`, if non-`nil`, directs `TAB` to choose the shortest possible completion if the usual Emacs completion algorithm cannot add even a single character. `comint-completion-autolist`, if non-`nil`, says to list all the possible completions whenever completion is not exact.

Command completion normally considers only executable files. If you set `shell-completion-execonly` to `nil`, it considers nonexecutable files as well.

The variable `shell-completion-fignore` specifies a list of file name extensions to ignore in Shell mode completion. The default setting is `nil`, but some users prefer `("~" "#" "%")` to ignore file names ending in '`~`', '`#`' or '`%`'. Other related Comint modes use the variable `comint-completion-fignore` instead.

Some implementation details of the shell command completion may also be found in the lisp documentation of the `shell-dynamic-complete-command` function.

You can configure the behavior of '`pushd`'. Variables control whether '`pushd`' behaves like '`cd`' if no argument is given (`shell-pushd-tohome`), pop rather than rotate with a numeric argument (`shell-pushd-dextract`), and only add directories to the directory stack if they are not already on it (`shell-pushd-dunique`). The values you choose should match the underlying shell, of course.

31.4.8 Emacs Terminal Emulator

To run a subshell in a text terminal emulator, use `M-x term`. This creates (or reuses) a buffer named `*terminal*`, and runs a subshell with input coming from your keyboard, and output going to that buffer.

The terminal emulator uses Term mode, which has two input modes. In *line mode*, Term basically acts like Shell mode (see Section 31.4.3 [Shell Mode], page 385). In *char mode*, each character is sent directly to the subshell, as terminal input; the sole exception is the terminal escape character, which by default is `C-c` (see Section 31.4.9 [Term Mode], page 392). Any echoing of your input is the responsibility of the subshell; any terminal output from the subshell goes into the buffer, advancing point.

Some programs (such as Emacs itself) need to control the appearance of the terminal screen in detail. They do this by emitting special control codes. Term mode recognizes and handles ANSI-standard VT100-style escape sequences, which are accepted by most modern terminals, including `xterm`. (Hence, you can actually run Emacs inside an Emacs Term window.)

The `term` face specifies the default appearance of text in the terminal emulator (the default is the same appearance as the `default` face). When terminal control codes are used to change the appearance of text, these are represented in the terminal emulator by the faces `term-color-black`, `term-color-red`, `term-color-green`, `term-color-yellow` `term-color-blue`, `term-color-magenta`, `term-color-cyan`, `term-color-white`, `term-color-underline`, and `term-color-bold`. See Section 11.8 [Faces], page 74.

You can also Term mode to communicate with a device connected to a serial port. See Section 31.4.11 [Serial Terminal], page 393.

The file name used to load the subshell is determined the same way as for Shell mode. To make multiple terminal emulators, rename the buffer `*terminal*` to something different using `M-x rename-uniquely`, just as with Shell mode.

Unlike Shell mode, Term mode does not track the current directory by examining your input. But some shells can tell Term what the current directory is. This is done automatically by `bash` version 1.15 and later.

31.4.9 Term Mode

The terminal emulator uses Term mode, which has two input modes. In line mode, Term basically acts like Shell mode (see Section 31.4.3 [Shell Mode], page 385). In char mode, each character is sent directly to the subshell, except for the Term escape character, normally `C-c`.

To switch between line and char mode, use these commands:

`C-c C-j` Switch to line mode (`term-line-mode`). Do nothing if already in line mode.

`C-c C-k` Switch to char mode (`term-char-mode`). Do nothing if already in char mode.

The following commands are only available in char mode:

`C-c C-c` Send a literal `C-c` to the sub-shell.

`C-c char` This is equivalent to `C-x char` in normal Emacs. For example, `C-c o` invokes the global binding of `C-x o`, which is normally 'other-window'.

Term mode has a page-at-a-time feature. When enabled, it makes output pause at the end of each screenful:

`C-c C-q` Toggle the page-at-a-time feature. This command works in both line and char modes. When the feature is enabled, the mode-line displays the word 'page', and each time Term receives more than a screenful of output, it pauses and displays '**MORE**' in the mode-line. Type SPC to display the next screenful of output, or ? to see your other options. The interface is similar to the `more` program.

31.4.10 Remote Host Shell

You can login to a remote computer, using whatever commands you would from a regular terminal (e.g., using the `telnet` or `rlogin` commands), from a Term window.

A program that asks you for a password will normally suppress echoing of the password, so the password will not show up in the buffer. This will happen just as if you were using a real terminal, if the buffer is in char mode. If it is in line mode, the password is temporarily visible, but will be erased when you hit return. (This happens automatically; there is no special password processing.)

When you log in to a different machine, you need to specify the type of terminal you're using, by setting the `TERM` environment variable in the environment for the remote login command. (If you use bash, you do that by writing the variable assignment before the remote login command, without a separating comma.) Terminal types 'ansi' or 'vt100' will work on most systems.

31.4.11 Serial Terminal

If you have a device connected to a serial port of your computer, you can communicate with it by typing M-x `serial-term`. This command asks for a serial port name and speed, and switches to a new Term mode buffer. Emacs communicates with the serial device through this buffer just like it does with a terminal in ordinary Term mode.

The speed of the serial port is measured in bits per second. The most common speed is 9600 bits per second. You can change the speed interactively by clicking on the mode line.

A serial port can be configured even more by clicking on "8N1" in the mode line. By default, a serial port is configured as "8N1", which means that each byte consists of 8 data bits, No parity check bit, and 1 stopbit.

If the speed or the configuration is wrong, you cannot communicate with your device and will probably only see garbage output in the window.

31.5 Using Emacs as a Server

Various programs can invoke your choice of editor to edit a particular piece of text. For instance, version control programs invoke an editor to enter version control logs (see Section 25.1 [Version Control], page 281), and the Unix `mail` utility invokes an editor to enter a message to send. By convention, your choice of editor is specified by the environment variable `EDITOR`. If you set `EDITOR` to 'emacs', Emacs would be invoked, but in an inconvenient way—by starting a new Emacs process. This is inconvenient because the new Emacs process doesn't share buffers, a command history, or other kinds of information with any existing Emacs process.

You can solve this problem by setting up Emacs as an *edit server*, so that it "listens" for external edit requests and acts accordingly. There are two ways to start an Emacs server:

- Run the command `server-start` in an existing Emacs process: either type M-x `server-start`, or put the expression (`server-start`) in your init file (see Section 33.4 [Init File], page 437). The existing Emacs process is the server; when you exit Emacs, the server dies with the Emacs process.

- Run Emacs as a *daemon*, using the '`--daemon`' command-line option. See Section C.2 [Initial Options], page 480. When Emacs is started this way, it calls `server-start` after initialization, and returns control to the calling terminal instead of opening an initial frame; it then waits in the background, listening for edit requests.

Either way, once an Emacs server is started, you can use a shell command called `emacsclient` to connect to the Emacs process and tell it to visit a file. You can then set the `EDITOR` environment variable to 'emacsclient', so that external programs will use the existing Emacs process for editing.[4]

You can run multiple Emacs servers on the same machine by giving each one a unique "server name", using the variable `server-name`. For example, `M-x set-variable RET server-name RET foo RET` sets the server name to 'foo'. The `emacsclient` program can specify a server by name, using the '`-s`' option (see Section 31.5.2 [emacsclient Options], page 395).

If you have defined a server by a unique server name, it is possible to connect to the server from another Emacs instance and evaluate Lisp expressions on the server, using the `server-eval-at` function. For instance, `(server-eval-at "foo" '(+ 1 2))` evaluates the expression `(+ 1 2)` on the 'foo' server, and returns `3`. (If there is no server with that name, an error is signaled.) Currently, this feature is mainly useful for developers.

31.5.1 Invoking `emacsclient`

The simplest way to use the `emacsclient` program is to run the shell command '`emacsclient file`', where *file* is a file name. This connects to an Emacs server, and tells that Emacs process to visit *file* in one of its existing frames—either a graphical frame, or one in a text terminal (see Chapter 18 [Frames], page 162). You can then select that frame to begin editing.

If there is no Emacs server, the `emacsclient` program halts with an error message. If the Emacs process has no existing frame—which can happen if it was started as a daemon (see Section 31.5 [Emacs Server], page 393)—then Emacs opens a frame on the terminal in which you called `emacsclient`.

You can also force `emacsclient` to open a new frame on a graphical display, or on a text terminal, using the '`-c`' and '`-t`' options. See Section 31.5.2 [emacsclient Options], page 395.

If you are running on a single text terminal, you can switch between `emacsclient`'s shell and the Emacs server using one of two methods: (i) run the Emacs server and `emacsclient` on different virtual terminals, and switch to the Emacs server's virtual terminal after calling `emacsclient`; or (ii) call `emacsclient` from within the Emacs server itself, using Shell mode (see Section 31.4.2 [Interactive Shell], page 384) or Term mode (see Section 31.4.9 [Term Mode], page 392); `emacsclient` blocks only the subshell under Emacs, and you can still use Emacs to edit the file.

When you finish editing *file* in the Emacs server, type `C-x #` (`server-edit`) in its buffer. This saves the file and sends a message back to the `emacsclient` program, telling it to exit. Programs that use `EDITOR` usually wait for the "editor"—in this case `emacsclient`—to exit before doing something else.

You can also call `emacsclient` with multiple file name arguments: '`emacsclient file1 file2 ...`' tells the Emacs server to visit *file1*, *file2*, and so forth. Emacs selects the buffer

---

[4] Some programs use a different environment variable; for example, to make TeX use 'emacsclient', set the `TEXEDIT` environment variable to 'emacsclient +%d %s'.

visiting *file1*, and buries the other buffers at the bottom of the buffer list (see Chapter 16 [Buffers], page 147). The `emacsclient` program exits once all the specified files are finished (i.e., once you have typed `C-x #` in each server buffer).

Finishing with a server buffer also kills the buffer, unless it already existed in the Emacs session before the server was asked to create it. However, if you set `server-kill-new-buffers` to `nil`, then a different criterion is used: finishing with a server buffer kills it if the file name matches the regular expression `server-temp-file-regexp`. This is set up to distinguish certain "temporary" files.

Each `C-x #` checks for other pending external requests to edit various files, and selects the next such file. You can switch to a server buffer manually if you wish; you don't have to arrive at it with `C-x #`. But `C-x #` is the way to tell `emacsclient` that you are finished.

If you set the value of the variable `server-window` to a window or a frame, `C-x #` always displays the next server buffer in that window or in that frame.

31.5.2 `emacsclient` Options

You can pass some optional arguments to the `emacsclient` program, such as:

        emacsclient -c +12 *file1* +4:3 *file2*

The '+*line*' or '+*line*:*column*' arguments specify line numbers, or line and column numbers, for the next file argument. These behave like the command line arguments for Emacs itself. See Section C.1 [Action Arguments], page 478.

The other optional arguments recognized by `emacsclient` are listed below:

'`-a` *command*'
'`--alternate-editor=`*command*'

> Specify a command to run if `emacsclient` fails to contact Emacs. This is useful when running `emacsclient` in a script.
>
> As a special exception, if *command* is the empty string, then `emacsclient` starts Emacs in daemon mode (as `emacs --daemon`) and then tries connecting again.
>
> The environment variable `ALTERNATE_EDITOR` has the same effect as the '`-a`' option. If both are present, the latter takes precedence.

'`-c`'
> Create a new graphical *client frame*, instead of using an existing Emacs frame. See below for the special behavior of `C-x C-c` in a client frame. If Emacs cannot create a new graphical frame (e.g., if it cannot connect to the X server), it tries to create a text terminal client frame, as though you had supplied the '`-t`' option instead.
>
> On MS-Windows, a single Emacs session cannot display frames on both graphical and text terminals, nor on multiple text terminals. Thus, if the Emacs server is running on a text terminal, the '`-c`' option, like the '`-t`' option, creates a new frame in the server's current text terminal. See Section G.1 [Windows Startup], page 505.
>
> If you omit a filename argument while supplying the '`-c`' option, the new frame displays the `*scratch*` buffer by default. You can customize this behavior with the variable `initial-buffer-choice` (see Section 3.1 [Entering Emacs], page 14).

'-F *alist*'
'--frame-parameters=*alist*'

>Set the parameters for a newly-created graphical frame (see Section 18.11 [Frame Parameters], page 172).

'-d *display*'
'--display=*display*'

>Tell Emacs to open the given files on the X display *display* (assuming there is more than one X display available).

'-e'
'--eval'   Tell Emacs to evaluate some Emacs Lisp code, instead of visiting some files. When this option is given, the arguments to `emacsclient` are interpreted as a list of expressions to evaluate, *not* as a list of files to visit.

'-f *server-file*'
'--server-file=*server-file*'

>Specify a *server file* for connecting to an Emacs server via TCP.

>An Emacs server usually uses an operating system feature called a "local socket" to listen for connections. Some operating systems, such as Microsoft Windows, do not support local sockets; in that case, the server communicates with `emacsclient` via TCP.

>When you start a TCP Emacs server, Emacs creates a *server file* containing the TCP information to be used by `emacsclient` to connect to the server. The variable `server-auth-dir` specifies the directory containing the server file; by default, this is `~/.emacs.d/server/`. To tell `emacsclient` to connect to the server over TCP with a specific server file, use the '-f' or '--server-file' option, or set the `EMACS_SERVER_FILE` environment variable.

'-n'
'--no-wait'

>Let `emacsclient` exit immediately, instead of waiting until all server buffers are finished. You can take as long as you like to edit the server buffers within Emacs, and they are *not* killed when you type `C-x #` in them.

'--parent-id *id*'

>Open an `emacsclient` frame as a client frame in the parent X window with id *id*, via the XEmbed protocol. Currently, this option is mainly useful for developers.

'-q'
'--quiet'   Do not let `emacsclient` display messages about waiting for Emacs or connecting to remote server sockets.

'-s *server-name*'
'--socket-name=*server-name*'

>Connect to the Emacs server named *server-name*. The server name is given by the variable `server-name` on the Emacs server. If this option is omitted, `emacsclient` connects to the first server it finds. (This option is not supported on MS-Windows.)

'-t'
'--tty'
'-nw'   Create a new client frame on the current text terminal, instead of using an
               existing Emacs frame. This behaves just like the '-c' option, described above,
               except that it creates a text terminal frame (see Section 18.19 [Non-Window
               Terminals], page 175).

               On MS-Windows, '-t' behaves just like '-c' if the Emacs server is using the
               graphical display, but if the Emacs server is running on a text terminal, it
               creates a new frame in the current text terminal.

The new graphical or text terminal frames created by the '-c' or '-t' options are considered *client frames*. Any new frame that you create from a client frame is also considered
a client frame. If you type C-x C-c (save-buffers-kill-terminal) in a client frame, that
command does not kill the Emacs session as it normally does (see Section 3.2 [Exiting],
page 15). Instead, Emacs deletes the client frame; furthermore, if the client frame has an
emacsclient waiting to regain control (i.e., if you did not supply the '-n' option), Emacs
deletes all other frames of the same client, and marks the client's server buffers as finished,
as though you had typed C-x # in all of them. If it so happens that there are no remaining
frames after the client frame(s) are deleted, the Emacs session exits.

As an exception, when Emacs is started as a daemon, all frames are considered client
frames, and C-x C-c never kills Emacs. To kill a daemon session, type M-x kill-emacs.

Note that the '-t' and '-n' options are contradictory: '-t' says to take control of the
current text terminal to create a new client frame, while '-n' says not to take control of the
text terminal. If you supply both options, Emacs visits the specified files(s) in an existing
frame rather than a new client frame, negating the effect of '-t'.

31.6 Printing Hard Copies

Emacs provides commands for printing hardcopies of either an entire buffer or part of one.
You can invoke the printing commands directly, as detailed below, or using the 'File' menu
on the menu bar.

Aside from the commands described in this section, you can also print hardcopies from
Dired (see Section 27.7 [Operating on Files], page 320) and the diary (see Section 28.10.1
[Displaying the Diary], page 341). You can also "print" an Emacs buffer to HTML with
the command M-x htmlfontify-buffer, which converts the current buffer to a HTML
file, replacing Emacs faces with CSS-based markup. Furthermore, Org mode allows you
to "print" Org files to a variety of formats, such as PDF (see Section 22.9 [Org Mode],
page 222).

M-x print-buffer
               Print hardcopy of current buffer with page headings containing the file name
               and page number.

M-x lpr-buffer
               Print hardcopy of current buffer without page headings.

M-x print-region
               Like print-buffer but print only the current region.

`M-x lpr-region`

> Like `lpr-buffer` but print only the current region.

On most operating system, the above hardcopy commands submit files for printing by calling the `lpr` program. To change the printer program, customize the variable `lpr-command`. To specify extra switches to give the printer program, customize the list variable `lpr-switches`. Its value should be a list of option strings, each of which should start with '`-`' (e.g., the option string `"-w80"` specifies a line width of 80 columns). The default is the empty list, `nil`.

To specify the printer to use, set the variable `printer-name`. The default, `nil`, specifies the default printer. If you set it to a printer name (a string), that name is passed to `lpr` with the '`-P`' switch; if you are not using `lpr`, you should specify the switch with `lpr-printer-switch`.

The variable `lpr-headers-switches` similarly specifies the extra switches to use to make page headers. The variable `lpr-add-switches` controls whether to supply '`-T`' and '`-J`' options (suitable for `lpr`) to the printer program: `nil` means don't add them (this should be the value if your printer program is not compatible with `lpr`).

31.6.1 PostScript Hardcopy

These commands convert buffer contents to PostScript, either printing it or leaving it in another Emacs buffer.

`M-x ps-print-buffer`

> Print hardcopy of the current buffer in PostScript form.

`M-x ps-print-region`

> Print hardcopy of the current region in PostScript form.

`M-x ps-print-buffer-with-faces`

> Print hardcopy of the current buffer in PostScript form, showing the faces used in the text by means of PostScript features.

`M-x ps-print-region-with-faces`

> Print hardcopy of the current region in PostScript form, showing the faces used in the text.

`M-x ps-spool-buffer`

> Generate and spool a PostScript image for the current buffer text.

`M-x ps-spool-region`

> Generate and spool a PostScript image for the current region.

`M-x ps-spool-buffer-with-faces`

> Generate and spool a PostScript image for the current buffer, showing the faces used.

`M-x ps-spool-region-with-faces`

> Generate and spool a PostScript image for the current region, showing the faces used.

`M-x ps-despool`

> Send the spooled PostScript to the printer.

`M-x handwrite`
>   Generate/print PostScript for the current buffer as if handwritten.

The `ps-print-buffer` and `ps-print-region` commands print buffer contents in Post-Script form. One command prints the entire buffer; the other, just the region. The commands `ps-print-buffer-with-faces` and `ps-print-region-with-faces` behave similarly, but use PostScript features to show the faces (fonts and colors) of the buffer text.

Interactively, when you use a prefix argument (`C-u`), the command prompts the user for a file name, and saves the PostScript image in that file instead of sending it to the printer.

The commands whose names have 'spool' instead of 'print', generate the PostScript output in an Emacs buffer instead of sending it to the printer.

Use the command `ps-despool` to send the spooled images to the printer. This command sends the PostScript generated by '`-spool-`' commands (see commands above) to the printer. With a prefix argument (`C-u`), it prompts for a file name, and saves the spooled PostScript image in that file instead of sending it to the printer.

`M-x handwrite` is more frivolous. It generates a PostScript rendition of the current buffer as a cursive handwritten document. It can be customized in group `handwrite`. This function only supports ISO 8859-1 characters.

31.6.2 Variables for PostScript Hardcopy

All the PostScript hardcopy commands use the variables `ps-lpr-command` and `ps-lpr-switches` to specify how to print the output. `ps-lpr-command` specifies the command name to run, `ps-lpr-switches` specifies command line options to use, and `ps-printer-name` specifies the printer. If you don't set the first two variables yourself, they take their initial values from `lpr-command` and `lpr-switches`. If `ps-printer-name` is nil, `printer-name` is used.

The variable `ps-print-header` controls whether these commands add header lines to each page—set it to `nil` to turn headers off.

If your printer doesn't support colors, you should turn off color processing by setting `ps-print-color-p` to `nil`. By default, if the display supports colors, Emacs produces hardcopy output with color information; on black-and-white printers, colors are emulated with shades of gray. This might produce illegible output, even if your screen colors only use shades of gray.

Alternatively, you can set `ps-print-color-p` to `black-white` to print colors on black/white printers.

By default, PostScript printing ignores the background colors of the faces, unless the variable `ps-use-face-background` is non-`nil`. This is to avoid unwanted interference with the zebra stripes and background image/text.

The variable `ps-paper-type` specifies which size of paper to format for; legitimate values include `a4`, `a3`, `a4small`, `b4`, `b5`, `executive`, `ledger`, `legal`, `letter`, `letter-small`, `statement`, `tabloid`. The default is `letter`. You can define additional paper sizes by changing the variable `ps-page-dimensions-database`.

The variable `ps-landscape-mode` specifies the orientation of printing on the page. The default is `nil`, which stands for "portrait" mode. Any non-`nil` value specifies "landscape" mode.

The variable `ps-number-of-columns` specifies the number of columns; it takes effect in both landscape and portrait mode. The default is 1.

The variable `ps-font-family` specifies which font family to use for printing ordinary text. Legitimate values include `Courier`, `Helvetica`, `NewCenturySchlbk`, `Palatino` and `Times`. The variable `ps-font-size` specifies the size of the font for ordinary text. It defaults to 8.5 points.

Emacs supports more scripts and characters than a typical PostScript printer. Thus, some of the characters in your buffer might not be printable using the fonts built into your printer. You can augment the fonts supplied with the printer with those from the GNU Intlfonts package, or you can instruct Emacs to use Intlfonts exclusively. The variable `ps-multibyte-buffer` controls this: the default value, `nil`, is appropriate for printing ASCII and Latin-1 characters; a value of `non-latin-printer` is for printers which have the fonts for ASCII, Latin-1, Japanese, and Korean characters built into them. A value of `bdf-font` arranges for the BDF fonts from the Intlfonts package to be used for *all* characters. Finally, a value of `bdf-font-except-latin` instructs the printer to use built-in fonts for ASCII and Latin-1 characters, and Intlfonts BDF fonts for the rest.

To be able to use the BDF fonts, Emacs needs to know where to find them. The variable `bdf-directory-list` holds the list of directories where Emacs should look for the fonts; the default value includes a single directory `/usr/local/share/emacs/fonts/bdf`.

Many other customization variables for these commands are defined and described in the Lisp files `ps-print.el` and `ps-mule.el`.

31.6.3 Printing Package

The basic Emacs facilities for printing hardcopy can be extended using the Printing package. This provides an easy-to-use interface for choosing what to print, previewing PostScript files before printing, and setting various printing options such as print headers, landscape or portrait modes, duplex modes, and so forth. On GNU/Linux or Unix systems, the Printing package relies on the `gs` and `gv` utilities, which are distributed as part of the GhostScript program. On MS-Windows, the `gstools` port of Ghostscript can be used.

To use the Printing package, add `(require 'printing)` to your init file (see Section 33.4 [Init File], page 437), followed by `(pr-update-menus)`. This function replaces the usual printing commands in the menu bar with a 'Printing' submenu that contains various printing options. You can also type `M-x pr-interface RET`; this creates a *Printing Interface* buffer, similar to a customization buffer, where you can set the printing options. After selecting what and how to print, you start the print job using the 'Print' button (click `Mouse-2` on it, or move point over it and type `RET`). For further information on the various options, use the 'Interface Help' button.

31.7 Sorting Text

Emacs provides several commands for sorting text in the buffer. All operate on the contents of the region. They divide the text of the region into many *sort records*, identify a *sort key* for each record, and then reorder the records into the order determined by the sort keys. The records are ordered so that their keys are in alphabetical order, or, for numeric sorting, in numeric order. In alphabetic sorting, all upper-case letters 'A' through 'Z' come before lower-case 'a', in accordance with the ASCII character sequence.

The various sort commands differ in how they divide the text into sort records and in which part of each record is used as the sort key. Most of the commands make each line a separate sort record, but some commands use paragraphs or pages as sort records. Most of the sort commands use each entire sort record as its own sort key, but some use only a portion of the record as the sort key.

M-x sort-lines

> Divide the region into lines, and sort by comparing the entire text of a line. A numeric argument means sort into descending order.

M-x sort-paragraphs

> Divide the region into paragraphs, and sort by comparing the entire text of a paragraph (except for leading blank lines). A numeric argument means sort into descending order.

M-x sort-pages

> Divide the region into pages, and sort by comparing the entire text of a page (except for leading blank lines). A numeric argument means sort into descending order.

M-x sort-fields

> Divide the region into lines, and sort by comparing the contents of one field in each line. Fields are defined as separated by whitespace, so the first run of consecutive non-whitespace characters in a line constitutes field 1, the second such run constitutes field 2, etc.

> Specify which field to sort by with a numeric argument: 1 to sort by field 1, etc. A negative argument means count fields from the right instead of from the left; thus, minus 1 means sort by the last field. If several lines have identical contents in the field being sorted, they keep the same relative order that they had in the original buffer.

M-x sort-numeric-fields

> Like M-x sort-fields except the specified field is converted to an integer for each line, and the numbers are compared. '10' comes before '2' when considered as text, but after it when considered as a number. By default, numbers are interpreted according to sort-numeric-base, but numbers beginning with '0x' or '0' are interpreted as hexadecimal and octal, respectively.

M-x sort-columns

> Like M-x sort-fields except that the text within each line used for comparison comes from a fixed range of columns. See below for an explanation.

M-x reverse-region

> Reverse the order of the lines in the region. This is useful for sorting into descending order by fields or columns, since those sort commands do not have a feature for doing that.

For example, if the buffer contains this:

```
On systems where clash detection (locking of files being edited) is
implemented, Emacs also checks the first time you modify a buffer
whether the file has changed on disk since it was last visited or
saved.  If it has, you are asked to confirm that you want to change
```

```
        the buffer.
```

applying M-x sort-lines to the entire buffer produces this:

```
        On systems where clash detection (locking of files being edited) is
        implemented, Emacs also checks the first time you modify a buffer
        saved.  If it has, you are asked to confirm that you want to change
        the buffer.
        whether the file has changed on disk since it was last visited or
```

where the upper-case 'O' sorts before all lower-case letters. If you use C-u 2 M-x sort-fields instead, you get this:

```
        implemented, Emacs also checks the first time you modify a buffer
        saved.  If it has, you are asked to confirm that you want to change
        the buffer.
        On systems where clash detection (locking of files being edited) is
        whether the file has changed on disk since it was last visited or
```

where the sort keys were 'Emacs', 'If', 'buffer', 'systems' and 'the'.

M-x sort-columns requires more explanation. You specify the columns by putting point at one of the columns and the mark at the other column. Because this means you cannot put point or the mark at the beginning of the first line of the text you want to sort, this command uses an unusual definition of "region": all of the line point is in is considered part of the region, and so is all of the line the mark is in, as well as all the lines in between.

For example, to sort a table by information found in columns 10 to 15, you could put the mark on column 10 in the first line of the table, and point on column 15 in the last line of the table, and then run sort-columns. Equivalently, you could run it with the mark on column 15 in the first line and point on column 10 in the last line.

This can be thought of as sorting the rectangle specified by point and the mark, except that the text on each line to the left or right of the rectangle moves along with the text inside the rectangle. See Section 9.5 [Rectangles], page 60.

Many of the sort commands ignore case differences when comparing, if sort-fold-case is non-nil.

31.8 Editing Binary Files

There is a special major mode for editing binary files: Hexl mode. To use it, use M-x hexl-find-file instead of C-x C-f to visit the file. This command converts the file's contents to hexadecimal and lets you edit the translation. When you save the file, it is converted automatically back to binary.

You can also use M-x hexl-mode to translate an existing buffer into hex. This is useful if you visit a file normally and then discover it is a binary file.

Ordinary text characters overwrite in Hexl mode. This is to reduce the risk of accidentally spoiling the alignment of data in the file. There are special commands for insertion. Here is a list of the commands of Hexl mode:

C-M-d   Insert a byte with a code typed in decimal.

C-M-o   Insert a byte with a code typed in octal.

C-M-x   Insert a byte with a code typed in hex.

C-x [Move to the beginning of a 1k-byte "page".

C-x]	Move to the end of a 1k-byte "page".
M-g	Move to an address specified in hex.
M-j	Move to an address specified in decimal.
C-c C-c	Leave Hexl mode, going back to the major mode this buffer had before you invoked `hexl-mode`.

Other Hexl commands let you insert strings (sequences) of binary bytes, move by `shorts` or `ints`, etc.; type `C-h a hexl-RET` for details.

31.9 Saving Emacs Sessions

Use the desktop library to save the state of Emacs from one session to another. Once you save the Emacs *desktop*—the buffers, their file names, major modes, buffer positions, and so on—then subsequent Emacs sessions reload the saved desktop. By default, the desktop also tries to save the frame and window configuration. To disable this, set `desktop-restore-frames` to `nil`. (See that variable's documentation for some related options that you can customize to fine-tune this behavior.)

You can save the desktop manually with the command `M-x desktop-save`. You can also enable automatic saving of the desktop when you exit Emacs, and automatic restoration of the last saved desktop when Emacs starts: use the Customization buffer (see Section 33.1 [Easy Customization], page 412) to set `desktop-save-mode` to `t` for future sessions, or add this line in your init file (see Section 33.4 [Init File], page 437):

```
(desktop-save-mode 1)
```

When `desktop-save-mode` is active and the desktop file exists, Emacs auto-saves it every `desktop-auto-save-timeout` seconds, if that is non-`nil` and non-zero.

If you turn on `desktop-save-mode` in your init file, then when Emacs starts, it looks for a saved desktop in the current directory. (More precisely, it looks in the directories specified by *desktop-path*, and uses the first desktop it finds.) Thus, you can have separate saved desktops in different directories, and the starting directory determines which one Emacs reloads. You can save the current desktop and reload one saved in another directory by typing `M-x desktop-change-dir`. Typing `M-x desktop-revert` reverts to the desktop previously reloaded.

Specify the option '`--no-desktop`' on the command line when you don't want it to reload any saved desktop. This turns off `desktop-save-mode` for the current session. Starting Emacs with the '`--no-init-file`' option also disables desktop reloading, since it bypasses the init file, where `desktop-save-mode` is usually turned on.

By default, all the buffers in the desktop are restored at one go. However, this may be slow if there are a lot of buffers in the desktop. You can specify the maximum number of buffers to restore immediately with the variable `desktop-restore-eager`; the remaining buffers are restored "lazily", when Emacs is idle.

Type `M-x desktop-clear` to empty the Emacs desktop. This kills all buffers except for internal ones, and clears the global variables listed in `desktop-globals-to-clear`. If you want this to preserve certain buffers, customize the variable `desktop-clear-preserve-buffers-regexp`, whose value is a regular expression matching the names of buffers not to kill.

If you want to save minibuffer history from one session to another, use the `savehist` library.

31.10 Recursive Editing Levels

A *recursive edit* is a situation in which you are using Emacs commands to perform arbitrary editing while in the middle of another Emacs command. For example, when you type `C-r` inside of a `query-replace`, you enter a recursive edit in which you can change the current buffer. On exiting from the recursive edit, you go back to the `query-replace`. See Section 12.10.4 [Query Replace], page 105.

Exiting the recursive edit means returning to the unfinished command, which continues execution. The command to exit is `C-M-c` (`exit-recursive-edit`).

You can also *abort* the recursive edit. This is like exiting, but also quits the unfinished command immediately. Use the command `C-]` (`abort-recursive-edit`) to do this. See Section 34.1 [Quitting], page 443.

The mode line shows you when you are in a recursive edit by displaying square brackets around the parentheses that always surround the major and minor mode names. Every window's mode line shows this in the same way, since being in a recursive edit is true of Emacs as a whole rather than any particular window or buffer.

It is possible to be in recursive edits within recursive edits. For example, after typing `C-r` in a `query-replace`, you may type a command that enters the debugger. This begins a recursive editing level for the debugger, within the recursive editing level for `C-r`. Mode lines display a pair of square brackets for each recursive editing level currently in progress.

Exiting the inner recursive edit (such as with the debugger `c` command) resumes the command running in the next level up. When that command finishes, you can then use `C-M-c` to exit another recursive editing level, and so on. Exiting applies to the innermost level only. Aborting also gets out of only one level of recursive edit; it returns immediately to the command level of the previous recursive edit. If you wish, you can then abort the next recursive editing level.

Alternatively, the command `M-x top-level` aborts all levels of recursive edits, returning immediately to the top-level command reader. It also exits the minibuffer, if it is active.

The text being edited inside the recursive edit need not be the same text that you were editing at top level. It depends on what the recursive edit is for. If the command that invokes the recursive edit selects a different buffer first, that is the buffer you will edit recursively. In any case, you can switch buffers within the recursive edit in the normal manner (as long as the buffer-switching keys have not been rebound). You could probably do all the rest of your editing inside the recursive edit, visiting files and all. But this could have surprising effects (such as stack overflow) from time to time. So remember to exit or abort the recursive edit when you no longer need it.

In general, we try to minimize the use of recursive editing levels in GNU Emacs. This is because they constrain you to "go back" in a particular order—from the innermost level toward the top level. When possible, we present different activities in separate buffers so that you can switch between them as you please. Some commands switch to a new major mode which provides a command to switch back. These approaches give you more flexibility to go back to unfinished tasks in the order you choose.

31.11 Hyperlinking and Navigation Features

The following subsections describe convenience features for handling URLs and other types of links occurring in Emacs buffer text.

31.11.1 Following URLs

`M-x browse-url RET` *url* `RET`
> Load a URL into a Web browser.

The Browse-URL package allows you to easily follow URLs from within Emacs. Most URLs are followed by invoking a web browser; '`mailto:`' URLs are followed by invoking the `compose-mail` Emacs command to send mail to the specified address (see Chapter 29 [Sending Mail], page 350).

The command `M-x browse-url` prompts for a URL, and follows it. If point is located near a plausible URL, that URL is offered as the default. The Browse-URL package also provides other commands which you might like to bind to keys, such as `browse-url-at-point` and `browse-url-at-mouse`.

You can customize Browse-URL's behavior via various options in the `browse-url` Customize group. In particular, the option `browse-url-mailto-function` lets you define how to follow '`mailto:`' URLs, while `browse-url-browser-function` lets you define how to follow other types of URLs. For more information, view the package commentary by typing `C-h P browse-url RET`.

31.11.2 Activating URLs

`M-x goto-address-mode`
> Activate URLs and e-mail addresses in the current buffer.

You can make Emacs mark out URLs specially in the current buffer, by typing `M-x goto-address-mode`. When this buffer-local minor mode is enabled, it finds all the URLs in the buffer, highlights them, and turns them into clickable buttons. You can follow the URL by typing `C-c RET` (`goto-address-at-point`) while point is on its text; or by clicking with `Mouse-2`, or by clicking `Mouse-1` quickly (see Section 18.3 [Mouse References], page 164). Following a URL is done by calling `browse-url` as a subroutine (see Section 31.11.1 [Browse-URL], page 405).

It can be useful to add `goto-address-mode` to mode hooks and hooks for displaying an incoming message (e.g., `rmail-show-message-hook` for Rmail, and `mh-show-mode-hook` for MH-E). This is not needed for Gnus, which has a similar feature of its own.

31.11.3 Finding Files and URLs at Point

The FFAP package replaces certain key bindings for finding files, such as `C-x C-f`, with commands that provide more sensitive defaults. These commands behave like the ordinary ones when given a prefix argument. Otherwise, they get the default file name or URL from the text around point. If what is found in the buffer has the form of a URL rather than a file name, the commands use `browse-url` to view it (see Section 31.11.1 [Browse-URL], page 405).

This feature is useful for following references in mail or news buffers, `README` files, `MANIFEST` files, and so on. For more information, view the package commentary by typing `C-h P ffap RET`.

To enable FFAP, type `M-x ffap-bindings`. This makes the following key bindings, and also installs hooks for additional FFAP functionality in Rmail, Gnus and VM article buffers.

`C-x C-f` *filename* `RET`

        Find *filename*, guessing a default from text around point (`find-file-at-point`).

`C-x C-r`   `ffap-read-only`, analogous to `find-file-read-only`.

`C-x C-v`   `ffap-alternate-file`, analogous to `find-alternate-file`.

`C-x d` *directory* `RET`

        Start Dired on *directory*, defaulting to the directory name at point (`dired-at-point`).

`C-x C-d`   `ffap-list-directory`, analogous to `list-directory`.

`C-x 4 f`   `ffap-other-window`, analogous to `find-file-other-window`.

`C-x 4 r`   `ffap-read-only-other-window`, analogous to `find-file-read-only-other-window`.

`C-x 4 d`   `ffap-dired-other-window`, like `dired-other-window`.

`C-x 5 f`   `ffap-other-frame`, analogous to `find-file-other-frame`.

`C-x 5 r`   `ffap-read-only-other-frame`, analogous to `find-file-read-only-other-frame`.

`C-x 5 d`   `ffap-dired-other-frame`, analogous to `dired-other-frame`.

`M-x ffap-next`

        Search buffer for next file name or URL, then find that file or URL.

`S-Mouse-3`

        `ffap-at-mouse` finds the file guessed from text around the position of a mouse click.

`C-S-Mouse-3`

        Display a menu of files and URLs mentioned in current buffer, then find the one you select (`ffap-menu`).

31.12 Other Amusements

The `animate` package makes text dance (e.g., `M-x animate-birthday-present`).

`M-x blackbox`, `M-x mpuz` and `M-x 5x5` are puzzles. `blackbox` challenges you to determine the location of objects inside a box by tomography. `mpuz` displays a multiplication puzzle with letters standing for digits in a code that you must guess—to guess a value, type a letter and then the digit you think it stands for. The aim of `5x5` is to fill in all the squares.

`M-x bubbles` is a game in which the object is to remove as many bubbles as you can in the smallest number of moves.

`M-x decipher` helps you to cryptanalyze a buffer which is encrypted in a simple monoalphabetic substitution cipher.

M-x dissociated-press scrambles the text in the current Emacs buffer, word by word or character by character, writing its output to a buffer named *Dissociation*. A positive argument tells it to operate character by character, and specifies the number of overlap characters. A negative argument tells it to operate word by word, and specifies the number of overlap words. Dissociated Press produces results fairly like those of a Markov chain, but is however, an independent, ignoriginal invention; it techniquitously copies several consecutive characters from the sample text between random jumps, unlike a Markov chain which would jump randomly after each word or character. Keep dissociwords out of your documentation, if you want it to be well userenced and properbose.

M-x dunnet runs an text-based adventure game.

If you want a little more personal involvement, try M-x gomoku, which plays the game Go Moku with you.

If you are a little bit bored, you can try M-x hanoi. If you are considerably bored, give it a numeric argument. If you are very, very bored, try an argument of 9. Sit back and watch.

M-x life runs Conway's "Life" cellular automaton.

M-x landmark runs a relatively non-participatory game in which a robot attempts to maneuver towards a tree at the center of the window based on unique olfactory cues from each of the four directions.

M-x morse-region converts the text in the region to Morse code; M-x unmorse-region converts it back. M-x nato-region converts the text in the region to NATO phonetic alphabet; M-x denato-region converts it back.

M-x pong, M-x snake and M-x tetris are implementations of the well-known Pong, Snake and Tetris games.

M-x solitaire plays a game of solitaire in which you jump pegs across other pegs.

The command M-x zone plays games with the display when Emacs is idle.

Finally, if you find yourself frustrated, try describing your problems to the famous psychotherapist Eliza. Just do M-x doctor. End each input by typing RET twice.

32 Emacs Lisp Packages

Emacs includes a facility that lets you easily download and install *packages* that implement additional features. Each package is a separate Emacs Lisp program, sometimes including other components such as an Info manual.

`M-x list-packages` brings up a buffer named `*Packages*` with a list of all packages. You can install or uninstall packages via this buffer. See Section 32.1 [Package Menu], page 408.

The command `C-h P` (`describe-package`) prompts for the name of a package, and displays a help buffer describing the attributes of the package and the features that it implements.

By default, Emacs downloads packages from a *package archive* maintained by the Emacs developers and hosted by the GNU project. Optionally, you can also download packages from archives maintained by third parties. See Section 32.2 [Package Installation], page 409.

For information about turning an Emacs Lisp program into an installable package, See Section "Packaging" in *The Emacs Lisp Reference Manual*. For information about finding third-party packages and other Emacs Lisp extensions, See Section "Packages that do not come with Emacs" in *GNU Emacs FAQ*.

32.1 The Package Menu Buffer

The command `M-x list-packages` brings up the *package menu*. This is a buffer listing all the packages that Emacs knows about, one on each line, with the following information:

- The package name (e.g., 'auctex').
- The package's version number (e.g., '11.86').
- The package's status—normally one of 'available' (can be downloaded from the package archive), 'installed', or 'built-in' (included in Emacs by default).

  The status can also be 'new'. This is equivalent to 'available', except that it means the package became newly available on the package archive after your last invocation of `M-x list-packages`. In other instances, a package may have the status 'held', 'disabled', or 'obsolete'. See Section 32.2 [Package Installation], page 409.

- A short description of the package.

The `list-packages` command accesses the network, to retrieve the list of available packages from the package archive server. If the network is unavailable, it falls back on the most recently retrieved list.

The following commands are available in the package menu:

h   Print a short message summarizing how to use the package menu (`package-menu-quick-help`).

?

RET   Display a help buffer for the package on the current line (`package-menu-describe-package`), similar to the help window displayed by the `C-h P` command (see Chapter 32 [Packages], page 408).

i   Mark the package on the current line for installation (`package-menu-mark-install`). If the package status is 'available', this adds an 'I' character to the start of the line; typing x (see below) will download and install the package.

d   Mark the package on the current line for deletion (`package-menu-mark-delete`). If the package status is 'installed', this adds a 'D' character to the start of the line; typing x (see below) will delete the package. See Section 32.3 [Package Files], page 411, for information about what package deletion entails.

u   Remove any installation or deletion mark previously added to the current line by an i or d command.

U   Mark all package with a newer available version for "upgrading" (`package-menu-mark-upgrades`). This places an installation mark on the new available versions, and a deletion mark on the old installed versions.

x   Download and install all packages marked with i, and their dependencies; also, delete all packages marked with d (`package-menu-execute`). This also removes the marks.

r   Refresh the package list (`package-menu-refresh`). This fetches the list of available packages from the package archive again, and recomputes the package list.

f   Filter the package list (`package-menu-filter`). This prompts for a keyword (e.g., 'games'), then shows only the packages that relate to that keyword. To restore the full package list, type q.

For example, you can install a package by typing i on the line listing that package, followed by x.

32.2 Package Installation

Packages are most conveniently installed using the package menu (see Section 32.1 [Package Menu], page 408), but you can also use the command M-x package-install. This prompts for the name of a package with the 'available' status, then downloads and installs it.

A package may *require* certain other packages to be installed, because it relies on functionality provided by them. When Emacs installs such a package, it also automatically downloads and installs any required package that is not already installed. (If a required package is somehow unavailable, Emacs signals an error and stops installation.) A package's requirements list is shown in its help buffer.

By default, packages are downloaded from a single package archive maintained by the Emacs developers. This is controlled by the variable `package-archives`, whose value is a list of package archives known to Emacs. Each list element must have the form (*id* . *location*), where *id* is the name of a package archive and *location* is the HTTP address or directory name of the package archive. You can alter this list if you wish to use third party package archives—but do so at your own risk, and use only third parties that you think you can trust!

The maintainers of package archives can increase the trust that you can have in their packages by *signing* them. They generate a private/public pair of cryptographic keys, and use the private key to create a *signature file* for each package. With the public key, you can use the signature files to verify who created the package, and that it has not been modified. A valid signature is not a cast-iron guarantee that a package is not malicious, so you should still exercise caution. Package archives should provide instructions on how you can obtain their public key. One way is to download the key from a server such as `http://pgp.mit.edu/`. Use `M-x package-import-keyring` to import the key into Emacs. Emacs stores package keys in the `gnupg` subdirectory of `package-user-dir`. The public key for the GNU package archive is distributed with Emacs, in the `etc/package-keyring.gpg`. Emacs uses it automatically.

If the user option `package-check-signature` is non-`nil`, Emacs attempts to verify signatures when you install packages. If the option has the value `allow-unsigned`, you can still install a package that is not signed. If you use some archives that do not sign their packages, you can add them to the list `package-unsigned-archives`.

For more information on cryptographic keys and signing, see *The GNU Privacy Guard Manual*. Emacs comes with an interface to GNU Privacy Guard, see Section "EasyPG" in *Emacs EasyPG Assistant Manual*.

If you have more than one package archive enabled, and some of them offer different versions of the same package, you may find the option `package-pinned-packages` useful. You can add package/archive pairs to this list, to ensure that the specified package is only ever downloaded from the specified archive.

Once a package is downloaded and installed, it is *loaded* into the current Emacs session. Loading a package is not quite the same as loading a Lisp library (see Section 24.8 [Lisp Libraries], page 276); its effect varies from package to package. Most packages just make some new commands available, while others have more wide-ranging effects on the Emacs session. For such information, consult the package's help buffer.

By default, Emacs also automatically loads all installed packages in subsequent Emacs sessions. This happens at startup, after processing the init file (see Section 33.4 [Init File], page 437). As an exception, Emacs does not load packages at startup if invoked with the '-q' or '--no-init-file' options (see Section C.2 [Initial Options], page 480).

To disable automatic package loading, change the variable `package-enable-at-startup` to `nil`.

The reason automatic package loading occurs after loading the init file is that user options only receive their customized values after loading the init file, including user options which affect the packaging system. In some circumstances, you may want to load packages explicitly in your init file (usually because some other code in your init file depends on a package). In that case, your init file should call the function `package-initialize`. It is up to you to ensure that relevant user options, such as `package-load-list` (see below), are set up prior to the `package-initialize` call. You should also set `package-enable-at-startup` to `nil`, to avoid loading the packages again after processing the init file. Alternatively, you may choose to completely inhibit package loading at startup, and invoke the command `M-x package-initialize` to load your packages manually.

For finer control over package loading, you can use the variable `package-load-list`. Its value should be a list. A list element of the form (*name version*) tells Emacs to load version *version* of the package named *name*. Here, *version* should be a version string (corresponding to a specific version of the package), or `t` (which means to load any installed version), or `nil` (which means no version; this "disables" the package, preventing it from being loaded).

A list element can also be the symbol `all`, which means to load the latest installed version of any package not named by the other list elements. The default value is just `'(all)`.

For example, if you set `package-load-list` to `'((muse "3.20") all)`, then Emacs only loads version 3.20 of the 'muse' package, plus any installed version of packages other than 'muse'. Any other version of 'muse' that happens to be installed will be ignored. The 'muse' package will be listed in the package menu with the 'held' status.

32.3 Package Files and Directory Layout

Each package is downloaded from the package archive in the form of a single *package file*—either an Emacs Lisp source file, or a tar file containing multiple Emacs Lisp source and other files. Package files are automatically retrieved, processed, and disposed of by the Emacs commands that install packages. Normally, you will not need to deal directly with them, unless you are making a package (see Section "Packaging" in *The Emacs Lisp Reference Manual*). Should you ever need to install a package directly from a package file, use the command `M-x package-install-file`.

Once installed, the contents of a package are placed in a subdirectory of `~/.emacs.d/elpa/` (you can change the name of that directory by changing the variable `package-user-dir`). The package subdirectory is named *name-version*, where *name* is the package name and *version* is its version string.

In addition to `package-user-dir`, Emacs looks for installed packages in the directories listed in `package-directory-list`. These directories are meant for system administrators to make Emacs packages available system-wide; Emacs itself never installs packages there. The package subdirectories for `package-directory-list` are laid out in the same way as in `package-user-dir`.

Deleting a package (see Section 32.1 [Package Menu], page 408) involves deleting the corresponding package subdirectory. This only works for packages installed in `package-user-dir`; if told to act on a package in a system-wide package directory, the deletion command signals an error.

33 Customization

This chapter describes some simple methods to customize the behavior of Emacs.

Apart from the methods described here, see Appendix D [X Resources], page 493 for information about using X resources to customize Emacs, and see Chapter 14 [Keyboard Macros], page 114 for information about recording and replaying keyboard macros. Making more far-reaching and open-ended changes involves writing Emacs Lisp code; see *The Emacs Lisp Reference Manual*.

33.1 Easy Customization Interface

Emacs has many *settings* which you can change. Most settings are *customizable variables* (see Section 33.2 [Variables], page 420), which are also called *user options*. There is a huge number of customizable variables, controlling numerous aspects of Emacs behavior; the variables documented in this manual are listed in [Variable Index], page 568. A separate class of settings are the *faces*, which determine the fonts, colors, and other attributes of text (see Section 11.8 [Faces], page 74).

To browse and alter settings (both variables and faces), type M-x customize. This creates a *customization buffer*, which lets you navigate through a logically organized list of settings, edit and set their values, and save them permanently.

33.1.1 Customization Groups

Customization settings are organized into *customization groups*. These groups are collected into bigger groups, all the way up to a master group called Emacs.

M-x customize creates a customization buffer that shows the top-level Emacs group. It looks like this, in part:

```
For help, see [Easy Customization] in the [Emacs manual].

---------------------------------------- [ Search ]

Operate on all settings in this buffer:
[ Revert... ] [ Apply ] [ Apply and Save ]


Emacs group: Customization of the One True Editor.
     [State]: visible group members are all at standard values.
     See also [Manual].

[Editing] : Basic text editing facilities.
[Convenience] : Convenience features for faster editing.

more second-level groups
```

The main part of this buffer shows the 'Emacs' customization group, which contains several other groups ('Editing', 'Convenience', etc.). The contents of those groups are not listed here, only one line of documentation each.

The *state* of the group indicates whether setting in that group has been edited, set or saved. See Section 33.1.3 [Changing a Variable], page 413.

Most of the customization buffer is read-only, but it includes some *editable fields* that you can edit. For example, at the top of the customization buffer is an editable field for searching for settings (see Section 33.1.2 [Browsing Custom], page 413). There are also *buttons* and *links*, which you can activate by either clicking with the mouse, or moving point there and typing RET. For example, the group names like '[Editing]' are links; activating one of these links brings up the customization buffer for that group.

In the customizable buffer, you can type TAB (widget-forward) to move forward to the next button or editable field. S-TAB (widget-backward) moves back to the previous button or editable field.

33.1.2 Browsing and Searching for Settings

From the top-level customization buffer created by M-x customize, you can follow the links to the subgroups of the 'Emacs' customization group. These subgroups may contain settings for you to customize; they may also contain further subgroups, dealing with yet more specialized subsystems of Emacs. As you navigate the hierarchy of customization groups, you should find some settings that you want to customize.

If you are interested in customizing a particular setting or customization group, you can go straight there with the commands M-x customize-option, M-x customize-face, or M-x customize-group. See Section 33.1.6 [Specific Customization], page 417.

If you don't know exactly what groups or settings you want to customize, you can search for them using the editable search field at the top of each customization buffer. Here, you can type in a search term—either one or more words separated by spaces, or a regular expression (see Section 12.6 [Regexps], page 97). Then type RET in the field, or activate the 'Search' button next to it, to switch to a customization buffer containing groups and settings that match those terms. Note, however, that this feature only finds groups and settings that are loaded in the current Emacs session.

If you don't want customization buffers to show the search field, change the variable custom-search-field to nil.

The command M-x customize-apropos is similar to using the search field, except that it reads the search term(s) using the minibuffer. See Section 33.1.6 [Specific Customization], page 417.

M-x customize-browse is another way to browse the available settings. This command creates a special customization buffer which shows only the names of groups and settings, in a structured layout. You can show the contents of a group, in the same buffer, by invoking the '[+]' button next to the group name. When the group contents are shown, the button changes to '[-]'; invoking that hides the group contents again. Each group or setting in this buffer has a link which says '[Group]', '[Option]' or '[Face]'. Invoking this link creates an ordinary customization buffer showing just that group, option, or face; this is the way to change settings that you find with M-x customize-browse.

33.1.3 Changing a Variable

Here is an example of what a variable, or user option, looks like in the customization buffer:

```
[Hide] Kill Ring Max: 60
   [State]: STANDARD.
   Maximum length of kill ring before oldest elements are thrown away.
```

The first line shows that the variable is named kill-ring-max, formatted as 'Kill Ring Max' for easier viewing. Its value is '60'. The button labeled '[Hide]', if activated, hides the variable's value and state; this is useful to avoid cluttering up the customization buffer with very long values (for this reason, variables that have very long values may start out hidden). If you use the '[Hide]' button, it changes to '[Show Value]', which you can activate to reveal the value and state. On a graphical display, the '[Hide]' and '[Show Value]' buttons are replaced with graphical triangles pointing downwards and rightwards respectively.

The line after the variable name indicates the *customization state* of the variable: in this example, 'STANDARD' means you have not changed the variable, so its value is the default one. The '[State]' button gives a menu of operations for customizing the variable.

Below the customization state is the documentation for the variable. This is the same documentation that would be shown by the C-h v command (see Section 33.2.1 [Examining], page 421). If the documentation is more than one line long, only one line may be shown. If so, that line ends with a '[More]' button; activate this to see the full documentation.

To enter a new value for 'Kill Ring Max', just move point to the value and edit it. For example, type M-d to delete the '60' and type in another number. As you begin to alter the text, the '[State]' line will change:

```
[State]: EDITED, shown value does not take effect until you
         set or save it.
```

Editing the value does not make it take effect right away. To do that, you must *set* the variable by activating the '[State]' button and choosing 'Set for Current Session'. Then the variable's state becomes:

```
[State]: SET for current session only.
```

You don't have to worry about specifying a value that is not valid; the 'Set for Current Session' operation checks for validity and will not install an unacceptable value.

While editing certain kinds of values, such as file names, directory names, and Emacs command names, you can perform completion with C-M-i (widget-complete), or the equivalent keys M-TAB or ESC TAB. This behaves much like minibuffer completion (see Section 5.4 [Completion], page 28).

Typing RET on an editable value field moves point forward to the next field or button, like TAB. You can thus type RET when you are finished editing a field, to move on to the next button or field. To insert a newline within an editable field, use C-o or C-q C-j.

For some variables, there is only a fixed set of legitimate values, and you are not allowed to edit the value directly. Instead, a '[Value Menu]' button appears before the value; activating this button presents a choice of values. For a boolean "on or off" value, the button says '[Toggle]', and flips the value. After using the '[Value Menu]' or '[Toggle]' button, you must again set the variable to make the chosen value take effect.

Some variables have values with complex structure. For example, the value of minibuffer-frame-alist is an association list. Here is how it appears in the customization buffer:

```
[Hide] Minibuffer Frame Alist:
[INS] [DEL] Parameter: width
            Value: 80
[INS] [DEL] Parameter: height
            Value: 2
[INS]
  [ State ]: STANDARD.
```

```
Alist of parameters for the initial minibuffer frame. [Hide]
[...more lines of documentation...]
```

In this case, each association in the list consists of two items, one labeled 'Parameter' and one labeled 'Value'; both are editable fields. You can delete an association from the list with the '[DEL]' button next to it. To add an association, use the '[INS]' button at the position where you want to insert it; the very last '[INS]' button inserts at the end of the list.

When you set a variable, the new value takes effect only in the current Emacs session. To save the value for future sessions, use the '[State]' button and select the 'Save for Future Sessions' operation. See Section 33.1.4 [Saving Customizations], page 416.

You can also restore the variable to its standard value by using the '[State]' button and selecting the 'Erase Customization' operation. There are actually four reset operations:

'Undo Edits'
> If you have modified but not yet set the variable, this restores the text in the customization buffer to match the actual value.

'Reset to Saved'
> This restores the value of the variable to the last saved value, and updates the text accordingly.

'Erase Customization'
> This sets the variable to its standard value. Any saved value that you have is also eliminated.

'Set to Backup Value'
> This sets the variable to a previous value that was set in the customization buffer in this session. If you customize a variable and then reset it, which discards the customized value, you can get the discarded value back again with this operation.

Sometimes it is useful to record a comment about a specific customization. Use the 'Add Comment' item from the '[State]' menu to create a field for entering the comment.

Near the top of the customization buffer are two lines of buttons:

```
[Set for Current Session] [Save for Future Sessions]
[Undo Edits] [Reset to Saved] [Erase Customization]   [Exit]
```

Each of the first five buttons performs the stated operation—set, save, reset, etc.—on all the settings in the buffer that could meaningfully be affected. They do not operate on settings that are hidden, nor on subgroups that are hidden or not visible in the buffer.

The command C-c C-c (Custom-set) is equivalent to using the '[Set for Current Session]' button. The command C-x C-s (Custom-save) is like using the '[Save for Future Sessions]' button.

The '[Exit]' button switches out of the customization buffer, and buries the buffer at the bottom of the buffer list. To make it kill the customization buffer instead, change the variable custom-buffer-done-kill to t.

33.1.4 Saving Customizations

In the customization buffer, you can *save* a customization setting by choosing the 'Save for Future Sessions' choice from its '[State]' button. The C-x C-s (Custom-save) command, or the '[Save for Future Sessions]' button at the top of the customization buffer, saves all applicable settings in the buffer.

Saving works by writing code to a file, usually your initialization file (see Section 33.4 [Init File], page 437). Future Emacs sessions automatically read this file at startup, which sets up the customizations again.

You can choose to save customizations somewhere other than your initialization file. To make this work, you must add a couple of lines of code to your initialization file, to set the variable custom-file to the name of the desired file, and to load that file. For example:

```
(setq custom-file "~/.emacs-custom.el")
(load custom-file)
```

You can even specify different customization files for different Emacs versions, like this:

```
(cond ((< emacs-major-version 22)
       ;; Emacs 21 customization.
       (setq custom-file "~/.custom-21.el"))
      ((and (= emacs-major-version 22)
            (< emacs-minor-version 3))
       ;; Emacs 22 customization, before version 22.3.
       (setq custom-file "~/.custom-22.el"))
      (t
       ;; Emacs version 22.3 or later.
       (setq custom-file "~/.emacs-custom.el")))
```

```
(load custom-file)
```

If Emacs was invoked with the -q or --no-init-file options (see Section C.2 [Initial Options], page 480), it will not let you save your customizations in your initialization file. This is because saving customizations from such a session would wipe out all the other customizations you might have on your initialization file.

33.1.5 Customizing Faces

You can customize faces (see Section 11.8 [Faces], page 74), which determine how Emacs displays different types of text. Customization groups can contain both variables and faces.

For example, in programming language modes, source code comments are shown with font-lock-comment-face (see Section 11.12 [Font Lock], page 78). In a customization buffer, that face appears like this:

```
[Hide] Font Lock Comment Face:[sample]
   [State] : STANDARD.
   Font Lock mode face used to highlight comments.
   [ ] Font Family: --
   [ ] Font Foundry: --
   [ ] Width: --
   [ ] Height: --
   [ ] Weight: --
   [ ] Slant: --
   [ ] Underline: --
```

```
[ ] Overline: --
[ ] Strike-through: --
[ ] Box around text: --
[ ] Inverse-video: --
[X] Foreground: Firebrick     [Choose]   (sample)
[ ] Background: --
[ ] Stipple: --
[ ] Inherit: --
[Hide Unused Attributes]
```

The first three lines show the name, '[State]' button, and documentation for the face. Below that is a list of *face attributes*. In front of each attribute is a checkbox. A filled checkbox, '[X]', means that the face specifies a value for this attribute; an empty checkbox, '[ ]', means that the face does not specify any special value for the attribute. You can activate a checkbox to specify or unspecify its attribute.

A face does not have to specify every single attribute; in fact, most faces only specify a few attributes. In the above example, `font-lock-comment-face` only specifies the foreground color. Any unspecified attribute is taken from the special face named `default`, whose attributes are all specified. The `default` face is the face used to display any text that does not have an explicitly-assigned face; furthermore, its background color attribute serves as the background color of the frame.

The '`Hide Unused Attributes`' button, at the end of the attribute list, hides the unspecified attributes of the face. When attributes are being hidden, the button changes to '[Show All Attributes]', which reveals the entire attribute list. The customization buffer may start out with unspecified attributes hidden, to avoid cluttering the interface.

When an attribute is specified, you can change its value in the usual ways.

Foreground and background colors can be specified using either color names or RGB triplets (see Section 11.9 [Colors], page 75). You can also use the '[Choose]' button to switch to a list of color names; select a color with RET in that buffer to put the color name in the value field.

Setting, saving and resetting a face work like the same operations for variables (see Section 33.1.3 [Changing a Variable], page 413).

A face can specify different appearances for different types of displays. For example, a face can make text red on a color display, but use a bold font on a monochrome display. To specify multiple appearances for a face, select '`For All Kinds of Displays`' in the menu you get from invoking '[State]'.

33.1.6 Customizing Specific Items

`M-x customize-option RET` *option* `RET`
`M-x customize-variable RET` *option* `RET`
> Set up a customization buffer for just one user option, *option*.

`M-x customize-face RET` *face* `RET`
> Set up a customization buffer for just one face, *face*.

`M-x customize-group RET` *group* `RET`
> Set up a customization buffer for just one group, *group*.

`M-x customize-apropos RET` *regexp* `RET`
> Set up a customization buffer for all the settings and groups that match *regexp*.

M-x customize-changed RET *version* RET

> Set up a customization buffer with all the settings and groups whose meaning has changed since Emacs version *version*.

M-x customize-saved

> Set up a customization buffer containing all settings that you have saved with customization buffers.

M-x customize-unsaved

> Set up a customization buffer containing all settings that you have set but not saved.

If you want to customize a particular user option, type M-x customize-option. This reads the variable name, and sets up the customization buffer with just that one user option. When entering the variable name into the minibuffer, completion is available, but only for the names of variables that have been loaded into Emacs.

Likewise, you can customize a specific face using M-x customize-face. You can set up a customization buffer for a specific customization group using M-x customize-group.

M-x customize-apropos prompts for a search term—either one or more words separated by spaces, or a regular expression—and sets up a customization buffer for all *loaded* settings and groups with matching names. This is like using the search field at the top of the customization buffer (see Section 33.1.1 [Customization Groups], page 412).

When you upgrade to a new Emacs version, you might want to consider customizing new settings, and settings whose meanings or default values have changed. To do this, use M-x customize-changed and specify a previous Emacs version number using the minibuffer. It creates a customization buffer which shows all the settings and groups whose definitions have been changed since the specified version, loading them if necessary.

If you change settings and then decide the change was a mistake, you can use two commands to revisit your changes. Use M-x customize-saved to customize settings that you have saved. Use M-x customize-unsaved to customize settings that you have set but not saved.

33.1.7 Custom Themes

Custom themes are collections of settings that can be enabled or disabled as a unit. You can use Custom themes to switch easily between various collections of settings, and to transfer such collections from one computer to another.

A Custom theme is stored as an Emacs Lisp source file. If the name of the Custom theme is *name*, the theme file is named *name*-theme.el. See Section 33.1.8 [Creating Custom Themes], page 419, for the format of a theme file and how to make one.

Type M-x customize-themes to switch to a buffer named *Custom Themes*, which lists the Custom themes that Emacs knows about. By default, Emacs looks for theme files in two locations: the directory specified by the variable custom-theme-directory (which defaults to ~/.emacs.d/), and a directory named etc/themes in your Emacs installation (see the variable data-directory). The latter contains several Custom themes which are distributed with Emacs, which customize Emacs's faces to fit various color schemes. (Note, however, that Custom themes need not be restricted to this purpose; they can be used to customize variables too.)

If you want Emacs to look for Custom themes in some other directory, add the directory name to the list variable `custom-theme-load-path`. Its default value is `(custom-theme-directory t)`; here, the symbol `custom-theme-directory` has the special meaning of the value of the variable `custom-theme-directory`, while `t` stands for the built-in theme directory `etc/themes`. The themes listed in the `*Custom Themes*` buffer are those found in the directories specified by `custom-theme-load-path`.

In the `*Custom Themes*` buffer, you can activate the checkbox next to a Custom theme to enable or disable the theme for the current Emacs session. When a Custom theme is enabled, all of its settings (variables and faces) take effect in the Emacs session. To apply the choice of theme(s) to future Emacs sessions, type `C-x C-s` (`custom-theme-save`) or use the '`[Save Theme Settings]`' button.

When you first enable a Custom theme, Emacs displays the contents of the theme file and asks if you really want to load it. Because loading a Custom theme can execute arbitrary Lisp code, you should only say yes if you know that the theme is safe; in that case, Emacs offers to remember in the future that the theme is safe (this is done by saving the theme file's SHA-256 hash to the variable `custom-safe-themes`; if you want to treat all themes as safe, change its value to `t`). Themes that come with Emacs (in the `etc/themes` directory) are exempt from this check, and are always considered safe.

Setting or saving Custom themes actually works by customizing the variable `custom-enabled-themes`. The value of this variable is a list of Custom theme names (as Lisp symbols, e.g., `tango`). Instead of using the `*Custom Themes*` buffer to set `custom-enabled-themes`, you can customize the variable using the usual customization interface, e.g., with `M-x customize-option`. Note that Custom themes are not allowed to set `custom-enabled-themes` themselves.

Any customizations that you make through the customization buffer take precedence over theme settings. This lets you easily override individual theme settings that you disagree with. If settings from two different themes overlap, the theme occurring earlier in `custom-enabled-themes` takes precedence. In the customization buffer, if a setting has been changed from its default by a Custom theme, its '`State`' display shows '`THEMED`' instead of '`STANDARD`'.

You can enable a specific Custom theme in the current Emacs session by typing `M-x load-theme`. This prompts for a theme name, loads the theme from the theme file, and enables it. If a theme file has been loaded before, you can enable the theme without loading its file by typing `M-x enable-theme`. To disable a Custom theme, type `M-x disable-theme`.

To see a description of a Custom theme, type `?` on its line in the `*Custom Themes*` buffer; or type `M-x describe-theme` anywhere in Emacs and enter the theme name.

33.1.8 Creating Custom Themes

You can define a Custom theme using an interface similar to the customization buffer, by typing `M-x customize-create-theme`. This switches to a buffer named `*Custom Theme*`. It also offers to insert some common Emacs faces into the theme (a convenience, since Custom themes are often used to customize faces). If you answer no, the theme will initially contain no settings.

Near the top of the `*Custom Theme*` buffer are editable fields where you can enter the theme's name and description. The name can be anything except '`user`'. The description is the one that will be shown when you invoke M-x describe-theme for the theme. Its first line should be a brief one-sentence summary; in the buffer made by M-x customize-themes, this sentence is displayed next to the theme name.

To add a new setting to the theme, use the '[Insert Additional Face]' or '[Insert Additional Variable]' buttons. Each button reads a face or variable name using the minibuffer, with completion, and inserts a customization entry for the face or variable. You can edit the variable values or face attributes in the same way as in a normal customization buffer. To remove a face or variable from the theme, uncheck the checkbox next to its name.

After specifying the Custom theme's faces and variables, type C-x C-s (custom-theme-write) or use the buffer's '[Save Theme]' button. This saves the theme file, named *name*-theme.el where *name* is the theme name, in the directory named by custom-theme-directory.

From the *Custom Theme* buffer, you can view and edit an existing Custom theme by activating the '[Visit Theme]' button and specifying the theme name. You can also add the settings of another theme into the buffer, using the '[Merge Theme]' button. You can import your non-theme settings into a Custom theme by using the '[Merge Theme]' button and specifying the special theme named 'user'.

A theme file is simply an Emacs Lisp source file, and loading the Custom theme works by loading the Lisp file. Therefore, you can edit a theme file directly instead of using the *Custom Theme* buffer. See Section "Custom Themes" in *The Emacs Lisp Reference Manual*, for details.

33.2 Variables

A *variable* is a Lisp symbol which has a value. The symbol's name is also called the *variable name*. A variable name can contain any characters that can appear in a file, but most variable names consist of ordinary words separated by hyphens.

The name of the variable serves as a compact description of its role. Most variables also have a *documentation string*, which describes what the variable's purpose is, what kind of value it should have, and how the value will be used. You can view this documentation using the help command C-h v (describe-variable). See Section 33.2.1 [Examining], page 421.

Emacs uses many Lisp variables for internal record keeping, but the most interesting variables for a non-programmer user are those meant for users to change—these are called *customizable variables* or *user options* (see Section 33.1 [Easy Customization], page 412). In the following sections, we will describe other aspects of Emacs variables, such as how to set them outside Customize.

Emacs Lisp allows any variable (with a few exceptions) to have any kind of value. However, many variables are meaningful only if assigned values of a certain type. For example, only numbers are meaningful values for kill-ring-max, which specifies the maximum length of the kill ring (see Section 9.2.2 [Earlier Kills], page 55); if you give kill-ring-max a string value, commands such as C-y (yank) will signal an error. On the other hand, some variables don't care about type; for instance, if a variable has one effect for nil values and another effect for "non-nil" values, then any value that is not the symbol nil induces the second effect, regardless of its type (by convention, we usually use the value t—a symbol which stands for "true"—to specify a non-nil value). If you set a variable using the customization buffer, you need not worry about giving it an invalid type: the customization buffer usually only allows you to enter meaningful values. When in doubt, use `C-h v` (`describe-variable`) to check the variable's documentation string to see kind of value it expects (see Section 33.2.1 [Examining], page 421).

33.2.1 Examining and Setting Variables

`C-h v` *var* `RET`

> Display the value and documentation of variable *var* (`describe-variable`).

`M-x set-variable RET` *var* `RET` *value* `RET`

> Change the value of variable *var* to *value*.

To examine the value of a variable, use `C-h v` (`describe-variable`). This reads a variable name using the minibuffer, with completion, and displays both the value and the documentation of the variable. For example,

        C-h v fill-column RET

displays something like this:

        fill-column is a variable defined in 'C source code'.
        fill-column's value is 70

        Automatically becomes buffer-local when set.
        This variable is safe as a file local variable if its value
        satisfies the predicate 'integerp'.

        Documentation:
        Column beyond which automatic line-wrapping should happen.
        Interactively, you can set the local value with C-x f.

        You can customize this variable.

The line that says "You can customize the variable" indicates that this variable is a user option. `C-h v` is not restricted to user options; it allows non-customizable variables too.

The most convenient way to set a specific customizable variable is with `M-x set-variable`. This reads the variable name with the minibuffer (with completion), and then reads a Lisp expression for the new value using the minibuffer a second time (you can insert the old value into the minibuffer for editing via `M-n`). For example,

        M-x set-variable RET fill-column RET 75 RET

sets `fill-column` to 75.

`M-x set-variable` is limited to customizable variables, but you can set any variable with a Lisp expression like this:

        (setq fill-column 75)

To execute such an expression, type `M-:` (`eval-expression`) and enter the expression in the minibuffer (see Section 24.9 [Lisp Eval], page 278). Alternatively, go to the `*scratch*` buffer, type in the expression, and then type `C-j` (see Section 24.10 [Lisp Interaction], page 279).

Setting variables, like all means of customizing Emacs except where otherwise stated, affects only the current Emacs session. The only way to alter the variable in future sessions is to put something in your initialization file (see Section 33.4 [Init File], page 437).

33.2.2 Hooks

Hooks are an important mechanism for customizing Emacs. A hook is a Lisp variable which holds a list of functions, to be called on some well-defined occasion. (This is called *running the hook*.) The individual functions in the list are called the *hook functions* of the hook. For example, the hook `kill-emacs-hook` runs just before exiting Emacs (see Section 3.2 [Exiting], page 15).

Most hooks are *normal hooks*. This means that when Emacs runs the hook, it calls each hook function in turn, with no arguments. We have made an effort to keep most hooks normal, so that you can use them in a uniform way. Every variable whose name ends in '`-hook`' is a normal hook.

A few hooks are *abnormal hooks*. Their names end in '`-functions`', instead of '`-hook`' (some old code may also use the deprecated suffix '`-hooks`'). What makes these hooks abnormal is the way its functions are called—perhaps they are given arguments, or perhaps the values they return are used in some way. For example, `find-file-not-found-functions` is abnormal because as soon as one hook function returns a non-`nil` value, the rest are not called at all (see Section 15.2 [Visiting], page 123). The documentation of each abnormal hook variable explains how its functions are used.

You can set a hook variable with `setq` like any other Lisp variable, but the recommended way to add a function to a hook (either normal or abnormal) is to use `add-hook`, as shown by the following examples. See Section "Hooks" in *The Emacs Lisp Reference Manual*, for details.

Most major modes run one or more *mode hooks* as the last step of initialization. Mode hooks are a convenient way to customize the behavior of individual modes; they are always normal. For example, here's how to set up a hook to turn on Auto Fill mode in Text mode and other modes based on Text mode:

```
(add-hook 'text-mode-hook 'auto-fill-mode)
```

This works by calling `auto-fill-mode`, which enables the minor mode when no argument is supplied (see Section 20.2 [Minor Modes], page 200). Next, suppose you don't want Auto Fill mode turned on in LaTeX mode, which is one of the modes based on Text mode. You can do this with the following additional line:

```
(add-hook 'latex-mode-hook (lambda () (auto-fill-mode -1)))
```

Here we have used the special macro `lambda` to construct an anonymous function (see Section "Lambda Expressions" in *The Emacs Lisp Reference Manual*), which calls `auto-fill-mode` with an argument of `-1` to disable the minor mode. Because LaTeX mode runs `latex-mode-hook` after running `text-mode-hook`, the result leaves Auto Fill mode disabled.

Here is a more complex example, showing how to use a hook to customize the indentation of C code:

```
(setq my-c-style
  '((c-comment-only-line-offset . 4)
```

```
(c-cleanup-list . (scope-operator
                   empty-defun-braces
                   defun-close-semi))))

(add-hook 'c-mode-common-hook
  (lambda () (c-add-style "my-style" my-c-style t)))
```

Major mode hooks also apply to other major modes *derived* from the original mode
(see Section "Derived Modes" in *The Emacs Lisp Reference Manual*). For instance, HTML
mode is derived from Text mode (see Section 22.11 [HTML Mode], page 228); when HTML
mode is enabled, it runs `text-mode-hook` before running `html-mode-hook`. This provides
a convenient way to use a single hook to affect several related modes. In particular, if you
want to apply a hook function to any programming language mode, add it to `prog-mode-hook`; Prog mode is a major mode that does little else than to let other major modes inherit
from it, exactly for this purpose.

It is best to design your hook functions so that the order in which they are executed
does not matter. Any dependence on the order is asking for trouble. However, the order is
predictable: the hook functions are executed in the order they appear in the hook.

If you play with adding various different versions of a hook function by calling `add-hook`
over and over, remember that all the versions you added will remain in the hook variable
together. You can clear out individual functions by calling `remove-hook`, or do (setq
hook-variable nil) to remove everything.

If the hook variable is buffer-local, the buffer-local variable will be used instead of the
global variable. However, if the buffer-local variable contains the element `t`, the global hook
variable will be run as well.

33.2.3 Local Variables

M-x make-local-variable RET *var* RET
> Make variable *var* have a local value in the current buffer.

M-x kill-local-variable RET *var* RET
> Make variable *var* use its global value in the current buffer.

M-x make-variable-buffer-local RET *var* RET
> Mark variable *var* so that setting it will make it local to the buffer that is
> current at that time.

Almost any variable can be made *local* to a specific Emacs buffer. This means that its
value in that buffer is independent of its value in other buffers. A few variables are always
local in every buffer. Every other Emacs variable has a *global* value which is in effect in all
buffers that have not made the variable local.

`M-x make-local-variable` reads the name of a variable and makes it local to the current
buffer. Changing its value subsequently in this buffer will not affect others, and changes in
its global value will not affect this buffer.

`M-x make-variable-buffer-local` marks a variable so it will become local automatically whenever it is set. More precisely, once a variable has been marked in this way, the
usual ways of setting the variable automatically do `make-local-variable` first. We call
such variables *per-buffer* variables. Many variables in Emacs are normally per-buffer; the

variable's document string tells you when this is so. A per-buffer variable's global value is normally never effective in any buffer, but it still has a meaning: it is the initial value of the variable for each new buffer.

Major modes (see Section 20.1 [Major Modes], page 199) always make variables local to the buffer before setting the variables. This is why changing major modes in one buffer has no effect on other buffers. Minor modes also work by setting variables—normally, each minor mode has one controlling variable which is non-`nil` when the mode is enabled (see Section 20.2 [Minor Modes], page 200). For many minor modes, the controlling variable is per buffer, and thus always buffer-local. Otherwise, you can make it local in a specific buffer like any other variable.

A few variables cannot be local to a buffer because they are always local to each display instead (see Section 18.10 [Multiple Displays], page 171). If you try to make one of these variables buffer-local, you'll get an error message.

`M-x kill-local-variable` makes a specified variable cease to be local to the current buffer. The global value of the variable henceforth is in effect in this buffer. Setting the major mode kills all the local variables of the buffer except for a few variables specially marked as *permanent locals*.

To set the global value of a variable, regardless of whether the variable has a local value in the current buffer, you can use the Lisp construct `setq-default`. This construct is used just like `setq`, but it sets variables' global values instead of their local values (if any). When the current buffer does have a local value, the new global value may not be visible until you switch to another buffer. Here is an example:

```
(setq-default fill-column 75)
```

`setq-default` is the only way to set the global value of a variable that has been marked with `make-variable-buffer-local`.

Lisp programs can use `default-value` to look at a variable's default value. This function takes a symbol as argument and returns its default value. The argument is evaluated; usually you must quote it explicitly. For example, here's how to obtain the default value of `fill-column`:

```
(default-value 'fill-column)
```

33.2.4 Local Variables in Files

A file can specify local variable values to use when editing the file with Emacs. Visiting the file checks for local variable specifications; it automatically makes these variables local to the buffer, and sets them to the values specified in the file.

33.2.4.1 Specifying File Variables

There are two ways to specify file local variable values: in the first line, or with a local variables list. Here's how to specify them in the first line:

```
-*- mode: modename; var: value; ... -*-
```

You can specify any number of variable/value pairs in this way, each pair with a colon and semicolon. The special variable/value pair `mode: modename;`, if present, specifies a major mode. The *values* are used literally, and not evaluated.

You can use `M-x add-file-local-variable-prop-line` instead of adding entries by hand. This command prompts for a variable and value, and adds them to the first line in the appropriate way. M-x delete-file-local-variable-prop-line prompts for a variable, and deletes its entry from the line. The command M-x copy-dir-locals-to-file-locals-prop-line copies the current directory-local variables to the first line (see Section 33.2.5 [Directory Variables], page 427).

Here is an example first line that specifies Lisp mode and sets two variables with numeric values:

```
;; -*- mode: Lisp; fill-column: 75; comment-column: 50; -*-
```

Aside from mode, other keywords that have special meanings as file variables are coding, unibyte, and eval. These are described below.

In shell scripts, the first line is used to identify the script interpreter, so you cannot put any local variables there. To accommodate this, Emacs looks for local variable specifications in the *second* line if the first line specifies an interpreter. The same is true for man pages which start with the magic string ''\"' to specify a list of troff preprocessors (not all do, however).

Apart from using a '-*-' line, you can define file local variables using a *local variables list* near the end of the file. The start of the local variables list should be no more than 3000 characters from the end of the file, and must be on the last page if the file is divided into pages.

If a file has both a local variables list and a '-*-' line, Emacs processes *everything* in the '-*-' line first, and *everything* in the local variables list afterward. The exception to this is a major mode specification. Emacs applies this first, wherever it appears, since most major modes kill all local variables as part of their initialization.

A local variables list starts with a line containing the string 'Local Variables:', and ends with a line containing the string 'End:'. In between come the variable names and values, one set per line, like this:

```
/* Local Variables:  */
/* mode: c           */
/* comment-column: 0 */
/* End:              */
```

In this example, each line starts with the prefix '/*' and ends with the suffix '*/'. Emacs recognizes the prefix and suffix by finding them surrounding the magic string 'Local Variables:', on the first line of the list; it then automatically discards them from the other lines of the list. The usual reason for using a prefix and/or suffix is to embed the local variables list in a comment, so it won't confuse other programs that the file is intended for. The example above is for the C programming language, where comments start with '/*' and end with '*/'.

Instead of typing in the local variables list directly, you can use the command M-x add-file-local-variable. This prompts for a variable and value, and adds them to the list, adding the 'Local Variables:' string and start and end markers as necessary. The command M-x delete-file-local-variable deletes a variable from the list. M-x copy-dir-locals-to-file-locals copies directory-local variables to the list (see Section 33.2.5 [Directory Variables], page 427).

As with the '-*-' line, the variables in a local variables list are used literally, and are not evaluated first. If you want to split a long string value across multiple lines of the file, you can use backslash-newline, which is ignored in Lisp string constants; you should put the prefix and suffix on each line, even lines that start or end within the string, as they will be stripped off when processing the list. Here is an example:

```
# Local Variables:
# compile-command: "cc foo.c -Dfoo=bar -Dhack=whatever \
#   -Dmumble=blaah"
# End:
```

Some "variable names" have special meanings in a local variables list:

- **mode** enables the specified major mode.

- **eval** evaluates the specified Lisp expression (the value returned by that expression is ignored).

- **coding** specifies the coding system for character code conversion of this file. See Section 19.5 [Coding Systems], page 183.

- **unibyte** says to load or compile a file of Emacs Lisp in unibyte mode, if the value is **t**. See Section "Disabling Multibyte Characters" in *GNU Emacs Lisp Reference Manual*.

These four keywords are not really variables; setting them in any other context has no special meaning.

Do not use the **mode** keyword for minor modes. To enable or disable a minor mode in a local variables list, use the **eval** keyword with a Lisp expression that runs the mode command (see Section 20.2 [Minor Modes], page 200). For example, the following local variables list enables Eldoc mode (see Section 23.6.3 [Lisp Doc], page 253) by calling **eldoc-mode** with no argument (calling it with an argument of 1 would do the same), and disables Font Lock mode (see Section 11.12 [Font Lock], page 78) by calling **font-lock-mode** with an argument of -1.

```
;; Local Variables:
;; eval: (eldoc-mode)
;; eval: (font-lock-mode -1)
;; End:
```

Note, however, that it is often a mistake to specify minor modes this way. Minor modes represent individual user preferences, and it may be inappropriate to impose your preferences on another user who might edit the file. If you wish to automatically enable or disable a minor mode in a situation-dependent way, it is often better to do it in a major mode hook (see Section 33.2.2 [Hooks], page 422).

Use the command M-x normal-mode to reset the local variables and major mode of a buffer according to the file name and contents, including the local variables list if any. See Section 20.3 [Choosing Modes], page 202.

33.2.4.2 Safety of File Variables

File-local variables can be dangerous; when you visit someone else's file, there's no telling what its local variables list could do to your Emacs. Improper values of the **eval** "variable", and other variables such as **load-path**, could execute Lisp code you didn't intend to run.

Therefore, whenever Emacs encounters file local variable values that are not known to be safe, it displays the file's entire local variables list, and asks you for confirmation before setting them. You can type **y** or **SPC** to put the local variables list into effect, or **n** to ignore it. When Emacs is run in batch mode (see Section C.2 [Initial Options], page 480), it can't really ask you, so it assumes the answer `n`.

Emacs normally recognizes certain variable/value pairs as safe. For instance, it is safe to give `comment-column` or `fill-column` any integer value. If a file specifies only known-safe variable/value pairs, Emacs does not ask for confirmation before setting them. Otherwise, you can tell Emacs to record all the variable/value pairs in this file as safe, by typing `!` at the confirmation prompt. When Emacs encounters these variable/value pairs subsequently, in the same file or others, it will assume they are safe.

Some variables, such as `load-path`, are considered particularly *risky*: there is seldom any reason to specify them as local variables, and changing them can be dangerous. If a file contains only risky local variables, Emacs neither offers nor accepts `!` as input at the confirmation prompt. If some of the local variables in a file are risky, and some are only potentially unsafe, you can enter `!` at the prompt. It applies all the variables, but only marks the non-risky ones as safe for the future. If you really want to record safe values for risky variables, do it directly by customizing 'safe-local-variable-values' (see Section 33.1 [Easy Customization], page 412).

The variable `enable-local-variables` allows you to change the way Emacs processes local variables. Its default value is `t`, which specifies the behavior described above. If it is `nil`, Emacs simply ignores all file local variables. `:safe` means use only the safe values and ignore the rest. Any other value says to query you about each file that has local variables, without trying to determine whether the values are known to be safe.

The variable `enable-local-eval` controls whether Emacs processes `eval` variables. The three possibilities for the variable's value are `t`, `nil`, and anything else, just as for `enable-local-variables`. The default is `maybe`, which is neither `t` nor `nil`, so normally Emacs does ask for confirmation about processing `eval` variables.

As an exception, Emacs never asks for confirmation to evaluate any `eval` form if that form occurs within the variable `safe-local-eval-forms`.

33.2.5 Per-Directory Local Variables

Sometimes, you may wish to define the same set of local variables to all the files in a certain directory and its subdirectories, such as the directory tree of a large software project. This can be accomplished with *directory-local variables*.

The usual way to define directory-local variables is to put a file named `.dir-locals.el`[1] in a directory. Whenever Emacs visits any file in that directory or any of its subdirectories, it will apply the directory-local variables specified in `.dir-locals.el`, as though they had been defined as file-local variables for that file (see Section 33.2.4 [File Variables], page 424). Emacs searches for `.dir-locals.el` starting in the directory of the visited file, and moving up the directory tree. To avoid slowdown, this search is skipped for remote files. If needed, the search can be extended for remote files by setting the variable `enable-remote-dir-locals` to `t`.

The `.dir-locals.el` file should hold a specially-constructed list, which maps major mode names (symbols) to alists (see Section "Association Lists" in *The Emacs Lisp Refer-*

---

[1] On MS-DOS, the name of this file should be `_dir-locals.el`, due to limitations of the DOS filesystems. If the filesystem is limited to 8+3 file names, the name of the file will be truncated by the OS to `_dir-loc.el`.

ence Manual). Each alist entry consists of a variable name and the directory-local value to assign to that variable, when the specified major mode is enabled. Instead of a mode name, you can specify 'nil', which means that the alist applies to any mode; or you can specify a subdirectory name (a string), in which case the alist applies to all files in that subdirectory.

Here's an example of a .dir-locals.el file:

```
((nil . ((indent-tabs-mode . t)
         (fill-column . 80)))
 (c-mode . ((c-file-style . "BSD")
            (subdirs . nil)))
 ("src/imported"
  . ((nil . ((change-log-default-name
              . "ChangeLog.local")))))))
```

This sets 'indent-tabs-mode' and fill-column for any file in the directory tree, and the indentation style for any C source file. The special subdirs element is not a variable, but a special keyword which indicates that the C mode settings are only to be applied in the current directory, not in any subdirectories. Finally, it specifies a different ChangeLog file name for any file in the src/imported subdirectory.

Instead of editing the .dir-locals.el file by hand, you can use the command M-x add-dir-local-variable. This prompts for a mode or subdirectory name, and for variable and value, and adds the entry defining the directory-local variable. M-x delete-dir-local-variable deletes an entry. M-x copy-file-locals-to-dir-locals copies the file-local variables in the current file into .dir-locals.el.

Another method of specifying directory-local variables is to define a group of variables/value pairs in a *directory class*, using the dir-locals-set-class-variables function; then, tell Emacs which directories correspond to the class by using the dir-locals-set-directory-class function. These function calls normally go in your initialization file (see Section 33.4 [Init File], page 437). This method is useful when you can't put .dir-locals.el in a directory for some reason. For example, you could apply settings to an unwritable directory this way:

```
(dir-locals-set-class-variables 'unwritable-directory
  '((nil . ((some-useful-setting . value)))))

(dir-locals-set-directory-class
   "/usr/include/" 'unwritable-directory)
```

If a variable has both a directory-local and file-local value specified, the file-local value takes effect. Unsafe directory-local variables are handled in the same way as unsafe file-local variables (see Section 33.2.4.2 [Safe File Variables], page 426).

Directory-local variables also take effect in certain buffers that do not visit a file directly but perform work within a directory, such as Dired buffers (see Chapter 27 [Dired], page 315).

33.3 Customizing Key Bindings

This section describes *key bindings*, which map keys to commands, and *keymaps*, which record key bindings. It also explains how to customize key bindings, which is done by editing your init file (see Section 33.3.6 [Init Rebinding], page 432).

33.3.1 Keymaps

As described in Section 2.3 [Commands], page 12, each Emacs command is a Lisp function whose definition provides for interactive use. Like every Lisp function, a command has a function name, which usually consists of lower-case letters and hyphens.

A *key sequence* (*key*, for short) is a sequence of *input events* that have a meaning as a unit. Input events include characters, function keys and mouse buttons—all the inputs that you can send to the computer. A key sequence gets its meaning from its *binding*, which says what command it runs.

The bindings between key sequences and command functions are recorded in data structures called *keymaps*. Emacs has many of these, each used on particular occasions.

The *global* keymap is the most important keymap because it is always in effect. The global keymap defines keys for Fundamental mode (see Section 20.1 [Major Modes], page 199); most of these definitions are common to most or all major modes. Each major or minor mode can have its own keymap which overrides the global definitions of some keys.

For example, a self-inserting character such as g is self-inserting because the global keymap binds it to the command `self-insert-command`. The standard Emacs editing characters such as C-a also get their standard meanings from the global keymap. Commands to rebind keys, such as `M-x global-set-key`, work by storing the new binding in the proper place in the global map (see Section 33.3.5 [Rebinding], page 431).

Most modern keyboards have function keys as well as character keys. Function keys send input events just as character keys do, and keymaps can have bindings for them. Key sequences can mix function keys and characters. For example, if your keyboard has a `Home` function key, Emacs can recognize key sequences like `C-x Home`. You can even mix mouse events with keyboard events, such as `S-down-mouse-1`.

On text terminals, typing a function key actually sends the computer a sequence of characters; the precise details of the sequence depends on the function key and on the terminal type. (Often the sequence starts with `ESC [`.) If Emacs understands your terminal type properly, it automatically handles such sequences as single input events.

33.3.2 Prefix Keymaps

Internally, Emacs records only single events in each keymap. Interpreting a key sequence of multiple events involves a chain of keymaps: the first keymap gives a definition for the first event, which is another keymap, which is used to look up the second event in the sequence, and so on. Thus, a prefix key such as `C-x` or `ESC` has its own keymap, which holds the definition for the event that immediately follows that prefix.

The definition of a prefix key is usually the keymap to use for looking up the following event. The definition can also be a Lisp symbol whose function definition is the following keymap; the effect is the same, but it provides a command name for the prefix key that can be used as a description of what the prefix key is for. Thus, the binding of `C-x` is the symbol `Control-X-prefix`, whose function definition is the keymap for `C-x` commands. The definitions of `C-c`, `C-x`, `C-h` and `ESC` as prefix keys appear in the global map, so these prefix keys are always available.

Aside from ordinary prefix keys, there is a fictitious "prefix key" which represents the menu bar; see Section "Menu Bar" in *The Emacs Lisp Reference Manual*, for special information about menu bar key bindings. Mouse button events that invoke pop-up menus are also prefix keys; see Section "Menu Keymaps" in *The Emacs Lisp Reference Manual*, for more details.

Some prefix keymaps are stored in variables with names:

- `ctl-x-map` is the variable name for the map used for characters that follow `C-x`.
- `help-map` is for characters that follow `C-h`.
- `esc-map` is for characters that follow `ESC`. Thus, all Meta characters are actually defined by this map.
- `ctl-x-4-map` is for characters that follow `C-x 4`.
- `mode-specific-map` is for characters that follow `C-c`.

33.3.3 Local Keymaps

So far, we have explained the ins and outs of the global map. Major modes customize Emacs by providing their own key bindings in *local keymaps*. For example, C mode overrides `TAB` to make it indent the current line for C code. Minor modes can also have local keymaps; whenever a minor mode is in effect, the definitions in its keymap override both the major mode's local keymap and the global keymap. In addition, portions of text in the buffer can specify their own keymaps, which override all other keymaps.

A local keymap can redefine a key as a prefix key by defining it as a prefix keymap. If the key is also defined globally as a prefix, its local and global definitions (both keymaps) effectively combine: both definitions are used to look up the event that follows the prefix key. For example, if a local keymap defines `C-c` as a prefix keymap, and that keymap defines `C-z` as a command, this provides a local meaning for `C-c C-z`. This does not affect other sequences that start with `C-c`; if those sequences don't have their own local bindings, their global bindings remain in effect.

Another way to think of this is that Emacs handles a multi-event key sequence by looking in several keymaps, one by one, for a binding of the whole key sequence. First it checks the minor mode keymaps for minor modes that are enabled, then it checks the major mode's keymap, and then it checks the global keymap. This is not precisely how key lookup works, but it's good enough for understanding the results in ordinary circumstances.

33.3.4 Minibuffer Keymaps

The minibuffer has its own set of local keymaps; they contain various completion and exit commands.

- `minibuffer-local-map` is used for ordinary input (no completion).
- `minibuffer-local-ns-map` is similar, except that `SPC` exits just like `RET`.
- `minibuffer-local-completion-map` is for permissive completion.
- `minibuffer-local-must-match-map` is for strict completion and for cautious completion.
- `minibuffer-local-filename-completion-map` and `minibuffer-local-filename-must-match-map` are like the two previous ones, but they are specifically for file name completion. They do not bind `SPC`.

33.3.5 Changing Key Bindings Interactively

The way to redefine an Emacs key is to change its entry in a keymap. You can change the global keymap, in which case the change is effective in all major modes (except those that have their own overriding local bindings for the same key). Or you can change a local keymap, which affects all buffers using the same major mode.

In this section, we describe how to rebind keys for the present Emacs session. See Section 33.3.6 [Init Rebinding], page 432, for a description of how to make key rebindings affect future Emacs sessions.

M-x global-set-key RET *key* *cmd* RET
>   Define *key* globally to run *cmd*.

M-x local-set-key RET *key* *cmd* RET
>   Define *key* locally (in the major mode now in effect) to run *cmd*.

M-x global-unset-key RET *key*
>   Make *key* undefined in the global map.

M-x local-unset-key RET *key*
>   Make *key* undefined locally (in the major mode now in effect).

For example, the following binds C-z to the shell command (see Section 31.4.2 [Interactive Shell], page 384), replacing the normal global definition of C-z:

>   M-x global-set-key RET C-z shell RET

The global-set-key command reads the command name after the key. After you press the key, a message like this appears so that you can confirm that you are binding the key you want:

>   Set key C-z to command:

You can redefine function keys and mouse events in the same way; just type the function key or click the mouse when it's time to specify the key to rebind.

You can rebind a key that contains more than one event in the same way. Emacs keeps reading the key to rebind until it is a complete key (that is, not a prefix key). Thus, if you type C-f for *key*, that's the end; it enters the minibuffer immediately to read *cmd*. But if you type C-x, since that's a prefix, it reads another character; if that is 4, another prefix character, it reads one more character, and so on. For example,

>   M-x global-set-key RET C-x 4 $ spell-other-window RET

redefines C-x 4 $ to run the (fictitious) command spell-other-window.

You can remove the global definition of a key with global-unset-key. This makes the key *undefined*; if you type it, Emacs will just beep. Similarly, local-unset-key makes a key undefined in the current major mode keymap, which makes the global definition (or lack of one) come back into effect in that major mode.

If you have redefined (or undefined) a key and you subsequently wish to retract the change, undefining the key will not do the job—you need to redefine the key with its standard definition. To find the name of the standard definition of a key, go to a Fundamental mode buffer in a fresh Emacs and use C-h c. The documentation of keys in this manual also lists their command names.

If you want to prevent yourself from invoking a command by mistake, it is better to disable the command than to undefine the key. A disabled command is less work to invoke when you really want to. See Section 33.3.11 [Disabling], page 437.

33.3.6 Rebinding Keys in Your Init File

If you have a set of key bindings that you like to use all the time, you can specify them in your initialization file by writing Lisp code. See Section 33.4 [Init File], page 437, for a description of the initialization file.

There are several ways to write a key binding using Lisp. The simplest is to use the `kbd` function, which converts a textual representation of a key sequence—similar to how we have written key sequences in this manual—into a form that can be passed as an argument to `global-set-key`. For example, here's how to bind C-z to the `shell` command (see Section 31.4.2 [Interactive Shell], page 384):

```
(global-set-key (kbd "C-z") 'shell)
```

The single-quote before the command name, `shell`, marks it as a constant symbol rather than a variable. If you omit the quote, Emacs would try to evaluate `shell` as a variable. This probably causes an error; it certainly isn't what you want.

Here are some additional examples, including binding function keys and mouse events:

```
(global-set-key (kbd "C-c y") 'clipboard-yank)
(global-set-key (kbd "C-M-q") 'query-replace)
(global-set-key (kbd "<f5>") 'flyspell-mode)
(global-set-key (kbd "C-<f5>") 'linum-mode)
(global-set-key (kbd "C-<right>") 'forward-sentence)
(global-set-key (kbd "<mouse-2>") 'mouse-save-then-kill)
```

Instead of using `kbd`, you can use a Lisp string or vector to specify the key sequence. Using a string is simpler, but only works for ASCII characters and Meta-modified ASCII characters. For example, here's how to bind C-x M-l to `make-symbolic-link` (see Section 15.10 [Misc File Ops], page 140):

```
(global-set-key "\C-x\M-l" 'make-symbolic-link)
```

To put TAB, RET, ESC, or DEL in the string, use the Emacs Lisp escape sequences '\t', '\r', '\e', and '\d' respectively. Here is an example which binds C-x TAB to `indent-rigidly` (see Chapter 21 [Indentation], page 205):

```
(global-set-key "\C-x\t" 'indent-rigidly)
```

When the key sequence includes function keys or mouse button events, or non-ASCII characters such as C-= or H-a, you can use a vector to specify the key sequence. Each element in the vector stands for an input event; the elements are separated by spaces and surrounded by a pair of square brackets. If a vector element is a character, write it as a Lisp character constant: '?' followed by the character as it would appear in a string. Function keys are represented by symbols (see Section 33.3.8 [Function Keys], page 433); simply write the symbol's name, with no other delimiters or punctuation. Here are some examples:

```
(global-set-key [?\C-=] 'make-symbolic-link)
(global-set-key [?\M-\C-=] 'make-symbolic-link)
(global-set-key [?\H-a] 'make-symbolic-link)
(global-set-key [f7] 'make-symbolic-link)
```

```
(global-set-key [C-mouse-1] 'make-symbolic-link)
```

You can use a vector for the simple cases too:

```
(global-set-key [?\C-z ?\M-l] 'make-symbolic-link)
```

Language and coding systems may cause problems with key bindings for non-ASCII characters. See Section 33.4.5 [Init Non-ASCII], page 442.

As described in Section 33.3.3 [Local Keymaps], page 430, major modes and minor modes can define local keymaps. These keymaps are constructed when the mode is used for the first time in a session. If you wish to change one of these keymaps, you must use the *mode hook* (see Section 33.2.2 [Hooks], page 422).

For example, Texinfo mode runs the hook `texinfo-mode-hook`. Here's how you can use the hook to add local bindings for C-c n and C-c p in Texinfo mode:

```
(add-hook 'texinfo-mode-hook
          (lambda ()
            (define-key texinfo-mode-map "\C-cp"
                        'backward-paragraph)
            (define-key texinfo-mode-map "\C-cn"
                        'forward-paragraph)))
```

33.3.7 Modifier Keys

The default key bindings in Emacs are set up so that modified alphabetical characters are case-insensitive. In other words, C-A does the same thing as C-a, and M-A does the same thing as M-a. This concerns only alphabetical characters, and does not apply to "shifted" versions of other keys; for instance, C-@ is not the same as C-2.

A `Control`-modified alphabetical character is always considered case-insensitive: Emacs always treats C-A as C-a, C-B as C-b, and so forth. The reason for this is historical.

For all other modifiers, you can make the modified alphabetical characters case-sensitive when you customize Emacs. For instance, you could make M-a and M-A run different commands.

Although only the `Control` and `META` modifier keys are commonly used, Emacs supports three other modifier keys. These are called `Super`, `Hyper` and `Alt`. Few terminals provide ways to use these modifiers; the key labeled `Alt` on most keyboards usually issues the `META` modifier, not `Alt`. The standard key bindings in Emacs do not include any characters with these modifiers. However, you can customize Emacs to assign meanings to them. The modifier bits are labeled as 's-', 'H-' and 'A-' respectively.

Even if your keyboard lacks these additional modifier keys, you can enter it using C-x @: C-x @ h adds the "hyper" flag to the next character, C-x @ s adds the "super" flag, and C-x @ a adds the "alt" flag. For instance, C-x @ h C-a is a way to enter Hyper-Control-a. (Unfortunately, there is no way to add two modifiers by using C-x @ twice for the same character, because the first one goes to work on the C-x.)

33.3.8 Rebinding Function Keys

Key sequences can contain function keys as well as ordinary characters. Just as Lisp characters (actually integers) represent keyboard characters, Lisp symbols represent function keys. If the function key has a word as its label, then that word is also the name of the corresponding Lisp symbol. Here are the conventional Lisp names for common function keys:

`LEFT, UP, RIGHT, DOWN`
>   Cursor arrow keys.

`Begin, End, Home, next, prior`
>   Other cursor repositioning keys.

`select, print, execute, backtab`
`insert, undo, redo, clearline`
`insertline, deleteline, insertchar, deletechar`
>   Miscellaneous function keys.

`f1, f2, ... f35`
>   Numbered function keys (across the top of the keyboard).

`kp-add, kp-subtract, kp-multiply, kp-divide`
`kp-backtab, kp-space, kp-tab, kp-enter`
`kp-separator, kp-decimal, kp-equal`
>   Keypad keys (to the right of the regular keyboard), with names or punctuation.

`kp-0, kp-1, ... kp-9`
>   Keypad keys with digits.

`kp-f1, kp-f2, kp-f3, kp-f4`
>   Keypad PF keys.

These names are conventional, but some systems (especially when using X) may use different names. To make certain what symbol is used for a given function key on your terminal, type `C-h c` followed by that key.

See Section 33.3.6 [Init Rebinding], page 432, for examples of binding function keys.

Many keyboards have a "numeric keypad" on the right hand side. The numeric keys in the keypad double up as cursor motion keys, toggled by a key labeled 'Num Lock'. By default, Emacs translates these keys to the corresponding keys in the main keyboard. For example, when 'Num Lock' is on, the key labeled '8' on the numeric keypad produces `kp-8`, which is translated to 8; when 'Num Lock' is off, the same key produces `kp-up`, which is translated to `UP`. If you rebind a key such as 8 or `UP`, it affects the equivalent keypad key too. However, if you rebind a 'kp-' key directly, that won't affect its non-keypad equivalent. Note that the modified keys are not translated: for instance, if you hold down the `META` key while pressing the '8' key on the numeric keypad, that generates `M-kp-8`.

Emacs provides a convenient method for binding the numeric keypad keys, using the variables `keypad-setup`, `keypad-numlock-setup`, `keypad-shifted-setup`, and `keypad-numlock-shifted-setup`. These can be found in the 'keyboard' customization group (see Section 33.1 [Easy Customization], page 412). You can rebind the keys to perform other tasks, such as issuing numeric prefix arguments.

33.3.9 Named ASCII Control Characters

`TAB, RET, BS, LFD, ESC` and `DEL` started out as names for certain ASCII control characters, used so often that they have special keys of their own. For instance, `TAB` was another name for `C-i`. Later, users found it convenient to distinguish in Emacs between these keys and the "same" control characters typed with the `Ctrl` key. Therefore, on most modern terminals, they are no longer the same: `TAB` is different from `C-i`.

Emacs can distinguish these two kinds of input if the keyboard does. It treats the "special" keys as function keys named `tab`, `return`, `backspace`, `linefeed`, `escape`, and `delete`. These function keys translate automatically into the corresponding ASCII characters *if* they have no bindings of their own. As a result, neither users nor Lisp programs need to pay attention to the distinction unless they care to.

If you do not want to distinguish between (for example) `TAB` and `C-i`, make just one binding, for the ASCII character `TAB` (octal code 011). If you do want to distinguish, make one binding for this ASCII character, and another for the "function key" `tab`.

With an ordinary ASCII terminal, there is no way to distinguish between `TAB` and `C-i` (and likewise for other such pairs), because the terminal sends the same character in both cases.

33.3.10 Rebinding Mouse Buttons

Emacs uses Lisp symbols to designate mouse buttons, too. The ordinary mouse events in Emacs are *click* events; these happen when you press a button and release it without moving the mouse. You can also get *drag* events, when you move the mouse while holding the button down. Drag events happen when you finally let go of the button.

The symbols for basic click events are `mouse-1` for the leftmost button, `mouse-2` for the next, and so on. Here is how you can redefine the second mouse button to split the current window:

```
(global-set-key [mouse-2] 'split-window-below)
```

The symbols for drag events are similar, but have the prefix 'drag-' before the word 'mouse'. For example, dragging the first button generates a `drag-mouse-1` event.

You can also define bindings for events that occur when a mouse button is pressed down. These events start with 'down-' instead of 'drag-'. Such events are generated only if they have key bindings. When you get a button-down event, a corresponding click or drag event will always follow.

If you wish, you can distinguish single, double, and triple clicks. A double click means clicking a mouse button twice in approximately the same place. The first click generates an ordinary click event. The second click, if it comes soon enough, generates a double-click event instead. The event type for a double-click event starts with 'double-': for example, `double-mouse-3`.

This means that you can give a special meaning to the second click at the same place, but it must act on the assumption that the ordinary single click definition has run when the first click was received.

This constrains what you can do with double clicks, but user interface designers say that this constraint ought to be followed in any case. A double click should do something similar to the single click, only "more so". The command for the double-click event should perform the extra work for the double click.

If a double-click event has no binding, it changes to the corresponding single-click event. Thus, if you don't define a particular double click specially, it executes the single-click command twice.

Emacs also supports triple-click events whose names start with 'triple-'. Emacs does not distinguish quadruple clicks as event types; clicks beyond the third generate additional triple-click events. However, the full number of clicks is recorded in the event list, so if you know Emacs Lisp you can distinguish if you really want to (see Section "Click Events" in *The Emacs Lisp Reference Manual*). We don't recommend distinct meanings for more than three clicks, but sometimes it is useful for subsequent clicks to cycle through the same set of three meanings, so that four clicks are equivalent to one click, five are equivalent to two, and six are equivalent to three.

Emacs also records multiple presses in drag and button-down events. For example, when you press a button twice, then move the mouse while holding the button, Emacs gets a 'double-drag-' event. And at the moment when you press it down for the second time, Emacs gets a 'double-down-' event (which is ignored, like all button-down events, if it has no binding).

The variable `double-click-time` specifies how much time can elapse between clicks and still allow them to be grouped as a multiple click. Its value is in units of milliseconds. If the value is `nil`, double clicks are not detected at all. If the value is `t`, then there is no time limit. The default is 500.

The variable `double-click-fuzz` specifies how much the mouse can move between clicks and still allow them to be grouped as a multiple click. Its value is in units of pixels on windowed displays and in units of 1/8 of a character cell on text-mode terminals; the default is 3.

The symbols for mouse events also indicate the status of the modifier keys, with the usual prefixes 'C-', 'M-', 'H-', 's-', 'A-' and 'S-'. These always precede 'double-' or 'triple-', which always precede 'drag-' or 'down-'.

A frame includes areas that don't show text from the buffer, such as the mode line and the scroll bar. You can tell whether a mouse button comes from a special area of the screen by means of dummy "prefix keys". For example, if you click the mouse in the mode line, you get the prefix key `mode-line` before the ordinary mouse-button symbol. Thus, here is how to define the command for clicking the first button in a mode line to run `scroll-up-command`:

        (global-set-key [mode-line mouse-1] 'scroll-up-command)

Here is the complete list of these dummy prefix keys and their meanings:

`mode-line`

> The mouse was in the mode line of a window.

`vertical-line`

> The mouse was in the vertical line separating side-by-side windows. (If you use scroll bars, they appear in place of these vertical lines.)

`vertical-scroll-bar`

> The mouse was in a vertical scroll bar. (This is the only kind of scroll bar Emacs currently supports.)

`menu-bar`   The mouse was in the menu bar.

`header-line`

> The mouse was in a header line.

You can put more than one mouse button in a key sequence, but it isn't usual to do so.

33.3.11 Disabling Commands

Disabling a command means that invoking it interactively asks for confirmation from the user. The purpose of disabling a command is to prevent users from executing it by accident; we do this for commands that might be confusing to the uninitiated.

Attempting to invoke a disabled command interactively in Emacs displays a window containing the command's name, its documentation, and some instructions on what to do immediately; then Emacs asks for input saying whether to execute the command as requested, enable it and execute it, or cancel. If you decide to enable the command, you must then answer another question—whether to do this permanently, or just for the current session. (Enabling permanently works by automatically editing your initialization file.) You can also type ! to enable *all* commands, for the current session only.

The direct mechanism for disabling a command is to put a non-**nil** **disabled** property on the Lisp symbol for the command. Here is the Lisp program to do this:

```
(put 'delete-region 'disabled t)
```

If the value of the **disabled** property is a string, that string is included in the message displayed when the command is used:

```
(put 'delete-region 'disabled
     "It's better to use 'kill-region' instead.\n")
```

You can make a command disabled either by editing the initialization file directly, or with the command **M-x disable-command**, which edits the initialization file for you. Likewise, **M-x enable-command** edits the initialization file to enable a command permanently. See Section 33.4 [Init File], page 437.

If Emacs was invoked with the **-q** or **--no-init-file** options (see Section C.2 [Initial Options], page 480), it will not edit your initialization file. Doing so could lose information because Emacs has not read your initialization file.

Whether a command is disabled is independent of what key is used to invoke it; disabling also applies if the command is invoked using **M-x**. However, disabling a command has no effect on calling it as a function from Lisp programs.

33.4 The Emacs Initialization File

When Emacs is started, it normally tries to load a Lisp program from an *initialization file*, or *init file* for short. This file, if it exists, specifies how to initialize Emacs for you. Emacs looks for your init file using the filenames `~/.emacs`, `~/.emacs.el`, or `~/.emacs.d/init.el`; you can choose to use any one of these three names (see Section 33.4.4 [Find Init], page 442). Here, `~/` stands for your home directory.

You can use the command line switch '**-q**' to prevent loading your init file, and '**-u**' (or '**--user**') to specify a different user's init file (see Section C.2 [Initial Options], page 480).

There can also be a *default init file*, which is the library named **default.el**, found via the standard search path for libraries. The Emacs distribution contains no such library; your site may create one for local customizations. If this library exists, it is loaded whenever you start Emacs (except when you specify '**-q**'). But your init file, if any, is loaded first; if it sets **inhibit-default-init** non-nil, then **default** is not loaded.

Your site may also have a *site startup file*; this is named **site-start.el**, if it exists. Like **default.el**, Emacs finds this file via the standard search path for Lisp libraries. Emacs loads this library before it loads your init file. To inhibit loading of this library, use the option '--no-site-file'. See Section C.2 [Initial Options], page 480. We recommend against using `site-start.el` for changes that some users may not like. It is better to put them in `default.el`, so that users can more easily override them.

You can place `default.el` and `site-start.el` in any of the directories which Emacs searches for Lisp libraries. The variable `load-path` (see Section 24.8 [Lisp Libraries], page 276) specifies these directories. Many sites put these files in a subdirectory named `site-lisp` in the Emacs installation directory, such as `/usr/local/share/emacs/site-lisp`.

Byte-compiling your init file is not recommended (see Section "Byte Compilation" in *the Emacs Lisp Reference Manual*). It generally does not speed up startup very much, and often leads to problems when you forget to recompile the file. A better solution is to use the Emacs server to reduce the number of times you have to start Emacs (see Section 31.5 [Emacs Server], page 393). If your init file defines many functions, consider moving them to a separate (byte-compiled) file that you load in your init file.

If you are going to write actual Emacs Lisp programs that go beyond minor customization, you should read the *Emacs Lisp Reference Manual*.

33.4.1 Init File Syntax

The init file contains one or more Lisp expressions. Each of these consists of a function name followed by arguments, all surrounded by parentheses. For example, (`setq fill-column 60`) calls the function `setq` to set the variable `fill-column` (see Section 22.5 [Filling], page 212) to 60.

You can set any Lisp variable with `setq`, but with certain variables `setq` won't do what you probably want in the `.emacs` file. Some variables automatically become buffer-local when set with `setq`; what you want in `.emacs` is to set the default value, using `setq-default`. Some customizable minor mode variables do special things to enable the mode when you set them with Customize, but ordinary `setq` won't do that; to enable the mode in your `.emacs` file, call the minor mode command. The following section has examples of both of these methods.

The second argument to `setq` is an expression for the new value of the variable. This can be a constant, a variable, or a function call expression. In `.emacs`, constants are used most of the time. They can be:

Numbers: Numbers are written in decimal, with an optional initial minus sign.

Strings: Lisp string syntax is the same as C string syntax with a few extra features. Use a double-quote character to begin and end a string constant.

In a string, you can include newlines and special characters literally. But often it is cleaner to use backslash sequences for them: '\n' for newline, '\b' for backspace, '\r' for carriage return, '\t' for tab, '\f' for formfeed (control-L), '\e' for escape, '\\' for a backslash, '\"' for a double-quote, or '\ooo' for the character whose octal code is *ooo*. Backslash and double-quote are the only characters for which backslash sequences are mandatory.

'\C-' can be used as a prefix for a control character, as in '\C-s' for ASCII control-S, and '\M-' can be used as a prefix for a Meta character, as in '\M-a' for META-A or '\M-\C-a' for Ctrl-META-A.

See Section 33.4.5 [Init Non-ASCII], page 442, for information about including non-ASCII in your init file.

Characters:

Lisp character constant syntax consists of a '?' followed by either a character or an escape sequence starting with '\'. Examples: ?x, ?\n, ?\", ?\). Note that strings and characters are not interchangeable in Lisp; some contexts require one and some contexts require the other.

See Section 33.4.5 [Init Non-ASCII], page 442, for information about binding commands to keys which send non-ASCII characters.

True: t stands for 'true'.

False: nil stands for 'false'.

Other Lisp objects:

Write a single-quote (') followed by the Lisp object you want.

33.4.2 Init File Examples

Here are some examples of doing certain commonly desired things with Lisp expressions:

- Add a directory to the variable `load-path`. You can then put Lisp libraries that are not included with Emacs in this directory, and load them with M-x `load-library`. See Section 24.8 [Lisp Libraries], page 276.

```
(add-to-list 'load-path "/path/to/lisp/libraries")
```

- Make `TAB` in C mode just insert a tab if point is in the middle of a line.

```
(setq c-tab-always-indent nil)
```

Here we have a variable whose value is normally `t` for 'true' and the alternative is `nil` for 'false'.

- Make searches case sensitive by default (in all buffers that do not override this).

```
(setq-default case-fold-search nil)
```

This sets the default value, which is effective in all buffers that do not have local values for the variable (see Section 33.2.3 [Locals], page 423). Setting `case-fold-search` with `setq` affects only the current buffer's local value, which is probably not what you want to do in an init file.

- Specify your own email address, if Emacs can't figure it out correctly.

```
(setq user-mail-address "cheney@torture.gov")
```

Various Emacs packages, such as Message mode, consult `user-mail-address` when they need to know your email address. See Section 29.2 [Mail Headers], page 351.

- Make Text mode the default mode for new buffers.

```
(setq-default major-mode 'text-mode)
```

Note that `text-mode` is used because it is the command for entering Text mode. The single-quote before it makes the symbol a constant; otherwise, `text-mode` would be treated as a variable name.

- Set up defaults for the Latin-1 character set which supports most of the languages of Western Europe.

  ```
  (set-language-environment "Latin-1")
  ```

- Turn off Line Number mode, a global minor mode.

  ```
  (line-number-mode 0)
  ```

- Turn on Auto Fill mode automatically in Text mode and related modes (see Section 33.2.2 [Hooks], page 422).

  ```
  (add-hook 'text-mode-hook 'auto-fill-mode)
  ```

- Load the installed Lisp library named `foo` (actually a file `foo.elc` or `foo.el` in a standard Emacs directory).

  ```
  (load "foo")
  ```

  When the argument to `load` is a relative file name, not starting with '/' or '~', `load` searches the directories in `load-path` (see Section 24.8 [Lisp Libraries], page 276).

- Load the compiled Lisp file `foo.elc` from your home directory.

  ```
  (load "~/foo.elc")
  ```

  Here a full file name is used, so no searching is done.

- Tell Emacs to find the definition for the function `myfunction` by loading a Lisp library named `mypackage` (i.e., a file `mypackage.elc` or `mypackage.el`):

  ```
  (autoload 'myfunction "mypackage" "Do what I say." t)
  ```

  Here the string `"Do what I say."` is the function's documentation string. You specify it in the `autoload` definition so it will be available for help commands even when the package is not loaded. The last argument, `t`, indicates that this function is interactive; that is, it can be invoked interactively by typing `M-x myfunction RET` or by binding it to a key. If the function is not interactive, omit the `t` or use `nil`.

- Rebind the key `C-x l` to run the function `make-symbolic-link` (see Section 33.3.6 [Init Rebinding], page 432).

  ```
  (global-set-key "\C-xl" 'make-symbolic-link)
  ```

  or

  ```
  (define-key global-map "\C-xl" 'make-symbolic-link)
  ```

  Note once again the single-quote used to refer to the symbol `make-symbolic-link` instead of its value as a variable.

- Do the same thing for Lisp mode only.

  ```
  (define-key lisp-mode-map "\C-xl" 'make-symbolic-link)
  ```

- Redefine all keys which now run `next-line` in Fundamental mode so that they run `forward-line` instead.

  ```
  (substitute-key-definition 'next-line 'forward-line
                             global-map)
  ```

- Make `C-x C-v` undefined.

  ```
  (global-unset-key "\C-x\C-v")
  ```

  One reason to undefine a key is so that you can make it a prefix. Simply defining `C-x C-v` *anything* will make `C-x C-v` a prefix, but `C-x C-v` must first be freed of its usual non-prefix definition.

- Make '$' have the syntax of punctuation in Text mode. Note the use of a character constant for '$'.

```
(modify-syntax-entry ?\$ "." text-mode-syntax-table)
```

- Enable the use of the command `narrow-to-region` without confirmation.

```
(put 'narrow-to-region 'disabled nil)
```

- Adjusting the configuration to various platforms and Emacs versions.

Users typically want Emacs to behave the same on all systems, so the same init file is right for all platforms. However, sometimes it happens that a function you use for customizing Emacs is not available on some platforms or in older Emacs versions. To deal with that situation, put the customization inside a conditional that tests whether the function or facility is available, like this:

```
(if (fboundp 'blink-cursor-mode)
    (blink-cursor-mode 0))
```

```
(if (boundp 'coding-category-utf-8)
    (set-coding-priority '(coding-category-utf-8)))
```

You can also simply disregard the errors that occur if the function is not defined.

```
(condition case ()
    (set-face-background 'region "grey75")
  (error nil))
```

A `setq` on a variable which does not exist is generally harmless, so those do not need a conditional.

33.4.3 Terminal-specific Initialization

Each terminal type can have a Lisp library to be loaded into Emacs when it is run on that type of terminal. For a terminal type named *termtype*, the library is called `term/termtype` and it is found by searching the directories `load-path` as usual and trying the suffixes '.elc' and '.el'. Normally it appears in the subdirectory `term` of the directory where most Emacs libraries are kept.

The usual purpose of the terminal-specific library is to map the escape sequences used by the terminal's function keys onto more meaningful names, using `input-decode-map` (or `function-key-map` before it). See the file `term/lk201.el` for an example of how this is done. Many function keys are mapped automatically according to the information in the Termcap data base; the terminal-specific library needs to map only the function keys that Termcap does not specify.

When the terminal type contains a hyphen, only the part of the name before the first hyphen is significant in choosing the library name. Thus, terminal types 'aaa-48' and 'aaa-30-rv' both use the library `term/aaa`. The code in the library can use (getenv "TERM") to find the full terminal type name.

The library's name is constructed by concatenating the value of the variable `term-file-prefix` and the terminal type. Your `.emacs` file can prevent the loading of the terminal-specific library by setting `term-file-prefix` to `nil`.

Emacs runs the hook `tty-setup-hook` at the end of initialization, after both your `.emacs` file and any terminal-specific library have been read in. Add hook functions to this hook if you wish to override part of any of the terminal-specific libraries and to define initializations for terminals that do not have a library. See Section 33.2.2 [Hooks], page 422.

33.4.4 How Emacs Finds Your Init File

Normally Emacs uses the environment variable HOME (see Section C.4.1 [General Variables], page 483) to find .emacs; that's what '~' means in a file name. If .emacs is not found inside ~/ (nor .emacs.el), Emacs looks for ~/.emacs.d/init.el (which, like ~/.emacs.el, can be byte-compiled).

However, if you run Emacs from a shell started by su, Emacs tries to find your own .emacs, not that of the user you are currently pretending to be. The idea is that you should get your own editor customizations even if you are running as the super user.

More precisely, Emacs first determines which user's init file to use. It gets your user name from the environment variables LOGNAME and USER; if neither of those exists, it uses effective user-ID. If that user name matches the real user-ID, then Emacs uses HOME; otherwise, it looks up the home directory corresponding to that user name in the system's data base of users.

33.4.5 Non-ASCII Characters in Init Files

Language and coding systems may cause problems if your init file contains non-ASCII characters, such as accented letters, in strings or key bindings.

If you want to use non-ASCII characters in your init file, you should put a '-*-coding: *coding-system*-*-' tag on the first line of the init file, and specify a coding system that supports the character(s) in question. See Section 19.6 [Recognize Coding], page 185. This is because the defaults for decoding non-ASCII text might not yet be set up by the time Emacs reads those parts of your init file which use such strings, possibly leading Emacs to decode those strings incorrectly. You should then avoid adding Emacs Lisp code that modifies the coding system in other ways, such as calls to set-language-environment.

To bind non-ASCII keys, you must use a vector (see Section 33.3.6 [Init Rebinding], page 432). The string syntax cannot be used, since the non-ASCII characters will be interpreted as meta keys. For instance:

```
(global-set-key [?char] 'some-function)
```

Type C-q, followed by the key you want to bind, to insert *char*.

Warning: if you change the keyboard encoding, or change between multibyte and unibyte mode, or anything that would alter which code C-q would insert for that character, this key binding may stop working. It is therefore advisable to use one and only one coding system, for your init file as well as the files you edit. For example, don't mix the 'latin-1' and 'latin-9' coding systems.

34 Dealing with Common Problems

If you type an Emacs command you did not intend, the results are often mysterious. This chapter tells what you can do to cancel your mistake or recover from a mysterious situation. Emacs bugs and system crashes are also considered.

34.1 Quitting and Aborting

C-g
C-Break (MS-DOS only)
> Quit: cancel running or partially typed command.

C-]   Abort innermost recursive editing level and cancel the command which invoked
        it (`abort-recursive-edit`).

ESC ESC ESC
> Either quit or abort, whichever makes sense (`keyboard-escape-quit`).

M-x top-level
> Abort all recursive editing levels that are currently executing.

C-/
C-x u
C-_   Cancel a previously made change in the buffer contents (`undo`).

There are two ways of canceling a command before it has finished: *quitting* with `C-g`, and *aborting* with `C-]` or `M-x top-level`. Quitting cancels a partially typed command, or one which is still running. Aborting exits a recursive editing level and cancels the command that invoked the recursive edit (see Section 31.10 [Recursive Edit], page 404).

Quitting with `C-g` is the way to get rid of a partially typed command, or a numeric argument that you don't want. Furthermore, if you are in the middle of a command that is running, `C-g` stops the command in a relatively safe way. For example, if you quit out of a kill command that is taking a long time, either your text will *all* still be in the buffer, or it will *all* be in the kill ring, or maybe both. If the region is active, `C-g` deactivates the mark, unless Transient Mark mode is off (see Section 8.7 [Disabled Transient Mark], page 50). If you are in the middle of an incremental search, `C-g` behaves specially; it may take two successive `C-g` characters to get out of a search. See Section 12.1 [Incremental Search], page 90, for details.

On MS-DOS, the character `C-Break` serves as a quit character like `C-g`. The reason is that it is not feasible, on MS-DOS, to recognize `C-g` while a command is running, between interactions with the user. By contrast, it *is* feasible to recognize `C-Break` at all times. See Section "MS-DOS Keyboard" in *Specialized Emacs Features*.

`C-g` works by setting the variable `quit-flag` to `t` the instant `C-g` is typed; Emacs Lisp checks this variable frequently, and quits if it is non-`nil`. `C-g` is only actually executed as a command if you type it while Emacs is waiting for input. In that case, the command it runs is `keyboard-quit`.

On a text terminal, if you quit with `C-g` a second time before the first `C-g` is recognized, you activate the "emergency escape" feature and return to the shell. See Section 34.2.8 [Emergency Escape], page 448.

There are some situations where you cannot quit. When Emacs is waiting for the operating system to do something, quitting is impossible unless special pains are taken for the particular system call within Emacs where the waiting occurs. We have done this for the system calls that users are likely to want to quit from, but it's possible you will encounter a case not handled. In one very common case—waiting for file input or output using NFS— Emacs itself knows how to quit, but many NFS implementations simply do not allow user programs to stop waiting for NFS when the NFS server is hung.

Aborting with C-] (`abort-recursive-edit`) is used to get out of a recursive editing level and cancel the command which invoked it. Quitting with C-g does not do this, and could not do this, because it is used to cancel a partially typed command *within* the recursive editing level. Both operations are useful. For example, if you are in a recursive edit and type C-u 8 to enter a numeric argument, you can cancel that argument with C-g and remain in the recursive edit.

The sequence ESC ESC ESC (`keyboard-escape-quit`) can either quit or abort. (We defined it this way because ESC means "get out" in many PC programs.) It can cancel a prefix argument, clear a selected region, or get out of a Query Replace, like C-g. It can get out of the minibuffer or a recursive edit, like C-]. It can also get out of splitting the frame into multiple windows, as with C-x 1. One thing it cannot do, however, is stop a command that is running. That's because it executes as an ordinary command, and Emacs doesn't notice it until it is ready for the next command.

The command M-x top-level is equivalent to "enough" C-] commands to get you out of all the levels of recursive edits that you are in; it also exits the minibuffer if it is active. C-] gets you out one level at a time, but M-x top-level goes out all levels at once. Both C-] and M-x top-level are like all other commands, and unlike C-g, in that they take effect only when Emacs is ready for a command. C-] is an ordinary key and has its meaning only because of its binding in the keymap. See Section 31.10 [Recursive Edit], page 404.

C-/ (`undo`) is not strictly speaking a way of canceling a command, but you can think of it as canceling a command that already finished executing. See Section 13.1 [Undo], page 109, for more information about the undo facility.

34.2 Dealing with Emacs Trouble

This section describes how to recognize and deal with situations in which Emacs does not work as you expect, such as keyboard code mixups, garbled displays, running out of memory, and crashes and hangs.

See Section 34.3 [Bugs], page 448, for what to do when you think you have found a bug in Emacs.

34.2.1 If DEL Fails to Delete

Every keyboard has a large key, usually labeled BACKSPACE, which is ordinarily used to erase the last character that you typed. In Emacs, this key is supposed to be equivalent to DEL.

When Emacs starts up on a graphical display, it determines automatically which key should be DEL. In some unusual cases, Emacs gets the wrong information from the system, and BACKSPACE ends up deleting forwards instead of backwards.

Some keyboards also have a `Delete` key, which is ordinarily used to delete forwards. If this key deletes backward in Emacs, that too suggests Emacs got the wrong information— but in the opposite sense.

On a text terminal, if you find that `BACKSPACE` prompts for a Help command, like `Control-h`, instead of deleting a character, it means that key is actually sending the 'BS' character. Emacs ought to be treating `BS` as `DEL`, but it isn't.

In all of those cases, the immediate remedy is the same: use the command `M-x normal-erase-is-backspace-mode`. This toggles between the two modes that Emacs supports for handling `DEL`, so if Emacs starts in the wrong mode, this should switch to the right mode. On a text terminal, if you want to ask for help when `BS` is treated as `DEL`, use `F1`; `C-?` may also work, if it sends character code 127.

To fix the problem in every Emacs session, put one of the following lines into your initialization file (see Section 33.4 [Init File], page 437). For the first case above, where `BACKSPACE` deletes forwards instead of backwards, use this line to make `BACKSPACE` act as `DEL`:

```
(normal-erase-is-backspace-mode 0)
```

For the other two cases, use this line:

```
(normal-erase-is-backspace-mode 1)
```

Another way to fix the problem for every Emacs session is to customize the variable `normal-erase-is-backspace`: the value `t` specifies the mode where `BS` or `BACKSPACE` is `DEL`, and `nil` specifies the other mode. See Section 33.1 [Easy Customization], page 412.

34.2.2 Recursive Editing Levels

Recursive editing levels are important and useful features of Emacs, but they can seem like malfunctions if you do not understand them.

If the mode line has square brackets '`[...]`' around the parentheses that contain the names of the major and minor modes, you have entered a recursive editing level. If you did not do this on purpose, or if you don't understand what that means, you should just get out of the recursive editing level. To do so, type `M-x top-level`. See Section 31.10 [Recursive Edit], page 404.

34.2.3 Garbage on the Screen

If the text on a text terminal looks wrong, the first thing to do is see whether it is wrong in the buffer. Type `C-l` to redisplay the entire screen. If the screen appears correct after this, the problem was entirely in the previous screen update. (Otherwise, see the following section.)

Display updating problems often result from an incorrect terminfo entry for the terminal you are using. The file `etc/TERMS` in the Emacs distribution gives the fixes for known problems of this sort. `INSTALL` contains general advice for these problems in one of its sections. If you seem to be using the right terminfo entry, it is possible that there is a bug in the terminfo entry, or a bug in Emacs that appears for certain terminal types.

34.2.4 Garbage in the Text

If C-l shows that the text is wrong, first type C-h l to see what commands you typed to produce the observed results. Then try undoing the changes step by step using C-x u, until it gets back to a state you consider correct.

If a large portion of text appears to be missing at the beginning or end of the buffer, check for the word 'Narrow' in the mode line. If it appears, the text you don't see is probably still present, but temporarily off-limits. To make it accessible again, type C-x n w. See Section 11.5 [Narrowing], page 73.

34.2.5 Running out of Memory

If you get the error message 'Virtual memory exceeded', save your modified buffers with C-x s. This method of saving them has the smallest need for additional memory. Emacs keeps a reserve of memory which it makes available when this error happens; that should be enough to enable C-x s to complete its work. When the reserve has been used, '!MEM FULL!' appears at the beginning of the mode line, indicating there is no more reserve.

Once you have saved your modified buffers, you can exit this Emacs session and start another, or you can use M-x kill-some-buffers to free space in the current Emacs job. If this frees up sufficient space, Emacs will refill its memory reserve, and '!MEM FULL!' will disappear from the mode line. That means you can safely go on editing in the same Emacs session.

Do not use M-x buffer-menu to save or kill buffers when you run out of memory, because the Buffer Menu needs a fair amount of memory itself, and the reserve supply may not be enough.

34.2.6 When Emacs Crashes

Emacs is not supposed to crash, but if it does, it produces a *crash report* prior to exiting. The crash report is printed to the standard error stream. If Emacs was started from a graphical desktop on a GNU or Unix system, the standard error stream is commonly redirected to a file such as ~/.xsession-errors, so you can look for the crash report there. On MS-Windows, the crash report is written to a file named emacs_backtrace.txt in the current directory of the Emacs process, in addition to the standard error stream.

The format of the crash report depends on the platform. On some platforms, such as those using the GNU C Library, the crash report includes a *backtrace* describing the execution state prior to crashing, which can be used to help debug the crash. Here is an example for a GNU system:

```
Fatal error 11: Segmentation fault
Backtrace:
emacs[0x5094e4]
emacs[0x4ed3e6]
emacs[0x4ed504]
/lib64/libpthread.so.0[0x375220efe0]
/lib64/libpthread.so.0(read+0xe)[0x375220e08e]
emacs[0x509af6]
emacs[0x5acc26]
 ...
```

The number '11' is the system signal number corresponding to the crash—in this case a segmentation fault. The hexadecimal numbers are program addresses, which can be associated with source code lines using a debugging tool. For example, the GDB command 'list *0x509af6' prints the source-code lines corresponding to the 'emacs[0x509af6]' entry. If your system has the addr2line utility, the following shell command outputs a backtrace with source-code line numbers:

```
sed -n 's/.*\[\(.*\)]$/\1/p' backtrace |
    addr2line -C -f -i -p -e bindir/emacs-binary
```

Here, *backtrace* is the name of a text file containing a copy of the backtrace, *bindir* is the name of the directory that contains the Emacs executable, and *emacs-binary* is the name of the Emacs executable file, normally emacs on GNU and Unix systems and emacs.exe on MS-Windows and MS-DOS. Omit the -p option if your version of addr2line is too old to have it.

Optionally, Emacs can generate a *core dump* when it crashes, on systems that support core files. A core dump is a file containing voluminous data about the state of the program prior to the crash, usually examined by loading it into a debugger such as GDB. On many platforms, core dumps are disabled by default, and you must explicitly enable them by running the shell command 'ulimit -c unlimited' (e.g., in your shell startup script).

34.2.7 Recovery After a Crash

If Emacs or the computer crashes, you can recover the files you were editing at the time of the crash from their auto-save files. To do this, start Emacs again and type the command M-x recover-session.

This command initially displays a buffer which lists interrupted session files, each with its date. You must choose which session to recover from. Typically the one you want is the most recent one. Move point to the one you choose, and type C-c C-c.

Then recover-session considers each of the files that you were editing during that session; for each such file, it asks whether to recover that file. If you answer y for a file, it shows the dates of that file and its auto-save file, then asks once again whether to recover that file. For the second question, you must confirm with yes. If you do, Emacs visits the file but gets the text from the auto-save file.

When recover-session is done, the files you've chosen to recover are present in Emacs buffers. You should then save them. Only this—saving them—updates the files themselves.

As a last resort, if you had buffers with content which were not associated with any files, or if the autosave was not recent enough to have recorded important changes, you can use the etc/emacs-buffer.gdb script with GDB (the GNU Debugger) to retrieve them from a core dump–provided that a core dump was saved, and that the Emacs executable was not stripped of its debugging symbols.

As soon as you get the core dump, rename it to another name such as core.emacs, so that another crash won't overwrite it.

To use this script, run gdb with the file name of your Emacs executable and the file name of the core dump, e.g., 'gdb /usr/bin/emacs core.emacs'. At the (gdb) prompt, load the recovery script: 'source /usr/src/emacs/etc/emacs-buffer.gdb'. Then type the command ybuffer-list to see which buffers are available. For each buffer, it lists a buffer number. To save a buffer, use ysave-buffer; you specify the buffer number, and the file name to write that buffer into. You should use a file name which does not already exist; if the file does exist, the script does not make a backup of its old contents.

34.2.8 Emergency Escape

On text terminals, the *emergency escape* feature suspends Emacs immediately if you type C-g a second time before Emacs can actually respond to the first one by quitting. This is so you can always get out of GNU Emacs no matter how badly it might be hung. When things are working properly, Emacs recognizes and handles the first C-g so fast that the second one won't trigger emergency escape. However, if some problem prevents Emacs from handling the first C-g properly, then the second one will get you back to the shell.

When you resume Emacs after a suspension caused by emergency escape, it asks two questions before going back to what it had been doing:

```
Auto-save? (y or n)
Abort (and dump core)? (y or n)
```

Answer each one with y or n followed by RET.

Saying y to 'Auto-save?' causes immediate auto-saving of all modified buffers in which auto-saving is enabled. Saying n skips this.

Saying y to 'Abort (and dump core)?' causes Emacs to crash, dumping core. This is to enable a wizard to figure out why Emacs was failing to quit in the first place. Execution does not continue after a core dump.

If you answer this question n, Emacs execution resumes. With luck, Emacs will ultimately do the requested quit. If not, each subsequent C-g invokes emergency escape again.

If Emacs is not really hung, just slow, you may invoke the double C-g feature without really meaning to. Then just resume and answer n to both questions, and you will get back to the former state. The quit you requested will happen by and by.

Emergency escape is active only for text terminals. On graphical displays, you can use the mouse to kill Emacs or switch to another program.

On MS-DOS, you must type C-Break (twice) to cause emergency escape—but there are cases where it won't work, when system call hangs or when Emacs is stuck in a tight loop in C code.

34.3 Reporting Bugs

If you think you have found a bug in Emacs, please report it. We cannot promise to fix it, or always to agree that it is a bug, but we certainly want to hear about it. The same applies for new features you would like to see added. The following sections will help you to construct an effective bug report.

34.3.1 Reading Existing Bug Reports and Known Problems

Before reporting a bug, if at all possible please check to see if it is already known about. Indeed, it may already have been fixed in a later release of Emacs, or in the development version. Here is a list of the main places you can read about known issues:

- The etc/PROBLEMS file; type C-h C-p to read it. This file contains a list of particularly well-known issues that have been encountered in compiling, installing and running Emacs. Often, there are suggestions for workarounds and solutions.

- Some additional user-level problems can be found in Section "Bugs and problems" in *GNU Emacs FAQ*.

- The GNU Bug Tracker at `http://debbugs.gnu.org`. Emacs bugs are filed in the tracker under the 'emacs' package. The tracker records information about the status of each bug, the initial bug report, and the follow-up messages by the bug reporter and Emacs developers. You can search for bugs by subject, severity, and other criteria.

  Instead of browsing the bug tracker as a webpage, you can browse it from Emacs using the `debbugs` package, which can be downloaded via the Package Menu (see Chapter 32 [Packages], page 408). This package provides the command `M-x debbugs-gnu` to list bugs, and `M-x debbugs-gnu-search` to search for a specific bug. User tags, applied by the Emacs maintainers, are shown by `M-x debbugs-gnu-usertags`.

- The 'bug-gnu-emacs' mailing list (also available as the newsgroup 'gnu.emacs.bug'). You can read the list archives at `http://lists.gnu.org/mailman/listinfo/bug-gnu-emacs`. This list works as a "mirror" of the Emacs bug reports and follow-up messages which are sent to the bug tracker. It also contains old bug reports from before the bug tracker was introduced (in early 2008).

  If you like, you can subscribe to the list. Be aware that its purpose is to provide the Emacs maintainers with information about bugs and feature requests, so reports may contain fairly large amounts of data; spectators should not complain about this.

- The 'emacs-pretest-bug' mailing list. This list is no longer used, and is mainly of historical interest. At one time, it was used for bug reports in development (i.e., not yet released) versions of Emacs. You can read the archives for 2003 to mid 2007 at `http://lists.gnu.org/archive/html/emacs-pretest-bug/`. Nowadays, it is an alias for 'bug-gnu-emacs'.

- The 'emacs-devel' mailing list. Sometimes people report bugs to this mailing list. This is not the main purpose of the list, however, and it is much better to send bug reports to the bug list. You should not feel obliged to read this list before reporting a bug.

34.3.2 When Is There a Bug

If Emacs accesses an invalid memory location ("segmentation fault"), or exits with an operating system error message that indicates a problem in the program (as opposed to something like "disk full"), then it is certainly a bug.

If the Emacs display does not correspond properly to the contents of the buffer, then it is a bug. But you should check that features like buffer narrowing (see Section 11.5 [Narrowing], page 73), which can hide parts of the buffer or change how it is displayed, are not responsible.

Taking forever to complete a command can be a bug, but you must make sure that it is really Emacs's fault. Some commands simply take a long time. Type `C-g` (`C-Break` on MS-DOS) and then `C-h l` to see whether the input Emacs received was what you intended to type; if the input was such that you *know* it should have been processed quickly, report a bug. If you don't know whether the command should take a long time, find out by looking in the manual or by asking for assistance.

If a command you are familiar with causes an Emacs error message in a case where its usual definition ought to be reasonable, it is probably a bug.

If a command does the wrong thing, that is a bug. But be sure you know for certain what it ought to have done. If you aren't familiar with the command, it might actually be working right. If in doubt, read the command's documentation (see Section 7.2 [Name Help], page 39).

A command's intended definition may not be the best possible definition for editing with. This is a very important sort of problem, but it is also a matter of judgment. Also, it is easy to come to such a conclusion out of ignorance of some of the existing features. It is probably best not to complain about such a problem until you have checked the documentation in the usual ways, feel confident that you understand it, and know for certain that what you want is not available. Ask other Emacs users, too. If you are not sure what the command is supposed to do after a careful reading of the manual, check the index and glossary for any terms that may be unclear.

If after careful rereading of the manual you still do not understand what the command should do, that indicates a bug in the manual, which you should report. The manual's job is to make everything clear to people who are not Emacs experts—including you. It is just as important to report documentation bugs as program bugs.

If the built-in documentation for a function or variable disagrees with the manual, one of them must be wrong; that is a bug.

34.3.3 Understanding Bug Reporting

When you decide that there is a bug, it is important to report it and to report it in a way which is useful. What is most useful is an exact description of what commands you type, starting with the shell command to run Emacs, until the problem happens.

The most important principle in reporting a bug is to report *facts*. Hypotheses and verbal descriptions are no substitute for the detailed raw data. Reporting the facts is straightforward, but many people strain to posit explanations and report them instead of the facts. If the explanations are based on guesses about how Emacs is implemented, they will be useless; meanwhile, lacking the facts, we will have no real information about the bug. If you want to actually *debug* the problem, and report explanations that are more than guesses, that is useful—but please include the raw facts as well.

For example, suppose that you type `C-x C-f /glorp/baz.ugh RET`, visiting a file which (you know) happens to be rather large, and Emacs displays 'I feel pretty today'. The bug report would need to provide all that information. You should not assume that the problem is due to the size of the file and say, "I visited a large file, and Emacs displayed 'I feel pretty today'." This is what we mean by "guessing explanations". The problem might be due to the fact that there is a 'z' in the file name. If this is so, then when we got your report, we would try out the problem with some "large file", probably with no 'z' in its name, and not see any problem. There is no way we could guess that we should try visiting a file with a 'z' in its name.

You should not even say "visit a file" instead of `C-x C-f`. Similarly, rather than saying "if I have three characters on the line", say "after I type `RET A B C RET C-p`", if that is the way you entered the text.

If possible, try quickly to reproduce the bug by invoking Emacs with `emacs -Q` (so that Emacs starts with no initial customizations; see Section C.2 [Initial Options], page 480), and repeating the steps that you took to trigger the bug. If you can reproduce the bug this way, that rules out bugs in your personal customizations. Then your bug report should begin by stating that you started Emacs with `emacs -Q`, followed by the exact sequence of steps for reproducing the bug. If possible, inform us of the exact contents of any file that is needed to reproduce the bug.

Some bugs are not reproducible from `emacs -Q`; some are not easily reproducible at all. In that case, you should report what you have—but, as before, please stick to the raw facts about what you did to trigger the bug the first time.

If you have multiple issues that you want to report, please make a separate bug report for each.

34.3.4 Checklist for Bug Reports

Before reporting a bug, first try to see if the problem has already been reported (see Section 34.3.1 [Known Problems], page 448).

If you are able to, try the latest release of Emacs to see if the problem has already been fixed. Even better is to try the latest development version. We recognize that this is not easy for some people, so do not feel that you absolutely must do this before making a report.

The best way to write a bug report for Emacs is to use the command `M-x report-emacs-bug`. This sets up a mail buffer (see Chapter 29 [Sending Mail], page 350) and automatically inserts *some* of the essential information. However, it cannot supply all the necessary information; you should still read and follow the guidelines below, so you can enter the other crucial information by hand before you send the message. You may feel that some of the information inserted by `M-x report-emacs-bug` is not relevant, but unless you are absolutely sure it is best to leave it, so that the developers can decide for themselves.

When you have finished writing your report, type `C-c C-c` and it will be sent to the Emacs maintainers at `bug-gnu-emacs@gnu.org`. (If you want to suggest an improvement or new feature, use the same address.) If you cannot send mail from inside Emacs, you can copy the text of your report to your normal mail client (if your system supports it, you can type `C-c M-i` to have Emacs do this for you) and send it to that address. Or you can simply send an email to that address describing the problem.

Your report will be sent to the 'bug-gnu-emacs' mailing list, and stored in the GNU Bug Tracker at `http://debbugs.gnu.org`. Please include a valid reply email address, in case we need to ask you for more information about your report. Submissions are moderated, so there may be a delay before your report appears.

You do not need to know how the Gnu Bug Tracker works in order to report a bug, but if you want to, you can read the tracker's online documentation to see the various features you can use.

All mail sent to the 'bug-gnu-emacs' mailing list is also gatewayed to the 'gnu.emacs.bug' newsgroup. The reverse is also true, but we ask you not to post bug reports (or replies) via the newsgroup. It can make it much harder to contact you if we need to ask for more information, and it does not integrate well with the bug tracker.

If your data is more than 500,000 bytes, please don't include it directly in the bug report; instead, offer to send it on request, or make it available by ftp and say where.

To enable maintainers to investigate a bug, your report should include all these things:

- The version number of Emacs. Without this, we won't know whether there is any point in looking for the bug in the current version of GNU Emacs.

  `M-x report-emacs-bug` includes this information automatically, but if you are not using that command for your report you can get the version number by typing `M-x emacs-version RET`. If that command does not work, you probably have something other than GNU Emacs, so you will have to report the bug somewhere else.

- The type of machine you are using, and the operating system name and version number (again, automatically included by `M-x report-emacs-bug`). `M-x emacs-version RET` provides this information too. Copy its output from the `*Messages*` buffer, so that you get it all and get it accurately.

- The operands given to the `configure` command when Emacs was installed (automatically included by `M-x report-emacs-bug`).

- A complete list of any modifications you have made to the Emacs source. (We may not have time to investigate the bug unless it happens in an unmodified Emacs. But if you've made modifications and you don't tell us, you are sending us on a wild goose chase.)

  Be precise about these changes. A description in English is not enough—send a context diff for them.

  Adding files of your own, or porting to another machine, is a modification of the source.

- Details of any other deviations from the standard procedure for installing GNU Emacs.

- The complete text of any files needed to reproduce the bug.

  If you can tell us a way to cause the problem without visiting any files, please do so. This makes it much easier to debug. If you do need files, make sure you arrange for us to see their exact contents. For example, it can matter whether there are spaces at the ends of lines, or a newline after the last line in the buffer (nothing ought to care whether the last line is terminated, but try telling the bugs that).

- The precise commands we need to type to reproduce the bug. If at all possible, give a full recipe for an Emacs started with the '`-Q`' option (see Section C.2 [Initial Options], page 480). This bypasses your personal customizations.

  One way to record the input to Emacs precisely is to write a dribble file. To start the file, use the `M-x open-dribble-file RET` command. From then on, Emacs copies all your input to the specified dribble file until the Emacs process is killed. Be aware that sensitive information (such as passwords) may end up recorded in the dribble file.

- For possible display bugs, the terminal type (the value of environment variable `TERM`), the complete termcap entry for the terminal from `/etc/termcap` (since that file is not identical on all machines), and the output that Emacs actually sent to the terminal.

  The way to collect the terminal output is to execute the Lisp expression

      (open-termscript "~/termscript")

  using `M-:` or from the `*scratch*` buffer just after starting Emacs. From then on, Emacs copies all terminal output to the specified termscript file as well, until the Emacs process is killed. If the problem happens when Emacs starts up, put this expression into your Emacs initialization file so that the termscript file will be open when Emacs displays the screen for the first time.

Be warned: it is often difficult, and sometimes impossible, to fix a terminal-dependent bug without access to a terminal of the type that stimulates the bug.

- If non-ASCII text or internationalization is relevant, the locale that was current when you started Emacs. On GNU/Linux and Unix systems, or if you use a Posix-style shell such as Bash, you can use this shell command to view the relevant values:

```
echo LC_ALL=$LC_ALL LC_COLLATE=$LC_COLLATE LC_CTYPE=$LC_CTYPE \
    LC_MESSAGES=$LC_MESSAGES LC_TIME=$LC_TIME LANG=$LANG
```

Alternatively, use the `locale` command, if your system has it, to display your locale settings.

You can use the `M-!` command to execute these commands from Emacs, and then copy the output from the *Messages* buffer into the bug report. Alternatively, `M-x getenv RET LC_ALL RET` will display the value of `LC_ALL` in the echo area, and you can copy its output from the *Messages* buffer.

- A description of what behavior you observe that you believe is incorrect. For example, "The Emacs process gets a fatal signal", or, "The resulting text is as follows, which I think is wrong."

Of course, if the bug is that Emacs gets a fatal signal, then one can't miss it. But if the bug is incorrect text, the maintainer might fail to notice what is wrong. Why leave it to chance?

Even if the problem you experience is a fatal signal, you should still say so explicitly. Suppose something strange is going on, such as, your copy of the source is out of sync, or you have encountered a bug in the C library on your system. (This has happened!) Your copy might crash and the copy here might not. If you *said* to expect a crash, then when Emacs here fails to crash, we would know that the bug was not happening. If you don't say to expect a crash, then we would not know whether the bug was happening—we would not be able to draw any conclusion from our observations.

- If the bug is that the Emacs Manual or the Emacs Lisp Reference Manual fails to describe the actual behavior of Emacs, or that the text is confusing, copy in the text from the manual which you think is at fault. If the section is small, just the section name is enough.

- If the manifestation of the bug is an Emacs error message, it is important to report the precise text of the error message, and a backtrace showing how the Lisp program in Emacs arrived at the error.

To get the error message text accurately, copy it from the *Messages* buffer into the bug report. Copy all of it, not just part.

To make a backtrace for the error, use `M-x toggle-debug-on-error` before the error happens (that is to say, you must give that command and then make the bug happen). This causes the error to start the Lisp debugger, which shows you a backtrace. Copy the text of the debugger's backtrace into the bug report. See Section "Edebug" in *the Emacs Lisp Reference Manual*, for information on debugging Emacs Lisp programs with the Edebug package.

This use of the debugger is possible only if you know how to make the bug happen again. If you can't make it happen again, at least copy the whole error message.

If Emacs appears to be stuck in an infinite loop or in a very long operation, typing `C-g` with the variable `debug-on-quit` non-`nil` will start the Lisp debugger and show a backtrace. This backtrace is useful for debugging such long loops, so if you can produce it, copy it into the bug report.

If you cannot get Emacs to respond to C-g (e.g., because inhibit-quit is set), then you can try sending the signal specified by debug-on-event (default SIGUSR2) from outside Emacs to cause it to enter the debugger.

- Check whether any programs you have loaded into the Lisp world, including your initialization file, set any variables that may affect the functioning of Emacs. Also, see whether the problem happens in a freshly started Emacs without loading your initialization file (start Emacs with the -Q switch to prevent loading the init files). If the problem does *not* occur then, you must report the precise contents of any programs that you must load into the Lisp world in order to cause the problem to occur.

- If the problem does depend on an init file or other Lisp programs that are not part of the standard Emacs system, then you should make sure it is not a bug in those programs by complaining to their maintainers first. After they verify that they are using Emacs in a way that is supposed to work, they should report the bug.

- If you wish to mention something in the GNU Emacs source, show the line of code with a few lines of context. Don't just give a line number.

  The line numbers in the development sources don't match those in your sources. It would take extra work for the maintainers to determine what code is in your version at a given line number, and we could not be certain.

- Additional information from a C debugger such as GDB might enable someone to find a problem on a machine which he does not have available. If you don't know how to use GDB, please read the GDB manual—it is not very long, and using GDB is easy. You can find the GDB distribution, including the GDB manual in online form, in most of the same places you can find the Emacs distribution. To run Emacs under GDB, you should switch to the src subdirectory in which Emacs was compiled, then do 'gdb emacs'. It is important for the directory src to be current so that GDB will read the .gdbinit file in this directory.

  However, you need to think when you collect the additional information if you want it to show what causes the bug.

  For example, many people send just a backtrace, but that is not very useful by itself. A simple backtrace with arguments often conveys little about what is happening inside GNU Emacs, because most of the arguments listed in the backtrace are pointers to Lisp objects. The numeric values of these pointers have no significance whatever; all that matters is the contents of the objects they point to (and most of the contents are themselves pointers).

  To provide useful information, you need to show the values of Lisp objects in Lisp notation. Do this for each variable which is a Lisp object, in several stack frames near the bottom of the stack. Look at the source to see which variables are Lisp objects, because the debugger thinks of them as integers.

  To show a variable's value in Lisp syntax, first print its value, then use the user-defined GDB command pr to print the Lisp object in Lisp syntax. (If you must use another debugger, call the function debug_print with the object as an argument.) The pr command is defined by the file .gdbinit, and it works only if you are debugging a running process (not with a core dump).

To make Lisp errors stop Emacs and return to GDB, put a breakpoint at `Fsignal`.

For a short listing of Lisp functions running, type the GDB command `xbacktrace`.

The file `.gdbinit` defines several other commands that are useful for examining the data types and contents of Lisp objects. Their names begin with '`x`'. These commands work at a lower level than `pr`, and are less convenient, but they may work even when `pr` does not, such as when debugging a core dump or when Emacs has had a fatal signal.

More detailed advice and other useful techniques for debugging Emacs are available in the file `etc/DEBUG` in the Emacs distribution. That file also includes instructions for investigating problems whereby Emacs stops responding (many people assume that Emacs is "hung", whereas in fact it might be in an infinite loop).

To find the file `etc/DEBUG` in your Emacs installation, use the directory name stored in the variable `data-directory`.

Here are some things that are not necessary in a bug report:

- A description of the envelope of the bug—this is not necessary for a reproducible bug.

  Often people who encounter a bug spend a lot of time investigating which changes to the input file will make the bug go away and which changes will not affect it.

  This is often time-consuming and not very useful, because the way we will find the bug is by running a single example under the debugger with breakpoints, not by pure deduction from a series of examples. You might as well save time by not searching for additional examples. It is better to send the bug report right away, go back to editing, and find another bug to report.

  Of course, if you can find a simpler example to report *instead* of the original one, that is a convenience. Errors in the output will be easier to spot, running under the debugger will take less time, etc.

  However, simplification is not vital; if you can't do this or don't have time to try, please report the bug with your original test case.

- A core dump file.

  Debugging the core dump might be useful, but it can only be done on your machine, with your Emacs executable. Therefore, sending the core dump file to the Emacs maintainers won't be useful. Above all, don't include the core file in an email bug report! Such a large message can be extremely inconvenient.

- A system-call trace of Emacs execution.

  System-call traces are very useful for certain special kinds of debugging, but in most cases they give little useful information. It is therefore strange that many people seem to think that *the* way to report information about a crash is to send a system-call trace. Perhaps this is a habit formed from experience debugging programs that don't have source code or debugging symbols.

  In most programs, a backtrace is normally far, far more informative than a system-call trace. Even in Emacs, a simple backtrace is generally more informative, though to give full information you should supplement the backtrace by displaying variable values and printing them as Lisp objects with `pr` (see above).

- A patch for the bug.

  A patch for the bug is useful if it is a good one. But don't omit the other information that a bug report needs, such as the test case, on the assumption that a patch is sufficient. We might see problems with your patch and decide to fix the problem another way, or we might not understand it at all. And if we can't understand what bug you are trying to fix, or why your patch should be an improvement, we mustn't install it.

- A guess about what the bug is or what it depends on.

  Such guesses are usually wrong. Even experts can't guess right about such things without first using the debugger to find the facts.

34.3.5 Sending Patches for GNU Emacs

If you would like to write bug fixes or improvements for GNU Emacs, that is very helpful. When you send your changes, please follow these guidelines to make it easy for the maintainers to use them. If you don't follow these guidelines, your information might still be useful, but using it will take extra work. Maintaining GNU Emacs is a lot of work in the best of circumstances, and we can't keep up unless you do your best to help.

- Send an explanation with your changes of what problem they fix or what improvement they bring about. For a fix for an existing bug, it is best to reply to the relevant discussion on the 'bug-gnu-emacs' list, or the bug entry in the GNU Bug Tracker at http://debbugs.gnu.org. Explain why your change fixes the bug.

- Always include a proper bug report for the problem you think you have fixed. We need to convince ourselves that the change is right before installing it. Even if it is correct, we might have trouble understanding it if we don't have a way to reproduce the problem.

- Include all the comments that are appropriate to help people reading the source in the future understand why this change was needed.

- Don't mix together changes made for different reasons. Send them *individually*.

  If you make two changes for separate reasons, then we might not want to install them both. We might want to install just one. If you send them all jumbled together in a single set of diffs, we have to do extra work to disentangle them—to figure out which parts of the change serve which purpose. If we don't have time for this, we might have to ignore your changes entirely.

  If you send each change as soon as you have written it, with its own explanation, then two changes never get tangled up, and we can consider each one properly without any extra work to disentangle them.

- Send each change as soon as that change is finished. Sometimes people think they are helping us by accumulating many changes to send them all together. As explained above, this is absolutely the worst thing you could do.

  Since you should send each change separately, you might as well send it right away. That gives us the option of installing it immediately if it is important.

- Use 'diff -c' to make your diffs. Diffs without context are hard to install reliably. More than that, they are hard to study; we must always study a patch to decide whether we want to install it. Unidiff format is better than contextless diffs, but not as easy to read as '-c' format.

  If you have GNU diff, use 'diff -c -F'^[_a-zA-Z0-9$]+ *('' when making diffs of C code. This shows the name of the function that each change occurs in.

- Avoid any ambiguity as to which is the old version and which is the new. Please make the old version the first argument to diff, and the new version the second argument. And please give one version or the other a name that indicates whether it is the old version or your new changed one.

- Write the change log entries for your changes. This is both to save us the extra work of writing them, and to help explain your changes so we can understand them.

  The purpose of the change log is to show people where to find what was changed. So you need to be specific about what functions you changed; in large functions, it's often helpful to indicate where within the function the change was.

  On the other hand, once you have shown people where to find the change, you need not explain its purpose in the change log. Thus, if you add a new function, all you need to say about it is that it is new. If you feel that the purpose needs explaining, it probably does—but put the explanation in comments in the code. It will be more useful there.

  Please look at the change log entries of recent commits to see what sorts of information to put in, and to learn the style that we use. See Section 25.2 [Change Log], page 297.

- When you write the fix, keep in mind that we can't install a change that would break other systems. Please think about what effect your change will have if compiled on another type of system.

  Sometimes people send fixes that *might* be an improvement in general—but it is hard to be sure of this. It's hard to install such changes because we have to study them very carefully. Of course, a good explanation of the reasoning by which you concluded the change was correct can help convince us.

  The safest changes are changes to the configuration files for a particular machine. These are safe because they can't create new bugs on other machines.

  Please help us keep up with the workload by designing the patch in a form that is clearly safe to install.

34.4 Contributing to Emacs Development

If you would like to work on improving Emacs, please contact the maintainers at emacs-devel@gnu.org. You can ask for suggested projects or suggest your own ideas.

If you have already written an improvement, please tell us about it. If you have not yet started work, it is useful to contact emacs-devel@gnu.org before you start; it might be possible to suggest ways to make your extension fit in better with the rest of Emacs.

The development version of Emacs can be downloaded from the repository where it is actively maintained by a group of developers. See the Emacs project page http://savannah.gnu.org/projects/emacs/ for details.

For more information on how to contribute, see the etc/CONTRIBUTE file in the Emacs distribution.

34.5 How To Get Help with GNU Emacs

If you need help installing, using or changing GNU Emacs, there are two ways to find it:

- Send a message to the mailing list help-gnu-emacs@gnu.org, or post your request on newsgroup gnu.emacs.help. (This mailing list and newsgroup interconnect, so it does not matter which one you use.)

- Look in the service directory (`http://www.fsf.org/resources/service/`) for someone who might help you for a fee.

Appendix A GNU GENERAL PUBLIC LICENSE

Version 3, 29 June 2007

Copyright © 2007 Free Software Foundation, Inc. `http://fsf.org/`

Everyone is permitted to copy and distribute verbatim copies of this license document, but changing it is not allowed.

Preamble

The GNU General Public License is a free, copyleft license for software and other kinds of works.

The licenses for most software and other practical works are designed to take away your freedom to share and change the works. By contrast, the GNU General Public License is intended to guarantee your freedom to share and change all versions of a program—to make sure it remains free software for all its users. We, the Free Software Foundation, use the GNU General Public License for most of our software; it applies also to any other work released this way by its authors. You can apply it to your programs, too.

When we speak of free software, we are referring to freedom, not price. Our General Public Licenses are designed to make sure that you have the freedom to distribute copies of free software (and charge for them if you wish), that you receive source code or can get it if you want it, that you can change the software or use pieces of it in new free programs, and that you know you can do these things.

To protect your rights, we need to prevent others from denying you these rights or asking you to surrender the rights. Therefore, you have certain responsibilities if you distribute copies of the software, or if you modify it: responsibilities to respect the freedom of others.

For example, if you distribute copies of such a program, whether gratis or for a fee, you must pass on to the recipients the same freedoms that you received. You must make sure that they, too, receive or can get the source code. And you must show them these terms so they know their rights.

Developers that use the GNU GPL protect your rights with two steps: (1) assert copyright on the software, and (2) offer you this License giving you legal permission to copy, distribute and/or modify it.

For the developers' and authors' protection, the GPL clearly explains that there is no warranty for this free software. For both users' and authors' sake, the GPL requires that modified versions be marked as changed, so that their problems will not be attributed erroneously to authors of previous versions.

Some devices are designed to deny users access to install or run modified versions of the software inside them, although the manufacturer can do so. This is fundamentally incompatible with the aim of protecting users' freedom to change the software. The systematic pattern of such abuse occurs in the area of products for individuals to use, which is precisely where it is most unacceptable. Therefore, we have designed this version of the GPL to prohibit the practice for those products. If such problems arise substantially in other domains, we stand ready to extend this provision to those domains in future versions of the GPL, as needed to protect the freedom of users.

Finally, every program is threatened constantly by software patents. States should not allow patents to restrict development and use of software on general-purpose computers, but in those that do, we wish to avoid the special danger that patents applied to a free program could make it effectively proprietary. To prevent this, the GPL assures that patents cannot be used to render the program non-free.

The precise terms and conditions for copying, distribution and modification follow.

TERMS AND CONDITIONS

0. Definitions.

   "This License" refers to version 3 of the GNU General Public License.

   "Copyright" also means copyright-like laws that apply to other kinds of works, such as semiconductor masks.

   "The Program" refers to any copyrightable work licensed under this License. Each licensee is addressed as "you". "Licensees" and "recipients" may be individuals or organizations.

   To "modify" a work means to copy from or adapt all or part of the work in a fashion requiring copyright permission, other than the making of an exact copy. The resulting work is called a "modified version" of the earlier work or a work "based on" the earlier work.

   A "covered work" means either the unmodified Program or a work based on the Program.

   To "propagate" a work means to do anything with it that, without permission, would make you directly or secondarily liable for infringement under applicable copyright law, except executing it on a computer or modifying a private copy. Propagation includes copying, distribution (with or without modification), making available to the public, and in some countries other activities as well.

   To "convey" a work means any kind of propagation that enables other parties to make or receive copies. Mere interaction with a user through a computer network, with no transfer of a copy, is not conveying.

   An interactive user interface displays "Appropriate Legal Notices" to the extent that it includes a convenient and prominently visible feature that (1) displays an appropriate copyright notice, and (2) tells the user that there is no warranty for the work (except to the extent that warranties are provided), that licensees may convey the work under this License, and how to view a copy of this License. If the interface presents a list of user commands or options, such as a menu, a prominent item in the list meets this criterion.

1. Source Code.

   The "source code" for a work means the preferred form of the work for making modifications to it. "Object code" means any non-source form of a work.

   A "Standard Interface" means an interface that either is an official standard defined by a recognized standards body, or, in the case of interfaces specified for a particular programming language, one that is widely used among developers working in that language.

The "System Libraries" of an executable work include anything, other than the work as a whole, that (a) is included in the normal form of packaging a Major Component, but which is not part of that Major Component, and (b) serves only to enable use of the work with that Major Component, or to implement a Standard Interface for which an implementation is available to the public in source code form. A "Major Component", in this context, means a major essential component (kernel, window system, and so on) of the specific operating system (if any) on which the executable work runs, or a compiler used to produce the work, or an object code interpreter used to run it.

The "Corresponding Source" for a work in object code form means all the source code needed to generate, install, and (for an executable work) run the object code and to modify the work, including scripts to control those activities. However, it does not include the work's System Libraries, or general-purpose tools or generally available free programs which are used unmodified in performing those activities but which are not part of the work. For example, Corresponding Source includes interface definition files associated with source files for the work, and the source code for shared libraries and dynamically linked subprograms that the work is specifically designed to require, such as by intimate data communication or control flow between those subprograms and other parts of the work.

The Corresponding Source need not include anything that users can regenerate automatically from other parts of the Corresponding Source.

The Corresponding Source for a work in source code form is that same work.

2. Basic Permissions.

All rights granted under this License are granted for the term of copyright on the Program, and are irrevocable provided the stated conditions are met. This License explicitly affirms your unlimited permission to run the unmodified Program. The output from running a covered work is covered by this License only if the output, given its content, constitutes a covered work. This License acknowledges your rights of fair use or other equivalent, as provided by copyright law.

You may make, run and propagate covered works that you do not convey, without conditions so long as your license otherwise remains in force. You may convey covered works to others for the sole purpose of having them make modifications exclusively for you, or provide you with facilities for running those works, provided that you comply with the terms of this License in conveying all material for which you do not control copyright. Those thus making or running the covered works for you must do so exclusively on your behalf, under your direction and control, on terms that prohibit them from making any copies of your copyrighted material outside their relationship with you.

Conveying under any other circumstances is permitted solely under the conditions stated below. Sublicensing is not allowed; section 10 makes it unnecessary.

3. Protecting Users' Legal Rights From Anti-Circumvention Law.

No covered work shall be deemed part of an effective technological measure under any applicable law fulfilling obligations under article 11 of the WIPO copyright treaty adopted on 20 December 1996, or similar laws prohibiting or restricting circumvention of such measures.

When you convey a covered work, you waive any legal power to forbid circumvention of technological measures to the extent such circumvention is effected by exercising rights under this License with respect to the covered work, and you disclaim any intention to limit operation or modification of the work as a means of enforcing, against the work's users, your or third parties' legal rights to forbid circumvention of technological measures.

4. Conveying Verbatim Copies.

You may convey verbatim copies of the Program's source code as you receive it, in any medium, provided that you conspicuously and appropriately publish on each copy an appropriate copyright notice; keep intact all notices stating that this License and any non-permissive terms added in accord with section 7 apply to the code; keep intact all notices of the absence of any warranty; and give all recipients a copy of this License along with the Program.

You may charge any price or no price for each copy that you convey, and you may offer support or warranty protection for a fee.

5. Conveying Modified Source Versions.

You may convey a work based on the Program, or the modifications to produce it from the Program, in the form of source code under the terms of section 4, provided that you also meet all of these conditions:

a. The work must carry prominent notices stating that you modified it, and giving a relevant date.

b. The work must carry prominent notices stating that it is released under this License and any conditions added under section 7. This requirement modifies the requirement in section 4 to "keep intact all notices".

c. You must license the entire work, as a whole, under this License to anyone who comes into possession of a copy. This License will therefore apply, along with any applicable section 7 additional terms, to the whole of the work, and all its parts, regardless of how they are packaged. This License gives no permission to license the work in any other way, but it does not invalidate such permission if you have separately received it.

d. If the work has interactive user interfaces, each must display Appropriate Legal Notices; however, if the Program has interactive interfaces that do not display Appropriate Legal Notices, your work need not make them do so.

A compilation of a covered work with other separate and independent works, which are not by their nature extensions of the covered work, and which are not combined with it such as to form a larger program, in or on a volume of a storage or distribution medium, is called an "aggregate" if the compilation and its resulting copyright are not used to limit the access or legal rights of the compilation's users beyond what the individual works permit. Inclusion of a covered work in an aggregate does not cause this License to apply to the other parts of the aggregate.

6. Conveying Non-Source Forms.

You may convey a covered work in object code form under the terms of sections 4 and 5, provided that you also convey the machine-readable Corresponding Source under the terms of this License, in one of these ways:

a. Convey the object code in, or embodied in, a physical product (including a physical distribution medium), accompanied by the Corresponding Source fixed on a durable physical medium customarily used for software interchange.

b. Convey the object code in, or embodied in, a physical product (including a physical distribution medium), accompanied by a written offer, valid for at least three years and valid for as long as you offer spare parts or customer support for that product model, to give anyone who possesses the object code either (1) a copy of the Corresponding Source for all the software in the product that is covered by this License, on a durable physical medium customarily used for software interchange, for a price no more than your reasonable cost of physically performing this conveying of source, or (2) access to copy the Corresponding Source from a network server at no charge.

c. Convey individual copies of the object code with a copy of the written offer to provide the Corresponding Source. This alternative is allowed only occasionally and noncommercially, and only if you received the object code with such an offer, in accord with subsection 6b.

d. Convey the object code by offering access from a designated place (gratis or for a charge), and offer equivalent access to the Corresponding Source in the same way through the same place at no further charge. You need not require recipients to copy the Corresponding Source along with the object code. If the place to copy the object code is a network server, the Corresponding Source may be on a different server (operated by you or a third party) that supports equivalent copying facilities, provided you maintain clear directions next to the object code saying where to find the Corresponding Source. Regardless of what server hosts the Corresponding Source, you remain obligated to ensure that it is available for as long as needed to satisfy these requirements.

e. Convey the object code using peer-to-peer transmission, provided you inform other peers where the object code and Corresponding Source of the work are being offered to the general public at no charge under subsection 6d.

A separable portion of the object code, whose source code is excluded from the Corresponding Source as a System Library, need not be included in conveying the object code work.

A "User Product" is either (1) a "consumer product", which means any tangible personal property which is normally used for personal, family, or household purposes, or (2) anything designed or sold for incorporation into a dwelling. In determining whether a product is a consumer product, doubtful cases shall be resolved in favor of coverage. For a particular product received by a particular user, "normally used" refers to a typical or common use of that class of product, regardless of the status of the particular user or of the way in which the particular user actually uses, or expects or is expected to use, the product. A product is a consumer product regardless of whether the product has substantial commercial, industrial or non-consumer uses, unless such uses represent the only significant mode of use of the product.

"Installation Information" for a User Product means any methods, procedures, authorization keys, or other information required to install and execute modified versions of a covered work in that User Product from a modified version of its Corresponding Source.

The information must suffice to ensure that the continued functioning of the modified object code is in no case prevented or interfered with solely because modification has been made.

If you convey an object code work under this section in, or with, or specifically for use in, a User Product, and the conveying occurs as part of a transaction in which the right of possession and use of the User Product is transferred to the recipient in perpetuity or for a fixed term (regardless of how the transaction is characterized), the Corresponding Source conveyed under this section must be accompanied by the Installation Information. But this requirement does not apply if neither you nor any third party retains the ability to install modified object code on the User Product (for example, the work has been installed in ROM).

The requirement to provide Installation Information does not include a requirement to continue to provide support service, warranty, or updates for a work that has been modified or installed by the recipient, or for the User Product in which it has been modified or installed. Access to a network may be denied when the modification itself materially and adversely affects the operation of the network or violates the rules and protocols for communication across the network.

Corresponding Source conveyed, and Installation Information provided, in accord with this section must be in a format that is publicly documented (and with an implementation available to the public in source code form), and must require no special password or key for unpacking, reading or copying.

7. Additional Terms.

"Additional permissions" are terms that supplement the terms of this License by making exceptions from one or more of its conditions. Additional permissions that are applicable to the entire Program shall be treated as though they were included in this License, to the extent that they are valid under applicable law. If additional permissions apply only to part of the Program, that part may be used separately under those permissions, but the entire Program remains governed by this License without regard to the additional permissions.

When you convey a copy of a covered work, you may at your option remove any additional permissions from that copy, or from any part of it. (Additional permissions may be written to require their own removal in certain cases when you modify the work.) You may place additional permissions on material, added by you to a covered work, for which you have or can give appropriate copyright permission.

Notwithstanding any other provision of this License, for material you add to a covered work, you may (if authorized by the copyright holders of that material) supplement the terms of this License with terms:

a. Disclaiming warranty or limiting liability differently from the terms of sections 15 and 16 of this License; or

b. Requiring preservation of specified reasonable legal notices or author attributions in that material or in the Appropriate Legal Notices displayed by works containing it; or

c. Prohibiting misrepresentation of the origin of that material, or requiring that modified versions of such material be marked in reasonable ways as different from the original version; or

d. Limiting the use for publicity purposes of names of licensors or authors of the material; or

e. Declining to grant rights under trademark law for use of some trade names, trademarks, or service marks; or

f. Requiring indemnification of licensors and authors of that material by anyone who conveys the material (or modified versions of it) with contractual assumptions of liability to the recipient, for any liability that these contractual assumptions directly impose on those licensors and authors.

All other non-permissive additional terms are considered "further restrictions" within the meaning of section 10. If the Program as you received it, or any part of it, contains a notice stating that it is governed by this License along with a term that is a further restriction, you may remove that term. If a license document contains a further restriction but permits relicensing or conveying under this License, you may add to a covered work material governed by the terms of that license document, provided that the further restriction does not survive such relicensing or conveying.

If you add terms to a covered work in accord with this section, you must place, in the relevant source files, a statement of the additional terms that apply to those files, or a notice indicating where to find the applicable terms.

Additional terms, permissive or non-permissive, may be stated in the form of a separately written license, or stated as exceptions; the above requirements apply either way.

8. Termination.

You may not propagate or modify a covered work except as expressly provided under this License. Any attempt otherwise to propagate or modify it is void, and will automatically terminate your rights under this License (including any patent licenses granted under the third paragraph of section 11).

However, if you cease all violation of this License, then your license from a particular copyright holder is reinstated (a) provisionally, unless and until the copyright holder explicitly and finally terminates your license, and (b) permanently, if the copyright holder fails to notify you of the violation by some reasonable means prior to 60 days after the cessation.

Moreover, your license from a particular copyright holder is reinstated permanently if the copyright holder notifies you of the violation by some reasonable means, this is the first time you have received notice of violation of this License (for any work) from that copyright holder, and you cure the violation prior to 30 days after your receipt of the notice.

Termination of your rights under this section does not terminate the licenses of parties who have received copies or rights from you under this License. If your rights have been terminated and not permanently reinstated, you do not qualify to receive new licenses for the same material under section 10.

9. Acceptance Not Required for Having Copies.

You are not required to accept this License in order to receive or run a copy of the Program. Ancillary propagation of a covered work occurring solely as a consequence of using peer-to-peer transmission to receive a copy likewise does not require acceptance.

However, nothing other than this License grants you permission to propagate or modify any covered work. These actions infringe copyright if you do not accept this License. Therefore, by modifying or propagating a covered work, you indicate your acceptance of this License to do so.

10. Automatic Licensing of Downstream Recipients.

Each time you convey a covered work, the recipient automatically receives a license from the original licensors, to run, modify and propagate that work, subject to this License. You are not responsible for enforcing compliance by third parties with this License.

An "entity transaction" is a transaction transferring control of an organization, or substantially all assets of one, or subdividing an organization, or merging organizations. If propagation of a covered work results from an entity transaction, each party to that transaction who receives a copy of the work also receives whatever licenses to the work the party's predecessor in interest had or could give under the previous paragraph, plus a right to possession of the Corresponding Source of the work from the predecessor in interest, if the predecessor has it or can get it with reasonable efforts.

You may not impose any further restrictions on the exercise of the rights granted or affirmed under this License. For example, you may not impose a license fee, royalty, or other charge for exercise of rights granted under this License, and you may not initiate litigation (including a cross-claim or counterclaim in a lawsuit) alleging that any patent claim is infringed by making, using, selling, offering for sale, or importing the Program or any portion of it.

11. Patents.

A "contributor" is a copyright holder who authorizes use under this License of the Program or a work on which the Program is based. The work thus licensed is called the contributor's "contributor version".

A contributor's "essential patent claims" are all patent claims owned or controlled by the contributor, whether already acquired or hereafter acquired, that would be infringed by some manner, permitted by this License, of making, using, or selling its contributor version, but do not include claims that would be infringed only as a consequence of further modification of the contributor version. For purposes of this definition, "control" includes the right to grant patent sublicenses in a manner consistent with the requirements of this License.

Each contributor grants you a non-exclusive, worldwide, royalty-free patent license under the contributor's essential patent claims, to make, use, sell, offer for sale, import and otherwise run, modify and propagate the contents of its contributor version.

In the following three paragraphs, a "patent license" is any express agreement or commitment, however denominated, not to enforce a patent (such as an express permission to practice a patent or covenant not to sue for patent infringement). To "grant" such a patent license to a party means to make such an agreement or commitment not to enforce a patent against the party.

If you convey a covered work, knowingly relying on a patent license, and the Corresponding Source of the work is not available for anyone to copy, free of charge and under the terms of this License, through a publicly available network server or other readily accessible means, then you must either (1) cause the Corresponding Source to be so available, or (2) arrange to deprive yourself of the benefit of the patent license for this particular work, or (3) arrange, in a manner consistent with the requirements of this License, to extend the patent license to downstream recipients. "Knowingly relying" means you have actual knowledge that, but for the patent license, your conveying the covered work in a country, or your recipient's use of the covered work in a country, would infringe one or more identifiable patents in that country that you have reason to believe are valid.

If, pursuant to or in connection with a single transaction or arrangement, you convey, or propagate by procuring conveyance of, a covered work, and grant a patent license to some of the parties receiving the covered work authorizing them to use, propagate, modify or convey a specific copy of the covered work, then the patent license you grant is automatically extended to all recipients of the covered work and works based on it.

A patent license is "discriminatory" if it does not include within the scope of its coverage, prohibits the exercise of, or is conditioned on the non-exercise of one or more of the rights that are specifically granted under this License. You may not convey a covered work if you are a party to an arrangement with a third party that is in the business of distributing software, under which you make payment to the third party based on the extent of your activity of conveying the work, and under which the third party grants, to any of the parties who would receive the covered work from you, a discriminatory patent license (a) in connection with copies of the covered work conveyed by you (or copies made from those copies), or (b) primarily for and in connection with specific products or compilations that contain the covered work, unless you entered into that arrangement, or that patent license was granted, prior to 28 March 2007.

Nothing in this License shall be construed as excluding or limiting any implied license or other defenses to infringement that may otherwise be available to you under applicable patent law.

12. No Surrender of Others' Freedom.

If conditions are imposed on you (whether by court order, agreement or otherwise) that contradict the conditions of this License, they do not excuse you from the conditions of this License. If you cannot convey a covered work so as to satisfy simultaneously your obligations under this License and any other pertinent obligations, then as a consequence you may not convey it at all. For example, if you agree to terms that obligate you to collect a royalty for further conveying from those to whom you convey the Program, the only way you could satisfy both those terms and this License would be to refrain entirely from conveying the Program.

13. Use with the GNU Affero General Public License.

Notwithstanding any other provision of this License, you have permission to link or combine any covered work with a work licensed under version 3 of the GNU Affero General Public License into a single combined work, and to convey the resulting work. The terms of this License will continue to apply to the part which is the covered work, but the special requirements of the GNU Affero General Public License, section 13, concerning interaction through a network will apply to the combination as such.

14. Revised Versions of this License.

The Free Software Foundation may publish revised and/or new versions of the GNU General Public License from time to time. Such new versions will be similar in spirit to the present version, but may differ in detail to address new problems or concerns.

Each version is given a distinguishing version number. If the Program specifies that a certain numbered version of the GNU General Public License "or any later version" applies to it, you have the option of following the terms and conditions either of that numbered version or of any later version published by the Free Software Foundation. If the Program does not specify a version number of the GNU General Public License, you may choose any version ever published by the Free Software Foundation.

If the Program specifies that a proxy can decide which future versions of the GNU General Public License can be used, that proxy's public statement of acceptance of a version permanently authorizes you to choose that version for the Program.

Later license versions may give you additional or different permissions. However, no additional obligations are imposed on any author or copyright holder as a result of your choosing to follow a later version.

15. Disclaimer of Warranty.

THERE IS NO WARRANTY FOR THE PROGRAM, TO THE EXTENT PERMITTED BY APPLICABLE LAW. EXCEPT WHEN OTHERWISE STATED IN WRITING THE COPYRIGHT HOLDERS AND/OR OTHER PARTIES PROVIDE THE PROGRAM "AS IS" WITHOUT WARRANTY OF ANY KIND, EITHER EXPRESSED OR IMPLIED, INCLUDING, BUT NOT LIMITED TO, THE IMPLIED WARRANTIES OF MERCHANTABILITY AND FITNESS FOR A PARTICULAR PURPOSE. THE ENTIRE RISK AS TO THE QUALITY AND PERFORMANCE OF THE PROGRAM IS WITH YOU. SHOULD THE PROGRAM PROVE DEFECTIVE, YOU ASSUME THE COST OF ALL NECESSARY SERVICING, REPAIR OR CORRECTION.

16. Limitation of Liability.

IN NO EVENT UNLESS REQUIRED BY APPLICABLE LAW OR AGREED TO IN WRITING WILL ANY COPYRIGHT HOLDER, OR ANY OTHER PARTY WHO MODIFIES AND/OR CONVEYS THE PROGRAM AS PERMITTED ABOVE, BE LIABLE TO YOU FOR DAMAGES, INCLUDING ANY GENERAL, SPECIAL, INCIDENTAL OR CONSEQUENTIAL DAMAGES ARISING OUT OF THE USE OR INABILITY TO USE THE PROGRAM (INCLUDING BUT NOT LIMITED TO LOSS OF DATA OR DATA BEING RENDERED INACCURATE OR LOSSES SUSTAINED BY YOU OR THIRD PARTIES OR A FAILURE OF THE PROGRAM TO OPERATE WITH ANY OTHER PROGRAMS), EVEN IF SUCH HOLDER OR OTHER PARTY HAS BEEN ADVISED OF THE POSSIBILITY OF SUCH DAMAGES.

17. Interpretation of Sections 15 and 16.

If the disclaimer of warranty and limitation of liability provided above cannot be given local legal effect according to their terms, reviewing courts shall apply local law that most closely approximates an absolute waiver of all civil liability in connection with the Program, unless a warranty or assumption of liability accompanies a copy of the Program in return for a fee.

END OF TERMS AND CONDITIONS

How to Apply These Terms to Your New Programs

If you develop a new program, and you want it to be of the greatest possible use to the public, the best way to achieve this is to make it free software which everyone can redistribute and change under these terms.

To do so, attach the following notices to the program. It is safest to attach them to the start of each source file to most effectively state the exclusion of warranty; and each file should have at least the "copyright" line and a pointer to where the full notice is found.

```
one line to give the program's name and a brief idea of what it does.
Copyright (C) year name of author

This program is free software: you can redistribute it and/or modify
it under the terms of the GNU General Public License as published by
the Free Software Foundation, either version 3 of the License, or (at
your option) any later version.

This program is distributed in the hope that it will be useful, but
WITHOUT ANY WARRANTY; without even the implied warranty of
MERCHANTABILITY or FITNESS FOR A PARTICULAR PURPOSE.  See the GNU
General Public License for more details.

You should have received a copy of the GNU General Public License
along with this program.  If not, see http://www.gnu.org/licenses/.
```

Also add information on how to contact you by electronic and paper mail.

If the program does terminal interaction, make it output a short notice like this when it starts in an interactive mode:

```
program Copyright (C) year name of author
This program comes with ABSOLUTELY NO WARRANTY; for details type 'show w'.
This is free software, and you are welcome to redistribute it
under certain conditions; type 'show c' for details.
```

The hypothetical commands 'show w' and 'show c' should show the appropriate parts of the General Public License. Of course, your program's commands might be different; for a GUI interface, you would use an "about box".

You should also get your employer (if you work as a programmer) or school, if any, to sign a "copyright disclaimer" for the program, if necessary. For more information on this, and how to apply and follow the GNU GPL, see http://www.gnu.org/licenses/.

The GNU General Public License does not permit incorporating your program into proprietary programs. If your program is a subroutine library, you may consider it more useful to permit linking proprietary applications with the library. If this is what you want to do, use the GNU Lesser General Public License instead of this License. But first, please read http://www.gnu.org/philosophy/why-not-lgpl.html.

Appendix B GNU Free Documentation License

Version 1.3, 3 November 2008

Copyright © 2000, 2001, 2002, 2007, 2008 Free Software Foundation, Inc.
`http://fsf.org/`

Everyone is permitted to copy and distribute verbatim copies
of this license document, but changing it is not allowed.

0. PREAMBLE

The purpose of this License is to make a manual, textbook, or other functional and useful document *free* in the sense of freedom: to assure everyone the effective freedom to copy and redistribute it, with or without modifying it, either commercially or non-commercially. Secondarily, this License preserves for the author and publisher a way to get credit for their work, while not being considered responsible for modifications made by others.

This License is a kind of "copyleft", which means that derivative works of the document must themselves be free in the same sense. It complements the GNU General Public License, which is a copyleft license designed for free software.

We have designed this License in order to use it for manuals for free software, because free software needs free documentation: a free program should come with manuals providing the same freedoms that the software does. But this License is not limited to software manuals; it can be used for any textual work, regardless of subject matter or whether it is published as a printed book. We recommend this License principally for works whose purpose is instruction or reference.

1. APPLICABILITY AND DEFINITIONS

This License applies to any manual or other work, in any medium, that contains a notice placed by the copyright holder saying it can be distributed under the terms of this License. Such a notice grants a world-wide, royalty-free license, unlimited in duration, to use that work under the conditions stated herein. The "Document", below, refers to any such manual or work. Any member of the public is a licensee, and is addressed as "you". You accept the license if you copy, modify or distribute the work in a way requiring permission under copyright law.

A "Modified Version" of the Document means any work containing the Document or a portion of it, either copied verbatim, or with modifications and/or translated into another language.

A "Secondary Section" is a named appendix or a front-matter section of the Document that deals exclusively with the relationship of the publishers or authors of the Document to the Document's overall subject (or to related matters) and contains nothing that could fall directly within that overall subject. (Thus, if the Document is in part a textbook of mathematics, a Secondary Section may not explain any mathematics.) The relationship could be a matter of historical connection with the subject or with related matters, or of legal, commercial, philosophical, ethical or political position regarding them.

The "Invariant Sections" are certain Secondary Sections whose titles are designated, as being those of Invariant Sections, in the notice that says that the Document is released under this License. If a section does not fit the above definition of Secondary then it is not allowed to be designated as Invariant. The Document may contain zero Invariant Sections. If the Document does not identify any Invariant Sections then there are none.

The "Cover Texts" are certain short passages of text that are listed, as Front-Cover Texts or Back-Cover Texts, in the notice that says that the Document is released under this License. A Front-Cover Text may be at most 5 words, and a Back-Cover Text may be at most 25 words.

A "Transparent" copy of the Document means a machine-readable copy, represented in a format whose specification is available to the general public, that is suitable for revising the document straightforwardly with generic text editors or (for images composed of pixels) generic paint programs or (for drawings) some widely available drawing editor, and that is suitable for input to text formatters or for automatic translation to a variety of formats suitable for input to text formatters. A copy made in an otherwise Transparent file format whose markup, or absence of markup, has been arranged to thwart or discourage subsequent modification by readers is not Transparent. An image format is not Transparent if used for any substantial amount of text. A copy that is not "Transparent" is called "Opaque".

Examples of suitable formats for Transparent copies include plain ASCII without markup, Texinfo input format, LaTeX input format, SGML or XML using a publicly available DTD, and standard-conforming simple HTML, PostScript or PDF designed for human modification. Examples of transparent image formats include PNG, XCF and JPG. Opaque formats include proprietary formats that can be read and edited only by proprietary word processors, SGML or XML for which the DTD and/or processing tools are not generally available, and the machine-generated HTML, PostScript or PDF produced by some word processors for output purposes only.

The "Title Page" means, for a printed book, the title page itself, plus such following pages as are needed to hold, legibly, the material this License requires to appear in the title page. For works in formats which do not have any title page as such, "Title Page" means the text near the most prominent appearance of the work's title, preceding the beginning of the body of the text.

The "publisher" means any person or entity that distributes copies of the Document to the public.

A section "Entitled XYZ" means a named subunit of the Document whose title either is precisely XYZ or contains XYZ in parentheses following text that translates XYZ in another language. (Here XYZ stands for a specific section name mentioned below, such as "Acknowledgements", "Dedications", "Endorsements", or "History".) To "Preserve the Title" of such a section when you modify the Document means that it remains a section "Entitled XYZ" according to this definition.

The Document may include Warranty Disclaimers next to the notice which states that this License applies to the Document. These Warranty Disclaimers are considered to be included by reference in this License, but only as regards disclaiming warranties: any other implication that these Warranty Disclaimers may have is void and has no effect on the meaning of this License.

2. VERBATIM COPYING

You may copy and distribute the Document in any medium, either commercially or noncommercially, provided that this License, the copyright notices, and the license notice saying this License applies to the Document are reproduced in all copies, and that you add no other conditions whatsoever to those of this License. You may not use technical measures to obstruct or control the reading or further copying of the copies you make or distribute. However, you may accept compensation in exchange for copies. If you distribute a large enough number of copies you must also follow the conditions in section 3.

You may also lend copies, under the same conditions stated above, and you may publicly display copies.

3. COPYING IN QUANTITY

If you publish printed copies (or copies in media that commonly have printed covers) of the Document, numbering more than 100, and the Document's license notice requires Cover Texts, you must enclose the copies in covers that carry, clearly and legibly, all these Cover Texts: Front-Cover Texts on the front cover, and Back-Cover Texts on the back cover. Both covers must also clearly and legibly identify you as the publisher of these copies. The front cover must present the full title with all words of the title equally prominent and visible. You may add other material on the covers in addition. Copying with changes limited to the covers, as long as they preserve the title of the Document and satisfy these conditions, can be treated as verbatim copying in other respects.

If the required texts for either cover are too voluminous to fit legibly, you should put the first ones listed (as many as fit reasonably) on the actual cover, and continue the rest onto adjacent pages.

If you publish or distribute Opaque copies of the Document numbering more than 100, you must either include a machine-readable Transparent copy along with each Opaque copy, or state in or with each Opaque copy a computer-network location from which the general network-using public has access to download using public-standard network protocols a complete Transparent copy of the Document, free of added material. If you use the latter option, you must take reasonably prudent steps, when you begin distribution of Opaque copies in quantity, to ensure that this Transparent copy will remain thus accessible at the stated location until at least one year after the last time you distribute an Opaque copy (directly or through your agents or retailers) of that edition to the public.

It is requested, but not required, that you contact the authors of the Document well before redistributing any large number of copies, to give them a chance to provide you with an updated version of the Document.

4. MODIFICATIONS

You may copy and distribute a Modified Version of the Document under the conditions of sections 2 and 3 above, provided that you release the Modified Version under precisely this License, with the Modified Version filling the role of the Document, thus licensing distribution and modification of the Modified Version to whoever possesses a copy of it. In addition, you must do these things in the Modified Version:

A. Use in the Title Page (and on the covers, if any) a title distinct from that of the Document, and from those of previous versions (which should, if there were any, be listed in the History section of the Document). You may use the same title as a previous version if the original publisher of that version gives permission.

B. List on the Title Page, as authors, one or more persons or entities responsible for authorship of the modifications in the Modified Version, together with at least five of the principal authors of the Document (all of its principal authors, if it has fewer than five), unless they release you from this requirement.

C. State on the Title page the name of the publisher of the Modified Version, as the publisher.

D. Preserve all the copyright notices of the Document.

E. Add an appropriate copyright notice for your modifications adjacent to the other copyright notices.

F. Include, immediately after the copyright notices, a license notice giving the public permission to use the Modified Version under the terms of this License, in the form shown in the Addendum below.

G. Preserve in that license notice the full lists of Invariant Sections and required Cover Texts given in the Document's license notice.

H. Include an unaltered copy of this License.

I. Preserve the section Entitled "History", Preserve its Title, and add to it an item stating at least the title, year, new authors, and publisher of the Modified Version as given on the Title Page. If there is no section Entitled "History" in the Document, create one stating the title, year, authors, and publisher of the Document as given on its Title Page, then add an item describing the Modified Version as stated in the previous sentence.

J. Preserve the network location, if any, given in the Document for public access to a Transparent copy of the Document, and likewise the network locations given in the Document for previous versions it was based on. These may be placed in the "History" section. You may omit a network location for a work that was published at least four years before the Document itself, or if the original publisher of the version it refers to gives permission.

K. For any section Entitled "Acknowledgements" or "Dedications", Preserve the Title of the section, and preserve in the section all the substance and tone of each of the contributor acknowledgements and/or dedications given therein.

L. Preserve all the Invariant Sections of the Document, unaltered in their text and in their titles. Section numbers or the equivalent are not considered part of the section titles.

M. Delete any section Entitled "Endorsements". Such a section may not be included in the Modified Version.

N. Do not retitle any existing section to be Entitled "Endorsements" or to conflict in title with any Invariant Section.

O. Preserve any Warranty Disclaimers.

If the Modified Version includes new front-matter sections or appendices that qualify as Secondary Sections and contain no material copied from the Document, you may at your option designate some or all of these sections as invariant. To do this, add their titles to the list of Invariant Sections in the Modified Version's license notice. These titles must be distinct from any other section titles.

You may add a section Entitled "Endorsements", provided it contains nothing but endorsements of your Modified Version by various parties—for example, statements of peer review or that the text has been approved by an organization as the authoritative definition of a standard.

You may add a passage of up to five words as a Front-Cover Text, and a passage of up to 25 words as a Back-Cover Text, to the end of the list of Cover Texts in the Modified Version. Only one passage of Front-Cover Text and one of Back-Cover Text may be added by (or through arrangements made by) any one entity. If the Document already includes a cover text for the same cover, previously added by you or by arrangement made by the same entity you are acting on behalf of, you may not add another; but you may replace the old one, on explicit permission from the previous publisher that added the old one.

The author(s) and publisher(s) of the Document do not by this License give permission to use their names for publicity for or to assert or imply endorsement of any Modified Version.

5. COMBINING DOCUMENTS

You may combine the Document with other documents released under this License, under the terms defined in section 4 above for modified versions, provided that you include in the combination all of the Invariant Sections of all of the original documents, unmodified, and list them all as Invariant Sections of your combined work in its license notice, and that you preserve all their Warranty Disclaimers.

The combined work need only contain one copy of this License, and multiple identical Invariant Sections may be replaced with a single copy. If there are multiple Invariant Sections with the same name but different contents, make the title of each such section unique by adding at the end of it, in parentheses, the name of the original author or publisher of that section if known, or else a unique number. Make the same adjustment to the section titles in the list of Invariant Sections in the license notice of the combined work.

In the combination, you must combine any sections Entitled "History" in the various original documents, forming one section Entitled "History"; likewise combine any sections Entitled "Acknowledgements", and any sections Entitled "Dedications". You must delete all sections Entitled "Endorsements."

6. COLLECTIONS OF DOCUMENTS

You may make a collection consisting of the Document and other documents released under this License, and replace the individual copies of this License in the various documents with a single copy that is included in the collection, provided that you follow the rules of this License for verbatim copying of each of the documents in all other respects.

You may extract a single document from such a collection, and distribute it individually under this License, provided you insert a copy of this License into the extracted document, and follow this License in all other respects regarding verbatim copying of that document.

7. AGGREGATION WITH INDEPENDENT WORKS

A compilation of the Document or its derivatives with other separate and independent documents or works, in or on a volume of a storage or distribution medium, is called an "aggregate" if the copyright resulting from the compilation is not used to limit the legal rights of the compilation's users beyond what the individual works permit. When the Document is included in an aggregate, this License does not apply to the other works in the aggregate which are not themselves derivative works of the Document.

If the Cover Text requirement of section 3 is applicable to these copies of the Document, then if the Document is less than one half of the entire aggregate, the Document's Cover Texts may be placed on covers that bracket the Document within the aggregate, or the electronic equivalent of covers if the Document is in electronic form. Otherwise they must appear on printed covers that bracket the whole aggregate.

8. TRANSLATION

Translation is considered a kind of modification, so you may distribute translations of the Document under the terms of section 4. Replacing Invariant Sections with translations requires special permission from their copyright holders, but you may include translations of some or all Invariant Sections in addition to the original versions of these Invariant Sections. You may include a translation of this License, and all the license notices in the Document, and any Warranty Disclaimers, provided that you also include the original English version of this License and the original versions of those notices and disclaimers. In case of a disagreement between the translation and the original version of this License or a notice or disclaimer, the original version will prevail.

If a section in the Document is Entitled "Acknowledgements", "Dedications", or "History", the requirement (section 4) to Preserve its Title (section 1) will typically require changing the actual title.

9. TERMINATION

You may not copy, modify, sublicense, or distribute the Document except as expressly provided under this License. Any attempt otherwise to copy, modify, sublicense, or distribute it is void, and will automatically terminate your rights under this License.

However, if you cease all violation of this License, then your license from a particular copyright holder is reinstated (a) provisionally, unless and until the copyright holder explicitly and finally terminates your license, and (b) permanently, if the copyright holder fails to notify you of the violation by some reasonable means prior to 60 days after the cessation.

Moreover, your license from a particular copyright holder is reinstated permanently if the copyright holder notifies you of the violation by some reasonable means, this is the first time you have received notice of violation of this License (for any work) from that copyright holder, and you cure the violation prior to 30 days after your receipt of the notice.

Termination of your rights under this section does not terminate the licenses of parties who have received copies or rights from you under this License. If your rights have been terminated and not permanently reinstated, receipt of a copy of some or all of the same material does not give you any rights to use it.

10. FUTURE REVISIONS OF THIS LICENSE

The Free Software Foundation may publish new, revised versions of the GNU Free Documentation License from time to time. Such new versions will be similar in spirit to the present version, but may differ in detail to address new problems or concerns. See http://www.gnu.org/copyleft/.

Each version of the License is given a distinguishing version number. If the Document specifies that a particular numbered version of this License "or any later version" applies to it, you have the option of following the terms and conditions either of that specified version or of any later version that has been published (not as a draft) by the Free Software Foundation. If the Document does not specify a version number of this License, you may choose any version ever published (not as a draft) by the Free Software Foundation. If the Document specifies that a proxy can decide which future versions of this License can be used, that proxy's public statement of acceptance of a version permanently authorizes you to choose that version for the Document.

11. RELICENSING

"Massive Multiauthor Collaboration Site" (or "MMC Site") means any World Wide Web server that publishes copyrightable works and also provides prominent facilities for anybody to edit those works. A public wiki that anybody can edit is an example of such a server. A "Massive Multiauthor Collaboration" (or "MMC") contained in the site means any set of copyrightable works thus published on the MMC site.

"CC-BY-SA" means the Creative Commons Attribution-Share Alike 3.0 license published by Creative Commons Corporation, a not-for-profit corporation with a principal place of business in San Francisco, California, as well as future copyleft versions of that license published by that same organization.

"Incorporate" means to publish or republish a Document, in whole or in part, as part of another Document.

An MMC is "eligible for relicensing" if it is licensed under this License, and if all works that were first published under this License somewhere other than this MMC, and subsequently incorporated in whole or in part into the MMC, (1) had no cover texts or invariant sections, and (2) were thus incorporated prior to November 1, 2008.

The operator of an MMC Site may republish an MMC contained in the site under CC-BY-SA on the same site at any time before August 1, 2009, provided the MMC is eligible for relicensing.

ADDENDUM: How to use this License for your documents

To use this License in a document you have written, include a copy of the License in the document and put the following copyright and license notices just after the title page:

```
Copyright (C)  year  your name.
Permission is granted to copy, distribute and/or modify this document
under the terms of the GNU Free Documentation License, Version 1.3
or any later version published by the Free Software Foundation;
with no Invariant Sections, no Front-Cover Texts, and no Back-Cover
Texts.  A copy of the license is included in the section entitled ''GNU
Free Documentation License''.
```

If you have Invariant Sections, Front-Cover Texts and Back-Cover Texts, replace the "with...Texts." line with this:

```
with the Invariant Sections being list their titles, with
the Front-Cover Texts being list, and with the Back-Cover Texts
being list.
```

If you have Invariant Sections without Cover Texts, or some other combination of the three, merge those two alternatives to suit the situation.

If your document contains nontrivial examples of program code, we recommend releasing these examples in parallel under your choice of free software license, such as the GNU General Public License, to permit their use in free software.

Appendix C Command Line Arguments for Emacs Invocation

Emacs supports command line arguments to request various actions when invoking Emacs. These are for compatibility with other editors and for sophisticated activities. We don't recommend using them for ordinary editing (See Section 31.5 [Emacs Server], page 393, for a way to access an existing Emacs job from the command line).

Arguments starting with '-' are *options*, and so is '+*linenum*'. All other arguments specify files to visit. Emacs visits the specified files while it starts up. The last file specified on the command line becomes the current buffer; the other files are also visited in other buffers. As with most programs, the special argument '--' says that all subsequent arguments are file names, not options, even if they start with '-'.

Emacs command options can specify many things, such as the size and position of the X window Emacs uses, its colors, and so on. A few options support advanced usage, such as running Lisp functions on files in batch mode. The sections of this chapter describe the available options, arranged according to their purpose.

There are two ways of writing options: the short forms that start with a single '-', and the long forms that start with '--'. For example, '-d' is a short form and '--display' is the corresponding long form.

The long forms with '--' are easier to remember, but longer to type. However, you don't have to spell out the whole option name; any unambiguous abbreviation is enough. When a long option takes an argument, you can use either a space or an equal sign to separate the option name and the argument. Thus, you can write either '--display sugar-bombs:0.0' or '--display=sugar-bombs:0.0'. We recommend an equal sign because it makes the relationship clearer, and the tables below always show an equal sign.

Most options specify how to initialize Emacs, or set parameters for the Emacs session. We call them *initial options*. A few options specify things to do, such as loading libraries or calling Lisp functions. These are called *action options*. These and file names together are called *action arguments*. The action arguments are stored as a list of strings in the variable `command-line-args`. (Actually, when Emacs starts up, `command-line-args` contains all the arguments passed from the command line; during initialization, the initial arguments are removed from this list when they are processed, leaving only the action arguments.)

C.1 Action Arguments

Here is a table of action arguments:

'*file*'
'--file=*file*'
'--find-file=*file*'
'--visit=*file*'

>   Visit *file* using `find-file`. See Section 15.2 [Visiting], page 123.

>   When Emacs starts up, it displays the startup buffer in one window, and the buffer visiting *file* in another window (see Chapter 17 [Windows], page 156). If you supply more than one file argument, the displayed file is the last one specified on the command line; the other files are visited but their buffers are not shown.

If the startup buffer is disabled (see Section 3.1 [Entering Emacs], page 14), then *file* is visited in a single window if one file argument was supplied; with two file arguments, Emacs displays the files in two different windows; with more than two file argument, Emacs displays the last file specified in one window, plus a Buffer Menu in a different window (see Section 16.5 [Several Buffers], page 151). To inhibit using the Buffer Menu for this, change the variable `inhibit-startup-buffer-menu` to `t`.

'+*linenum file*'

> Visit *file* using `find-file`, then go to line number *linenum* in it.

'+*linenum*:*columnnum file*'

> Visit *file* using `find-file`, then go to line number *linenum* and put point at column number *columnnum*.

'-l *file*'
'--load=*file*'

> Load a Lisp library named *file* with the function `load`. If *file* is not an absolute file name, Emacs first looks for it in the current directory, then in the directories listed in `load-path` (see Section 24.8 [Lisp Libraries], page 276).
>
> **Warning:** If previous command-line arguments have visited files, the current directory is the directory of the last file visited.

'-L *dir*'
'--directory=*dir*'

> Prepend directory *dir* to the variable `load-path`. If you specify multiple '-L' options, Emacs preserves the relative order; i.e., using '-L /foo -L /bar' results in a `load-path` of the form (`"/foo" "/bar"` ...). If *dir* begins with ':', Emacs removes the ':' and appends (rather than prepends) the remainder to `load-path`. (On MS Windows, use ';' instead of ':'; i.e., use the value of `path-separator`.)

'-f *function*'
'--funcall=*function*'

> Call Lisp function *function*. If it is an interactive function (a command), it reads the arguments interactively just as if you had called the same function with a key sequence. Otherwise, it calls the function with no arguments.

'--eval=*expression*'
'--execute=*expression*'

> Evaluate Lisp expression *expression*.

'--insert=*file*'

> Insert the contents of *file* into the buffer that is current when this command-line argument is processed. Usually, this is the `*scratch*` buffer (see Section 24.10 [Lisp Interaction], page 279), but if arguments earlier on the command line visit files or switch buffers, that might be a different buffer. The effect of this command-line argument is like what `M-x insert-file` does (see Section 15.10 [Misc File Ops], page 140).

'--kill'   Exit from Emacs without asking for confirmation.

'--help'   Print a usage message listing all available options, then exit successfully.

'--version'
          Print Emacs version, then exit successfully.

C.2 Initial Options

The initial options specify parameters for the Emacs session. This section describes the more general initial options; some other options specifically related to the X Window System appear in the following sections.

Some initial options affect the loading of the initialization file. Normally, Emacs first loads `site-start.el` if it exists, then your own initialization file if it exists, and finally the default initialization file `default.el` if it exists (see Section 33.4 [Init File], page 437). Certain options prevent loading of some of these files or substitute other files for them.

'-chdir *directory*'
'--chdir=*directory*'
          Change to *directory* before doing anything else. This is mainly used by session management in X so that Emacs starts in the same directory as it stopped. This makes desktop saving and restoring easier.

'-t *device*'
'--terminal=*device*'
          Use *device* as the device for terminal input and output. This option implies '--no-window-system'.

'-d *display*'
'--display=*display*'
          Use the X Window System and use the display named *display* to open the initial Emacs frame. See Section C.5 [Display X], page 487, for more details.

'-nw'
'--no-window-system'
          Don't communicate directly with the window system, disregarding the DISPLAY environment variable even if it is set. This means that Emacs uses the terminal from which it was launched for all its display and input.

'-batch'
'--batch'   Run Emacs in *batch mode*. Batch mode is used for running programs written in Emacs Lisp from shell scripts, makefiles, and so on. To invoke a Lisp program, use the '-batch' option in conjunction with one or more of '-l', '-f' or '--eval' (see Section C.1 [Action Arguments], page 478). See Section C.3 [Command Example], page 482, for an example.

          In batch mode, Emacs does not display the text being edited, and the standard terminal interrupt characters such as C-z and C-c have their usual effect. Emacs functions that normally print a message in the echo area will print to either the standard output stream (stdout) or the standard error stream (stderr) instead. (To be precise, functions like prin1, princ and print print to stdout, while message and error print to stderr.) Functions that normally read keyboard input from the minibuffer take their input from the terminal's standard input stream (stdin) instead.

'--batch' implies '-q' (do not load an initialization file), but `site-start.el` is loaded nonetheless. It also causes Emacs to exit after processing all the command options. In addition, it disables auto-saving except in buffers for which auto-saving is explicitly requested, and when saving files it omits the `fsync` system call unless otherwise requested.

'--script *file*'

Run Emacs in batch mode, like '--batch', and then read and execute the Lisp code in *file*.

The normal use of this option is in executable script files that run Emacs. They can start with this text on the first line

```
#!/usr/bin/emacs --script
```

which will invoke Emacs with '--script' and supply the name of the script file as *file*. Emacs Lisp then treats the '#!' on this first line as a comment delimiter.

'-q'
'--no-init-file'

Do not load any initialization file (see Section 33.4 [Init File], page 437). When Emacs is invoked with this option, the Customize facility does not allow options to be saved (see Section 33.1 [Easy Customization], page 412). This option does not disable loading `site-start.el`.

'--no-site-file'

Do not load `site-start.el` (see Section 33.4 [Init File], page 437). The '-Q' option does this too, but other options like '-q' do not.

'--no-site-lisp'

Do not include the `site-lisp` directories in `load-path` (see Section 33.4 [Init File], page 437). The '-Q' option does this too.

'--no-splash'

Do not display a startup screen. You can also achieve this effect by setting the variable `inhibit-startup-screen` to non-`nil` in your initialization file (see Section 3.1 [Entering Emacs], page 14).

'-Q'
'--quick'   Start emacs with minimum customizations. This is similar to using '-q', '--no-site-file', '--no-site-lisp', and '--no-splash' together. This also stops Emacs from processing X resources by setting `inhibit-x-resources` to `t` (see Section D.1 [Resources], page 493).

'-daemon'
'--daemon'

Start Emacs as a daemon—after Emacs starts up, it starts the Emacs server and disconnects from the terminal without opening any frames. You can then use the `emacsclient` command to connect to Emacs for editing. See Section 31.5 [Emacs Server], page 393, for information about using Emacs as a daemon.

'-daemon=*SERVER-NAME*'

Start emacs in background as a daemon, and use *SERVER-NAME* as the server name.

'--no-desktop'

> Do not reload any saved desktop. See Section 31.9 [Saving Emacs Sessions], page 403.

'-u *user*'
'--user=*user*'

> Load *user*'s initialization file instead of your own[1].

'--debug-init'

> Enable the Emacs Lisp debugger for errors in the init file. See Section "Entering the Debugger on an Error" in *The GNU Emacs Lisp Reference Manual*.

C.3 Command Argument Example

Here is an example of using Emacs with arguments and options. It assumes you have a Lisp program file called `hack-c.el` which, when loaded, performs some useful operation on the current buffer, expected to be a C program.

```
emacs --batch foo.c -l hack-c -f save-buffer >& log
```

This says to visit `foo.c`, load `hack-c.el` (which makes changes in the visited file), save `foo.c` (note that `save-buffer` is the function that C-x C-s is bound to), and then exit back to the shell (because of '--batch'). '--batch' also guarantees there will be no problem redirecting output to `log`, because Emacs will not assume that it has a display terminal to work with.

C.4 Environment Variables

The *environment* is a feature of the operating system; it consists of a collection of variables with names and values. Each variable is called an *environment variable*; environment variable names are case-sensitive, and it is conventional to use upper case letters only. The values are all text strings.

What makes the environment useful is that subprocesses inherit the environment automatically from their parent process. This means you can set up an environment variable in your login shell, and all the programs you run (including Emacs) will automatically see it. Subprocesses of Emacs (such as shells, compilers, and version control programs) inherit the environment from Emacs, too.

Inside Emacs, the command M-x getenv reads the name of an environment variable, and prints its value in the echo area. M-x setenv sets a variable in the Emacs environment, and C-u M-x setenv removes a variable. (Environment variable substitutions with '$' work in the value just as in file names; see [File Names with $], page 122.) The variable `initial-environment` stores the initial environment inherited by Emacs.

The way to set environment variables outside of Emacs depends on the operating system, and especially the shell that you are using. For example, here's how to set the environment variable ORGANIZATION to 'not very much' using Bash:

```
export ORGANIZATION="not very much"
```

and here's how to do it in csh or tcsh:

---

[1] This option has no effect on MS-Windows.

```
setenv ORGANIZATION "not very much"
```

When Emacs is using the X Window System, various environment variables that control X work for Emacs as well. See the X documentation for more information.

C.4.1 General Variables

Here is an alphabetical list of environment variables that have special meanings in Emacs. Most of these variables are also used by some other programs. Emacs does not require any of these environment variables to be set, but it uses their values if they are set.

CDPATH   Used by the `cd` command to search for the directory you specify, when you specify a relative directory name.

DBUS_SESSION_BUS_ADDRESS

Used by D-Bus when Emacs is compiled with it. Usually, there is no need to change it. Setting it to a dummy address, like 'unix:path=/dev/null', suppresses connections to the D-Bus session bus as well as autolaunching the D-Bus session bus if not running yet.

EMACSDATA

Directory for the architecture-independent files that come with Emacs. This is used to initialize the variable `data-directory`.

EMACSDOC   #vindex EMACSDOC, environment variable Directory for the documentation string file, which is used to initialize the Lisp variable `doc-directory`.

EMACSLOADPATH

#vindex EMACSLOADPATH, environment variable A colon-separated list of directories[2] to search for Emacs Lisp files. If set, it modifies the usual initial value of the `load-path` variable (see Section 24.8 [Lisp Libraries], page 276). An empty element stands for the default value of `load-path`; e.g., using 'EMACSLOADPATH="/tmp:"' adds /tmp to the front of the default `load-path`. To specify an empty element in the middle of the list, use 2 colons in a row, as in 'EMACSLOADPATH="/tmp::/foo"'.

EMACSPATH

A colon-separated list of directories to search for executable files. If set, Emacs uses this in addition to PATH (see below) when initializing the variable `exec-path` (see Section 31.4 [Shell], page 383).

EMAIL   Your email address; used to initialize the Lisp variable `user-mail-address`, which the Emacs mail interface puts into the 'From' header of outgoing messages (see Section 29.2 [Mail Headers], page 351).

ESHELL   Used for shell-mode to override the SHELL environment variable (see Section 31.4.2 [Interactive Shell], page 384).

HISTFILE   The name of the file that shell commands are saved in between logins. This variable defaults to ~/.bash_history if you use Bash, to ~/.sh_history if you use ksh, and to ~/.history otherwise.

---

[2] Here and below, whenever we say "colon-separated list of directories", it pertains to Unix and GNU/Linux systems. On MS-DOS and MS-Windows, the directories are separated by semi-colons instead, since DOS/Windows file names might include a colon after a drive letter.

HOME   The location of your files in the directory tree; used for expansion of file names starting with a tilde (~). On MS-DOS, it defaults to the directory from which Emacs was started, with '/bin' removed from the end if it was present. On Windows, the default value of HOME is the `Application Data` subdirectory of the user profile directory (normally, this is `C:/Documents and Settings/`*username*`/Application Data`, where *username* is your user name), though for backwards compatibility `C:/` will be used instead if a `.emacs` file is found there.

HOSTNAME   The name of the machine that Emacs is running on.

INFOPATH   A colon-separated list of directories in which to search for Info files.

LC_ALL
LC_COLLATE
LC_CTYPE
LC_MESSAGES
LC_MONETARY
LC_NUMERIC
LC_TIME
LANG   The user's preferred locale. The locale has six categories, specified by the environment variables LC_COLLATE for sorting, LC_CTYPE for character encoding, LC_MESSAGES for system messages, LC_MONETARY for monetary formats, LC_NUMERIC for numbers, and LC_TIME for dates and times. If one of these variables is not set, the category defaults to the value of the LANG environment variable, or to the default 'C' locale if LANG is not set. But if LC_ALL is specified, it overrides the settings of all the other locale environment variables.

            On MS-Windows, if LANG is not already set in the environment when Emacs starts, Emacs sets it based on the system-wide default language, which you can set in the 'Regional Settings' Control Panel on some versions of MS-Windows.

            The value of the LC_CTYPE category is matched against entries in `locale-language-names`, `locale-charset-language-names`, and `locale-preferred-coding-systems`, to select a default language environment and coding system. See Section 19.2 [Language Environments], page 179.

LOGNAME   The user's login name. See also USER.

MAIL   The name of your system mail inbox.

NAME   Your real-world name. This is used to initialize the variable **user-full-name** (see Section 29.2 [Mail Headers], page 351).

NNTPSERVER
            The name of the news server. Used by the mh and Gnus packages.

ORGANIZATION
            The name of the organization to which you belong. Used for setting the 'Organization:' header in your posts from the Gnus package.

PATH   A colon-separated list of directories containing executable files. This is used to initialize the variable **exec-path** (see Section 31.4 [Shell], page 383).

PWD   If set, this should be the default directory when Emacs was started.

REPLYTO   If set, this specifies an initial value for the variable `mail-default-reply-to` (see Section 29.2 [Mail Headers], page 351).

SAVEDIR   The name of a directory in which news articles are saved by default. Used by the Gnus package.

SHELL   The name of an interpreter used to parse and execute programs run from inside Emacs.

SMTPSERVER
              The name of the outgoing mail server. This is used to initialize the variable `smtpmail-smtp-server` (see Section 29.4.1 [Mail Sending], page 353).

TERM   The type of the terminal that Emacs is using. This variable must be set unless Emacs is run in batch mode. On MS-DOS, it defaults to 'internal', which specifies a built-in terminal emulation that handles the machine's own display.

TERMCAP   The name of the termcap library file describing how to program the terminal specified by TERM. This defaults to `/etc/termcap`.

TMPDIR
TMP
TEMP   These environment variables are used to initialize the variable `temporary-file-directory`, which specifies a directory in which to put temporary files (see Section 15.3.2 [Backup], page 127). Emacs tries to use TMPDIR first. If that is unset, Emacs normally falls back on `/tmp`, but on MS-Windows and MS-DOS it instead falls back on TMP, then TEMP, and finally `c:/temp`.

TZ   This specifies the current time zone and possibly also daylight saving time information. On MS-DOS, if TZ is not set in the environment when Emacs starts, Emacs defines a default value as appropriate for the country code returned by DOS. On MS-Windows, Emacs does not use TZ at all.

USER   The user's login name. See also LOGNAME. On MS-DOS, this defaults to 'root'.

VERSION_CONTROL
              Used to initialize the `version-control` variable (see Section 15.3.2.1 [Backup Names], page 128).

C.4.2 Miscellaneous Variables

These variables are used only on particular configurations:

COMSPEC   On MS-DOS and MS-Windows, the name of the command interpreter to use when invoking batch files and commands internal to the shell. On MS-DOS this is also used to make a default value for the SHELL environment variable.

NAME   On MS-DOS, this variable defaults to the value of the USER variable.

EMACSTEST
              On MS-DOS, this specifies a file to use to log the operation of the internal terminal emulator. This feature is useful for submitting bug reports.

EMACSCOLORS

> On MS-DOS, this specifies the screen colors. It is useful to set them this way, since otherwise Emacs would display the default colors momentarily when it starts up.
>
> The value of this variable should be the two-character encoding of the foreground (the first character) and the background (the second character) colors of the default face. Each character should be the hexadecimal code for the desired color on a standard PC text-mode display. For example, to get blue text on a light gray background, specify 'EMACSCOLORS=17', since 1 is the code of the blue color and 7 is the code of the light gray color.
>
> The PC display usually supports only eight background colors. However, Emacs switches the DOS display to a mode where all 16 colors can be used for the background, so all four bits of the background color are actually used.

PRELOAD_WINSOCK

> On MS-Windows, if you set this variable, Emacs will load and initialize the network library at startup, instead of waiting until the first time it is required.

emacs_dir

> On MS-Windows, emacs_dir is a special environment variable, which indicates the full path of the directory in which Emacs is installed. If Emacs is installed in the standard directory structure, it calculates this value automatically. It is not much use setting this variable yourself unless your installation is non-standard, since unlike other environment variables, it will be overridden by Emacs at startup. When setting other environment variables, such as EMACSLOADPATH, you may find it useful to use emacs_dir rather than hard-coding an absolute path. This allows multiple versions of Emacs to share the same environment variable settings, and it allows you to move the Emacs installation directory, without changing any environment or registry settings.

C.4.3 The MS-Windows System Registry

On MS-Windows, the installation program addpm.exe adds values for emacs_dir, EMACSLOADPATH, EMACSDATA, EMACSPATH, EMACSDOC, SHELL and TERM to the HKEY_LOCAL_MACHINE section of the system registry, under /Software/GNU/Emacs. It does this because there is no standard place to set environment variables across different versions of Windows. Running addpm.exe is no longer strictly necessary in recent versions of Emacs, but if you are upgrading from an older version, running addpm.exe ensures that you do not have older registry entries from a previous installation, which may not be compatible with the latest version of Emacs.

When Emacs starts, as well as checking the environment, it also checks the System Registry for those variables and for HOME, LANG and PRELOAD_WINSOCK.

To determine the value of those variables, Emacs goes through the following procedure. First, the environment is checked. If the variable is not found there, Emacs looks for registry keys by that name under /Software/GNU/Emacs; first in the HKEY_CURRENT_USER section of the registry, and if not found there, in the HKEY_LOCAL_MACHINE section. Finally, if Emacs still cannot determine the values, compiled-in defaults are used.

In addition to the environment variables above, you can also add many of the settings which on X belong in the `.Xdefaults` file (see Appendix D [X Resources], page 493) to the `/Software/GNU/Emacs` registry key.

C.5 Specifying the Display Name

The environment variable `DISPLAY` tells all X clients, including Emacs, where to display their windows. Its value is set by default in ordinary circumstances, when you start an X server and run jobs locally. You can specify the display yourself; one reason to do this is if you want to log into another system and run Emacs there, and have the window displayed at your local terminal.

`DISPLAY` has the syntax '*host*:*display*.*screen*', where *host* is the host name of the X Window System server machine, *display* is an arbitrarily-assigned number that distinguishes your server (X terminal) from other servers on the same machine, and *screen* is a field that allows an X server to control multiple terminal screens. The period and the *screen* field are optional. If included, *screen* is usually zero.

For example, if your host is named '`glasperle`' and your server is the first (or perhaps the only) server listed in the configuration, your `DISPLAY` is '`glasperle:0.0`'.

You can specify the display name explicitly when you run Emacs, either by changing the `DISPLAY` variable, or with the option '`-d `*display*' or '`--display=`*display*'. Here is an example:

```
emacs --display=glasperle:0 &
```

You can inhibit the use of the X window system with the '`-nw`' option. Then Emacs uses its controlling text terminal for display. See Section C.2 [Initial Options], page 480.

Sometimes, security arrangements prevent a program on a remote system from displaying on your local system. In this case, trying to run Emacs produces messages like this:

```
Xlib:  connection to "glasperle:0.0" refused by server
```

You might be able to overcome this problem by using the `xhost` command on the local system to give permission for access from your remote machine.

C.6 Font Specification Options

You can use the command line option '`-fn `*font*' (or '`--font`', which is an alias for '`-fn`') to specify a default font:

'`-fn `*font*'
'`--font=`*font*'
> Use *font* as the default font.

When passing a font name to Emacs on the command line, you may need to "quote" it, by enclosing it in quotation marks, if it contains characters that the shell treats specially (e.g., spaces). For example:

```
emacs -fn "DejaVu Sans Mono-12"
```

See Section 18.8 [Fonts], page 168, for details about font names and other ways to specify the default font.

C.7 Window Color Options

You can use the following command-line options to specify the colors to use for various parts of the Emacs display. Colors may be specified using either color names or RGB triplets (see Section 11.9 [Colors], page 75).

'-fg color'
'--foreground-color=color'

> Specify the foreground color, overriding the color specified by the default face (see Section 11.8 [Faces], page 74).

'-bg color'
'--background-color=color'

> Specify the background color, overriding the color specified by the default face.

'-bd color'
'--border-color=color'

> Specify the color of the border of the X window. This has no effect if Emacs is compiled with GTK+ support.

'-cr color'
'--cursor-color=color'

> Specify the color of the Emacs cursor which indicates where point is.

'-ms color'
'--mouse-color=color'

> Specify the color for the mouse cursor when the mouse is in the Emacs window.

'-r'
'-rv'
'--reverse-video'

> Reverse video—swap the foreground and background colors.

'--color=mode'

> Set the color support mode when Emacs is run on a text terminal. This option overrides the number of supported colors that the character terminal advertises in its termcap or terminfo database. The parameter mode can be one of the following:

> 'never'
> 'no'   Don't use colors even if the terminal's capabilities specify color support.

> 'default'
> 'auto'   Same as when --color is not used at all: Emacs detects at startup whether the terminal supports colors, and if it does, turns on colored display.

> 'always'
> 'yes'
> 'ansi8'   Turn on the color support unconditionally, and use color commands specified by the ANSI escape sequences for the 8 standard colors.

'*num*'
>   Use color mode for *num* colors. If *num* is -1, turn off color support (equivalent to '`never`'); if it is 0, use the default color support for this terminal (equivalent to '`auto`'); otherwise use an appropriate standard mode for *num* colors. Depending on your terminal's capabilities, Emacs might be able to turn on a color mode for 8, 16, 88, or 256 as the value of *num*. If there is no mode that supports *num* colors, Emacs acts as if *num* were 0, i.e., it uses the terminal's default color support mode.

>   If *mode* is omitted, it defaults to *ansi8*.

For example, to use a coral mouse cursor and a slate blue text cursor, enter:

```
emacs -ms coral -cr 'slate blue' &
```

You can reverse the foreground and background colors through the '`-rv`' option or with the X resource '`reverseVideo`'.

The '`-fg`', '`-bg`', and '`-rv`' options function on text terminals as well as on graphical displays.

C.8 Options for Window Size and Position

Here is a list of the command-line options for specifying size and position of the initial Emacs frame:

'`-g `*widthxheight*[{+-}*xoffset*{+-}*yoffset*]]'
'`--geometry=`*widthxheight*[{+-}*xoffset*{+-}*yoffset*]]'
>   Specify the size *width* and *height* (measured in character columns and lines), and positions *xoffset* and *yoffset* (measured in pixels). The *width* and *height* parameters apply to all frames, whereas *xoffset* and *yoffset* only to the initial frame.

'`-fs`'
'`--fullscreen`'
>   Specify that width and height should be that of the screen. Normally no window manager decorations are shown. (After starting Emacs, you can toggle this state using `F11`, `toggle-frame-fullscreen`.)

'`-mm`'
'`--maximized`'
>   Specify that the Emacs frame should be maximized. This normally means that the frame has window manager decorations. (After starting Emacs, you can toggle this state using `M-F10`, `toggle-frame-maximized`.)

'`-fh`'
'`--fullheight`'
>   Specify that the height should be the height of the screen.

'`-fw`'
'`--fullwidth`'
>   Specify that the width should be the width of the screen.

In the '--geometry' option, {+-} means either a plus sign or a minus sign. A plus sign before *xoffset* means it is the distance from the left side of the screen; a minus sign means it counts from the right side. A plus sign before *yoffset* means it is the distance from the top of the screen, and a minus sign there indicates the distance from the bottom. The values *xoffset* and *yoffset* may themselves be positive or negative, but that doesn't change their meaning, only their direction.

Emacs uses the same units as xterm does to interpret the geometry. The *width* and *height* are measured in characters, so a large font creates a larger frame than a small font. (If you specify a proportional font, Emacs uses its maximum bounds width as the width unit.) The *xoffset* and *yoffset* are measured in pixels.

You do not have to specify all of the fields in the geometry specification. If you omit both *xoffset* and *yoffset*, the window manager decides where to put the Emacs frame, possibly by letting you place it with the mouse. For example, '164x55' specifies a window 164 columns wide, enough for two ordinary width windows side by side, and 55 lines tall.

The default frame width is 80 characters and the default height is 40 lines. You can omit either the width or the height or both. If you start the geometry with an integer, Emacs interprets it as the width. If you start with an 'x' followed by an integer, Emacs interprets it as the height. Thus, '81' specifies just the width; 'x45' specifies just the height.

If you start with '+' or '-', that introduces an offset, which means both sizes are omitted. Thus, '-3' specifies the *xoffset* only. (If you give just one offset, it is always *xoffset*.) '+3-3' specifies both the *xoffset* and the *yoffset*, placing the frame near the bottom left of the screen.

You can specify a default for any or all of the fields in your X resource file (see Section D.1 [Resources], page 493), and then override selected fields with a '--geometry' option.

Since the mode line and the echo area occupy the last 2 lines of the frame, the height of the initial text window is 2 less than the height specified in your geometry. In non-X-toolkit versions of Emacs, the menu bar also takes one line of the specified number. But in the X toolkit version, the menu bar is additional and does not count against the specified height. The tool bar, if present, is also additional.

Enabling or disabling the menu bar or tool bar alters the amount of space available for ordinary text. Therefore, if Emacs starts up with a tool bar (which is the default), and handles the geometry specification assuming there is a tool bar, and then your initialization file disables the tool bar, you will end up with a frame geometry different from what you asked for. To get the intended size with no tool bar, use an X resource to specify "no tool bar" (see Section D.2 [Table of Resources], page 494); then Emacs will already know there's no tool bar when it processes the specified geometry.

When using one of '--fullscreen', '--maximized', '--fullwidth' or '--fullheight', some window managers require you to set the variable frame-resize-pixelwise to a non-nil value to make a frame appear truly "maximized" or "fullscreen".

Some window managers have options that can make them ignore both program-specified and user-specified positions. If these are set, Emacs fails to position the window correctly.

C.9 Internal and External Borders

An Emacs frame has an internal border and an external border. The internal border is an extra strip of the background color around the text portion of the frame. Emacs itself draws the internal border. The external border is added by the window manager outside the frame; depending on the window manager you use, it may contain various boxes you can click on to move or iconify the window.

'-ib *width*'
'--internal-border=*width*'
> Specify *width* as the width of the internal border (between the text and the main border), in pixels.

'-bw *width*'
'--border-width=*width*'
> Specify *width* as the width of the main border, in pixels.

When you specify the size of the frame, that does not count the borders. The frame's position is measured from the outside edge of the external border.

Use the '-ib *n*' option to specify an internal border *n* pixels wide. The default is 1. Use '-bw *n*' to specify the width of the external border (though the window manager may not pay attention to what you specify). The default width of the external border is 2.

C.10 Frame Titles

An Emacs frame may or may not have a specified title. The frame title, if specified, appears in window decorations and icons as the name of the frame. If an Emacs frame has no specified title, the default title has the form '*invocation-name@machine*' (if there is only one frame) or the selected window's buffer name (if there is more than one frame).

You can specify a title for the initial Emacs frame with a command line option:

'-T *title*'
'--title=*title*'
> Specify *title* as the title for the initial Emacs frame.

The '--name' option (see Section D.1 [Resources], page 493) also specifies the title for the initial Emacs frame.

C.11 Icons

'-iconic'
'--iconic'
> Start Emacs in an iconified ("minimized") state.

'-nbi'
'--no-bitmap-icon'
> Disable the use of the Emacs icon.

Most window managers allow you to "iconify" (or "minimize") an Emacs frame, hiding it from sight. Some window managers replace iconified windows with tiny "icons", while others remove them entirely from sight. The '-iconic' option tells Emacs to begin running in an iconified state, rather than showing a frame right away. The text frame doesn't appear until you deiconify (or "un-minimize") it.

By default, Emacs uses an icon containing the Emacs logo. On desktop environments such as Gnome, this icon is also displayed in other contexts, e.g., when switching into an

Emacs frame. The '-nbi' or '--no-bitmap-icon' option tells Emacs to let the window manager choose what sort of icon to use—usually just a small rectangle containing the frame's title.

C.12 Other Display Options

'--parent-id *id*'

> Open Emacs as a client X window via the XEmbed protocol, with *id* as the parent X window id. Currently, this option is mainly useful for developers.

'-vb'
'--vertical-scroll-bars'

> Enable vertical scroll bars.

'-lsp *pixels*'
'--line-spacing=*pixels*'

> Specify *pixels* as additional space to put between lines, in pixels.

'-nbc'
'--no-blinking-cursor'

> Disable the blinking cursor on graphical displays.

'-D'
'--basic-display'

> Disable the menu-bar, the tool-bar, the scroll-bars, and tool tips, and turn off the blinking cursor. This can be useful for making a test case that simplifies debugging of display problems.

The '--xrm' option (see Section D.1 [Resources], page 493) specifies additional X resource values.

Appendix D X Options and Resources

You can customize some X-related aspects of Emacs behavior using X resources, as is usual for programs that use X.

When Emacs is compiled with GTK+ support, the appearance of various graphical widgets, such as the menu-bar, scroll-bar, and dialog boxes, is determined by "GTK resources". When Emacs is built without GTK+ support, the appearance of these widgets is determined by additional X resources.

On MS-Windows, you can customize some of the same aspects using the system registry (see Section C.4.3 [MS-Windows Registry], page 486).

D.1 X Resources

Programs running under the X Window System organize their user options under a hierarchy of classes and resources. You can specify default values for these options in your *X resource file*, usually named `~/.Xdefaults` or `~/.Xresources`. Changes in this file do not take effect immediately, because the X server stores its own list of resources; to update it, use the command `xrdb`—for instance, '`xrdb ~/.Xdefaults`'.

(MS-Windows systems do not support X resource files; on such systems, Emacs looks for X resources in the Windows Registry, first under the key '`HKEY_CURRENT_USER\SOFTWARE\GNU\Emacs`', which affects only the current user and override the system-wide settings, and then under the key '`HKEY_LOCAL_MACHINE\SOFTWARE\GNU\Emacs`', which affects all users of the system. The menu and scroll bars are native widgets on MS-Windows, so they are only customizable via the system-wide settings in the Display Control Panel. You can also set resources using the '`-xrm`' command line option, as explained below.)

Each line in the X resource file specifies a value for one option or for a collection of related options. The order in which the lines appear in the file does not matter. Each resource specification consists of a *program name* and a *resource name*. Case distinctions are significant in each of these names. Here is an example:

        emacs.cursorColor: dark green

The program name is the name of the executable file to which the resource applies. For Emacs, this is normally '`emacs`'. To specify a definition that applies to all instances of Emacs, regardless of the name of the Emacs executable, use '`Emacs`'.

The resource name is the name of a program setting. For instance, Emacs recognizes a '`cursorColor`' resource that controls the color of the text cursor.

Resources are grouped into named classes. For instance, the '`Foreground`' class contains the '`cursorColor`', '`foreground`' and '`pointerColor`' resources (see Section D.2 [Table of Resources], page 494). Instead of using a resource name, you can use a class name to specify the default value for all resources in that class, like this:

        emacs.Foreground: dark green

Emacs does not process X resources at all if you set the variable `inhibit-x-resources` to a non-`nil` value. If you invoke Emacs with the '`-Q`' (or '`--quick`') command-line option, `inhibit-x-resources` is automatically set to `t` (see Section C.2 [Initial Options], page 480).

D.2 Table of X Resources for Emacs

This table lists the X resource names that Emacs recognizes, excluding those that control the appearance of graphical widgets like the menu bar:

background (class `Background`)

>   Background color (see Section 11.9 [Colors], page 75).

bitmapIcon (class `BitmapIcon`)

>   Tell the window manager to display the Emacs icon if 'on'; don't do so if 'off'. See Section C.11 [Icons X], page 491, for a description of the icon.

cursorColor (class `Foreground`)

>   Text cursor color. If this resource is specified when Emacs starts up, Emacs sets its value as the background color of the `cursor` face (see Section 11.8 [Faces], page 74).

cursorBlink (class `CursorBlink`)

>   If the value of this resource is 'off' or 'false' or '0' at startup, Emacs disables Blink Cursor mode (see Section 11.20 [Cursor Display], page 86).

font (class `Font`)

>   Font name for the `default` face (see Section 18.8 [Fonts], page 168). You can also specify a fontset name (see Section 19.13 [Fontsets], page 192).

fontBackend (class `FontBackend`)

>   Comma-delimited list of backend(s) to use for drawing fonts, in order of precedence. For instance, the value 'x,xft' tells Emacs to draw fonts using the X core font driver, falling back on the Xft font driver if that fails. Normally, you should leave this resource unset, in which case Emacs tries using all available font backends.

foreground (class `Foreground`)

>   Default foreground color for text.

geometry (class `Geometry`)

>   Window size and position. The value should be a size and position specification, of the same form as in the '-g' or '--geometry' command-line option (see Section C.8 [Window Size X], page 489).

>   The size applies to all frames in the Emacs session, but the position applies only to the initial Emacs frame (or, in the case of a resource for a specific frame name, only that frame).

>   Be careful not to specify this resource as 'emacs*geometry', as that may affect individual menus as well as the main Emacs frame.

fullscreen (class `Fullscreen`)

>   The desired fullscreen size. The value can be one of `fullboth`, `maximized`, `fullwidth` or `fullheight`, which correspond to the command-line options '-fs', '-mm', '-fw', and '-fh' (see Section C.8 [Window Size X], page 489). Note that this applies to the initial frame only.

lineSpacing (class `LineSpacing`)

>   Additional space between lines, in pixels.

`menuBar` (class `MenuBar`)

> If the value of this resource is 'off' or 'false' or '0', Emacs disables Menu Bar mode at startup (see Section 18.14 [Menu Bars], page 173).

`pointerColor` (class `Foreground`)

> Color of the mouse cursor. This has no effect in many graphical desktop environments, as they do not let Emacs change the mouse cursor this way.

`title` (class `Title`)

> Name to display in the title bar of the initial Emacs frame.

`toolBar` (class `ToolBar`)

> If the value of this resource is 'off' or 'false' or '0', Emacs disables Tool Bar mode at startup (see Section 18.15 [Tool Bars], page 173).

`useXIM` (class `UseXIM`)

> Disable use of X input methods (XIM) if 'false' or 'off'. This is only relevant if your Emacs is built with XIM support. It might be useful to turn off XIM on slow X client/server links.

`verticalScrollBars` (class `ScrollBars`)

> Give frames scroll bars if 'on'; don't have scroll bars if 'off'.

You can also use X resources to customize individual Emacs faces (see Section 11.8 [Faces], page 74). For example, setting the resource '`face.attributeForeground`' is equivalent to customizing the '`foreground`' attribute of the face *face*. However, we recommend customizing faces from within Emacs, instead of using X resources. See Section 33.1.5 [Face Customization], page 416.

D.3 GTK resources

If Emacs is compiled with GTK+ toolkit support, the simplest way to customize its GTK+ widgets (e.g., menus, dialogs, tool bars and scroll bars) is to choose an appropriate GTK+ theme, for example with the GNOME theme selector.

In GTK+ version 2, you can also use *GTK+ resources* to customize the appearance of GTK+ widgets used by Emacs. These resources are specified in either the file `~/.emacs.d/gtkrc` (for Emacs-specific GTK+ resources), or `~/.gtkrc-2.0` (for general GTK+ resources). We recommend using `~/.emacs.d/gtkrc`, since GTK+ seems to ignore `~/.gtkrc-2.0` when running GConf with GNOME. Note, however, that some GTK themes may override customizations in `~/.emacs.d/gtkrc`; there is nothing we can do about this. GTK+ resources do not affect aspects of Emacs unrelated to GTK+ widgets, such as fonts and colors in the main Emacs window; those are governed by normal X resources (see Section D.1 [Resources], page 493).

The following sections describe how to customize GTK+ resources for Emacs. For details about GTK+ resources, see the GTK+ API document at `http://developer.gnome.org/gtk2/stable/gtk2-Resource-Files.html`.

In GTK+ version 3, GTK+ resources have been replaced by a completely different system. The appearance of GTK+ widgets is now determined by CSS-like style files: `gtk-3.0/gtk.css` in the GTK+ installation directory, and `~/.themes/theme/gtk-3.0/gtk.css` for local style settings (where *theme* is the name of the current GTK+ theme). Therefore, the description of GTK+ resources in this section does not apply to GTK+ 3. For details about the GTK+ 3 styling system, see `http://developer.gnome.org/gtk3/3.0/GtkCssProvider.html`.

D.3.1 GTK Resource Basics

In a GTK+ 2 resource file (usually `~/.emacs.d/gtkrc`), the simplest kinds of resource settings simply assign a value to a variable. For example, putting the following line in the resource file changes the font on all GTK+ widgets to 'courier-12':

```
gtk-font-name = "courier 12"
```

Note that in this case the font name must be supplied as a GTK font pattern (also called a *Pango font name*), not as a Fontconfig-style font name or XLFD. See Section 18.8 [Fonts], page 168.

To customize widgets you first define a *style*, and then apply the style to the widgets. Here is an example that sets the font for menus ('#' characters indicate comments):

```
# Define the style 'my_style'.
style "my_style"
{
  font_name = "helvetica bold 14"
}


# Specify that widget type '*emacs-menuitem*' uses 'my_style'.
widget "*emacs-menuitem*" style "my_style"
```

The widget name in this example contains wildcards, so the style is applied to all widgets matching '*emacs-menuitem*'. The widgets are named by the way they are contained, from the outer widget to the inner widget. Here is another example that applies 'my_style' specifically to the Emacs menu bar:

```
widget "Emacs.pane.menubar.*" style "my_style"
```

Here is a more elaborate example, showing how to change the parts of the scroll bar:

```
style "scroll"
{
  fg[NORMAL] = "red"      # Arrow color.
  bg[NORMAL] = "yellow"   # Thumb and background around arrow.
  bg[ACTIVE] = "blue"     # Trough color.
  bg[PRELIGHT] = "white"  # Thumb color when the mouse is over it.
}


widget "*verticalScrollBar*" style "scroll"
```

D.3.2 GTK widget names

A GTK+ widget is specified by a *widget name* and a *widget class*. The widget name refers to a specific widget (e.g., 'emacs-menuitem'), while the widget class refers to a collection of similar widgets (e.g., 'GtkMenuItem'). A widget always has a class, but need not have a name.

Absolute names are sequences of widget names or widget classes, corresponding to hierarchies of widgets embedded within other widgets. For example, if a GtkWindow named top contains a GtkVBox named box, which in turn contains a GtkMenuBar called menubar, the absolute class name of the menu-bar widget is GtkWindow.GtkVBox.GtkMenuBar, and its absolute widget name is top.box.menubar.

GTK+ resource files can contain two types of commands for specifying widget appearances:

widget   specifies a style for widgets based on the class name, or just the class.

widget_class
        specifies a style for widgets based on the class name.

See the previous subsection for examples of using the `widget` command; the `widget_class` command is used similarly. Note that the widget name/class and the style must be enclosed in double-quotes, and these commands must be at the top level in the GTK+ resource file.

As previously noted, you may specify a widget name or class with shell wildcard syntax: '*' matches zero or more characters and '?' matches one character. This example assigns a style to all widgets:

```
widget "*" style "my_style"
```

D.3.3 GTK Widget Names in Emacs

The GTK+ widgets used by an Emacs frame are listed below:

Emacs (class GtkWindow)

      pane (class GtkVBox)

            menubar (class GtkMenuBar)

                [menu item widgets]

            [unnamed widget] (class GtkHandleBox)

                emacs-toolbar (class GtkToolbar)

                    [tool bar item widgets]

            emacs (class GtkFixed)

                verticalScrollBar (class GtkVScrollbar)

The contents of Emacs windows are drawn in the `emacs` widget. Note that even if there are multiple Emacs windows, each scroll bar widget is named `verticalScrollBar`.

For example, here are two different ways to set the menu bar style:

```
widget "Emacs.pane.menubar.*" style "my_style"
widget_class "GtkWindow.GtkVBox.GtkMenuBar.*" style "my_style"
```

For GTK+ dialogs, Emacs uses a widget named `emacs-dialog`, of class `GtkDialog`. For file selection, Emacs uses a widget named `emacs-filedialog`, of class `GtkFileSelection`.

Because the widgets for pop-up menus and dialogs are free-standing windows and not "contained" in the `Emacs` widget, their GTK+ absolute names do not start with 'Emacs'. To customize these widgets, use wildcards like this:

```
widget "*emacs-dialog*" style "my_dialog_style"
widget "*emacs-filedialog* style "my_file_style"
widget "*emacs-menuitem* style "my_menu_style"
```

If you want to apply a style to all menus in Emacs, use this:

```
widget_class "*Menu*" style "my_menu_style"
```

D.3.4 GTK styles

Here is an example of two GTK+ style declarations:

```
pixmap_path "/usr/share/pixmaps:/usr/include/X11/pixmaps"

style "default"
{
  font_name = "helvetica 12"

  bg[NORMAL] = { 0.83, 0.80, 0.73 }
  bg[SELECTED] = { 0.0, 0.55, 0.55 }
  bg[INSENSITIVE] = { 0.77, 0.77, 0.66 }
  bg[ACTIVE] = { 0.0, 0.55, 0.55 }
  bg[PRELIGHT] = { 0.0, 0.55, 0.55 }

  fg[NORMAL] = "black"
  fg[SELECTED] = { 0.9, 0.9, 0.9 }
  fg[ACTIVE] = "black"
  fg[PRELIGHT] = { 0.9, 0.9, 0.9 }

  base[INSENSITIVE] = "#777766"
  text[INSENSITIVE] = { 0.60, 0.65, 0.57 }

  bg_pixmap[NORMAL] = "background.xpm"
  bg_pixmap[INSENSITIVE] = "background.xpm"
  bg_pixmap[ACTIVE] = "background.xpm"
  bg_pixmap[PRELIGHT] = "<none>"

}

style "ruler" = "default"
{
  font_name = "helvetica 8"
}
```

The style 'ruler' inherits from 'default'. This way you can build on existing styles. The syntax for fonts and colors is described below.

As this example shows, it is possible to specify several values for foreground and background depending on the widget's *state*. The possible states are:

NORMAL   This is the default state for widgets.

ACTIVE   This is the state for a widget that is ready to do something. It is also for the trough of a scroll bar, i.e., bg[ACTIVE] = "red" sets the scroll bar trough to red. Buttons that have been pressed but not released yet ("armed") are in this state.

PRELIGHT This is the state for a widget that can be manipulated, when the mouse pointer is over it—for example when the mouse is over the thumb in the scroll bar or over a menu item. When the mouse is over a button that is not pressed, the button is in this state.

SELECTED This is the state for data that has been selected by the user. It can be selected text or items selected in a list. This state is not used in Emacs.

INSENSITIVE

> This is the state for widgets that are visible, but they can not be manipulated in the usual way—for example, buttons that can't be pressed, and disabled menu items. To display disabled menu items in yellow, use `fg[INSENSITIVE] = "yellow"`.

Here are the things that can go in a style declaration:

`bg[state] = color`

> This specifies the background color for the widget. Note that editable text doesn't use `bg`; it uses `base` instead.

`base[state] = color`

> This specifies the background color for editable text. In Emacs, this color is used for the background of the text fields in the file dialog.

`bg_pixmap[state] = "pixmap"`

> This specifies an image background (instead of a background color). *pixmap* should be the image file name. GTK can use a number of image file formats, including XPM, XBM, GIF, JPEG and PNG. If you want a widget to use the same image as its parent, use '`<parent>`'. If you don't want any image, use '`<none>`'. '`<none>`' is the way to cancel a background image inherited from a parent style.

> You can't specify the file by its absolute file name. GTK looks for the pixmap file in directories specified in `pixmap_path`. `pixmap_path` is a colon-separated list of directories within double quotes, specified at the top level in a `gtkrc` file (i.e., not inside a style definition; see example above):
>
>   pixmap_path "/usr/share/pixmaps:/usr/include/X11/pixmaps"

`fg[state] = color`

> This specifies the foreground color for widgets to use. It is the color of text in menus and buttons, and the color for the arrows in the scroll bar. For editable text, use `text`.

`text[state] = color`

> This is the color for editable text. In Emacs, this color is used for the text fields in the file dialog.

`font_name = "font"`

> This specifies the font for text in the widget. *font* is a GTK-style (or Pango) font name, like '`Sans Italic 10`'. See Section 18.8 [Fonts], page 168. The names are case insensitive.

There are three ways to specify a color: a color name, an RGB triplet, or a GTK-style RGB triplet. See Section 11.9 [Colors], page 75, for a description of color names and RGB triplets. Color names should be enclosed with double quotes, e.g., '`"red"`'. RGB triplets should be written without double quotes, e.g., '`#ff0000`'. GTK-style RGB triplets have the form `{ r, g, b }`, where *r*, *g* and *b* are either integers in the range 0–65535 or floats in the range 0.0–1.0.

Appendix E Emacs 23 Antinews

For those users who live backwards in time, here is information about downgrading to Emacs version 23.4. We hope you will enjoy the greater simplicity that results from the absence of many Emacs 24.5 features.

- Support for displaying and editing "bidirectional" text has been removed. Text is now always displayed on the screen in a single consistent direction—left to right—regardless of the underlying script. Similarly, `C-f` and `C-b` always move the text cursor to the right and left respectively. Also, `RIGHT` and `LEFT` are now equivalent to `C-f` and `C-b`, as you might expect, rather than moving forward or backward based on the underlying "paragraph direction".

   Users of "right-to-left" languages, like Arabic and Hebrew, may adapt by reading and/or editing text in left-to-right order.

- The Emacs Lisp package manager has been removed. Instead of using a "user interface" (`M-x list-packages`), additional Lisp packages must now be installed by hand, which is the most flexible and "Lispy" method anyway. Typically, this just involves editing your init file to add the package installation directory to the load path and defining some autoloads; see each package's commentary section and/or README file for details.

- The option `delete-active-region` has been deleted. When the region is active, typing `DEL` or `Delete` no longer deletes the text in the region; it deletes a single character instead.

- We have reworked how Emacs handles the clipboard and the X primary selection. Commands for killing and yanking, like `C-w` and `C-y`, use the primary selection and not the clipboard, so you can use these commands without interfering with "cutting" or "pasting" in other programs. The 'Cut'/'Copy'/'Paste' menu items are bound to separate clipboard commands, not to the same commands as `C-w`/`M-w`/`C-y`.

   Selecting text by dragging with the mouse now puts the text in the kill ring, in addition to the primary selection. But note that selecting an active region with `C-SPC` does *not* alter the kill ring nor the primary selection, even though the text highlighting is visually identical.

- In Isearch, `C-y` and `M-y` are no longer bound to `isearch-yank-kill` and `isearch-yank-pop` respectively. Instead, `C-y` yanks the rest of the current line into the search string (`isearch-yank-line`), whereas `M-y` does `isearch-yank-kill`. The mismatch with the usual meanings of `C-y` and `M-y` is unintended.

- Various completion features have been simplified. The option `completion-category-overrides` has been removed, so Emacs uses a single consistent scheme to generate completions, instead of using a separate scheme for (say) buffer name completion. Several major modes, such as Shell mode, now implement their own inline completion commands instead of using `completion-at-point`.

- We have removed several options for controlling how windows are used, such as `display-buffer-base-action`, `display-buffer-alist`, `window-combination-limit`, and `window-combination-resize`.

- The command `M-x customize-themes` has been removed. Emacs no longer comes with pre-defined themes (you can write your own).

- Emacs no longer adapts various aspects of its display to GTK+ settings, opting instead for a uniform toolkit-independent look. GTK+ scroll bars are placed on the left, the same position as non-GTK+ X scroll bars. Emacs no longer refers to GTK+ to set the default `region` face, nor for drawing tooltips.

- Setting the option `delete-by-moving-to-trash` to a non-`nil` value now causes all file deletions to use the system trash, even temporary files created by Lisp programs; furthermore, the `M-x delete-file` and `M-x delete-directory` commands no longer accept prefix arguments to force true deletion.

- On GNU/Linux and Unix, the default method for sending mail (as specified by `send-mail-function`) is to use the `sendmail` program. Emacs no longer asks for a delivery method the first time you try to send mail, trusting instead that the system is configured for mail delivery, as it ought to be.

- Several VC features have been removed, including the `C-x v +` and `C-x v m` commands for pulling and merging on distributed version control systems, and the ability to view inline log entries in the log buffers made by `C-x v L`.

- To keep up with decreasing computer memory capacity and disk space, many other functions and files have been eliminated in Emacs 23.4.

Appendix F Emacs and Mac OS / GNUstep

This section describes the peculiarities of using Emacs built with the GNUstep libraries on GNU/Linux or other operating systems, or on Mac OS X with native window system support. On Mac OS X, Emacs can be built either without window system support, with X11, or with the Cocoa interface; this section only applies to the Cocoa build. This does not support versions of Mac OS X earlier than 10.4.

For various historical and technical reasons, Emacs uses the term 'Nextstep' internally, instead of "Cocoa" or "Mac OS X"; for instance, most of the commands and variables described in this section begin with 'ns-', which is short for 'Nextstep'. NeXTstep was an application interface released by NeXT Inc during the 1980s, of which Cocoa is a direct descendant. Apart from Cocoa, there is another NeXTstep-style system: GNUstep, which is free software. As of this writing, Emacs GNUstep support is alpha status (see Section F.4 [GNUstep Support], page 504), but we hope to improve it in the future.

F.1 Basic Emacs usage under Mac OS and GNUstep

By default, the alt and option keys are the same as Meta. The Mac Cmd key is the same as Super, and Emacs provides a set of key bindings using this modifier key that mimic other Mac / GNUstep applications (see Section F.3 [Mac / GNUstep Events], page 503). You can change these bindings in the usual way (see Section 33.3 [Key Bindings], page 428).

The variable ns-right-alternate-modifier controls the behavior of the right alt and option keys. These keys behave like the left-hand keys if the value is left (the default). A value of control, meta, alt, super, or hyper makes them behave like the corresponding modifier keys; a value to left means be the same key as ns-alternate-modifier; a value of none tells Emacs to ignore them.

S-Mouse-1 adjusts the region to the click position, just like Mouse-3 (mouse-save-then-kill); it does not pop up a menu for changing the default face, as S-Mouse-1 normally does (see Section 11.11 [Text Scale], page 78). This change makes Emacs behave more like other Mac / GNUstep applications.

When you open or save files using the menus, or using the Cmd-o and Cmd-S bindings, Emacs uses graphical file dialogs to read file names. However, if you use the regular Emacs key sequences, such as C-x C-f, Emacs uses the minibuffer to read file names.

On GNUstep, in an X-windows environment you need to use Cmd-c instead of one of the C-w or M-w commands to transfer text to the X primary selection; otherwise, Emacs will use the "clipboard" selection. Likewise, Cmd-y (instead of C-y) yanks from the X primary selection instead of the kill-ring or clipboard.

F.1.1 Grabbing environment variables

Many programs which may run under Emacs, like latex or man, depend on the settings of environment variables. If Emacs is launched from the shell, it will automatically inherit these environment variables and its subprocesses will inherit them from it. But if Emacs is launched from the Finder it is not a descendant of any shell, so its environment variables haven't been set, which often causes the subprocesses it launches to behave differently than they would when launched from the shell.

For the PATH and MANPATH variables, a system-wide method of setting PATH is recommended on Mac OS X 10.5 and later, using the `/etc/paths` files and the `/etc/paths.d` directory.

F.2 Mac / GNUstep Customization

There are a few customization options that are specific to the Nextstep port. For example, they affect things such as the modifier keys and the fullscreen behavior. To see all such options, use `M-x customize-group RET ns RET`.

F.2.1 Font and Color Panels

The standard Mac / GNUstep font and color panels are accessible via Lisp commands. The Font Panel may be accessed with `M-x ns-popup-font-panel`. It will set the default font in the frame most recently used or clicked on.

You can bring up a color panel with `M-x ns-popup-color-panel` and drag the color you want over the Emacs face you want to change. Normal dragging will alter the foreground color. Shift dragging will alter the background color. To discard the settings, create a new frame and close the altered one.

Useful in this context is the listing of all faces obtained by `M-x list-faces-display`.

In Mac OS X 10.5 and later, Emacs uses a Core Text based font backend by default. If you prefer the older font style, enter the following at the command-line before starting Emacs:

```
% defaults write org.gnu.Emacs FontBackend ns
```

F.3 Windowing System Events under Mac OS / GNUstep

Nextstep applications receive a number of special events which have no X equivalent. These are sent as specially defined "keys", which do not correspond to any sequence of keystrokes. Under Emacs, these "key" events can be bound to functions just like ordinary keystrokes. Here is a list of these events.

`ns-open-file`

> This event occurs when another Nextstep application requests that Emacs open a file. A typical reason for this would be a user double-clicking a file in the Finder application. By default, Emacs responds to this event by opening a new frame and visiting the file in that frame (`ns-find-file`). As an exception, if the selected buffer is the `*scratch*` buffer, Emacs visits the file in the selected frame.

> You can change how Emacs responds to a `ns-open-file` event by changing the variable `ns-pop-up-frames`. Its default value, 'fresh', is what we have just described. A value of `t` means to always visit the file in a new frame. A value of `nil` means to always visit the file in an existing frame.

`ns-open-temp-file`

> This event occurs when another application requests that Emacs open a temporary file. By default, this is handled by just generating a `ns-open-file` event, the results of which are described above.

`ns-open-file-line`

> Some applications, such as ProjectBuilder and gdb, request not only a particular file, but also a particular line or sequence of lines in the file. Emacs handles this by visiting that file and highlighting the requested line (`ns-open-file-select-line`).

`ns-drag-file`

> This event occurs when a user drags files from another application into an Emacs frame. The default behavior is to insert the contents of all the dragged files into the current buffer (`ns-insert-files`). The list of dragged files is stored in the variable `ns-input-file`.

`ns-drag-color`

> This event occurs when a user drags a color from the color well (or some other source) into an Emacs frame. The default behavior is to alter the foreground color of the area the color was dragged onto (`ns-set-foreground-at-mouse`). If this event is issued with a `Shift` modifier, Emacs changes the background color instead (`ns-set-background-at-mouse`). The name of the dragged color is stored in the variable `ns-input-color`.

`ns-change-font`

> This event occurs when the user selects a font in a Nextstep font panel (which can be opened with `Cmd-t`). The default behavior is to adjust the font of the selected frame (`ns-respond-to-changefont`). The name and size of the selected font are stored in the variables `ns-input-font` and `ns-input-fontsize`, respectively.

`ns-power-off`

> This event occurs when the user logs out and Emacs is still running, or when 'Quit Emacs' is chosen from the application menu. The default behavior is to save all file-visiting buffers.

Emacs also allows users to make use of Nextstep services, via a set of commands whose names begin with '`ns-service-`' and end with the name of the service. Type `M-x ns-service-TAB` to see a list of these commands. These functions either operate on marked text (replacing it with the result) or take a string argument and return the result as a string. You can also use the Lisp function `ns-perform-service` to pass arbitrary strings to arbitrary services and receive the results back. Note that you may need to restart Emacs to access newly-available services.

F.4 GNUstep Support

Emacs can be built and run under GNUstep, but there are still issues to be addressed. Interested developers should contact `emacs-devel@gnu.org`.

Appendix G Emacs and Microsoft Windows/MS-DOS

This section describes peculiarities of using Emacs on Microsoft Windows. Some of these peculiarities are also relevant to Microsoft's older MS-DOS "operating system" (also known as "MS-DOG"). However, Emacs features that are relevant *only* to MS-DOS are described in a separate manual (see Section "MS-DOS" in *Specialized Emacs Features*).

The behavior of Emacs on MS-Windows is reasonably similar to what is documented in the rest of the manual, including support for long file names, multiple frames, scroll bars, mouse menus, and subprocesses. However, a few special considerations apply, and they are described here.

G.1 How to Start Emacs on MS-Windows

There are several ways of starting Emacs on MS-Windows:

1. From the desktop shortcut icon: either double-click the left mouse button on the icon, or click once, then press `RET`. The desktop shortcut should specify as its "Target" (in the "Properties" of the shortcut) the full absolute file name of `runemacs.exe`, *not* of `emacs.exe`. This is because `runemacs.exe` hides the console window that would have been created if the target of the shortcut were `emacs.exe` (which is a console program, as far as Windows is concerned). If you use this method, Emacs starts in the directory specified by the shortcut. To control where that is, right-click on the shortcut, select "Properties", and in the "Shortcut" tab modify the "Start in" field to your liking.

2. From the Command Prompt window, by typing `emacs RET` at the prompt. The Command Prompt window where you did that will not be available for invoking other commands until Emacs exits. In this case, Emacs will start in the current directory of the Windows shell.

3. From the Command Prompt window, by typing `runemacs RET` at the prompt. The Command Prompt window where you did that will be immediately available for invoking other commands. In this case, Emacs will start in the current directory of the Windows shell.

4. Via `emacsclient.exe` or `emacsclientw.exe`, which allow you to invoke Emacs from other programs, and to reuse a running Emacs process for serving editing jobs required by other programs. See Section 31.5 [Emacs Server], page 393. The difference between `emacsclient.exe` and `emacsclientw.exe` is that the former is a console program, while the latter is a Windows GUI program. Both programs wait for Emacs to signal that the editing job is finished, before they exit and return control to the program that invoked them. Which one of them to use in each case depends on the expectations of the program that needs editing services. If that program is itself a console (text-mode) program, you should use `emacsclient.exe`, so that any of its messages and prompts appear in the same command window as those of the invoking program. By contrast, if the invoking program is a GUI program, you will be better off using `emacsclientw.exe`, because `emacsclient.exe` will pop up a command window if it is invoked from a GUI program. A notable situation where you would want `emacsclientw.exe` is when you right-click on a file in the Windows Explorer and select "Open With" from the pop-up menu. Use the '`--alternate-editor=`' or '`-a`' options if Emacs might not be running (or not running as a server) when `emacsclient` is invoked—that will always give you

an editor. When invoked via `emacsclient`, Emacs will start in the current directory of the program that invoked `emacsclient`.

Note that, due to limitations of MS-Windows, Emacs cannot have both GUI and text-mode frames in the same session. It also cannot open text-mode frames on more than a single *Command Prompt* window, because each Windows program can have only one console at any given time. For these reasons, if you invoke `emacsclient` with the `-c` option, and the Emacs server runs in a text-mode session, Emacs will always create a new text-mode frame in the same *Command Prompt* window where it was started; a GUI frame will be created only if the server runs in a GUI session. Similarly, if you invoke `emacsclient` with the `-t` option, Emacs will create a GUI frame if the server runs in a GUI session, or a text-mode frame when the session runs in text mode in a *Command Prompt* window. See Section 31.5.2 [emacsclient Options], page 395.

G.2 Text Files and Binary Files

GNU Emacs uses newline characters to separate text lines. This is the convention used on GNU, Unix, and other Posix-compliant systems.

By contrast, MS-DOS and MS-Windows normally use carriage-return linefeed, a two-character sequence, to separate text lines. (Linefeed is the same character as newline.) Therefore, convenient editing of typical files with Emacs requires conversion of these end-of-line (EOL) sequences. And that is what Emacs normally does: it converts carriage-return linefeed into newline when reading files, and converts newline into carriage-return linefeed when writing files. The same mechanism that handles conversion of international character codes does this conversion also (see Section 19.5 [Coding Systems], page 183).

One consequence of this special format-conversion of most files is that character positions as reported by Emacs (see Section 4.9 [Position Info], page 22) do not agree with the file size information known to the operating system.

In addition, if Emacs recognizes from a file's contents that it uses newline rather than carriage-return linefeed as its line separator, it does not perform EOL conversion when reading or writing that file. Thus, you can read and edit files from GNU and Unix systems on MS-DOS with no special effort, and they will retain their Unix-style end-of-line convention after you edit them.

The mode line indicates whether end-of-line translation was used for the current buffer. If MS-DOS end-of-line translation is in use for the buffer, the MS-Windows build of Emacs displays a backslash '\' after the coding system mnemonic near the beginning of the mode line (see Section 1.3 [Mode Line], page 8). If no EOL translation was performed, the string '(Unix)' is displayed instead of the backslash, to alert you that the file's EOL format is not the usual carriage-return linefeed.

To visit a file and specify whether it uses DOS-style or Unix-style end-of-line, specify a coding system (see Section 19.9 [Text Coding], page 188). For example, `C-x RET c unix RET C-x C-f foobar.txt` visits the file `foobar.txt` without converting the EOLs; if some line ends with a carriage-return linefeed pair, Emacs will display '^M' at the end of that line. Similarly, you can direct Emacs to save a buffer in a specified EOL format with the `C-x RET f` command. For example, to save a buffer with Unix EOL format, type `C-x RET f unix RET C-x C-s`. If you visit a file with DOS EOL conversion, then save it with Unix EOL format, that effectively converts the file to Unix EOL style, like the `dos2unix` program.

When you use NFS, Samba, or some other similar method to access file systems that reside on computers using GNU or Unix systems, Emacs should not perform end-of-line translation on any files in these file systems—not even when you create a new file. To request this, designate these file systems as *untranslated* file systems by calling the function `add-untranslated-filesystem`. It takes one argument: the file system name, including a drive letter and optionally a directory. For example,

        (add-untranslated-filesystem "Z:")

designates drive Z as an untranslated file system, and

        (add-untranslated-filesystem "Z:\\foo")

designates directory `\foo` on drive Z as an untranslated file system.

Most often you would use `add-untranslated-filesystem` in your `.emacs` file, or in `site-start.el` so that all the users at your site get the benefit of it.

To countermand the effect of `add-untranslated-filesystem`, use the function `remove-untranslated-filesystem`. This function takes one argument, which should be a string just like the one that was used previously with `add-untranslated-filesystem`.

Designating a file system as untranslated does not affect character set conversion, only end-of-line conversion. Essentially, it directs Emacs to create new files with the Unix-style convention of using newline at the end of a line. See Section 19.5 [Coding Systems], page 183.

G.3 File Names on MS-Windows

MS-Windows and MS-DOS normally use a backslash, '\', to separate name units within a file name, instead of the slash used on other systems. Emacs on MS-DOS/MS-Windows permits use of either slash or backslash, and also knows about drive letters in file names.

On MS-DOS/MS-Windows, file names are case-insensitive, so Emacs by default ignores letter-case in file names during completion.

The variable `w32-get-true-file-attributes` controls whether Emacs should issue additional system calls to determine more accurately file attributes in primitives like `file-attributes` and `directory-files-and-attributes`. These additional calls are needed to report correct file ownership, link counts and file types for special files such as pipes. Without these system calls, file ownership will be attributed to the current user, link counts will be always reported as 1, and special files will be reported as regular files.

If the value of this variable is `local` (the default), Emacs will issue these additional system calls only for files on local fixed drives. Any other non-`nil` value means do this even for removable and remote volumes, where this could potentially slow down Dired and other related features. The value of `nil` means never issue those system calls. Non-`nil` values are more useful on NTFS volumes, which support hard links and file security, than on FAT, FAT32, and exFAT volumes.

Unlike Unix, MS-Windows file systems restrict the set of characters that can be used in a file name. The following characters are not allowed:

- Shell redirection symbols '<', '>', and '|'.
- Colon ':' (except after the drive letter).
- Forward slash '/' and backslash '\' (except as directory separators).
- Wildcard characters '*' and '?'.

- Control characters whose codepoints are 1 through 31 decimal. In particular, newlines in file names are not allowed.

- The null character, whose codepoint is zero (this limitation exists on Unix filesystems as well).

In addition, referencing any file whose name matches a DOS character device, such as NUL or LPT1 or PRN or CON, with or without any file-name extension, will always resolve to those character devices, in any directory. Therefore, only use such file names when you want to use the corresponding character device.

G.4 Emulation of ls on MS-Windows

Dired normally uses the external program ls to produce the directory listing displayed in Dired buffers (see Chapter 27 [Dired], page 315). However, MS-Windows and MS-DOS systems don't come with such a program, although several ports of GNU ls are available. Therefore, Emacs on those systems *emulates* ls in Lisp, by using the ls-lisp.el package. While ls-lisp.el provides a reasonably full emulation of ls, there are some options and features peculiar to that emulation; for more details, see the documentation of the variables whose names begin with ls-lisp.

G.5 HOME and Startup Directories on MS-Windows

The Windows equivalent of HOME is the *user-specific application data directory*. The actual location depends on the Windows version; typical values are C:\Documents and Settings*username*\Application Data on Windows 2000/XP/2K3, C:\Users*username*\AppData\Roaming on Windows Vista/7/2008, and either C:\WINDOWS\Application Data or C:\WINDOWS\Profiles*username*\Application Data on Windows 9X/ME. If this directory does not exist or cannot be accessed, Emacs falls back to C:\ as the default value of HOME.

You can override this default value of HOME by explicitly setting the environment variable HOME to point to any directory on your system. HOME can be set either from the command shell prompt or from 'Properties' dialog of 'My Computer'. HOME can also be set in the system registry, see Section C.4.3 [MS-Windows Registry], page 486.

For compatibility with older versions of Emacs[1], if there is a file named .emacs in C:\, the root directory of drive C:, and HOME is set neither in the environment nor in the Registry, Emacs will treat C:\ as the default HOME location, and will not look in the application data directory, even if it exists. Note that only .emacs is looked for in C:\; the older name _emacs (see below) is not. This use of C:\.emacs to define HOME is deprecated.

Whatever the final place is, Emacs sets the internal value of the HOME environment variable to point to it, and it will use that location for other files and directories it normally looks for or creates in your home directory.

You can always find out what Emacs thinks is your home directory's location by typing C-x d ~/ RET. This should present the list of files in the home directory, and show its full name on the first line. Likewise, to visit your init file, type C-x C-f ~/.emacs RET (assuming the file's name is .emacs).

---

[1] Older versions of Emacs didn't check the application data directory.

The home directory is where your init file is stored. It can have any name mentioned in Section 33.4 [Init File], page 437.

Because MS-DOS does not allow file names with leading dots, and older Windows systems made it hard to create files with such names, the Windows port of Emacs supports an init file name _emacs, if such a file exists in the home directory and .emacs does not. This name is considered obsolete.

G.6 Keyboard Usage on MS-Windows

This section describes the Windows-specific features related to keyboard input in Emacs.

Many key combinations (known as "keyboard shortcuts") that have conventional uses in MS-Windows programs conflict with traditional Emacs key bindings. (These Emacs key bindings were established years before Microsoft was founded.) Examples of conflicts include C-c, C-x, C-z, C-a, and W-SPC. You can redefine some of them with meanings more like the MS-Windows meanings by enabling CUA Mode (see Section 9.6 [CUA Bindings], page 62).

See Info file emacs, node 'Windows Keyboard', for information about additional Windows-specific variables in this category.

The variable w32-apps-modifier controls the effect of the Apps key (usually located between the right Alt and the right Ctrl keys). Its value can be one of the symbols hyper, super, meta, alt, control, or shift for the respective modifier, or nil to appear as the key apps. The default is nil.

The variable w32-lwindow-modifier determines the effect of the left Windows key (usually labeled with start and the Windows logo). If its value is nil (the default), the key will produce the symbol lwindow. Setting it to one of the symbols hyper, super, meta, alt, control, or shift will produce the respective modifier. A similar variable w32-rwindow-modifier controls the effect of the right Windows key, and w32-scroll-lock-modifier does the same for the ScrLock key. If these variables are set to nil, the right Windows key produces the symbol rwindow and ScrLock produces the symbol scroll.

Emacs compiled as a native Windows application normally turns off the Windows feature that tapping the Alt key invokes the Windows menu. The reason is that the Alt serves as META in Emacs. When using Emacs, users often press the META key temporarily and then change their minds; if this has the effect of bringing up the Windows menu, it alters the meaning of subsequent commands. Many users find this frustrating.

You can re-enable Windows's default handling of tapping the Alt key by setting w32-pass-alt-to-system to a non-nil value.

G.7 Mouse Usage on MS-Windows

This section describes the Windows-specific variables related to the mouse.

The variable w32-mouse-button-tolerance specifies the time interval, in milliseconds, for faking middle mouse button press on 2-button mice. If both mouse buttons are depressed within this time interval, Emacs generates a middle mouse button click event instead of a double click on one of the buttons.

If the variable w32-pass-extra-mouse-buttons-to-system is non-nil, Emacs passes the fourth and fifth mouse buttons to Windows.

The variable `w32-swap-mouse-buttons` controls which of the 3 mouse buttons generates the `mouse-2` events. When it is `nil` (the default), the middle button generates `mouse-2` and the right button generates `mouse-3` events. If this variable is non-`nil`, the roles of these two buttons are reversed.

G.8 Subprocesses on Windows 9X/ME and Windows NT/2K/XP

Emacs compiled as a native Windows application (as opposed to the DOS version) includes full support for asynchronous subprocesses. In the Windows version, synchronous and asynchronous subprocesses work fine on both Windows 9X/ME and Windows NT/2K/XP as long as you run only 32-bit Windows applications. However, when you run a DOS application in a subprocess, you may encounter problems or be unable to run the application at all; and if you run two DOS applications at the same time in two subprocesses, you may have to reboot your system.

Since the standard command interpreter (and most command line utilities) on Windows 9X are DOS applications, these problems are significant when using that system. But there's nothing we can do about them; only Microsoft can fix them.

If you run just one DOS application subprocess, the subprocess should work as expected as long as it is "well-behaved" and does not perform direct screen access or other unusual actions. If you have a CPU monitor application, your machine will appear to be 100% busy even when the DOS application is idle, but this is only an artifact of the way CPU monitors measure processor load.

You must terminate the DOS application before you start any other DOS application in a different subprocess. Emacs is unable to interrupt or terminate a DOS subprocess. The only way you can terminate such a subprocess is by giving it a command that tells its program to exit.

If you attempt to run two DOS applications at the same time in separate subprocesses, the second one that is started will be suspended until the first one finishes, even if either or both of them are asynchronous.

If you can go to the first subprocess, and tell it to exit, the second subprocess should continue normally. However, if the second subprocess is synchronous, Emacs itself will be hung until the first subprocess finishes. If it will not finish without user input, then you have no choice but to reboot if you are running on Windows 9X. If you are running on Windows NT/2K/XP, you can use a process viewer application to kill the appropriate instance of NTVDM instead (this will terminate both DOS subprocesses).

If you have to reboot Windows 9X in this situation, do not use the **Shutdown** command on the **Start** menu; that usually hangs the system. Instead, type **Ctrl-Alt-DEL** and then choose **Shutdown**. That usually works, although it may take a few minutes to do its job.

The variable `w32-quote-process-args` controls how Emacs quotes the process arguments. Non-`nil` means quote with the " character. If the value is a character, Emacs uses that character to escape any quote characters that appear; otherwise it chooses a suitable escape character based on the type of the program.

G.9 Printing and MS-Windows

Printing commands, such as `lpr-buffer` (see Section 31.6 [Printing], page 397) and `ps-print-buffer` (see Section 31.6.1 [PostScript], page 398) work in MS-DOS and MS-Windows by sending the output to one of the printer ports, if a Posix-style `lpr` program is unavailable. The same Emacs variables control printing on all systems, but in some cases they have different default values on MS-DOS and MS-Windows.

Emacs on MS Windows attempts to determine your default printer automatically (using the function `default-printer-name`). But in some rare cases this can fail, or you may wish to use a different printer from within Emacs. The rest of this section explains how to tell Emacs which printer to use.

If you want to use your local printer, then set the Lisp variable `lpr-command` to `""` (its default value on Windows) and `printer-name` to the name of the printer port—for example, `"PRN"`, the usual local printer port, or `"LPT2"`, or `"COM1"` for a serial printer. You can also set `printer-name` to a file name, in which case "printed" output is actually appended to that file. If you set `printer-name` to `"NUL"`, printed output is silently discarded (sent to the system null device).

You can also use a printer shared by another machine by setting `printer-name` to the UNC share name for that printer—for example, `"//joes_pc/hp4si"`. (It doesn't matter whether you use forward slashes or backslashes here.) To find out the names of shared printers, run the command 'net view' from the command prompt to obtain a list of servers, and 'net view *server-name*' to see the names of printers (and directories) shared by that server. Alternatively, click the 'Network Neighborhood' icon on your desktop, and look for machines that share their printers via the network.

If the printer doesn't appear in the output of 'net view', or if setting `printer-name` to the UNC share name doesn't produce a hardcopy on that printer, you can use the 'net use' command to connect a local print port such as `"LPT2"` to the networked printer. For example, typing `net use LPT2: \\joes_pc\hp4si`[2] causes Windows to *capture* the LPT2 port and redirect the printed material to the printer connected to the machine `joes_pc`. After this command, setting `printer-name` to `"LPT2"` should produce the hardcopy on the networked printer.

With some varieties of Windows network software, you can instruct Windows to capture a specific printer port such as `"LPT2"`, and redirect it to a networked printer via the `Control Panel->Printers` applet instead of 'net use'.

If you set `printer-name` to a file name, it's best to use an absolute file name. Emacs changes the working directory according to the default directory of the current buffer, so if the file name in `printer-name` is relative, you will end up with several such files, each one in the directory of the buffer from which the printing was done.

If the value of `printer-name` is correct, but printing does not produce the hardcopy on your printer, it is possible that your printer does not support printing plain text (some cheap printers omit this functionality). In that case, try the PostScript print commands, described below.

---

[2] Note that the 'net use' command requires the UNC share name to be typed with the Windows-style backslashes, while the value of `printer-name` can be set with either forward- or backslashes.

The commands `print-buffer` and `print-region` call the `pr` program, or use special switches to the `lpr` program, to produce headers on each printed page. MS-DOS and MS-Windows don't normally have these programs, so by default, the variable `lpr-headers-switches` is set so that the requests to print page headers are silently ignored. Thus, `print-buffer` and `print-region` produce the same output as `lpr-buffer` and `lpr-region`, respectively. If you do have a suitable `pr` program (for example, from GNU Coreutils), set `lpr-headers-switches` to `nil`; Emacs will then call `pr` to produce the page headers, and print the resulting output as specified by `printer-name`.

Finally, if you do have an `lpr` work-alike, you can set the variable `lpr-command` to `"lpr"`. Then Emacs will use `lpr` for printing, as on other systems. (If the name of the program isn't `lpr`, set `lpr-command` to the appropriate value.) The variable `lpr-switches` has its standard meaning when `lpr-command` is not `""`. If the variable `printer-name` has a string value, it is used as the value for the `-P` option to `lpr`, as on Unix.

A parallel set of variables, `ps-lpr-command`, `ps-lpr-switches`, and `ps-printer-name` (see Section 31.6.2 [PostScript Variables], page 399), defines how PostScript files should be printed. These variables are used in the same way as the corresponding variables described above for non-PostScript printing. Thus, the value of `ps-printer-name` is used as the name of the device (or file) to which PostScript output is sent, just as `printer-name` is used for non-PostScript printing. (There are two distinct sets of variables in case you have two printers attached to two different ports, and only one of them is a PostScript printer.)

The default value of the variable `ps-lpr-command` is `""`, which causes PostScript output to be sent to the printer port specified by `ps-printer-name`; but `ps-lpr-command` can also be set to the name of a program which will accept PostScript files. Thus, if you have a non-PostScript printer, you can set this variable to the name of a PostScript interpreter program (such as Ghostscript). Any switches that need to be passed to the interpreter program are specified using `ps-lpr-switches`. (If the value of `ps-printer-name` is a string, it will be added to the list of switches as the value for the `-P` option. This is probably only useful if you are using `lpr`, so when using an interpreter typically you would set `ps-printer-name` to something other than a string so it is ignored.)

For example, to use Ghostscript for printing on the system's default printer, put this in your `.emacs` file:

```
(setq ps-printer-name t)
(setq ps-lpr-command "D:/gs6.01/bin/gswin32c.exe")
(setq ps-lpr-switches '("-q" "-dNOPAUSE" "-dBATCH"
                        "-sDEVICE=mswinpr2"
                        "-sPAPERSIZE=a4"))
```

(This assumes that Ghostscript is installed in the `D:/gs6.01` directory.)

G.10 Specifying Fonts on MS-Windows

Starting with Emacs 23, fonts are specified by their name, size and optional properties. The format for specifying fonts comes from the fontconfig library used in modern Free desktops:

```
[Family[-PointSize]][:Option1=Value1[:Option2=Value2[...]]]
```

The old XLFD based format is also supported for backwards compatibility.

Emacs 23 and later supports a number of font backends. Currently, the `gdi` and `uniscribe` backends are supported on Windows. The `gdi` font backend is available on all versions of Windows, and supports all fonts that are natively supported by Windows. The `uniscribe` font backend is available on Windows 2000 and later, and supports TrueType and OpenType fonts. Some languages requiring complex layout can only be properly supported by the Uniscribe backend. By default, both backends are enabled if supported, with `uniscribe` taking priority over `gdi`. To override that and use the GDI backend even if Uniscribe is available, invoke Emacs with the `-xrm Emacs.fontBackend:gdi` command-line argument, or add a `Emacs.fontBackend` resource with the value `gdi` in the Registry under either the 'HKEY_CURRENT_USER\SOFTWARE\GNU\Emacs' or the 'HKEY_LOCAL_MACHINE\SOFTWARE\GNU\Emacs' key (see Section D.1 [Resources], page 493).

Optional properties common to all font backends on MS-Windows are:

weight
: Specifies the weight of the font. Special values `light`, `medium`, `demibold`, `bold`, and `black` can be specified without `weight=` (e.g., `Courier New-12:bold`). Otherwise, the weight should be a numeric value between 100 and 900, or one of the named weights in `font-weight-table`. If unspecified, a regular font is assumed.

slant
: Specifies whether the font is italic. Special values `roman`, `italic` and `oblique` can be specified without `slant=` (e.g., `Courier New-12:italic`). Otherwise, the slant should be a numeric value, or one of the named slants in `font-slant-table`. On Windows, any slant above 150 is treated as italics, and anything below as roman.

family
: Specifies the font family, but normally this will be specified at the start of the font name.

pixelsize
: Specifies the font size in pixels. This can be used instead of the point size specified after the family name.

adstyle
: Specifies additional style information for the font. On MS-Windows, the values `mono`, `sans`, `serif`, `script` and `decorative` are recognized. These are most useful as a fallback with the font family left unspecified.

registry
: Specifies the character set registry that the font is expected to cover. Most TrueType and OpenType fonts will be Unicode fonts that cover several national character sets, but you can narrow down the selection of fonts to those that support a particular character set by using a specific registry from `w32-charset-info-alist` here.

spacing
: Specifies how the font is spaced. The `p` spacing specifies a proportional font, and `m` or `c` specify a monospaced font.

foundry
: Not used on Windows, but for informational purposes and to prevent problems with code that expects it to be set, is set internally to `raster` for bitmapped fonts, `outline` for scalable fonts, or `unknown` if the type cannot be determined as one of those.

Options specific to `GDI` fonts:

script
: Specifies a Unicode subrange the font should support.

  The following scripts are recognized on Windows: `latin`, `greek`, `coptic`, `cyrillic`, `armenian`, `hebrew`, `arabic`, `syriac`, `nko`, `thaana`, `devanagari`,

> bengali, gurmukhi, gujarati, oriya, tamil, telugu, kannada, malayam, sinhala, thai, lao, tibetan, myanmar, georgian, hangul, ethiopic, cherokee, canadian-aboriginal, ogham, runic, khmer, mongolian, symbol, braille, han, ideographic-description, cjk-misc, kana, bopomofo, kanbun, yi, byzantine-musical-symbol, musical-symbol, and mathematical.

antialias

> Specifies the antialiasing method. The value `none` means no antialiasing, `standard` means use standard antialiasing, `subpixel` means use subpixel antialiasing (known as Cleartype on Windows), and `natural` means use subpixel antialiasing with adjusted spacing between letters. If unspecified, the font will use the system default antialiasing.

G.11 Miscellaneous Windows-specific features

This section describes miscellaneous Windows-specific features.

The variable `w32-use-visible-system-caret` is a flag that determines whether to make the system caret visible. The default when no screen reader software is in use is `nil`, which means Emacs draws its own cursor to indicate the position of point. A non-`nil` value means Emacs will indicate point location with the system caret; this facilitates use of screen reader software, and is the default when such software is detected when running Emacs. When this variable is non-`nil`, other variables affecting the cursor display have no effect.

See Info file `emacs`, node 'Windows Misc', for information about additional Windows-specific variables in this category.

The GNU Manifesto

The GNU Manifesto which appears below was written by Richard Stallman at the beginning of the GNU project, to ask for participation and support. For the first few years, it was updated in minor ways to account for developments, but now it seems best to leave it unchanged as most people have seen it.

Since that time, we have learned about certain common misunderstandings that different wording could help avoid. Footnotes added in 1993 help clarify these points.

For up-to-date information about available GNU software, please see our web site, http://www.gnu.org. For software tasks and other ways to contribute, see http://www.gnu.org/help.

What's GNU? Gnu's Not Unix!

GNU, which stands for Gnu's Not Unix, is the name for the complete Unix-compatible software system which I am writing so that I can give it away free to everyone who can use it.[1] Several other volunteers are helping me. Contributions of time, money, programs and equipment are greatly needed.

So far we have an Emacs text editor with Lisp for writing editor commands, a source level debugger, a yacc-compatible parser generator, a linker, and around 35 utilities. A shell (command interpreter) is nearly completed. A new portable optimizing C compiler has compiled itself and may be released this year. An initial kernel exists but many more features are needed to emulate Unix. When the kernel and compiler are finished, it will be possible to distribute a GNU system suitable for program development. We will use TEX as our text formatter, but an nroff is being worked on. We will use the free, portable X window system as well. After this we will add a portable Common Lisp, an Empire game, a spreadsheet, and hundreds of other things, plus on-line documentation. We hope to supply, eventually, everything useful that normally comes with a Unix system, and more.

GNU will be able to run Unix programs, but will not be identical to Unix. We will make all improvements that are convenient, based on our experience with other operating systems. In particular, we plan to have longer file names, file version numbers, a crashproof file system, file name completion perhaps, terminal-independent display support, and perhaps eventually a Lisp-based window system through which several Lisp programs and ordinary Unix programs can share a screen. Both C and Lisp will be available as system programming languages. We will try to support UUCP, MIT Chaosnet, and Internet protocols for communication.

---

[1] The wording here was careless. The intention was that nobody would have to pay for *permission* to use the GNU system. But the words don't make this clear, and people often interpret them as saying that copies of GNU should always be distributed at little or no charge. That was never the intent; later on, the manifesto mentions the possibility of companies providing the service of distribution for a profit. Subsequently I have learned to distinguish carefully between "free" in the sense of freedom and "free" in the sense of price. Free software is software that users have the freedom to distribute and change. Some users may obtain copies at no charge, while others pay to obtain copies—and if the funds help support improving the software, so much the better. The important thing is that everyone who has a copy has the freedom to cooperate with others in using it.

GNU is aimed initially at machines in the 68000/16000 class with virtual memory, because they are the easiest machines to make it run on. The extra effort to make it run on smaller machines will be left to someone who wants to use it on them.

To avoid horrible confusion, please pronounce the 'G' in the word 'GNU' when it is the name of this project.

Why I Must Write GNU

I consider that the golden rule requires that if I like a program I must share it with other people who like it. Software sellers want to divide the users and conquer them, making each user agree not to share with others. I refuse to break solidarity with other users in this way. I cannot in good conscience sign a nondisclosure agreement or a software license agreement. For years I worked within the Artificial Intelligence Lab to resist such tendencies and other inhospitalities, but eventually they had gone too far: I could not remain in an institution where such things are done for me against my will.

So that I can continue to use computers without dishonor, I have decided to put together a sufficient body of free software so that I will be able to get along without any software that is not free. I have resigned from the AI lab to deny MIT any legal excuse to prevent me from giving GNU away.

Why GNU Will Be Compatible with Unix

Unix is not my ideal system, but it is not too bad. The essential features of Unix seem to be good ones, and I think I can fill in what Unix lacks without spoiling them. And a system compatible with Unix would be convenient for many other people to adopt.

How GNU Will Be Available

GNU is not in the public domain. Everyone will be permitted to modify and redistribute GNU, but no distributor will be allowed to restrict its further redistribution. That is to say, proprietary modifications will not be allowed. I want to make sure that all versions of GNU remain free.

Why Many Other Programmers Want to Help

I have found many other programmers who are excited about GNU and want to help.

Many programmers are unhappy about the commercialization of system software. It may enable them to make more money, but it requires them to feel in conflict with other programmers in general rather than feel as comrades. The fundamental act of friendship among programmers is the sharing of programs; marketing arrangements now typically used essentially forbid programmers to treat others as friends. The purchaser of software must choose between friendship and obeying the law. Naturally, many decide that friendship is more important. But those who believe in law often do not feel at ease with either choice. They become cynical and think that programming is just a way of making money.

By working on and using GNU rather than proprietary programs, we can be hospitable to everyone and obey the law. In addition, GNU serves as an example to inspire and a banner to rally others to join us in sharing. This can give us a feeling of harmony which is impossible if we use software that is not free. For about half the programmers I talk to, this is an important happiness that money cannot replace.

How You Can Contribute

I am asking computer manufacturers for donations of machines and money. I'm asking individuals for donations of programs and work.

One consequence you can expect if you donate machines is that GNU will run on them at an early date. The machines should be complete, ready to use systems, approved for use in a residential area, and not in need of sophisticated cooling or power.

I have found very many programmers eager to contribute part-time work for GNU. For most projects, such part-time distributed work would be very hard to coordinate; the independently-written parts would not work together. But for the particular task of replacing Unix, this problem is absent. A complete Unix system contains hundreds of utility programs, each of which is documented separately. Most interface specifications are fixed by Unix compatibility. If each contributor can write a compatible replacement for a single Unix utility, and make it work properly in place of the original on a Unix system, then these utilities will work right when put together. Even allowing for Murphy to create a few unexpected problems, assembling these components will be a feasible task. (The kernel will require closer communication and will be worked on by a small, tight group.)

If I get donations of money, I may be able to hire a few people full or part time. The salary won't be high by programmers' standards, but I'm looking for people for whom building community spirit is as important as making money. I view this as a way of enabling dedicated people to devote their full energies to working on GNU by sparing them the need to make a living in another way.

Why All Computer Users Will Benefit

Once GNU is written, everyone will be able to obtain good system software free, just like air.[2]

This means much more than just saving everyone the price of a Unix license. It means that much wasteful duplication of system programming effort will be avoided. This effort can go instead into advancing the state of the art.

Complete system sources will be available to everyone. As a result, a user who needs changes in the system will always be free to make them himself, or hire any available programmer or company to make them for him. Users will no longer be at the mercy of one programmer or company which owns the sources and is in sole position to make changes.

Schools will be able to provide a much more educational environment by encouraging all students to study and improve the system code. Harvard's computer lab used to have the policy that no program could be installed on the system if its sources were not on public display, and upheld it by actually refusing to install certain programs. I was very much inspired by this.

---

[2] This is another place I failed to distinguish carefully between the two different meanings of "free." The statement as it stands is not false—you can get copies of GNU software at no charge, from your friends or over the net. But it does suggest the wrong idea.

Finally, the overhead of considering who owns the system software and what one is or is not entitled to do with it will be lifted.

Arrangements to make people pay for using a program, including licensing of copies, always incur a tremendous cost to society through the cumbersome mechanisms necessary to figure out how much (that is, which programs) a person must pay for. And only a police state can force everyone to obey them. Consider a space station where air must be manufactured at great cost: charging each breather per liter of air may be fair, but wearing the metered gas mask all day and all night is intolerable even if everyone can afford to pay the air bill. And the TV cameras everywhere to see if you ever take the mask off are outrageous. It's better to support the air plant with a head tax and chuck the masks.

Copying all or parts of a program is as natural to a programmer as breathing, and as productive. It ought to be as free.

Some Easily Rebutted Objections to GNU's Goals

"Nobody will use it if it is free, because that means they can't rely on any support."

"You have to charge for the program to pay for providing the support."

If people would rather pay for GNU plus service than get GNU free without service, a company to provide just service to people who have obtained GNU free ought to be profitable.[3]

We must distinguish between support in the form of real programming work and mere handholding. The former is something one cannot rely on from a software vendor. If your problem is not shared by enough people, the vendor will tell you to get lost.

If your business needs to be able to rely on support, the only way is to have all the necessary sources and tools. Then you can hire any available person to fix your problem; you are not at the mercy of any individual. With Unix, the price of sources puts this out of consideration for most businesses. With GNU this will be easy. It is still possible for there to be no available competent person, but this problem cannot be blamed on distribution arrangements. GNU does not eliminate all the world's problems, only some of them.

Meanwhile, the users who know nothing about computers need handholding: doing things for them which they could easily do themselves but don't know how.

Such services could be provided by companies that sell just hand-holding and repair service. If it is true that users would rather spend money and get a product with service, they will also be willing to buy the service having got the product free. The service companies will compete in quality and price; users will not be tied to any particular one. Meanwhile, those of us who don't need the service should be able to use the program without paying for the service.

"You cannot reach many people without advertising, and you must charge for the program to support that."

"It's no use advertising a program people can get free."

There are various forms of free or very cheap publicity that can be used to inform numbers of computer users about something like GNU. But it may be true that one can reach more

---

[3] Several such companies now exist.

microcomputer users with advertising. If this is really so, a business which advertises the service of copying and mailing GNU for a fee ought to be successful enough to pay for its advertising and more. This way, only the users who benefit from the advertising pay for it.

On the other hand, if many people get GNU from their friends, and such companies don't succeed, this will show that advertising was not really necessary to spread GNU. Why is it that free market advocates don't want to let the free market decide this?[4]

"My company needs a proprietary operating system to get a competitive edge."

GNU will remove operating system software from the realm of competition. You will not be able to get an edge in this area, but neither will your competitors be able to get an edge over you. You and they will compete in other areas, while benefiting mutually in this one. If your business is selling an operating system, you will not like GNU, but that's tough on you. If your business is something else, GNU can save you from being pushed into the expensive business of selling operating systems.

I would like to see GNU development supported by gifts from many manufacturers and users, reducing the cost to each.[5]

"Don't programmers deserve a reward for their creativity?"

If anything deserves a reward, it is social contribution. Creativity can be a social contribution, but only in so far as society is free to use the results. If programmers deserve to be rewarded for creating innovative programs, by the same token they deserve to be punished if they restrict the use of these programs.

"Shouldn't a programmer be able to ask for a reward for his creativity?"

There is nothing wrong with wanting pay for work, or seeking to maximize one's income, as long as one does not use means that are destructive. But the means customary in the field of software today are based on destruction.

Extracting money from users of a program by restricting their use of it is destructive because the restrictions reduce the amount and the ways that the program can be used. This reduces the amount of wealth that humanity derives from the program. When there is a deliberate choice to restrict, the harmful consequences are deliberate destruction.

The reason a good citizen does not use such destructive means to become wealthier is that, if everyone did so, we would all become poorer from the mutual destructiveness. This is Kantian ethics; or, the Golden Rule. Since I do not like the consequences that result if everyone hoards information, I am required to consider it wrong for one to do so. Specifically, the desire to be rewarded for one's creativity does not justify depriving the world in general of all or part of that creativity.

"Won't programmers starve?"

I could answer that nobody is forced to be a programmer. Most of us cannot manage to get any money for standing on the street and making faces. But we are not, as a result, condemned to spend our lives standing on the street making faces, and starving. We do something else.

---

[4] The Free Software Foundation raises most of its funds from a distribution service, although it is a charity rather than a company. If *no one* chooses to obtain copies by ordering from the FSF, it will be unable to do its work. But this does not mean that proprietary restrictions are justified to force every user to pay. If a small fraction of all the users order copies from the FSF, that is sufficient to keep the FSF afloat. So we ask users to choose to support us in this way. Have you done your part?

[5] A group of computer companies recently pooled funds to support maintenance of the GNU C Compiler.

But that is the wrong answer because it accepts the questioner's implicit assumption: that without ownership of software, programmers cannot possibly be paid a cent. Supposedly it is all or nothing.

The real reason programmers will not starve is that it will still be possible for them to get paid for programming; just not paid as much as now.

Restricting copying is not the only basis for business in software. It is the most common basis because it brings in the most money. If it were prohibited, or rejected by the customer, software business would move to other bases of organization which are now used less often. There are always numerous ways to organize any kind of business.

Probably programming will not be as lucrative on the new basis as it is now. But that is not an argument against the change. It is not considered an injustice that sales clerks make the salaries that they now do. If programmers made the same, that would not be an injustice either. (In practice they would still make considerably more than that.)

"Don't people have a right to control how their creativity is used?"

"Control over the use of one's ideas" really constitutes control over other people's lives; and it is usually used to make their lives more difficult.

People who have studied the issue of intellectual property rights[6] carefully (such as lawyers) say that there is no intrinsic right to intellectual property. The kinds of supposed intellectual property rights that the government recognizes were created by specific acts of legislation for specific purposes.

For example, the patent system was established to encourage inventors to disclose the details of their inventions. Its purpose was to help society rather than to help inventors. At the time, the life span of 17 years for a patent was short compared with the rate of advance of the state of the art. Since patents are an issue only among manufacturers, for whom the cost and effort of a license agreement are small compared with setting up production, the patents often do not do much harm. They do not obstruct most individuals who use patented products.

The idea of copyright did not exist in ancient times, when authors frequently copied other authors at length in works of non-fiction. This practice was useful, and is the only way many authors' works have survived even in part. The copyright system was created expressly for the purpose of encouraging authorship. In the domain for which it was invented—books, which could be copied economically only on a printing press—it did little harm, and did not obstruct most of the individuals who read the books.

All intellectual property rights are just licenses granted by society because it was thought, rightly or wrongly, that society as a whole would benefit by granting them. But in any particular situation, we have to ask: are we really better off granting such license? What kind of act are we licensing a person to do?

The case of programs today is very different from that of books a hundred years ago. The fact that the easiest way to copy a program is from one neighbor to another, the

---

[6] In the 80s I had not yet realized how confusing it was to speak of "the issue" of "intellectual property." That term is obviously biased; more subtle is the fact that it lumps together various disparate laws which raise very different issues. Nowadays I urge people to reject the term "intellectual property" entirely, lest it lead others to suppose that those laws form one coherent issue. The way to be clear is to discuss patents, copyrights, and trademarks separately. See http://www.gnu.org/philosophy/not-ipr.xhtml for more explanation of how this term spreads confusion and bias.

fact that a program has both source code and object code which are distinct, and the fact that a program is used rather than read and enjoyed, combine to create a situation in which a person who enforces a copyright is harming society as a whole both materially and spiritually; in which a person should not do so regardless of whether the law enables him to.

"Competition makes things get done better."

The paradigm of competition is a race: by rewarding the winner, we encourage everyone to run faster. When capitalism really works this way, it does a good job; but its defenders are wrong in assuming it always works this way. If the runners forget why the reward is offered and become intent on winning, no matter how, they may find other strategies—such as, attacking other runners. If the runners get into a fist fight, they will all finish late.

Proprietary and secret software is the moral equivalent of runners in a fist fight. Sad to say, the only referee we've got does not seem to object to fights; he just regulates them ("For every ten yards you run, you can fire one shot"). He really ought to break them up, and penalize runners for even trying to fight.

"Won't everyone stop programming without a monetary incentive?"

Actually, many people will program with absolutely no monetary incentive. Programming has an irresistible fascination for some people, usually the people who are best at it. There is no shortage of professional musicians who keep at it even though they have no hope of making a living that way.

But really this question, though commonly asked, is not appropriate to the situation. Pay for programmers will not disappear, only become less. So the right question is, will anyone program with a reduced monetary incentive? My experience shows that they will.

For more than ten years, many of the world's best programmers worked at the Artificial Intelligence Lab for far less money than they could have had anywhere else. They got many kinds of non-monetary rewards: fame and appreciation, for example. And creativity is also fun, a reward in itself.

Then most of them left when offered a chance to do the same interesting work for a lot of money.

What the facts show is that people will program for reasons other than riches; but if given a chance to make a lot of money as well, they will come to expect and demand it. Low-paying organizations do poorly in competition with high-paying ones, but they do not have to do badly if the high-paying ones are banned.

"We need the programmers desperately. If they demand that we stop helping our neighbors, we have to obey."

You're never so desperate that you have to obey this sort of demand. Remember: millions for defense, but not a cent for tribute!

"Programmers need to make a living somehow."

In the short run, this is true. However, there are plenty of ways that programmers could make a living without selling the right to use a program. This way is customary now because it brings programmers and businessmen the most money, not because it is the only way to make a living. It is easy to find other ways if you want to find them. Here are a number of examples.

A manufacturer introducing a new computer will pay for the porting of operating systems onto the new hardware.

The sale of teaching, hand-holding and maintenance services could also employ programmers.

People with new ideas could distribute programs as freeware[7], asking for donations from satisfied users, or selling hand-holding services. I have met people who are already working this way successfully.

Users with related needs can form users' groups, and pay dues. A group would contract with programming companies to write programs that the group's members would like to use.

All sorts of development can be funded with a Software Tax:

Suppose everyone who buys a computer has to pay x percent of the price as a software tax. The government gives this to an agency like the NSF to spend on software development.

But if the computer buyer makes a donation to software development himself, he can take a credit against the tax. He can donate to the project of his own choosing—often, chosen because he hopes to use the results when it is done. He can take a credit for any amount of donation up to the total tax he had to pay.

The total tax rate could be decided by a vote of the payers of the tax, weighted according to the amount they will be taxed on.

The consequences:

- The computer-using community supports software development.
- This community decides what level of support is needed.
- Users who care which projects their share is spent on can choose this for themselves.

In the long run, making programs free is a step toward the post-scarcity world, where nobody will have to work very hard just to make a living. People will be free to devote themselves to activities that are fun, such as programming, after spending the necessary ten hours a week on required tasks such as legislation, family counseling, robot repair and asteroid prospecting. There will be no need to be able to make a living from programming.

We have already greatly reduced the amount of work that the whole society must do for its actual productivity, but only a little of this has translated itself into leisure for workers because much nonproductive activity is required to accompany productive activity. The main causes of this are bureaucracy and isometric struggles against competition. Free software will greatly reduce these drains in the area of software production. We must do this, in order for technical gains in productivity to translate into less work for us.

---

[7] Subsequently we have discovered the need to distinguish between "free software" and "freeware". The term "freeware" means software you are free to redistribute, but usually you are not free to study and change the source code, so most of it is not free software. See `http://www.gnu.org/philosophy/words-to-avoid.html` for more explanation.

Glossary

Abbrev   An abbrev is a text string that expands into a different text string when present in the buffer. For example, you might define a few letters as an abbrev for a long phrase that you want to insert frequently. See Chapter 26 [Abbrevs], page 309.

Aborting   Aborting means getting out of a recursive edit (q.v.). The commands `C-]` and `M-x top-level` are used for this. See Section 34.1 [Quitting], page 443.

Active Region
              Setting the mark (q.v.) at a position in the text also activates it. When the mark is active, we call the region an active region. See Chapter 8 [Mark], page 45.

Alt   Alt is the name of a modifier bit that a keyboard input character may have. To make a character Alt, type it while holding down the `Alt` key. Such characters are given names that start with `Alt-` (usually written `A-` for short). (Note that many terminals have a key labeled `Alt` that is really a `META` key.) See Section 2.1 [User Input], page 11.

Argument   See [Glossary—Numeric Argument], page 538.

ASCII character
              An ASCII character is either an ASCII control character or an ASCII printing character. See Section 2.1 [User Input], page 11.

ASCII control character
              An ASCII control character is the Control version of an upper-case letter, or the Control version of one of the characters '`@[\]^_?`'.

ASCII printing character
              ASCII letters, digits, space, and the following punctuation characters: '`!@#$%^&*()_-+=|\~`{}[]:;"'<>,.?/`'.

Auto Fill Mode
              Auto Fill mode is a minor mode (q.v.) in which text that you insert is automatically broken into lines of a given maximum width. See Section 22.5 [Filling], page 212.

Auto Saving
              Auto saving is the practice of periodically saving the contents of an Emacs buffer in a specially-named file, so that the information will be preserved if the buffer is lost due to a system error or user error. See Section 15.5 [Auto Save], page 133.

Autoloading
              Emacs can automatically load Lisp libraries when a Lisp program requests a function from those libraries. This is called 'autoloading'. See Section 24.8 [Lisp Libraries], page 276.

Backtrace   A backtrace is a trace of a series of function calls showing how a program arrived at a certain point. It is used mainly for finding and correcting bugs (q.v.). Emacs can display a backtrace when it signals an error or when you type C-g (see [Glossary—Quitting], page 539). See Section 34.3.4 [Checklist], page 451.

Backup File

A backup file records the contents that a file had before the current editing session. Emacs makes backup files automatically to help you track down or cancel changes you later regret making. See Section 15.3.2 [Backup], page 127.

Balancing Parentheses

Emacs can balance parentheses (or other matching delimiters) either manually or automatically. You do manual balancing with the commands to move over parenthetical groupings (see Section 23.4.2 [Moving by Parens], page 248). Automatic balancing works by blinking or highlighting the delimiter that matches the one you just inserted, or inserting the matching delimiter for you (see Section 23.4.3 [Matching Parens], page 248).

Balanced Expressions

A balanced expression is a syntactically recognizable expression, such as a symbol, number, string constant, block, or parenthesized expression in C. See Section 23.4.1 [Expressions], page 246.

Balloon Help

See [Glossary—Tooltips], page 543.

Base Buffer

A base buffer is a buffer whose text is shared by an indirect buffer (q.v.).

Bidirectional Text

Some human languages, such as English, are written from left to right. Others, such as Arabic, are written from right to left. Emacs supports both of these forms, as well as any mixture of them—this is 'bidirectional text'. See Section 19.19 [Bidirectional Editing], page 197.

Bind   To bind a key sequence means to give it a binding (q.v.). See Section 33.3.5 [Rebinding], page 431.

Binding   A key sequence gets its meaning in Emacs by having a binding, which is a command (q.v.), a Lisp function that is run when you type that sequence. See Section 2.3 [Commands], page 12. Customization often involves rebinding a character to a different command function. The bindings of all key sequences are recorded in the keymaps (q.v.). See Section 33.3.1 [Keymaps], page 429.

Blank Lines

Blank lines are lines that contain only whitespace. Emacs has several commands for operating on the blank lines in the buffer. See Section 4.7 [Blank Lines], page 21.

Bookmark   Bookmarks are akin to registers (q.v.) in that they record positions in buffers to which you can return later. Unlike registers, bookmarks persist between Emacs sessions. See Section 10.8 [Bookmarks], page 67.

Border   A border is a thin space along the edge of the frame, used just for spacing, not for displaying anything. An Emacs frame has an ordinary external border, outside of everything including the menu bar, plus an internal border that surrounds the text windows, their scroll bars and fringes, and separates them from the menu bar and tool bar. You can customize both borders with options and resources (see Section C.9 [Borders X], page 490). Borders are not the same as fringes (q.v.).

Buffer   The buffer is the basic editing unit; one buffer corresponds to one text being edited. You normally have several buffers, but at any time you are editing only one, the 'current buffer', though several can be visible when you are using multiple windows or frames (q.v.). Most buffers are visiting (q.v.) some file. See Chapter 16 [Buffers], page 147.

Buffer Selection History

Emacs keeps a buffer selection history that records how recently each Emacs buffer has been selected. This is used for choosing a buffer to select. See Chapter 16 [Buffers], page 147.

Bug   A bug is an incorrect or unreasonable behavior of a program, or inaccurate or confusing documentation. Emacs developers treat bug reports, both in Emacs code and its documentation, very seriously and ask you to report any bugs you find. See Section 34.3 [Bugs], page 448.

Button Down Event

A button down event is the kind of input event (q.v.) generated right away when you press down on a mouse button. See Section 33.3.10 [Mouse Buttons], page 435.

By Default

See [Glossary—Default], page 528.

Byte Compilation

See [Glossary—Compilation], page 526.

C-   C- in the name of a character is an abbreviation for Control. See Section 2.1 [User Input], page 11.

C-M-   C-M- in the name of a character is an abbreviation for Control-Meta. If your terminal lacks a real META key, you type a Control-Meta character by typing ESC and then typing the corresponding Control character. See Section 2.1 [User Input], page 11.

Case Conversion

Case conversion means changing text from upper case to lower case or vice versa. See Section 22.6 [Case], page 216.

Character   Characters form the contents of an Emacs buffer. Also, key sequences (q.v.) are usually made up of characters (though they may include other input events as well). See Section 2.1 [User Input], page 11.

Character Set

Emacs supports a number of character sets, each of which represents a particular alphabet or script. See Chapter 19 [International], page 177.

Character Terminal
:   See [Glossary—Text Terminal], page 543.

Click Event
:   A click event is the kind of input event (q.v.) generated when you press a mouse button and release it without moving the mouse. See Section 33.3.10 [Mouse Buttons], page 435.

Client
:   See [Glossary—Server], page 542.

Clipboard
:   A clipboard is a buffer provided by the window system for transferring text between applications. On the X Window System, the clipboard is provided in addition to the primary selection (q.v.); on MS-Windows and Mac, the clipboard is used *instead* of the primary selection. See Section 9.3.1 [Clipboard], page 57.

Coding System
:   A coding system is an encoding for representing text characters in a file or in a stream of information. Emacs has the ability to convert text to or from a variety of coding systems when reading or writing it. See Section 19.5 [Coding Systems], page 183.

Command
:   A command is a Lisp function specially defined to be able to serve as a key binding in Emacs. When you type a key sequence (q.v.), its binding (q.v.) is looked up in the relevant keymaps (q.v.) to find the command to run. See Section 2.3 [Commands], page 12.

Command History
:   See [Glossary—Minibuffer History], page 537.

Command Name
:   A command name is the name of a Lisp symbol that is a command (see Section 2.3 [Commands], page 12). You can invoke any command by its name using M-x (see Chapter 6 [Running Commands by Name], page 36).

Comment
:   A comment is text in a program which is intended only for humans reading the program, and which is specially marked so that it will be ignored when the program is loaded or compiled. Emacs offers special commands for creating, aligning and killing comments. See Section 23.5 [Comments], page 249.

Common Lisp
:   Common Lisp is a dialect of Lisp (q.v.) much larger and more powerful than Emacs Lisp. Emacs provides a subset of Common Lisp in the CL package. See Section "Overview" in *Common Lisp Extensions*.

Compilation
:   Compilation is the process of creating an executable program from source code. Emacs has commands for compiling files of Emacs Lisp code (see Section "Byte Compilation" in *the Emacs Lisp Reference Manual*) and programs in C and other languages (see Section 24.1 [Compilation], page 261).

Complete Key
:   A complete key is a key sequence that fully specifies one action to be performed by Emacs. For example, X and C-f and C-x m are complete keys. Complete

keys derive their meanings from being bound (q.v.) to commands (q.v.). Thus, X is conventionally bound to a command to insert 'X' in the buffer; C-x m is conventionally bound to a command to begin composing a mail message. See Section 2.2 [Keys], page 11.

Completion

Completion is what Emacs does when it automatically expands an abbreviation for a name into the entire name. Completion is done for minibuffer (q.v.) arguments when the set of possible valid inputs is known; for example, on command names, buffer names, and file names. Completion usually occurs when TAB, SPC or RET is typed. See Section 5.4 [Completion], page 28.

Continuation Line

When a line of text is longer than the width of the window, it normally (but see [Glossary—Truncation], page 544) takes up more than one screen line when displayed. We say that the text line is continued, and all screen lines used for it after the first are called continuation lines. See Section 4.8 [Continuation Lines], page 22. A related Emacs feature is 'filling' (q.v.).

Control Character

A control character is a character that you type by holding down the Ctrl key. Some control characters also have their own keys, so that you can type them without using Ctrl. For example, RET, TAB, ESC and DEL are all control characters. See Section 2.1 [User Input], page 11.

Copyleft   A copyleft is a notice giving the public legal permission to redistribute and modify a program or other work of art, but requiring modified versions to carry similar permission. Copyright is normally used to keep users divided and helpless; with copyleft we turn that around to empower users and encourage them to cooperate.

The particular form of copyleft used by the GNU project is called the GNU General Public License. See Appendix A [Copying], page 459.

Ctrl   The Ctrl or "control" key is what you hold down in order to enter a control character (q.v.). See [Glossary—C-], page 525.

Current Buffer

The current buffer in Emacs is the Emacs buffer on which most editing commands operate. You can select any Emacs buffer as the current one. See Chapter 16 [Buffers], page 147.

Current Line

The current line is the line that point is on (see Section 1.1 [Point], page 6).

Current Paragraph

The current paragraph is the paragraph that point is in. If point is between two paragraphs, the current paragraph is the one that follows point. See Section 22.3 [Paragraphs], page 210.

Current Defun

The current defun is the defun (q.v.) that point is in. If point is between defuns, the current defun is the one that follows point. See Section 23.2 [Defuns], page 241.

Cursor   The cursor is the rectangle on the screen which indicates the position (called point; q.v.) at which insertion and deletion takes place. The cursor is on or under the character that follows point. Often people speak of 'the cursor' when, strictly speaking, they mean 'point'. See Section 1.1 [Point], page 6.

Customization
                Customization is making minor changes in the way Emacs works, to reflect your preferences or needs. It is often done by setting variables (see Section 33.2 [Variables], page 420) or faces (see Section 33.1.5 [Face Customization], page 416), or by rebinding key sequences (see Section 33.3.1 [Keymaps], page 429).

Cut and Paste
                See [Glossary—Killing], page 535, and [Glossary—Yanking], page 545.

Daemon   A daemon is a standard term for a system-level process that runs in the background. Daemons are often started when the system first starts up. When Emacs runs in daemon-mode, it runs in the background and does not open a display. You can then connect to it with the `emacsclient` program. See Section 31.5 [Emacs Server], page 393.

Default Argument
                The default for an argument is the value that will be assumed if you do not specify one. When the minibuffer is used to read an argument, the default argument is used if you just type `RET`. See Chapter 5 [Minibuffer], page 26.

Default   A default is the value that is used for a certain purpose when you do not explicitly specify a value to use.

Default Directory
                When you specify a file name that does not start with '/' or '~', it is interpreted relative to the current buffer's default directory. (On MS systems, file names that start with a drive letter 'x:' are treated as absolute, not relative.) See Section 5.2 [Minibuffer File], page 26.

Defun   A defun is a major definition at the top level in a program. The name 'defun' comes from Lisp, where most such definitions use the construct `defun`. See Section 23.2 [Defuns], page 241.

DEL   `DEL` is a character that runs the command to delete one character of text before the cursor. It is typically either the `Delete` key or the `BACKSPACE` key, whichever one is easy to type. See Section 4.3 [Erasing], page 19.

Deletion   Deletion means erasing text without copying it into the kill ring (q.v.). The alternative is killing (q.v.). See Chapter 9 [Killing], page 52.

Deletion of Files
                Deleting a file means erasing it from the file system. (Note that some systems use the concept of a "trash can", or "recycle bin", to allow you to "undelete" files.) See Section 15.10 [Miscellaneous File Operations], page 140.

Deletion of Messages
                Deleting a message (in Rmail, and other mail clients) means flagging it to be eliminated from your mail file. Until you expunge (q.v.) the Rmail file, you can

still undelete the messages you have deleted. See Section 30.4 [Rmail Deletion], page 361.

Deletion of Windows

Deleting a window means eliminating it from the screen. Other windows expand to use up the space. The text that was in the window is not lost, and you can create a new window with the same dimensions as the old if you wish. See Chapter 17 [Windows], page 156.

Directory   File directories are named collections in the file system, within which you can place individual files or subdirectories. They are sometimes referred to as "folders". See Section 15.7 [Directories], page 136.

Directory Local Variable

A directory local variable is a local variable (q.v.) that applies to all the files within a certain directory. See Section 33.2.5 [Directory Variables], page 427.

Dired   Dired is the Emacs facility that displays the contents of a file directory and allows you to "edit the directory", performing operations on the files in the directory. See Chapter 27 [Dired], page 315.

Disabled Command

A disabled command is one that you may not run without special confirmation. The usual reason for disabling a command is that it is confusing for beginning users. See Section 33.3.11 [Disabling], page 437.

Down Event

Short for 'button down event' (q.v.).

Drag Event

A drag event is the kind of input event (q.v.) generated when you press a mouse button, move the mouse, and then release the button. See Section 33.3.10 [Mouse Buttons], page 435.

Dribble File

A dribble file is a file into which Emacs writes all the characters that you type on the keyboard. Dribble files can be used to make a record for debugging Emacs bugs. Emacs does not make a dribble file unless you tell it to. See Section 34.3 [Bugs], page 448.

Echo Area   The echo area is the bottom line of the screen, used for echoing the arguments to commands, for asking questions, and showing brief messages (including error messages). The messages are stored in the buffer *Messages* so you can review them later. See Section 1.2 [Echo Area], page 7.

Echoing   Echoing is acknowledging the receipt of input events by displaying them (in the echo area). Emacs never echoes single-character key sequences; longer key sequences echo only if you pause while typing them.

Electric   We say that a character is electric if it is normally self-inserting (q.v.), but the current major mode (q.v.) redefines it to do something else as well. For example, some programming language major modes define particular delimiter characters to reindent the line, or insert one or more newlines in addition to self-insertion.

End Of Line

> End of line is a character or a sequence of characters that indicate the end of a text line. On GNU and Unix systems, this is a newline (q.v.), but other systems have other conventions. See Section 19.5 [Coding Systems], page 183. Emacs can recognize several end-of-line conventions in files and convert between them.

Environment Variable

> An environment variable is one of a collection of variables stored by the operating system, each one having a name and a value. Emacs can access environment variables set by its parent shell, and it can set variables in the environment it passes to programs it invokes. See Section C.4 [Environment], page 482.

EOL   See [Glossary—End Of Line], page 529.

Error   An error occurs when an Emacs command cannot execute in the current circumstances. When an error occurs, execution of the command stops (unless the command has been programmed to do otherwise) and Emacs reports the error by displaying an error message (q.v.).

Error Message

> An error message is output displayed by Emacs when you ask it to do something impossible (such as, killing text forward when point is at the end of the buffer), or when a command malfunctions in some way. Such messages appear in the echo area, accompanied by a beep.

ESC   ESC is a character used as a prefix for typing Meta characters on keyboards lacking a META key. Unlike the META key (which, like the SHIFT key, is held down while another character is typed), you press the ESC key as you would press a letter key, and it applies to the next character you type.

Expression

> See [Glossary—Balanced Expression], page 524.

Expunging

> Expunging an Rmail, Gnus newsgroup, or Dired buffer is an operation that truly discards the messages or files you have previously flagged for deletion.

Face   A face is a style of displaying characters. It specifies attributes such as font family and size, foreground and background colors, underline and strike-through, background stipple, etc. Emacs provides features to associate specific faces with portions of buffer text, in order to display that text as specified by the face attributes. See Section 11.8 [Faces], page 74.

File Local Variable

> A file local variable is a local variable (q.v.) specified in a given file. See Section 33.2.4 [File Variables], page 424, and [Glossary—Directory Local Variable], page 529.

File Locking

> Emacs uses file locking to notice when two different users start to edit one file at the same time. See Section 15.3.4 [Interlocking], page 130.

File Name A file name is a name that refers to a file. File names may be relative or absolute; the meaning of a relative file name depends on the current directory, but an absolute file name refers to the same file regardless of which directory is current. On GNU and Unix systems, an absolute file name starts with a slash (the root directory) or with '~/' or '~*user*/' (a home directory). On MS-Windows/MS-DOS, an absolute file name can also start with a drive letter and a colon, e.g., 'd:'.

Some people use the term "pathname" for file names, but we do not; we use the word "path" only in the term "search path" (q.v.).

File-Name Component

A file-name component names a file directly within a particular directory. On GNU and Unix systems, a file name is a sequence of file-name components, separated by slashes. For example, foo/bar is a file name containing two components, 'foo' and 'bar'; it refers to the file named 'bar' in the directory named 'foo' in the current directory. MS-DOS/MS-Windows file names can also use backslashes to separate components, as in foo\bar.

Fill Prefix   The fill prefix is a string that should be expected at the beginning of each line when filling is done. It is not regarded as part of the text to be filled. See Section 22.5 [Filling], page 212.

Filling   Filling text means adjusting the position of line-breaks to shift text between consecutive lines, so that all the lines are approximately the same length. See Section 22.5 [Filling], page 212. Some other editors call this feature "line wrapping".

Font Lock   Font Lock is a mode that highlights parts of buffer text in different faces, according to the syntax. Some other editors refer to this as "syntax highlighting". For example, all comments (q.v.) might be colored red. See Section 11.12 [Font Lock], page 78.

Fontset   A fontset is a named collection of fonts. A fontset specification lists character sets and which font to use to display each of them. Fontsets make it easy to change several fonts at once by specifying the name of a fontset, rather than changing each font separately. See Section 19.13 [Fontsets], page 192.

Formfeed Character

See [Glossary—Page], page 538.

Frame   A frame is a rectangular cluster of Emacs windows. Emacs starts out with one frame, but you can create more. You can subdivide each frame into Emacs windows (q.v.). When you are using a window system (q.v.), more than one frame can be visible at the same time. See Chapter 18 [Frames], page 162. Some other editors use the term "window" for this, but in Emacs a window means something else.

Free Software

Free software is software that gives you the freedom to share, study and modify it. Emacs is free software, part of the GNU project (q.v.), and distributed under a copyleft (q.v.) license called the GNU General Public License. See Appendix A [Copying], page 459.

Free Software Foundation

> The Free Software Foundation (FSF) is a charitable foundation dedicated to promoting the development of free software (q.v.). For more information, see the FSF website (`http://fsf.org/`).

Fringe   On a graphical display (q.v.), there's a narrow portion of the frame (q.v.) between the text area and the window's border. These "fringes" are used to display symbols that provide information about the buffer text (see Section 11.14 [Fringes], page 81). Emacs displays the fringe using a special face (q.v.) called `fringe`. See Section 11.8 [Faces], page 74.

FSF   See [Glossary—Free Software Foundation], page 531.

FTP   FTP is an acronym for File Transfer Protocol. This is one standard method for retrieving remote files (q.v.).

Function Key

> A function key is a key on the keyboard that sends input but does not correspond to any character. See Section 33.3.8 [Function Keys], page 433.

Global   Global means "independent of the current environment; in effect throughout Emacs". It is the opposite of local (q.v.). Particular examples of the use of 'global' appear below.

Global Abbrev

> A global definition of an abbrev (q.v.) is effective in all major modes that do not have local (q.v.) definitions for the same abbrev. See Chapter 26 [Abbrevs], page 309.

Global Keymap

> The global keymap (q.v.) contains key bindings that are in effect everywhere, except when overridden by local key bindings in a major mode's local keymap (q.v.). See Section 33.3.1 [Keymaps], page 429.

Global Mark Ring

> The global mark ring records the series of buffers you have recently set a mark (q.v.) in. In many cases you can use this to backtrack through buffers you have been editing, or in which you have found tags (see [Glossary—Tags Table], page 543). See Section 8.5 [Global Mark Ring], page 49.

Global Substitution

> Global substitution means replacing each occurrence of one string by another string throughout a large amount of text. See Section 12.10 [Replace], page 103.

Global Variable

> The global value of a variable (q.v.) takes effect in all buffers that do not have their own local (q.v.) values for the variable. See Section 33.2 [Variables], page 420.

GNU   GNU is a recursive acronym for GNU's Not Unix, and it refers to a Unix-compatible operating system which is free software (q.v.). See [Manifesto], page 515. GNU is normally used with Linux as the kernel since Linux works better than the GNU kernel. For more information, see the GNU website (`http://www.gnu.org/`).

Graphic Character

Graphic characters are those assigned pictorial images rather than just names. All the non-Meta (q.v.) characters except for the Control (q.v.) characters are graphic characters. These include letters, digits, punctuation, and spaces; they do not include RET or ESC. In Emacs, typing a graphic character inserts that character (in ordinary editing modes). See Section 4.1 [Inserting Text], page 16.

Graphical Display

A graphical display is one that can display images and multiple fonts. Usually it also has a window system (q.v.).

Highlighting

Highlighting text means displaying it with a different foreground and/or background color to make it stand out from the rest of the text in the buffer.

Emacs uses highlighting in several ways. It highlights the region whenever it is active (see Chapter 8 [Mark], page 45). Incremental search also highlights matches (see Section 12.1 [Incremental Search], page 90). See [Glossary—Font Lock], page 531.

Hardcopy   Hardcopy means printed output. Emacs has various commands for printing the contents of Emacs buffers. See Section 31.6 [Printing], page 397.

HELP   HELP is the Emacs name for C-h or F1. You can type HELP at any time to ask what options you have, or to ask what a command does. See Chapter 7 [Help], page 37.

Help Echo   Help echo is a short message displayed in the echo area (q.v.) when the mouse pointer is located on portions of display that require some explanations. Emacs displays help echo for menu items, parts of the mode line, tool-bar buttons, etc. On graphical displays, the messages can be displayed as tooltips (q.v.). See Section 18.17 [Tooltips], page 174.

Home Directory

Your home directory contains your personal files. On a multi-user GNU or Unix system, each user has his or her own home directory. When you start a new login session, your home directory is the default directory in which to start. A standard shorthand for your home directory is '~'. Similarly, '~user' represents the home directory of some other user.

Hook   A hook is a list of functions to be called on specific occasions, such as saving a buffer in a file, major mode activation, etc. By customizing the various hooks, you can modify Emacs's behavior without changing any of its code. See Section 33.2.2 [Hooks], page 422.

Hyper   Hyper is the name of a modifier bit that a keyboard input character may have. To make a character Hyper, type it while holding down the Hyper key. Such characters are given names that start with Hyper- (usually written H- for short). See Section 2.1 [User Input], page 11.

Iff   "Iff" means "if and only if". This terminology comes from mathematics. Try to avoid using this term in documentation, since many are unfamiliar with it and mistake it for a typo.

Inbox   An inbox is a file in which mail is delivered by the operating system. Rmail
               transfers mail from inboxes to Rmail files in which the mail is then stored per-
               manently or until explicitly deleted. See Section 30.5 [Rmail Inbox], page 362.

Incremental Search
               Emacs provides an incremental search facility, whereby Emacs begins searching
               for a string as soon as you type the first character. As you type more characters,
               it refines the search. See Section 12.1 [Incremental Search], page 90.

Indentation
               Indentation means blank space at the beginning of a line. Most programming
               languages have conventions for using indentation to illuminate the structure
               of the program, and Emacs has special commands to adjust indentation. See
               Chapter 21 [Indentation], page 205.

Indirect Buffer
               An indirect buffer is a buffer that shares the text of another buffer, called its
               base buffer (q.v.). See Section 16.6 [Indirect Buffers], page 153.

Info   Info is the hypertext format used by the GNU project for writing documenta-
               tion.

Input Event
               An input event represents, within Emacs, one action taken by the user on
               the terminal. Input events include typing characters, typing function keys,
               pressing or releasing mouse buttons, and switching between Emacs frames. See
               Section 2.1 [User Input], page 11.

Input Method
               An input method is a system for entering non-ASCII text characters by typ-
               ing sequences of ASCII characters (q.v.). See Section 19.3 [Input Methods],
               page 181.

Insertion   Insertion means adding text into the buffer, either from the keyboard or from
               some other place in Emacs.

Interlocking
               See [Glossary—File Locking], page 530.

Isearch   See [Glossary—Incremental Search], page 534.

Justification
               Justification means adding extra spaces within lines of text in order to adjust
               the position of the text edges. See Section 22.5.2 [Fill Commands], page 213.

Key Binding
               See [Glossary—Binding], page 524.

Keyboard Macro
               Keyboard macros are a way of defining new Emacs commands from sequences
               of existing ones, with no need to write a Lisp program. You can use a macro
               to record a sequence of commands, then play them back as many times as you
               like. See Chapter 14 [Keyboard Macros], page 114.

Keyboard Shortcut

A keyboard shortcut is a key sequence (q.v.) that invokes a command. What some programs call "assigning a keyboard shortcut", Emacs calls "binding a key sequence". See [Glossary—Binding], page 524.

Key Sequence

A key sequence (key, for short) is a sequence of input events (q.v.) that are meaningful as a single unit. If the key sequence is enough to specify one action, it is a complete key (q.v.); if it is not enough, it is a prefix key (q.v.). See Section 2.2 [Keys], page 11.

Keymap   The keymap is the data structure that records the bindings (q.v.) of key sequences to the commands that they run. For example, the global keymap binds the character C-n to the command function next-line. See Section 33.3.1 [Keymaps], page 429.

Keyboard Translation Table

The keyboard translation table is an array that translates the character codes that come from the terminal into the character codes that make up key sequences.

Kill Ring The kill ring is where all text you have killed (see [Glossary—Killing], page 535) recently is saved. You can reinsert any of the killed text still in the ring; this is called yanking (q.v.). See Section 9.2 [Yanking], page 55.

Killing   Killing means erasing text and saving it on the kill ring so it can be yanked (q.v.) later. Some other systems call this "cutting". Most Emacs commands that erase text perform killing, as opposed to deletion (q.v.). See Chapter 9 [Killing], page 52.

Killing a Job

Killing a job (such as, an invocation of Emacs) means making it cease to exist. Any data within it, if not saved in a file, is lost. See Section 3.2 [Exiting], page 15.

Language Environment

Your choice of language environment specifies defaults for the input method (q.v.) and coding system (q.v.). See Section 19.2 [Language Environments], page 179. These defaults are relevant if you edit non-ASCII text (see Chapter 19 [International], page 177).

Line Wrapping

See [Glossary—Filling], page 531.

Lisp   Lisp is a programming language. Most of Emacs is written in a dialect of Lisp, called Emacs Lisp, which is extended with special features that make it especially suitable for text editing tasks.

List   A list is, approximately, a text string beginning with an open parenthesis and ending with the matching close parenthesis. In C mode and other non-Lisp modes, groupings surrounded by other kinds of matched delimiters appropriate to the language, such as braces, are also considered lists. Emacs has special commands for many operations on lists. See Section 23.4.2 [Moving by Parens], page 248.

Local   Local means "in effect only in a particular context"; the relevant kind of context is a particular function execution, a particular buffer, or a particular major mode. It is the opposite of 'global' (q.v.). Specific uses of 'local' in Emacs terminology appear below.

Local Abbrev
                  A local abbrev definition is effective only if a particular major mode is selected. In that major mode, it overrides any global definition for the same abbrev. See Chapter 26 [Abbrevs], page 309.

Local Keymap
                  A local keymap is used in a particular major mode; the key bindings (q.v.) in the current local keymap override global bindings of the same key sequences. See Section 33.3.1 [Keymaps], page 429.

Local Variable
                  A local value of a variable (q.v.) applies to only one buffer. See Section 33.2.3 [Locals], page 423.

M-   M- in the name of a character is an abbreviation for Meta, one of the modifier keys that can accompany any character. See Section 2.1 [User Input], page 11.

M-C-   M-C- in the name of a character is an abbreviation for Control-Meta; it means the same thing as 'C-M-' (q.v.).

M-x   M-x is the key sequence that is used to call an Emacs command by name. This is how you run commands that are not bound to key sequences. See Chapter 6 [Running Commands by Name], page 36.

Mail   Mail means messages sent from one user to another through the computer system, to be read at the recipient's convenience. Emacs has commands for composing and sending mail, and for reading and editing the mail you have received. See Chapter 29 [Sending Mail], page 350. See Chapter 30 [Rmail], page 359, for one way to read mail with Emacs.

Mail Composition Method
                  A mail composition method is a program runnable within Emacs for editing and sending a mail message. Emacs lets you select from several alternative mail composition methods. See Section 29.7 [Mail Methods], page 357.

Major Mode
                  The Emacs major modes are a mutually exclusive set of options, each of which configures Emacs for editing a certain sort of text. Ideally, each programming language has its own major mode. See Section 20.1 [Major Modes], page 199.

Margin   The space between the usable part of a window (including the fringe) and the window edge.

Mark   The mark points to a position in the text. It specifies one end of the region (q.v.), point being the other end. Many commands operate on all the text from point to the mark. Each buffer has its own mark. See Chapter 8 [Mark], page 45.

Mark Ring

> The mark ring is used to hold several recent previous locations of the mark, in case you want to move back to them. Each buffer has its own mark ring; in addition, there is a single global mark ring (q.v.). See Section 8.4 [Mark Ring], page 48.

Menu Bar   The menu bar is a line at the top of an Emacs frame. It contains words you can click on with the mouse to bring up menus, or you can use a keyboard interface to navigate it. See Section 18.14 [Menu Bars], page 173.

Message   See [Glossary—Mail], page 536.

Meta   Meta is the name of a modifier bit which you can use in a command character. To enter a meta character, you hold down the Meta key while typing the character. We refer to such characters with names that start with Meta- (usually written M- for short). For example, M-< is typed by holding down Meta and at the same time typing < (which itself is done, on most terminals, by holding down SHIFT and typing ,). See Section 2.1 [User Input], page 11.

> On some terminals, the Meta key is actually labeled Alt or Edit.

Meta Character

> A Meta character is one whose character code includes the Meta bit.

Minibuffer The minibuffer is the window that appears when necessary inside the echo area (q.v.), used for reading arguments to commands. See Chapter 5 [Minibuffer], page 26.

Minibuffer History

> The minibuffer history records the text you have specified in the past for minibuffer arguments, so you can conveniently use the same text again. See Section 5.5 [Minibuffer History], page 32.

Minor Mode

> A minor mode is an optional feature of Emacs, which can be switched on or off independently of all other features. Each minor mode has a command to turn it on or off. Some minor modes are global (q.v.), and some are local (q.v.). See Section 20.2 [Minor Modes], page 200.

Minor Mode Keymap

> A minor mode keymap is a keymap that belongs to a minor mode and is active when that mode is enabled. Minor mode keymaps take precedence over the buffer's local keymap, just as the local keymap takes precedence over the global keymap. See Section 33.3.1 [Keymaps], page 429.

Mode Line

> The mode line is the line at the bottom of each window (q.v.), giving status information on the buffer displayed in that window. See Section 1.3 [Mode Line], page 8.

Modified Buffer

> A buffer (q.v.) is modified if its text has been changed since the last time the buffer was saved (or since it was created, if it has never been saved). See Section 15.3 [Saving], page 126.

Moving Text
  Moving text means erasing it from one place and inserting it in another. The usual way to move text is by killing (q.v.) it and then yanking (q.v.) it. See Chapter 9 [Killing], page 52.

MULE
  Prior to Emacs 23, MULE was the name of a software package which provided a *MULtilingual Enhancement* to Emacs, by adding support for multiple character sets (q.v.). MULE was later integrated into Emacs, and much of it was replaced when Emacs gained internal Unicode support in version 23.

  Some parts of Emacs that deal with character set support still use the MULE name. See Chapter 19 [International], page 177.

Multibyte Character
  A multibyte character is a character that takes up several bytes in a buffer. Emacs uses multibyte characters to represent non-ASCII text, since the number of non-ASCII characters is much more than 256. See Section 19.1 [International Chars], page 177.

Named Mark
  A named mark is a register (q.v.), in its role of recording a location in text so that you can move point to that location. See Chapter 10 [Registers], page 64.

Narrowing Narrowing means creating a restriction (q.v.) that limits editing in the current buffer to only a part of the text. Text outside that part is inaccessible for editing (or viewing) until the boundaries are widened again, but it is still there, and saving the file saves it all. See Section 11.5 [Narrowing], page 73.

Newline Control-J characters in the buffer terminate lines of text and are therefore also called newlines. See [Glossary—End Of Line], page 529.

nil nil is a value usually interpreted as a logical "false". Its opposite is t, interpreted as "true".

Numeric Argument
  A numeric argument is a number, specified before a command, to change the effect of the command. Often the numeric argument serves as a repeat count. See Section 4.10 [Arguments], page 23.

Overwrite Mode
  Overwrite mode is a minor mode. When it is enabled, ordinary text characters replace the existing text after point rather than pushing it to one side. See Section 20.2 [Minor Modes], page 200.

Package A package is a collection of Lisp code that you download and automatically install from within Emacs. Packages provide a convenient way to add new features. See Chapter 32 [Packages], page 408.

Page A page is a unit of text, delimited by formfeed characters (ASCII control-L, code 014) at the beginning of a line. Some Emacs commands are provided for moving over and operating on pages. See Section 22.4 [Pages], page 211.

Paragraph Paragraphs are the medium-size unit of human-language text. There are special Emacs commands for moving over and operating on paragraphs. See Section 22.3 [Paragraphs], page 210.

Parsing   We say that certain Emacs commands parse words or expressions in the text being edited. Really, all they know how to do is find the other end of a word or expression.

Point   Point is the place in the buffer at which insertion and deletion occur. Point is considered to be between two characters, not at one character. The terminal's cursor (q.v.) indicates the location of point. See Section 1.1 [Point], page 6.

Prefix Argument
           See [Glossary—Numeric Argument], page 538.

Prefix Key
           A prefix key is a key sequence (q.v.) whose sole function is to introduce a set of longer key sequences. C-x is an example of prefix key; any two-character sequence starting with C-x is therefore a legitimate key sequence. See Section 2.2 [Keys], page 11.

Primary Selection
           The primary selection is one particular X selection (q.v.); it is the selection that most X applications use for transferring text to and from other applications.

           The Emacs kill commands set the primary selection and the yank command uses the primary selection when appropriate. See Chapter 9 [Killing], page 52.

Prompt   A prompt is text used to ask you for input. Displaying a prompt is called prompting. Emacs prompts always appear in the echo area (q.v.). One kind of prompting happens when the minibuffer is used to read an argument (see Chapter 5 [Minibuffer], page 26); the echoing that happens when you pause in the middle of typing a multi-character key sequence is also a kind of prompting (see Section 1.2 [Echo Area], page 7).

Query-Replace
           Query-replace is an interactive string replacement feature provided by Emacs. See Section 12.10.4 [Query Replace], page 105.

Quitting   Quitting means canceling a partially typed command or a running command, using C-g (or C-BREAK on MS-DOS). See Section 34.1 [Quitting], page 443.

Quoting   Quoting means depriving a character of its usual special significance. The most common kind of quoting in Emacs is with C-q. What constitutes special significance depends on the context and on convention. For example, an "ordinary" character as an Emacs command inserts itself; so in this context, a special character is any character that does not normally insert itself (such as DEL, for example), and quoting it makes it insert itself as if it were not special. Not all contexts allow quoting. See Section 4.1 [Inserting Text], page 16.

Quoting File Names
           Quoting a file name turns off the special significance of constructs such as '$', '~' and ':'. See Section 15.14 [Quoted File Names], page 143.

Read-Only Buffer
           A read-only buffer is one whose text you are not allowed to change. Normally Emacs makes buffers read-only when they contain text which has a special

significance to Emacs; for example, Dired buffers. Visiting a file that is write-protected also makes a read-only buffer. See Chapter 16 [Buffers], page 147.

Rectangle   A rectangle consists of the text in a given range of columns on a given range of lines. Normally you specify a rectangle by putting point at one corner and putting the mark at the diagonally opposite corner. See Section 9.5 [Rectangles], page 60.

Recursive Editing Level

A recursive editing level is a state in which part of the execution of a command involves asking you to edit some text. This text may or may not be the same as the text to which the command was applied. The mode line indicates recursive editing levels with square brackets ('[' and ']'). See Section 31.10 [Recursive Edit], page 404.

Redisplay   Redisplay is the process of correcting the image on the screen to correspond to changes that have been made in the text being edited. See Chapter 1 [Screen], page 6.

Regexp   See [Glossary—Regular Expression], page 540.

Region   The region is the text between point (q.v.) and the mark (q.v.). Many commands operate on the text of the region. See Chapter 8 [Mark], page 45.

Register   Registers are named slots in which text, buffer positions, or rectangles can be saved for later use. See Chapter 10 [Registers], page 64. A related Emacs feature is 'bookmarks' (q.v.).

Regular Expression

A regular expression is a pattern that can match various text strings; for example, 'a[0-9]+' matches 'a' followed by one or more digits. See Section 12.6 [Regexps], page 97.

Remote File

A remote file is a file that is stored on a system other than your own. Emacs can access files on other computers provided that they are connected to the same network as your machine, and (obviously) that you have a supported method to gain access to those files. See Section 15.13 [Remote Files], page 142.

Repeat Count

See [Glossary—Numeric Argument], page 538.

Replacement

See [Glossary—Global Substitution], page 532.

Restriction

A buffer's restriction is the amount of text, at the beginning or the end of the buffer, that is temporarily inaccessible. Giving a buffer a nonzero amount of restriction is called narrowing (q.v.); removing a restriction is called widening (q.v.). See Section 11.5 [Narrowing], page 73.

RET   RET is a character that in Emacs runs the command to insert a newline into the text. It is also used to terminate most arguments read in the minibuffer (q.v.). See Section 2.1 [User Input], page 11.

Reverting   Reverting means returning to the original state. Emacs lets you revert a buffer by re-reading its file from disk. See Section 15.4 [Reverting], page 132.

Saving   Saving a buffer means copying its text into the file that was visited (q.v.) in that buffer. This is the way text in files actually gets changed by your Emacs editing. See Section 15.3 [Saving], page 126.

Scroll Bar   A scroll bar is a tall thin hollow box that appears at the side of a window. You can use mouse commands in the scroll bar to scroll the window. The scroll bar feature is supported only under windowing systems. See Section 18.12 [Scroll Bars], page 172.

Scrolling   Scrolling means shifting the text in the Emacs window so as to see a different part of the buffer. See Section 11.1 [Scrolling], page 69.

Searching   Searching means moving point to the next occurrence of a specified string or the next match for a specified regular expression. See Chapter 12 [Search], page 90.

Search Path
             A search path is a list of directory names, to be used for searching for files for certain purposes. For example, the variable `load-path` holds a search path for finding Lisp library files. See Section 24.8 [Lisp Libraries], page 276.

Secondary Selection
             The secondary selection is one particular X selection (q.v.); some X applications can use it for transferring text to and from other applications. Emacs has special mouse commands for transferring text using the secondary selection. See Section 9.3.3 [Secondary Selection], page 58.

Selected Frame
             The selected frame is the one your input currently operates on. See Chapter 18 [Frames], page 162.

Selected Window
             The selected window is the one your input currently operates on. See Section 17.1 [Basic Window], page 156.

Selecting a Buffer
             Selecting a buffer means making it the current (q.v.) buffer. See Section 16.1 [Select Buffer], page 147.

Selection   Windowing systems allow an application program to specify selections whose values are text. A program can also read the selections that other programs have set up. This is the principal way of transferring text between window applications. Emacs has commands to work with the primary (q.v.) selection and the secondary (q.v.) selection, and also with the clipboard (q.v.).

Self-Documentation
             Self-documentation is the feature of Emacs that can tell you what any command does, or give you a list of all commands related to a topic you specify. You ask for self-documentation with the help character, `C-h`. See Chapter 7 [Help], page 37.

Self-Inserting Character

> A character is self-inserting if typing that character inserts that character in the buffer. Ordinary printing and whitespace characters are self-inserting in Emacs, except in certain special major modes.

Sentences   Emacs has commands for moving by or killing by sentences. See Section 22.2 [Sentences], page 209.

Server   Within Emacs, you can start a 'server' process, which listens for connections from 'clients'. This offers a faster alternative to starting several Emacs instances. See Section 31.5 [Emacs Server], page 393, and [Glossary—Daemon], page 528.

Sexp   A sexp (short for "s-expression") is the basic syntactic unit of Lisp in its textual form: either a list, or Lisp atom. Sexps are also the balanced expressions (q.v.) of the Lisp language; this is why the commands for editing balanced expressions have 'sexp' in their name. See Section 23.4.1 [Expressions], page 246.

Simultaneous Editing

> Simultaneous editing means two users modifying the same file at once. Simultaneous editing, if not detected, can cause one user to lose his or her work. Emacs detects all cases of simultaneous editing, and warns one of the users to investigate. See Section 15.3.4 [Simultaneous Editing], page 130.

SPC   SPC is the space character, which you enter by pressing the space bar.

Speedbar   The speedbar is a special tall frame that provides fast access to Emacs buffers, functions within those buffers, Info nodes, and other interesting parts of text within Emacs. See Section 18.9 [Speedbar], page 171.

Spell Checking

> Spell checking means checking correctness of the written form of each one of the words in a text. Emacs can use various external spelling-checker programs to check the spelling of parts of a buffer via a convenient user interface. See Section 13.4 [Spelling], page 111.

String   A string is a kind of Lisp data object that contains a sequence of characters. Many Emacs variables are intended to have strings as values. The Lisp syntax for a string consists of the characters in the string with a '"' before and another '"' after. A '"' that is part of the string must be written as '\"' and a '\' that is part of the string must be written as '\\'. All other characters, including newline, can be included just by writing them inside the string; however, backslash sequences as in C, such as '\n' for newline or '\241' using an octal character code, are allowed as well.

String Substitution

> See [Glossary—Global Substitution], page 532.

Syntax Highlighting

> See [Glossary—Font Lock], page 531.

Syntax Table

The syntax table tells Emacs which characters are part of a word, which characters balance each other like parentheses, etc. See Section "Syntax Tables" in *The Emacs Lisp Reference Manual*.

Super   Super is the name of a modifier bit that a keyboard input character may have. To make a character Super, type it while holding down the `SUPER` key. Such characters are given names that start with `Super-` (usually written `s-` for short). See Section 2.1 [User Input], page 11.

Suspending

Suspending Emacs means stopping it temporarily and returning control to its parent process, which is usually a shell. Unlike killing a job (q.v.), you can later resume the suspended Emacs job without losing your buffers, unsaved edits, undo history, etc. See Section 3.2 [Exiting], page 15.

`TAB`   `TAB` is the tab character. In Emacs it is typically used for indentation or completion.

Tags Table

A tags table is a file that serves as an index to the function definitions in one or more other files. See Section 25.3 [Tags], page 299.

Termscript File

A termscript file contains a record of all characters sent by Emacs to the terminal. It is used for tracking down bugs in Emacs redisplay. Emacs does not make a termscript file unless you tell it to. See Section 34.3 [Bugs], page 448.

Text   'Text' has two meanings (see Chapter 22 [Text], page 208):

- Data consisting of a sequence of characters, as opposed to binary numbers, executable programs, and the like. The basic contents of an Emacs buffer (aside from the text properties, q.v.) are always text in this sense.
- Data consisting of written human language (as opposed to programs), or following the stylistic conventions of human language.

Text Terminal

A text terminal, or character terminal, is a display that is limited to displaying text in character units. Such a terminal cannot control individual pixels it displays. Emacs supports a subset of display features on text terminals.

Text Properties

Text properties are annotations recorded for particular characters in the buffer. Images in the buffer are recorded as text properties; they also specify formatting information. See Section 22.13.3 [Editing Format Info], page 231.

Theme   A theme is a set of customizations (q.v.) that give Emacs a particular appearance or behavior. For example, you might use a theme for your favorite set of faces (q.v.).

Tool Bar   The tool bar is a line (sometimes multiple lines) of icons at the top of an Emacs frame. Clicking on one of these icons executes a command. You can think of this as a graphical relative of the menu bar (q.v.). See Section 18.15 [Tool Bars], page 173.

Tooltips   Tooltips are small windows displaying a help echo (q.v.) text, which explains parts of the display, lists useful options available via mouse clicks, etc. See Section 18.17 [Tooltips], page 174.

Top Level   Top level is the normal state of Emacs, in which you are editing the text of the file you have visited. You are at top level whenever you are not in a recursive editing level (q.v.) or the minibuffer (q.v.), and not in the middle of a command. You can get back to top level by aborting (q.v.) and quitting (q.v.). See Section 34.1 [Quitting], page 443.

Transient Mark Mode
                The default behavior of the mark (q.v.) and region (q.v.), in which setting the mark activates it and highlights the region, is called Transient Mark mode. In GNU Emacs 23 and onwards, it is enabled by default. See Section 8.7 [Disabled Transient Mark], page 50.

Transposition
                Transposing two units of text means putting each one into the place formerly occupied by the other. There are Emacs commands to transpose two adjacent characters, words, balanced expressions (q.v.) or lines (see Section 13.2 [Transpose], page 110).

Trash Can   See [Glossary—Deletion of Files], page 528.

Truncation
                Truncating text lines in the display means leaving out any text on a line that does not fit within the right margin of the window displaying it. See Section 4.8 [Continuation Lines], page 22, and [Glossary—Continuation Line], page 527.

TTY   See [Glossary—Text Terminal], page 543.

Undoing   Undoing means making your previous editing go in reverse, bringing back the text that existed earlier in the editing session. See Section 13.1 [Undo], page 109.

Unix   Unix is a class of multi-user computer operating systems with a long history. There are several implementations today. The GNU project (q.v.) aims to develop a complete Unix-like operating system that is free software (q.v.).

User Option
                A user option is a face (q.v.) or a variable (q.v.) that exists so that you can customize Emacs by setting it to a new value. See Section 33.1 [Easy Customization], page 412.

Variable   A variable is an object in Lisp that can store an arbitrary value. Emacs uses some variables for internal purposes, and has others (known as 'user options'; q.v.) just so that you can set their values to control the behavior of Emacs. The variables used in Emacs that you are likely to be interested in are listed in the Variables Index in this manual (see [Variable Index], page 568). See Section 33.2 [Variables], page 420, for information on variables.

Version Control
                Version control systems keep track of multiple versions of a source file. They provide a more powerful alternative to keeping backup files (q.v.). See Section 25.1 [Version Control], page 281.

Visiting   Visiting a file means loading its contents into a buffer (q.v.) where they can be edited. See Section 15.2 [Visiting], page 123.

Whitespace
                Whitespace is any run of consecutive formatting characters (space, tab, newline, and backspace).

Widening   Widening is removing any restriction (q.v.) on the current buffer; it is the opposite of narrowing (q.v.). See Section 11.5 [Narrowing], page 73.

Window   Emacs divides a frame (q.v.) into one or more windows, each of which can display the contents of one buffer (q.v.) at any time. See Chapter 1 [Screen], page 6, for basic information on how Emacs uses the screen. See Chapter 17 [Windows], page 156, for commands to control the use of windows. Some other editors use the term "window" for what we call a 'frame' (q.v.) in Emacs.

Window System
                A window system is software that operates on a graphical display (q.v.), to subdivide the screen so that multiple applications can have their] own windows at the same time. All modern operating systems include a window system.

Word Abbrev
                See [Glossary—Abbrev], page 523.

Word Search
                Word search is searching for a sequence of words, considering the punctuation between them as insignificant. See Section 12.3 [Word Search], page 95.

Yanking   Yanking means reinserting text previously killed (q.v.). It can be used to undo a mistaken kill, or for copying or moving text. Some other systems call this "pasting". See Section 9.2 [Yanking], page 55.

Key (Character) Index

N

O

P

Q

Command and Function Index

C

T

U

V

W

X

Y

Z

Variable Index

Concept Index

B

C

D

E

L

M

T

X

Y

Z

www.ingramcontent.com/pod-product-compliance
Lightning Source LLC
LaVergne TN
LVHW060131070326
832902LV00018B/2752